Essentials of INTERNATIONAL RELATIONS

SEVENTH EDITION

Essentials of
INTERNATIONAL RELATIONS

SEVENTH EDITION

KAREN A. MINGST

UNIVERSITY OF KENTUCKY

IVAN M. ARREGUÍN-TOFT

BOSTON UNIVERSITY

W. W. NORTON & COMPANY

NEW YORK · LONDON

Editor: Peter Lesser
Assistant Editor: Samantha Held
Project Editor: Katie Callahan
Managing Editor, College: Marian Johnson
Managing Editor, College Digital Media: Kim Yi
Associate Director of Production, College: Ben Reynolds
Media Editor: Spencer Richardson-Jones
Media Project Editor: Marcus Van Harpen
Media Assistant Editor: Michael Jaoui
Marketing Manager, Political Science: Erin Brown
Design Director: Hope Miller Goodell
Book design by: Faceout Studio
Photo Editor: Catherine Abelman
Permissions Clearing: Elizabeth Trammell
Permissions Manager: Megan Schindel
Composition: Westchester Publishing Services
Manufacturing: Transcontinental

Permission to use copyrighted material is included in the credits section of this book, which begins on p. A27.

Library of Congress Cataloging-in-Publication Data

Names: Mingst, Karen A., 1947– author. | Arreguín-Toft, Ivan M.
Title: Essentials of international relations / Karen A. Mingst, University of Kentucky,
    Ivan M. Arreguín-Toft, Boston University.
Description: Seventh edition. | New York : W. W. Norton & Company, [2017] | Includes
    bibliographical references and index.
Identifiers: LCCN 2016013756 | **ISBN 9780393283402 (pbk.)**
Subjects: LCSH: International relations.
Classification: LCC JZ1305 .M56 2016 | DDC 327—dc23 LC record available at https://lccn.loc.gov
    /2016013756

W. W. Norton & Company, Inc., 500 Fifth Avenue, New York, NY 10110
wwnorton.com
W. W. Norton & Company Ltd., Castle House, 75/76 Wells Street, London W1T 3QT

1 2 3 4 5 6 7 8 9 0

CONTENTS

Figures, Tables, and Maps

FIGURES

TABLES

MAPS

ABOUT THE AUTHORS

Karen A. Mingst is Professor Emeritus at the Patterson School of Diplomacy and International Commerce at the University of Kentucky. She holds a Ph.D. in political science from the University of Wisconsin. A specialist in international organization, international law, and international political economy, Professor Mingst has conducted research in Western Europe, West Africa, and Yugoslavia. She is the author or editor of seven books and numerous academic articles.

Ivan M. Arreguín-Toft is Assistant Professor of International Relations at Boston University, where he teaches introductory international relations, among other courses. He holds a Ph.D. in political science from the University of Chicago. Professor Arreguín-Toft is a specialist in security studies, asymmetric conflict, and cyber warfare. He is most recently the recipient of a U.S. Fulbright grant to Norway.

PREFACE

Brief textbooks are now commonplace in International Relations. This textbook was originally written to be not only smart and brief, but also, in the words of Roby Harrington of W. W. Norton, to include "a clear sense of what's essential and what's not." We are pleased that this book's treatment of the essential concepts and information has stood the test of time.

This seventh edition of *Essentials of International Relations*, published more than fifteen years after the first, preserves the overall structure of earlier editions. Students need a brief history of international relations to understand why we study the subject and how current scholarship is informed by what has preceded it. This background is provided in Chapters 1 and 2. Theories provide interpretative frameworks for understanding what is happening in the world, and levels of analysis—the international system, the state, and the individual—help us further organize and conceptualize the material. In Chapters 3–7, we present competing theories and use them to illustrate how each level of analysis can be applied and how international organizations, international law, and nongovernmental organizations are viewed. Then the major issues of the twenty-first century—security, economics, human rights, and transnational issues—are presented and analyzed in Chapters 8–11.

This fully revised seventh edition is enhanced by the addition of new material on terrorism, cybersecurity, and nuclear threats to security; the continuing impact of China, India, and other states on the functioning of finance and trade in the global economy; and the challenges posed by the Eurozone and the refugee crisis to the future of the European Union. Refugees and internally displaced persons are discussed as human rights and humanitarian issues. The challenges of climate change and the increasing persistence of global health threats like Ebola are also new additions.

The rich pedagogical program of previous editions has been revised based on suggestions from adopters and reviewers:

- Each chapter is introduced with a new story "ripped from the headlines," selected to help students apply the concepts discussed in the chapter to a contemporary problem. Later in each chapter, these headlines are discussed in the new **Behind the Headlines** features using the concepts and ideas from the text. Topics include the Palestinian efforts to acquire statehood; the human cost of climate change; and Russia, Syria, and the international system.
- The popular **Global Perspectives** features have been updated with new perspectives—including cyber security as viewed from Great Britain, the Eurozone crisis viewed from Greece, the view from a rising state like India, and the view from the Vatican. This feature encourages students to consider a specific issue from the vantage point of a particular state.
- End-of-chapter review materials include **discussion questions** and a list of **key terms** from the chapter to help students remember, apply, and synthesize what they have learned.
- **Theory in Brief** boxes, **In Focus** boxes, and numerous maps, figures, and tables appear throughout the text to summarize key ideas.

Many of these changes have been made at the suggestion of expert reviewers, primarily faculty who have taught the book in the classroom. While it is impossible to act on every suggestion (not all the critics themselves agree), we have carefully studied the various recommendations and thank the reviewers for taking time to offer critiques. We thank the following reviewers for their input on this new edition: Baktybek Abdrisaev, Utah Valley University; Benjamin Appel, Michigan State University; Dlynn Armstrong-Williams, University of North Georgia; Mark Baron, University of Calgary; Michael Beckley, Tufts University; Celeste Beesley, Brigham Young University; Tabitha Benney, University of Utah; Cynthia A. Botteron, Shippensburg University; John W. Dietrich, Bryant University; Kathryn Fisher, National Defense University; Andrea B. Haupt, Santa Barbara City College; Cynthia Horne, Western Washington University; Paul E. Lenze, Jr., Northern Arizona University; Heather Elko McKibben, University of California, Davis; Lyle Stevens, Iowa Central Community College; Kendall Stiles, Brigham Young University; and Bradford Young, Snow College.

In this edition, Karen Mingst owes special thanks to her husband, Robert Stauffer. He has always provided both space and encouragement, as well as holding up more than one-half of the marriage bargain. Yet he keeps asking, just as our adult kids, Ginger and Brett, do—another book, another edition! Our toddler grandson, Quintin, has not yet mastered the dimension of time and space! He exemplifies the importance of the "here and now."

In this edition, Ivan Arreguín-Toft owes thanks to a number of people; especially to my wife Monica Toft, and to my children Sam and Ingrid Toft. I also owe great thanks to Roby Harrington, whose sage advice and unflappable optimism invariably catalyze my best efforts. Finally, I owe a special debt of gratitude to Karen Mingst, whose pedagogical vision, and strength and clarity of intention are matched only by her willingness to critically challenge herself and me in the complicated and rewarding task of continuing to produce the world's most compact, engaging, and comprehensive international relations textbook.

We have been fortunate to have several editors from W. W. Norton who have shepherded various editions: Ann Shin, editor of the first four editions, knows this book as well as its authors. She has always been a constant fountain of ideas and enthusiasm. Lisa Camner McKay made constructive suggestions and rather quickly came to understand our individual and collective strengths and weaknesses. Pete Lesser has been the calm point person on this edition, taking a personal interest in developing new features, keeping us on task and time, and offering his own formidable editing skills along the way. And Samantha Held has expertly directed the editorial process in an expeditious fashion. In short, many talented, professional, and delightful people contributed to the making of this edition, which we feel is the best so far. And for that, we remain always grateful.

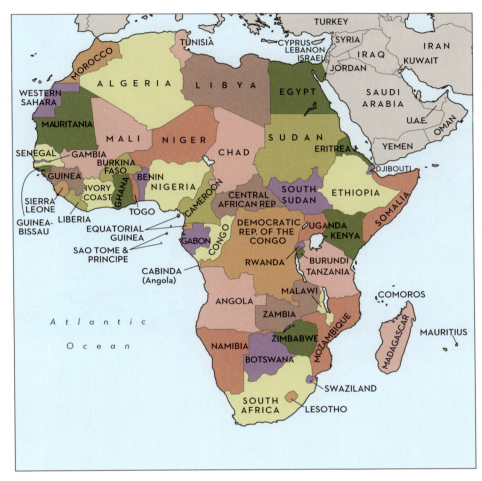

AFRICA

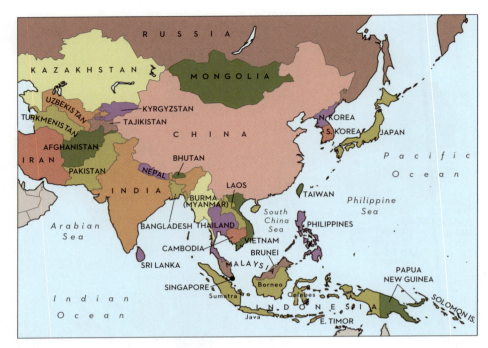

ASIA

EUROPE

NORTH AMERICA

CENTRAL AND SOUTH AMERICA

North
America

Europe

*Pacific
Ocean*

*Atlantic
Ocean*

Central
and
South America

THE WORLD

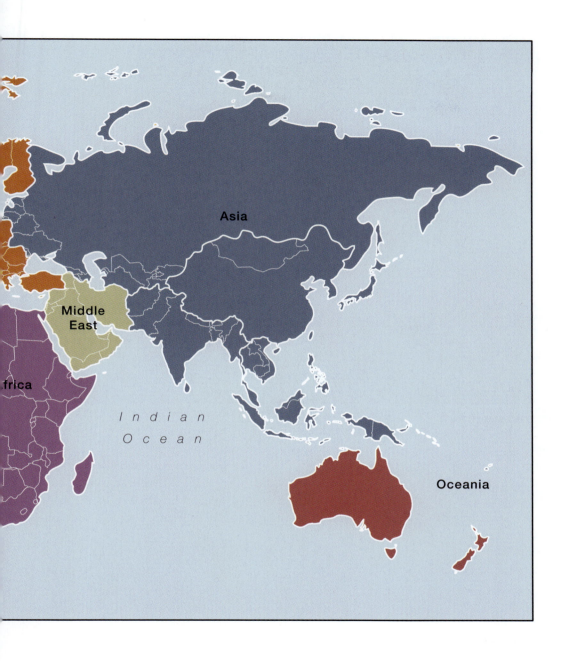

THE MIDDLE EAST

Macedonian police clash with migrants on the Greek side of the border in August 2015. Europe's migrant crisis and images like this one have dominated global news headlines since mid-2015, as an increasing number of refugees from countries like Syria, Afghanistan, and Iraq have come to Europe seeking asylum.

APPROACHES TO INTERNATIONAL RELATIONS

Martin Dempsey, former chairman of the Joint Chiefs of Staff, remarked in 2012 that the world has become "more dangerous than it has ever been." If we listen to the 24-hour news cycle and social media, we are flooded with reports of the Islamic State gunning down Parisians and blowing up ancient archeological sites; drones hitting unintended Pakistani targets; men, women, and children clinging to rickety boats, fleeing conflict and economic hardship; and thousands in Haiti, the Philippines, and Indonesia fleeing natural disasters. Vivid pictures make those events appear to be happening everywhere, perhaps just next door. And Dempsey, responsible for keeping the United States safe, is all too aware of the threats at the door.

Yet psychologist Steven Pinker, author of *The Better Angels of Our Nature: Why Violence Has Declined*, concluded in 2011 that "we may be living in the most peaceful era in our species' existence." Dempsey and Pinker agree that the number of interstate wars has declined, as have the number of deaths caused by such wars. Since the end of the Cold War, civil wars, too, have declined. If all this is true, why can one person be optimistic about our ability to live together more peacefully and another be more pessimistic? Are the authors coming at the question from different theoretical positions? Are they examining different data, using different time periods?

Your place in the world is complicated. You are a member of a family; your father or mother may work for a multinational corporation; you may be a member of a non-governmental organization (NGO), supporting a particular cause that you hold dear; you may be member of a church, synagogue, or mosque, or an ethnic group whose members span the globe; your state may be composed of different local units having responsibilities for issues with transnational significance; your state may have diplomatic relations and trades with states across the globe, may participate in the activities of international NGOs, and may be a member of numerous intergovernmental organizations. The variety of actors in international relations includes not just the 193 states recognized in the world today, their leaders, and government bureaucracies, but also municipalities, for-profit and not-for-profit private organizations, international organizations, and you.

International relations, as a subfield of political science, is the study of the interactions among the various actors that participate in international politics. It is the study of the behaviors of these actors as they participate individually and together in international political processes. International relations is also an interdisciplinary field of inquiry, using concepts and substance from history, economics, and anthropology, as well as political science.

How can we begin to study this multifaceted phenomenon called international relations? How can we begin to think theoretically about what appear to be disconnected events? How can we begin to answer the foundational questions of international relations: What are the characteristics of human nature and the state? What is the relationship between the individual and society? How is the international system organized? In this book, we will help you answer these questions, and many more.

LEARNING OBJECTIVES

- Understand how international relations affects you in your daily life.

- Explain why we study international relations theory.

- Analyze how history and philosophy have been used to study international relations.

- Describe the contribution of behavioralism in international relations.

- Explain how and why alternative approaches have challenged traditional approaches in international relations.

Non-governmental organizations and their members often respond to issues of international significance. Here, volunteers from NGOs operating in Lebanon distribute aid to Syrian refugees in Al-Masri refugee camp in October 2014.

Thinking Theoretically

Political scientists develop theories or frameworks both to understand the causes of events that occur in international relations every day and to answer the foundational questions in the field. Although there are many contending theories, four of the more prominent theories are developed in this book: realism and neorealism, liberalism and neoliberal institutionalism, radical perspectives whose origins lie in Marxism, and constructivism.

In brief, realism posits that states exist in an anarchic international system; that is, there is no overarching hierarchical authority. Each state bases its policies on an interpretation of its national interest defined in terms of power. The structure of the international system is determined by the distribution of power among states. In contrast, liberalism is historically rooted in several philosophical traditions that posit that human nature is basically good. Individuals form groups and, later, states. States generally cooperate and follow international norms and procedures that they have agreed to support. Radical theory is rooted in economics. Actions of individuals are largely determined by economic class; the state is an agent of international capitalism; and the international system is highly stratified, dominated by an international capitalist system.

IN FOCUS

FOUNDATIONAL QUESTIONS OF INTERNATIONAL RELATIONS

- How can human nature be characterized?

- What is the relationship between the individual and society?

- What are the characteristics and role of the state?

- How is the international system organized?

And international relations constructivists, in contrast to both realists and liberals, argue that the key structures in the state system are not material but instead are social and dependent on ideas. The interests of states are not fixed but are malleable and ever-changing. All four of these theories are subject to different interpretations by scholars who analyze international relations. Those theories help us describe, explain, and predict. These different theoretical approaches help us see international relations from different viewpoints. As political scientist Stephen Walt explains, "No single approach can capture all the complexity of contemporary world politics. Therefore, we are better off with a diverse array of competing ideas rather than a single theoretical orthodoxy. Competition between theories helps reveal their strengths and weaknesses and spurs subsequent refinements, while revealing flaws in conventional wisdom."[1] We will explore these competing ideas, and their strengths and weaknesses, in the remainder of this book.

Developing the Answers

How do political scientists find information to assess the accuracy, relevancy, and potency of their theories? The tools they use to answer the foundational questions of their field include history, philosophy, and the scientific method.

History

Inquiry in international relations often begins with history. Without any historical background, many of today's key issues are incomprehensible. History tells us that the periodic bombings in Israel by Hamas are part of a dispute over territory between Arabs and Jews, a dispute having its origins in biblical times and its modern roots in the establishment of the state of Israel in 1948. Sudan's 20-year civil war between the Muslim north and Christian/animist south and the Darfur crisis beginning in 2003 are both products of the central government's long-standing neglect of marginalized areas, exacerbated by religious differences and magnified by natural disasters. Without that historical background, we cannot debate the appropriate solution in the Arab-Israeli dispute, nor can we understand why the establishment of the Republic of South Sudan in 2011 did not lead to a solution for the Darfur crisis.

Thus, history provides a crucial background for the study of international relations. History has been so fundamental to the study of international relations that there was no separate international relations subfield until the early twentieth century. Before that time, especially in Europe and the United States, international relations was studied under the umbrella of diplomatic history in most academic institutions. Having knowledge of both diplomatic history and national histories remains critical for students of international relations.

History invites its students to acquire detailed knowledge of specific events, but it also can be used to test generalizations. Having deciphered patterns from the past, students of history can begin to explain the relationships among various events. For example, having historically documented the cases when wars occur and described the patterns leading up to war, the diplomatic historian can seek explanations for, or causes of, war. The ancient Greek historian Thucydides (c. 460–401 BCE), in *History of the Peloponnesian War*, used this approach. Distinguishing between the underlying and the immediate causes of wars, Thucydides found that what made that war inevitable was the growth of Athenian power. As Athens's power increased, Sparta, Athens's greatest rival, feared losing its own power. Thus, the changing distribution of power was the underlying cause of the Peloponnesian War.[2]

Many scholars following in Thucydides's footsteps use history in similar ways. But those using history must be wary because it is not always clear what history attempts to teach us. We often rely on analogies, comparing, for example, the 2003 Iraq War to the Vietnam War. In both cases, the United States fought a lengthy war against a little understood, often unidentifiable enemy. In both, the United States adopted the strategy of supporting state building so that the central government could continue the fight, a policy labeled *Vietnamization* and *Iraqization* in the respective conflicts. The policy led to a quagmire in both places when American domestic support waned and the United States withdrew. Yet differences are also evident; no analogies are perfect. Vietnam has a long history and a strong sense of national identity, forged by wars against both the Chinese and French. Iraq, in contrast, is a relatively new state with significant ethnic and religious divisions, whose various groups seek a variety of different objectives. In Vietnam, the goal was defense of the U.S. ally South Vietnam against the communist north, backed by the Soviet Union. In Iraq, the goal was first to oust Saddam Hussein, who was suspected of building weapons of mass destruction, and second, to create a democratic Iraq that would eventually lead the region to greater

Scholars often draw on history to help understand world politics. When the United States invaded Iraq first in the 1991 Gulf War and then in the 2003 Iraq War, some observers raised comparisons to the Vietnam War, when many Americans protested U.S. involvement. However, there were also significant differences between these events.

stability.[3] In both, although we cannot ignore history, neither can we draw simple "lessons" from historical analogies.

Analogies are incomplete. Lessons are often drawn that reflect one's theoretical orientation. Realists might draw the lesson from both Vietnam and Iraq that the United States did not use all of its military might; political actors constrained military actions; otherwise, the outcome may have been different. Liberals might conclude that the United States should have never been involved since the homeland was not directly affected and one country's ability to construct or reconstruct another state is limited. What lessons can we draw from the United States' acquiescence to the Soviet takeover of Crimea in 2014? Was this another Munich, when the allies appeased Germany at the early stages of World War II? Or was this an affirmation of national self-determination since the Crimeans, mostly ethnic Russians, voted to secede from Ukraine and rejoin Russia? Was the Joint Comprehensive Plan of Action, the 2015 agreement between the western powers and Iran setting limits on Iran's nuclear program, another Munich or a Helsinki moment? [4] Helsinki refers to the 1975 accord officially ratifying post–World War II borders and advocating for respect of human rights. History offers no clear-cut lesson or guidance.

Philosophy

Philosophy can help us answer questions in international relations. Much classical philosophy focuses on the state and its leaders—the basic building blocks of international relations—as well as on methods of analysis. For example, the ancient Greek philosopher Plato (c. 427–347 BCE), in *The Republic*, concluded that in the "perfect state," the people who should govern are those who are superior in the ways of philosophy and war. Plato called these ideal rulers "philosopher-kings."[5] Though not directly discussing international relations, Plato introduced two ideas seminal to the discipline: class analysis and dialectical reasoning, both of which were bases for later Marxist analysts. Radicals like Marxists see economic class as the major divider in domestic and international politics; Chapters 3 and 9 will explore this viewpoint in depth. Marxists also acknowledge the importance of dialectical reasoning—that is, reasoning from a dialogue or conversation that leads to the discovery of contradictions in the original assertions and in political reality. In contemporary Marxist terms, such analysis reveals the contradiction between global and local policies, whereby, for example, local-level textile workers lose their jobs to foreign competition and are replaced by high-technology industries.

Just as Plato's contributions to contemporary thinking were both substantive and methodological, the contributions of his student, the philosopher Aristotle (384–322 BCE), lay both in substance (the search for an ideal domestic political system) and in method. Analyzing 168 constitutions, Aristotle looked at the similarities and differences among states, becoming the first writer to use the comparative method of analysis. He concluded that states rise and fall largely because of internal factors—a conclusion still debated in the twenty-first century.[6]

After the classical era, many of the philosophers of relevance to international relations focused on the foundational questions of the discipline. The English philosopher Thomas Hobbes (1588–1679), in *Leviathan*, imagined a state of nature, a world without governmental authority or civil order, where men rule by passions, living with the constant uncertainty of their own security. To Hobbes, the life of man is solitary, selfish, and even brutish. Extrapolating to the international level, in the absence of international authority, society is in a "state of nature," or **anarchy**. States in this anarchic condition act as man does in the state of nature. For Hobbes, the solution to the dilemma is a unitary state—a leviathan—where power is centrally and absolutely controlled.[7]

The French philosopher Jean-Jacques Rousseau (1712–78) addressed the same set of questions but, having been influenced by the Enlightenment, saw a different solution. In "Discourse on the Origin and Foundations of Inequality among Men," Rousseau described the state of nature as an egocentric world, with man's primary concern being self-preservation—not unlike Hobbes's description of the state of nature.

Rousseau posed the dilemma in terms of the story of the stag and the hare. In a hunting society, each individual must keep to his assigned task so the hunters can find and trap the stag for food for the whole group. However, if a hare happens to pass nearby, an individual might well follow the hare, hoping to get his next meal quickly and caring little for how his actions will affect the group. Rousseau drew an analogy between these hunters and states. Do states follow short-term self-interest, like the hunter who follows the hare? Or do they recognize the benefits of a common interest?[8] Rousseau's solution to the dilemma posed by the stag and the hare was different from Hobbes's leviathan. Rousseau's preference was for the creation of smaller communities in which the "general will" could be attained. Indeed, according to Rousseau, it is "only the general will," not a leviathan, that can "direct the forces of the state according to the purpose for which it was instituted, which is the common good."[9] In Rousseau's vision, "each of us places his person and all his power in common under the supreme direction of the general will; and as one we receive each member as an indivisible part of the whole."[10]

Still another philosophical view of the characteristics of international society was set forth by the German philosopher Immanuel Kant (1724–1804), in both *Idea for a Universal History* and *Perpetual Peace*. Kant envisioned a federation of states as a means to achieve peace, a world order in which man is able to live without fear of war. Sovereignties would remain intact, but the new federal order would be both preferable to a "super-leviathan" and more effective and realistic than Rousseau's small communities. Kant's analysis was based on a vision of human beings that was different from that of either Rousseau or Hobbes. In his view, though man is admittedly selfish, he can learn new ways of cosmopolitanism and universalism.[11]

The tradition laid down by these philosophers has contributed to the development of international relations by calling attention to fundamental relationships: those between the individual and society, between individuals *in* society, and between societies. These philosophers had varied, often competing, visions of what these relationships were and what they ought to be. (See Table 1.1.) The early philosophers have led contemporary international relations scholars to the examination of the characteristics of leaders, to the recognition of the importance of the internal dimensions of the state, to the analogy of the state and nature, and to descriptions of an international community. History and philosophy permit us to delve into foundational questions—the nature of people and the broad characteristics of the state and of international society. They allow us to speculate on the **normative** (or moral) elements in political life: What *should be* the role of the state? What *ought to be* the norms in international society? How *might* international society be structured to achieve order? When *is* war just? Should economic resources be redistributed? Should human rights be universalized?[12] Philosophical methods may not be useful for helping us answer specific questions; they may tell us what *should* be done, providing the normative guide, but philosophy generally

TABLE 1.1	CONTRIBUTIONS OF PHILOSOPHERS TO INTERNATIONAL RELATIONS THEORY
Plato (427–347 BCE) Greek	Argued that the life force in man is intelligent. Only a few people can have insight into what is good; society should submit to the authority of these philosopher-kings. Many of these ideas are developed in *The Republic*.
Aristotle (384–322 BCE) Greek	Addressed the problem of order in the individual Greek city-state. The first to use the comparative method of research, observing multiple points in time and suggesting explanations for the patterns found.
Thomas Hobbes (1588–1679) English	In *Leviathan* described life in a state of nature as solitary, selfish, and brutish. Individuals and society can escape from the state of nature through a unitary state, a leviathan.
Jean-Jacques Rousseau (1712–78) French	In "Discourse on the Origin and Foundations of Inequality among Men," described the state of nature in both national and international society. Argued that the solution to the state of nature is the social contract, whereby individuals gather in small communities where the "general will" is realized.
Immanuel Kant (1724–1804) German	Associated with the idealist or utopian school of thought. In *Idea for a Universal History* and *Perpetual Peace*, advocated a world federation of republics bound by the rule of law.

does not help us make or implement policy. Nevertheless, both history and philosophy are key tools for international relations scholars.

The Scientific Method: Behavioralism

In the 1950s, some scholars began to draw upon one understanding of the nature of humans and on history to develop a more scientific approach to the study of international relations. They built upon the philosophical assumption that man tends to act in predictable ways. If individuals act in predictable ways, might not states do the same? Are there recurrent patterns to how states behave? Are there subtle patterns to diplomatic history? Are states as power hungry as some philosophers would have us believe? How can we explain empirical findings? Can we use those findings to predict the future?

Behavioralism proposes that individuals, both alone and in groups, act in patterned ways. The task of the behavioral scientist is to suggest plausible hypotheses regarding those patterned actions and to systematically and empirically test those hypotheses. Using the tools of the scientific method to describe and explain human behavior, these scholars hope to predict future behavior. Many will be satisfied, however, with being able to explain patterns, because prediction in the social sciences remains an uncertain enterprise.

The Correlates of War project permits us to see the application of behavioralism. Beginning in 1963 at the University of Michigan, the political scientist J. David Singer and his historian colleague Melvin Small investigated one of the fundamental questions in international relations: Why is there war?[13] Motivated by the normative philosophical concern with how peace can be achieved, the two scholars chose an empirical methodological approach. Rather than focusing on one "big" war that changed the tide of history, as Thucydides did, they sought to find patterns among a number of different wars. Believing that generalizable patterns may be found across all wars, Singer and Small turned to statistical data to discover the patterns.

The initial task of the Correlates of War project was to collect data on international wars between 1865 and 1965 in which 1,000 or more deaths had been reported in a 12-month period. For each of the 93 wars that fit these criteria, the researchers found data on its magnitude, severity, and intensity, as well as the frequency of war over time. This data-collection process proved a much larger task than Singer and Small had anticipated, employing a bevy of researchers and graduate students.

Once the wars were codified, the second task was to generate specific, testable hypotheses that might explain the outbreak of war. Is there a relationship between the number of alliance commitments in the international system and the number of wars that are fought? Is there a relationship between the number of great powers in the international system and the number of wars? Is there a relationship between the number of wars over time and the severity of the conflicts? Which factors are *most* correlated over time with the outbreak of war? And how are these factors related to each other? What is the correlation between international system–level factors—such as the existence of international organizations—and the outbreak of war? Although answering these questions will never *prove* that a particular factor is the cause of war, the answers could suggest some high-level correlations that merit theoretical explanation. That is the goal of this research project and many others following in the behavioralist scientific tradition.

Another example of research in the behavioral tradition can be found in human rights literature. The question many scholars probe is why countries violate human rights treaties. Is it because states never intended to follow the provisions? Is signing onto treaties just cheap talk? Is it because there is no threat of direct international enforcement? Or is it because states often lack the capacity to implement new standards? Sociologist Wade M. Cole began with a hypothesis, unlike the Correlates of War project, which began with data collection, that "noncompliance with international treaty obligations is neither willful or premediated."[14] Rather, it depends on a state's bureaucratic efficiency. Using data from each independent variable of state bureaucratic efficiency and dependent variables of state empowerment and physical integrity rights data found in the Cingranelli-Richards (CIRI) Human Rights Dataset, Cole uses sophisticated statistical models that confirm his expectations. Improvements in a state's empowerment and physical-integrity rights after the signing of the International Covenant on Civil and Political Rights depend on state capacity.

Yet methodological problems occur in both projects. The Correlates of War database looks at all international wars, irrespective of the different political, military, social, and technological contexts. Can wars of the late 1800s be explained by the same factors as the wars of the new millennium? Answering that question has led subsequent researchers to expand the data set to include militarized interstate disputes, conflicts that do not involve a full-scale war. And those data include not only international and civil wars but also regional internal, intercommunal, and nonstate wars.[15] The human rights study also involves major problems of measurement and operationalization of key variables. How can one measure concepts like state's empowerment and state capacity? Many different indicators need to be combined. And data may not be available for all states across all the time periods studied. In each case, alternative explanations need to be investigated. Such studies are never an end in themselves, only a means to improve explanation and to provide other scholars with hypotheses that warrant further testing.

Disillusionment with behavioral approaches has taken several forms. First, data have to be selected and compiled. Different data may lead to substantially different conclusions. Witness the contrasting assessments on the question of whether there has been a decline in global violence, whether the world is, in fact, more peaceful. Second, some critics suggest that attention to data and methods has overwhelmed the substance of their research. Few would doubt the importance of Singer and Small's initial excursion into the causes of war, but even the researchers themselves admitted losing sight of the important questions in their quest to compile data and hone research methods. Some scholars, still within the behavioral orientation, suggest simplifying esoteric methods to refocus on the substantive questions. Third, to still others, many of the foundational questions—the nature of humanity and society—are neglected by behavioralists because they are not easily testable by empirical methods. These critics suggest returning to the philosophical roots of international relations. Most scholars remain firmly committed to behavioralism and the scientific method, pointing to the slow incremental progress that has been made in explaining the interactions of states.

⚫ BEHIND THE HEADLINES

Is the World Becoming More Peaceful?

Headlines such as "The Decline in Global Violence: Reality or Myth?" or "Is the World Becoming More Peaceful?" pique our interest.[a] As we saw at the beginning of the chapter, former chairman of the Joint Chiefs of Staff Martin Dempsey and psychologist Steven Pinker (and no doubt many others) come to quite different answers to these questions. What explains the differences in their perspectives?

Pinker argues that the world was much more violent in the past. Violence in Pinker's analysis includes all types of violence—murder, tribal warfare, slavery, executions, rape. His "past" is centuries. He cites statistics showing that tribal warfare was nine times as deadly as twentieth-century warfare and the murder rate in Medieval Europe was 30 times more than it is today. Slavery, he points out, existed for thousands of years, having declined only in the last 50 years. And, in his view, the numbers affected by the violence needed to be compared to the relative size of the population at the time. So while the numbers of deaths and violent acts today may be larger, they are much smaller compared to the size of the population: in the seventeenth century, the "wars of religion" killed about 2 percent of the population in the warring states, while in the twentieth century, the deadliest century in absolute numbers, just 0.7 percent of the people died in battle. Comparing the past with more contemporary data, Pinker sees a decline in wars between great powers. World Wars I and II represent spikes from what is generally a downward trend. Post 1946, there has been a decline in deaths on a per capita basis in all different kinds of wars: colonial wars, civil wars, internationalized civil wars, genocide, as well as interstate conflicts.

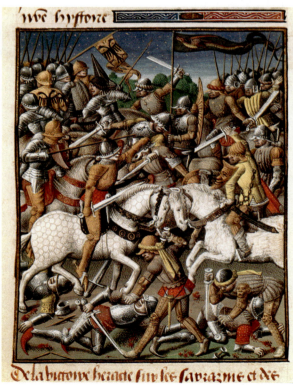

People argue that our world is more peaceful than it was centuries ago. Is that true? How do we know?

Dempsey, and certainly many others in the policy community, see a different reality. The total number of armed conflicts of all types tripled from the 1950s to the 1990s. And though most were relatively low-intensity conflicts with limited fatalities and wartime fatalities have declined dramatically—from 240 battle-related deaths per million of the world's population in 1950 to less than 10 per million in 2007—the numbers are still too high if you are responsible for the lives of others. Those that see today's world as overly violent question the reliability of the data from earlier centuries. Do we really know that in hunter-gather societies, warfare was responsible for 15 percent of fatalities as Pinker asserts? Many anthropologists claim that no evidence suggests that the earliest human societies were warlike. And we actually have had no reliable data about murder rates and rates of organized crime in most developing countries until only very recently, yet Pinker's argument includes all those types of violence.

Pinker's explanation for the decline in violence is that while individuals may still be inclined toward revenge, sadism, and violence, other forces—"better angels"—are steering people in another direction. Governments and better education implore people to control their impulses and negotiate with others. Democratization helps; democratic states are less likely to fight each other. Free trade helps; those who trade are less likely to fight. International institutions help; member states are less likely to fight each other.

Examining past trends should help us predict the future. Dempsey and others would more than likely see a bleak future. They predict future confrontations in not only the Middle East but also East Asia, where nationalism in China, Japan, and others is coming to a head. Pinker himself makes no predictions about the future, although if his argument is correct, then despite people's deepest urges, the future should become even more peaceful.

FOR CRITICAL ANALYSIS

1. **Based on what you know so far, who has the better argument about whether our world is more peaceful today—Dempsey or Pinker? What kind of evidence would strengthen each of their arguments?**

2. **In your opinion, is it important to debate these questions? Why or why not?**

a. See Human Security Report Project, "The Decline in Global Violence: Reality or Myth?" (March 3, 2014) and Carnegie Council for Ethics in International Affairs, "Is the World Becoming More Peaceful?" (Sept. 27, 2012).

Does choosing one method over another make a difference in the research findings? Although there are few systematic comparisons, evidence suggests that in human rights research, the findings do tend to vary by method.[16] Qualitative researchers in the historical and philosophical tradition, often employing case studies of a specific human rights issue over a long period, generally find progress in human rights records. And they find that new human rights norms have emerged. In contrast, behavioral researchers, in general, find less evidence of changes in state behavior. Usually drawing on large "N" studies, including many states over decades when data are available, researchers find only marginal improvements in a state's human rights record. What explains these divergent findings? Differences in operationalization, issues, periods, and availability of data are all responsible for the difference in findings. This divergence has led researchers to plead for more mixed-method research. Multi-method projects can help us overcome the disturbing finding that different methods lead to different substantive conclusions.

Alternative Approaches

Some international relations scholars are dissatisfied with using history, philosophy, or behavioral tools. Constructivists have turned to discourse analysis to answer the foundational questions of international relations. To trace how ideas shape identities, constructivists analyze culture, norms, procedures, and social practices. They probe how identities are shaped and change over time. They use texts, interviews, and archival material, and they research local practices by riding public transportation and standing in lines. By using multiple sets of data, they create thick description. The case studies found in Peter Katzenstein's edited volume *The Culture of National Security* use this approach. Drawing on analyses of Soviet foreign policy at the end of the Cold War, German and Japanese security policy from militarism to antimilitarism, and Arab national identity, the authors search for security interests defined by actors who are responding to changing cultural factors. These studies show how social and cultural factors shape national security policy in ways that contradict realist or liberal expectations.[17]

The postmodernists seek to deconstruct the basic concepts of the field, such as the state, the nation, rationality, and realism, by searching texts (or sources) for hidden meanings underneath the surface, in the subtext. Once those hidden meanings are revealed, the postmodernists seek to replace the once-orderly picture with disorder, to replace the dichotomies with multiple portraits. Cynthia Weber, for example, argues that sovereignty (the independence of a state) is neither well defined nor consistently grounded. Digging below the surface of sovereignty, going beyond evaluations of the traditional philosophers, she has discovered that conceptualizations of sovereignty are constantly shifting, depending on the exigencies of the moment and the values of different communities. The multiple meanings of sovereignty are conditioned by time, place, and historical circumstances.[18] More specifically, Karen T. Litfin shows how norms of sovereignty are shifting to address ecological destruction, although the process remains a contested one.[19] These analyses have profound implications for the theory and practice of international relations, which are rooted in state sovereignty and accepted practices that reinforce sovereignty. They challenge conventional understandings.

Postmodernists also seek to find the voices of "the others," those individuals who have been disenfranchised and marginalized in international relations. Christine Sylvester illustrates her approach with a discussion of the Greenham Common Peace Camp, a group of mostly women who in the early 1980s walked more than 100 miles to a British air force base to protest plans to deploy missiles at the base. Although the marchers were ignored by the media—and thus were "voiceless"—they maintained a politics of resistance, recruiting other political action groups near the camp and engaging members of the military stationed at the base. In 1988, when the Intermediate Range Nuclear Force Treaty was signed, dismantling the missiles, the women moved to another protest site, drawing public attention to Britain's role in the nuclear era.[20] Scholars in this tradition also probe how the voiceless *dalit* (or untouchables) have fought for rights in South Asia, how the disabled have found a voice in international forums, and how some, like children born of rape, have not found a voice.[21]

No important question of international relations today can be answered with exclusive reliance on any one method. History, whether in the form of an extended case study (Peloponnesian War) or a study of multiple wars (Correlates of War or militarized interstate disputes), provides useful answers. Philosophical traditions offer both cogent reasoning and the framework for the major discussions of the day. But behavioral methods dominate because they are increasingly using mixed methods, combining the best of social-science methods and other approaches. And the newer methods of discourse analysis, thick description, and postmodernism provide an even richer base from which the international relations scholar can draw.

In Sum: Making Sense of International Relations

How can we, as students, begin to make sense of international political events in our daily lives? How have scholars of international relations helped us make sense of the world around us? This chapter has introduced the major theories of international relations, including the realist, liberal, radical, and constructivist approaches.

TABLE 1.2	TOOLS FOR STUDYING INTERNATIONAL RELATIONS
TOOL	**METHOD**
History	Examines individual or multiple cases
Philosophy	Develops rationales from core texts and analytical thinking
Behavioralism	Finds patterns in human behavior and state behavior using empirical methods, grounded in scientific method
Alternatives	Deconstructs major concepts and uses discourse analysis to build thick description; finds voices of "others"

These theories provide frameworks for asking and answering core foundational questions. To answer these questions, international relations scholars turn to many other disciplines, including history, philosophy, behavioral psychology, and critical studies (see Table 1.2). International relations is a pluralistic and eclectic discipline.

To understand the development of international relations theory, we need to examine general historical trends for developments in the state and the international system, particularly events in Europe during the nineteenth and twentieth centuries. This "stuff" of diplomatic history is the subject of Chapter 2. Chapter 3 is designed to help us think about the development of international relations theoretically through several frameworks—liberalism, realism, radicalism, and constructivism. Chapters 4, 5, and 6 examine the levels of analysis in international relations. Thus, Chapter 4 examines the international system; Chapter 5, the state; and Chapter 6, the individual. Each of these chapters is organized around the theoretical frameworks, as we compare liberal, realist, and radical descriptions and explanations, augmented, when appropriate, with constructivism. Chapter 7 explores and analyzes the roles of international organizations, international law, and nongovernmental actors. The last four chapters study the major issues of international relations: in Chapter 8, war and strife; in Chapter 9, international political economy; in Chapter 10, human rights; and in Chapter 11, the transnational issues of the twenty-first century.

Discussion Questions

1. A respected family member picks up this book and sees the word *theory* in the first chapter. She is skeptical about the value of theory. Explain to her the utility of developing a theoretical perspective.

2. Philosophy is your passion, but you find international relations moderately interesting. How can you integrate your passion with this pragmatic interest? What questions can you explore?

3. You are a history major skilled in researching the historical archives. Suggest two research projects that you might undertake to further your understanding of international relations.

4. How can the study of international relations be made more scientific? What are the problems with doing so?

Key Terms

anarchy (p. 9)

behavioralism (p. 12)

international relations (p. 4)

normative (p. 10)

02

Visits to the Yasukuni Shrine by Japanese politicians are always controversial for Chinese and Koreans who suffered at the hands of Japan's military aggression. The shrine commemorates those who died in the service of the Empire of Japan, including those convicted of war crimes at Nanking during World War II.

THE HISTORICAL CONTEXT OF CONTEMPORARY INTERNATIONAL RELATIONS

The morning of December 12, 1937, dawned cold in China's new capital, Nanking. Chinese soldiers, weak and demoralized, watched as soldiers of Imperial Japan maneuvered heavy guns into position for an assault on the city. The Japanese attacked from three directions, supported by heavy artillery and aerial bombardment. Some Chinese troops dropped their weapons and ran, others stripped off their uniforms and tried to blend in as civilians, while still others resolved to fight on, beyond the city.

The next day, Japan's army entered Nanking; all hell broke loose. Chinese soldiers who raised their hands and knelt in surrender were simply executed. Many more were bayonetted or beheaded. Women and girls as young as six or seven were raped. Thousands were raped and gang raped each day, and usually murdered afterward. The rapes, murders, executions, torture, and humiliation of thousands of human beings were witnessed by an international community of journalists, missionaries, and businesspeople who maintained delegations in China's capital. Their letters of complaint to Japanese authorities went unanswered. By January 1938, about one month after the carnage had begun, the Japanese Army had purportedly murdered a staggering 300,000 noncombatants.

For the Chinese today, the "Massacre" or "Rape of Nanking" is never forgotten. The fact that Japanese officials honoring the war dead visit the Yasukuni Shrine today angers the Chinese, who are forced to remember those horrible events.

Students of international relations need to understand the events and trends of the past. Theorists recognize that historical circumstances have shaped core concepts in the field—concepts such as the state, the nation, sovereignty, power, and balance of power. It will prove difficult to understand the contemporary politics of the Koreas, China, and Japan, for example, without understanding how the peoples of each present-day state remember the events of World War II.

In large part, the roots of the contemporary international system are found in Europe-centered Western civilization. Of course, great civilizations thrived in other parts of the world, too. India and China, among others, had extensive, vibrant civilizations long before the historical events covered here. But the European emphasis is justified because for better or worse, in both theory and practice, contemporary international relations is rooted in the European experience. In this chapter, we will begin by looking at Europe in the period immediately preceding and following the Thirty Years' War (1618–48). We then consider Europe's relationship with the rest of the world during the nineteenth century, and we conclude with an analysis of the major transitions during the twentieth and early twenty-first centuries.

LEARNING OBJECTIVES

- Analyze which historical periods have most influenced the development of international relations.

- Describe the historical origins of the state.

- Understand why international relations scholars use the Treaties of Westphalia as a benchmark.

- Explain the historical origins of the European balance-of-power system.

- Explain how the Cold War became a series of confrontations between the United States and the Soviet Union.

- Analyze the key events that have shaped the post–Cold War world and the first two decades of the new millennium.

The Emergence of the Westphalian System

Most international relations theorists locate the origins of the contemporary states system in Europe in 1648, the year the **Treaties of Westphalia** ended the Thirty Years' War. These treaties marked the end of rule by religious authority in Europe and the emergence of secular authorities. With secular authority came the principle that has provided the foundation for international relations ever since then: the notion of the territorial integrity of states—legally equal and sovereign participants in an international system.

The formulation of **sovereignty**—a core concept in contemporary international relations—was one of the most important intellectual developments leading to the Westphalian revolution. Much of the development of the notion is found in the writings of the French philosopher Jean Bodin (1530–96). To Bodin, sovereignty is the "absolute and perpetual power vested in a commonwealth."[1] It resides not in an individual but in a state; thus, it is perpetual. It is "the distinguishing mark of the sovereign that he cannot in any way be subject to the commands of another, for it is he who makes law for the subject, abrogates law already made, and amends obsolete law."[2]

Although, ideally, sovereignty is absolute, in reality, according to Bodin, it is not without limits. Leaders are limited by divine law and natural law: "All the princes on earth are subject to the laws of God and of nature." They are also limited by the type of regime—"the constitutional laws of the realm"—be it a monarchy, an aristocracy, or a democracy. And lastly, leaders are limited by covenants, contracts with promises to the people within the commonwealth, and treaties with other states, though there is no supreme arbiter in relations among states.[3] Thus, Bodin provided the conceptual glue of sovereignty that would emerge with the Westphalian agreement.

The Thirty Years' War devastated Europe. The war, which had begun as a religious dispute between Catholics and Protestants, ended due to mutual exhaustion and bankruptcy. Princes and mercenary armies ravaged the central European countryside, fought frequent battles and undertook ruinous sieges, and plundered the civilian population to secure supplies while in the field. But the treaties that ended the conflict had three key impacts on the practice of international relations.

First, the Treaties of Westphalia embraced the notion of sovereignty. With one stroke, virtually all the small states in central Europe attained sovereignty. The Holy Roman Empire was dead. Monarchs—and not a supranational chruch—gained the authority to decide which version of Christianity was appropriate for their subjects. With the pope and the emperor stripped of this power, the notion of the territorial state came into focus and people increasingly accepted it as normal. The Treaties not only legitimized territoriality and the right of *states*—as the sovereign, territorially contiguous principalities increasingly came to be known—to choose their own religion, but the Treaties also established that states had the right to determine their own domestic policies, free from external pressure and with full jurisdiction in their own geographic space. The Treaties thus introduced the principle of noninterference in the affairs of other states.

Second, because the leaders of Europe's most powerful countries had seen the devastation wrought by mercenaries in war, after the Treaties of Westphalia, these countries sought to establish their own permanent national militaries. The growth of such forces led to increasingly centralized control, since the state had to collect taxes to pay for these militaries and leaders assumed absolute control over the troops. The state with a national army emerged as a powerful force—its sovereignty acknowledged and its secular base firmly established. And that state's power increased. Larger territorial units gained an advantage as armaments became more standardized and more lethal.

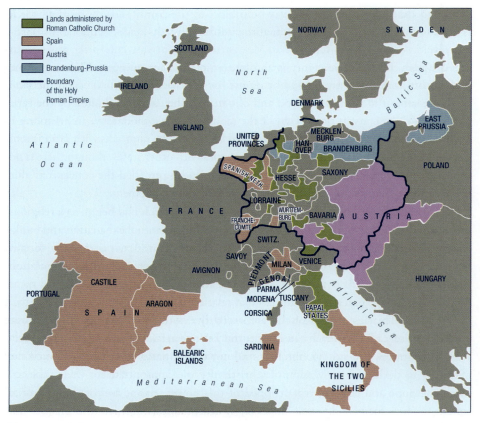

Europe, c. 1648

IN FOCUS   KEY DEVELOPMENTS AFTER WESTPHALIA

- Concept and practice of sovereignty develops.

- Capitalist economic system emerges (stable expectations facilitate long-term investment).

- Centralized control of institutions to facilitate the creation and maintenance of military; military power grows.

Third, the Treaties of Westphalia established a core group of states that dominated the world until the beginning of the nineteenth century: Austria, Russia, Prussia, England, France, and the United Provinces (the area now comprising the Netherlands). Those in the west—England, France, and the United Provinces—underwent an economic revival under the aegis of liberal capitalism, whereas those in the east—Prussia and Russia—reverted to feudal practices. In the west, private enterprise was encouraged. States improved their infrastructure to facilitate commerce, and great trading companies and banks emerged. In contrast, in the east, serfs remained on the land, and economic development was stifled. Yet in both regions, states led by a monarch with absolute power (called "absolutist" states) dominated, with Louis XIV ruling in France (1643–1715), Peter the Great in Russia (1682–1725), and Frederick II in Prussia (1740–86).

The most important social theorist of the time was the Scottish economist Adam Smith (1723–90). In *An Inquiry into the Nature and Causes of the Wealth of Nations,* Smith argued that the notion of a market should apply to all social orders. Individuals— laborers, owners, investors, consumers—should be permitted to pursue their own interests, unfettered by all but the most modest state regulations. According to Smith, each individual acts rationally to maximize her or his own interests. With groups of individuals pursuing their interests, economic efficiency is enhanced, and more goods and services are produced and consumed. At the aggregate level, the wealth of the state and that of the international system are similarly enhanced. What makes the system work is the so-called invisible hand of the market: when individuals pursue their rational self-interests, the system (the market) operates in a way that benefits everyone.[4] Smith's explication of how competing units enable market capitalism to ensure economic vitality has had a profound effect on states' economic policies and political choices, which we will explore in Chapter 9. But other ideas of the period would also dramatically alter governance in the nineteenth, twentieth, and twenty-first centuries.

Europe in the Nineteenth Century

Two revolutions ushered in the nineteenth century—the American Revolution (1773–1785) against British rule and the French Revolution (1789) against absolutist rule. Both revolutions were the product of Enlightenment thinking as well as social-contract theory. Enlightenment thinkers saw individuals as rational, capable of understanding the laws governing them and capable of working to improve their condition in society.

The Aftermath of Revolution: Core Principles

Two core principles emerged in the aftermath of the American and French revolutions. The first was that absolutist rule is subject to limits imposed by man. In *Two Treatises of Government,* the English philosopher John Locke (1632–1704) attacked absolute power and the notion of the divine right of kings. Locke argued that the state is a beneficial institution created by rational men to protect both their natural rights (life, liberty, and property) and their self-interests. Men freely enter into this political arrangement, agreeing to establish government to ensure natural rights for all. The crux of Locke's argument is that political power ultimately rests with the people, rather than with a leader or monarch. The monarch derives **legitimacy** from the consent of the governed.[5]

The second core principle was **nationalism**, wherein a people comes to identify with a common past, language, customs, and territory. Individuals who share such characteristics are motivated to participate actively in the political process as a **nation**. For example, during the French Revolution, a patriotic appeal was made to the *French* masses to defend the French *nation* and its new ideals. This appeal forged an emotional link between the people and the state, regardless of social class. These two principles—legitimacy and nationalism—arose out of the American and French revolutions to provide the foundation for politics in the nineteenth and twentieth centuries.

The Napoleonic Wars

The political impact of nationalism in Europe was profound. The nineteenth century opened with war in Europe on an unprecedented scale. France's status as a revolutionary power made it an enticing target of other European states intent on stamping out the contagious idea of government by popular consent. In addition, France appeared disorganized and weak, stemming from years of internal conflict. As a result, following its revolution, France became embroiled in an escalating series of wars with Austria, Britain, and Prussia, which culminated in the rise of a "low-born" Corsican artillery officer named Napoleon Bonaparte to leader of the French military and, eventually, to the rank of emperor of France.

Napoleon, with help from other talented officers, set about reorganizing and regularizing the French military. Making skillful use of French national zeal, Napoleon fielded large, well-armed, and passionately motivated armies. Modest changes in technology—in particular, more efficient cultivation of the potato—made possible the advent of a *magazine* system; this system meant war supplies could be stored in pre-positioned locations along likely campaign routes so troops could retrieve them on the move and avoid having to stop and forage for food. In combination with nationalism, the magazine system made it possible for the French to field larger, more mobile, and more reliable armies that could employ innovative tactics unavailable to the smaller professional armies of France's rivals, such as the highly regarded Prussian army. Through a series of famous battles, including those at Jena and Auerstedt (1806), in which Napoleon's armies shattered those of "invincible" Prussia, Napoleon was able to conquer nearly the whole of Europe in a few short years.

Yet the same nationalist fervor that brought about much of Napoleon's success also led to his downfall. In Spain and Russia, Napoleon's armies met nationalists who fought a different sort of war. Rather than facing French forces in direct confrontations, Spanish *guerrillas* used intimate local knowledge to mount hit-and-run attacks on French

The dramatic successes and failures of France's Napoleon Bonaparte illustrated both the power and the limits of nationalism, new military technology, and organization.

occupying forces. The Spanish guerrillas also enjoyed the support of Britain, whose unrivaled mastery of the seas meant the country could lend supplies and occasional expeditionary forces. When local French forces attempted to punish the Spanish into submission by barbarism (including looting, torture, rape, and execution of prisoners and suspected insurgents without trial), resistance to French occupation escalated. The cost to France was high, draining away talented soldiers and cash and damaging French morale far beyond Spain. When Napoleon invaded Russia in 1812 with an army numbering a staggering 422,000, the Russians also refused to give direct battle. Instead, they retreated toward their areas of supply, destroying all available food and shelter behind them in what came to be known as a "scorched earth" policy. The advancing French began to suffer from severe malnutrition, with the entire army slowly starving to death as it advanced to Moscow.

By the time the French reached the Russian capital, the government had already evacuated. The French army occupying Moscow had dwindled to a mere 110,000. Napoleon waited in vain for the tsar to surrender. After realizing the magnitude of his vulnerability, Napoleon attempted to return to France before Russia's harsh winter set in. But, it was already too late. By the time French troops crossed the original line of departure at the Nieman River, Napoleon's *Grande Armeé* had been reduced to a mere 10,000. The proud emperor's final defeat in 1815 by English and Prussian forces at the Battle of Waterloo (in present-day Belgium) was assured.

Peace at the Core of the European System

Following the defeat of Napoleon in 1815 and the establishment of peace by the Congress of Vienna, the five powers of Europe—Austria, Britain, France, Prussia, and Russia—known as the Concert of Europe, ushered in a period of relative peace in the international political system. These great powers fought no major wars after the defeat of Napoleon until the Crimean War in 1854, and in that war, both Austria and Prussia remained neutral. Other local wars of brief duration were fought, and in these, too, some of the five major powers remained neutral. Meeting more than 30 times before World War I at a series of ad hoc conferences, the Concert became a club of like-minded leaders. Through these meetings, these countries legitimized both the independence of new European states and the division of Africa among the colonial powers.

The fact that peace among great powers prevailed during this time seems surprising since major economic, technological, and political changes were radically altering power relationships. Industrialization, a critical development during the nineteenth century, was a double-edged sword. During the second half of the nineteenth century, the powers focused all attention on the processes of industrialization. Great Britain was the leader, outstripping all rivals in its output of coal, iron, and steel and the export of manufactured goods. In addition, Britain became the source of finance capital, the

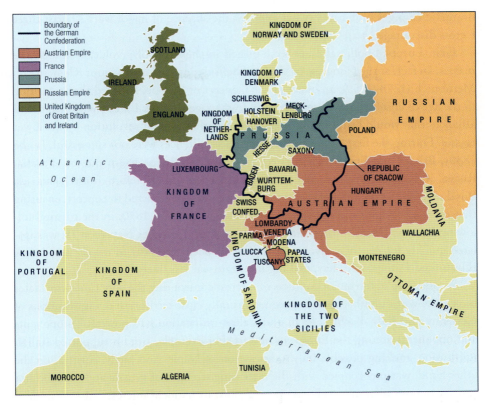

Europe, c. 1815

banker for the continent and, in the twentieth century, for the world. Industrialization spread through virtually all areas of western Europe as the masses flocked to the cities and entrepreneurs and middlemen scrambled for economic advantage. In addition, more than any other factor, industrialization led the middle classes to capture political power at the expense of the aristocratic classes. Unlike the aristocratic classes, the middle classes did not depend on land for wealth and power; their ability to invent, use, and improve industrial machines and processes gave them power. As machine power became indispensable to the security (think artillery, battleships) and prosperity (think merchant ships and railroads) of states, the middle classes began to seek more political power to match their contributions.

The population of Europe soared and commerce surged as transportation corridors across Europe and the globe were strengthened. Political changes were dramatic: Italy was unified in 1870; Germany was formed out of 39 different fragments in 1871; the United Kingdom of the Netherlands was divided into the Netherlands and Belgium in the 1830s; and the Ottoman Empire gradually disintegrated, leading to independence for Greece in 1829 and for Moldavia and Wallachia (Romania) in 1856. With such dramatic changes under way, what explains the absence of major war? At least three factors discouraged war.

First, Europe's political elites were united in their fear of revolution among the masses. In fact, at the Congress of Vienna, the Austrian diplomat Count Klemens von Metternich (1773–1859), architect of the Concert of Europe, believed that returning to the age of absolutism was the best way to manage Europe. Elites envisioned grand alliances that would bring European leaders together to fight revolution by the lower classes. During the first half of the century, these alliances were not successful. In the 1830s, Britain and France sided together against the three eastern powers (Prussia, Russia, and Austria). In 1848, all five powers faced demands for reform from the masses. But during the second half of the century, European leaders acted in concert, ensuring that mass revolutions did not spread from state to state. In 1870, in the turmoil following France's defeat in the Franco-Prussian War, the leader Napoleon III was isolated quickly for fear of a revolution that never occurred. Fear of revolt from below thus united European leaders, making interstate war less likely.

Second, two of the major conflicts of interest confronting the core European states took place within, rather than between, culturally close territories: the unifications of Germany and Italy. Both German and Italian unification had powerful proponents and opponents among the European powers. For example, Britain supported Italian unification, making possible Italy's annexation of Naples and Sicily. Austria, on the other hand, was preoccupied with the increasing strength of Prussia and thus did not actively oppose what may well have been against its national interest—the creation of two sizable neighbors out of myriad independent units. German unification was acceptable to Russia, as long as Russian interests in Poland were respected. German unification also got support from Britain's dominant middle class, which viewed a stronger Germany as a potential counterbalance to France. Thus, because the energies and resources of German and Italian peoples were concentrated on the struggle to form single contiguous territorial states, and because the precise impact of the newly unified states on the European balance of power was unknown, a wider war was averted.

The third factor in supporting peace in Europe was the complex and crucial phenomenon of imperialism-colonialism.

Imperialism and Colonialism in the European System before 1870

The discovery of the "new" world—as Europeans after 1492 called it—led to rapidly expanding communication between the Americas and Europe. The same blue-water navigation technology also made contact with Asia less costly and more frequent. The first to arrive in the new world were explorers seeking discovery, riches, and personal glory; merchants seeking raw materials and trade relations; and clerics seeking to convert "savages" to Christianity. But the staggering wealth they discovered, and the relative ease with which it could be acquired, led to increasing competition among European powers for territories in far-distant lands. Most of the European powers became empires and, once established, claimed as sovereign territory the lands indigenous peoples occupied. These empires are the origin of the term **imperialism**, the annexation of distant territory (most often by force) and its inhabitants to an empire. **Colonialism**, which often followed or accompanied imperialism, refers to the settling of people from a home country like Spain among indigenous peoples of a distant territory like Mexico. The two terms are thus subtly different; most but not all imperial powers settled their own citizens among the peoples whose territories they annexed, and some states established colonies but did not identify themselves as empires. Still, most scholars use the two terms interchangeably.

This process of annexation by conquest or treaty continued for 400 years. As the technology of travel and communications improved, and as Europeans developed vaccines and cures for tropical diseases, the costs to European powers of imposing their will on indigenous people continued to drop. Europeans were welcomed in some places but were resisted in most. In most cases, Europeans overcame that resistance with very little cost or risk. They met spears with machine guns and horses with heavy artillery. In the dawning machine age, it became more common to target indigenous civilians deliberately, often with near genocidal results. By the close of the nineteenth century, almost the whole of the globe was "ruled" by European states. Great Britain was the largest and most successful of the imperial powers, but even small states, such as Portugal and the Netherlands, maintained important colonies abroad.

The process also led to the establishment of a "European" identity. European states enjoyed a solidarity among themselves, based on their being European, Christian, "civilized," and white. These traits differentiated an "us"—white Christian Europeans—from an "other"—the rest of the world. With the rise of mass literacy and increasing contact with the colonial world due to industrialization, Europeans more than ever saw their commonalities, the uniqueness of being "European." This identity was, in part, a return to the same kind of unity felt under the Roman Empire and Roman law, a secular form of medieval Christendom, and a larger Europe as Kant and Rousseau had envisioned (see Chapter 1). The Congress of Vienna and the Concert of Europe gave more concrete form to these beliefs. The flip side of these beliefs was the ongoing exploration, conquest, and exploitation of peoples in the non-European world and the subsequent establishment of colonies there.

The Industrial Revolution provided the European states with the military and economic capacity to engage in territorial expansion. Some imperial states were motivated by economic gains, seeking new external markets for manufactured goods and obtaining, in turn, raw materials to fuel their industrial growth. For others, the motivation was cultural and religious—to spread the Christian faith and the ways of white "civilization" to the "dark" continent and beyond. For still others, the motivation was political. Since the European balance of power prevented direct confrontation in Europe, European state rivalries were played out in Africa and Asia.

Two important questions follow. First, why did territorial expansion only happen in Asia and Africa and not Latin America? Second, how did Germany and Italy—two European powers who unified late— react to having so few of their own colonies as compared to, say, Portugal, a much smaller state? Latin America was "protected" from late-nineteenth-century European colonial and imperial attention by the Monroe Doctrine—the U.S. policy of defending the Western Hemisphere from European interference.

In the nineteenth century, explorers often paved the way for the colonization of African and Asian lands by European powers. Here, a French expedition seeks to stake a claim in central Africa.

As to Italy and Germany, once they unified and industrialized, many within each state felt that to have international respect (and to guarantee cheap imports of raw materials), both states "needed" to annex or colonize countries in Asia or Africa. Italy attempted to conquer and colonize Ethiopia, a Christian empire in the horn of Africa, but suffered a humiliating defeat at the Battle of Adowa in 1896.

To mollify Germany's imperial ambitions, during the Congress of Berlin in 1885, the major powers divided up Africa, "giving" Germany a sphere of influence in east Africa (Tanganyika), west Africa (Cameroon and Togo), and southern Africa (Southwest Africa). European imperialism seemed to provide a convenient outlet for Germany's aspirations as a great power, without endangering the delicate balance of power within Europe itself. By the end of the nineteenth century, 85 percent of Africa was under the control of European states.

In Asia, only Japan and Siam (Thailand) were not under direct European or U.S. influence. China is an excellent example of the extent of external domination. Under the Qing dynasty, which began in the seventeenth century, China had slowly been losing political, economic, and military power for several hundred years. During the nine-

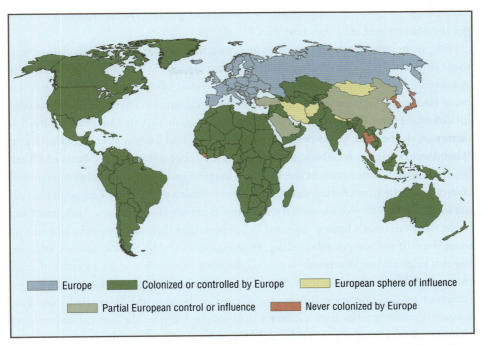

Europe | **Colonized or controlled by Europe** | **European sphere of influence**
Partial European control or influence | **Never colonized by Europe**

This map shows every country that has been under European control at any point from the 1500s to the 1960s. The United States, Mexico, and most of Latin America became independent of Europe in the eighteenth and nineteenth centuries, respectively, but much of the rest of the world remained under colonial control until after World War II.

teenth century, British merchants began to trade with China for tea, silk, and porcelain, often paying for these products with smuggled opium. In 1842, the British defeated China in the Opium War, forcing China to cede various political and territorial rights to foreigners through a series of unequal treaties. European states and Japan were able to occupy large portions of Chinese territory, claiming to have exclusive trading rights in particular regions. Foreign powers exercised separate "spheres of influence" in China. By 1914, Europeans had colonized four-fifths of the world, and still controlled much of it.

The United States eventually became an imperial power as well. Having won the 1898 Spanish-American War, pushing the Spanish out of the Philippines, Puerto Rico, Cuba, and other small islands, the United States acquired its own small empire.

The struggle for economic power led to heedless exploitation of colonial areas, particularly in Africa and Asia. One striking aspect of the contest between the Europeans and the peoples they encountered in Africa and Asia is that European weapons and communications technology proved very difficult for indigenous peoples to resist. European states and their militaries became accustomed to winning battles against vastly more numerous adversaries, and often attributed their ability to do so to their military technology. As one famous apologist for colonialism put it: "Thank God that we have got the Maxim gun, and they have not."[6]

But, as the nineteenth century drew to a close, the assumption that imperialist countries could cheaply control vast stretches of distant territory containing large numbers of aggrieved or oppressed people with only a few colonial officers and administrators was being challenged with increasing frequency. For Great Britain, the world's most successful colonial power, the future of colonialism was clearly signaled by Britain's Pyrrhic victory in the Second Anglo-Boer War (1899–1902; also known as the South African War). British soldiers fought, against Boer commandos (white descendants of Dutch immigrants to South Africa in the 1820s), a lengthy and bitter counterinsurgency war that claimed the lives of more than 20,000 Boer women and children through the failure of the British to provide sanitary internment conditions, sufficient food, and fresh water. The war, which Britain expected to last no longer than three months and cost no more than 10 million pounds sterling, ended up costing 230 million pounds and lasting two years and eight months. It proved the most expensive war, by an order of magnitude, in British colonial history. The war was largely unpopular in Europe and led to increased tensions between Britain and Germany, because the Boers had purchased advanced infantry rifles from Germany and sought German diplomatic and military intervention during the war. However, the five European powers had still not fought major wars directly against each other.

In sum, much of the competition, rivalry, and tension traditionally marking relations among Europe's states could be acted out far beyond Europe itself. Europeans raced to acquire colonies to achieve increased status, wealth, and power vis-à-vis their rivals. Europeans could imagine themselves as bringing the light of civilization to the "dark" regions of the world, while at the same time acquiring the material resources (mineral wealth and "native levies") they might need in a future war in Europe. Each colonial power understood it might take years to accumulate sufficient resources to gain an advantage in a major European war. Therefore, each state maintained an interest in managing crises so conflicts of interest would not escalate to all-out war. Thus, the "safety valve" of colonialism both reinforced European unity and identity and prevented the buildup of tension in Europe.

By the end of the nineteenth century, however, the toll of political rivalry and economic competition had become destabilizing. Germany's unification, rapid industrialization, and population growth led to an escalation of tension that could not be assuaged in time to prevent war. In 1870, France and Germany fought a major war, in which France suffered defeat. Through a humiliating peace treaty, France was forced to surrender the long-contested provinces of Alsace and Lorraine, which became part of the new Germany. The war and the simmering resentments to which it gave birth were mere harbingers of conflicts to come. In addition, the legacy of colonialism, which had served to defuse tension in Europe, laid the groundwork for enduring resentment of

Europeans by many Asians and Africans; this resentment continues to complicate peace, humanitarian work, and development operations in these areas of the world to this day.

Balance of Power

During the nineteenth century, colonialism, the common interests of conservative European elites, and distraction over the troubled unifications of German and Italian principalities seemed to promote a long peace in Europe. But this condition of relative peace was underpinned by another factor as well: a **balance of power**. The independent European states, each with relatively equal power, feared the emergence of any predominant state (**hegemon**) among them. As a result, they formed alliances to counteract any potentially more powerful faction, thus creating a balance of power. The idea behind a balance of power is simple. States will hesitate to start a war with an adversary whose power to fight and win wars is relatively balanced (*symmetrical*), because the risk of defeat is high. When one state or coalition of states is much more powerful than its adversaries (*asymmetrical*), war is relatively more likely. The treaties signed after 1815 were designed not only to quell revolution from below but also to prevent the emergence of a hegemon, such as France had become under Napoleon. Britain or Russia, at least later in the century, could have assumed a dominant leadership position—Britain because of its economic capability and naval prowess, and Russia because of its relative geographic isolation and extraordinary manpower. However, neither sought to exert hegemonic power; each one's respective capacity to effect a balance of power in Europe was declining and the status quo was acceptable to both states.

Britain and Russia did play different roles, however, in the balance of power. Britain most often played the role of off-shore balancer; for example, it intervened on behalf of the Greeks in their struggle for independence from the Turks in the late 1820s, on behalf of the Belgians during their war of independence against Holland in 1830, on behalf of Turkey against Russia in the Crimean War in 1854–56, and again in the Russo-Turkish War in 1877–78. Thus, Britain ensured that power in Europe remained relatively balanced. Russia's role was as a builder of alliances. The Holy Alliance of 1815 kept Austria, Prussia, and Russia united against revolutionary France, and Russia used its claim on Poland to build a bond with Prussia. Russian interests in the Dardanelles, the strategic waterway linking the Mediterranean Sea and the Black Sea, and in Constantinople (today's Istanbul) overlapped with those of Britain. Thus, these two states, located at the margins of Europe, played key roles in making the balance-of-power system work.

During the last three decades of the nineteenth century, the Concert of Europe frayed, beginning with the Franco-Prussian War (1870) and the Russian invasion of Turkey (Russo-Turkish War, 1877–78). Alliances began to solidify as the balance-of-power system began to weaken. The advent of the railroad gave continental powers such

IN FOCUS

KEY DEVELOPMENTS IN NINETEENTH-CENTURY EUROPE

- From revolutions emerge two concepts: the idea that legitimate rule requires (some) consent of the governed, and nationalism.

- A system managed by the balance of power brings relative peace to Europe. Elites are united in fear of the masses, and domestic concerns are more important than foreign policy.

- European imperialism in Asia and Africa helps to maintain the European balance of power.

- The balance of power breaks down due to imperial Germany's too-rapid growth and the increasing rigidity of alliances, resulting in World War I.

as Germany and Austria-Hungary an enhanced level of economic and strategic mobility equal to that of maritime powers such as Britain. This change reduced Britain's ability to balance power on the continent. Russia, for its part, began to fall markedly behind in the industrialization race, and its relatively few railroads meant that its massive manpower advantage would be less and less able to reach a battlefield in time to determine an outcome. So Russia's power began to wane compared with that of France, Germany, and Austria-Hungary.

The Breakdown: Solidification of Alliances

By the waning years of the nineteenth century, the balance-of-power system had weakened. Whereas alliances previously had been flexible and fluid, now alliances became increasingly rigid. Two camps emerged: the Triple Alliance (Germany, Austria-Hungary, and Italy) in 1882 and the Dual Alliance (France and Russia) in 1893. In 1902, Britain broke from the "balancer" role, joining in a naval alliance with Japan to forestall Russian and Japanese collaboration in China. This alliance marked a significant turn: for the first time, a European state (Great Britain) turned to an Asian one (Japan) to thwart a European power (Russia). And, in 1904, Britain joined with France in an alliance called the Entente Cordiale.

In that same year, Russia and Japan went to war (the Russo-Japanese War) in a contest Europeans widely expected to result in a Japanese defeat. After all, the Japanese had come late to industrialization, and although Japan's naval forces looked impressive on paper, their opponents would be white Europeans. But Russia's industrial backwardness would affect it severely. As the war opened, Japanese forces surrounded a key Russian fortress at Port Arthur. Russia's lack of sufficient railroads meant it could not reinforce its forces in the Far East by rail, so it attempted to relieve the siege by sending a naval flotilla from its Baltic home ports 18,000 miles away. But after a very costly Japanese assault, Port Arthur was captured while the Russian fleet was still at sea. In May 1905, the Russian and Japanese fleets clashed in Tsushima Bay, and the result was perhaps the greatest naval defeat in history: Russia lost eight battleships, some 5,000 sailors were killed, and another 5,000 were captured as prisoners of war. The Japanese lost three torpedo boats and 116 sailors. The impact of Japan's victory would extend far beyond the defeat of Russia in the Far East. An Asian power's defeat of a white colonial power seriously compromised a core ideological foundation of colonialism—that whites were inherently superior to nonwhites. The Russian defeat spurred Japanese expansion and caused Germany to discount Russia's ability to interfere with German ambitions in Europe. Russia's defeat severely compromised the legitimacy of the tsar, setting in motion a revolution that, after 1917, was to topple the Russian empire and replace it with the Union of Soviet Socialist Republics (USSR, or the Soviet Union).

The final collapse of the balance-of-power system came with World War I. Germany's rapid rise in power intensified the destabilizing impact of the hardening of alliances at the turn of the twentieth century. By 1912, Germany had exceeded France and Britain in both heavy industrial output and population growth. Germany also feared Russian efforts to modernize its relatively sparse railroad network. Being "latecomers" to the core of European power, and having defeated France in the Franco-Prussian War (1870), many Germans felt that Germany had not received the diplomatic recognition and status it deserved. This lack of recognition in part explains why Germany encouraged Austria-Hungary to crush Serbia following the assassination of Archduke Franz Ferdinand (heir to the throne of the Austro-Hungarian Empire), who was shot in Sarajevo in June 1914. Like most of Europe's leaders at the time, Germany's leaders believed war made the state and its citizens stronger, and that backing down after a humiliation would only encourage further humiliations. Besides, the outcome of a local war between Austria-Hungary and Serbia was certain to be a quick victory for Germany's most important ally.

But under the tight system of alliances, the fateful shot set off a chain reaction. What Germany had hoped would remain a local war soon escalated to a continental war, once Russia's tsar ordered a premobilization of Russian forces. And once German troops crossed into Belgium (thus violating British-guaranteed Belgian neutrality), that continental war escalated to a world war when Britain sided with France and Russia. The Ottoman Empire, long a rival with Russia, entered the war on the side of Germany and Austria-Hungary. Both sides anticipated a short, decisive war (over by Christmas), but this did not happen. Germany's Schlieffen Plan—its strategy for a decisive victory in a two-front war against Russia and France—failed almost immediately, leading to a

Europe, 1914

ghastly stalemate. Between 1914 and 1918, soldiers from more than a dozen countries endured the persistent degradation of trench warfare and the horrors of poison gas. The "Great War," as it came to be known, saw the introduction of aerial bombing and unrestricted submarine warfare as well. Britain's naval blockade of Germany caused widespread suffering and privation for German civilians. More than 8.5 million soldiers and 1.5 million civilians lost their lives. Germany, Austria-Hungary, the Ottoman Empire, and Russia were defeated, while Britain and France—two of the three "victors"— were seriously weakened. Only the United States, a late entrant into the war, emerged relatively unscathed. The defeat and subsequent dismemberment of the Ottoman Empire by France and Britain—which created new states subject to control and manipulation by both—continues to affect interstate peace in the Middle East to this day.

The Interwar Years and World War II

The end of World War I saw critical changes in international relations. First, three European empires were strained and finally broke up during or near the end of World

War I. With those empires went the conservative social order of Europe; in its place emerged a proliferation of nationalisms. Russia exited the war in 1917, as revolution raged within its territory. The tsar was overthrown and eventually replaced by not only a new leader (Vladimir Ilyich Lenin) but also a new ideology—Communism—that would have profound implications for international politics during the remainder of the twentieth century. The Austro-Hungarian and Ottoman Empires disintegrated. Austria-Hungary was replaced by Austria, Hungary, Czechoslovakia, part of Yugoslavia, and part of Romania. The Ottoman Empire was also reconfigured. Having gradually weakened throughout the nineteenth century, its defeat resulted in the final overthrow of the Ottomans. Arabia rose against Ottoman rule, and British forces occupied Palestine (including Jerusalem) and Baghdad. Turkey became the largest of the successor states that emerged from the disintegration of the Ottoman Empire.

The end of the empires accelerated and intensified nationalisms. In fact, one of President Woodrow Wilson's Fourteen Points in the treaty ending World War I called for self-determination, the right of national groups to self-rule. Technological innovations in the printing industry and a mass audience, now literate, stimulated the nationalism of these various groups (for example, Austrians and Hungarians). Now it was easy and cheap to publish material in the multitude of different European languages and so offer differing interpretations of history and national life.

A second critical change was that Germany emerged from World War I an even more dissatisfied power. Germany had been defeated on the battlefield, but German forces ended the war in occupation of enemy territory. What's more, German leaders had not been honest with the German people. Many German newspapers had been predicting a major breakthrough and victory right up until the armistice of November 11, 1918, so the myth grew that the German military had been "stabbed in the back" by "liberals" (and later Jews) in Berlin. Even more devastating was the fact that the Treaty of Versailles, which formally ended the war, made the subsequent generation of Germans pay the entire economic cost of the war through reparations—$32 billion for wartime damages. As Germany printed more money to pay its reparations, Germans suffered from hyperinflation, causing widespread impoverishment of the middle and working classes. Finally, Germany was no longer allowed to have a standing military, and French and British troops occupied its most productive industrialized region, the Ruhr Valley. Bitterness over these harsh penalties provided the climate for the emergence of conservatives such as the National Socialist Worker's Party (Nazis for short), led by Adolf Hitler. Hitler publicly dedicated himself to righting the "wrongs" imposed on the German people after World War I.

Third, enforcement of the Treaty of Versailles was given to the ultimately unsuccessful **League of Nations**, the intergovernmental organization designed to prevent all future interstate wars. But the organization itself did not have the political weight, the legal instruments, or the legitimacy to carry out the task. The political weight of the League was weakened by the fact that the United States—whose president Woodrow Wilson had been the League's principal architect—itself refused to join, retreating instead to an isolationist foreign policy. Nor did Russia join, nor were any of the vanquished states of the war permitted to participate. The League's legal authority was weak, and the instruments it had for enforcing the peace proved ineffective.

Fourth, the blueprint for a peaceful international order enshrined in Wilson's Fourteen Points failed. Wilson had called for open diplomacy—"open covenants of peace, openly arrived at, after which there shall be no private international understandings of any kind but diplomacy shall proceed always frankly and in public view."[7] Point three was a reaffirmation of economic liberalism, the removal of economic barriers among all the nations consenting to the peace. The League, a "general association of nations" that would ensure war never occurred again, would maintain order. But these principles were not adopted. In the words of historian E. H. Carr, "The characteristic feature of the twenty years between 1919 and 1939 was the abrupt descent from the visionary hopes of the first decade to the grim despair of the second, from a utopia which took little account of reality to a reality from which every element of utopia was rigorously excluded."[8] Liberalism and its utopian and idealist elements were replaced by realism as the dominant international-relations theory—a fundamentally divergent theoretical perspective. (See Chapter 3.)

The world from which these realists emerged was a turbulent one. The German economy imploded; the U.S. stock market plummeted; and the world economy sputtered, and then collapsed. Japan marched into Manchuria in 1931 and into the rest of China in 1937; Italy overran Ethiopia in 1935; fascism, liberalism, and communism clashed.

IN FOCUS

KEY DEVELOPMENTS IN THE INTERWAR YEARS

- Three empires collapse: Russia by revolution, the Austro-Hungarian Empire by dismemberment, and the Ottoman Empire by external wars and internal turmoil. These collapses lead to a resurgence of nationalisms.

- German dissatisfaction with the World War I settlement (Versailles Treaty) leads to the rise of Fascism in Germany. Germany finds allies in Italy and Japan.

- A weak League of Nations is unable to respond to Japanese, Italian, and German aggression. Nor can it prevent or reverse widespread economic depression.

World War II

In the view of most Europeans and many in the United States, Germany, and in particular Adolf Hitler, started World War II. But Japan and Italy also played major roles in the breakdown of interstate order in the 1930s. In 1931, Japan staged the Mukden incident as a pretext for assaulting China and annexing Manchuria. The Japanese invasion of China was marked by horrifying barbarity against the Chinese people, including the rape, murder, and torture of Chinese civilians, and by the increasing inability of Japan's civilian government to restrain its generals in China. Japan's record in Korea was equally brutal. Japan's reputation for savagery against noncombatants in China reached its peak in the Rape of Nanking, discussed at the beginning of the chapter. When news of the massacres and rapes reached the United States—itself already embroiled in a dispute with Japan over Japan's prior conduct in China—a diplomatic crisis ensued, the result of which was war, when Japanese forces attacked the U.S. Seventh Fleet at Pearl Harbor in December 1941.

But Nazi Germany, the **Third Reich**, proved to be the greatest challenge to the nascent interstate order that followed World War I. Adolf Hitler had come to power with a promise to restore Germany's economy and national pride. The core of his economic policies, however, was an over-investment in armaments production. Germany could not actually pay for the foodstuff and raw materials needed to maintain the pace of production, so it bullied its neighbors—mostly much weaker new states to the east, such as Bulgaria, Hungary, and Romania—into ruinous (for the weaker states) trade deals. As one economic historian of the period put it: "The process was circular. The economic crisis itself was largely caused by the extreme pace of German rearmament. One way out would have been to slacken that pace: when that was rejected, Germany was in a position where she was arming in order to expand, and then had to expand in order to continue to arm."[9] But once the other European powers realized how far behind they were, they used every diplomatic opportunity to delay confronting Germany until they themselves might have a chance to succeed. For these and other reasons, including the economic damage both Britain and France suffered in World War I, Britain and France did little to halt Germany's resurgence.

The Third Reich's fascism effectively mobilized the masses in support of the state. It capitalized on the idea that war and conflict were noble activities from which ultimately superior civilizations would be formed. It drew strength from the belief that certain racial groups were superior and others inferior, and it mobilized the disenchanted and the economically weak on behalf of its cause. In autumn 1938, Britain agreed to let Germany occupy the westernmost region of Czechoslovakia, in the hope of averting a general war, or at least delaying war until Britain's defense preparations could be sufficiently strengthened. But this was a false hope. In spring 1939, the Third Reich annexed the remainder of Czechoslovakia, and in September 1939, after having

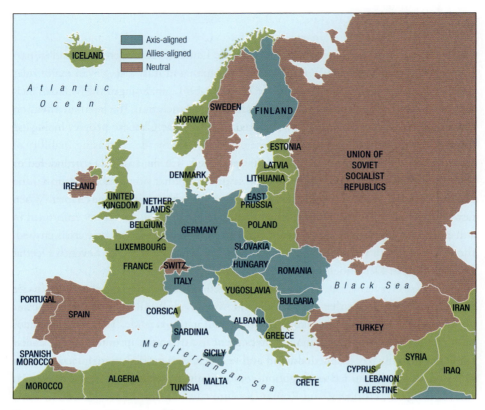

Europe, showing alliances as of 1939

signed a peace treaty with the Soviet Union that divided Poland between them, German forces stormed into Poland from the west while Soviet forces assaulted from the east. Hitler's real intent was to secure his eastern flank against a Soviet threat while he assaulted Norway, Denmark, the Netherlands, and, ultimately, France (intending to force Britain into neutrality). His grand plan then called for Germany to turn east and conquer the Soviet Union. Poland was quickly overcome, but because Britain and France had guaranteed Polish security, the invasion prompted a declaration of war: World War II had begun.

In 1940, Hitler set his plans into motion and succeeded in a series of rapid conquests, culminating in the defeat of France in May. In the late summer and fall, after being repeatedly rebuffed in its efforts to coerce Britain into neutrality, the Third Reich prepared to invade and the Battle of Britain ensued. Fought almost entirely in the air, Britain eventually won the battle with a combination of extreme courage, resourcefulness, and luck; and Hitler was forced to turn east with a hostile Britain at his back. In June 1941, the Third Reich undertook the most ambitious land invasion in history: Operation Barbarossa—its long-planned yet ill-fated invasion of the Soviet Union. This surprise attack led the Soviet Union to join sides with Britain and France.

The power of fascism—in German, Italian, and Japanese versions—led to an uneasy alliance between the communist Soviet Union and the liberal United States, Great Britain, and France, among others (the Allies). That alliance sought to check the Axis powers (Germany, Italy, and Japan), by force if necessary. Thus, during World War II, those fighting against the Axis powers acted in unison, regardless of their ideological disagreements.

At the end of the war in 1945, the Allies prevailed. Italy had already surrendered in September 1943, and the Third Reich and imperial Japan lay in ruins. In Europe, the Soviet Union paid the highest price for the Third Reich's aggression, and, with some justification, considered itself the victor in Europe, with help from the United States and Britain. In the Pacific, the United States, China, and Korea paid the highest price for Japan's aggression. With some justification, the United States considered itself the victor in the Pacific. Two other features of World War II demand attention as well.

First, the Third Reich's military invasion of Poland, the Baltic states, and the Soviet Union was followed by organized killing teams whose sole aim was the mass murder of human beings, regardless of their support for, or resistance to, the German state. Jews in particular were singled out, but Nazi policy extended to gypsies (now called Roma), communists, homosexuals, and even ethnic Germans born with genetic defects such as a cleft palate or a club foot. In Germany, Poland, the Baltic states, Yugoslavia, and the Soviet Union, persons on target lists were forced to abandon their homes. Nazi captors forced these people to work in forced-labor camps under cruel conditions, then either slowly or rapidly murdered them. In East Asia, Japanese forces acted with similar cruelty against Chinese, Vietnamese, and Korean noncombatants. The Japanese often tortured victims or forced them to become subjects in gruesome experiments before murdering them. In many places, women were forced into brothels, or "comfort stations," as Japanese rhetoric of the day described them. The nearly unprecedented brutality of the Axis powers against noncombatants in areas of occupation during the war led to war crimes tribunals and, ultimately, to a major new feature of international politics following the war: the Geneva Conventions of 1948 and 1949. These conventions—which today have the force of international law—formally criminalized many abuses, including torture, murder, and food deprivation, all perpetrated against noncombatants in areas of German and Japanese occupation during World War II. The conventions are collectively known as international humanitarian law (IHL); however, because enforcement is largely voluntary, their effectiveness has often been called into question.

The Germans and Japanese were not the only forces for whom race was a factor in World War II. As documented by John Dower in his book *War without Mercy*, U.S., British, and Australian forces fighting in the Pacific tended to view the Japanese as "apes" or "monkey men." As a result, they rarely took prisoners and were more comfortable in undertaking massive strategic air assaults on Japanese cities. In the United States in 1942, citizens of Japanese descent were summarily deprived of their constitutional rights and interned for the duration of the war. In the Pacific theater, racism affected the conduct and strategies of armed forces on *both* sides.[10]

Second, although Germany surrendered unconditionally in May 1945, the war did not end until the Japanese surrender in August of that year. By this point in the war, Japan had no hope of winning. Japan had made it clear as early as January that it might be willing to surrender, so long as Allied forces did not try or imprison Emperor Hirohito. But the Allies had already agreed they would accept no less than unconditional surrender, so Japan prepared for an invasion by U.S. and possibly Soviet forces, hoping that the threat of massive Allied casualties might yet win it a chance to preserve the emperor from trial and punishment. Instead, on August 6, the United States dropped an atomic bomb on Hiroshima, and three days later, a second bomb on Nagasaki. The casualties were no greater than those experienced in fire-bombings of major Japanese cities earlier that year. But the new weapon, combined with a Soviet declaration of war on Japan the same day as the Nagasaki bombing (and Japanese calculation that the emperor might be spared), led to Japan's unconditional surrender on August 15, 1945.

The end of World War II resulted in a major redistribution of power. The victorious United States and Soviet Union emerged as the new world powers, though the USSR had been severely hurt by the war and remained economically crippled as compared to the United States. Yet what the USSR lacked in economic power, it gained from geopolitical proximity to the two places where the future of the international system would be decided: Western Europe and East Asia. The war also changed political boundaries. The Soviet Union virtually annexed the Baltic states (Latvia, Lithuania, and Estonia) and portions of Austria, Finland, Czechoslovakia, Poland, and Romania; Germany and Korea were divided; and Japan was ousted from much of Asia. Each of these changes contributed to the new international conflict: the **Cold War**.

The Cold War

The leaders of the victors of World War II—Britain's prime minister, Winston Churchill; the United States' president, Franklin Roosevelt; and the Soviet Union's premier, Joseph Stalin—planned during the war for a postwar order. Indeed, the Atlantic Charter of August 14, 1941, called for collaboration on economic issues and prepared for a permanent system of security. These plans were consolidated in 1943 and 1944 and came to fruition in the United Nations in 1945. Yet several other outcomes of World War II help explain the emergence of what we now call the Cold War.

Origins of the Cold War

The first and most important outcome of World War II was the emergence of two superpowers—the United States and the Soviet Union—as the primary actors in the international system, which resulted in the decline of Western Europe as the epicenter of international politics. The second outcome of the war was the intensification of fundamental incompatibilities between these two superpowers in both national interests and ideology. Differences surfaced immediately over geopolitical national interests. Having been invaded from the west on several occasions, including during World War II, the USSR used its newfound power to solidify its sphere of influence in Eastern Europe, specifically in Poland, Czechoslovakia, Hungary, Bulgaria, and Romania. The Soviet leadership believed that ensuring friendly (or at least weak) neighbors on its western borders was vital to the country's national interests. In the United States, there raged a debate between those favoring an aggressive rollback strategy—pushing the USSR back to its own borders—and those favoring a less-aggressive containment strategy. The diplomat and historian George Kennan published in *Foreign Affairs* the famous "X" telegram, in which he argued that because the Soviet Union would always feel military insecurity, it would conduct an aggressive foreign policy. Containing the Soviets, Kennan wrote, should therefore become the cornerstone of the United States' postwar foreign policy.[11]

The United States put the notion of containment into action in the Truman Doctrine of 1947. Justifying material support in Greece against the communists, President Harry Truman asserted, "I believe that it must be the policy of the United States to support free peoples who are resisting attempted subjugation by armed minorities or by outside pressures. I believe that we must assist free peoples to work out their own destinies in their own way."[12] Containment as policy—essentially, the use of espionage, economic pressure, and forward-deployed military resources—emerged from a comparative asymmetry of forces in Europe. After the Third Reich's surrender, U.S. and British forces rapidly demobilized and went home, whereas the Soviet army did not. In 1948, the Soviets blocked western transportation corridors to Berlin, the German capital—which had been divided into sectors by the Potsdam Conference of 1945; the United States then realized that even as the sole state in possession of atomic weapons, it did not possess the power to coerce the Soviet Union into retreating to its pre–World War II borders. And, in August 1949, the Soviets successfully tested their first atomic bomb. Thus, containment, based on U.S. geostrategic interests and a growing recognition that attempting rollback would likely lead to another world war, became the fundamental doctrine of U.S. foreign policy during the Cold War.

The United States and the Soviet Union also had major ideological differences. The United States' democratic liberalism was based on a social system that accepted the worth and value of the individual; a political system that depended on the participation of individuals in the electoral process; and an economic system, **capitalism**, that provided opportunities to individuals to pursue what was economically rational with minimal government interference. At the international level, this translated into support for other democratic regimes and support of liberal capitalist institutions and processes, including, most critically, free trade.

Soviet communist ideology also influenced that country's conception of the international system and state practices. The failure of the Revolutions of 1848 cast Marxist theory into crisis; Marxism insisted that peasants and workers would spontaneously rise up and overthrow their capitalist masters, but this had not happened. The crisis in Marxist theory was partly resolved by Vladimir Lenin's "vanguard of the proletariat" amendment, in which Lenin argued that the masses must be led or "sparked" by intellectuals who fully understand **socialism**. But the end result was a system in which any hope of achieving communism—a utopian vision in which the state withered away along with poverty, war, sexism, and the like—had to be led from the top down. This result meant that to the United States and its liberal allies, the Soviet system looked like a dictatorship, bent on aggressively exporting dictatorship under the guise of worldwide socialist revolution. Popular sovereignty vanished in every state allied to the Soviet Union (e.g., Czechoslovakia, Hungary, Romania, Lithuania, Latvia, Estonia, Poland, and so on). For their part, Soviet leaders felt themselves surrounded by a hostile capitalist camp and argued that the Soviet Union "must not weaken but must in every way strengthen its state, the state organs, the organs of the intelligence service, the army, if that country does not want to be smashed by the capitalist environment."[13]

These "bottom up," "top down" differences were exacerbated by mutual misperceptions. Once distrustful, each side tended to view the other side's policies as necessarily threatening. For example, the formation of the **North Atlantic Treaty Organization** (or **NATO**) became a contentious worldwide issue. On the Western side, NATO represented a desperate effort to defend indefensible Western Europe from the fully mobilized Soviet Army; while from the Soviet perspective, NATO seemed clearly an aggressive military alliance aimed at depriving the USSR of the fruits of its victory over the Third Reich. When the USSR reacted in ways it took to be defensive, Britain and the United States interpreted these actions as dangerous escalations.

The third outcome of the end of World War II was the collapse of the colonial system, a development few foresaw. The defeat of Japan and Germany meant the immediate end of their respective empires. The other colonial powers, faced with the reality of their economically and politically weakened position, and confronted with newly powerful indigenous movements for independence, were spurred by the United Nations Charter's endorsement of the principle of national self-determination. These movements were equipped with leftover small arms from World War II, led by talented commanders employing indirect defense strategies such as "revolutionary" guerrilla warfare,

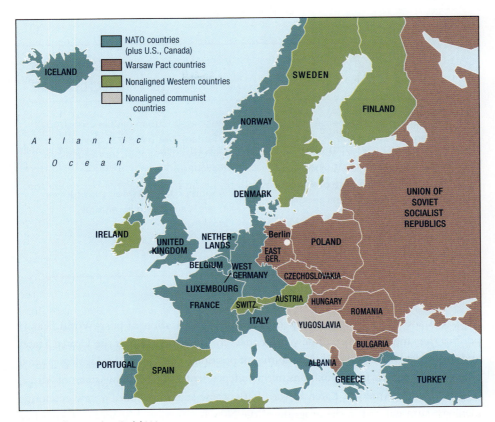

Europe during the Cold War

and inspired to great self-sacrifice by the ideals of nationalism. Victorious powers were forced—by local resistance, their own decline, or by pressure from the United States, to grant independence to their former colonies, starting with Britain, which granted India independence in 1947. It took the military defeat of France in Indochina in the early 1950s to bring decolonization to that part of the world. African states, too, became independent between 1957 and 1963.

The fourth outcome was the realization that the differences between the two emergent superpowers would be played out indirectly, on third-party stages, rather than through direct confrontation. Both rivals came to believe the risks of a direct military confrontation were too great. The "loss" of any potential ally, no matter how poor or distant, might begin a cumulative process leading to a significant shift in the balance of power. Thus, the Cold War resulted in the globalization of conflict to all continents. International relations became truly global.

Other parts of the world did not merely react to U.S. and Soviet Cold War imperatives: they developed new ideologies or recast the dominant discourse of Europe in

IN FOCUS

KEY DEVELOPMENTS IN THE COLD WAR

- Two superpowers emerge—the United States and the Soviet Union. They are divided by national interests, ideologies, and mutual misperceptions. These divisions are projected into different geographic areas.

- A series of crises occurs—Berlin blockade (1948–49), Korean War

(1950–53), Cuban missile crisis (1962), Vietnam War (1965–73), Soviet military intervention in Afghanistan (1979–89).

- A long peace between superpower rivals is sustained by mutual deterrence.

ways that addressed their own experiences. The globalization of post–World War II politics thus meant the rise of new contenders for power. Although the United States and the Soviet Union retained their dominant positions, new alternative ideologies acted as powerful magnets for populations in the independent and developing states of Africa, Asia, and Latin America. Later, in the 1970s, these states advanced a new economic ideology, summarized in the program of the New International Economic Order (see Chapter 9).

The Cold War as a Series of Confrontations

We can characterize the Cold War itself (1945–89) as 45 years of overall high-level tension and competition between the superpowers but with no direct military conflict. The advent of nuclear weapons created a **deterrence** stalemate in which each side acted, at times reluctantly, with increasing caution. As nuclear technology advanced, both sides realized that a nuclear war would likely result in the destruction of each power beyond hope of recovery. This state of affairs was called "mutual assured destruction"—aptly underlined by its acronym: MAD. Though each superpower tended to back down from particular confrontations—either because its national interest was not sufficiently strong to risk a nuclear confrontation, or because its ideological resolve wavered in light of military realities—several confrontations very nearly escalated to war.

The Cold War, then, can be understood as a series of confrontations. Most were between proxies (North Korea versus South Korea, North Vietnam versus South Vietnam, Ethiopia versus Somalia) that, in all likelihood, neither the United States nor the Soviet Union had intended to escalate as they did. Thus, the Cold War comprised not only superpower confrontations but also confrontations between two blocs of states: the non-communist bloc (the United States, with Canada, Australia, most of Western Europe [allied in NATO], South Korea, Japan, and the Philippines); and the communist bloc (the Soviet Union, with its **Warsaw Pact** allies in Eastern Europe, North Korea, Vietnam, and the People's Republic of China, along with Cuba). Over the life of the Cold War, these blocs loosened, and states sometimes took positions different from that of the dominant power. But for much of this time, bloc politics operated. Table 2.1 shows a timeline of major events related to the Cold War.

One of the high-level, direct confrontations between the superpowers took place in Germany. Germany had been divided immediately after World War II into zones of occupation. The United States, France, and Great Britain administered the western portion; the Soviet Union, the eastern. Berlin, Germany's capital, was similarly divided but lay within Soviet-controlled East Germany. In 1948, the Soviet Union blocked land access to Berlin, prompting the United States and Britain to airlift supplies for 13 months. In 1949, the separate states of West and East Germany were declared. In 1961, East Germany erected the Berlin Wall around the West German

TABLE 2.1	IMPORTANT EVENTS OF THE COLD WAR
1945–48	Soviet Union establishes communist regimes in Eastern Europe.
1947	Announcement of Truman Doctrine; United States proposes Marshall Plan for the rebuilding of Europe.
1948–49	Soviets blockade Berlin; United States and Allies carry out airlift.
1949	Soviets test atomic bomb, ending U.S. nuclear monopoly. Chinese communists under Mao win civil war, establish People's Republic of China. United States and Allies establish NATO.
1950–53	Korean War.
1957	Soviets launch the satellite *Sputnik*, causing anxiety in the West and catalyzing superpower scientific competition.
1960–63	Congo crisis and UN action to fill power vacuum.
1962	Cuban missile crisis, nuclear war narrowly averted.

(CONTINUED)

1965	United States begins large-scale intervention in Vietnam.
1967	Israel defeats Egypt, Syria, and Jordan in the Six-Day War. Glassboro summit signals détente, loosening of tensions between the superpowers.
1968	Czech government liberalization halted by Soviet invasion. Nuclear Nonproliferation Treaty (NPT) signed.
1972	U.S. President Nixon visits China and Soviet Union. United States and Soviet Union sign strategic arms limitation treaty (SALT I).
1973	Yom Kippur War between Israel and Arab states leads to global energy crisis.
1975	Proxy and anticolonial wars fought in Angola, Mozambique, Ethiopia, and Somalia. South Vietnam falls to communist North Vietnam.
1979	United States and Soviet Union sign SALT II (but U.S. Senate fails to ratify it). Soviet Union invades Afghanistan. Shah of Iran (a major U.S. ally) overthrown in Islamic revolution. Israel and Egypt sign a peace treaty.
1981–89	Reagan Doctrine provides basis for U.S. support of "anticommunist" forces in Nicaragua and Afghanistan.
1985	Gorbachev starts economic and political reforms in Soviet Union.
1989	Peaceful revolutions in Eastern Europe replace communist governments. Berlin Wall is dismantled. Soviet Union withdraws from Afghanistan.
1990	Germany reunified.
1991	Resignation of Gorbachev. Soviet Union collapses.
1992–93	Russia and other former Soviet republics become independent states.

portion of the city to stem the tide of East Germans trying to leave the troubled state. U.S. president John F. Kennedy responded by visiting the city and declaring, "Ich bin ein Berliner" (improper German for the sentiment "I am a Berliner"), committing the United States to the security of the Federal Republic of Germany at any cost. Not surprisingly, the dismantling of that same wall in November 1989 became the most iconic symbol of the end of the Cold War.

The Cold War in Asia and Latin America

China, Indochina, and especially Korea became the symbols of the Cold War in Asia. In 1946, after years of bitter and heroic fighting against the Japanese occupation, communists throughout Asia attempted to take control of their respective states following Japan's surrender. In China, the wartime alliance between the Kuomintang (non-communist Chinese nationalists) and Mao Zedong's "Peoples Liberation Army" dissolved into renewed civil war, in which the United States attempted to support the Kuomintang with large shipments of arms and military equipment. By 1949, however, the Kuomintang had been defeated, and its leaders fled to the island of Formosa (now Taiwan). With the addition of one-fourth of the world's population to the communist bloc, U.S. interests in Japan and the Philippines now seemed directly threatened.

In 1946, in what was then French Indochina (an amalgamation of the contemporary states of Cambodia, Laos, and Vietnam), Ho Chi Minh raised the communist flag over Hanoi, declaring Vietnam to be an independent state. The French quickly returned to take Indochina back, but though French forces fought bravely and with great skill, they proved unable to defeat the communists (known as the Viet Minh). In 1954, after having laid a trap for the Viet Minh in a fortified town called Dien Bien Phu, the French were themselves trapped and decisively defeated. France abandoned Indochina; a peace treaty signed in Geneva that same year divided Indochina into the political entities of Laos, Cambodia, and Vietnam, with Vietnam being divided into two zones: North Vietnam and South Vietnam.

After having spent years seeking support from the USSR to unify the Korean peninsula under communist rule, North Korean leader Kim Il-Sung finally persuaded Joseph Stalin to lend him the tanks, heavy artillery, and combat support aircraft needed to conquer non-communist South Korea. On June 25, 1950, communist North Korean forces crossed the frontier into South Korea and rapidly overwhelmed the South's defenders. The North Korean offensive quickly captured Seoul, South Korea's capital, and then forced the retreat of the few surviving South Korean and American armed forces all the way to the outskirts of the port city of Pusan. In one of the most dramatic military reversals in history, U.S. forces—fighting for the first time under the auspices of the United Nations because of North Korea's "unprovoked aggression" and violations of international law—landed a surprise force at Inchon. Within days, the U.S.

forces cut off and then routed the North Korean forces. By mid-October, UN forces had captured North Korea's capital, Pyongyang, and by the end of the month, the destruction of North Korea's military was nearly complete.

Yet the war did not end. Against the wishes of U.S. president Harry Truman, U.S. General Douglas MacArthur ordered his victorious troops—now overconfident of victory and spread thin—to finish off the defeated North Koreans, who by this time were encamped very close to the border with communist China. The Chinese had warned they would intervene if their territory was approached too closely, and in November, they did. The relatively poorly equipped but more numerous and highly motivated Chinese soldiers attacked the UN forces, causing the longest retreat of U.S. armed forces in American history. The two sides then became mired in a stalemate that finally ended in an armistice in 1953. But, as with the Berlin crisis, numerous diplomatic skirmishes followed the armistice over the years—provoked by the basing of U.S. troops in South Korea, the use of the demilitarized zone between the north and the south, and North Korean attempts to become a nuclear power; even after the end of the Cold War, the last is still a source of conflict today.

The 1962 Cuban missile crisis was a high-profile direct confrontation between the superpowers in another area of the world. The United States viewed the Soviet Union's installation of nuclear missiles in Cuba as a direct threat to its territory: no weapons of a powerful enemy had ever been located so close to U.S. shores. The way in which the crisis was resolved suggests unequivocally that neither party sought a direct confrontation, but once the crisis became public, neither side could back down and global thermonuclear war became a very real possibility. The United States chose to blockade Cuba—another example of containment strategy in action—to prevent the arrival of additional Soviet missiles. The U.S. president, John F. Kennedy, rejected the more aggressive actions the U.S. military favored, such as a land invasion of Cuba or air strikes on missile sites. Through behind-the-scenes, unofficial contacts in Washington and direct communication between Kennedy and Soviet premier Nikita Khruschev, the Soviets agreed to remove the missiles from Cuba and the United States agreed to remove similarly capable missiles from Turkey. The crisis was defused, and war was averted.

Vietnam provided a test of a different kind. The Cold War was also played out there, not in one dramatic crisis but in an extended civil war. Communist North Vietnam and its Chinese and Soviet allies were pitted against the "free world"—South Vietnam, allied with the United States and assorted supporters including South Korea, the Philippines, and Thailand. To most U.S. policy makers in the late 1950s and early 1960s, Vietnam was yet another test of the containment doctrine: communist influence must be stopped, they argued, before it spread like a chain of falling dominos through the rest of Southeast Asia and beyond (hence the term **domino effect**). Thus, the United States supported the South Vietnamese dictators Ngo Dinh Diem and later Nguyen Van Thieu against the rival communist regime of Ho Chi Minh in the north, which

For the United States, Vietnam became a symbol of the Cold War rivalries in Asia. The United States supported the South Vietnamese forces against the communist regime in the north. Here, a female Vietcong guerrilla prepares to fire an anti-tank rifle during the Tet Offensive of 1968.

was underwritten by both the People's Republic of China and the Soviet Union. But, as the South Vietnamese government and military faltered on their own, the United States stepped up its military support, increasing the number of its troops on the ground and escalating the air war over the north.

In the early stages, the United States was confident of victory; after all, a superpower with all its military hardware and technically skilled labor force could surely beat a poorly trained Vietcong guerrilla force. American policy makers were quickly disillusioned, however, as communist forces proved adept at avoiding the massive technical firepower of U.S. forces, and a corrupt South Vietnamese leadership siphoned away many of the crucial resources needed to win its more vital struggle for popular legitimacy. As U.S. casualties mounted, with no prospects for victory in sight, the U.S. public grew disenchanted. Should the U.S. use all of its conventional military capability to prevent the "fall" of South Vietnam and stave off the domino effect? Should the U.S. fight until victory was guaranteed for liberalism and capitalism, or should it extricate itself from this unpopular quagmire? Should the U.S. capitulate to the forces of ideological communism? These questions, posed in both geostrategic and ideological terms, defined the middle years of the Cold War, from the Vietnam War's slow beginning in

the late 1950s until the dramatic departure of U.S. officials from the South Vietnamese capital, Saigon, in 1975, symbolized by U.S. helicopters leaving the U.S. embassy
roof while dozens of desperate Vietnamese tried to grab on to the boarding ladders
and escape with them.

The U.S. effort to avert a communist takeover in South Vietnam failed, yet contrary to expectations, the domino effect did not occur. Cold War alliances were shaken
on both sides: the friendship between the Soviet Union and China had long before
degenerated into a geostrategic fight and a struggle over the proper form of communism,
especially in Third World countries. But the Soviet bloc was left relatively unscathed
by the Vietnam War. The U.S.-led Western alliance was seriously jeopardized, as several
allies (including Canada) strongly opposed U.S. policy toward Vietnam. The bipolar
structure of the Cold War–era international system was coming apart. Confidence in
military alternatives was shaken in the United States, undermining for more than a
decade the United States' ability to commit itself militarily. The power of the United
States was supposed to be righteous power, but in Vietnam, it was neither victorious in
its outcome nor righteous in its effects.

Was the Cold War Really Cold?

It was not always the case that when one of the superpowers acted, the other side
responded. In some cases, the other side chose not to act, or at least not to respond in
kind, even though it might have escalated the conflict. Usually this was out of concern
for escalating a conflict to a major war. For example, the Soviet Union invaded Hungary
in 1956 and Czechoslovakia in 1968, both sovereign states and allies in the Warsaw
Pact. Under other circumstances, the United States might have responded with coun-
terforce, but while it verbally condemned these aggressive Soviet actions, the actions
themselves went unchecked. In 1956, the United States, preoccupied with the Suez
Canal crisis, kept quiet, aware that it was ill prepared to respond militarily. In 1968, the
United States was mired in Vietnam and beset by domestic turmoil and a presidential
election. The United States was also relatively complacent, although angry, when the
Soviets invaded Afghanistan in 1979. The Soviets likewise kept quiet when the United
States took aggressive action within the U.S. sphere of influence, invading Grenada
in 1983 and Panama in 1989. Thus, during the Cold War, even blatantly aggressive
actions by one of the superpowers did not always lead to a response by the other.

Many of the events of the Cold War involved the United States and the Soviet Union
only indirectly; proxies often fought in their place. Nowhere was this so true as in the
Middle East. For both the United States and the Soviet Union, the Middle East was a
region of vital importance because of its natural resources (including an estimated one-
third of the world's oil), its strategic position as a transportation hub between Asia and
Europe, and its cultural significance as the cradle of three of the world's major reli-

gions. Not surprisingly, following the establishment of Israel in 1948 and its diplomatic recognition (first by the United States), the region was the scene of a superpower confrontation by proxy between the U.S.-supported Israel and the Soviet-backed Arab states Syria, Iraq, and Egypt. During the Six-Day War in 1967, Israel crushed the Soviet-equipped Arabs in six short days, seizing the strategic territories of the Golan Heights, Gaza, and the West Bank. During the Yom Kippur War of 1973, which the Egyptians had planned as a limited war, the Israeli victory was not so overwhelming, because the United States and the Soviets negotiated a cease-fire before more damage could be done. But throughout the Cold War, these "hot" wars were followed by guerrilla actions supported by all parties. As long as the basic balance of power was maintained between Israel (and the United States) on one side and the Arabs (and the Soviets) on the other, the region was left alone; when that balance was threatened, the superpowers acted through proxies to maintain the balance. Other controversies also plagued the region, as evidenced by events after the end of the Cold War.

In parts of the world that were of less strategic importance to the two superpowers, confrontation through proxies was even more regular during the Cold War. Africa and Latin America present many examples of such events. When the colonialist Belgians abruptly left the Congo in 1960, civil war broke out as various contending factions sought to take power and bring order out of the chaos. One of the contenders, the Congolese premier Patrice Lumumba (1925–61), appealed to the Soviets for help in fighting the Western-backed insurgents and received both diplomatic support and military supplies. However, Lumumba was dismissed by the Congolese president, Joseph Kasavubu, an ally of the United States. Still others, such as Moïse Tshombe, leader of the copper-rich Katanga province, who was also closely identified with Western interests, fought for control. The three-year civil war could have become another protracted proxy war between the United States and the Soviet Union. However, the United Nations averted such a confrontation by sending in peacekeepers, whose primary purpose was to stabilize a transition government and prevent the superpowers from making the Congo yet another violent arena of the Cold War.

In Latin America, too, participants in civil wars were able to transform their struggles into Cold War confrontations by proxy, thereby gaining military equipment and technical expertise from one of the superpowers. In most cases, Latin American states were led by governments beholden to wealthy elites who maintained a virtual monopoly on the country's wealth (such as the coffee industry in El Salvador). When popular protest against corruption and injustice escalated to violence, Communist Cuba was often asked to support these armed movements, and in response, the United States tended to support the incumbent governments—even those whose record of human rights abuses against their own citizens had been well established. In Nicaragua, for example, after communists called Sandinistas captured the government from its dictator in 1979, the Ronald Reagan administration supported an insurgency known as the

"Contras" in an attempt to reverse what it feared would be a "communist foothold" in Latin America. Such proxy warfare enabled the superpowers to project power and support geostrategic interests (e.g., oil in Angola, transportation routes around the Horn, the Monroe Doctrine in Latin America) and ideologies without directly confronting one another and risking major or thermonuclear war.

In sum, the Cold War was really only relatively cold in Europe, and very warm, or even hot, in other places. In Asia, the Middle East, Africa, and Latin America, over 40 million people lost their lives in superpower proxy wars from 1946 to 1990.

But the Cold War was also "fought" and moderated in words, at **summits** (meetings between leaders), and in treaties. Some Cold War summits were relatively successful: the 1967 Glassboro summit between U.S. and Soviet leaders began the loosening of tensions known as **détente**. Others, however, did not produce results. Treaties between the two parties placed self-imposed limitations on nuclear arms. For example, the first Strategic Arms Limitations Treaty (SALT I), in 1972, placed an absolute ceiling on the numbers of intercontinental ballistic missiles (ICBMs), deployed nuclear warheads, and multiple independently targetable reentry vehicles (MIRVs); and limited the number of antiballistic missile sites each superpower maintained. So the superpowers did enjoy periods of accommodation, when they could agree on principles and policies.

The Immediate Post–Cold War Era

The fall of the Berlin Wall in 1989 symbolized the end of the Cold War, but its actual end was gradual. The Soviet premier at the time, Mikhail Gorbachev, and other Soviet reformers had set in motion two domestic processes—*glasnost* (political openness) and *perestroika* (economic restructuring)—as early as the mid-1980s. *Glasnost*, combined with a new technology—the videocassette player—made it possible for the first time since the October Revolution for average Soviet citizens to compare their living standards with those of their Western counterparts. The comparison proved dramatically unfavorable. It also opened the door to criticism of the political system, culminating in the emergence of a multiparty system and the massive reorientation of the once-monopolistic Communist Party. *Perestroika* undermined the foundation of the planned economy, an essential part of the communist system. At the outset, Gorbachev and his reformers sought to save the system, but once initiated, these reforms led to the dissolution of the Warsaw Pact, Gorbachev's resignation in December 1991, and the disintegration of the Soviet Union itself in 1992–93.

Gorbachev's domestic reforms also led to changes in the orientation of Soviet foreign policy. Needing to extricate the country from the political quagmire and economic drain of the Soviet war in Afghanistan while seeking to save face, Gorbachev suggested that the permanent members of the UN Security Council "could become guarantors of regional security."[14] Afghanistan was a test case, where a small group of UN observers monitored and verified the withdrawal of more than 100,000 Soviet troops in 1988 and 1989—an action that would have been impossible during the height of the Cold War. Similarly, the Soviets agreed to and supported the 1988 withdrawal of Cuban troops from Angola. The Soviet Union had retreated from international commitments near its borders, as well as others farther abroad. Most important, the Soviets agreed to cooperate in multilateral activities to preserve regional security.

The first post–Cold War test of the so-called new world order came in response to Iraq's invasion and annexation of Kuwait in August 1990. Despite its long-standing support for Iraq, the Soviet Union (and later Russia), along with the four other permanent members of the UN Security Council, agreed first to implement economic sanctions against Iraq. Then they agreed in a Security Council resolution to support the means to restore the status quo—to oust Iraq from Kuwait with a multinational military force. Finally, they supported sending the UN Iraq-Kuwait Observer Mission to monitor the zone and permitted the UN to undertake humanitarian intervention and create safe havens for the Kurdish and Shiite populations of Iraq. Although forging a consensus on each of these actions (or in the case of China, convincing it to abstain) was difficult, the coalition held—a unity unthinkable during the Cold War.

The 1990s were marked by the struggle of former allies and enemies to find new identities and interests in more complex world. As the threat of World War III vanished, what was the purpose of an organization such as NATO? What was the purpose or focus of state foreign policy to be if not the deterrence of aggression by other states? The United States and Israel, for example, were unparalleled in their capacity to

---

IN FOCUS

KEY DEVELOPMENTS IN THE IMMEDIATE POST-COLD WAR ERA

- Changes are made in Soviet/Russian foreign policy, with the withdrawals from Afghanistan and Angola in the late 1980s, monitored by the United Nations.

- Iraqi invasion of Kuwait in 1990 and the multilateral response unite the former Cold War adversaries.

- *Glasnost* and *perestroika* continue in Russia, as reorganized in 1992–93.

- The former Yugoslavia disintegrates into independent states; civil war ensues in Bosnia and Kosovo, leading to UN and NATO intervention.

- Widespread ethnic conflict arises in central and western Africa, Central Asia, and the Indian subcontinent.

Explaining the End of the Cold War:
A View from the Former Soviet Union

Many scholars of American diplomatic history attribute the end of the Cold War to policies the United States initiated: the buildup of a formidable military capable of winning either a nuclear or conventional war against the Soviet Union and the development of the strongest, most diversified economy the world has ever known. However, those within the Soviet Union perceived the events leading to the end of the Cold War differently.

The predominant viewpoint in the former Soviet Union is that the explanation for the end of the Cold War can be found in a very long and complex chain of domestic developments in the Soviet Union itself. Political, economic, and demographic factors led to what seemed to be an abrupt disintegration of the Soviet Union and hence the end of the Cold War. International relations theorists did not predict it; perhaps they were not looking at domestic factors within the Soviet state itself and did not have a sufficiently long historical perspective.

The political dominance and authority of the Communist Party, the main ideological pillar of the Soviet Union, had significantly eroded by the late 1980s. The revelation of Joseph Stalin's horrific crimes against the Soviet people, especially ethnic minorities, intensified animosity in the far-flung parts of the Soviet empire. Many of the smaller republics and subnational regions bore a grudge against the central government for forced Russification, the resettlement of certain minorities, and other atrocities such as induced famines in Russia and Ukraine in the early 1930s. Increasingly open discussion of such events undermined the ideological fervor of the common population and shook their trust in the "people's government."

During the 1960s, some Soviet leaders saw stagnation in the economic, technological, and agricultural spheres. Internal critics of the regime blamed the top-level political leadership, which had become ossified. The policy of lifelong appointments to leading posts, a policy that remained in effect until the mid-1980s, meant that political appointees stayed in their posts for 20 or more years, regardless of their performance. There were few efforts to reform and modernize the system, and younger people had little opportunity to exercise political leadership. These failures in leadership, exemplified by the poor economy, led to widespread discontent and resentment in all layers of the society.

Moreover, the Soviet Union was a very ethnically diverse state, consisting of 15 major republics, some of which also contained "autonomous" republics and regions, inhabited by hundreds of ethnicities. Although the Soviet Union had benefitted economically from extracting resources found in the far reaches of its territories, the costs of keeping the empire together were high. Subsidies flowed to the outer regions at the expense of the Soviet state. With growing economic discontent and the erosion of the ideology promoted by the Communist Party, local nationalist movements started to fill the ideological vacuum by the late 1980s.

Before the mid-1980s, the inherent distortions and inefficiencies of the Soviet planned economy were partially offset by the profits from the energy sector based on oil and gas exports. However, the Soviet industrial and agricultural sectors lagged behind, inefficient and uncompetitive. Technological development stagnated, too. The sharp decline in world oil prices in the 1980s compounded the problems. The resulting rationing of basic food products and the poor quality of domestically manufactured products totally discredited the socialist economic model and added to the general discontent. The declining state budget could no longer bear the burden of the arms race with the United States, finance an expensive war in Afghanistan, and keep the increasingly fractured empire within its orbit.

The interplay of all these factors came to a climax when Mikhail Gorbachev took power in 1985. Acknowledging the urgent need for change, he launched ambitious domestic reforms collectively referred to as *perestroika*, literally, "restructuring" of economic relations, including stepping back from central planning and curbing government subsidies. *Glasnost* was the political component, an "opening" that relaxed censorship and encouraged democratization. In foreign policy, "New Thinking" meant improving relations with the United States and the possibility of the coexistence of the capitalist and socialist systems through shared human values. The underlying reasons for most of these domestic changes were economic. Reducing military expenditures and gaining access to Western loans became critical for the survival of the troubled state.

The rapid dissolution of the Eastern bloc led to a dramatic shift in the balance of power in the international system. Rising nationalist movements and local liberal forces gained momentum and won significant representation in the local parliaments after the first competitive elections in the former Socialist republics.

Mikhail Gorbachev addresses the Russian parliament in 1991.

Eventually, Russia became one of the first to declare independence and affirm sovereignty, with the rest of the republics following suit in the "sovereignty parade" in 1991. The de facto dissolution of the Soviet Union marked an important chapter in the history of the Cold War, but given recent events in Russia and Ukraine—especially the annexation by force of Crimea—we cannot yet say that the collapse of the Soviet Union is the Cold War's final chapter.

FOR CRITICAL ANALYSIS

1. How can we balance the traditional view that Western economic and military dominance caused a Soviet "defeat" with the Soviet view that internal weaknesses and contractions were primarily to blame?

2. *Glasnost* was supposed to make it possible for Soviet citizens to share information, but it also made it possible for them to compare their own lives with those beyond the USSR. How might this development have affected the legitimacy of the Communist Party?

3. If states "learn" from their own mistakes and achievements as well as those of other states, what might a state like China have learned from the collapse of the USSR?

fight and win interstate wars. But who might these other states be? What role might armed forces specialized to win interstate wars play in substate violence? Yugoslavia's violent disintegration played itself out over the entire decade, despite Western attempts to resolve the conflict peacefully. At the same time, the world witnessed ethnic tension and violence in central Africa. Genocide in Rwanda and Burundi was effectively ignored by the international community. And, despite U.S. military primacy, Russia maintains enough military power and political influence to prevent U.S. intervention in ethnic hostilities in the Transcaucasus region.

These dual realities converged and diverged throughout the 1990s and continue to do so today. The disintegration of Yugoslavia culminated in an American-led war against Serbia to halt attacks on the ethnic Albanian population in Kosovo. The 78-day air war by NATO against Serbia ended with the capitulation of the Serbs and international administration of the province of Kosovo. The war also severely challenged core principles of international law: technically, the action of NATO in Kosovo was a violation of Serbian sovereignty. Yet NATO's leaders held that Serb rapes, lootings, and murders constituted a greater harm: violating the principle of sovereignty was less than the harm of allowing Serbians to murder and torture Kosovar Albanians. The repercussions affect international politics to this day.

Clearly, the end of the Cold War in the 1990s denotes a major change in international relations, the end of one historical era and the beginning of another. The overwhelming military power of the United States, combined with its economic power, appeared to many to usher in an era of U.S. primacy in international affairs to a degree not matched even by the Romans or Alexander the Great. The United States seemed able to impose its will on other states, even against the strong objections of its allies. Yet this moment of primacy now appears doubtful; it proved insufficient to deter or prevent ethnic conflict, civil wars, and human rights abuses from occurring, whether in Somalia, Rwanda, or the former Yugoslavia. And many threats, like terrorism, cyber security, and the global financial crisis of 2008, have shown themselves, by their very nature, to demand *multilateral* engagement: no single state, however, powerful, can remain secure against these threats on its own.

The New Millennium: The First Two Decades

Perhaps the biggest change in interstate politics following the end of the Cold War was the puzzling elevation of terrorism—once a relatively minor threat—from a law-enforcement problem to a vital national security interest (and therefore a military problem). On September 11, 2001, the world witnessed lethal, psychologically disruptive, and economically devastating terrorist attacks organized and funded by Al Qaeda against New York City and Washington, D.C. These attacks, directed by Osama bin Laden, set into motion a U.S.-led global "war on terrorism." Buoyed by an outpouring of support from around the world and by the first-ever invocation of Article V of the NATO Charter, which declares an attack on one NATO member to be an attack on all, the United States undertook to lead an ad hoc coalition to combat terrorist organizations with global reach. As discussed in Chapter 8, this new **war on terrorism** combines many elements into multiple campaigns in different countries. Many countries have arrested known terrorists and their supporters and frozen their monetary assets. In October 2001, the United States launched a war in Afghanistan to oust the Taliban regime, which was providing safe haven to Osama bin Laden's Al Qaeda organization and a base from which it freely planned, organized, and trained operatives to carry out a global terror campaign against the United States and its allies.

Following an initially successful campaign in Afghanistan in 2001 and 2002, called Operation Enduring Freedom, that specifically targeted terrorists and their supporters and paved the way for popular elections, the United States broke from its allies. Convinced that Iraq maintained a clandestine **weapons of mass destruction (WMD)** program and posed a continued threat by backing terrorist organizations, the United States attempted to build support in the United Nations for authorization to remove Saddam Hussein forcibly from power and find the hidden WMD. When the United Nations refused to back this request, the United States built its own coalition, including key ally Great Britain. This coalition destroyed the Iraqi military and overthrew Iraq's government in 2003. No weapons of mass destruction were found, but additional justifications for the invasion were offered, including promoting democracy for Iraq's three main peoples—Kurds, Sunni Arabs, and Shia Arabs—within a single state. Fighting in Iraq continues today, although Hussein himself was executed in 2006 and U.S. combat forces have withdrawn. Iraq remains riven by sectarian conflict, and its U.S.-built and trained armed forces have suffered repeated defeats and setbacks since the United States withdrew in 2011. Iraq, Syria, and Lebanon now face a new and barbarous group calling itself the "Islamic State." Sadly, then, Iraq's future stability and the fate of its long-suffering people remains unclear.

In an important way, Operation Enduring Freedom set a very dangerous precedent. If the United States and its allies could invade Afghanistan to punish or preempt terrorism, why couldn't it also invade any other state that hosted terrorists? After the defeat of the Taliban in 2001, much of the Taliban's leadership escaped across the poorly controlled border between Afghanistan and Pakistan's Northwest Territories. But Pakistan was a formal U.S. ally, and extremely sensitive to any perceived slights to its sovereignty. This situation created a dilemma that is not unique to U.S.–Pakistan relations. If the United States is now to succeed in stabilizing Afghanistan, it must have the help of Pakistan to eliminate the sanctuary it gives to groups the United States and its allies consider terrorists. Yet Pakistan currently lacks both the capacity, and possibly the will, either to close the border between Pakistan and Afghanistan or to stop the groups in its territory from attacking Afghan forces within Afghanistan. If the United States attempts to use its own resources to achieve its objectives, Pakistan will vehemently resist. Thus, the "war on terror" poses tricky dilemmas for U.S. policy makers.

Even after the economic downturns following the September 11 terrorist attacks and the financial crisis of 2008, the U.S. military and economy remain the strongest in the world. Yet despite this strength, citizens of the United States do not feel secure. The global war against terrorism is far from over and appears no nearer to victory. The issue of whether U.S. power will be balanced by an emerging power (or coalition of powers) is also far from resolved. And although the U.S. military is still

---

IN FOCUS

KEY DEVELOPMENTS IN THE FIRST TWO DECADES OF THE NEW MILLENNIUM

- Al Qaeda terrorist network commits terrorist acts against the homeland of the United States and U.S. interests abroad; U.S. and coalition forces respond militarily in Afghanistan and Iraq.

- Terrorist attacks occur in Saudi Arabia, Spain, Great Britain, Nigeria, and France.

- A financial crisis in the United States in 2008 devastates its economy and rapidly spreads to other countries.

- In the spring of 2011, Tunisia becomes the first in a series of Arab countries in which a popular uprising topples a long-established dictator. The outcome of this so-called Arab Spring remains indeterminate.

- In 2014, China's military budget expands, making it the second largest after the United States. China also begins dredging operations to support its ambitious territorial claims in the South China Sea. Tensions between China, its neighbors, and the United States escalate.

- In February 2014, soldiers in uniforms with no national insignia begin occupying key government and communications facilities in Crimea. In March, Crimea votes overwhelmingly to rejoin Russia, a move that is unsettling to Europeans and states bordering Russia.

- In June 2014, the Islamic State declares itself to be a worldwide caliphate with Abu Bakr al-Baghdadi as its caliph and lays claim to territory containing more than ten million people in Iraq and Syria. The United States and a coalition of Arab partner states have so far failed to defeat the IS or seriously impair its territorial control.

held in high esteem within the United States, the war in Afghanistan—all but a few U.S. military advisors were withdrawn in 2014—became widely unpopular.

Contemporary events continue to hold surprises. In December 2010, a local protest by a single man in Tunisia sparked a massive social protest against the cruelty and corruption of Tunisia's long-standing dictator, Zine al-Abidine Ben Ali. In January 2011, Ben Ali was overthrown and fled to exile in Saudi Arabia. But protest against corrupt and brutal Arab leaders did not stop there. Soon popular protests broke out in Egypt, Libya, Yemen, Bahrain, and later Syria. Egypt's leader, Hosni Mubarak, was taken by surprise and faced a choice of mass murder of protestors or stepping down. With Egypt's military refusing to kill protestors, Mubarak was forced to step down. The fate of Libya's dictator, Muammar Qaddafi, was more

Protesters in Tunisia attack the office of the prime minister using a coffin draped in the Tunisian flag in January 2011. Many authoritarian governments in the Middle East faced popular uprisings during the Arab Spring.

severe: after having been forced from power by a rebellion actively supported by France and the United States, Qaddafi was captured and later murdered by his captors.

The ultimate fate of what we now think of as the "Arab Spring" of 2011 remains unclear; in Bahrain protest was brutally suppressed, and in Syria, Bashar al Assad's efforts to stay in power against widespread social protest have led to his forces killing more than 70,000 of Syria's own citizens and a massive refugee crisis. In Egypt, "democracy" has proven elusive as the fall of Mubarak was followed by the election of Muhammad Morsi (leader of an unpopular religious party), then his ouster by the Egyptian military, and now a provisional government run, essentially, by Egypt's military. The Arab Spring is nevertheless remarkable for two reasons. First, it gave lie to the claims of radical and militant Islamists (such as Al Qaeda) that only through Islamic revolution, terror attacks on "the West," and the reestablishment of strict Islamic law could Arab dictators be overthrown. Second, the combined might of secret services and militaries failed to resist the power of young people armed with mobile phones, courage, and conviction.

::: BEHIND THE HEADLINES

Why Can't a Powerful State like Japan Use Armed Force Abroad?

In early 2015, two Japanese journalists were beheaded by the Islamic State (IS). The IS recorded and posted the executions—beheadings—in graphic detail on the Internet, shocking and angering Japan and the world. Many, including Japan's Prime Minister Shinzo Abe, called for Japan to respond with military force. Yet the headline "Beheadings Frame a New Debate About Restraints on Japan's Military"[a] calls our attention to "restraints" on Japan's military. What are these restraints? Where did they come from? Why do they matter?

Japan is a constitutional democracy now, but it was not always so. Japan's constitution was largely modeled on that of the United States, because the United States was the chief victor and occupier of Japan after Japan's surrender in World War II. Although Japan was, and remains, a powerful advanced-industrial state with a skilled population and the world's third largest economy in terms of gross domestic product, its postwar constitution contained several unusual provisions and con-

Japan's Maritime Defense Forces remain the key military force in Japan today. Like contemporary Britain, another advanced-industrial island nation, Japan has a small army and maintains considerable naval capability to guard its sea lanes of communication for commerce purposes. Discussions over whether to increase the size of the army and to allow it to deploy abroad remain controversial.

straints. Chief among these is the prohibition against the use of Japanese armed forces abroad (contained in Article 9). So, except for humanitarian operations, Japan's defense forces are currently prohibited from deploying abroad.

Japan's historical experience constrains contemporary actions. Many historians argue that during World War II, Japan's enemies and the victims of its military campaigns came to understand Japan's aggression and brutal conduct in wartime occupation as a *national* or *race* characteristic, rather than as bad leadership. The Rape of Nanking described at the beginning of the chapter is an example of the horrors during that time. This history is why a *constitutional* constraint on the use of Japan's armed forces abroad seemed sensible to many in 1945. This contrasts with the case of Germany's Third Reich, the other major aggressor in World War II. In that case, blame largely fell on Germany's leader, Adolf Hitler, although many believed that something in German culture made Germans more warlike and brutal as a nation. Constraints, too, were put on the German military under the new constitution. Are these constraints still relevant?

Times do change; norms change. Should constitutions change with them? If so, how and how quickly? There is an ongoing debate in both Japan and Germany over this question. In the case of Japan, is the restraint on use of military force abroad still a useful way to protect its citizens from terrorism or other abuses committed outside of Japan? Does this restraint on the use of military force diminish Japan's power more generally? When can Japan become a "normal" state again—one able to protect its national interest like other states do?

FOR CRITICAL ANALYSIS

1. Should Japan be trusted to send its armed forces abroad today? Why or why not?

2. How long should the consequences of historical events affect current political decisions and institutions?

3. What are some factors that would encourage a nation to move beyond historical lessons?

a. Martin Fackler, "Beheadings Frame a New Debate About Restraints on Japan's Military," *New York Times,* February 3, 2015.

Four additional recent developments merit attention. First, "China's peaceful rise" was a term first used by China's leadership in 2003; it was meant to frame China's growing economic, military, and diplomatic power as something that would not provoke fear and insecurity in China's neighbors. Yet since 2014, China has been expanding its military at a very high rate, making it the world's second largest military budget behind the United States. In addition, in 2014, China began the practice of dredging large quantities of sand onto fragile coral reefs in the disputed waters of the Spratly Islands. These islands are a critical strategic resource for Vietnam, the Philippines, Malaysia, and Taiwan, who have each responded with their own dredging programs, though on a much smaller scale. If China's "peaceful rise" was intended to allay regional or international concerns about rising Chinese power, China's military spending and dredging have had the opposite effect. In October 2015, the U.S. Navy sent the guided missile destroyer USS *Lassen* to within 12 nautical miles of one of these artificial islands in protest, and tensions in the area—which not only traverses key shipping routes but is said to contain vast energy resources—have continued to rise.

Second, in 2014, the Russian Federation invaded Ukraine—an independent sovereign state—and then annexed the Ukrainian province of Crimea (along with its strategically important port of Sevastopol). The action was undertaken not by Russian Federation soldiers in Russian uniform, but by Russian soldiers (often special forces) wearing uniforms without insignia (a practice now called **hybrid warfare**). This tactic enabled both the Russian government and NATO and EU representatives to support the argument that no violation of international law had actually taken place, although outside of Russia, no credible authorities believe this assertion. What is perhaps most dangerous about Russian foreign policy in Ukraine is not its annexation of Crimea as such, but the precedent the action has set. In a move reminiscent of Germany's claims about Sudeten Germans in 1938, Russia argued that its citizens in Crimea and Ukraine were being physically threatened after the legitimate government of Ukraine had fallen in a coup. NATO members Poland, Slovakia, the Czech Republic, Estonia, Latvia, and Lithuania are concerned that Russia might use similar tactics to bring down their governments and annex large portions of their respective territories.

Third, Germany has been the European Union's most reliable engine of economic productivity and growth, but since 2009, the economic health and even long-term sustainability of the Eurozone has come into question. Fellow EU members Greece, Portugal, Ireland, Spain, and Cyprus have proved unable to repay or refinance their government debt. This inability has led to serious political tensions between Germany and the "northern tier" of Eurozone states. The wealthier nations have come under pressure to forgive the debt. And the debtor states claim that whatever the causes of their economic problems, allowing them to go bankrupt would destroy the European Union and, by extension perhaps, the relative peace that Europeans have come to expect.

These issues—along with closely linked issues of migration and refugees—are covered in greater detail in Chapters 7, 9, and 10.

Fourth, the weakening of powerful dictators in the Arab Spring also gave rise to the Islamic State (IS), sometimes called ISIS (Islamic State in Iraq and Syria) or ISIL (Islamic State in Iraq and the Levant), which has affected Syria, Lebanon, and Iraq, but also Iran and even Europe (many refugees from the region have sought asylum in Europe). Beyond its naked brutality (including the deliberate and systematic rape of non-Muslim girls in areas it controls) and religious conservatism (it relies on very narrow and, to most Islamic scholars, incorrect interpretations of the Koran and sayings of the Prophet), the IS has gained and maintained large swathes of territory in Iraq and Syria, and has systematically destroyed cultural heritage sites in territories it occupies asserting that these represent idol worship. We discuss the IS further in Chapter 8.

Beyond what appear to be the emergence of old-style realpolitik conflicts for all states in the new millennium, two additional major issues remain moving forward: (1) Will the **transnational** issues of the first decade—important issues that cross state boundaries, such as religion, organized crime, communicable disease, the environment, cyber security, and terrorism—become easier to redress or harder? (2) Toward what ends should states devote their national energies: military, economic, cultural, diplomatic, and political? Will containing or rooting out terrorism become the new national aim of states? Will it be preventing global environmental catastrophe? Will it be finding a way to overcome increasing income inequality worldwide? It remains to be seen which national and international goals will dominate the political landscape as the twenty-first century advances, and who will lead the way.

In Sum: Learning from History

Will the new millennium world be characterized by increasing cooperation among the great powers, or will the era be one of conflict among states or over new ideas? Do recent conflicts of interest in North Africa, the South China Sea, and Russia's geographic periphery signal a return to the multipolar system of the nineteenth century? Or is the entire concept of polarity an anachronism? How can we begin to predict what the future will bring or how it will characterize the current era? How will changing state identities and the interaction of nonstate actors and organizations affect the interests and capabilities of states moving forward?

We have taken the first step toward answering these questions by looking to the past. Our examination of the development of contemporary international relations has focused on how core concepts of international relations have emerged and evolved over time, most notably the state, sovereignty, the nation, balance of power, and the international system. Each concept developed within a specific historical context, providing the building blocks for contemporary international relations. The state is well established, but its sovereignty may be eroding from without and from within. The principal characteristics of the contemporary international system are in the process of changing as Cold War bipolarity ends.

Moreover, we have seen that the way peoples and their leaders remember events dramatically affects their sense of the legitimacy of any given cause or action. China's remembrance of the Rape of Nanking in 1937 and its feeling that Japan has never satisfactorily acknowledged its racist brutality in China during World War II still complicate China-Japan relations today. And Iran's memories of U.S. and British support for the former Shah of Iran (whom Iran considers an evil dictator), and their recent invasions of two predominantly Muslim states—Iraq and Afghanistan—strongly affect Iran's views on acquiring an independent nuclear deterrent. Thus, understanding historical events is a good way to understand the motives of *contemporary* leaders and the peoples they lead.

To help us further understand the trends of the past and how they influence contemporary thinking, we turn to theory. Theory gives order to analysis; it provides generalized explanations for specific events. In Chapter 3, we will look at competing theories of international relations. These theories view the past from quite different perspectives.

Discussion Questions

1. The Treaties of Westphalia are often viewed as the beginning of modern international relations. Why are they a useful benchmark? What factors does this benchmark ignore?

2. Colonization by the great powers of Europe has officially ended. However, the effects of the colonial era linger. Explain with specific examples.

3. The Cold War has ended. Discuss two current events in which Cold War politics persist.

4. The developments of international relations as a discipline have been closely identified with the history of Western Europe and the United States. With this civilizational bias, what might we be missing?

Key Terms

balance of power (p. 35)

capitalism (p. 46)

Cold War (p. 44)

colonialism (p. 31)

containment (p. 45)

détente (p. 56)

deterrence (p. 48)

domino effect (p. 52)

hegemon (p. 35)

hybrid warfare (p. 66)

imperialism (p. 31)

League of Nations (p. 39)

legitimacy (p. 26)

nation (p. 26)

nationalism (p. 26)

North Atlantic Treaty Organization (NATO) (p. 46)

rollback (p. 45)

socialism (p. 46)

sovereignty (p. 23)

summits (p. 56)

superpowers (p. 45)

Third Reich (p. 41)

transnational (p. 67)

Treaties of Westphalia (p. 23)

war on terrorism (p. 61)

Warsaw Pact (p. 49)

weapons of mass destruction (WMD) (p. 61)

O3

U.S. Army captain Kristen Griest and U.S. Army first lieutenant Shaye Haver congratulate each other on successfully completing the U.S. Army's ranger qualification course. On August 21, 2015, the two became the first women in U.S. history to graduate from the elite course, meeting the same standards as the 94 men who graduated with them.

INTERNATIONAL RELATIONS THEORIES

On March 20, 2005, a 23-year-old U.S. Army National Guard sergeant named Leigh Ann Hester responded to her convoy's ambush by anti-Iraqi insurgents by leading her team in a counterattack. Her actions saved the convoy and killed 27 insurgents, wounded six, and captured one. Hester's leadership was not only brave, it was also smart. By moving her team across the ambush's kill zone, Hester's team was able to attack the insurgent positions from the side with devastating effect. Because of her leadership, Sergeant Hester was awarded the third-highest medal for valor in combat, the Silver Star, in June 2005, making her only the second woman since World War II to receive the honor.

More women fought and died in the U.S.-led military intervention in Iraq (2003–2011) than in all the wars since World War II put together. This is true even though American women were not allowed to serve in combat units until December 2015, when U.S. secretary of defense Ashton Carter formally overturned this long-standing ruling. Because armies no longer fight only on front lines with relatively safe rear areas, these women lost their lives in Iraq and Afghanistan. Today, and for the foreseeable future, soldiers and marines on the ground face threats of imminent action from any direction and at any time.

Women serving in combat areas are often exposed to the same risks and engage in the same reactions as their male counterparts do. Yet they suffer discrimination both in service and after, as well as a very high risk of sexual assault while serving. Many female veterans of Iraq were surprised to find that when they returned home, they were not respected as the men were for their service. As one rightfully angry female U.S. Army veteran put it: "War doesn't give a damn what your job is, we're getting killed anyway . . . We're getting blown up right alongside the guys. We're manning whatever weapons we can get our little hands on. We're in combat!"[1] The plight of women in the U.S. armed forces is not unique, but it highlights a deeper theoretical critique of contemporary and historical international relations and foreign policy. What is the source of the long-standing ban on women serving in combat roles in the military? How does limiting women's roles in the military affect our views of women's potential as leaders in other pursuits? Would world politics look different if women and men were given equal opportunities worldwide, and if so, how? International relations theories offer answers.

LEARNING OBJECTIVES

- Explain the value of studying international relations from a theoretical perspective.

- Understand why scholars pay attention to the levels-of-analysis problem.

- Explain the central tenets of realism, liberalism, radicalism, and constructivism. Understand the feminist critiques of each perspective.

- Analyze contemporary international events using different theoretical perspectives.

Thinking Theoretically

A **theory** is a set of propositions and concepts that combine to explain phenomena by specifying the relationships among the propositions. Theory's ultimate goal is to predict phenomena. Good theories can explain events across space (e.g., it works just as well in Argentina as it does in Morocco) and time (e.g., it works just as well today as it did in the tenth century). Good theories generate testable **hypotheses**: specific *falsifiable* statements questioning a particular relationship among two or more variables.

By testing groups of interrelated hypotheses, theories are either refuted or supported and refined—but never conclusively "proven"—and new relationships are found that demand subsequent testing.

A famous example of a powerful theory from the natural sciences is Charles Darwin's theory of evolution. Darwin's theory of natural selection and his concept of survival of the fittest explain what had previously been puzzling variation in the coloration and beak shapes of identical species of birds in different environments. We say that Darwin's theory is powerful because it has survived many challenges; its logic is consistent, even with evidence unavailable to Darwin at the time he formulated his theory. The theory is therefore very general in the sense that it can explain seemingly unique variations across space and time. Yet in neither natural nor social sciences do we ever consider theories to be "proven" or "settled" or "fact." Theories, whether Darwin's or Albert Einstein's or Kenneth Waltz's, can always be overturned or refuted by new evidence or better theory. Theories are therefore *not* explanations that scientists "believe in." Rather, we say they are stronger or weaker, or more or less supported.

Moving from description to explanation to theory, and from theory to testable hypotheses, is not an entirely linear process. Although theory depends on a logical

The destruction of a statue of Saddam Hussein in Baghdad became a symbol of his regime's defeat in 2003 by a U.S.-led coalition. Theory can help us understand why Saddam risked war with a more powerful country and why the United States chose to invade Iraq.

deduction of hypotheses from assumptions and a testing of the hypotheses as more and more data are collected in the empirical world, we often must revise or adjust theories. This process is, in part, a creative exercise, in which we must be tolerant of ambiguity, concerned about probabilities, and distrustful of absolutes.

International relations (IR) theories come in various forms. In this chapter, we introduce four general theories, or theoretical perspectives, in the study of international relations: realism (and neorealism), liberalism (and neoliberal institutionalism), radicalism (in this case, Marxism), and social constructivism. The attempt to explain such important and complex things as war, peace, oppression, economic development, and crisis remains ambitious; explanations require constant testing and revision. Before we examine these theories more closely, we apply three levels of analysis—a tool IR theorists use to manage the bewildering complexity of the empirical world—to the 2003 U.S. and coalition invasion of Iraq.

Theory and the Levels of Analysis

The United States and its coalition partners invaded Iraq in 2003. Understanding why and when the invasion happened may prove critical in challenging contemporary IR theory—and in preventing future wars. What then is our best explanation of the invasion? We can organize the list of possible explanations according to three **levels of analysis** (see Figure 3.1). Dividing the analysis of international politics into levels helps orient our questions and suggests the appropriate type of evidence to explore. Paying attention to levels of analysis helps us make logical deductions and enables us to explore all categories of explanation.

A categorization first used by Kenneth Waltz and later amplified by J. David Singer offers three different sources of explanations. If the *individual level* is the focus, then the personality, perceptions, choices, and activities of individual decision makers (e.g., Saddam Hussein and George W. Bush) and individual participants (e.g., Defense Secretary Donald Rumsfeld and Saddam's sons) provide the explanation. If the *state level*, or domestic factors, is the focus, then the explanation is derived from characteristics of the state: the type of government (e.g., democratic or authoritarian), the type of economic system (e.g., capitalist or socialist), interest groups within the country, or even the national interest. If the *international system level* is the focus, then the explanation rests with the characteristics of that system (such as the distribution of "power") or with international and regional organizations and their relative strengths and weaknesses.[2]

Box 3.1 on p. 76 categorizes possible explanations for the Iraq War according to these three levels of analysis. Of course, explanations from all three levels probably contributed to the United States' decision to invade Iraq in 2003. The purpose of theory

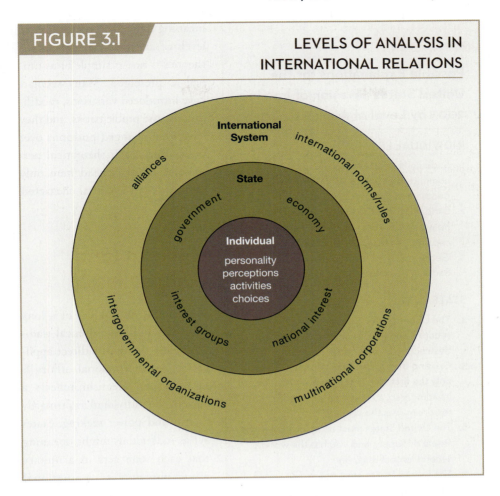

FIGURE 3.1

LEVELS OF ANALYSIS IN
INTERNATIONAL RELATIONS

is to guide us toward an understanding of which of these various ideas are necessary and sufficient to explain the invasion.

Although most international relations scholars acknowledge the utility of paying attention to levels of analysis, they differ on how many levels are useful in explaining events. Most political scientists apply between three and six levels. Although adding more layers may provide more descriptive context, it makes explanation and prediction more difficult. The most important differentiation in theory must be made between the international level and the domestic level. In this book, we will use the three levels explained earlier: individual, state, and international system.

Good theory, then, should effectively explain phenomena at a particular level of analysis; better theory should also offer explanations across different levels of analysis. The general theories outlined in the rest of this chapter are all comprehensive,

BOX 3.1

Possible Explanations for the United States' Invasion of Iraq in 2003 by Level of Analysis

INDIVIDUAL LEVEL

1. Saddam Hussein was an evil leader who committed atrocities against his own people and defied the West.
2. Saddam Hussein was irrational; otherwise, he would have capitulated to the superior capability of the U.S. and British coalition.
3. George W. Bush and his advisers targeted Saddam Hussein and Iraq in 2001.

STATE LEVEL

4. The United States must protect its national security, and Iraq's weapons of mass destruction threatened U.S. security.
5. Ousting the Taliban from Afghanistan was only the first step in the war on terrorism; invading Iraq, a known supporter of terrorism, was the second.
6. The United States must be assured of a stable oil supply, and Iraq has the world's second largest reserves.
7. The United States must not permit states that support terrorism or terrorist groups access to destructive weapons.
8. It is in the U.S. national interest to build a progressive Arab regime in the Middle East.

INTERNATIONAL SYSTEM LEVEL

9. UN resolutions condemning Iraq had to be enforced to maintain the legitimacy of the United Nations.
10. A unipolar international system is uniquely capable of responding to perceived threats to the stability of the system, and the U.S. invasion was one manifestation of this capability.
11. There is an international moral imperative for humanitarian intervention—to oust evil leaders and install democratic regimes.

meaning they incorporate all three levels of analysis. Yet each of the theories is not as simple or as unified as presented. Many scholars have introduced variations, modifications, and problematics, and they have even changed positions over time. Thus, each theoretical perspective is introduced here only in terms of its essential characteristics.

Realism (and Neorealism)

Realism is the product of a long historical and philosophical tradition, even though its direct application to international affairs is more recent. Realism reflects a view of the individual as primarily fearful and power seeking. States act as individuals might, meaning that each state acts in a unitary way in pursuit of its own **national interest**, defined in terms of power. *Power,* in turn, is primarily thought of in terms of the material resources necessary to physically harm or coerce other states: in other words, to fight and win wars. These states exist in an anarchic international system, a characterization in which the term *anarchy* highlights the absence of an authoritative hierarchy (i.e., a single state powerful enough to conquer all other states). Under this condition of anarchy, realists argue that states in the international system can rely only on themselves. Their most important concern is to increase their own relative power. They can do so by means of two logical pathways: (1) war (and conquest) or (2) balance (either *dividing* the power of real or potential rivals by means of alliance politics or economic sanctions, or *multiplying* their own power by raising armies, or manufacturing fearsome weaponry).

The Roots of Realism

At least four of the essential assumptions of realism are found in Thucydides's *History of the Peloponnesian War*.[3] First, for Thucydides, the state (in this case, Athens and Sparta) is the *principal actor* in war and in politics in general, just as today's realists posit. Although other actors, such as international institutions, may participate, their impact on the system is marginal.

Second, the state is assumed to be a **unitary actor**. Although Thucydides includes fascinating debates among different officials from the same state, he argues that once a state decides to go to war or capitulate, it speaks and acts with one voice. No subnational actors are trying to overturn the government's decision or subvert the state's interests.

Third, decision makers acting in the name of the state are assumed to be **rational actors**. Like most educated Greeks, Thucydides believed that individuals are essentially rational beings who make decisions by weighing the strengths and weaknesses of various options against the goal to be achieved. Thucydides admitted that potential impediments to rational decision making exist, including wishful thinking by leaders, confusing intentions and national interests, and misperceiving the characteristics of the counterpart decision maker. But the core notion—that rational decision making leads to the pursuit of the national interest—remains. Likewise for modern realists, rational decisions advance the national interest—the interests of the state—however ambiguously that national interest is formulated.

Fourth, Thucydides, like contemporary realists, was concerned with security issues—the state's need to protect itself from enemies both foreign and domestic. A state augments its security by increasing its domestic capacities, strengthening its economic prowess, and forming alliances with other states based on similar interests. In fact, Thucydides found that before and during the Peloponnesian War, fear of rivals motivated states to join alliances, a rational decision by their leaders. In perhaps the most famous section of *History of the Peloponnesian War*, the Melian dialogue, Thucydides summarized a key tenet of realist thinking: "[T]he strong do what they can and the weak suffer what they must." More generally, do states have rights based on the conception of an international ethical or moral order, as liberals suggest? Or is a state's power, in the absence of an international authority, the deciding factor?

Thucydides did not identify all the tenets of what we think of as realism today. Indeed, the tenets and rationale of realism have unfolded over centuries, and not all realists agree on what they are. For example, six centuries after Thucydides lived, the Christian bishop and philosopher Saint Augustine (354–430) added a fundamental assumption of realism, arguing that humanity is flawed, egoistic, and selfish, although not predetermined to be so. Augustine blames war on these basic characteristics of humanity.[4] Although subsequent realists dispute Augustine's biblical explanation for humanity's flawed, selfish nature, few realists dispute the fact that humans are basically power seeking and self-absorbed.

The central tenet virtually all realist theorists accept is that the chief constraint on "better" state behavior—especially enduring peace—is that states exist in an anarchic international system. This tenet was forcefully articulated by Thomas Hobbes (see Chapter 1), who lived and wrote during one of history's greatest periods of turmoil (the Thirty Years' War, 1618–48, and the English Civil Wars, 1641–51). Hobbes maintained that just as individuals in a hypothetical "state of nature" have the responsibility and the right to preserve themselves—including a right of violence against others—so too does each state in the international system. In his most famous treatise, *Leviathan*, Hobbes argued that the only cure for perpetual war within a state was the emergence of a single powerful prince who could overawe all others: a leviathan. Applying his arguments to relations among sovereigns, Hobbes depicted a condition of anarchy where the norm for states is "having their weapons pointing, and their eyes fixed on one another."[5] In the absence of an international sovereign to enforce rules, few rules or norms can restrain states. War—defined by Hobbes as a climate in which peace cannot be guaranteed—would be perpetual.

In sum, by the twentieth century, most of the central tenets of realism were well established. Given a system in which no single power was capable of imposing its will on all the others (anarchy), states in the system had to rely on self-help. Because even allies might, in a crisis, hesitate or refuse to come to an ally's aid, a state's only rational policy in a self-help world would be to seek power. According to one prominent post–World War II realist, international relations theorist Hans Morgenthau (1904–80), this idea explained why peace in the international system would always prove elusive.

Realism in the Twentieth and Twenty-First Centuries

In the aftermath of World War II, Morgenthau wrote the seminal synthesis of realism in international politics and offered what he argued was a methodological approach for testing this theory. For Morgenthau, just as for Thucydides, Augustine, and Hobbes, international politics is best characterized as a struggle for power. That struggle can be explained at the three levels of analysis: (1) the flawed individual in the state of nature struggles for self-preservation; (2) the autonomous and unitary state is constantly involved in power struggles, balancing power with power and reacting to preserve what is in the national interest; and (3) because the international system is anarchic—no higher power exists to defeat the competition—the struggle is perpetual. Because of the imperative to ensure a state's survival, leaders are driven by a morality quite different from that of ordinary individuals. Morality, for realists, is to be judged by the political consequences of a policy.[6]

Morgenthau's international relations textbook *Politics among Nations* became the realist bible in the years following World War II. Policy implications flowed naturally from the theory that the most effective technique for managing power is balance of power. Both George Kennan (1904–2005), a writer and chair of the state department's policy planning staff in the late 1940s and later the U.S. ambassador to the Soviet Union, and Henry Kissinger (b. 1923), a scholar, foreign policy adviser, and secretary of state to presidents Richard Nixon and Gerald Ford, are known to have based their policy recommendations on realist theory.

As we saw in Chapter 2, Kennan was one of the architects of the U.S. Cold War policy of containment, an interpretation of the balance of power. The goal of containment was to prevent Soviet power from extending into regions beyond that country's immediate, existing sphere of influence (Eastern Europe), thus balancing U.S. power against Soviet power. Containment was an important alternative to the competing strategy of "rollback," in which a combination of nuclear and conventional military threats would be used to force the Soviet Union out of Eastern Europe and, in particular, Germany. Kennan's keen analysis of Soviet intentions and his fear of uncontrolled escalation to a third world war ultimately led to the adoption of containment as U.S. foreign policy. During the 1970s, Kissinger encouraged the classic realist balance of power by supporting weaker powers such as China and Pakistan to exert leverage over the Soviet Union and to offset India's growing power, respectively. At the time, India was an ally of the Soviets.

Whereas realism appears to offer clear policy prescriptions, not all realists agree on what an ideal realist foreign policy might look like. Defensive realists observe that few if any major wars in the last century ended up benefiting the state or states that started them. Threatened states, they argue, tend to balance against aggressors, invariably overwhelming and reversing whatever initial gains were made.

Saddam Hussein's attempt to conquer and annex neighboring Kuwait in 1990 serves as a classic example. In August 1990, Iraq's armed forces quickly overwhelmed the paltry defenses of Kuwait, and Saddam's soldiers followed their victory with rape and looting. Before the invasion, Kuwait had been a little-known, oil-rich Arab state in which a repressive hereditary elite ruled over a population composed mainly of servants hired from surrounding Arab countries (in particular, Palestinian Arabs). However, although critics pointed out that Kuwait was itself a less-than-ideal candidate for rescue, Saddam's aggression provoked a powerful international reaction. In 1991, an international coalition of armed forces, led by the United States, invaded Kuwait and rapidly forced the retreat and later surrender of the Iraqi army. Iraq was forced to repay all the damages of its conquest, and its sovereignty was abridged by two "no-fly" zones, which offered some protection to Kurds in the north and Shia Muslims in the south from Saddam's harsh reprisals. Conquest, in other words, did not pay for Iraq.

For defensive realists, the outcome of Iraq's 1990 war forms part of a long historical pattern of effective (and inevitable) balancing. In this case, Saudi Arabia, the United States, and others supported Kuwait to balance against Iraq's regional power. As a result, defensive realists argue that states in the international system should pursue policies of restraint, whether through military, diplomatic, or economic channels. Such defensive moderate postures can be pursued without leading to dangerous levels of mistrust among states and, more importantly, without fear of unintended or uncontrolled escalation to counterproductive wars.

Offensive realists, by contrast, note that periodically demonstrating a willingness to engage in war, though perhaps costly in the short run, may pay huge dividends in reputation enhancement later. They argue that the credible threat of conquest can often act as a motivation to alter a target state's interests, leading states that might have opposed the threatening state to ally with it in a process international relations theorists call **bandwagoning**. The logic is that the more power you have, the more power you get. Conquest, in other words, pays. States may thus pursue expansionist politics, building up their relative power positions and intimidating potential rivals into cooperation.

Consider the stunning case of Libya's decision in December 2003 to publicly acknowledge and then abandon its years-long efforts to acquire nuclear, chemical, and biological weapons, along with the vehicles to launch them. To an offensive realist, Libya's decision could well have been the result of the George W. Bush administration's decision to invade Iraq in March 2003, an invasion justified to halt Saddam's production or dissemination of weapons of mass destruction (WMD). After years of opposing the United States, Libya chose instead to bandwagon in the face of this demonstration of U.S. power. By offensive realist logic, the costs of the war against Iraq were at least partly redeemed by Libya's change of policy: conquest, or the credible threat of conquest, paid.

Thus, defensive and offensive realists have significant differences of view about appropriate foreign policy.[7] In fact, realism encompasses a family of related arguments, sharing common assumptions and premises. It is not a single, unified theory. Among the various reinterpretations of realism, the most important is **neorealism** (or structural realism), as delineated in Kenneth Waltz's *Theory of International Politics*.[8] Reasoning that lack of progress in social scientific theory of international politics was due to lack of theoretical rigor (especially in comparison to steady theoretical progress in the natural sciences), Waltz undertook this reinterpretation of classical realism to make political realism a more rigorous theory of international politics. Neorealists therefore propose general laws to explain events: they simplify explanations of behavior in anticipation of being better able to explain and predict trends.

Neorealists give precedence in their analyses to the structure of the international system as an explanatory factor, while traditional realists also attach importance to the characteristics of states and human nature. According to Waltz, the most important object of study is the structure of the international system. Attempting to understand the international system by reference to states is analogous, in Waltz's view, to attempting to understand a market by reference to individual firms: unproductive at best. Neorealism thus advances two normative arguments and one theoretical. The first normative argument is that we need theory to understand international politics (and that prior to the publication of Waltz's book, we had none), and the second is that his theory, neorealism, explains international politics since 1648, the date scholars cite for the advent of the state system. Waltz's theoretical argument is that the amount of peace and war in an anarchic international system depends critically on the distribution of power, described in terms of system structure.

Critics of classical realism noted that if the human desire for power, inscribed on states, was driving the recurrence of interstate war, how could we explain long periods of peace? Waltz argued that the distribution of power in the international system can be described as having one of three possible forms: (1) unipolar (where one state in the system has sufficient power to defeat all the others combined against it; we've never seen a true unipolar situation); (2) bipolar (where most of the system's power is divided between two states or coalitions of states; as between Rome and Carthage, or Athens and Sparta); and (3) multipolar (in which power is divided among three or more states or coalitions of states, as in Europe in 1914). Thus, according to neorealists, the structure of the system and the distribution of power within it, rather than the characteristics of individual states, determine outcomes. This is why, in the neorealist view, the closer the overall distribution of power approaches unipolarity, the greater the likelihood (but never the certainty) of peace.[9]

This observation leads to another key question, the answers to which lie at the root of the disagreement between liberals and realists. Why, we might ask, have not two or more great powers ever cooperated to become a single leviathan, thus ending war? Neorealists posit two answers: first, cooperation is difficult under conditions of anarchy due to concerns over relative gains; and second, states in an anarchic system must be on constant guard against cheating.

The importance of relative power means that states hesitate to engage in cooperation if the benefits to be gained might be distributed unevenly among participating states. For example, if you and I are trading partners, and after each trade I gain $3.00 and you gain $1.50, we both gain in absolute terms. But, over time, I will accumulate more cash than you will; I might then use my advantage in wealth to coerce you. In a neorealist's

THEORY IN BRIEF	REALISM / NEOREALISM
KEY ACTORS	States (most powerful matter most)
VIEW OF THE INDIVIDUAL	Insecure, selfish, power-seeking
VIEW OF THE STATE	Insecure, selfish, unitary, power-seeking as evidence of rationality
VIEW OF THE INTERNATIONAL SYSTEM	Anarchic (implies perpetual threat of war); more stable as distribution of power approaches unipolarity
BELIEFS ABOUT CHANGE	Possibility of perpetual peace logically precluded; emphasis shifted to managing the frequency and intensity of war
MAJOR THEORISTS	Thucydides, Saint Augustine, Hobbes, Morgenthau, Waltz, Gilpin, Mearsheimer

balance-of-power world, a state's survival depends on its having more power than other states. Thus, all power, and gains in power, is viewed in relative rather than absolute terms.[10]

Neorealists are also concerned with cheating. States may be tempted to cheat on agreements so they can gain a relative advantage over other states. Fear that other states will renege on existing cooperative agreements is especially potent in the military realm, in which changes in weaponry might result in a major shift in the balance of power. Self-interest provides a powerful incentive for one state to take advantage of another. The awareness that such incentives exist, combined with states' rational desire to protect their own interests, tends to preclude long-term cooperation among states. As the popular paraphrase of Britain's Lord Palmerston (1784–1865) puts it, "Nations have no permanent friends or allies, only permanent interests."

Scholars have developed other interpretations of realism as well. Although neorealism simplifies the classical realist theory and focuses on a few core concepts (system structure and balance of power), other reinterpretations add increased complexity to realism. In *War and Change in World Politics*, Robert Gilpin offers one such reinterpretation. Accepting the realist assumptions that states are the principal actors, decision makers are basically rational, and the international system structure plays a key role in determining power, Gilpin examines 2,400 years of history, finding that "the distribution of power among states constitutes the principal form of control in every international system."[11] What Gilpin adds is the notion of dynamism, of history as a series of cycles—cycles of the birth, expansion, and demise of dominant powers.

Whereas classical realism offers no satisfactory rationale for the decline of powers, Gilpin finds the answer in economic power. Hegemons decline because of three processes: the increasingly marginal returns of controlling an empire, a state-level phenomenon; the tendency for economic hegemons to consume more over time and invest less, also a state-level phenomenon; and the diffusion of technology, a system-level phenomenon through which new powers challenge the hegemon. As Gilpin explains, "disequilibrium replaces equilibrium, and the world moves toward a new round of hegemonic conflict."[12]

In short, there is no single tradition of political realism; there are "realisms." Although each is predicated on a key group of assumptions, each attaches different importance to the various core propositions. Yet what unites proponents of realist theory—their emphasis on the unitary state in an anarchic international system, and a threat of war that can be managed but never done away with—distinguishes them clearly from both the liberals and the radicals.

Liberalism and Neoliberal Institutionalism

Liberalism holds that human nature is basically good and that people can improve their moral and material conditions, thus making societal progress—including lasting peace—possible. Bad or evil human behavior, such as injustice and war, is the product of inadequate or corrupt social institutions and misunderstandings among leaders. Thus, liberals believe that injustice, war, and aggression are not inevitable but can be moderated or even eliminated through institutional reform or collective action. According to liberal thinking, the expansion of human freedom is best achieved in democracies and through well-regulated market capitalism.

The Roots of Liberalism

The origins of liberal theory are found in eighteenth-century Enlightenment optimism, nineteenth-century political and economic liberalism, and twentieth-century Wilsonian idealism. The contribution of the Enlightenment to liberalism rests on the Greek idea that individuals are rational human beings, able to understand the universally applicable laws governing both nature and human society. Understanding such laws means that people have the capacity to improve their condition by creating a just society. If a just society is not attained, then the fault rests with inadequate institutions, the result of a corrupt environment.

The writings of the French philosopher Charles-Louis de Secondat, Baron de La Brède et de Montesquieu (1689–1755), reflect Enlightenment thinking. He argued that human nature is not defective, but rather, problems arise as humanity enters civil society and forms separate nations. War is a product of society, not an attribute inherent in individuals. To overcome defects in society, education is imperative; it prepares one for civil life. Groups of states are united according to the law of nations, which regulates conduct even during war. Montesquieu optimistically stated that "different nations ought in time of peace to do one another all the good they can, and in time of war as little harm as possible, without prejudicing their real interests."[13]

Likewise, the writings of Immanuel Kant (1724–1804) form the core of Enlightenment beliefs. According to Kant, international anarchy can be overcome through a particular kind of collective action—a federation of republics in which sovereignties would be left intact. Like other liberal philosophers, Kant's argument held out the possibility of transcending the limitations of anarchy in the international system and the withering away of war. Unlike others, however, Kant's philosophy did not assume or require moral actors. On the contrary, Kant assumed that states would act in self-interested ways and that the repeated interaction of self-interested states would eventually lead to an expanding zone of peace, *in spite of that self-interest*. As he famously put it, what is required for the emergence of perpetual peace is not moral angels, but "rational devils."[14]

Nineteenth-century liberalism took the rationalism of the Enlightenment and reformulated it by adding a preference for democracy over aristocracy and for free trade over national economic self-sufficiency. Sharing the Enlightenment's optimistic view of human nature, nineteenth-century liberalism saw humanity as capable of satisfying its natural needs and wants in rational ways. These needs and wants could be met most efficiently when each individual pursued his or her own freedom and autonomy in a democratic state, unfettered by excessive governmental restrictions. Likewise, political freedoms are most easily achieved in capitalist states, where rational and acquisitive human beings can improve their own conditions, maximizing both individual and collective economic growth and economic welfare. Free markets must be allowed to flourish, and governments must permit the free flow of trade and commerce. Liberal theorists believe that free trade and commerce create interdependencies among states, thus raising the cost of war and reducing its likelihood.

Twentieth-century idealism also contributed to liberalism, finding its greatest adherent in U.S. president Woodrow Wilson. Wilson authored the covenant of the League of Nations—hence the term *Wilsonian idealism*. The basic proposition of Wilson's idealism is that war is preventable through the collective action of states; more than half of the League covenant's 26 provisions focused on preventing war. The covenant even included a provision legitimizing the notion of **collective security**, whereby aggression by one state would be countered by automatic and collective reaction, embodied in a "league of nations."

Thus, the League of Nations illustrated the importance that liberals place on the potential of international institutions to deal with war and the opportunity for collective problem solving in a multilateral forum. Liberals also place faith in international law and legal instruments such as mediation, arbitration, and international courts. Still other liberals think that all war can be eliminated through disarmament. Whatever the specific prescriptive solution, the basis of liberalism remains firmly embedded in the belief in the rationality of human beings, the irreducibility of the human condition to the individual (unlike realists, who model human insecurity on an isolated human being, liberals observe that humans exist everywhere in *society*), and that through learning and education, humans can develop institutions capable of ensuring and advancing human welfare.

During the interwar period, when the League of Nations proved incapable of maintaining collective security, and during World War II, when atrocities made many question the basic goodness of humanity, liberalism came under intense criticism. *Was* humankind inherently good? How could an institution fashioned under the best assumptions have failed so miserably? Liberalism as a theoretical perspective fell out of favor, replaced by realism and its preferred solution to the scourge of war: a balance of power.

Neoliberal Institutionalism

Since the 1970s, however, liberalism has been revived under the rubric of **neoliberal institutionalism**. Neoliberal institutionalists such as the political scientists Robert Axelrod and Robert O. Keohane ask *why* states choose to cooperate most of the time, even under the anarchic conditions of the international system. One answer is found in the simple but important story of the prisoner's dilemma.[15]

The **prisoner's dilemma** is the story of two prisoners who are interrogated separately for an alleged crime. The police have enough evidence to convict both prisoners on a minor charge but need a confession to convict them on a major charge. An interrogator tells each prisoner that if one testifies against the other (defects) and the other stays silent (cooperates), the one who defects will go free, but the one who cooperates will get a one-year prison term. If both defect, both will get three-month prison terms. If neither defects (i.e., they both cooperate and stay silent), both will receive one-month prison terms for the minor charge. Let's say that both prisoners defect. Each will serve a longer sentence than if they had cooperated and kept silent. Why didn't each prisoner cooperate? So long as the game is played once, neither prisoner can be certain of what the other will do, so each chooses to testify against the other (defect) because each will be better off *regardless of what the other prisoner decides*. Two important points follow. First, the prisoner's dilemma is actually not a dilemma, because so long as the game is structured as it is, any rational prisoner would choose to defect: it is the only sure way of minimizing the possibility of disaster (a full year in jail). Second, the prisoner's dilemma is famous as an illustrative game because it highlights how the

French president François Hollande and German chancellor Angela Merkel attend a celebration of the peaceful Franco-German relationship that has endured since the end of World
War II. Liberal theorists believe France's and Germany's joint membership in numerous
international organizations, including the UN, NATO, and the European Union, has supported
this long peace.

structure of an interaction can intervene between intention and outcome to explain
unintended (or harmful) outcomes. It is an effectively realist story, which emphasizes
how the structure of interactions limit the possibility of peace through cooperation.
But neoliberal institutionalists added a startling question: Why assume a single round of
play?

If the prisoner's dilemma interaction is played repeatedly, the likelihood of reciprocity (known in game theory parlance as "tit for tat") makes it rational for each prisoner
to cooperate rather than defect. If either prisoner testified against the other in a first
round, then in a second round, that prisoner could expect retaliation. As more rounds
are played, rational players understand they can maximize their expected benefit by
cooperating, and over time, cooperation becomes their preferred or dominant strategy. Similarly, states in the international system are not faced with a one-time round
of "play": they confront each other repeatedly on a wide range of issues. Unlike classical liberals, neoliberal institutionalists do not believe that individuals naturally cooperate out of an innate characteristic of humanity. The prisoner's dilemma provides
neoliberal institutionalists with a rationale for mutual cooperation in an environment
where no international authority mandates such cooperation.

Neoliberal institutionalists arrive at the same prediction that liberals do—cooperation—but their explanation for why cooperation occurs is different. For classical liberals, cooperation emerges from humanity's establishing and reforming institutions that permit cooperative interactions and prohibit coercive actions. For neoliberal institutionalists, cooperation emerges because when actors have continuous interactions with each other, it is in their *self-interest* to cooperate. Institutions help prevent cheating in other ways: they reduce transaction costs (costs incurred in making an exchange), reduce opportunity costs (the costs of alternative possibilities), and improve the flow of information—all benefits of cooperation.

Two other additions to neoliberal institutionalist thought also explain cooperation. First, cooperation in one issue area may spill over into other areas. Thus, cooperation on trade may over time lead to cooperation on security. Second, theorists such as Robert Keohane argue that institutional cooperation can deepen to the point where it may be said to have inertia: whatever the original conditions of its establishment, once established, institutional cooperation can exist and even flourish—even if those initial conditions vanish. Consider NATO: it was founded after World War II to prevent Europe from being bullied or conquered by the Soviet Union, yet the Soviet Union disintegrated in 1991. Why then does NATO still exist? Neoliberal institutionalists would argue that the cooperation that originally made NATO possible and effective deepened over time to become an end in itself.

For neoliberal institutionalists, security is essential, just as it is for realists. But as theorists like G. John Ikenberry argue, realism cannot explain the duration of postwar stability following the collapse of the Soviet Union, while neoliberal institutionalism can.[16] Institutions such as NATO and the European Union's Common Foreign and Security Policy provide a guaranteed framework of interactions, and thus incorporate a powerful expectation of repeated interactions. The implication of these repeated interactions is increased cooperation, not only on security issues but across a whole range of international issues including economics and trade, human rights (a classic liberal concern), the environment, immigration, and transnational crime.[17] Thus, for neoliberals, institutions are critical: they facilitate, widen, and deepen cooperation by building on common interests, thus maximizing the gains for all parties. Institutions help shape state preferences, solidifying cooperative relationships.

Liberalism Today

With the end of the Cold War in the 1990s, liberalism as a general theoretical perspective has achieved new credibility. Two particular areas stand out. First, researchers of the so-called democratic peace (discussed in more detail in Chapter 5) have been trying to explain an empirical puzzle: although on balance, democratic states are as warlike as authoritarian states, democratic states never attack *each other*. The question

THEORY IN BRIEF	LIBERALISM / NEOLIBERAL INSTITUTIONALISM
KEY ACTORS	States, nongovernmental groups, international organizations
VIEW OF THE INDIVIDUAL	Basically good; social; capable of cooperating
VIEW OF THE STATE	States are selfish; have relationships (enduring friends and rivals); can be good (democratic-liberal) or bad (authoritarian-autarkic)
VIEW OF THE INTERNATIONAL SYSTEM	Anarchy abridged by interdependence among actors; an international order
BELIEFS ABOUT CHANGE	Self-interest managed by structure (institutions) leads to possibility of perpetual peace
MAJOR THEORISTS	Montesquieu, Kant, Wilson, Keohane, Doyle, Ikenberry

is: Why? Various liberal explanations provide potential answers. One argument is that the democratic process inhibits aggression; leaders in democracies hear from a multiplicity of voices that tend to restrain decision makers and therefore lessen the chance of war. Another argument is that transnational and international institutions that bind democracies together through dense networks act to constrain behavior. These explanations are based on liberal theorizing. The policy implications are clear: replacing dictators with democratic governments could reduce the likelihood of interstate war, a net benefit to every state in the system of states.

Second, the scholar and former policy analyst Francis Fukuyama sees not just a revival but also a victory for international liberalism following the end of the Cold War. He admits that some groups, such as Palestinians and Israelis, and Armenians and Azeris, will continue to have grievances against one another. But the frequency of large-scale conflict has been declining over the last 20 years. For the first time, Fukuyama argues, the possibility exists for the "universalization of Western liberal democracy as the final form of human governance."[18] Indeed, the political scientist John Mueller makes the liberal argument even more strongly. Just as dueling and slavery, once acceptable practices, have become morally unacceptable, nations of the developed world increasingly see war as immoral and repugnant. The terrifying moments of World Wars I and II have led to the obsolescence of war, says Mueller (see Chapter 8).[19] And Mueller's observation that war is going out of fashion has recently been expanded by two other scholars, Steven Pinker and Joshua Goldstein. Pinker, a scholar of cognitive and evolutionary psychology, argues that not only has war gone out of fashion, but violence of all sorts is also disappearing. Goldstein's analysis shows that the frequency and intensity of war between states has dropped precipitously in the past four decades, so much so that he has argued that "the war against war has been won."[20]

Liberalism, then, has provided the major counterpoint to realism. Although these two theories differ in many respects, they both assume that actors are basically rational and that states are the most important international actors, and both conceptualize power in material terms.

The Radical Perspective

Radicalism offers a third theoretical perspective on international relations. Whereas agreement is widespread concerning the appropriate assignment of the liberal and realist labels, no such agreement exists about the label *radicalism*, which for some carries unavoidable negative connotations. We use the term today in its more neutral sense of "a sharp *departure* from the norm," and, in this case, one such norm is the state as a necessary form of political association. Radicals, such as anarchists and Marxists, problematize the state itself. Their idea that the state is the *problem* is part of what sets them so dramatically apart from realists and liberals.

The writings of Karl Marx (1818–83) are fundamental to all radical thought, even though his theories did not directly address many contemporary issues. Marx based his theory of the evolution of capitalism on economic class conflict: the capitalism of nineteenth-century Europe emerged out of the earlier feudal system. According to Marx, in the capitalist system, private interests control labor and market exchanges, creating bondages from which certain classes try to free themselves. Note that Marx and his partner Friedrich Engels borrowed the notion of "class" from Europe's social classes (upper classes, the aristocracy; middle classes, guildsmen; and lower classes, peasants and laborers) but reimagined them as two economic classes: a bourgeoisie—which owns all means of production—and a proletariat—exploited labor. A clash inevitably arises between the controlling, capitalist bourgeois class and the controlled proletariat. A new socialist order is born from this violent clash, which the proletariat must inevitably win after a period of revolutionary struggle.[21]

A group of core beliefs unites those espousing a radical, mostly Marxist, perspective. The first set of radical beliefs is found in historical analysis. Whereas for most realists and liberals, history provides various data points from which to glean appropriate generalizations, radicals see historical analysis as revealing necessary outcomes. Of special relevance is the history of the production process. During the evolution of the production process from feudalism to capitalism, new patterns of social relations developed. Radicals are concerned most with explaining the relationships among the means of production, social relations, and power.

Basing their analyses of history on the importance of the production process, most radical theorists also assume the primacy of economics for explaining virtually all other phenomena. Along with the theories' different ideas about the necessity of states, this clearly differentiates radicalism from either realism or liberalism. For liberals, economic interdependence is one possible explanation for international cooperation, but only one among many factors. For realists, economic factors are one of the ingredients of power, one component of the international structure. In neither theory, though, is economics the determining factor. Both realists and liberals accept that the *state* is the primary unit of analysis. In radicalism, on the other hand, economic factors (for Marxists, it is class) assume primary importance.

A different group of radical beliefs centers on the structure of the global system. That structure, in Marxist thinking, is hierarchical and is largely the by-product of imperialism, or the expansion of certain economic forms into other areas of the world. The British economist John A. Hobson (1858–1940) theorized that expansion occurs because of three conditions in the more developed states: overproduction of goods and services, underconsumption by workers and the lower classes because of low wages, and oversavings by the upper classes and the bourgeoisie. To solve these three economic problems, developed states historically have expanded abroad, and radicals argue that developed countries still see expansion as a solution. Goods find new markets in under-developed regions, workers' wages are kept low because of foreign competition, and savings are profitably invested in new markets rather than in improving the lot of the workers. Imperialism leads to rivalry among the developed countries.[22] Critically, for radicals, the turmoil that follows from worker exploitation is disciplined by state intervention on behalf of the bourgeoisie class. States as such become an obstacle to workers being treated as human beings.

For radicals, imperialism produces the hierarchical international system, which offers opportunities to some states, organizations, and individuals, but imposes significant constraints on behavior for others. Developed countries can expand, enabling them to sell goods and export surplus wealth that they cannot use at home. Simultaneously, the developing countries are increasingly constrained by, and dependent on, the actions of the developed world. Hobson, who condemned imperialism as irrational, risky, and potentially conflictual, did not see it as necessarily inevitable. But, whereas free-market capitalists maintain that equilibrium will be found through the market, most radicals drawing on Marx's analysis critique capitalism as inevitably leading to crises.

Radical theorists emphasize the techniques of domination and suppression that arise from the uneven economic development inherent in the capitalist system. Uneven development empowers and enables the dominant states to exploit the underdogs; the dynamics of capitalism and economic expansion make such exploitation necessary if the top dogs are to maintain their position and the capitalist structure is to survive. Whereas realists see balancing the power of other states to fight and win wars as the mechanism for gaining and maintaining power, Marxists and radicals view the economic techniques of domination and suppression as the means of power in the world; the choices for the underdog are few and ineffective.

One latter-day school of radicalism recognizes that capitalists can apply additional, more sophisticated techniques of control to developing markets. Contemporary radicals such as **dependency theorists** attribute primary importance in exerting such fundamental control to the role of **multinational corporations (MNCs)** and international banks based in developed countries. These organizations are seen as key players in establishing and maintaining dependency relationships; they are agents of penetration, not benign actors, as liberals would characterize them, or marginal actors, as realists would. These organizations can forge transnational relationships with elites in the developing countries, so that domestic elites in both exploiter and exploited countries are tightly linked in a symbiotic relationship.

Dependency theorists, particularly those from Latin America (Raul Prebisch, Enzo Faletto, Fernando Henrique Cardoso), believe that options for states on the periphery are few. Since the basic terms of trade are unequal, these states have few external options. Nor do they have many internal options, because their internal constraints, land tenure and social and class structures, are just as real.[23] Thus, like the realists, dependency theorists are fairly pessimistic about the possibility of change.

THEORY IN BRIEF	RADICALISM / DEPENDENCY THEORY
KEY ACTORS	Social classes, transnational elites, multinational corporations
VIEW OF THE INDIVIDUAL	Actions determined by economic class interests
VIEW OF THE STATE	An agent of the structure of international capitalism and the executing agent of the bourgeoisie
VIEW OF THE INTERNATIONAL SYSTEM	Highly stratified; dominated by international capitalist system
BELIEFS ABOUT CHANGE	Radical change inevitable
MAJOR THEORISTS	Marx, Hobson, Lenin, Prebisch

Finally, virtually all radical theorists, regardless of their specific emphases, are normative in their orientation. They evaluate the hierarchical capitalist structure as "bad" and its methods as invariably exploitative. They have clear normative and activist positions about what should be done to ameliorate inequalities among both individuals and states—ranging from forming radical organizations Leninists support, to making more incremental changes dependency theorists might suggest.

In some quarters, radicalism has been discredited as an international relations theory. Radicalism cannot explain why cooperation began to emerge between capitalist and socialist states even before the end of the Cold War. And it cannot explain obvious divisiveness among noncapitalist states. For example, in 1948, communist Yugoslavia and the USSR dramatically split over the former's refusal to submit important domestic and foreign policy decisions for Stalin's approval. Radicalism also can't explain why and how some developing countries such as India have successfully adopted a capitalist approach and escaped from economic and political dependency. Radicalism could not have predicted such developments. And radicalism, just like liberalism and realism, did not foresee or predict the demise of the Soviet Union, arguably one of the most significant changes in the twentieth century. Each theory, despite claims of comprehensiveness, has significant shortcomings.

In other circles, radicalism has survived as a theory of economic determinism and as a force advocating major change in the international system's structure. Its critique of market capitalism's tendency to cause income inequality is as vibrant as ever. Radicalism helps us understand the role of economic forces, both within and between states, and to explain the dynamics of late-twentieth-century economic globalization and the 2008 economic crisis, as Chapter 9 discusses.

Social Constructivism

A late-twentieth-century addition to international relations, **constructivism**, has returned international relations scholars to foundational questions, including the nature of the state and the concepts of sovereignty, identity, and citizenship. In addition, constructivism has opened new substantive areas to inquiry, such as the roles of gender and ethnicity, which have been largely absent from other international relations theories. Yet like liberalism, realism, and radicalism, constructivism is not a uniform theory. Indeed, some scholars question whether it is a substantive theory at all. That said, most constructivists do share a number of core ideas.

Constructivism's major theoretical proposition is that neither objects nor concepts have any necessary, fixed, or objective meaning; rather, their meanings are *constructed* through social interaction. In other words, we bring meaning to objects, not

Constructivism explains how ideas such as "crimes against humanity" can evolve into powerful international norms and laws. The precedent for war crimes trials established at Nuremberg after World War II has since been replicated around the world.

the other way around. By extension, state conduct is shaped by elite beliefs, identities, and social norms. Individuals and collectivities forge, shape, and change culture through ideas and practices. State and national interests are the result of the social identities of these actors. Thus, the objects of study are the norms and practices of individuals and the collectivity.[24] Ted Hopf offers a simple analogy:

> The scenario is a fire in a theater where all run for the exits. But absent knowledge of social practices of constitutive norms, structure, even in this seemingly overdetermined circumstance, is still indeterminate. Even in a theater with just one door, while all run for that exit, who goes first? Are they the strongest or the disabled, the women or the children, the aged or the infirm, or is it just a mad dash? Determining the outcome will require knowing more about the situation than about the distribution of material power or the structure of authority. One will need to know about the culture, norms, institutions, procedures, rules, and social practices that constitute the actors and the structure alike.[25]

Note that had realist logic been employed to predict the outcome of Hopf's fire-in-a-theater example, or, say, the demographic composition of the *Titanic*'s lifeboats in 1912, realist assumptions about the value placed on one's own survival and self-interests, and about relative power, would have caused an incorrect prediction. In real life, the strong sometimes yield to the weak, rather than forcing the weak to "suffer what they must." That is why the *Titanic*'s lifeboats were not filled with strong men, but with the ship's physically weakest passengers: women and children.

Constructivists thus dispute the idea that material structures have a necessary, fixed, or inherent meaning. Alexander Wendt, one of the best-known constructivists, argues that, on its own, a political structure—whether one of anarchy or a particular distribution of material capabilities—cannot tell us much of interest: "It does not predict whether two states will be friends or foes, will recognize each other's sovereignty, will have dynastic ties, will have revisionist or status quo powers, and so on."[26] Many constructivists emphasize normative structures. What we need to know is identity, and identities change because of cooperative behavior and learning. Whether a system is anarchic depends on the distribution of identities, not the distribution of military capabilities, as realists would have us believe. If a state identifies only with itself, then the system may *be* anarchic. If a state identifies with other states, then there is no anarchy. In short, "anarchy is what states make of it."[27]

Like the realists and neoliberal institutionalists, constructivists see power as important. But whereas the former see power in primarily material terms (military, economic, political), constructivists also see power in discursive terms—the power of ideas, culture, and language. Thus, to constructivists, power includes such ideas as legitimacy; states may alter their actions so other members of the international community will view them as legitimate. Power exists in every exchange among actors, and the goal of constructivists is to find the sources of that power. Their unique contribution may well be in elucidating the sources of power in ideas and in showing how ideas shape and change identity. An example of constructivist contributions can be seen in the discussion of sovereignty. Constructivists see sovereignty not as an absolute but as a contested concept. They point out that states have never had exclusive control over territory. State sovereignty has always been challenged and is being challenged continuously by new institutional forms and new national needs.

Constructivist theory offers different explanations of change. Change can occur through diffusion of ideas or the internationalization of norms, as well as through socialization, when one adopts the identities of peer groups. These explanations help us understand that ideas are spread both within a national setting and cross-nationally. This is how democracy is diffused, how ideas about human rights protection have been internationalized, and how such states as the new members of the European Union become socialized into the community's norms and practices. Put another way, realism and lib-

THEORY IN BRIEF   CONSTRUCTIVISM

KEY ACTORS	People, elites, cultures
VIEW OF THE INDIVIDUAL	Key component in creation of meaning; bound by education, socialization, and culture
VIEW OF THE STATE	An artifact whose significance is socially constructed through discourse
VIEW OF THE INTERNATIONAL SYSTEM	An artifact whose significance is socially constructed through discourse
BELIEFS ABOUT CHANGE	Possible by means of discourse: "[anarchy] [war] [peace] is what we make of it"
MAJOR THEORISTS	Foucault, Derrida, Kratochwil, Hopf, Wendt

eralism each have a more difficult time explaining the advent, spread, and real-world *impact* of ideas and norms such as taboos against land mines or the "responsibility to protect" (see Chapter 8). Thus, constructivism does *not* reduce to mere conversation and blathery, but helps provide strong explanations of shifts in our understanding of objects that have an impact on real human lives, just as realism, liberalism, and radicalism do.

But also like realism, liberalism, and radicalism, constructivism has its shortcomings. Until recently, constructivism remained mainly a powerful tool of criticism rather than a program capable of explaining outcomes in the real world. This situation is changing, however. Throughout this textbook, examples of constructivist scholarship will allow you to see this approach in use so that you can make your own judgments concerning this crucial and still relatively new theoretical perspective.

Feminist Critiques of IR Theory

Feminists offer a variety of critiques of the four international relations theories. Many of the critiques share core propositions. Chief among them is the proposition that the world would be a better place—more just, more peaceful, more prosperous—if women were given more space to define, describe, and lead in domestic and international affairs (these being linked in most feminist IR theory). Thus, both realist and liberal feminists argue for greater participation of women in national and international decision making, and in economic life. Liberal feminists, for example, call for developing organizational policies that affect women, especially the role of women in economic development, women as victims of crime and discrimination, and women in situations of armed conflict. For too long, states have neglected these issues.

Radical feminists critique international relations theories as well. Unlike other radicals, who point to the structure of the international economic system as determinant of international relations, radical feminists define the problem as overarching patriarchy. The patriarchal system permeates national and international systems; for example, making war seem desirable or rational. Until this system is changed, war will always be more likely, and women will always be in a subservient position—the victims of a neoliberal capitalist model of economic governance, exposing poor women to the ravages of global competition.

Feminist critics are also found among social constructivists, postmodernists, and critical theorists. To these feminists, studying gender involves more than just counting women in elite positions or cataloging programs targeting women. Just as constructivists more broadly assert, the meaning of things is established, supported, and changed through a process of social interaction called discourse.

According to J. Ann Tickner, for example, classical realism is based on a very limited—indeed, *masculine*—notion of both human nature and power. She argues that human nature is not fixed and unalterable; it is multidimensional and contextual. Power cannot be equated exclusively with physical control and domination. Tickner thinks that all international relations theory must be reoriented toward a more inclusive notion of power, in which power is the ability to act in concert (not just in conflict) or to engage in a symbiotic relationship (instead of outright competition). In other words, power can also be a concept of connection rather than one only of autonomy.[28]

For Tickner, as well as many other feminist scholars, such as Cynthia Enloe and Christine Sylvester, discourse has been dominated by a narrowly male perspective. This domination affects not only the issues IR theorists and policy makers consider important, but also the very standards by which a given policy is thought to be effective or ineffective. For example, if we want to understand violent conflict in terms of intensity, we may think that the number of combatants killed constitutes a sound measure of how important a given conflict is. Yet feminist IR scholars have pointed to rape as a serious cost of conflict that does not often result in a physical death. By privileging deaths in conflict over rape, we discount the true costs and consequences of a violent conflict such as a civil or interstate war. Paying little attention to the voices of women affects the kinds of questions we ask and the way we evaluate the answers.

Tickner has also pointed to the masculinization of many aims of foreign policy. For example, to the extent males tend to frame problems as dichotomous, gender suggests a hierarchy of associations that often result in states giving unwarranted or coun-terproductive priority to armed conflict as the core meaning of "security." Some countries are "feminine" or "childlike," and therefore in need of guidance or disci-pline from "masculine" or "grown up" states (e.g., Britain or Germany). This situation creates incentives to intervene (rescue fantasies) and, at the same time, channels the forms of "effective" intervention to military force at the high (masculine) end, and dip-lomatic or economic intervention at the low (feminine) end.

Other feminists, such as Cynthia Enloe, have argued that contrary to Tickner's assertion that women have been absent from international politics, they have in fact been key participants.[29] The problem, according to Enloe, is that their participation goes almost entirely unnoticed (and, she might add, unrewarded). Enloe calls atten-tion to the ways that the domestic roles for women condition our understanding of their potential as leaders and agenda-setters in international politics.

Even today, we see a strong gap between women's potential and women's *visible* par-ticipation and leadership in international politics as compared to men. Perhaps, then, the strongest argument is that, just as in science, technology, mathematics, and engi-neering, the core values of justice, peace, and prosperity, which both sexes share, can-not help but be advanced by the active participation and leadership of more women. And international relations theories can benefit from the various critiques that femi-nists of all theoretical persuasions offer.

Theory in Action: Analyzing the 2003 Iraq War

The contending theoretical perspectives discussed in the preceding sections see the world and even specific events quite differently. What theorists and policy makers choose to see, what they each seek to explain, and what implications they draw—all these elements of analysis vary, even though the facts of an event seem identical. Analyzing the 2003 Iraq War by applying these different theories allows us to compare and contrast them in action.

Realist Perspectives

Realist interpretations of the 2003 Iraq War would focus on state-level and international-level factors. Realists see the international system as anarchic: no international authority governs and few states, other than the United States, are able and willing to act to rid the world of the Iraq threat. Iraq posed a security threat to the United States with its supposed stockpiles of weapons of mass destruction; the United States therefore saw a need to eliminate those weapons and, at the same time, to ensure a stable oil supply to the West. The only way to achieve these objectives was to oust Saddam's Baathist

::: **BEHIND THE HEADLINES**

The Effectiveness of Female Marines in Combat: A Fair Test?

In September 2015, *The Marine Corps Times* reported on the results of a critical experiment: an attempt to objectively assess whether women could perform as well as men in combat roles. In the article, "Mixed-Gender Teams Come Up Short in Marines' Infantry Experiment,"[a] we learned that the teams the marines assessed were in infantry, armor, and artillery units, and they were a mix of men and women. In all but the artillery units, all-male teams outperformed the mixed teams. All five services— army, navy, marines, air force, and coast guard—are facing a defense department mandate to open all jobs to women by January 1, 2016, or ask for a specific exception to the mandate by showing it would harm combat effectiveness. But the experiment the marines ran points to a conclusion that adding women to the team hurts combat effectiveness. What then should the U.S. Marine Corps commandant do? And was the test fair in the first place?

In trying to address these important questions, international relations theory can help. Realist IR theory, for example, focuses our attention on state power—in particular, the power to fight and win wars. A realist explanation would note that the experience of the males who lead all state militaries would predispose them to view the inclusion of females in combat roles as a risk, resulting in opposition to full inclusion of females in combat roles and, in testing, deliberate bias. Realists would not oppose women serving in combat if it could be shown that the net effect of full inclusion was either neutral or positive; in that event, a state's relative power would be enhanced.

Liberal IR theory would likely divide on the question of women in combat roles. On the one hand, liberal theorists would note that eco-nomic development is enhanced dramatically in states that have included women fully in politics, economics, and social life (and hurt when women are subjected to systematic discrimination). To the extent that economic power is an important aspect of trade and cooperation, liberals would support an unbiased examination of the net effect of allowing women to serve in combat. On the other hand, liberals might observe that both the frequency and intensity of interstate war has dropped so low that any modest decrease in military combat effectiveness (or increase) resulting from full inclusion of women does not matter that much. Conflict between states has moved away from war, even in the developing world, and so the consequences of risking full inclusion are negligible either way.

Constructivist and feminist IR theories offer much more direct insight. For constructivists, who focus much on identity, bias must ultimately come down to the costs of males surrendering their view of "maleness" as protective. That identity has served to fill the ranks of militaries since ancient times. If women can demonstrate that, as a class, they are not in need of protection, then by extension, males would lose that important component of their identity as men.

Various feminist international relations theories offer perhaps the most focused insights into both questions—what the U.S. Marine Corps commandant might do, and whether the test was fair. First, if we are comparing women and men, are we considering how socialization to effort and physical body types matter? If males have been essentially "training" from a young age, through sports and employment, for the physical tasks asked of them and females haven't, the test is biased. Second, most of the injuries female marines suffered were related to movement with very heavy rifleman's assault packs, but the physiology and bone structure of most males and females differ in key ways. Were these packs designed for women? Were their boots? If not, the test was biased. Third, a feminist international relations theorist would note that, even if the marines had done all they could to simulate the kinds of tasks their combat teams would need to face in real war, the simulations likely *don't* take into account the positive capabilities women might bring to a team that could be missing in an all-male team. For example, we have evidence that males fight harder when near females and that the ability to tolerate heat, cold, pain, and hunger tend to differ between the sexes. Without addressing potentially positive gender contributions, female marines and mixed units will appear to be less effective, when in reality, combat mixed-gender teams might enjoy a net benefit in effectiveness. But perhaps the biggest theoretical insight a feminist IR theorist might make is that so long as service roles exist

U.S. Marine lance corporal Stephanie Robertson, a member of a female engagement team (FET), speaks with local civilians during an engagement mission in Marjah, Afghanistan, in August 2010. The FET is attached to infantry battalions throughout Afghanistan to aid in engaging the female populace in support of the International Security Assistance Force (ISAF). The ISAF was disbanded in December 2014 with some troops remaining behind in an advisory capacity.

in a hierarchy favoring males, women in the service will continue to be thought of as second-class leaders and team members.

FOR CRITICAL ANALYSIS

1. Why is it important for us to think through the issue of women in combat, not just in the United States, but more broadly?

2. If mixed combat units perform combat simulation tests less effectively than all-male combat units, does it follow that an all-female unit would also prove less effective? Why or why not?

3. Do you agree or disagree with the argument that it remains critical for all jobs in the world's militaries to be open to women who qualify, because discrimination in the armed services affects our understanding of women's leadership and teamwork potential in other domains, such as work and politics? Develop your argument.

a. Hope Hodge Seck, "Mixed-Gender Teams Come Up Short in Marines' Infantry Experiment," *Marine Corps Times*, September 10, 2015, www.marinecorpstimes.com/story/military/2015/09/10/mixed-gender-teams-come-up-short-marines-infantry-experiment/71979146.

regime from power in Iraq. Having escalated its threats and amassed its troops on Iraq's borders to coerce the regime into giving up power, the United States had no choice but to act militarily when that coercion failed.

Yet not all realists agree that the policy the United States pursued was the correct one. Realists are engaging in an interesting discussion about whether the U.S. operation was necessary. John Mearsheimer, an offensive realist, and Stephen Walt, a defensive realist, have jointly argued that the war was not necessary. Before the war began, they wrote that U.S. military power could deter any threat Saddam posed, even his possible attainment of nuclear weapons. They further argued that, even if the war went well and had positive long-term consequences, it would be unnecessary and could engender long-term animosity toward the United States, both in the Middle East and around the world. The policy of deterrence the United States employed had worked previously and could have continued to work.[30]

But other realist theorists, as well as President George W. Bush, believed that Saddam was not being effectively deterred. The Bush administration argued that Saddam's use of chemical weapons against the Kurds in the past meant that it was probable he would use these weapons to threaten the United States. This perceived threat influenced the Bush administration's decision to invade. In addition, some realists in the Bush administration argued that a forceful response to Saddam's flouting of his obligations to the international community (his government was in violation of agreements it had signed as part of the settlement that ended the first Gulf War in 1991) would deter other enemies of the United States and its allies from actions that harmed U.S. and allied interests. Perhaps a dramatic show of force could also curtail what the administration referred to as state-sponsored terrorism. Realists clearly can draw different policy prescriptions from theory.

Liberal Perspectives

A liberal view of the 2003 Iraq War would utilize all three levels of analysis. With respect to the individual level, Saddam was clearly an abusive leader whose atrocities against his own population were made evident in the aftermath of the war, with the discovery of mass graves. He was aggressive not only against domestic opponents of his regime but also against other peoples within the region; he even supported some terrorist activities against enemies in the West. With respect to the state level, liberals would emphasize the characteristics of the Iraqi regime—mainly its authoritarian nature—and the notion that replacement by a democracy would decrease the coercive threat of the Iraqi state and enhance stability in the Middle East. A democratic Iraq would be a beacon for other nascent democracies nearby. The fact that many liberals believed that Saddam's regime had acquired, or was very close to acquiring, weapons of mass destruction only added to the urgency of regime change. With respect to the international level, liberals would emphasize that Iraq was not conforming to its obligations under various UN Security Council resolutions. Thus, the international community had an obligation to support sanctions and continue inspections and, failing that, undertake collective action, fighting a war to punish Saddam's regime and allow an alternative government to take root.

Why did the international community not respond as some liberals would have predicted? U.S. inability to win the endorsement of the UN Security Council for collective action can be attributed to the fact that some members of the council, including France and Russia, and some other powerful states, including Germany, believed that containment of the Iraqi regime was sufficient, evidence of weapons of mass destruction was lacking, and that immediate action was not necessary in light of the higher priority given to fighting Al Qaeda in Afghanistan. Liberals' predictions of restraint in the face of allies' skepticism proved wrong in Iraq in 2003, but later received strong support in British and U.S. deliberations, in 2013, over whether to intervene militarily in Syria.

Radical Perspectives

A radical interpretation of the Iraq War would tend to focus mainly on the international system structure and the economic interests of states. That system structure, for radicals, is embedded in the historical colonial system and its contemporary legacies. Radicals hold that political colonialism spawned an imperialist system in which the economic needs of the capitalist states were paramount. In the Middle East, that meant imperialist action by the West to secure oil resources. In the nineteenth-century colonial era, imperialism was state organized; today, imperialism is practiced by multinational corporations. In this view, the instability of the oil supply coming from Iraq explains the U.S. invasion of Iraq in 2003. Many radicals (and many in the Arab world) believe that the United States invaded to gain control of Iraq's oil. They point to the fact that one of the United States' first military objectives was the seizure of the Rumaila oil field in southern Iraq. U.S. troops protected oil fields all over the country, even when civil disorder and looting of precious cultural monuments went unchecked. The U.S. forces prioritized restarting the oil pipelines over providing for the basic needs of the Iraqi people.

Radicals, especially dependency theorists, would not be at all surprised that the core states of the capitalist system—the United States and its allies—responded with force when Iraq threatened their critical interests in oil. Nor would they expect the end of the Cold War to make any difference in the structure of the system. The major changes in international power relationships that radicals seek—and predict—have not yet come.

Canadian Views of Foreign Military Intervention: Afghanistan and Beyond

State foreign policies tend to be rooted in a single theoretical perspective. Skeptics or dissenters often have a different theoretical perspective. Their justifications and the evidence they provide often reflect different international relations theories.

On October 7, 2001, just hours after U.S. and British planes began bombing targets in Afghan cities, Prime Minister Jean Chrétien announced that Canada would join the U.S. war in Afghanistan. In early 2002, regular military troops arrived in the country. These troops—between 2,500 and 2,800—soon became part of the International Security Assistance Force (ISAF). One key part of Canadian participation was its 330-person Kandahar Provincial Reconstruction Team (PRT), deployed to support reconstruction efforts. Between 2001 and 2011, 158 Canadian troops died in the cause, the third highest number of deaths of any foreign participating state. Given the rarity of foreign war casualties in Canada's history and Canada's relatively small population, the high casualties particularly affected Canadian views of the war in Afghanistan. Their experience contributed to Canada's decision to withdraw its combat forces completely by the end of 2011, a decision revised following U.S. president Barack Obama's later decision to keep U.S. forces in Afghanistan until 2014. Canada likewise extended its mission (for non-combat forces only), which ended on March 12, 2014.

In 2001, the Canadian defense minister provided unequivocal support for Canadian involvement in Afghanistan as the means to address the problem of terrorism. The discovery of the 2006 plot by an Al Qaeda cell to carry out attacks in Ottawa and Toronto reaffirmed the salience of the global terrorist threat to Canadian territory. Conservative prime minister Stephen Harper framed Canada's policy in realist terms: Canada's participation in Afghanistan, he argued, amounted to a projection of Canadian power in the national interest, which was to protect itself and support the United States, its closest ally. In Harper's view, these policies reaffirmed that Canada's security, borders, and economy are interdependent with those of the United States.

Liberals in Canada initially supported Canada's involvement in Afghanistan, for reasons beyond the terrorist threat. Would not the establishment of democratic institutions be a worthy goal? Doesn't Canada stand for human rights for women? Clearly, legitimate economic development and respect for human rights were severely compromised under the Taliban.

But liberals and conservatives alike proved disappointed by the rate of progress in Afghanistan. Representatives from the New Democratic Party, in particular, argued that reconstruction was being undermined by the counterinsurgency operations themselves. Women's groups pointed to few improvements in the emancipation of women—girls were still being attacked and sometimes maimed for attending school. Canada had finished few development projects of any importance. Liberals argued that the money would have been better spent on social programs at home. This lack of progress made the casualty figures more difficult to bear.

Radical dissatisfaction with Canadian policy focused on two arguments: (1) that Canadian involvement in what they viewed as America's war proved a sad illustration of the reluctance and unwillingness of the Canadian government to distance itself from the United States; and (2) that Canadian and international businesses profited from the war, especially Canada's large arms and mining industries.

Constructivists could point to the power of Canadian identity to explain the country's policies in Afghanistan. That identity revolves around Canada's global citizenship and its support of peacekeeping, multilateralism, NGOs, and human security issues. This identity remains strong, in spite of the fact that a past tradition of generous Canadian support, aid, and investment abroad has veered in the opposite direction.

Feminists might have the stronger argument: Canada's transition from a liberal ("girly") to a conservative ("manly") government in 2006 was marked by a shift from UN support (including humanitarian and peacekeeping missions) to a more active and aggressive search-and-destroy effort after 2006.

By 2009, both popular and political sentiment had shifted. The relatively high casualties and lack of progress toward well-intentioned political objectives meant that Canadians no longer supported a combat role for their troops. By 2013, Canadian involvement in Afghanistan was changed to strictly noncombat support. Canada remains rightly proud of its attempts to bring security and prosperity to Afghanistan, but perhaps should be even prouder of a political process that led to a bipartisan and well-reasoned decision to withdraw combat forces as gracefully as possible.

In October 2015, Canada transitioned back to a liberal government, and its current foreign policy preferences strongly reflect a return to

A newly arrived Syrian refugee family, sponsored by a local NGO called The Ripple Refugee Project, poses for photos in Toronto.

"prudence first" policy in military interventions, such as those currently under way in Syria and Iraq. In keeping with the policies of many European countries, Canada is increasingly exploring ways to conserve its aid resources and reduce military spending. As of December 2015, for example, Canada's new government has ordered the withdrawal of Canadian fighter aircraft from coalition airstrikes against the IS and extended an offer to resettle 25,000 Syrian refugees in Canada.

FOR CRITICAL ANALYSIS

1. Canada supported U.S. policy in Afghanistan, but not in Iraq. Which theory best explains the difference in the Canadian positions?

2. Which explanation of Canada's foreign policy do you find most convincing? Why?

Constructivist Perspectives

A constructivist view of the 2003 Iraq War would focus on several factors. Constructivist theorists would emphasize the social construction of threat: how U.S. policy makers constructed Saddam Hussein and the purported WMD as imminent threats to the United States, even though UN inspectors claimed that the weapons program had been dismantled. The "constructed" nature of the threat becomes evident when comparing Iraq to Israel or Great Britain, both of which possess sophisticated nuclear weapons but are not considered "threatening" and are in fact close allies. The rhetoric of the threat accelerated as Saddam was portrayed as an evil tyrant, having power beyond materialist considerations. Constructivists would also point to the importance of legitimacy. The United States recognized the need for legitimacy for its actions, being socialized into those norms. That explains the considerable effort the United States expended in trying to obtain UN Security Council approval for the invasion, though in the long run those efforts failed. In much constructivist thinking, international organizations such as the UN play a powerful legitimizing and socializing role in international relations. But in 2003, this construction of legitimacy was overwhelmed by the U.S., a single powerful state led by an administration highly critical of collective security. The Bush administration argued that the legitimacy of UN support—slow and demanding of compromise—was eclipsed by the greater legitimacy of doing the right thing quickly, even if on one's own.

In Sum: Seeing the World through Theoretical Lenses

Without theory, we are reduced to educated guesses on how to resolve crises or how to constructively advance human values such as justice and peace. How each of us sees international relations depends on our own theoretical lens. Do you see events through a realist framework? Are you inclined toward a liberal interpretation? Or do you adhere to a radical, constructivist, or perhaps feminist view of the world? These theoretical perspectives differ not only in whom they identify as key actors, but also in what counts as a threat or a benefit. They also differ in their views about the relative explanatory power of the individual, the state, and the international system—the three levels of analysis. Equally important, these perspectives support different views about the possibility and desirability of change—in particular war, peace, and development—in the international system.

In the next four chapters, we examine in more detail how each of these perspectives sees the international system, the state, the individual, and international organizations. We begin with the most general level of analysis—the international system.

Discussion Questions

1. Choose a current event in world politics. Describe and explain that event using the three levels of analysis.

2. A realist and a liberal are discussing the role of domestic politics in influencing international outcomes. Re-create that conversation, highlighting the differing perspectives.

3. Constructivists assert that the power of norms and ideas is continuously shaping and reshaping state behavior. Select a political idea—equality, democracy, or human rights. How has that idea changed over time? How has state behavior changed, if at all?

4. What feminist critique of international relations theory do you find the most convincing? Why?

Key Terms

bandwagoning (p. 80)

collective security (p. 84)

constructivism (p. 92)

dependency theorists (p. 91)

hypotheses (p. 72)

institutions (p. 83)

levels of analysis (p. 74)

liberalism (p. 83)

multinational corporations (MNCs) (p. 91)

national interest (p. 76)

neoliberal institutionalism (p. 85)

neorealism (p. 80)

prisoner's dilemma (p. 85)

radicalism (p. 89)

rational actors (p. 77)

realism (p. 76)

theory (p. 72)

unitary actor (p. 77)

04

Residents of Nawa, Syria, survey the aftermath of Russian airstrikes in late 2015. Russia has claimed it is carefully targeting radical Islamic opponents of Syria's President Bashar al Assad. Many international experts have disputed Russia's claims, arguing that Russian planes have used prohibited cluster bombs and otherwise injured many noncombatants in urban areas.

THE INTERNATIONAL SYSTEM

During the turmoil that followed the Arab Spring of 2011, several authoritarian Arab rulers were unseated. Street demonstrations confronted Syria's Bashar al Assad, and after his government's violent crackdown, these demonstrators were soon in open armed rebellion. Because governments in Europe and the United States believe that dictatorships such as Assad's are cruel and unjust, the United States and its allies, among others, supported some of the various rebel groups that aimed to depose Assad. As Syria descended into civil war, the government lost control of all but its westernmost territories and cities. In Syria's north, Kurdish fighters gained territory, and in 2013, the Islamic State gained control over the eastern half of Syria. In September 2015, the Russian Federation intervened and began air strikes against rebel forces in support of Assad, sometimes violating Turkish air space. In October, Russian President Vladimir Putin announced that his country would be sending "volunteers" into Syria to fight on the ground. Tensions between the Russian Federation and NATO were already high when Turkey shot down a Russian fighter jet in November 2015.

Observers of these events no doubt worry about how Russia's actions affect the international system. Will the intervention by Russia and the Western allies in Syria undermine the stability of the international system? Does the Russian intervention, coupled with Russian activities in Crimea and the Ukraine, indicate a change in the balance of power in the international system? Will a resurgent Russia alter the structure of the international system?

Each of the contending theoretical perspectives examined in Chapter 3 describes an international system. For realists and radicals, the concept of an international system is vital to their analyses, whereas for liberals—who focus much more of their analyses on key characteristics of states—the international system is less consequential. For constructivists, the concept of an international system is tied to notions of identity as derived from norms, ideas, and discourse.

To understand the *international* system, we must first clarify the notion of a system itself. Broadly defined, a **system** is an assemblage of units, objects, or parts united by some form of regular interaction. The concept of systems is essential to the physical and biological sciences; systems are composed of different interacting units, whether at the micro (cell, plant, animal) or the macro (natural ecosystem or global climate) level. Because these units interact, a change in one unit causes changes in the others. With their interacting parts, systems tend to respond in regularized ways; their actions have patterns. Boundaries separate one system from another, but exchanges can occur across these boundaries. A system can break down when changes within it become so significant that, in effect, a new system emerges. In this chapter, we look at how political science defines and views the international system, and how we can use the international system as a lens through which to analyze international political events.

LEARNING OBJECTIVES

- Explain why the concept of a system is a powerful descriptive and explanatory device.

- Understand the concepts that realists, liberals, radicals, and constructivists employ to analyze the international system.

- Describe how each of the contending theoretical perspectives explains change in the international system.

- Analyze the problems and/or weaknesses with the notion of the international system.

Contending Perspectives on the International System

In the 1950s, the behavioral revolution in the social sciences and the growing acceptance of political realism in international relations led scholars to conceptualize international politics as a system, using the language of systems theory. Beginning with the supposition that people act in regularized ways and that their patterns of interaction with each other are largely habitual, both realists and behavioralists made the conceptual leap that international politics is a system whose major actors are individual states.[1] This notion of a system is embedded in ideas of the major theoretical schools of international relations. Of particular interest to theorists is this question: How and why do conditions of periodic war and economic collapse turn into conditions of relative peace and sustainable economic development?

The International System According to Realists

Political realists have clear notions about the international system and its essential characteristics. All realists characterize the international system as anarchic. Its key feature is that states are all sovereign (meaning no other state may legitimately intervene in any other state's internal affairs) and, in this sense, equal. For realists, this anarchic structure has critical implications for the possibility of enduring peace among states. Realists argue that states should constantly seek power because, in an anarchic system, the only true guarantee of security must come from self-help. In addition, the power to conquer is the most relevant power. In doing so, states will inevitably come into conflict, whether their aim is simply self-preservation or, alternatively, to conquer others.

To characterize the possibilities of war and peace in the international system, realists rely on the concept of polarity. System polarity simply describes the distribution of capabilities among states in the international system by counting the number of "poles" (states or groups of states) where material power is concentrated. For neorealists in particular, the possibility of peace in the system depends simply on the number of poles: the fewer the poles, the more likely the system is to remain stable and peaceful (at least insofar as by "peace," we mean the absence of armed conflicts). There are only three types of system polarity: multipolarity, bipolarity, and unipolarity (see Figure 4.1).

A **multipolar** system is any system in which the distribution of the power to conquer is concentrated in more than two states. In the system preceding World War I, five states, Great Britain, Russia, Prussia, France, and Austria-Hungary, comprised a multipolar system that had evolved from the balance of power after the Napoleonic wars.

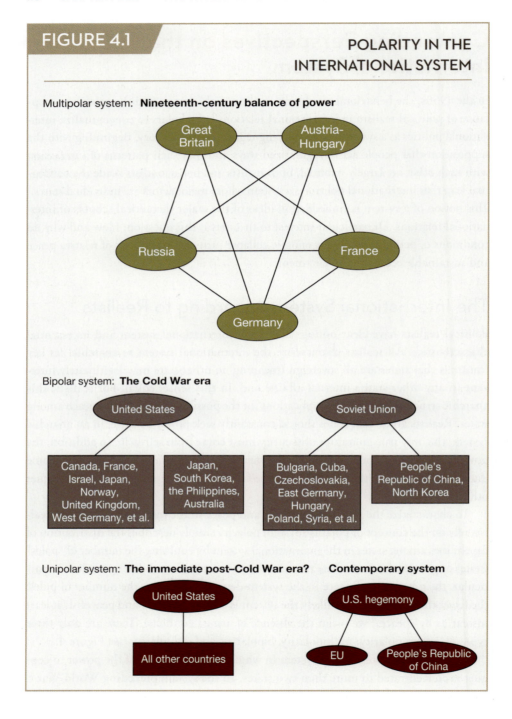

FIGURE 4.1

POLARITY IN THE
INTERNATIONAL SYSTEM

Multipolar system: **Nineteenth-century balance of power**

Bipolar system: **The Cold War era**

Unipolar system: **The immediate post–Cold War era?**   **Contemporary system**

In a stable multipolar system—a balance-of-power system—the essential norms are clear to each of the state actors. In systems in which these norms are shared and observed, alliances are formed for a specific purpose, have a short duration, and shift according to advantage rather than ideology. Any wars that do erupt are expected to be limited in nature, designed to preserve a balance of power. As we saw in Chapter 2, however, when an essential actor ignores the understood norms, the system may become unstable.

Bipolar systems are those in which the distribution of the power to conquer is concentrated in two states or coalitions of states. In the bipolar system of the Cold War, each of the blocs (the North Atlantic Treaty Organization, or NATO, and the Warsaw Pact) sought to negotiate rather than fight, and to fight proxy wars, rather than major wars, outside of Europe. In a bipolar system, alliances tend to be longer term, based on relatively permanent interests, not shifting ones. Unlike in a multipolar system, each bloc in a bipolar system is certain about the direction and magnitude of its biggest threat. In a tight bipolar system, international organizations either do not develop or are relatively ineffective, as the United Nations was during the height of the Cold War. In a looser bipolar system, international organizations may develop primarily to mediate between the two blocs, and individual states within the looser coalitions may try to use the international organizations for their own advantage. During much of the Cold War era, particularly in the 1950s and 1960s, the international system was bipolar—the United States, its European and Asian allies (NATO, and Japan, South Korea, South Vietnam [until 1975], the Philippines, and Australia, respectively) faced the Soviet Union and its European and Asian allies (the Warsaw Pact, and the People's Republic of China, North Korea, and North Vietnam, respectively; and after 1962, Cuba). But over the course of the Cold War, the relative tightness or looseness of the bipolar system shifted, as powerful states such as the People's Republic of China, India, and France pursued independent paths.

A **unipolar** system is one in which the power to conquer all other states in the system combined resides within a single state. Realists of all sorts still disagree about whether the world has actually seen a true unipolar system (which, if it were to happen, would abrogate anarchy and its interstate conflict implications). But immediately after the Gulf War in 1991, many states, including the United States' closest allies and virtually all developing states, grew concerned that the international system *had* become unipolar. After all, its chief rival bloc—the USSR and Warsaw Pact—had collapsed, U.S. defense expenditures were greater than those of the next 15 states combined, and its economy was three times stronger than the next three economies combined. With that superiority, other states were worried there might be no effective counterweight to the power of the United States. This concern remains in the twenty-first century. There is little debate about whether the United States still commands overwhelming material capabilities, but there is much more discussion over whether the United States can translate those

The Berlin Wall, which divided Soviet-controlled East Berlin from Allied-controlled West Berlin,
was one symbol of the bipolar system that characterized the Cold War. Despite the tension
between the two poles, the Cold War stayed "cold," which some realists take as evidence
of the stability of a bipolar system.

capabilities into effective dominance. In relative terms, U.S. power is on the decline.
China, Japan, and the European Union are rising economically, as are Brazil and
India, even though U.S. dominance in military expenditures has gone largely unchallenged, save perhaps modestly by China and Russia. The trend clearly suggests that
not only is the global distribution of material power widening, but that material power
itself may be less important than many assume, especially as compared to other sorts
of power such as the power of ideas.

The type of international system in place at any given time has implications for system management and stability. Are certain polarities more manageable and hence
more stable than others are? Are wars more likely to occur in bipolar systems, multipolar
systems, or unipolar systems? These questions have dominated much of the discussion
among realists, but so far, studies of these relationships have proven inconclusive.

Bipolar systems are very difficult to regulate formally, because neither uncommitted states nor international organizations can reliably direct the behavior of either of the
two poles. Informal regulation may be easier. If either of the blocs is engaged in disruptive behavior, the consequences are immediately evident, especially if one of the blocs
gains in strength or position as a result. The neorealist theorist Kenneth Waltz, for one,

argues that because of this visibility, the bipolar international system is the most stable structure in the long run: the two sides are "able both to moderate the other's use of violence and to absorb possibly destabilizing changes that emanate from uses of violence that they do not or cannot control."[2] In such a system, a clear difference exists in how much power each pole holds compared with what other state actors hold. Because of the power disparity, each of the two poles can focus its activity almost exclusively on the other. Each can anticipate the other's actions and accurately predict its responses because of their history of repeated interactions. Each tries to preserve this balance of power to preserve itself and the bipolar system. In 2012, Waltz reprised a similar argument in "Why Iran Should Get the Bomb." He argues that Israel's nuclear capability is destabilizing the region: "If Iran goes nuclear, Israel and Iran will deter each other, as nuclear powers always have." That would bring stability.[3]

Pointing to the stability attained in the bipolar Cold War system, John Mearsheimer provoked controversy by suggesting that the world would miss the stability and predictability that the Cold War had forged. With the end of the Cold War bipolar system, Mearsheimer argued, more interstate conflicts would develop and hence more possibilities for war. He felt that deterrence would be more difficult and miscalculations more probable. He drew a clear policy implication: "The West has an interest in maintaining peace in Europe. It therefore has an interest in maintaining the Cold War order, and hence has an interest in the continuation of the Cold War confrontation; developments that threaten to end it are dangerous. . . . A complete end to the Cold War would create more problems than it would solve."[4] Most analysts did not agree with this provocative conclusion, partly because factors other than polarity can affect system stability. Yet others have pointed to the Russian Federation's recent forceful annexation of the Crimea from Ukraine as evidence that Russia's current president, Vladimir Putin, both understands the importance of bipolar rivalry for international stability and has begun taking steps to reenact that rivalry.

Of course, both bipolar and multipolar systems are, or can be, "balance of power" systems. According to realists, multipolar systems can be very stable so long as the system's key actors internalize norms of competition and cooperation. For neorealists, however, balance of power is more difficult in multipolar systems because they involve more inherent uncertainty about where and when a threat might emerge (including the threat of a given state ignoring important balance of power norms). For this reason, neorealists argue that bipolar systems are likely to be more peaceful. Again, the empirical evidence is mixed.

In contrast, hegemonic stability theorists claim that an approximation of unipolarity—hegemony—may be sufficient to create and maintain a stable international system. So long as the hegemon—a word coming from the Greek "to lead"—is able and willing to act, and act in ways that benefit those it leads as well as itself, enduring and prosperous peace can result. In *The Rise and Fall of the Great Powers*, historian Paul Kennedy argues that the hegemony of Britain in the nineteenth century and the

United States in the immediate post–World War II era led to the greatest stability.[5] Other proponents of this theory, such as Robert O. Keohane, contend that hegemonic states are willing to pay the price of enforcing norms, unilaterally if necessary, to ensure the continuation of the system that benefits them. When the hegemon loses material capability or is no longer willing to exercise its advantage in relative power, then system stability is jeopardized.[6]

It is clear, then, that realists do not entirely agree among themselves about the relationship between polarity and stability. Individual and group efforts to test this relationship have been inconclusive. The Correlates of War project (discussed in Chapter 1) did test two hypotheses flowing from the polarity-stability debate. J. David Singer and Melvin Small hypothesized that the greater the number of alliance commitments in the system, the more war the system will experience. They also hypothesized that the closer the system is to bipolarity, the more war it will experience. According to data between 1815 and 1945, however, neither argument was proven valid across the whole time span. During the nineteenth century, alliance commitments prevented war, whereas in the twentieth century, proliferating alliances seemed to cause war.[7] Other evidence from the 1970s suggests that although U.S. economic prowess declined in relative terms, the international system itself remained stable; system stability is not dependent solely on one power.[8]

Realists and International System Change

For realists, the nature of the change in the system can be reduced to the distribution of peace and war between great powers (small and medium powers matter less). If that structure affects the likelihood of war and peace in the system, then logically, any understanding of what causes structural change (e.g., in polarity) will result in an understanding of what makes war or peace more likely. Changes in either the number of major actors or the relative power of those actors may cause a fundamental change in the structure of the international system. According to realists, wars are most often responsible for such fundamental changes in power relationships. For example, World War II caused a relative decline of Great Britain and France, even though they were the victors. The war also signaled the end not only of Germany's and Japan's imperial aspirations but of their considerable military and economic capabilities as well. Their militaries were soundly defeated; their civil societies were destroyed and their infrastructures demolished. Two other powers emerged in dominant positions—the United States, now willing to assume the international role it had shunned after World War I, and the Soviet Union, buoyed by its victory, although economically weakened. The international system had fundamentally changed; the multipolar world had been replaced by a bipolar one.

Robert Gilpin, in *War and Change in World Politics,* sees another mechanism of system change: states grow at uneven rates because states respond differently to political, economic, and technological developments. Those uneven rates eventually lead to a redistribution of power and thus change the international system. For example, the rapidly industrializing East Asian states—South Korea, Taiwan, and Hong Kong (now part of China)—have responded to technological change the fastest. By responding rapidly and with single-mindedness, these states have improved their relative positions. Thus, the actions of a few can change the characteristics of the international system.[9]

Exogenous shifts in technology may also lead to a shift in the international political system. Technological advances—such as the instruments for oceanic navigation, the airplane for transatlantic crossings, satellites and rockets for the exploration of space, and cyber and Internet technology—have not only expanded the boundaries of accessible geographic space but also have brought about changes in the boundaries of the international political system. The same is true of global warming and the receding Arctic ice cap: previously unexplored territory and unnavigable waterways have created new strategic interests in the area, and states bordering the Arctic are not alone in seeking to establish territorial and economic interests there. These exogenous shifts changed the relative power of state actors, all reflecting different political interests and different cultural traditions.

Perhaps no technological change has had a stronger impact on the international system than the development of nuclear weapons and their use in warfare. Their destructiveness, their inability to discriminate between combatants and civilians, and their evident harm to future generations have led policy makers to reconsider the political utility of the power to destroy. During the Cold War, this led the superpowers to spar through non-nuclear proxies using conventional military technology, rather than fight directly, as Chapter 2 discussed. Since nuclear weapons have not been used in war since 1945, they are no longer seen as credible in some circles. Nevertheless, their use remains greatly feared. Efforts or threats by non-nuclear states to develop such weapons have provoked sharp resistance, such as when North Korea claimed to have tested a hydrogen bomb in January 2016. The nuclear states do not want a change in the status quo; in their view, nuclear proliferation, particularly in the hands of "rogue" states such as North Korea and Iran, leads to international system instability. That is why the Joint Comprehensive Plan of Action for Iran denuclearization—a compromise plan between Iran, P5+1 (the five permanent members of the UN Security Council plus Germany), and the EU in which Iran agreed to halt production of nuclear weapons in exchange for the lifting of costly economic sanctions—was pursued with such unity and vigor.

Thus, in the view of realists, international systems can change, yet the inherent bias among realist interpretations is for continuity. The reason is all states have an interest in preventing the one structural change that might abrogate the possibility of war in the system: unipolarity. The closer the system gets to a single actor exercising all the power in its own interests, the greater the incentives of actors in the system to countervail that actor. Put differently, we might say that most states prefer independence (sovereignty) and some risk of war, over a guarantee of peace under the absolute rule of a single state. Thus, in reality, the neorealist argument may reduce to the claim that because unipolarity will not actually happen, and unipolarity is necessary to suspend anarchy and war, we can never be entirely at peace in the international system but must always remain prepared to defend ourselves. This argument explains why, for realists, peace in the international system must prove elusive.

The International System According to Liberals

For liberals, the international system is less consequential as an explanatory level of analysis. Therefore, it is not surprising to find at least three different conceptions of the international system in liberal thinking.

The first conception sees the international system not as an unchanging structure, but rather as an interdependent system in which multiple and fluid interactions occur among different parties and where various actors learn from the interactions. Actors in this process include not only states but also international governmental organizations (such as the United Nations), nongovernmental organizations (such as Human Rights Watch), multinational corporations, and substate actors (such as parliaments and bureaucracies). With so many different kinds of actors interacting with all of the others, a plethora of national interests defines the liberal international system. Although security interests, so dominant for realists, are also important to liberals, other interests, such as economic and social issues, are considered, depending on the time and circumstance. In their book *Power and Interdependence,* the political scientists Robert Keohane and Joseph Nye describe the international system as an interdependent system in which the different actors are both sensitive to (affected by) and vulnerable to (suffering costly effects from) the actions of others. Interdependent systems have multiple channels connecting states; these channels exist among governmental elites, nongovernmental elites, and transnational organizations. Multiple issues and agendas arise in the interdependent system. Military force may be useful in some situations, but it is not useful for all issues.[10]

Negotiating and coordinating in the liberal international system often occurs through multilateralism. Multilateralism is based on core principles, one of which is the collective security system. Briefly, collective security rests on the idea that peace is indivisible: a war against one is a war against all, meaning that the international community is obligated to respond. That idea will be examined in greater detail in Chapter 8; it is a key liberal approach to war and strife. Thus, the possibility of coordinating behavior through multilateralism is a critical component of the liberal view of the international system.

A second liberal conception sees the international system in terms of a specific international order. Building on the tradition of Immanuel Kant and U.S. president

Woodrow Wilson, as Chapter 3 discussed, this view holds that a liberal international order governs arrangements among states by means of shared rules and principles, similar to the principles that realists see under varying conditions of polarity. But unlike the realists' principles, this order is an acknowledged order; it is not just patterned behavior or some interconnections. In this order, institutions play a key role. As John Ikenberrry in *After Victory* argues, the acknowledged goal of a dominant power in this international order is to establish rules that are "both durable and legitimate, but rules and arrangements that also serve the long-term interests of the leading state."[11] To do that, the dominant power limits its own autonomy and agrees to make credible commitments.

A third liberal view of the international system is held by neoliberal institutionalists. Neoliberal institutionalists see the international system as anarchic and acknowledge that each individual state acts in its own self-interest, similar to realist thinking. But neoliberal institutionalists draw different conclusions about state behavior in the international system. It may be a cooperative system, wherein states choose to cooperate because they realize that they will have future interactions with the same actors, as Chapter 3 explains. Those repeated interactions provide the motivation for states to create international institutions, which in turn moderate state behavior, providing a guaranteed framework for interactions and a context for bargaining. International institutions provide focal points for coordination and serve to make state commitments more credible by specifying what is expected, thereby encouraging states to establish reputations for compliance. Thus, for neoliberals, institutions have important and independent effects on interstate interactions, both by providing information and by framing actions, but they do not necessarily affect states' underlying motivations. The international system may be anarchic, but cooperation may emerge through institutions.

Liberals and International System Change

International relations theorists are often interested in answering different questions. As we just saw, for realists, the core questions surround the issue of whether war is something we are all stuck with, or something we can, through good policy, transcend and put behind us. Liberals, too, see the role of states, and peace, as critical features of the international system. Liberals see change as coming from several sources. First, changes in the international system may occur as the result of exogenous technological developments, that is, progress occurring independently, outside the control of actors in the system. For example, changes in communication and transportation are responsible for the increasing level of interdependence among states within the international system.

Second, change may occur because of changes in the relative importance of different issue areas. Although realists give primacy to issues of national security, liberals identify the relative importance of other issue areas. Specifically, in the last decades of the twentieth century, economic issues replaced national security issues as the leading topic of the international agenda. In the twenty-first century, transnational concerns such as human rights, the environment, and health have assumed a much more prominent role. These are fundamental changes in the international system, according to most liberal thinking.

Third, change may occur when new actors, including multinational corporations, nongovernmental organizations, or other participants in global civil society, augment or replace state actors. The various new actors may enter into new kinds of relationships and may alter both the international system and individual state behaviors. These types of changes are compatible with liberal thinking and are discussed by liberal writers. And, like their realist counterparts, liberal thinkers also acknowledge that change *may* occur in the overall power structure among the states. In contrast, radicals *advocate* major changes.

On the critical question of whether war is something we must live with, liberals are distinct from realists in arguing that a different feature of human nature—besides fear and greed—helps explain how we might transcend and eradicate war. In the liberal view, the economic or material self-interest of states can lead to cooperation, including cooperation across what were once considered zero-sum issues. For example, in the liberal view, cooperation to reduce tariff barriers to trade, after a while, may lead to cooperation on professional standards, immigration controls, and even, eventually, security cooperation. Change in the system, and in the likelihood of war in the system, then comes after decades, even centuries, of painstaking, at times reversed, but ultimately more comprehensive cooperation. In sum, whereas realist theory remains pessimistic about the possibilities of transcending perpetual war, liberal theory holds out an optimistic possibility of an evolution toward perpetual peace.

The International System According to Radicals

Whereas realists define the international system in terms of its polarity and stability, radicals seek to describe and explain the structure in totally different terms.

Radicals describe the structure of the international system by stratification. **Stratification** refers to the uneven—and relatively fixed—division of valued resources among different groups of states. The international system is stratified according to which states have valued resources, such as oil, military strength, or economic power. Stratification parallels a Marxist emphasis on social class within states: developed, wealthy, advanced-industrial capitalist states represent the bourgeoisie, and developing, poor, agrarian states represent the proletariat. Because, just as in the within-state critique of labor exploitation, the distribution of wealth is fixed and supported by violent force, stratification in the international system is the key to understanding the radicals' notion of the system and pathways to change (see Figure 4.2).

Different international systems have had varying degrees of stratification. Historically, system stratification is extensive. According to one set of measures, several of the world's powers (the United States, Japan, Germany, France, Britain, Russia, and China) account for about half of the world's total gross domestic product (GDP). The other 180 plus states share the other half. From the stratification of power and resources comes the division between the haves, loosely characterized as the **North**, and the have-nots, states largely located in the **South**. This distinction is vital to the discussion of international political economy found in Chapter 9.

Stratification of resources and hence influence has implications for a system's ability to regulate itself, as well as for system stability. When the dominant powers are challenged by those states just below them, the system may become highly unstable in terms of access to resources. For example, Germany's and Japan's attempts to obtain and reclaim resources during the 1930s led to World War II. Such a group of second-tier powers has the potential to win a confrontation, but the real underdogs in a severely stratified system do not (although they can cause major disruptions). The rising powers, especially those that are acquiring resources, seek first-tier status and are willing to fight wars to get it. If the challengers do not begin a war, the top powers may do so to quell the threat of a power displacement.

For Marxists, as well as most other radicals, crippling stratification in the international system is caused by capitalism. Capitalism structures and then *fixes* the

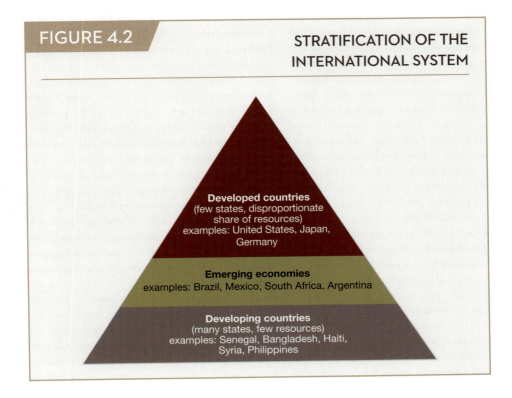

FIGURE 4.2   STRATIFICATION OF THE INTERNATIONAL SYSTEM

Developed countries
(few states, disproportionate share of resources)
examples: United States, Japan, Germany

Emerging economies
examples: Brazil, Mexico, South Africa, Argentina

Developing countries
(many states, few resources)
examples: Senegal, Bangladesh, Haiti, Syria, Philippines

Russia, Syria, and the International System

Russian air strikes against targets in Syria, its deployment of "volunteer" ground forces into the country (as highlighted in the *New York Times* headline "Kremlin Says Russian 'Volunteer' Forces Will Fight in Syria"),[a] and the escalating tension caused by the Turkish downing of a Russian bomber over its alleged incursion into Turkish air space all represent a complex and dangerous turn of events. The situation is complicated. Russia, a long-time ally of Syria, supports the Assad regime and Iran; it opposes the Islamic State and moderate rebels fighting the Syrian government. The United States supports Syrian Kurds, the moderate rebels, Saudi Arabia, and the Gulf states, but opposes the IS, the Assad regime, and Iran. Iran supports Assad but opposes the IS, Saudi Arabia, the Gulf states, and moderate rebels. Turkey supports the moderate rebels, Saudi Arabia, and its Gulf allies, but opposes Assad, the IS, Iran, and the Syrian Kurds. To counter Iranian influence, the Sunni Arab states like Saudi Arabia and Qatar fund and arm the Syrian rebels, but are increasingly alarmed by the IS and have joined the U.S.-led coalition against the IS. The situation is dangerous because the United States, France, and several regional states are flying combat air sorties over Syria both targeting the IS and supporting moderate rebel groups, while the Russian planes are targeting opponents of Assad and the IS. There is a real possibility that the various combatants might engage, increasing the likelihood of a military confrontation.

What explains Russia's military intervention in Syria? One possibility is that Russia's leaders are acting more assertively in the interstate system to increase domestic political support for the regime at a time when material and economic conditions in Russia are in decline. Russia's government launched military attacks in Syria, just as it had in Crimea and Ukraine, to continue to distract from its poor record of governance in Russia: low investment in national education, health care, and transportation infrastructure has caused many Russians to become resentful, and others to emigrate. Supporting Syria, its long-time ally, opens another military engagement far from home. Another possibility relates to Russia's long history of struggle with Islam-inspired insurgency. The fall of Chechnya in 1996 to nationalist insurgents—many of whom were Muslims—greatly compromised Russia's military reputation and emboldened nationalists and radical Muslims to attack Russia. By attacking "terrorists" opposing an allied leader in the Middle East, Russia not only distracts from its domestic and economic troubles, but also harms the reputation of radical fighters claiming Islam as their motivation, and at the same time, enhances its prestige as a great power with global reach.

Although Russia's foreign policy appears to be realist at its core—intervening militarily far from its shores to expand and defend its interests in the Middle East, and weakening the power of the United States and its allies in the same region—both constructivism and feminism offer alternative insights.

The argument that Russia's need to enhance its prestige may explain its actions is directly engaged by constructivism. Being a great power is not only about relative material power, a constructivist would argue, but also about the foreign policy "scripts" that attach to power. Great powers are expected to act in certain ways. An important sign of great power status is a willingness to threaten or use armed force abroad in pursuit of state interests. Thus, even though Russia's power is in decline in material terms, by *acting* according to the great power script, Russia's leaders make it possible for Russians to feel that their state (and they) are feared and therefore respected.

Feminist explanations of Russia's recent interventions are similar. Some feminist international relations theorists argue that the international system is profoundly gendered. States with more material power and a willingness to use power aggressively (e.g., Russia) are more masculine, and states with less material power or an unwillingness to use power aggressively are more feminine. Foreign policies follow: "feminine" states are more patient, and more apt to respond to crises or threats with diplomatic or economic resources than with military action. "Masculine" states are less patient, and more apt to respond to crises and threats with an aggressive use of military force. In this view, Russia's foreign policy helps to constitute it as a hypermasculinist state. Realism, constructivism, and feminist theory move in the same direction: power demands military action (as does a masculine identity), and military action implies power.

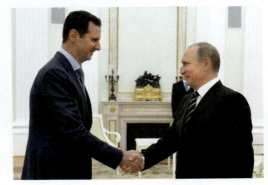

Russia's President Vladimir Putin (right) accompanies Syria's President Bashar al Assad in a show of support for Assad in late 2015. Russia has argued that a Western preference for justice over stability has led to dramatically increased injustice as many states in the Middle East and North Africa—such as Libya and Syria—are now beset by vicious civil wars, leading to widespread human suffering and massive refugee flows.

FOR CRITICAL ANALYSIS

1. Is Russia's military intervention a sign of its weakness or evidence of its resurgent strength?

2. If you were advising the United States, what would you recommend the president do in response to Russia's intervention? What role do you think the UN should have in that response?

a. Andrew E. Kraemer, Helene Cooper, and Ceylan Yeginsu, "Kremlin Says Russian 'Volunteer' Forces Will Fight in Syria," *New York Times*, Oct. 6, 2015.

With a GDP per capita of approximately $3,200, Nigeria is one of the "have-nots" in the radical understanding of the international system. Despite its wealth of natural resources, Nigeria has been unable to successfully develop out of poverty.

relationship between the advantaged and the disadvantaged, empowering the rich and disenfranchising the weak. Marxists assert that capitalism breeds its own instruments of domination. These include international institutions whose rules capitalist states structure to facilitate capitalist processes, multinational corporations whose headquarters are in capitalist states but whose loci of activity are in "dependent areas," and even individuals (often leaders) or classes (the national bourgeoisie) residing in weak states who are co-opted to participate in and perpetuate an economic system that places the masses in a permanently dependent position.

Radicals believe that the greatest amount of resentment will arise in systems where the stratification is most extreme. There, the poor are likely to be not only resentful but also aggressive, in large part because in such systems, the poor have so little to lose by resistance. They want change, but the rich have very little incentive to change their behavior. The call for the **New International Economic Order (NIEO)** was voiced by radicals (and some liberal reformers) in the 1970s in most developing countries. The poorer, developing states of the South, underdogs with a dearth of resources, sought fundamental changes that would enhance their economic development and control over their own natural resources, thus increasing their power relative to the North.

In short, radicals argue that great economic disparities are built into the structure of the international system and that this structure constrains all actions and interactions. But some radicals recognize that transitions may occur. The hegemonic Dutch of the eighteenth century were replaced by the British in the nineteenth century and the Americans in the twentieth. Change may occur in the semiperiphery and periphery, as states change their positions relative to each other. Capitalism goes through cycles of growth and expansion, as occurred during the age of colonialism and imperialism, followed by periods of contraction and decline. So capitalism itself is a dynamic force for change, though radicals do not view those changes in a positive light.

But can the capitalist system itself be changed? In other words, is system transformation—such as the change from the feudal to the capitalist system—possible? Here, radicals differ among themselves. In the original radical theories, the state had to be done away with if capitalism was to collapse and permit the laborers of the world a fair share of the world's wealth. One pathway was revolution—global revolution. As we saw in Chapter 2, however, in 1848, this revolutionary moment seemed to pass; since 1917, the promise of revolutions in Russia, China, and Cuba all seemed to stall, leaving permanent dictatorships in place. But today, we might wonder whether technology—in particular cyber and Internet technologies—might serve as an exogenous factor capable of forcing revolutionary change. If capitalist dominance is based on monopoly ownership of the means of production, as for example Marx and Engels claimed, and technology breaks this monopoly, perhaps putting the means of production into workers' hands, then capitalism might be undone, and with it, stratification and war. Already in the early part of this century, poor and desperate people all over the world have begun using mobile phone technology to coordinate dissent in their home countries, or to find pathways out of their deadly circumstances. But just as realists disagree among themselves about policy implications, radicals disagree about the likelihood that the system stratification they all abhor can be transcended.

The International System According to Constructivists

Constructivists argue that the whole concept of an international system is a European idea that, over time, became accepted as a natural fact (at least among Europeans and North Americans). They hold that we can explain nothing by international material structures alone. Martha Finnemore in *The Purpose of Intervention* suggests that there have been different international orders with changing purposes, different views of threat, and reliance on different ways to maintain order. She traces at least four European international orders: an eighteenth-century balance order; a nineteenth-century concert order; a sphere-of-influence system for much of the twentieth century; and, since the end of the Cold War, an evolving new order whose purposes are the promotion of liberal democracy, capitalism, and human rights. Constructivists agree with other theorists that power matters in the international system, but they propose that the meaning of "power" can change over time. As Finnemore writes, "[W]hat made 1815 a concert and 1950 a cold war was not the material distribution of capabilities but the shared meanings and interpretations participants imposed on those capabilities."[12]

Constructivists see not a material structure in the international system but rather a socially constructed process. While the prominent constructivist Alexander Wendt, in *Social Theory of International Politics,* agrees with the fundamental premise of realists that the system is anarchic, he contends that the whole notion of anarchy is socially constructed: anarchy is what states make of it.[13] The meaning of anarchy is not constant across geographic space or through time. Anarchy leads to no particular outcome unless we agree it does. States debate anarchy's meaning and in turn give it meaning. Neither sovereignty nor balance of power objectively exist. Thus, constructivists reject the notion that the international system exists objectively or gives rise to objective rules or principles.

Constructivists believe that what does change are norms, although not all norm changes will be transforming. Social norms can be changed through both actions of the collective and the efforts of charismatic individuals. Individuals matter in both realist and liberal theory, but they matter differently. For constructivists, they matter in how they affect discourse (how we frame and understand our world in talking, writing, and performing). Collectively, norms may change through coercion, but most likely, through international institutions, law, and social movements. So although material capabilities do matter in explaining change, just as realists and many liberals argue, "why one order emerges rather than another" can only be seen, Finnemore argues, "by examining the ideas, culture, and social purpose of the actors involved."[14]

Constructivists, then, are interested in understanding the major changes in the normative structure: how the use of force has evolved over time, how the view of who is human has changed, how ideas about democracy and human rights have internationalized, and how states have been socialized—or resisted socialization—in turn.

Advantages and Disadvantages of the International System as a Level of Analysis

For adherents of all theoretical perspectives, using the international system as a level of analysis has clear advantages. The language of systems theory allows comparison and contrasts between systems: we may compare the international system at one point in time with one at another point in time; compare international systems with internal state systems; or contrast political systems with social or even biological systems. How these various systems interact is the focus of both the social and the natural sciences.

For all the sciences, three of the most significant advantages to this level of analysis lie in the comprehensiveness of systems theory. First, important aspects of the whole are more difficult to understand by reference to their parts. If systems interest you, trying to understand them entirely by reference to their parts will prove misleading. Second, it enables scholars to organize the seemingly disjointed parts into a whole; it allows them to hypothesize about and then to test how the system's various parts, actors, and rules are related and to show how change in one part of the system causes changes in other parts. In this sense, the notion of a system is a significant research tool. Third, it facilitates theorizing about change.

In short, while analysis at the international systems level cannot explain events at the micro level—why a particular individual acts a certain way—it does allow plausible explanations at the more general level. For realists, generalizations derived from systems theory provide the fodder for prediction, the ultimate goal of all behavioral science. For liberals and radicals, these generalizations have definite normative implications; in the former case, they affirm movement toward a positive system, and, in the latter case, they confirm pessimistic assessments about the place of states in the economically determined international system.

But systems theory also has some glaring weaknesses and inadequacies. The emphasis at the international-system level means that politics is often neglected. The generalizations are broad and sometimes obvious. Who disputes that most states seek to maintain their relative capability or that most states prefer to negotiate rather than fight under all but a few circumstances? Who doubts that some states occupy a preeminent economic position that affects the status of all others?

International system theorists have always been hampered by the problem of boundaries. If they use the notion of the international system, do they mean the international *political* system? What factors lie outside the system? In fact, much realist theory systematically ignores this critical question by differentiating several different levels within the system but only one international-system-level construct. Liberals do better, differentiating factors external to the system and even incorporating those factors into their expanded notion of an interdependent international system. Yet, if we cannot clearly distinguish between what is inside and what is outside of the system, do we in fact have a system? Even more important, what shapes the system? What is the reciprocal relationship between international system constraints and unit (state) behavior? By way of contrast, constructivists do not acknowledge such boundaries. They argue that no natural or necessary distinction exists between the international system and the state or between international politics and domestic politics, and no distinction exists between endogenous and exogenous sources of change.

The International System: A View from China

Realists posit that the international system changes as great powers gain or lose power relative to other states. As China's economic and political power has grown, many scholars have speculated whether China will catch up to the United States, leading to a new bipolarity, or surpass the United States, becoming the new hegemon in a unipolar system. Chinese government officials have stated their intentions.

Following almost a century of seeing itself as a victim of the great powers and after decades of internal revolution when it was closed to the world, China is becoming a confident great power. The country wields increasing economic and political influence, using both bilateral and multilateral diplomacy. China's interests align quite closely with those of other major powers, although they are not parallel. The country now operates within the rules of the contemporary international system; it has become socialized into prevailing international norms.

The economic revolution in China, its embrace of free markets, and its opening to foreign investment and enterprise have led to almost four decades of unprecedented economic growth of more than 9 percent per year. As the world's second-largest economy, China has maintained that it is in China's interest to continue this "peaceful rise," or *zhongguo heping jueqi,* serving as a viable economic model for many states.

China's participation in world trade regimes has increased its global presence to the benefit of all parties. China's accession to the World Trade Organization (WTO) and its Free Trade Agreement with the United States have allowed it to maximize economic output while demonstrating to the world that it can adhere to WTO regulations, such as nondiscrimination policies and elimination of price controls. China is also now actively engaged in regional trade and economic agreements, particularly with South East Asian Nations (ASEAN) states and within the Asia-Pacific Economic Cooperation (APEC) forum. In 2015, China launched the Asian Infrastructure Investment Bank, a rival to the World Bank, the International Monetary Fund, and the Asian Development Bank. Headquartered in Beijing, more than 50 members have joined the bank, over the objections of both the United States and Japan.

China has acted responsibly toward both the advanced capitalist states and the developing world. China finances a large portion of American debt because of its large balance-of-trade surplus with the United States. During the 2008 international financial crisis, China refrained from putting pressure on the U.S. dollar and interest rates. To help rebalance the international economy, China is encouraging domestic consumption, increasing workers' pay, and allowing its currency to appreciate gradually. Even though China has geopolitical disputes with Japan, the economic ties between the two countries remain strong.

Like many other states, China needs natural resources. Thus, China has forged relationships with African countries by investing in infrastructure, technology, and raw materials. With trade of more than $210 billion, China is Africa's top business partner. Chinese private companies, businesses, and tourists are finding Africa fertile territory. Whereas the West colonized these lands and often stripped them of their resource wealth, China seeks a peaceful, mutually beneficial relationship. China does not interfere in the domestic affairs of other states or impose unwanted conditions on issues that are within the state's own responsibility.

Like all great powers, China has increased its military expenditures, although the United States spends six times more on defense than China spends. China will continue to modernize its nuclear forces and strengthen its second-strike abilities. It will develop cyberwarfare capabilities. But the threat posed by these advances may have been exaggerated by Western observers.

China has so far chosen not to use its military capabilities. Nor has China fought to expand its territory. But China will defend its national interest consistent with the One-China policy: the view that Tibet, Taiwan, and the islands in the South China Seas including Diaoyu are part of China. Since 2014, China has undertaken a new policy of dredging thousands of metric tons of sand onto coral reefs to create artificial islands in the Spratly Island group to strengthen its territorial claims. China will continue to oppose the designs of neighboring states, who consistently refute those claims.

China is building the capacity—mainly naval capacity—to deploy armed forces further and further abroad. China argues that as a global power with global interests—including economic development projects in Africa—its armed forces will need to be able to reach Chinese citizens when they are stranded or threatened abroad. Unlike its principal rival, China has not openly exercised its financial power, except to support regional and global economic stability. China has acted responsibly to try to solve major international issues like the North Korea nuclear standoff. China

China financed the construction of this stadium in Ndola, Zambia.

has benefited from the international order of the last decades and is committed to a stable continuation of that order. And like other powers, China is now exercising its soft power. Over 440 Confucius Institutes have been established in almost 100 countries to promote Chinese language, culture, and exchanges.

FOR CRITICAL ANALYSIS

1. Why does China have an interest in sustaining the contemporary international system, even if it does not dominate it?

2. Constructivists argue that changes in norms lead to system change. Has China internalized new norms? Or is it merely acting in its own self-interest, as realists would argue?

3. How would an offensive realist react to China's explanation of its role in the international system?

4. China has consistently argued in favor of sovereignty and noninterference in the domestic affairs of states. How does this position support China's international role?

Furthermore, the testing of systems theories is very difficult. In most cases, theorists are constrained by a lack of historical information. After all, few systems theorists besides some radical and cyclical theorists discuss systems predating 1648. In fact, most begin with the nineteenth century. Those using earlier time frames are constrained by both a poor grounding in history and glaring lapses in the historical record. Although these weaknesses are not fatal, they restrict scholars' ability to generalize their findings.

Perhaps the most fundamental critique is the attention paid to one international system in particular. Is not the idea of one international system really a Eurocentric notion? Here, the critics have a valid point. The idea of an international system evolved out of the state-centric, post-Westphalian world. In that world, the international system consisted of sovereign European states that shared common pre-Westphalian traditions: the Roman Empire, which had imposed order and unity by force on a large geographic expanse and used a common language, and the Christian tradition, as exemplified by the Catholic Church of the medieval era with its authority and law. From those common social roots, the idea of the international system arose. Some scholars, the so-called English school, call this system an **international society**, because it shares a common culture that was a foundation for common rules and institutions. According to two of the principal architects, the scholars Hedley Bull and Adam Watson, although the international system comprises a group of independent political communities, an international society is more than that. In an international society, the various actors communicate; they consent to common rules and institutions and recognize common interests. Actors in an international society share a common identity, a sense of "we-ness." Without such an identity, a society cannot exist.[15]

Yet were there not international systems—or more accurately international societies—beyond the European world? Perhaps those societies were based on other sets of rules and institutions. For example, various kingdoms flourished in China for centuries before unification in 200 BCE. Imperial China endured for 2,000 years, united around a common culture that the Chinese thought was the center of the universe. The Islamic peoples, too, shared a common identity as Islam spread across the Middle East to Africa, Asia, and even Europe. That social identity can be seen in the belief in the *umma*, or community of believers. The *umma* was symbolized by the institution of the caliphate, the Islamic political authority, and was an identity that overrode tribe, race, and even the state itself. That unity broke down in the division between Sunni and Shia, a dispute over who was the rightful successor to the Prophet Muhammad. Some advocate restoration of the caliphate as a renewal of Islamic civilization's former historical greatness, and the Islamic State proclaimed that restoration in 2014. International relations scholars have often paid too little attention to non-European international societies.

THEORY IN BRIEF

CONTENDING PERSPECTIVES ON THE INTERNATIONAL SYSTEM

	REALISM / NEOREALISM	LIBERALISM / NEOLIBERAL INSTITUTIONALISM	RADICALISM / DEPENDENCY THEORY	CONSTRUCTIVISM
CHARACTERIZATION	Anarchic	Three liberal interpretations: interdependence, international order, and neoliberal institutionalism	Highly stratified	International system exists as social construct
ACTORS	State is primary actor	States, international governmental institutions, nongovernmental organizations, substate actors	Capitalist states vs. developing states	Individuals matter; no differentiation between international and domestic
CONSTRAINTS	Polarity; distribution of power	Interdependence; institutions	Capitalism; stratification	Ongoing interactions
POSSIBILITY OF CHANGE	Slow change when the balance of power shifts	Low possibility of radical change; constant incremental change as actors are involved in new relationships	Radical change desired but limited by the capitalist structure	Emphasis on change in social norms and identities

As the European-based international system emerged as the most powerful and dominant one, how did other regions become part of it? Colonialism and the spread of capitalism by the European powers brought many areas into this system, as Chapter 2 traced.

Struggles persist among these different international societies. The political scientist Samuel Huntington identified these struggles as civilizational, positing that states and state interests were being transcended by cultures, the largest aggregation of which is civilizations. He believed civilizational differences would become the new basis of international conflict.[16] Thus, although the notion of one international system may reflect power realities from the nineteenth century to the early years of the twenty-first, that idea is disputed because of its Eurocentric bias, its neglect of the international systems of "others," and the empirical difficulties involved in differentiating the international system and its component parts.

In Sum: From the International System to the State

Of all the theoretical approaches, the international system level of analysis receives the most attention from realists and radicals. For realists, the defining characteristic of the international system is polarity; for radicals, it is stratification. In both perspectives, the international system constrains state behavior. Realists generally view such constraints as positive, depending on the distribution of power, whereas for radicals, the constraints are negative, preventing economically depressed states from achieving equality and justice. Liberals view the international system from a more neutral perspective as an arena and process for interaction. Constructivists take an evolutionary approach, emphasizing how changes in norms and ideas shape what the system means, seeing little differentiation between international and domestic systems and discounting the importance that other theorists attach to international system structure.

States and foreign policy decision makers operate within the confines of the international system. In the next chapter, we examine the state, models of state decision making, and challenges to the state.

Discussion Questions

1. Is the international system like physical or biological systems? How are these systems similar? How are they different?

2. Realists, liberals, radicals, and constructivists view sovereignty differently. Explain.

3. The realist view of the international system has been criticized as oriented to the status quo. To what extent is that critique valid? Is that characteristic desirable or not?

4. Neorealists and neoliberals agree on an essential characteristic of the international system. How do they disagree? Why is that disagreement important?

5. After the collapse of the Soviet Union, some theorists argued that Marxism had been discredited and was, in fact, dead. Do you think that argument is

true? How can radicalism help us explain some features of the international system?

6.   What kind of international system would you like to live in? Why?

Key Terms

bipolar (p. 111)

international society (p. 128)

multilateralism (p. 116)

multipolar (p. 109)

New International Economic Order
(NIEO) (p. 122)

North (p. 119)

South (p. 119)

stratification (p. 118)

system (p. 108)

unipolar (p. 111)

05

Palestinians unfurled their flag in celebration of Palestine's recognition by the United Nations as a nonmember observer state and the hanging of the flag at UN headquarters. Many gathered in Ramallah to watch a live broadcast of President Mahmoud Abbas's speech to the General Assembly on this occasion.

THE STATE

At the 2015 meeting of the UN General Assembly, the flags of Palestine and the Holy See, both nonmember observer states, were raised outside UN headquarters. The General Assembly approved this symbolic gesture at the request of Palestine, as part of an offensive to seek approval from various international bodies to gain broader recognition as a state. Previously, in 2012, reflecting the frustration of the majority of UN members as well as the Palestinian people, the United Nations General Assembly voted to upgrade the Palestinian Authority's status from nonmember observer entity to nonmember observer state—a recognition of de facto sovereign statehood. In 2015, Palestine won admission to the International Criminal Court and delivered accusations of Israeli war crimes to the court. But when Prime Minister Benjamin Netanyahu, in the heat of the 2015 election campaign, admitted that he would never agree to a Palestinian state, a member of the Palestine Liberation Organization's top decision-making body replied, "We will continue a diplomatic intifada. We have no other choice."

Why is achieving statehood so essential to Palestine's agenda? In the practice of international politics and in thinking about international relations, the state is central. Much of the history traced in Chapter 2 was the history of how the state emerged from the post-Westphalian framework and developed in tandem with sovereignty and the nation. Two of the theoretical perspectives—realism and liberalism—acknowledge the primacy of the state. Yet despite this emphasis on the state, it is inadequately conceptualized. As the scholar James Rosenau laments, "All too many studies posit the state as a symbol without content, as an actor whose nature, motives, and conduct are so self-evident as to obviate any need for precise conceptualizing. Often, in fact, the concept seems to be used as a residual category to explain that which is otherwise inexplicable in macro politics."[1] We need to do better. How do states behave in international relations, and why do they matter?

LEARNING OBJECTIVES

- Define the state, the major actor in international relations.

- Explain how the various theoretical perspectives view the state.

- Describe how political scientists measure state power.

- Explain the methods states use to exercise their power.

- Analyze how democracies behave differently from nondemocracies.

- Understand the models that help us explain how states make foreign policy decisions.

- Analyze the major contemporary challenges to the state.

The State and the Nation

For an entity to qualify as a **state**, it must meet four fundamental legal conditions, as outlined in the 1933 Montevideo Convention. First, a state must have a territorial base, with geographically defined boundaries. Second, a stable population must reside within its borders. Third, this population should owe allegiance to an entity government. Finally, other states must recognize this state diplomatically.

These legal criteria are not absolute; they are often subject to various interpretations. Most states do have a territorial base, though the precise borders are often disputed. Until the Palestinian Authority was given a measure of control over the West Bank, for instance, Palestine was not territorially based. Also, it is not officially rec-

Officers of the Philippine Marine Corps watch as a Chinese surveillance vessel cruises past Philippine-claimed territory in the Spratly Islands. China's building of small artificial islands in the South China Seas, an area contested by Vietnam, Malaysia, and the Philippines, signals its intention to extend territorial jurisdiction.

ognized as a state, despite its attempt to further its status in international bodies, as described above. Possessing territory is so important that states try to extend their territory. China, for example, asserts its claims in the South China Seas by dredging sand and building landmasses on reefs in the contested Spratly Islands, in an attempt to solidify access to oil and gas reserves.

Most states have a stable population, but migrant communities and nomadic peoples cross borders, as the Maasai peoples of Kenya and Tanzania do, undetected by state authorities. Most states have some type of institutional structure for governance, but whether the people are obedient to it can be unknown due to lack of information. Such a structure might also be problematic, if the government's institutional legitimacy is constantly questioned. A state need not have a particular form of government, but most of its people must acknowledge the legitimacy of that government. In 2010, the people of Egypt told the international community that they no longer recognized the legitimacy of the government led by Hosni Mubarak, leading to demonstrations and ultimately the downfall of his administration.

Finally, other states must recognize the state diplomatically. But, how many states' recognition does it take to fulfill this criterion? The Republic of Transkei—a tiny piece of real estate carved out of South Africa—was recognized by just one state, South Africa; that proved insufficient to give Transkei status as a state, and the territory was soon reincorporated into South Africa.

Some states are currently contested. In early 2008, Kosovo, once a semi-autonomous part of Yugoslavia and later a province of Serbia, declared independence from Serbia. It accepted a constitution and established a ministry of foreign affairs. In 2013, Facebook gave users the option to identify themselves as citizens of Kosovo, rather than Serbia, an act that Kosovar leaders hailed as raising the country's profile and reinforcing its independence. By the end of 2015, more than 100 states had recognized Kosovo's independence, but these states did not include Serbia, Russia, or five EU members, each battling their own insurgency, which they feared might seek independence.

Other de facto but unrecognized states include Abkhaza, Nagorno-Karabakh, and South Ossetia, among others. They are variously described as "quasi-countries teetering on the brink of statehood," which are in "the international community's prenatal ward" or, more simply, states in limbo land.[2] So although the legal conditions for statehood provide a yardstick, that measuring stick is not absolute.

The definition of a state differs from that of a **nation**. A nation is a group of people who share a set of characteristics. Do a people share a common history and heritage, a common language and set of customs, or similar lifestyles? If so, then the people make up a nation. At the core of the concept of a nation is the notion that people with commonalities owe their allegiance to the nation and to its legal representative, the state. This feeling of commonality, of people uniting together for a cause, provided the foundation for the French Revolution and spread to Central and South America and central Europe. Nationalism—the belief that nations should form their own states—propelled the formation of a unified Italy and Germany in the nineteenth century. The recognition of commonalities among people (and hence of differences from other groups) spread with new technologies and education. When the printing press became widely used, the masses could read in their national languages; with improved methods of transportation, people could travel, witnessing firsthand similarities and differences among other groups. With better communications, elites could use the media to promote unity or sometimes to exploit differences.

Some nations, like the Danes and Italians, formed their own states. That coincidence between state and nation, the **nation-state**, is the foundation for national self-determination, the idea that peoples sharing nationhood have a right to determine how and under what conditions they should live. Other nations are spread among several states. One of the largest groups of people without their own state is the Kurds. Thirty million people strong, scattered in the mountainous areas of Turkey (14.7 million), Syria (1.7 million), Iran (8.1 million), and Iraq (5.5 million), their language, Kurdish, is unrelated to either Arabic or Turkish, and most Kurds are Sunni Muslims. After World War I, the Kurds sought self-rule and an independent Kurdistan, but independence did not occur; the states in the region fought to keep the Kurds within their own boundaries, and the Kurds themselves were divided. But the new Iraq constitution following the 2003 Iraq War called for an autonomous Kurdistan Regional Government for the Kurds in Iraq, resulting in an economically vibrant area separate from the chaos in the rest of Iraq. And the 2011 Arab Spring offered new opportunities for Kurdish nationhood, as Syria was plunged into a civil war and the Kurds seized control of the Kurdish-majority regions. As one of the Kurdish leaders expressed, "All the facts on the ground encourage the Kurds to be independent. . . . Today, international powers can no longer resolve any issue in the Middle East without taking into account the interests of the Kurds."[3]

Still other states have within their borders several different nations—India, Russia, and South Africa are prominent examples. In the United States and Canada, a number of different Native American nations are a part of the state, as are multiple immigrant communities. The state and the nation do not always coincide. Yet over time in the latter cases, a common identity and nationality have been forged, even in the absence of religious, ethnic, or cultural similarity. In the case of the United States, national values reflecting commonly held ideas are expressed in public rituals, including reciting the Pledge of Allegiance, singing the national anthem, and volunteering in one's community.[4] Nation-states are both complex and constantly evolving.

Some of the hundreds of national subgroups around the world, which count over 900 million people, identify more with a particular culture or religion than with a particular state, often experiencing discrimination or persecution because of their identity. This situation is not new. The gradual disintegration of the Ottoman Empire between the 1830s and World War I reflected increasing ethnic demands for self-determination from Egypt and Greece to Albania, Montenegro, and Bulgaria.

Yet not all ethnonationalists aspire to the same goals. Some want recognition of a unique status, the right to speak and write a particular language or practice their religion, or special seats in representative bodies, as the Basques in Spain and France desire. Still other groups seek separation and the right to form their own state, as Catalonians in Spain expressed in the 2015 regional elections when separatists won in Catalonia, the wealthiest area of the country. And some prefer joining with another state that is populated by fellow ethnonationalists.

One persistent dispute over the state and nation involves the People's Republic of China (PRC) and Taiwan, also called the Republic of China (ROC). After World War II, Mao Zedong and his communist revolutionaries took over the territory and government of mainland China, forcing the former Nationalist government to flee to Taiwan, a small island about 100 miles to the southeast. Both governments claimed to represent the Chinese nation. For ideological and geopolitical reasons, the United States originally recognized the ROC, while the Soviet Union recognized the PRC. Over time, however, the growing political and economic power of the PRC meant that the ROC was sidelined; notably, in 1972, the PRC assumed China's permanent seat in the Security Council at the United Nations. Today, the PRC is recognized by 172 states, while the ROC is recognized by only 21 plus the Holy See. The PRC has always maintained that Taiwan is an inseparable part of China, a policy it calls "the One China policy," which the United States supports. The relationship between China and Taiwan became more complicated after democracy was established in Taiwan in 1990, since one major political party supports independence for Taiwan while the other supports a continuation of the status quo. The so-called China question, the conflict over the state and nation of China, continues today, even though the first top-level contact in 66 years occurred in late 2015 between President Xi Jinping of the mainland and President Ma Ying-jeou of Taiwan.

Disputes over state territories and the desires of nations to form their own states have been major sources of instability and even conflict since the end of colonialism in Africa and the Middle East, and most recently, after the breakups of the Soviet Union and Yugoslavia. Another of these intractable conflicts is that between Israeli Jews and Palestinian Arabs, who each claim the same territory. This conflict has been complicated by several factors—that Jews, Christians, Muslims, and Bahá'ís each claim certain land and monuments as sacred, the intense opposition from Arab states to the existence of the state of Israel, and Israel's gradual expansion of its territory through war and settlements. Since the founding of Israel in 1948, the Arab and Jewish peoples of Palestine have been involved in six interstate wars and three popular uprisings. Civilians on both sides have been harmed and killed, and many continue to live as refugees. Policy makers have debated several alternatives. Should Israel and the Palestinian territories be divided into two separate independent states? The complicated boundaries exacerbated by increasing number of Jewish settlers on the West Bank make that solution increasingly unlikely. Should the two nations be part of one multinational state? That would likely mean the end of the Jewish democratic state. Or, should the Palestinians focus on attaining rights other than self-determination—basic political and civil rights within the current structure?

Contending Conceptualizations of the State

Just as the nation is more than a historic entity, the state is more than a legal entity. There are numerous competing conceptualizations of the state, many of which emphasize ideas absent from the legalistic approach.

Other concepts of the state include the following: The state is a normative order, a symbol for a particular society and the beliefs that bind the people living within its borders. This entity also has a monopoly on the legitimate use of violence within a society. The state is a functional unit that assumes a number of important responsibilities, centralizing and unifying them. These perspectives of the state parallel the

Central Middle Eastern Region, 2016

general international relations theories discussed in Chapters 3 and 4. For two of these theoretical perspectives, the state is paramount.

The Realist View of the State

Realists generally hold a statist, or state-centric, view. They believe that the state is an autonomous actor constrained only by the structural anarchy of the international

Seeking Palestinian Statehood

Palestine has been contested territory for more than 2,000 years. Since the establishment of Israel in 1948, there have been numerous proposals for creating two states in the region—Israel for the Jews and Palestine for the Arabic Muslim peoples. But after six wars and numerous rounds of negotiations, no solution for dividing the territory that is compatible with the national interests of each entity has been found. So why did a recent headline declare, "Palestinian Leaders See Validation of Their Statehood Effort"[a]?

In recent years, Palestinian leaders have started an enhanced unilateral diplomatic offensive to achieve state status by a different route. Most states in Asia, Latin America, and Africa already recognize Palestine as a state, supporting the Palestinian people against what many perceive as domination by the Western-supported hegemony of the United States. In 2012, Palestine became a "nonmember observer state"—a recognition of de facto sovereign statehood, followed in 2015 by its admission to the International Criminal Court.

That strategy has begun in earnest. In 2015, Pope Francis praised Mahmoud Abbas, the president of the Palestinian Authority, as an "angel of peace." Then in June of the same year, the Vatican signed a treaty with the "state of Palestine," an endorsement of Palestine's bid for sovereignty and statehood and the Vatican's hope that relations between Israel and Palestine would improve.

Also in 2015, Palestinian authorities lobbied FIFA (Fédération Internationale de Football Association), the governing body of world soccer, to suspend Israel from that organization—a strategy that had previously been used to isolate South Africa during the apartheid era. While that proposal was subsequently rescinded, it set off another round of shuttle diplomacy, much as American diplomats have engaged in for decades to try to reach a peace agreement.

The legal criteria for statehood is well established: a defined territory, a government to which people are obedient, a people living in a confined space, and recognition by other states and international bodies. For the vast majority of new "states" seeking legal statehood, joining the United Nations is the legitimation of statehood. It was no problem for South Sudan to gain that status in 2011, at the end of the 20-year civil war in that country. But the Palestinian case is different. The United States, one of the permanent members of the UN Security Council with veto power, will not support Palestinian statehood since Israel strongly opposes the policy and the process. Thus, this impasse has led Palestine to seek statehood using a different strategy. What cannot be accomplished de jure (according to the law) may be achieved de facto (in fact).

Realists view the impasse as an example of each side acting on behalf of its national interest. Israel needs assurances that its security is firm and that its citizens will no longer be threatened by attacks from Palestinian territories. The United States supports its ally. Palestinians demand a territory and a space of their own, where their people may live peacefully as they have for millennia. While liberals may have placed faith in negotiations to solve the problem of two peoples on one land, decades of disappointments have led some to support this other approach. As constructivists would argue, the more Palestinian claims to statehood are legitimized by members of the international community, the more Palestine can act as a de jure state.

Palestinians plant an olive tree on land confiscated by Israel in the West Bank, which is claimed by both Israelis and Palestinians.

FOR CRITICAL ANALYSIS

1. Do you think Palestine can win over the international community using this strategy?

2. What should be the response of the United States, usually a strong supporter of Israel?

3. Would a one-state solution be a better alternative to solving this decades-old conflict?

a. Diaa Hadid, "Palestinian Leaders See Validation of Their Statehood Effort," *New York Times,* March 19, 2015.

IN FOCUS

THE REALIST VIEW OF THE STATE

The state is:

- an autonomous actor

- constrained only by the anarchy of the international system

- sovereign

- guided by a national interest that is defined in terms of power

system. The state enjoys sovereignty—the authority to govern matters that are within its own borders and that affect its people, economy, security, and form of government. As a sovereign entity, the state has a consistent set of goals—that is, a national interest—defined in terms of power. Different kinds of power translate into military power. Although power is of primary importance to realists, as we will see later in this chapter, ideas also matter in their estimation; ideology, for example, can determine the nature of the state, as with the North Korean state under communism. But in international relations, once the state (with power and ideas) acts, according to the realists, it does so as an autonomous, unitary actor.

An example of the realist interpretation of the state can be seen with respect to natural resources. States recognize certain strategic commodities as vital for their national security. Thus, states desire stability in the availability and prices of these commodities. They do what is possible so that they have a guaranteed supply. Oil is a key resource for the rapidly developing China. Thus, one high priority of the government is to forge strong relations with governments possessing petroleum resources, like Iran, Sudan, and Angola. China defends these states in international forums and provides foreign aid to guarantee consistent supply. China's creation of territory in the South China Sea to augment its own resources is another example of China acting in its national interest, consistent with a realist conception of the proper role of the state.

The Liberal View of the State

In the liberal view, the state enjoys sovereignty but is not an autonomous actor. Just as liberals believe the international system is a process occurring among many actors, they see the state as a pluralist arena whose function is to maintain the basic rules of the game. These rules ensure that various interests (both governmental and societal) compete fairly and effectively in the game of politics. There is no single explicit or consistent national interest; there are many. These interests often compete against

IN FOCUS   THE LIBERAL VIEW OF THE STATE

The state is:

- a process, involving contending interests
- a reflection of both governmental and societal interests
- the repository of multiple and changing national interests
- the possessor of fungible sources of power

each other within a pluralistic framework. A state's national interests change over time, reflecting the interests and relative power positions of competing groups inside and sometimes also outside the state.

With respect to natural resources, liberals believe that multiple national interests influence state actions: consumer groups desire oil at the lowest price possible; manufacturers, who depend on bulk supplies to run their factories, value a stable supply of oil, otherwise they risk losing their jobs; producers of oil, including domestic producers, want high prices, to make profits and have incentives to reinvest in drilling. The state itself reflects no consistent viewpoint about the oil; its task is to ensure that the "playing field is level" and that the procedural rules are the same for the various players in the market. The substantive outcome of the game—which group's interests predominate—changes depending on circumstances and is of little import to the state. There is no single or consistent national interest: at times, it is low consumer prices; at other times, stability of prices; and at still other times, high prices to stimulate domestic production. For liberals, the state provides the arena for groups, each with different self-interests, to find a common interest.

The Radical View of the State

Radicals offer two alternative views of the state, each emphasizing the role of capitalism and the capitalist class in the state's formation and functioning. The *instrumental* Marxist view sees the state as the executing agent of the bourgeoisie. The bourgeoisie reacts to direct societal pressures, especially to pressures from the capitalist class. The *structural* Marxist view sees the state as operating within the structure of the capitalist system. Within that system, the state is driven to expand, not because of the direct pressure of the capitalists but because of the imperatives of the capitalist system. In neither view is there a national interest: state behavior reflects economic goals. In neither

IN FOCUS

THE RADICAL VIEW OF THE STATE

The state is:

- the executing agent of the bourgeoisie

- influenced by pressures from the capitalist class

- constrained by the structure of the international capitalist system

---

case is real sovereignty possible, because the state is continually reacting to external and internal capitalist pressures.

In the radical perspective, a state's policy toward primary commodities reflects the interests of the owner capitalist class aligned with the bourgeoisie (in the instrumental Marxist view) and reflects the structure of the international capitalist system (in structural Marxist thinking). Both views would more than likely see the negotiating process as exploitative, where the weak (poor and dependent groups or states) are exploited for the advancement of strong capitalists or capitalist states. According to radical thinking, the international petroleum companies are the capitalists, aligned with hegemonic states. They are able to negotiate favorable prices, often to the detriment of weaker oil-producing states, such as Mexico. Radicals may explain U.S. and European military intervention in the Middle East in terms of protecting vital petroleum and natural gas resources, the source of power for the international capitalist class.

The Constructivist View of the State

Because constructivists see both national interests and national identities as social constructs, they conceptualize the state very differently from theorists who have other perspectives. To constructivists, national interests are neither material nor given. They are ideational and ever-changing and evolving, in response to both domestic factors and international norms and ideas. States share a variety of goals and values, which they are socialized into by international and nongovernmental organizations. Those norms can change state preferences, which in turn can influence state behavior. So, too, do states have multiple identities, including a shared understanding of national identity, which also changes, altering state preferences and hence state behavior. In short, the state "makes" the system and the system "makes" the state.[5]

IN FOCUS

THE CONSTRUCTIVIST VIEW OF THE STATE

The state is:

- a socially constructed entity

- the repository of national interests that change over time

- shaped by international norms that change preferences

- influenced by changing national interests that shape and reshape identities

- socialized by IGOs and NGOs

While constructivists may pay little heed to materialist conceptions of power defined in terms of oil resources, they may try to tease out how the identities of states are forged by having such a valuable resource. Saudi Arabia and the Gulf states have developed an identity based on a seemingly limitless, valuable resource. Oil permits them to merge that identity with their identity as Islamic states that export the faith to other countries.

Thus, each theory holds a different view about the state. These differences can be seen in four topic areas: the nature of state power (What is power? What are important sources of power?), the exercise of state power (the relative importance of different techniques of statecraft), how foreign policy is made (the statist versus the bureaucratic/organizational or pluralist approach to decision making), and the determinants of foreign policy (the relative importance of domestic versus international factors).

The Nature of State Power

States are critical actors because they have **power**, which is the ability not only to influence others but also to control outcomes to produce results that would not have occurred naturally. States have power with respect to each other and with respect to actors within the state. All theoretical perspectives acknowledge the importance of power, but each pays attention to different types of power. Realists, liberals, and radicals all conceptualize power in materialist terms, realists and radicals primarily in natural and tangible sources, while liberals also pay attention to intangible power sources. Constructivists emphasize the nonmaterialist sources found in the power of ideas, one of the intangible sources. All agree that power is multidimensional, dynamic, and situational.

Natural Sources of Power

Through the exercise of power, states have influence over others and can control the direction of policies and events. Whether power is effective at influencing outcomes depends, in part, on the **power potential** of each party. A state's power potential also depends on its natural sources of power, which are critical to both realist and radical perspectives. The three most important natural sources of power potential are geographic size and position, natural resources, and population.

Geographic size and position were the natural sources of power international relations theorists recognized first. A large geographic expanse gives a state automatic power potential (when we think of power, we think of large states—Russia, China, the United States, Australia, India, Canada, or Brazil, for instance). Long borders, however, may be a weakness: they must be defended, an expensive and often problematic task.

Two different views about the importance of geography in international relations emerged at the turn of the last century within the realist tradition. In the late 1890s, the naval officer and historian Alfred Mahan (1840–1914) wrote of the importance of controlling the sea. He argued that the state controlling the ocean routes controls the world. To Mahan, sovereignty over land was not as critical as having access to, and control over, sea routes.[6] In 1904, the British geographer Sir Halford Mackinder (1861–1947) countered this view. To Mackinder, the state that controlled the Eurasian geographic "heartland" had the most power: "He who rules Eastern Europe commands the Heartland of Eurasia; who rules the Heartland commands the World Island of Europe, Asia, and Africa, and who rules the World Island commands the world."[7]

Both views have empirical validity. British power in the eighteenth and nineteenth centuries was determined largely by its dominance on the seas, a power that allowed Britain to colonialize distant places, including India, much of Africa, and North and Central America. Russia's lack of easy access to the sea and its resultant inability to wield naval power has been viewed as a persistent weakness in that country's power potential. Control of key oceanic choke points—the Straits of Malacca, Gibraltar, and Hormuz; the Dardanelles; the Persian Gulf; and the Suez and Panama canals—is viewed as a positive indicator of power potential.

Yet geographic position in Mackinder's heartland of Eurasia has also proven to be a significant source of power potential. More than any other country, Germany has acted to secure its power through its control of the heartland of Eurasia, acting very clearly according to Mackinder's dictum, as interpreted by the German geographer Karl Haushofer (1869–1946). Haushofer, who had served in both the Bavarian and the German armies, was disappointed by Germany's loss in World War I. Arguing that Germany could become a powerful state if it could capture the Eurasian heartland, he set out to make geopolitics a legitimate area for academic inquiry. He founded an institute and a journal, thrusting himself into a position as the leading supporter and proponent of Nazi expansion.

But geographic power potential is magnified or constrained by natural resources, a second source of natural power. Controlling a large geographic expanse is not a positive ingredient of power unless that expanse contains natural resources. Petroleum-exporting states such as Kuwait, Qatar, and the United Arab Emirates, which are geographically small but have a crucial natural resource, have greater power potential than their sizes would suggest. States need oil and are ready to pay dearly for it, and will even go to war when access to it is denied. States that have such valuable natural resources, regardless of their geographic size, wield power over states that do not. The United States, Russia, and South Africa exert vast power potential because of their diverse natural resources—oil, copper, bauxite, vanadium, gold, and silver. Russia has leveraged its power from its control of natural resources to influence political outcomes in other states. For instance, Russia cut off natural gas supplies to Ukraine, thereby slowing supplies to Europe, which gets one-quarter of its gas through Ukraine. Mainland China, which supplies over 95 percent of the demand for so-called rare earth minerals essential in high-tech manufacturing, has been able to use its monopoly to deny access for political purposes and drive up prices. Yet China's monopoly is not assured as new mines in Australia, the United States, India, and Vietnam open. Even natural resource–based power may have its limits.

Of course, having a sought-after resource may prove a liability, making states targets for aggressive actions, as Kuwait soberly learned in 1990. Nor does the absence of natural resources mean that a state has no power potential; Japan is not rich in natural resources, but it has parlayed other elements of power to make itself an economic powerhouse.

Population is a third natural source of power. Sizable populations, such as those of China (1.4 billion people), India (1.3 billion), the United States (321 million), Indonesia (256 million), Brazil (204 million), and Russia (142 million), automatically give power potential, and often great power status, to a state. Although a large population produces a variety of goods and services, characteristics of that population (health status, age distribution, level of social services) may magnify or constrain state power. States with small, highly educated, skilled populations, such as Switzerland, Norway, Austria, and Singapore, can fill disproportionately large economic and political niches. States with large but relatively poor populations, such as Ethiopia, with 99 million people but a gross national product of only $550 per capita, can exercise less power. States with a declining population, like Russia, or a rapidly aging one, as in South Korea and Japan, may in the future suffer from a decline in this natural source of power, as Chapter 11 explains.

Both tangible and intangible sources can affect the degree to which these natural sources of power potential are translated into actual power. These sources are used to enhance, modify, or constrain power potential, as Figure 5.1 shows.

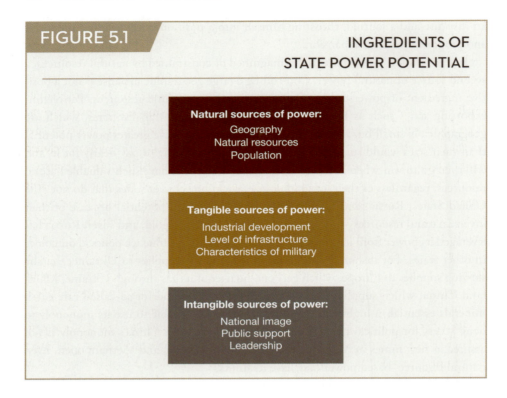

FIGURE 5.1

INGREDIENTS OF STATE POWER POTENTIAL

Natural sources of power:
Geography
Natural resources
Population

Tangible sources of power:
Industrial development
Level of infrastructure
Characteristics of military

Intangible sources of power:
National image
Public support
Leadership

Tangible Sources of Power

Among the tangible sources of power, industrial development, economic diversification, level of infrastructure, and characteristics of the military are among the most critical. With an advanced industrial capacity, the advantages and disadvantages of geography diminish. Air travel, for example, makes geographic expanse less of a barrier to commerce, yet at the same time, makes even large states militarily vulnerable. Industrialization modifies the importance of population, too. Large but poorly equipped armies are no match for small armies with advanced equipment. Industrialized states generally have higher educational levels and more advanced technology, and use capital more efficiently, all of which add to their tangible power potential.

Intangible Sources of Power

Intangible power sources—national image, quality of government, public support, leadership, and morale—may be as important as the tangible ones, although not to radicals, who emphasize material sources of power. People within states have images of their own state's power potential—images that translate into an intangible power ingredient. Canadians have typically viewed themselves as internationally responsible and eager to participate in multilateral peacekeeping missions, to provide generous foreign-aid packages, and to respond unselfishly to international emergencies. The state has acted on and, indeed, helped to shape that image, making Canada a more powerful actor than its small population (35 million) would otherwise dictate. But images can slowly change as policy positions change. In recent years, Canada's view of itself as "helpful fixer" has waned as its defense and development spending has lagged compared to other developed states, a trend that Prime Minister Justin Trudeau (elected in 2015) hopes to reverse.

The perception by other states of public support and cohesion is another intangible source of power. China's power was magnified during the leadership of Mao Zedong (1893–1976), when there appeared to be unprecedented public support for the communist leadership and a high degree of societal cohesion. A state government's actual support among its own population can also be a powerful mediator of state power. Israel's successful campaigns in the Middle East in the 1967 and 1973 wars can be attributed in large part to strong public support, including the willingness of Israeli citizens to pay the cost and die for their country when necessary.

When that public support is absent, particularly in democracies, the power potential of the state diminishes. Witness the U.S. loss in the Vietnam War, when challenges to, and disagreement with, the war effort undermined military effectiveness. Loss of public support may also inhibit authoritarian systems. In both the 1991 Gulf War and the 2003 Iraq War, Saddam Hussein's support from his own troops was woefully inadequate: many were not ready to die for the Iraqi regime and fled. In 2015, Iraqi soldiers once again dropped their weapons and discarded their uniforms when faced with the Islamic State onslaught. They were not ready to fight for the regime. Neither were the mercenaries Muammar Qaddafi hired ready to fight for Libya in 2011 as they left with their arms, making their way to West African states like Mali, ready to fight another day.

Leadership is another source of intangible power. Visionaries and charismatic leaders, such as India's Mohandas Gandhi, Germany's Otto von Bismarck, and Britain's Winston Churchill, were able to augment the power potential of their states by taking bold initiatives. Poor leaders, those who squander public resources and abuse the public's trust, such as Zimbabwe's Robert Mugabe, Iraq's Nouri al-Maliki, and Syria's Bashar al Assad, diminish the state's power capability and its capacity to exert power over the long term. Liberals, in particular, pay attention to leadership: good leaders can avoid resorting to war; bad leaders may not be able to prevent it.

More generally, states can exercise intangible power characteristics. Joseph S. Nye labeled such power **soft power**, the ability to attract others because of the legitimacy of the state's values or its policies.[8] Rather than exerting its natural and tangible power, such a state influences other states by being what it is. A state is able to co-opt others

Shanghai, China, has undergone a major transformation in the last 25 years as China's economy has developed rapidly from agricultural to industrial. With numerous sources of natural and tangible power, China today is considered one of the foremost powers in the world.

through the power of its example. For the United States, its soft power resources may include its model of functioning democracy and commitment to political and civil rights. Since 2007, China has tried to increase its soft power resources—its reputation as a defender of national sovereignty and its record of achievement in economic growth, as well as its traditional ancient cultures and its cuisine. But as one scholar found, despite its estimated $10 billion per year in its overseas publicity work, China has "very little influence on global cultural trends, minimal soft power, and a mixed-to-poor international image in public opinion polls."[9] Monocle Media ranks countries annually by a soft power index. Based on 50 factors, including number of cultural missions, number of Olympic medals, and quality of its architecture, Germany, Great Britain, the United States, France, and Japan lead in their soft power resources.

Critics disagree, however, about the effectiveness of soft power. Realists might argue that it is ineffective compared to hard power. Yet when coupled with the tangible, intangible power sources either augment a state's capacity or diminish its power. Liberals, who have a more expansive notion of power, would more than likely place greater importance on these intangible ingredients because several reflect domestic political processes. Yet different combinations of the sources of power may produce different outcomes. The NATO alliance's victory over Slobodan Milošević's Yugoslavian forces in 1999 and Libya in 2011 can be explained by the alliance's overwhelming natural sources of power coupled with its strong tangible sources of power. But how can we explain Afghanistan's victory over the Soviet Union in the early 1980s, or the North Vietnamese victory over the United States in the 1970s, or the Algerian victory over France in the early 1960s? In each case, a country with limited natural and tangible sources of power prevailed over those with strong natural and tangible power resources. In these cases, the intangible sources of power, including the willingness of the populations to continue fighting against overwhelming odds, explains victory by the objectively weaker side.[10] Success involves using various forms of state power. Nye calls that **smart power**, the combination of the hard power of coercion and payment with the soft power of persuasion and attraction, the appropriate combination depending on context.[11]

Constructivists, in contrast, offer a unique perspective on power. They argue that power includes more than the tangible and intangible sources. In addition, it includes the power of ideas and language—as distinguished from ideology, which fueled the unlikely victory of the objectively weaker side in the cases described earlier. State identities and nationalism are forged and changed through the power of ideas and norms.

States have various forms of power. But, as the case of India shows (see the Global Perspectives box p. 152–53), whether they can utilize this power depends, too, on a variety of factors, including a state's domestic capacity.

The Exercise of State Power

In all theoretical perspectives, power is not just to be possessed, it is to be used. States use a variety of techniques to translate power potential into effective power; namely, these techniques include diplomacy, economic statecraft, and force. In a particular situation, a state may begin with one approach and then try several others to influence the intended target. In other cases, a state may use several different techniques simultaneously. Which techniques political scientists think states emphasize varies across the theoretical perspectives. In addition, different types of states may make different choices.

The Art of Diplomacy

Traditional **diplomacy** entails states trying to influence the behavior of other actors by bargaining, negotiating, taking a specific action or refraining from such an action, or by appealing to the foreign public for support of a position.

According to Harold Nicolson, a British diplomat and writer, diplomacy usually begins with negotiation, through direct or indirect communication, in an attempt to

India: A View from a Rising State

India, a civilization thousands of years old, is a relatively young state. Established in 1947 following independence from Great Britain and partition from Pakistan, India is a state with many nations. With 22 official languages and 60 other spoken languages, it is home to Hindus, one of the largest Muslim populations in the world, as well as Christians, Sikhs, Buddhists, and Jains, among others. This diverse population, which historically was never united under a centralized government, poses unique opportunities and challenges in the twenty-first century.

India has unsurpassed power potential—a population of 1.3 billion people, with a young workforce; a large landmass protected by the Himalayan mountains and Indian Ocean; a major lane of commerce connecting the subcontinent to both Africa and South East Asia; and diverse natural resources, including the world's fourth largest deposits of coal and substantial deposits of iron ore, manganese, bauxite, and natural gas. Until recently, India's tangible sources of power lagged—industrialization was generally small scale; its level of infrastructure, with the exception of the railways, awful; its economy between the 1950s and 1980s struggled under socialist policies. At the same time, India's intangible power sources are the sophisticated intellectual and philosophical traditions which underpin its soft power, displayed in literature, academia, and movies.

India's democracy is anchored by a lively free press, an increasingly strong federal system able to accommodate diversity, and a history of strong leaders. The election of Narendra Modi in 2014 was path-breaking, marking the first time that the governing Bharatiya Janata Party could govern without building coalitions. And Modi, himself, represented the new democrat—he was not tied to any prominent family and was elected on his managerial record of economic success in an Indian state.

India is widely viewed as a "rising power"—an emerging power like the other members of the so-called BRICS countries (Brazil, Russia, India, China, South Africa). These states have the power potential, the tangible power, and the intangible resources to be emergent powers and perhaps great powers. To be sure, the specific attributes of each differ. For India, that label was given because key sectors of the Indian economy are leading economic growth and are competitive at the global level. The computer services and information-technology sectors are major global players in back-office outsourcing, used by major multinational corporations, international banks, and growing e-commerce companies. Indian growth rates have verged on 7.5 percent annually, though more normally they have been around 5 percent. Cell phones have penetrated the markets, giving 900 million people access to modern technology. Bangalore has become second only to Silicon Valley, California, for the high-tech industry, peopled by a growing middle class. India is also connected to an extraordinary diaspora that links it to many states and economies and influences India's global outlook.

India's globally competitive information technology and computer sector attracts people from all over the world to Bangalore, which hosts annual computing trade fairs and hackathons.

Despite its economic and technological growth, India faces major domestic challenges. Despite the high growth rates, it has the world's largest number of poor people—7 out of 10 households in the rural areas live on less than $4 a day. Although the urban communities are growing, still almost 70 percent lives in the rural areas, where social investments are deficient: public schools are of poor quality; infrastructure is inadequate; and access to clean water, electricity, all-weather roads, and basic sanitation is lacking. Thirty percent of the population lives below the poverty line. The government cannot deliver even basic services.

So can this "rising power" be a great power? India is a nuclear power and has been since 1974. India seeks membership on the UN Security Council—often seen as a symbol of becoming a great power. The globalization of Indian business completely overshadows the international ventures of the government. The state, with its strong military and police, surviving many challenges including terrorism and ethnonationalist movements, but with its difficult domestic economic agenda, is limited by its capacity to take on its share of global responsibilities.

FOR CRITICAL ANALYSIS

1. How do India's domestic issues prevent it from increasing influence in global affairs?

2. If you were an Indian leader in the private economic sector, what recommendations would you make to government authorities to advance the interests of India internationally?

3. Is the concept of a "rising power" useful in the study of international relations?

reach agreement. Parties may conduct this negotiation tacitly, with each party recognizing that a move in one direction leads the other to respond in a way that is strategic. The parties may conduct open, formal negotiations, where one side offers a formal proposal and the other responds; this process is generally repeated many times until the parties reach a compromise. In either case, reciprocity usually occurs, whereby each side responds to the other's moves in kind.

Yet for negotiations to be successful, each party needs to be credible; that is, each party needs to make believable statements, assume a likely position, and be able to back up its position by taking action. Well-intentioned and credible parties will have a higher probability of engaging in successful negotiations.

States seldom enter diplomatic bargaining or negotiations as power equals. Each state knows its own goals and power potential, of course, and has some idea of its opponent's goals and power potential, although information about the opponent may be imperfect, incomplete, or just wrong. Thus, although the outcome of the bargaining is almost always mutually beneficial (if not, why bother?), that outcome is not likely to please the parties equally. And the satisfaction of each party may change as new information is revealed or as conditions change over time.

Bargaining and negotiations are complex processes, complicated by at least two critical factors. First, most states carry out two levels of bargaining simultaneously: international bargaining between and among states, and the bargaining between the state's negotiators and its various domestic constituencies, both to reach a negotiating position and to ratify the agreement. The political scientist Robert Putnam refers to this as a "two-level game."[12]

The negotiations between the P5+1 and Iran over Iran's nuclear weapons programs illustrate the two-level game because each country conducted two sets of negotiations: one with the foreign states and the other within their own domestic political arena. Iran's negotiators had to satisfy the demands of Supreme Leader Ali Khamenei, whose strident words to the country's conservative constituency extolled Iran's sovereignty to make its own security choices, while at the same time keeping the United States and its partners hopeful that a compromise could be negotiated. The U.S. negotiators had to mollify the demands of their domestic opposition including members of the Republican Party, supporters of Israel, and the pro-Israel American Israel Public Affairs Committee (AIPAC), who opposed any negotiations with terrorist state Iran. What makes the game unusually complex is that "moves that are rational for one player at one board . . . may be impolitic for that same player at the other board."[13] The negotiator is the formal link between the two levels of negotiation. Realists see the two-level game as constrained primarily by the structure of the international system, whereas liberals more readily acknowledge domestic pressures and incentives.

Second, bargaining and negotiating are, in part, a culture-bound activity. Approaches to bargaining vary across cultures—a view accepted among liberals, who place importance on state differences. At least two styles of negotiations have been identified.[14] These two different styles may lead to contrasting outcomes. The more advanced industrialized states, like the United States, Great Britain, and Germany, favor discussion of concrete detail, eschewing grand philosophical debate, addressing concrete problems, and resolving specific issues before broader principles are crystallized. Other states, many in the developing world, argue in a deductive style—from general principles to particular applications. This approach may mask conflict over details until a later stage in the process. These differences in negotiating approaches can lead to stalemate or even, occasionally, negotiation failure.

The use of **public diplomacy** is an increasingly popular diplomatic technique in a communication-linked world. Public diplomacy involves targeting both foreign publics and elites, attempting to create an overall image that enhances a country's ability to achieve its diplomatic objectives. For instance, as secretary of state, Hillary Rodham Clinton traveled to more than 100 countries, highlighting the role of women and promoting values, democracy, and human rights. China's public diplomacy has used Confucius Institutes to promote Chinese language and culture worldwide.

Before and during the 2003 Iraq War, public diplomacy became a particularly useful diplomatic instrument. American administration officials not only made the case for war to the American people in news interviews and newspaper op-ed pieces but also lobbied friendly and opposing states, both directly in negotiations and indirectly through various media outlets, including independent Arab media such as the Qatar-funded Al Jazeera television network. The Department of State established the Middle East Radio Network, comprising both Radio Sawa and Alhurra. Radio Sawa broadcasts both Western and Middle Eastern popular music with periodic news briefs. The more controversial Alhurra, begun in 2004, has attracted much of the Iraqi market, and during the Arab Spring in Egypt, an estimated 25 percent of people living in Cairo and Alexandria listened to this news source. Al Jazeera remains the number one news source for an estimated 55 percent of the Arab world. States in the communication age clearly have another diplomatic instrument at their disposal, but whether public diplomacy changes "hearts and minds" is debatable.

Celebrity diplomacy is another form of public diplomacy, but celebrity diplomacy aims not only to influence the public but also to persuade decision makers. Celebrities like Bob Geldof, Bono, Angelina Jolie, and George Clooney are able to use their media access to support a particular cause, lobby for action, and speak directly to world leaders. No celebrity has been as effective as George Clooney and his work on behalf of the people of Darfur and South Sudan. Called a "21st-century statesman," Clooney has become an issue expert and privately funded a satellite to monitor military movements; he sees his role as helping "focus news media where they have abdicated their responsibility. We can't make policy, but we can 'encourage' politicians more than ever before."[15]

But diplomacy may need to encompass more than conducting negotiations and persuading the public. Negotiators may find they need to use other measures of state-craft, including positive incentives (such as diplomatic recognition or foreign aid in return for desired actions) and the threat of negative consequences (reduction or elimi-nation of foreign aid, severance of diplomatic ties, use of coercive force) if the target state continues to move in a specific direction. The tools of statecraft are not only dip-lomatic but also economic and military.

The liberal view is that talking, via all forms of diplomacy, is better than not talking to one's adversaries. Whatever the differences, liberals assert, discussion clarifies the issues, narrows differences, and encourages bargaining. Use of more forceful actions, like economic statecraft and use of military force, may make diplomacy less effective and should be a last resort. Realists are more skeptical about the value of diplomacy. While not ignoring some benefits, realists tend to see state goals as inherently con-flictual. Thus, to them, negotiations and diplomacy are apt to be effective only when backed by force, either economic or military.

Economic Statecraft

States use more than words to exercise power. They may use economic statecraft—both engagement (sometimes called positive sanctions) and **sanctions (or negative sanctions)**—to try to influence other states.[16] Engaging another state involves offer-ing a "carrot," enticing the target state to act in the desired way by rewarding moves it makes in the desired direction. The assumption is that positive incentives will lead the target state to change its behavior. Sanctions, however, may be imposed more often: threatening to act or actually taking actions that punish the target state for moves it makes in the direction not desired. The goal of using the "stick" (sanctions) may be to punish or reprimand the target state for actions taken or may be to try to change the future behavior of the target state. Table 5.1 provides examples of both positive engage-ment and negative sanctions.

Since the mid-1990s, states have increasingly imposed **smart sanctions**, including freezing assets of governments and/or individuals and imposing commodities sanc-tions (e.g., on oil, timber, or diamonds). Targeting has involved not just "what" but also "who" as the international community has tried to affect specific individuals and rebel groups, reduce ambiguity and loopholes, and avoid the high humanitarian costs of general sanctions. Despite these modifications, liberals are still wary of sanctions, believing instead that diplomacy is a more effective way for states to achieve interna-tional goals. Realist theorists, on the other hand, believe it is necessary in exercising power to resort to, or threaten to use, sanctions or force more regularly.

TABLE 5.1

INSTRUMENTS OF ECONOMIC STATECRAFT

Positive Engagement

THE ACTIVITY	EXAMPLE
Give the target state the same trading privileges given to your best trading partner (most-favored-nation [MFN] status) as incentive for policy change.	The United States granted MFN status to China, in spite of that country's poor human rights record.
Allow sensitive trade with target state, including militarily useful equipment.	France and Germany export equipment to Iran, even though Iran's government is hostile to the West.
Give corporations investment guarantees or tax breaks as incentives to invest in target state.	The United States offered insurance to U.S. companies willing to invest in post-apartheid South Africa.
Allow importation of target state's products into your country at best tariff rates.	Industrialized states allow imports from developing countries at lower tariff rates.

Negative Sanctions

THE SANCTION	EXAMPLE
Freeze target state's assets.	The United States froze Iranian assets during 1979 hostage crisis; Libyan assets, 2011 to present; Islamic State and al-Nusra Front assets, 2014 to present.
Arms embargo.	Sudan (militias), 2004 to present; Iran, 2006 to present; North Korea, 2006.
Export or import limits of selected technology and products.	Liberia (diamonds), 2001–2007; Côte d'Ivoire (diamonds), 2004–2014; Somalia (charcoal), 2012 to present.
Comprehensive sanctions.	Iraq, 1990–2003; Yugoslavia, 1992–1995.

A state's ability to use these instruments of economic statecraft depends on its power potential. States with a variety of power sources have more instruments at their disposal. Clearly, only economically well-endowed countries can grant licenses, offer investment guarantees, grant preferences to specific countries, house foreign assets, or boycott effectively. Radicals often point to this fact to illustrate the hegemony of the international capitalist system.

Although radicals disagree, liberals argue that developing states do have some leverage in economic statecraft under special circumstances. If a state or group of states controls a key resource whose production is limited, their power is strengthened. Among the primary commodities, petroleum has this potential, and it gave the Arab members of the Organization of the Petroleum Exporting Countries (OPEC) the ability to impose oil sanctions on the United States and the Netherlands when those two countries strongly supported Israel in the 1973 Arab-Israeli War.

The ability of sanctions to alter a target state's behavior appears mixed. South Africa illustrates a case of relative success in the use of economic sanctions. When the Reagan administration's "constructive engagement" policy failed to work, the U.S. Congress approved harsh sanctions against South Africa's apartheid regime in 1986, over a presidential veto. Under the Comprehensive Anti-Apartheid Act, the United States joined with other countries and the United Nations, which had already imposed economic sanctions. In 1992, the white-controlled South African regime announced a political opening that led to the end of apartheid and white-minority rule. Most commentators conclude that sanctions probably had an important effect on the regime's decision to change policy, but that was not the sole explanation.

Economic statecraft does not always lead to the intended outcome. In 1960, the United States imposed an economic, commercial, and financial embargo against Cuba, designed to punish the communist regime under Fidel Castro; those restrictions were strengthened and codified in 1992, making it the longest trade embargo in history. Only in 2000 were some of the restrictions relaxed for agribusiness and medicine. But, in late 2014, the Obama administration decided that sanctions had not worked and a new era of positive engagement would begin. Talking with Cuba's leaders and bureaucrats, re-opening the U.S. embassy in Havana, and using executive power to loosen a host of travel and commercial restrictions, including removing Cuba from the list of states sponsoring terrorism, would begin the engagement process. While only Congress can lift the economic embargo, the Obama administration embarked on a totally different strategy, to the consternation of some Florida-based older Cubans and many Republicans.

Iraq and Russia represent cases of ambiguous results for sanctioning, albeit for different reasons, and illustrate the difficulty in evaluating the policy's effectiveness. Between 1991 and 2003, Iraq was subject to comprehensive sanctions designed to pressure the Saddam Hussein regime to dismantle its weapons of mass destruction and ultimately to bring down the government. The sanctions may have achieved the first goal of driving the disarmament process and keeping most of Iraq's oil wealth out of the hands of Saddam Hussein. The more general goal of removing Saddam from power was not achieved; accomplishing that goal would require military action. We can also see ambiguous results in the sanctions the European Union and the United States imposed against Russia in 2014; these sanctions were in response to the Russian annexation of the Crimean Peninsula and in support for separatists in Ukraine. The Russian economy was clearly hurt; the economy shrunk in early 2015 by 2 percent, losing $26.8 billion in value. Russian officials acknowledged "meaningful" economic harm, but averred that the price was worth it. They would continue to support Ukrainian separatists, even if sanctions adversely affected their economy.

Sanctions the United States and the European Union took against Iran and its petrochemical and oil industries in 2011–13, designed to cut off that country from the international financial system, produced different results. Iran experienced an estimated $9 billion loss every quarter, leading to a dramatic decline in the value of its currency and weakening the Iranian economy, with direct effects on the population experiencing shortages in all sectors. That outcome may have led Iran to the negotiating table in 2014–15, although we cannot prove that was the cause or the reason for the final agreement.

So how successful are sanctions as a tool of statecraft? One empirical study of UN-imposed sanctions (62 cases) differentiates between various kinds of sanctions: sanctions that intend to change behavior; sanctions that constrain access to critical goods or funds; and sanctions that signal or stigmatize targets in support of international norms. The study found that sanctions were effective 22 percent of the time in achieving at least one of the three purposes. They were more effective in signaling or constraining a target than in coercing a change in behavior. In only 10 percent of the cases were sanctions effective in actually changing behavior.[17]

These findings suggest that while sanctions are typically viewed as a cheaper and easier tool for coercion and punishment than the use of armed force, they may be effective in limited cases. These outcomes have led realist theorists to conclude that states must use the threat of force to achieve their objective of changing the behavior of another state.

The Use of Force

Force (and the threat of force) is another critical instrument of statecraft and is central to realist thinking. Like economic statecraft, a state may use force or its threat either to get a target state to do something or to undo something that state has done—compellence—or to keep an adversary from doing something—deterrence.[18] Liberal theorists are more likely to advocate compellent strategies, moving cautiously to deterrence, whereas realists promote deterrence.

With the strategy of **compellence**, a state tries, by threatening to use force, to get another state to do something or to undo an act it has undertaken. The prelude to the 1991 Gulf War is an excellent example. The United States, the United Nations, and coalition members tried to get Saddam Hussein to change his actions using the compellent strategy of escalating threats. Iraq's invasion of Kuwait initially was widely condemned. Formal UN Security Council measures gave multilateral legitimacy to the condemnation. Next, Iraq's external economic assets were frozen and economic sanctions were imposed. Finally, U.S. and coalition military forces were mobilized and deployed, and specific deadlines were given for Iraq to withdraw from Kuwait. At each step of the compellent strategy of escalation, one message was communicated to Iraq: withdraw from Kuwait or more coercive actions will follow. The Western alliance followed a similar strategy to try to compel Serbia to stop abusing the human rights of Kosovar Albanians and to withdraw its military forces from the region. Compellence was also used before the 2003 Iraq War, when the United States and others threatened Saddam Hussein that if certain actions were not taken, then war would follow. Threats began when George W. Bush labeled Iraq a member of the "axis of evil"; they escalated when the United Nations found Iraq to be in material breach of a UN resolution. Then in March 2003, Great Britain, one of the coalition partners, gave Iraq ten days to comply with the UN resolution. And on March 17, the last compellent threat was issued: President George W. Bush gave Saddam's Baathist regime 48 hours to leave Iraq as its last chance to avert war. In all of these cases, it was necessary to resort to an invasion because compellence via an escalation of threats failed. Note that compellence ends once the use of force begins.

With the strategy of **deterrence**, states commit themselves to punishing a target state if that state takes an undesired action. Threats of actual war are used as an instrument of policy to dissuade a state from pursuing certain courses of action. If the target state does not take the undesired action, deterrence is successful and conflict is avoided. If it does choose to act, despite the deterrent threat, then the first state will presumably deliver a devastating blow.

Since the advent of nuclear weapons in 1945, deterrence has taken on a special meaning. Today, if a state chooses to resort to violence against a nuclear state, nuclear weapons might be launched against it in retaliation. If this happens, the cost of the aggression will be unacceptable, especially if both states have nuclear weapons—the viability of both societies would be at stake. Theoretically, therefore, states that recognize the destructive capability of nuclear weapons will be hesitant to take aggressive action. It is difficult for a state to know with absolute certainty that it could annihilate its adversary's nuclear capability in one go—called **first-strike capability**—and even the possibility that the adversary could respond with its **second-strike capability** would result in restraint. Deterrence is then successful.

For either compellence or deterrence to be effective, states must lay the ground-work. They must clearly and openly communicate their objectives and capabilities, be willing to make good on threats or fulfill promises, and have the capacity to follow through with their commitments. In short, a state's credibility is essential for compellence and deterrence. Yet this is not a one-sided, unilateral process; it is a strategic interaction where the behavior of each state is determined not only by each state's own behavior, but by the actions and responses of the other.

Compellence and deterrence can fail, however. If they do, states may go to war, but even during war, states have choices. They choose the type of weaponry (nuclear or nonnuclear, strategic or tactical, conventional or chemical and biological), the kind of targets (military or civilian, urban or rural), and the geographic locus (city, state, region) to be targeted. They may choose to respond in kind, to escalate, or to de-escalate. In war, both implicit and explicit negotiation takes place, over both how to fight the war and how to end it. We will return to a discussion of war in Chapter 8.

Democracy, Autocracy, and Foreign Policy

Although all states use diplomacy, the economy, and force to conduct foreign policy, do policy choices vary by type of government? Specifically, do democratic states conduct foreign policy and make policy choices that are any different from the choices and policies authoritarian states and leaders make? We might expect that in democratic states, the intangible sources of power—national image, public support, and leadership—would matter more, because the leaders are responsible to the public through elections. If that expectation is true, then does the foreign policy behavior of democratic states differ from the behavior of nondemocratic or authoritarian states?

This question has occupied philosophers, diplomatic historians, and political scientists for centuries. In *Perpetual Peace* (1795), Immanuel Kant argued that the spread of democracy would change international politics by eliminating war. He reasoned that the public would be very cautious in supporting war because they, the public, would likely suffer the most devastating effects. Thus, leaders would act in a restrained fashion and tend to abstain from war because of domestic constraints.[19] Since Kant's time, other explanations have been added to the **democratic-peace** hypothesis. Liberals point to the notion of shared domestic norms and joint membership in international institutions to explain peace among democracies. And because democratic states trade more with each other than with nondemocratic states, they prefer to benefit from those economic gains made during peacetime. Many of these ideas found resonance with Woodrow Wilson, a major advocate of the democratic peace. Realists, too, add to the democratic-peace explanation. By belonging to the same alliances, democratic states are more effective at practicing balance of power, decreasing the probability of war.

Political scientists have developed an extensive research agenda related to the democratic-peace theory. Are democracies more peaceful than nondemocracies are? Do democracies fight each other less than nondemocracies do? Do democracies fight nondemocracies more than they fight each other? Or is there a "capitalist peace"? Does capitalism explain the pacifying effects of democracy on interstate conflict? Gathering data on different kinds of warfare over several centuries, researchers have addressed these questions. One study has confirmed the hypothesis that democracies do not go to war against each other: since 1789, no wars have been fought strictly between independent states with democratically elected governments. Another study has found that wars involving democracies have tended to be less bloody but more protracted, although between 1816 and 1965, democratic governments were not noticeably more peaceable or passive. Other studies have shown that socioeconomic factors and globalization have a more important pacifying effect than that of democracy or economic interdependence.[20] But the evidence is not that clear-cut, and explanations are partial. Why are states in the middle of transitions to democracy more susceptible to conflict? How can we explain when democratic states have not gone to war? The choice not to go to war, after all, may have had little to do with their democratic character.

Why have some of the findings on the democratic peace been so divergent? Scholars who use the behavioral approach themselves point to some of the difficulties. Some researchers analyzing the democratic peace use different definitions of the key variables, democracy and war. Some researchers distinguish between liberal democracies (for example, the United States and Germany) and illiberal democracies (Yugoslavia in the late 1990s). Also, the data for war would be different if wars with fewer than 1,000 deaths were included, as they are in some studies. And other studies of the democratic peace examine different time periods. Such differences in research protocols might well lead to different research findings. Yet even with these qualifications, the basic finding from the research is that democracies do not engage in militarized disputes against each other. That finding *is* statistically significant—that is, it does not occur by random chance. Overall, democracies are not more pacific than nondemocracies are; democracies simply do not fight *each other*. In fact, autocracies are just as peaceful with each other as are democracies. State structure—whether a state is democratic or authoritarian—matters in its selection of foreign policy instruments only some of the time.

Models of Foreign Policy Decision Making

How do states actually make specific foreign policy decisions? Do democracies make foreign policy choices differently from the way nondemocracies do? How do the different theories view the decision-making process? Differences depend in large part on how we view subnational actors—interest groups, **nongovernmental organizations (NGOs)**, and businesses.

The Rational Model: The Realist Approach

Most policy makers, particularly during crises, and most realists begin with the rational model, which conceives of foreign policy as actions the national government chooses to maximize its strategic objectives. The state is assumed to be a unitary actor with established goals, a set of options, and an algorithm for deciding which option best meets its goals. The process is relatively straightforward, as Figure 5.2 shows. Taking as our case the 1996 incident in which the People's Republic of China (PRC) tested missiles by launching them over the Republic of China (ROC; Taiwan), a rational approach would view Taiwan's decision-making process about how to respond in the following manner (the numbers correspond to the numbered steps in Figure 5.2):

1. The PRC was testing missiles over the ROC in direct threat to the latter's national security.
2. The goal of both the ROC and its major supporter, the United States, was to stop the firings immediately.
3. The ROC decision makers had several options: do nothing; wait until after the upcoming elections; issue diplomatic protests; bring the issue to the UN Security Council; threaten or conduct military operations against the PRC; or threaten or use economic statecraft (cut trade, impose sanctions or embargoes).
4. The ROC leaders analyzed the benefits and costs of these options: the PRC would exercise its veto in the UN Security Council; any economic or military actions the ROC undertook were unlikely to be successful against the stronger adversary, potentially leading to the destruction of Taiwan.
5. The ROC, with U.S. support, chose diplomatic protest as a first step. Doing nothing clearly would have suggested that the missile testing was acceptable. Military action against the PRC might have led to disastrous consequences.

Crises such as the preceding example have a unique set of characteristics: decision makers are confronted by a surprising, threatening event; they have only a short time to make a decision about how to respond; often a limited number of decision makers are involved in top-secret proceedings; and there is little time for substate actors to have much influence. In these circumstances, using the rational model as a way to assess the other side's behavior is an appropriate choice.

In a noncrisis situation, when a state knows very little about the internal domestic processes of another state—as the United States knew little about mainland China

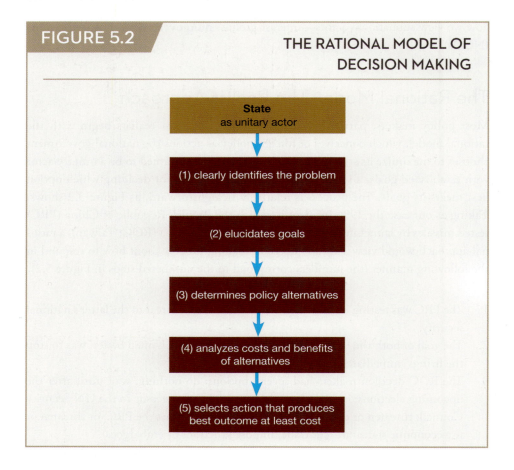

FIGURE 5.2

THE RATIONAL MODEL OF DECISION MAKING

State
as unitary actor

(1) clearly identifies the problem

(2) elucidates goals

(3) determines policy alternatives

(4) analyzes costs and benefits of alternatives

(5) selects action that produces best outcome at least cost

during the era of Mao Zedong—then decision makers have little alternative but to assume that the other state will follow the rational model. Indeed, in the absence of better information, most U.S. assessments of decisions the Soviet Union took during the Cold War were based on a rational model. Only after the opening of the Soviet governmental archives following the end of the Cold War did historians find that, in fact, the Soviets had no concrete plans for turning Poland, Hungary, Romania, or other East European states into communist dictatorships or socialist economies, as the United States had believed. The Soviets appear to have been guided by events happening in the region, not by specific ideological goals and rational plans.[21] The United States was incorrect in imputing the rational model to Soviet decision making, but in the absence of complete information, this was the least risky approach: the anarchy of the international system means a state assumes that its opponent engages in rational decision making.

The Bureaucratic/Organizational Model and the Pluralist Model: The Liberal Approaches

Not all decisions occur during crises, and not all decisions are taken with so little knowledge of domestic politics in other countries. In these instances, foreign policy decisions may be products of either subnational governmental organizations or bureaucracies—departments or ministries of government—the bureaucratic/organizational model, or decisions taken after bargaining conducted among domestic sources—the public, interest groups, mass movements, and multinational corporations—the pluralist model (see Figure 5.3).

In the first case, **organizational politics** emphasizes an organization's standard operating procedures and processes. Decisions arising from organizational processes depend heavily on precedents; major changes in policy are unlikely. Conflicts can occur when different subgroups within the organization have different goals and procedures. Often particular interest groups or NGOs have strongly influenced those different goals. In models of **bureaucratic politics**, members of the bureaucracy representing different interests negotiate decisions. Decisions determined by bureaucratic politics flow from the push and pull, or tug-of-war, among these departments, groups, or individuals. In either political scenario, the ultimate decision depends on the relative strength of the individual bureaucratic players or the organizations they represent.

In the second case, pluralist models, societal groups may play very important roles, especially in noncrisis situations and on particular issues, often economic ones. Societal groups have a variety of ways of forcing favorable decisions or constraining adverse decisions. They can mobilize the media and public opinion, lobby the government agencies responsible for making decisions, influence the appropriate representative bodies (e.g., the U.S. Congress, the French National Assembly, the Japanese Diet), organize transnational networks of people with comparable interests, and, in the case of high-profile heads of multinational corporations, make direct contacts with the highest governmental officials. Decisions made will reflect these diverse societal interests and strategies—a result that is particularly compatible with liberal thinking. Both trade and environmental policy are prominent examples of the bureaucratic/organizational model of decision making at work in noncrisis situations. Bureaucracies in the ministries of agriculture, industry, and labor in the case of trade, and environment, economics, and labor in the case of the environment, fight particularly hard within their own governments for policies favorable to their constituencies. Substate groups develop strong relationships with these ministries to ensure favorable outcomes. When time is no real constraint, informal bureaucratic groups and departments are free to mobilize. They hold meetings, hammering out positions that satisfy all the contending interests. The decisions reached are not always the most rational ones;

FIGURE 5.3 THE BUREAUCRATIC/ORGANIZATIONAL AND PLURALIST MODELS OF DECISION MAKING

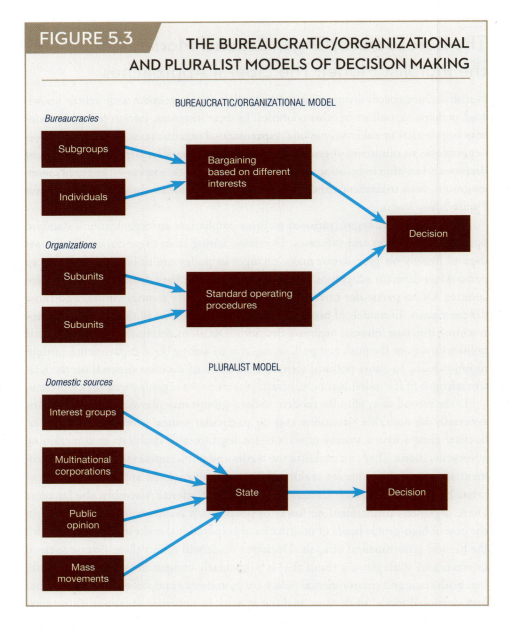

rather, the groups are content with **satisficing**—that is, settling for a decision that satisfies the different constituents without ostracizing any, even if the decision they reach is not the best possible outcome.

Liberals especially turn to this model of decision-making behavior in their analyses because, for them, the state is only the playing field; the actors are the competing interests in bureaucracies and organizations. The model is most relevant in large democratic countries, which usually have highly differentiated institutional structures for foreign policy decision making and where responsibility and jurisdiction are divided among several different units. But to use this model in policy-making circles to analyze or predict other states' behavior, or to use it to analyze decisions for scholarly purposes, one must have detailed knowledge of a country's foreign policy structures and bureaucracies.

The pluralist model is also compatible with liberal approaches. No one doubts the power of the rice farmer lobbies in both Japan and South Korea in preventing the importation of cheap, U.S. grown rice. No one denies the power of U.S. labor unions in supporting restrictions on the importation of products from developing countries. No one doubts the power of AIPAC in influencing much of U.S. policy toward the Arab-Israeli conflict. The movement to ban land mines in the 1990s is yet another example of a societally based pluralist foreign policy decision, a process reflecting democratic practices.

The bureaucratic/organizational and pluralist models require considerable knowledge of a country's foreign policy processes and are most applicable in noncrisis situations. Time is needed for bureaucracies to be called to the table, for organizations to bring their standard operating procedures, and for societal groups to organize. In a crisis, where time is of the essence and information about a country's foreign policy apparatus is absent, the rational model is the best alternative.

An Elite Model: A Radical Alternative

While both realists and liberals acknowledge that states have real choices in foreign policy, no matter which model explains their behavior, radicals see fewer real choices. In the radical view, capitalist states' interests are determined by the structure of the international system, and their decisions are dictated by the economic imperatives of the dominant class. Internal domestic elites have been co-opted by international capitalists. So in the elite model that radicals favor, multinational corporations play a key role in influencing the making of foreign policy.

A Constructivist Alternative

Constructivists hold that foreign policy decisions are based on two major factors. First is the country's strategic culture: the decision makers' interpretation of a country's historical experience, including philosophies, values, institutions, and understandings of its geography and development. Australia's strategic culture encompasses the geography-history trade-off: whether policy should be set by Australia's place in Asia-Pacific or by its history, its ties with Britain and the English-speaking world. Canada's strategic culture is shaped by its search for independence from the United States and its policies, made more problematic by geographic proximity and economic interdependence.

THEORY IN BRIEF

CONTENDING PERSPECTIVES ON STATE POWER AND POLICY

	REALISM/ NEOREALISM	LIBERALISM/ NEOLIBERAL INSTITUTIONALISM	RADICALISM/ DEPENDENCY THEORY	CONSTRUCTIVISM
NATURE OF STATE POWER	Emphasis on power as key concept in international relations; geography, natural resources, population especially important	Multiple power sources; tangible and intangible sources	Economic power organized around classes	Power subject to norm socialization
USING STATE POWER	Emphasis on coercive techniques of power; use of force acceptable	Broad range of power techniques; preference for noncoercive alternatives	Weak states have few instruments of power	Power is tool of elites for socializing societies through norms
HOW FOREIGN POLICY IS MADE	Emphasis on rational model of decision making; unitary state actor assumed once decision is made	Bureaucratic/ organizational and pluralist models of decision making	States have no real choices; decisions dictated by economic capitalist elites	Decisions based on norms that regulate policy sector
DETERMINANTS OF FOREIGN POLICY	Largely external/ international determinants	Largely domestic determinants	Largely external determinants; co-opted internal elements	External determinants in combination with domestic civil society

Second is the leaders' interpretation of the salient international norms. Acknowledging that leaders are socialized into the dominant international norms, they are inclined to build policies through processes open to domestic and international civil society, the mass media, and international partners. Foreign policy decisions are determined by leaders' beliefs that their actions are congruent with the international norms they have appropriated. Decisions may not be the same, as strategic cultures differ.[22] In short, constructivists take a holistic view of decision making, and the domestic and international factors are enmeshed.

Each alternative model offers a simplification of the foreign policy decision-making process. Each provides a window into how groups (both governmental and nongovernmental) influence the foreign policy process. But these models do not provide answers to other critical questions. They do not tell us the content of a specific decision or indicate the effectiveness with which the foreign policy was implemented.

Challenges to the State

The state, despite its centrality in international affairs, is facing challenges from the processes of globalization, religiously and ideologically based transnational movements, ethnonational movements, transnational crime, and fragile states (see Table 5.2). In each of these processes, new and intrusive technologies—e-mail, Facebook, Twitter, cell phones with cameras, direct satellite broadcasting, and worldwide television networks such as CNN—increasingly undermine the state's control over information and hence its control over its citizens, nongovernmental groups, and their activities. Both the Persian Gulf states and China have fought losing battles trying to "protect"

TABLE 5.2	CHALLENGES TO STATE POWER
FORCES	**EFFECTS ON THE STATE**
Globalization—political, economic, cultural	Undermines state sovereignty; interferes with state exercise of power; exacerbated by the rise of new media.
Transnational religious and ideological movements	Seek loyalty and commitment of individuals and groups beyond the state; change state behavior on a specific problem or issue.
Ethnonational movements	Seek own state; attempt to replace current government with one representing the interests of the movement.
Transnational crime	Challenges state authority.
Fragile states	Threaten lives of persons within states and security of other states in international system.

their populations from either crass Western values or dangerous political ideas transmitted through modern media. These new communication technologies have facilitated the organization of transnational and ethnonational movements and transnational crime, in many cases posing a challenge to the authority of the states.

Globalization

Externally, the state is buffeted by globalization, the growing integration of the world in terms of politics, economics, and culture, a process that undermines traditional state sovereignty. In political terms, states, an overwhelming number of which are now democracies, are confronted by transnational issues—environmental degradation, disease, crime, and intrusive technologies—that governments cannot manage alone, as Chapter 11 discusses. Increasingly, cooperative actions to address these issues require states to compromise their sovereignty. In the economic realm, states' financial markets are tied inextricably together; multinational corporations and the internationalization of production and consumption make it ever more difficult for states to regulate their own economic policies and make states more subject to international forces, as Chapter 9 discusses. Culturally, globalization has prompted both homogenization and differentiation. On the one hand, people around the world share a culture by watching the same cinema and listening to the same music. On the other, people are also eager to differentiate themselves within this homogenizing cultural force by maintaining local languages or pressing for local political and economic autonomy. An outgrowth of globalization has been both increasing democratization and the emerging power of transnational movements.

Transnational Religious and Ideological Movements

Transnational movements, particularly religious and ideological movements, have become political forces in their own right. Different religions have always existed, and their current numbers reveal the diversity (2.2 billion Christians; 1.6 billion Muslims; 1 billion Hindus; 376 million Buddhists; 14 million Jews). What has changed is that increasing democratization has emerged as a by-product of globalization, providing an opening for members of the same religion to organize transnationally and therefore increase their political influence. Now that groups can communicate with their adherents and compete for political power both within states and transnationally, some of them, antisecular and antimodern, pose stark challenges to state and international authorities.[23] More than 20 years ago, prominent political scientist Samuel Huntington predicted that the next great international conflict would be a "clash of civilizations" arising from underlying differences between Western liberal democracy and Islamic fundamentalism.[24] But he never predicted how complex those religious and political divides would become.

Extremist Islamic fundamentalism poses such a dual threat. Although Islamic extremists come from many different countries and support different strategies for reaching their end goal, believers are united in their belief that political and social authority should be based in the Koran. This movement presents both a basic critique of what is wrong in many secular states and a solution that calls for radical state transformation. Islamic extremists see a long-standing discrepancy between the political and economic aspirations of states and the actual conditions of uneven economic distribution and rule by corrupt elites. Extremist groups advocate violence as the means to overthrow these corrupt rulers and install religious authority in their place.

The fight by the Afghans and their Islamic supporters against the Soviet Union in the 1980s proved to be a galvanizing event for extremist

Political protests have become globalized, a result in part of new communication technology. Here, an Iranian living in Greece holds a poster with an image of a blood-drenched woman allegedly killed in protests in Tehran. The video became an Internet sensation, increasing pressure on the Iranian government.

Islamic fundamentalism. It brought together religiously committed yet politically and economically disaffected young Islamists from all over the world; fighting the "godless" enemy forged group cohesion, and fighting the better-equipped Soviet military allowed them to hone their guerrilla tactics. These *mujahideen* (holy warriors) gained confidence by beating the Soviets into retreat. When they returned to their homelands in Saudi Arabia, Egypt, and other parts of the Middle East, they were imbued with a mission—to wage *jihad* (holy war) against what they viewed as illegitimate regimes. During the fight in Afghanistan, Osama bin Laden, a Saudi national, emerged as a charismatic leader. When the Taliban assumed power in Afghanistan in 1996, bin Laden and what remained of the *mujahideen* formed Al Qaeda. Yet, as we will see in Chapter 8, Al Qaeda is just one of many Islamic fundamentalist groups, although its successful terrorist attacks on September 11, 2001, have made it one of the most widely known. But, since 2007, Al Qaeda has steadily lost popular support, and public-opinion polling in Muslim countries shows high rates of disapproval.[25]

What few commentators would have predicted is how the Sunni-Shia divide within Islam would become politicized and violent, affecting virtually all the conflicts in the Middle East today. Theologically, the divide is over who was the legitimate successor to the Prophet Muhammad. The divisions have existed for centuries, but violence among individuals was not significant. The 1979 Iranian Shiite revolution and the 2003 invasion of Iraq empowered majority Shiites over the Arab Sunni minority and caused the sectarian division to become political. It is the Islamic State which took the Shiites and moderate Sunnis to task. Announcing the formation of a new caliphate in 2014, the IS captured territory in Iraq and, joined by foreign fighters from more than 80 countries, established a capital in war-torn Syria. The IS has become a powerful force, hoping to bring grandeur, authority, and stability through the caliphate by capturing territory, exploiting resources in that territory to gain economic support, and establishing governance—with a strict legal system bringing swift justice to offenders and an educational and social service system. Instead of achieving these goals, however, it has killed those who oppose strict application of Islamic law, Shiites, and "infidels," nonbelievers from the West.

Although extremist Islamic fundamentalists, exemplified by the IS, are only a very small proportion of the more than 1.6 billion Muslims worldwide, theirs is still a powerful transnational movement and a challenge to states from Iraq, Syria, Saudi Arabia, Lebanon, Iran, and Yemen, to Nigeria, Chad, Cameroon, Algeria, and Libya, to the Philippines and Indonesia. Other extremist religious groups have also posed problems for state authority, though their small numbers have not meant a direct challenge to the state itself. These include both Christian extremist groups operating in the United States, like one affiliated with Timothy McVeigh, responsible for the Oklahoma City Federal Building bombing in 1995, and ultra-Orthodox Jewish extremist individuals and groups in Israel and the West Bank. The latter are motivated by several factors: some by the actions of the Israeli government, which has forced them to abandon illegal settlements; others seeking revenge for Palestinian killings of Israelis; and still others to voice opposition for social trends, exemplified by the 2015 stabbings during the Jerusalem Gay Pride Parade.

Not all transnational movements pose such direct challenges to the state. Indeed, many movements, rather than forming around major cleavages such as religion or ideology, as discussed earlier, develop around progressive goals such as the environment, human rights, and development, or around conservative goals such as opposition to abortion, family planning, or immigration. Often spurred by nongovernmental organizations that frame the issue and mobilize resources, these social movements want change, develop new approaches to problems, and push governments to take action. However, these movements do not generally undermine state sovereignty.

Ethnonational Movements

Another dramatic challenge to the state is found in **ethnonational movements**. The end of the Cold War witnessed the demise of multi-ethnic states, such as the Soviet Union and Yugoslavia, followed by the rise of democratic states in their stead. This political change, coupled with the communications revolution of fax technology, cell phones, and the Internet, has led to increasing demands by ethnonational movements. While the demands differ in degree and kind, each poses a threat to the viability and sovereignty of established states.

One of the more complex ethnonational movements with international implications involves Kashmir—a mountainous area at the intersection of India, Pakistan, and China—and the Kashmiris, a people who are overwhelmingly Muslim but who have traditionally been ruled by Hindus. When India (dominated by Hindus) and Pakistan (dominated by Muslims) separated into two independent states in 1947, the maharaja of Kashmir, Hari Singh, opted to join India, much to the displeasure of the majority population. In 1947–48, and again in 1965, India and Pakistan fought over the territory, which has been plagued ever since by tensions and periodic skirmishes. A Line of Control (LOC) was reestablished in 1972, dividing Kashmir into India-administered Kashmir to the east and south, with 9 million people, and Pakistan-administered Kashmir to the north and west, with 3 million people. In addition to the rival claims of India and Pakistan, since 1989, a growing violent separatist movement has fought against Indian rule in Kashmir. The Kashmiri ethnonational conflict has been particularly difficult because its factions are both fighting for control of territory and tied into the larger conflict between India and Pakistan. In 2003, India and Pakistan signed a cease-fire along their borders in Kashmir and established diplomatic ties, reopening transportation links. But despite rounds of Indo-Pakistani peace talks, the dispute continues. In 2007, a devastating train bombing ignited violence; in 2012, soldiers from both parties were killed in skirmishes; and in 2013, the boundary between Punjab (Pakistan) and Jammu and Kashmir (India) saw the worst flare-up in decades.

Ethnonationalist movements pose a challenge even to the strongest states. China has been confronted by ethnic uprisings within the Muslim Uighur minority in the Xinjiang Uighur Autonomous Region, its northwestern-most province, over the past several decades. Today, Xinjiang (a name the Uighurs find offensive), which makes up one-sixth of China's land area, is home to 20 million people and 13 ethnic groups. Of these, 45 percent are Uighurs and 40 percent are ethnic Han. The Uighurs migrated to the Chinese border region from the Mongolian steppe in the tenth century. They are a Turkic-speaking race that follows Sufi Islam, a branch of Sunni. Their diaspora is

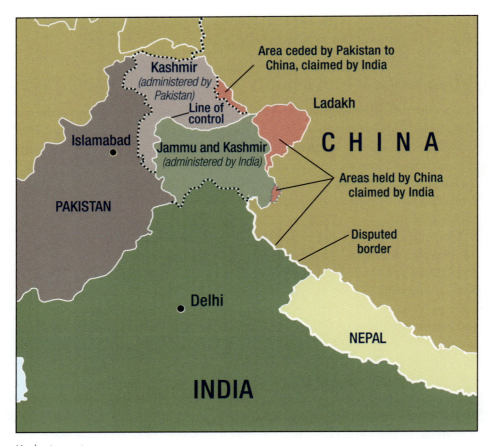

Kashmir, 2016
Note: The Line of Control separates the two sides in the Kashmir conflict.

centered in this area, but Uighurs also live in Kazakhstan, Kyrgyzstan, and Uzbekistan, with smaller numbers in Mongolia and Afghanistan. They have a long history of fighting for independence as Uighuristan or East Turkestan.

When vast mineral and oil deposits were found in Xinjiang in the 1950s, Han Chinese began to move into the region at the urging of the government, which promised the settlers infrastructure and jobs. But to the Uighurs, the ethnic Han Chinese migrants are colonists; Uighur Islamic faith, traditional language, and economic prosperity are being stifled by the official Han policies.

Following 9/11, the Chinese government began to refer to Uighurs and the East Turkestan Islamic Movement as terrorists. As more ethnic Han moved in, the Chinese have come to dominate media coverage and the confrontation has grown. In 2009, 200 people were killed and 2,000 people wounded in clashes between the two groups. In 2013, Muslim separatists killed several Chinese in the heart of Beijing. As Uighurs continue to join the IS, China sees the jihad peril, and greater repression only fuels Uighur radicalism.

Chinese policy toward minorities is one of official recognition, granting limited autonomy with an extensive effort at central control. Although only 9 percent of China's population consists of ethnic minorities, those minorities are spread across resource-rich areas. They are actually the majorities in the strategically important border areas of not only Xinjiang but also Tibet, Inner Mongolia, and Yunan. The Chinese government's suppressions of Tibet (in 1959 and 2008) and of Xinjiang demonstrate Beijing's determination to exert dominance and authority across the entire country, justifying repression in the name of suppressing terrorism. With increasing economic problems and growing economic inequities, the state may continue to be challenged by ethnic minorities.

Some ethnonational challenges lead to civil conflict and even war, as the case of Kashmir illustrates. The political scientist Jack Snyder has identified the causal mechanism whereby ethnic nationalists challenge the state based on the legitimacy of their language, culture, or religion. Particularly when countervailing state institutions are weak, elites within these ethnonational movements may be able to incite the masses to war.[26] Table 5.3 lists some of the ethnonational challengers in the world today.

TABLE 5.3 — ETHNONATIONAL CHALLENGERS, REPRESENTATIVE CASES

STATE(S)	ETHNONATIONAL GROUPS
People's Republic of China	Tibetans, Uighurs, Manchus
Burundi, Rwanda	Hutus, Tutsis
Syria, Iraq, Iran, Turkey	Kurds
Serbia, Macedonia	Albanians
Mexico, Guatemala	Maya, Zapotecs, Mixtecs
Burma, Thailand	Karen, Kachin, Shan, Rohingya
India	Kashmiris
Afghanistan	Pashtuns, Hazaras, Tajiks, Uzbeks, Turkmens
Georgia	Abkhaz, Ossetes

Transnational Crime

Nowhere is the challenge to the state more evident than in the rise of transnational crime—illicit activities made easier by globalization. Growing in value, extending in scope, and becoming highly specialized, these activities have been facilitated by more and faster transportation routes, rapid communication, and electronic financial networks. Transnational crime has led to the accelerating movement of illegal drugs, counterfeit goods, smuggled weapons, laundered money, trade in body parts, piracy, and trafficking in poor and exploited people. (Chapter 11 explores this situation further.) Organized around flexible networks and circuitous trafficking routes, and lubricated by electronic transfers of funds, transnational crime has created new businesses while distorting national and regional economies. States and governments are largely incapable of responding: rigid bureaucracies, laborious procedures, interbureaucratic fighting, and corrupt officials undermine states' efforts. In fact, some states—such as China, North Korea, and Nigeria—actively participate in these illicit activities or do nothing to stop them because key elites are making major profits.[27]

Other states such as Mexico have made concerted efforts to stop transnational crime. Since 2006, Mexico has undertaken a major effort to break up its drug cartels. That effort has escalated in increased violence. Between 2007 and 2014, more than 164,000 people have become victims of homicide, more than the combined deaths in Iraq and Afghanistan. An estimated 34 to 55 percent of these homicides can be attributed to the drug cartels. Organized crime-style killings remain a major threat. The 2014 killings of 43 teachers' college students by a local gang led to outrage in the country. A panel convened by the Inter-American Commission on Human Rights accused the government of hiding the presence of police and army in the area at the time. There are clearly questions about the government's complicity, either by commission or omission.

The Mexican case has transnational implications. Small arms smuggled into Mexico from the United States fuel the violence; gang violence crosses the border into American cities; American tourists are staying away from Mexican resorts, with adverse effects on the economy. Many states are finding it very difficult to control and punish the transgressors, undermining their own sovereignty and that of their neighbors.

Fragile States

Fragile states include those having several characteristics: an inability to exercise a monopoly on the legitimate use of force within its territory, make collective decisions because of the erosion of legitimate authority, interact with other states in the international system, or provide public services.[28] The notion of such a state entered the political lexicon in 1992 under the rubric of a failed state with Somalia as exemplary.

The Fund for Peace, in conjunction with *Foreign Policy,* publishes the Fragile State Index annually, based on 12 social, economic, and political indicators. South Sudan, Somalia, Central African Republic, Democratic Republic of the Congo, and Sudan are among the most fragile states. Whatever the term used—*fragile, failed, weak, dysfunctional states*—the implications are the same.

Fragile states pose an internal threat to the people residing within them. They fail to perform one of the state's vital functions—protection of its people from violence and crime. Political, civil, and economic rights of a fragile state's population are in continuous jeopardy. Such states are unable to serve their citizenry, one of the requisites of sovereignty.

Fragile states also pose an international threat, serving as hideaways for transnational terrorists, criminals, and pirates, as Somalia did when its functioning government ceased to exist in 1991. Since 2007, there have been attempts to rebuild that government with the African Union forces providing a modicum of security. A 2012 provisional constitution is supposed to lead to national elections in 2016. But given the difficulties in conducting traditional elections, elders from the four main Somali clans will act as representative electors. And Somaliland in the north has ignored the whole process, in practice becoming a de facto but unrecognized state. Libya in 2016 also approaches fragile state status: border security is nonexistent, facilitating refugee and migrant flows across the Mediterranean Sea; corruption is rampant; the coast guard, lacking adequate equipment, rarely leaves port. Warring militias represent the only law. There are at least three governments in different regions and tensions between tribes and Islamist militias. Each depends on different subnational loyalties and has allegiances to different international groups, including the IS. Plans for a UN-proposed unity government are unlikely in the near future.

In Sum: The State and Challenges Beyond

The centrality of the state in international politics cannot be disputed. In this chapter, we have conceptualized the state according to the contending theoretical perspectives. We have looked inside the state to describe the various forms of state power. We have discussed the ways states are able to use power through the diplomatic, economic, and coercive instruments of statecraft. We have explored the question of whether certain kinds of governments—democracies in particular—behave differently from nondemocracies. We have looked at actors within the state to identify different models of foreign policy decision making. And we have examined the ways in which globalization, transnational religious and ideological movements, ethnonationalist movements, transnational crime, and fragile states pose threats to state sovereignty and to the stability of the international system. Such movements, however, depend on individuals, who lead the challenge. Some are elites who are charismatic and powerful leaders in their own right. Some are part of a mass movement. We now turn to these individuals.

Discussion Questions

1. You are the leader of an emerging economy such as Indonesia. What tools of statecraft do you have at your disposal to influence your neighbors? What if, instead, you are the leader of a rising power like the People's Republic of China? What tools could you use?

2. Find two newspaper articles that suggest the use of soft power. How can you tell whether soft power "works"?

3. Ethnonationalist movements are a major source of state instability. Compare two recent cases of such conflict. How are the respective states addressing the issue? Are they addressing it at all?

4. Choose one state labeled as a fragile state. What recommendations can you make to turn the state into a viable one?

Key Terms

bureaucratic politics (p. 165)

celebrity diplomacy (p. 155)

compellence (p. 160)

democratic peace (p. 161)

deterrence (p. 160)

diplomacy (p. 151)

ethnonational movements (p. 173)

extremist Islamic fundamentalism
(p. 171)

first-strike capability (p. 160)

fragile states (p. 176)

nation (p. 136)

nation-state (p. 136)

nongovernmental organizations
(NGOs) (p. 163)

organizational politics (p. 165)

power (p. 145)

power potential (p. 146)

public diplomacy (p. 155)

sanctions (p. 156)

satisficing (p. 166)

second-strike capability (p. 160)

smart power (p. 151)

smart sanctions (p. 156)

soft power (p. 149)

state (p. 134)

transnational movements (p. 170)

06

North Korean officials sit in front of the portraits of former leaders Kim Il-Sung and Kim Jong-Il on the occasion of a military parade honoring the 100th birthday of the country's founder Kim Il-Sung. International relations scholars study the roles, personalities, and actions of leaders like the Kims to better explain their foreign policy behavior.

THE INDIVIDUAL

Vladimir Putin continues to fascinate and confound students of international politics, as have Germany's Adolf Hitler, Iraq's Saddam Hussein, Cuba's Fidel Castro, Venezuela's Hugo Chavez, and the Kims of North Korea, among others. Biographies abound detailing these leaders' childhoods, formative political experiences, personality characteristics, and idiosyncrasies. Will such probing help us explain the policies these people pursued? Or is the emphasis on one individual leader only a shortcut attempt to explain complex events? Are agents of the state acting in the national interest? Can individuals who do not hold official positions make a difference in international politics? Can individuals play a significant enough role that they should be considered as a third level of analysis, along with the state and international system?

Recall the possible explanations given in Chapter 3 for the United States' invasion of Iraq in 2003. One explanation pointed to the beliefs of President George W. Bush and his security advisers and to their response to Saddam Hussein, Hussein's personal characteristics, and his advisers. Clearly, one group of individuals that makes a difference to international relations is the group of leaders. But individuals holding more informal roles can also have a significant influence on international events, including war and peace, as well as international policies. For example, Srdja Popovic, a Serb activist and founder of CANVAS, the Centre for Applied Nonviolent Action and Strategies, has trained revolutionaries in 46 countries, including Georgia, Ukraine, Moldova, and Egypt. And Wangari Maathai, the late Kenyan environmentalist, founded the Green Belt Movement, which promotes environmental management. In this chapter, we explore the various roles both public and private individuals play in international relations.

LEARNING OBJECTIVES

- Describe which individuals matter most in international relations.

- Analyze what psychological factors have an impact on elite foreign policy decision making.

- Describe the roles private individuals play in international relations.

- Explain the roles mass publics play in foreign policy.

- Analyze how much individuals matter, according to the various theoretical perspectives.

Foreign Policy Elites: Individuals Who Matter

Do individuals who occupy official positions make a difference in the formation of foreign policy? How much of a difference do individuals make? The extent to which individuals matter differs by international relations theories. Liberals recognize that leaders do make a difference and individuals may be an appropriate level of analysis. Whenever a leadership change happens in a major power such as the United States, China, or Russia, speculation always arises about possible changes in the country's foreign policy. This speculation reflects the general belief that individual leaders and their personal characteristics do make a difference in foreign policy, and hence, in international relations. Ample empirical proof exists for this position.

The example of Soviet leader Mikhail Gorbachev illustrates the fact that individual leaders can effect real change. After coming to power in 1985, he began to frame the challenges confronting the Soviet Union differently, identifying the Soviet security problem as part of the larger problem of weakness in the Soviet economy. Through a process of trial and error, and by living through and then studying failures, Gorbachev realized that the economic system had to be reformed to improve the country's security. He then took action to implement major reforms. Although he eventually lost power, he is responsible for initiating broad economic foreign policy change, including extricating the Soviet Union from its war in Afghanistan. Constructivists who also recognize the importance of individuals credit the changes not only to Gorbachev as an individual but also to a network of Western-oriented policy entrepreneurs who promoted new ideas, which were then implemented.[1]

For realists, individuals are of little importance. This position comes from the realist assumption of a unitary actor. Thus, states are not differentiated by their government type or the personalities or styles of the leaders in office but by the relative power they hold in the international system. Hans J. Morgenthau explained as follows:

> The concept of national interest defined as power imposes intellectual discipline upon the observer, infuses rational order into the subject matter of politics, and thus makes the theoretical understanding of politics possible. On the side of the actor, it provides for rational discipline in action and creates the astounding continuity in foreign policy which makes American, British, or Russian foreign policy appear as an intelligible, rational continuum, by and large consistent with itself, regardless of the different motives, preferences, and intellectual and moral qualities of successive statesmen.[2]

Realists see individuals as constrained by the state they inhabit, and neorealists see them as constrained by the international system. Those are the most relevant levels of analysis. Radicals see individuals as constrained by the international system, namely international capitalism, and, for them, there is really only one relevant level of analysis.

Yet, sometimes, individual motives and preferences seem to make a difference. Gorbachev introduced *glasnost* and *perestroika* in the Soviet Union beginning in 1986. The Chinese leader Deng Xiaoping established himself as the architect of the new China after 1978. Under his socialist market economy, the state permitted limited private competition and gradually opened itself economically to the outside world. Were these individuals in fact responsible for these major changes, or did individual leaders just happen to be the right (or wrong) people at the time? Given the same situation, would different individuals have made different decisions, thus charting different courses through international relations?

With respect to elites, two questions are most pertinent to determining the role of individuals: When are the actions of individuals likely to have a greater or lesser effect on the course of events? And under what circumstances do actors' different personal characteristics cause them to behave differently?

The Impact of Elites: External Conditions

An individual's actions affect the course of events when at least one of several factors is present (see Figure 6.1). When political institutions are unstable, young, in crisis, or collapsed, leaders are able to provide powerful influences. Founding fathers, be they the United States' George Washington, India's Mohandas Gandhi, Russia's Vladimir Lenin, or South Africa's Nelson Mandela, have a great impact because they lead in the early years of their nations' lives, when institutions and practices are being established. Thus, Mandela's informal style and his genius for the gesture of reconciliation made the transition to a multiracial regime smoother. And Adolf Hitler, Franklin Roosevelt, Mikhail Gorbachev, and Vladimir Putin had more influence precisely because their states were in economic crises when they came to power.

Individuals also affect the course of events when they have few institutional constraints. In dictatorial or highly centralized regimes, top leaders are relatively free from domestic constraints, such as political opposition or societal inputs, and thus are able to chart courses and implement foreign policy relatively unfettered, as illustrated by the Soviet and Chinese examples. In younger and struggling democ-

Mohandas Gandhi tirelessly led a mass nonviolent movement for Indian independence from British rule. His actions helped to establish India as an independent state, with major international ramifications. Here, Gandhi visits the British prime minister's residence in London in 1931.

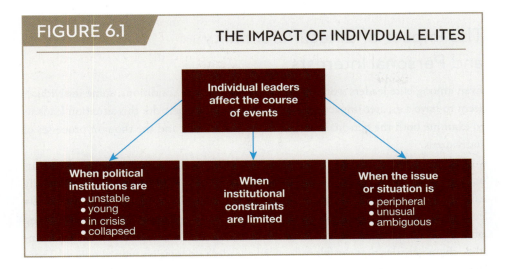

FIGURE 6.1

THE IMPACT OF INDIVIDUAL ELITES

Individual leaders affect the course of events

When political institutions are
- unstable
- young
- in crisis
- collapsed

When institutional constraints are limited

When the issue or situation is
- peripheral
- unusual
- ambiguous

racies, the institutions may not be well established. Indeed, Hamid Karzai of Afghanistan admitted that he relied "the very least" on his own governmental institutions, but rather, he depended on informal networks and ad hoc governance.[3]

In democratic regimes, too, top decision makers occasionally are able to change policy in a dramatic fashion. For example, U.S. president Richard Nixon in 1972 was able to engineer a complete foreign policy reversal in relations with the People's Republic of China, secretly sending his top foreign policy adviser, Henry Kissinger, for several meetings with the Chinese premier Zhou Enlai and his advisers. These moves were an unexpected change, given Nixon's Republican Party affiliation and prior anticommunist record. President Barack Obama in 2015 also announced an unexpected policy reversal, opening up dialogue with Cuba after almost five decades, and the administration negotiated a framework nuclear agreement with Iran after almost four decades of little contact. But such reversals may be the exception since many democratic leaders are constrained by bureaucracies and societal groups, as illustrated by some strong domestic opposition in the United States over both the Cuban "opening" and the Iran nuclear agreement.

The specifics of a situation also determine the extent to which individuals matter. Decision makers' personal characteristics have more influence on outcomes when the issue is peripheral rather than central, when the issue is not routine—that is, standard operating procedures are not available—or when the situation is ambiguous and information is unclear. Crisis situations, in particular when information is in short supply and standard operating procedures are inapplicable, create scenarios in which a decision maker's personal characteristics count most. Such a scenario arose during the Cuban missile crisis, when President John F. Kennedy's personal openness to alternatives and attention to group dynamics played a role in the resolution.

The Impact of Elites: Personality and Personal Interests

Even among elite leaders working amid similar external conditions, some individuals seem to have a greater impact on foreign policy than others do; this situation leads us to examine both the personal characteristics that matter and the thought processes of individuals.

Political psychologist Margaret Hermann has found a number of personality characteristics that affect foreign policy behaviors. Because top leaders do not generally take personality tests, Hermann used a different research strategy. She systematically collected spontaneous interviews and press conferences with 80 heads of state holding office in 38 countries between 1959 and 1968. From these data, she found key personality characteristics that she felt influenced a leader's orientation toward policy.[4] Those characteristics are listed in the top section of Figure 6.2.

These personality characteristics orient an individual's view of foreign affairs. Two orientations emerge from the personality traits. One group, leaders with high levels of nationalism, a strong belief in their own ability to control events, a strong need for power, low levels of conceptual complexity, and high levels of distrust of others, tend to develop an independent orientation to foreign affairs. The other group, leaders with low levels of nationalism, little belief in their ability to control events, a high need for affiliation, high levels of conceptual complexity, and low levels of distrust of others, tend toward a participatory orientation in foreign affairs. (The bottom of Figure 6.2 illustrates these orientations.) Then Hermann tested whether these personal characteristics and their respective orientations were related to the foreign policy style and the behavior of the leaders.

Both Hermann and subsequent researchers using the same schema have found that these characteristics and orientations matter. For example, one study analyzed the personality characteristics of the former British prime minister Tony Blair using Hermann's categories to organize Blair's foreign policy answers to questions posed in the House of Commons.[5] The researcher found that Blair had a strong belief in his own ability to control events and a high need for power, accompanied by a low conceptual complexity. These personality findings go a long way toward explaining British foreign policy toward the 2003 Iraq War, a policy that many in the government and the British public opposed. Thus, even in democracies, where institutional constraints are high, individual personality characteristics influence foreign policy orientation and behavior.

Political scientist Betty Glad has developed a profile of the former president Jimmy Carter that suggests how his personality characteristics played a key role in influencing the course of U.S. policy during the 1979–81 hostage crisis. The crisis began when Iranian militants kidnapped more than 60 Americans and held them for more than a

| FIGURE 6.2 | PERSONALITY CHARACTERISTICS OF LEADERS |

Personality Characteristics of Leaders

Nationalism: strong emotional ties to nation; emphasis on national honor and dignity

Perception of control: belief in ability to control events; high degree of control over situations; governments able to influence state and nation

Need for power: need to establish, maintain, and project power or influence over others

Need for affiliation: concern for establishing and maintaining friendly relationships with others

Conceptual complexity: ability to discuss with other people places, policies, ideas in a discerning way

Distrust of others: feelings of doubt, uneasiness about others; doubt about motives and actions of others

Foreign Policy Orientations

Independent leader: high in nationalism

high in perception of control

high in need for power

low in conceptual complexity

high in distrust of others

Participatory leader: low in nationalism

low in perception of control

high in need for affiliation

high in conceptual complexity

low in distrust of others

Source: Margaret G. Hermann, "Explaining Foreign Policy Behavior Using the Personal Characteristics of Political Leaders," *International Studies Quarterly* 24:1 (March 1980): 7–46.

year. Carter personalized the hostage taking. He was humiliated, obsessed, wanting above all to have *his* decisions vindicated. After an attempted helicopter rescue mission failed, he rationalized the failure as a "worthy effort," feeling that some action was better than no action. Glad points to Carter's personality characteristics: his difficulty in admitting that he made mistakes in this situation was based on his more general need to be right. In this instance, the psychic costs to the United States of its impotence in a crisis upon which the entire people and government focused for several months, as well as the political price Carter had to pay for that fixation, would make it particularly difficult for him to see where he had gone wrong.[6] Reflecting back over that period in 2015, citizen Carter lamented that if only had he sent in more helicopters, the rescue might have been successful and he would have been re-elected.

Personality characteristics affect the leadership of dictators perhaps more than that of democratic leaders because of the absence of effective institutional checks, as Glad has also investigated. She analyzed the personalities of tyrants—those who rule without attention to law, capitalize on grandiose self-presentations and projects, look for every advantage, and utilize cruel, often extreme tactics. Comparing Hitler, Stalin, and Saddam Hussein, she labels them as having malignant narcissism syndrome. Glad explains how "project over-reach and creation of new enemies leads to increasing vulnerability, a deepening of the paranoiac defense, and volatility in behavior."[7]

The late North Korean leader Kim Jong-Il (the "Dear Leader") and his father, Kim Il-Sung (the "Great Leader"), exhibited some of these same characteristics. Kim Il-Sung erected more than 34,000 monuments to himself during his 50-year rule, and his photo was prominently displayed in buildings and other public places. Likewise, Kim Jong-Il expressed his megalomania with gigantic pictures of himself, spending millions of dollars on spectacles with historical themes while millions of his people starved. One former CIA psychiatrist suggested that Kim Jong-Il was self-absorbed, lacked an ability to empathize, and was capable of "unconstrained aggression."[8]

Following Kim Jong-Il's death in 2011, North Korean propaganda immediately began to elevate his son, Kim Jong-Un, to deity, noting his talents and extraordinary deeds—all in an effort to legitimize the succession. Labeled the "Great Successor," Kim Jong-Un, like his father and grandfather, has consolidated power through a cult of personality. He is extolled as an "outstanding leader of the party, army, and people" and "a great person born in heaven"—attributes that serve to legitimate his succession.

Personality characteristics, then, partly determine what decisions individual leaders make. But individual leaders also have personal preferences, and they may have the ability to chart a policy course that reflects those personal preferences. The Global Perspectives box on p. 190–91 illustrates the preferences of Pope Francis and how he is charting new courses for the Catholic church, almost singlehandedly.

Individual Decision Making

Decisions that individual decision makers take may reflect the fact that they are confronted with the task of putting divergent information into an organized form. The rational model of decision making that we discussed in Chapter 5 suggests that the individual possesses all the relevant information, stipulates a goal, examines the relevant choices, and makes a decision that best achieves that goal. In actuality, however, individuals are not always rational decision makers. Confronted by information that is neither perfect nor complete, and often overwhelmed by a plethora of information and conditioned by personal experience, the decision maker selects, organizes, and evaluates incoming information about the surrounding world.

Individuals use a variety of psychological techniques to process and evaluate information. In perceiving and interpreting new and often contradictory information, individuals rely on existing perceptions, usually based on prior experiences. Such perceptions are the "screens" that enable individuals to process information selectively; these perceptions have an integrating function, permitting the individual to synthesize and interpret the information. Perceptions also serve an orienting function, providing guidance about future expectations and expediting planning for future contingencies. If those perceptions form a relatively integrated set of images, then they are called a **belief system**.

International relations scholars have devised methods to test the existence of elite perceptions, although research has not been conducted on many individuals because sufficient data are usually unavailable. Ole Holsti systematically analyzed 434 of the publicly available statements of Secretary of State John Foster Dulles concerning the Soviet Union during the years 1953–54. His research showed convincingly that Dulles held an unwavering image of the Soviet Union, focusing on atheism, totalitarianism, and communism. To Dulles, the Soviet people were good, but their leaders were bad; the state was good, the Communist party bad. This image was unvarying; the character of the Soviet Union did not change. Whether this perception, gleaned from Dulles's statements, affected U.S. decisions during the period cannot be stated with certainty. He was, after all, only one among a group of top leaders. Yet a plethora of decisions made during that time is consistent with his perception.[9]

The political scientists Harvey Starr and Stephen Walker both completed similar empirical research on Henry Kissinger.[10] Elucidating Kissinger's operational code (the rules he operated by) from his scholarly writings, Walker found that the conduct of the Vietnam War, orchestrated in large part by Kissinger between 1969 and 1973, was congruent with the premises of his operational code and his conception of mutually acceptable outcomes. He wanted to negotiate a mutual withdrawal of external forces

The Pope: A View from the Vatican

Ascending to the papacy in 2013, Pope Francis represents a number of firsts: the first Jesuit pope, the first from the Americas (Argentina), the first from the southern hemisphere, and the first non-European since 741. Taking the name of Francis after Saint Francis of Assisi, the Pope has followed the example of his namesake. He has shown his concern for the poor and weak and his disdain for an international system where unbridled capitalism has led to the unequal division of wealth. His approach is humble and welcoming to all peoples, the sick, the imprisoned, even those whose lifestyle is not accepted by official church doctrine. While espousing the traditional views of the church against homosexuality, abortion, and ordination of women, he has publicly stated that those individuals should be treated with love and respect.

Using both traditional church encyclicals and contemporary social media, the Pope speaks forcefully on the major issues of the day, as he did during his triumphant visit to the United States in the autumn of 2015. Those issues include criticizing excessive monetary ambitions and advocating for greater controls on financial markets and greater social justice. Using his personal popularity and charisma, he has appealed for and engaged in interfaith dialogue. During a 2014 trip to Jordan, he worked to bring Jews and Muslims into dialogue and sought closer relationships with the estranged Orthodox Churches of the east. In 2015, the Vatican signed a treaty with the "state of Palestine" following 15 years of negotiations and dialogue. The hope is that this development leads to better relations between Israel and the Palestinians and serves as an example of cooperation to other states in the Middle East.

In 2015, the Pope issued a 184-page papal encyclical to highlight the contemporary challenge of climate change. Drawing on the Bible, past papal encyclicals, and statements by other religious leaders from the Eastern Orthodox tradition and Islam, the Pope provided a critique of irresponsible development and excessive spending. He described the destruction to the environment caused by fossil fuels at the hands of humanity, warning of the grave environmental, economic, political, and social consequences—especially for the poor. His calls for social action in this encyclical give policymakers a moral justification for taking measures to address climate change. His call for every Catholic family to take in refugees is yet another illustration of leading by pleading with people to act morally.

The Pope, like other popes before him, has facilitated diplomatic initiatives and thus conducted track-two diplomacy. The Vatican has long aimed to help restore Cuba to the community of nations. Cardinal O'Malley of Boston, a confidant of Pope Francis, played a key role in getting the issue of Cuba and U.S. relations added to the agenda in the March 2014 meeting between President Obama and Pope Francis in Rome. Cardinal Jaime Ortega acted for Pope Francis, bringing him up to date on the critical issues. That meeting had been a follow

Pope Francis addressed poverty and climate change during his speech at the White House in September 2015 as part of his triumphant visit to the United States.

up from secret negotiations between U.S. and Cuban officials a year earlier in Canada. The timing was fortuitous—there were short-term pressures of the health of prisoners to be exchanged and there were long-term trends acknowledged, that the opposition of the generation of Cuban-Americans opposing any reconciliation until the end of communism was softening. The leaders of both countries acknowledged the personal role that the Pope played in the reconciliation process.

At the end, the Pope speaks as pope of the Catholic church worldwide with its 1.1 billion members and as sovereign of the Vatican City, the smallest internationally recognized independent state. His preferences are having a strong impact on Catholic Church policy and being used to pressure states to fashion policy based on ethical considerations.

FOR CRITICAL ANALYSIS

1. Using Hermann's personality characteristics, how would you describe Pope Francis?

2. Has Pope Francis been successful in influencing policy because of his individual personality and biography, or the fact that he speaks for the Catholic Church? How would a realist argue for one or the other?

and avoid negotiating about the internal structure of South Vietnam. He used enough force, combined with generous peace terms, so that North Vietnam was faced with an attractive peace settlement versus unpalatable alternatives—stalemate or escalation.

These elite mind-set studies were possible because these particular individuals left behind extensive written records from before, during, and after they held key policy-making positions. Since few leaders leave such a record, however, our ability to empirically reconstruct elite beliefs, perceptions, or operational codes is limited, as is our inability to state with certainty their influence on a specific decision. So often, both political scientists and historians publish interpretative biographies, based on reexamination of the historical record, as previously classified documents become available. Historian John Lewis Gaddis's authorized biography of George F. Kennan, architect of the containment doctrine discussed in Chapter 2, shows his strategic thinking, which had such an influence in American foreign policy, while Kennan and Costigliola, using Kennan's own detailed personal diaries, show his fragile, often despairing personality, a different perspective of the man and the roots of his thinking.[11] Henry Kissinger, strategist and policy maker during the Nixon presidency, is the subject of a new interpretative biography by Niall Ferguson. Refuting much of the literature that sees Kissinger as the quintessential realist, Ferguson, drawing on Kissinger's own private papers and the archives, finds him an idealist, not in the tradition of Woodrow Wilson or Immanuel Kant, but one who recognizes that realism could be paralyzing and morally vacuous. Principles of human freedom and choice matter more than pragmatism.[12]

For many leaders, such as Vladimir Putin, authoritative biographies do not exist, and some leaders may try to shape their personal image for political purposes. So, based on our knowledge at this time, is Putin a realist? an idealist? or just a pragmatist? (See Behind the Headlines box on p. 194–95.)

Information-Processing Mechanisms

Our images and perceptions of the world are continually bombarded by new, sometimes overwhelming, and often discordant information. Images and belief systems, however, are not generally changed, and almost never are they radically altered. Thus, individual elites use, usually unconsciously, several psychological mechanisms to process the information they encounter in the world. Table 6.1 on p. 196 summarizes these mechanisms.

First, individuals strive for **cognitive consistency**, ensuring that their beliefs fit together into a coherent whole. For example, individuals like to believe that the enemy of an enemy is a friend, and the enemy of a friend is an enemy. Because of the tendency to be cognitively consistent, individuals select or amplify information that supports existing beliefs and ignore or downplay contradictory information. For example, because both Great Britain and Argentina were friends of the United States prior to their war over the Falkland/Malvinas Islands in 1982, U.S. decision makers denied the seriousness of the conflict. They did not think that its ally would go to war with Argentina over barren islands thousands of miles from Britain's shores. However, the United States underestimated the strength of British public support for military action and misjudged the precarious domestic position of the Argentinian generals, who were trying to bolster their power by diverting attention to a popular external conflict.

Individuals also perceive and evaluate the world according to what they have learned from past events. They look for details of a present episode that look like those of a past one, perhaps ignoring the important differences. Such similar details are often referred to as an **evoked set**. During the 1956 Suez crisis, for instance, British prime minister Anthony Eden saw Egyptian president Gamal Abdel Nasser as another Hitler. Eden recalled Prime Minister Neville Chamberlain's failed effort to appease Hitler with the Munich agreement in 1938 and thus believed that Nasser, likewise, could not be appeased. Similar thinking led some American elites to describe Iraq as another Vietnam or to see the Soviet defeat in Afghanistan as that country's Vietnam, despite critical differences.

Individual perceptions are often shaped in terms of **mirror images**: Whereas one considers one's own actions good, moral, and just, the enemy's actions are automatically found to be evil, immoral, and unjust. Mirror imaging often exacerbates conflicts, making it even more difficult to resolve a contentious issue.

The psychological mechanisms that we have discussed so far affect the functioning of both individuals and small groups. But small groups themselves also have psychologically based dynamics that undermine the rational model. Psychologist Irving Janis called this dynamic **groupthink**. Groupthink, according to Janis, is "a mode of thinking that people engage in when they are deeply involved in a cohesive in-group, when members' strivings for unanimity override their motivation to realistically appraise alternative courses of action."[13] The dynamics of the group, which include the illusion of invulnerability and unanimity, excessive optimism, the belief in the group's own morality and the enemy's evil, and the pressure placed on dissenters to change their views, lead to groupthink.

During the Vietnam War, for example, a top group of U.S. decision makers, unified by bonds of friendship and loyalty, met in what they called the Tuesday lunch group. In the aftermath of President Lyndon Johnson's overwhelming electoral win in 1964, the group basked in self-confidence and optimism, rejecting pessimistic information about North Vietnam's military buildup. When information mounted about increasing South Vietnamese and American casualties and external stresses intensified, the group further closed ranks, its members taking solace in the security of the group. Individuals who did not share the group's thinking were both informally and formally removed from the group because their prognosis that the war effort was going badly was ignored.

Vladimir Putin: The Individual and His Policies

"Putin Is a Soviet Leader for the 21st Century," writes Maxim Trudolubov, editor of an independent Russian newspaper, in *The Moscow Times*. Putin's regime is "an attempt to strengthen the Soviet experiment and take it to its logical conclusion...improving upon the performance of former Soviet leaders Vladimir Lenin, Josef Stalin, Nikita Khrushchev, Leonid Brezhnev, Yury Andropov and Mikhail Gorbachev."[a] Ashton Carter, U.S. secretary of defense, thinks that Putin "says what he thinks; he couldn't be clearer. He regrets the demise of the Soviet Union. He wants respect for Russia's greatness. He wants a voice in the world. And he wants a nonthreatening neighborhood."[b] But is that all we need to know?

Putin's personal website reveals birth in 1952 to parents of humble origins, living an ordinary life in a communal apartment in Leningrad, today's St. Petersburg. An unmotivated and undistinguished student through the middle school years, he later began to take studies seriously and see a future. After earning a degree from Leningrad State University, he spent 16 years in the Soviet secret service, the KGB, where he was schooled in intelligence and counterintelligence. From 1985 to 1990, he was stationed with the KGB in East Germany, just as East Germany was unravelling. After resigning from the KGB, he spent six years in administration in his native city before moving to Moscow and rapidly rising through the ranks of Russian bureaucracy.

While Putin was the first post–World War II generation leader, he worked closely with the struggling Russian leadership. Then from 2000–2008, he was president of the Russian Federation; prime minister from 2008–12, and then president again starting in 2012.

Putin has carefully crafted a strong personal image—a 5-foot-7-inch bare chested, horse-backing riding, tiger wrestling, race car driving, hockey playing macho man. Yet in the same breath, he is viewed as a straight-shooting, pragmatic problem solver willing to respond to queries in an annual televised phone-in. He is viewed as a moral family man, an image skewed by a recent official divorce. The passage of a controversial law banning homosexual propaganda in 2013 and the failure of the government to prevent homophobic violence illustrate Putin's support of traditional values. He has established excellent relations with the various religious groups in Russia and shown strong support for the Orthodox Church, a purveyor of traditional Russian values. He supports the construction of a huge but controversial 82-foot monument in Moscow to St. Vladimir, Russia's patron saint, founder of both the Russian Orthodox Church and the modern Russian state. As a female member of his teenage fan club gloated, "Putin is like God to me. I perceive him as daddy. He is a perfect man—politician, sportsman, family man. I want my husband to be like him."

Much of Putin's personal image has manifested itself in policy positions. He has stood up to the West, saying no to NATO expansion. Seeing weakness in former leaders like Tsar Nicholas II and Mikhail Gorbachev, he has vowed never to bend to others. He responded to the travesty of Soviet leader Nikita Khrushchev's cession of Crimea to Ukraine in 1954 by retaking Crimea in 2014 to great popular acclaim. And, buoyed by high prices for Russia's oil exports, the real disposable income of Russians doubled between 1999 and 2006, with Putin taking credit.

An important culmination of Russia's reestablishment of a central role in international circles was the success of the Sochi Winter Olympic Games of 2014. Not only a triumph for Russia, it was also a major personal triumph for Putin, who oversaw all parts of the games. Equally as important to Putin's prestige was the awarding of the 2018 FIFA World Cup to Russia. Thus, when U.S. authorities indicted FIFA officials for corruption, Putin came to FIFA's defense, calling it "another blatant attempt by the United States to extend its jurisdiction to other states."

For standing up against the United States, and the West more generally, and for presiding over a period of relative political stability and economic growth, Putin's approval ratings have been above 80 percent for much of the era.

Realists see Putin as yet another leader who acts according to Russian historical national interests. As a former great power whose power has been diminished with the dissolution of the territory, Russia needs to reaffirm its rightful place among nations. Putin's actions are consistent with those interests.

Liberals would argue that leaders like Putin do make a difference, even though they may not explain all of Russia's policies. Putin's carefully crafted image and his use of the media, unprecedented in Russia, has enabled him to acquire greater power, and his personal success like the staging of the Olympics has become synonymous with the success of the nation.

Russian president Vladimir Putin greeting athletes at the Sochi Olympic Games, the scene of personal success and national prestige.

FOR CRITICAL ANALYSIS

1. Using Hermann's personality characteristics, how would you describe Vladimir Putin?

2. Why do you think Putin has emphasized traditional Russian values, despite wanting to move his country forward economically and technologically?

a. Maxim Trubolyubov, "Putin Is a Soviet Leader for the 21st Century," *Moscow Times*, March 23, 2015.

b. Ashton Carter, "The Scholar as Secretary. A Conversation with Ashton Carter," *Foreign Affairs* 94:5 (Sept./Oct. 2015): 75.

TABLE 6.1	PSYCHOLOGICAL MECHANISMS USED TO PROCESS INFORMATION	
TECHNIQUE	**EXPLANATION**	**EXAMPLE**
Cognitive Consistency	Tendency to accept information that is compatible with what has previously been accepted, often ignoring inconsistent information. Desire to be consistent in attitude.	Just prior to the Japanese attack on Pearl Harbor, military spotters saw unmarked planes approaching Hawaii. Not believing the evidence, they discounted the sightings.
Evoked Set	Details in a present situation that are similar to information gleaned from past situations. The tendency to look for an evoked set leads one to conclusions that are similar to those of the past.	During the Vietnam War, U.S. decision makers saw the Korean War as a precedent, although there were critical differences.
Mirror Image	Seeing in one's opponent the opposite of characteristics seen in oneself. Opponent is viewed as hostile and uncompromising, whereas one views oneself as friendly and compromising.	During the Cold War, U.S. elites and public viewed the Soviet Union in terms of their own mirror image: the United States was friendly, the Soviet Union hostile.
Groupthink	Thought process whereby small groups form consensus and resist criticism of that core position, often disregarding contradictory information.	During the U.S. planning for the Bay of Pigs operation against Cuba in 1961, opponents were ostracized from the planning group.
Satisficing	Tendency for groups to search for a "good enough" solution, rather than an optimal one.	Decision of NATO to bomb Kosovo in 1999 in an attempt to stop the ethnic cleansing against the Albanian Kosovars, rather than sending in ground troops.

While many studies exploring groupthink apply the concept to small groups during crises, recent work has expanded the application of groupthink to explaining long-term changes in ideas. One political scientist examines group decision making surrounding the decision of the Bush administration to see Saddam Hussein not just as a difficult dictator but also as a major threat to U.S. national security following 9/11. President George W. Bush, Vice President Dick Cheney, and Secretary of State Donald Rumsfeld drove policy, influencing the other members. Following the trauma of 9/11, there was increasing conformity of ideas consistent with the hawks. Moved by that cohesiveness, "the illusion of unanimity then involved little examination of alternative courses of action."[14] Mindguards controlled the flow of information, and dissenters self-censored.

Participants in small groups, then, are likely to employ the same psychological techniques, such as the evoked set and the mirror image, to process new incoming information at the individual level. But additional distorting tendencies affect small groups, such as the pressure for group conformity and solidarity. Larger groups seeking accommodation look for what is possible within the bounds of their situation, searching for a "good enough" solution, rather than an optimal one. Herbert Simon has labeled this trait *satisficing,* as introduced in Chapter 5.[15]

Political scientist Robert Jervis offers suggestions on how decision makers can safeguard their thinking and minimize mistakes due to various kinds of misperceptions.[16] They need to make their assumptions and beliefs as explicit as possible, be cognizant of the pitfall of interpreting data only as consistent with one's own theory, and be willing to consider information from different angles. Yet even this awareness does not necessarily lead to a rational model of decision making. It is not just the authoritarians (Robert Mugabe of Zimbabwe or Hun Sen of Cambodia) but also the visionaries (Tanzania's Julius Nyerere, India's Mohandas Gandhi), and the political pragmatists (Rwanda's Paul Kagame, Liberia's Ellen Johnson Sirleaf, or Germany's Angela Merkel), who make an impact on the basis of their perceptions and misperceptions.

Private Individuals

Although leaders holding formal positions have more opportunity not only to participate in but also to shape international relations, private individuals can and do play key roles. Private individuals, independent of any official role, may by virtue of circumstances, skills, or resources carry out independent actions in international relations. They are less bound by the rules of the game and institutional norms. Many of these individual voices can magnify their impact through social media, including Facebook, Twitter, and blogs. From Tunisia to Colombia, Iran, and China, individuals have used blogs and Facebook to expose grievances and corruption and organize protests and demonstrations in support of their individual position.

Individuals with financial resources are able to develop programs and support causes that governments are unwilling or unable to fund. The Bill and Melinda Gates Foundation, with resources of $60 billion, gives about $1 billion a year to international health programs for childhood immunizations, AIDS research, and to strengthen health and education programs. George Soros, a Hungarian-born American business-man, uses his immense fortune through the Open Society Foundation to support democracy and human rights in Eastern Europe and Central Asian states.

Some private individuals have stood for and supported specific causes, which has enhanced public knowledge of these issues. With celebrity status, they are able to effectively use the media and even gain an audience with public officials. These so-called celebrity diplomats, as discussed in Chapter 5, include George Clooney, well-known crusader for the people of Darfur; his wife, human rights lawyer Amal Clooney; and Angelina Jolie, a spokesperson for children, women, and refugees.

A few individuals become crusaders for a cause because of what they have achieved or stood for. No better example exists than Malala Yousafzai, the youngest ever recipi-ent, in 2014, of the Nobel Peace Prize. In 2009, blogging for the BBC, she gained a worldwide audience by describing the harsh life under the Taliban and condemning the discriminatory treatment of girls who were banned from public schools. In 2012, a gunman shot her for speaking out, elevating her status as a fighter for women's and children's rights. Using that celebrity status, she is able to lobby heads of state and delegates to the United Nations, as well as use the public media and her own founda-tion to promote the cause of education for girls. Her book *I Am Malala* and a recent documentary "He Named Me Malala" have won high accolades.[17]

There are other individual crusaders, as well. Mohamed Bouazizi, a Tunisian ven-dor, set himself on fire outside a government building after state authorities confis-cated his goods in 2010. The video posted on the Internet of his self-immolation was seen around the Arab world, not only leading to the overthrow of the Tunisian presi-dent, Zine al-Abidine Ben Ali, in the Jasmine Revolution but also providing the spark for the broader democratic opening in the Arab world, the Arab Spring.

Aung San Suu Kyi became yet a different symbol: the face of the opposition move-ment to the repressive military government of Myanmar (formerly Burma). Her father, General Aung San, negotiated that country's independence from Great Britain in 1947, becoming known as the father of modern-day Burma. His daughter's public acts began after the 1962 military coup. Defying a ban on political gatherings, she spoke to large crowds, demanding democratic government. Advocating nonviolence and civil disobe-dience, she traveled across the country, speaking to large audiences. In 1989, the gov-ernment placed her under house arrest, where she stayed for more than two decades.

Awarded the Nobel Peace Prize in 1991, Aung San Suu Kyi became an interna-tional symbol of the opposition, demanding both the release of political prisoners and broader political change. As a free individual, she rebuilt a political party and won election to the parliament. She made triumphant trips to Europe and the United States, yet the extent of her influence on top decision makers was unclear. In 2015, her political party won in a landslide election. Although constitutionally barred from the presidency, she intends to use her prestige and power gained from years of private resistance to govern as a public official.

Track-Two Diplomacy Use of Individuals

Private individuals increasingly play a role in so-called **track-two diplomacy**, particularly in the area of conflict resolution. Track-two diplomacy uses individuals outside of governments to carry out negotiations, resulting in success in some cases. In the spring of 1992, for example, Eritrea signed a declaration of independence, seceding from Ethiopia after years of both low- and high-intensity conflict. The foundation for the agreement was negotiated in numerous informal meetings in Atlanta, Georgia, and elsewhere, between the affected parties and former president Jimmy Carter, acting through the Carter Center's International Negotiation Network at Emory University. In the fall of 1993, the unexpected framework for reconciliation between Israel and the Palestine Liberation Organization was negotiated through track-two informal and formal processes initiated by Terje Larsen, a Norwegian sociologist, and Yossi Beilin of the opposition Labor Party in Israel. A series of preparatory negotiations was conducted over a five-month period in total secrecy. Beginning unofficially, the talks gradually evolved into official negotiations, building up trust in an informal atmosphere and setting the stage for an eventual agreement.[18]

Such high-level, track-two diplomatic efforts are not always well received. For example, Jimmy Carter's eleventh-hour dash in 1994 to meet with North Korea's Kim Il-Sung to discuss the latter's nuclear buildup was met by a barrage of probing questions. Was the U.S. government being preempted? For whom did Carter speak? Could the understandings become the basis of a formal intergovernmental agreement? Despite the misgivings and the eventual unraveling of North Korea's promises, Carter received the Nobel Peace Prize in 2002 for this and other efforts to promote peace around the world. Was this private citizen actually speaking on behalf of the U.S. administration?

Other types of track-two diplomacy involve the lengthier process of sustained dialogue. In some cases, unofficial individuals from different international groups are brought together in small problem-solving workshops so they can develop personal relationships and understanding of the problems from the perspective of others. It is hoped that these individuals will then seek to influence public opinion in their respective states, trying to reshape, and often rehumanize, the image of the opponent. This approach has been used to address the conflict between Protestants and Catholics in Northern Ireland and the Arab-Israeli dispute. Problem-solving workshops have been conducted over decades and cooperative activities encouraged. Systematic studies about their effectiveness have yet to be written.

Alternative critical and postmodernist approaches are attempting to draw mainstream theorists' attention to other less well-known and less-publicized stories, because they, too, are part of the fabric of international relations. Feminist writers in particular have sought to bring attention to the role of private individuals, especially women. In *Bananas, Beaches, and Bases*, political scientist Cynthia Enloe shows strikingly how "the personal is international" by documenting the many ways that women influence international relations. She points to women in economic roles participating in the international division of labor, as seamstresses, light-industry "girls," nannies, and fashion models. She also identifies women more directly involved in foreign policy —the women living around military bases, diplomatic wives, domestic servants, and women in international organizations.[19] Theirs are the untold stories of marginalized groups that critical theorists, postmodernists, and constructivists are increasingly bringing to light.

In 2009, former president Bill Clinton played an instrumental role in arranging the release of two American journalists being held by North Korea. Private individuals, including former leaders who no longer hold any government position, can sometimes shape international relations.

Mass Publics

Mass publics have the same psychological tendencies as elite individuals and small groups. They think in terms of perceptions and images, they see mirror images, and they use similar information-processing strategies. During the height of the Cold War, the United States and the Soviet Union were often seen as mirror images of each other: the one generous and peace loving; the other selfish and aggressive. Following the seizure of the U.S. embassy in Iran in 1979, public-opinion surveys showed the prevalence of mirror images. The United States (strong and brave) and its leader (safe and humane) were compared to Iran (weak and cowardly) and its leader Ayatollah Khomeini (dangerous and ruthless). Yet whether this public perception of Iran had an impact on top decision makers is unclear.[20]

Was President Carter's exclusive focus on the hostages because of the attention the public was paying to the hostages? Or did Carter's personality characteristics predispose him to focus so exclusively and so passionately on the hostages? The influence that mass publics have on foreign policy might be explained in three ways: by common traits they share with elites, mass public opinion actually influencing decision makers, or masses acting relatively independently.

Elites and Masses: Common Traits

First, it could be argued that elites and masses hold similar beliefs and act in similar ways because they share common psychological and biological characteristics. For example, individuals, like animals, are said to have an innate drive to gain, protect, and defend territory—the "territorial imperative." This, according to some, explains the preoccupation with securing territorial boundaries that groups feel belong to them. Israel's defense of its perceived ancestral homeland is opposed by the Palestinians' claim to the same territory. Individuals and societies also share the frustration-aggression syndrome: when societies become frustrated, just like individuals, they become aggressive. Frustration, of course, can arise from a number of different sources, including economic shocks such as those Germany suffered after World War I or those Russia experienced in the 1990s.

The problem with both the territorial imperative and the frustration-aggression notion is that even if all individuals and societies share these innate biological predispositions, not all leaders and all peoples act on these predispositions. So general predispositions of all societies, or the similarities in predispositions between elites and masses, cannot explain the extreme variation found in individual behavior and state behavior.

Another possibility is that elites and masses share common traits differentiated by gender. Male elites and masses possess characteristics common to each other, whereas female elites and masses share traits different from those of males. These differences can explain political behavior. One much-discussed difference is that males, both elites and masses, are power seeking, whereas women are consensus builders, more collaborative, and more inclined toward compromise. One study, for example, sees the direct implications of these gender differences for peace negotiations. Because women often come to the negotiating table with experience in civic activism, nongovernmental organizations, and citizen-empowering movements, they bring with them different attitudes and skill-sets. Women negotiators like Mary Robinson, UN special envoy for the Great Lakes region in Africa, have brought in local women's groups leaders in hopes of reaching better outcomes.[21] If there are differences in male and female attitudes and behavior, are these differences rooted in biology or are they learned from the culture? Most feminists, particularly the constructivists, contend that these differences are socially constructed products of culture and can thus be reconstructed over time. Yet, once again, these general predispositions, whatever their origin, cannot explain extreme variation in individual behavior.

The Impact of Public Opinion on Elites

The second possibility is that the masses have opinions and attitudes about foreign policy and international relations that are different from those of the elites. If public-opinion polls capture these differences, will the elites listen to these opinions? Will policy made by the elites reflect the public's attitudes? Sometimes a public's general foreign policy orientation reflects a perceived general mood of the population that leaders can detect. President George H. W. Bush was able to capitalize internationally on the positive public mood in the aftermath of victory in the 1991 Gulf War, although the domestic effect was short lived; he did not win reelection. Even leaders of authoritarian regimes pay attention to dominant moods, with Chinese leaders curbing corruption at the local and provincial level in response to public anger.

More often than not, however, publics do not express a single, dominant mood; top leaders are usually confronted with an array of public attitudes. These opinions are registered in elections, but elections are an imperfect measure of public opinion because they merely select individuals for office—individuals who may share voters' attitudes on some issues but not on others.

In most democratic regimes, public-opinion polling provides information about public attitudes. The European Union, for example, conducts the Eurobarometer, a scientific survey of public attitudes on a wide range of issues in European Union (EU) countries. Because the same questions are asked during different polls over time, state officials and the EU leadership can avail themselves of reliable data on public opinion. Likewise, the Latin American Public Opinion Project has conducted systematic surveys of Latin American citizens since the 1970s. And Afrobarometer polls conducted since 2000 chart citizen attitudes on governance and economics in almost 35 countries. But do leaders fashion policy with these attitudes in mind? Do elites change policy to reflect the preferences of the public? Data collected in 2014 on EU countries' attitudes toward immigrants reflect wide variance of opinion. In Greece, 86 percent supported fewer numbers of immigrants; in Spain, the number was 47 percent; Germany, 44 percent, and Poland 40 percent. In Germany, 14 percent supported more immigrants, while in Greece, only 1 percent did.[22] And, in the aftermath of the massive influx of refugees and asylum seekers in the summer of 2015, those opinion polls conducted just a year earlier are likely to be unreliable. No wonder the EU policy makers have had such difficulty in fashioning an EU-wide policy.

Evidence from the United States suggests that elites do care about the preferences of the public, although they do not always directly incorporate those attitudes into policy decisions. Presidents care about their popularity because it affects their ability to work; a president's popularity is enhanced if he or she follows the general mood of the masses or fights for generally popular policies. Such popularity gives the president more leeway to set a national agenda, but mass attitudes may not always be directly translated into policy.

Occasionally, and quite extraordinarily, the masses may vote directly on an issue with foreign policy significance. For example, many issues related to the European Union have been put to public referendum, including the Maastricht Treaty, the EU Constitution, and the Lisbon Treaty, as we will discuss in Chapter 7. In 2002, the Swiss people voted in a referendum to join the United Nations. In 2017, Britain will vote on whether, and under what conditions, the state will remain in the EU. These are rather rare instances of direct public input on a foreign policy decision.

Mass Actions and the Role of Elites

The third possibility is that the masses, uncontrolled by formal institutions, may occasionally act in ways that have a profound impact on international relations, regardless of anything that the elites do. At times, the masses, essentially appearing leaderless, take collective actions that have significant effects on the course of world politics. Individual acts of thousands fleeing East Germany led to the construction of the Berlin Wall in 1961. Twenty-eight years later, the spontaneous exodus of thousands of East Germans through Hungary and Austria led to the tearing down of the wall in 1989. The spontaneous movement of "boat people" fleeing Vietnam and the ragged ships leaving Cuba and Haiti for the U.S. coast resulted in changes in U.S. immigration policy. Currently, the spontaneous movement of Syrians and Iraqis fleeing their war-torn countries in masses has led to the refugee crisis in Europe. Several months of public demonstrations in Guatemala ultimately brought down that government in 2015, the people seeking an end to widespread corruption; but the relationship between the masses and leaders is not always so clear.

At other times, a small elite may have acted behind the scenes or even organized mass protests, as illustrated by the "people's putsch" during October 2000 against the Yugoslavian leader Slobodan Milošević. After 13 years of his rule, people from all walks of Serbian life joined 7,000 striking miners, crippled the economic system, blocked transportation routes, and descended on Belgrade, the capital. Aided by the new technology of the time—the cell phone—they were able to mobilize citizens from all over the country, driving tractors into the city, attacking the Parliament, and disrupting Milošević's radio and TV stations. But the opposition elite was behind the scenes, aiding in the mobilization of the masses for policy change, and as *Time* reported, "the Serbs took back their country and belatedly joined the democratic tide that swept away the rest of Eastern Europe's communist tyrants a decade ago."[23]

The people's revolution in Serbia against Milošević (the Bulldozer Revolution) proved to be a blueprint for action in other states of the post-communist world. In Georgia, in 2003, the Rose Revolution brought a new president to power and a political dynasty was broken. In Ukraine in 2004, the Orange Resolution brought into power an opposition leader, Viktor Yushchenko, who fled to Russia a decade later following the Euromaidan Revolution, named for the central square in Kiev where the demonstrators amassed. Although these events illustrate the power of the masses and of mass communications, opposition elites played a key role.

In the events of the Arab Spring, although galvanized by the public action of a Tunisian vendor, it was a group of young private citizens, led by Google executive Wael Ghonim in late 2010, who organized a Facebook and YouTube campaign, calling on over 130,000 followers for the ouster of the government of President Hosni Mubarak. They connected with human rights groups, raising the public awareness of the average Egyptian about governmental abuses. Collaborating with Mohammed ElBaradei (former director-general of the International Atomic Energy Agency and leader of an opposition political party), they became the voice behind the January 25, 2011, demonstration. Ghonim wrote, "This is Revolution 2.0. No one was a hero because everyone was a hero."[24]

The long-term impact of these revolutions, where the masses played a role with elite support, remains in doubt. In several color-revolution states, newly instituted reforms have been overturned, or the reforms weakened, and the NGOs that they spawned have been severely restricted. In Iran, a mass opposition challenging Iranian religious

Google executive Wael Ghonim used Facebook and YouTube to help organize anti-government protests in Egypt, demonstrating how private individuals can harness technology to challenge elites, ultimately leading to changes in domestic governance and international relations.

THEORY IN BRIEF

CONTENDING PERSPECTIVES ON THE INDIVIDUAL

	REALISM/ NEOREALISM	LIBERALISM/ NEOLIBERAL INSTITUTIONALISM	RADICALISM/ DEPENDENCY THEORY	CONSTRUCTIVISM
FOREIGN POLICY ELITES	Constrained by anarchic international system and national interests	Significant impact on international relations through choices made and personality factors	Constrained by international capitalist system	Shape popular understanding and incorporation of events and processes
PRIVATE INDIVIDUALS	Actions of private individuals have effect only in aggregate, as reflected in national interest	Secondary role, but may be involved in track-two diplomacy and may fund important initiatives	Individual capitalists may be influential	Actions of individuals less important than beliefs
MASS PUBLICS	Actions may be reflected in national interest	May affect international relations through mass actions that pressure state decision makers	Agents of potential revolutionary change	Agents of potential change through discourse

and political elites in the 2009 Green movement lost the election, and its momentum. And the future for democracy is unclear in Egypt and other Arab states. While new regimes have been voted into power, they face high expectations, steep challenges, and lingering societal opposition.

In Sum: Contending Perspectives on the Impact of Individuals

For liberals, the actions of individuals matter. Individual elites can make a difference: they have choices in the kinds of foreign policy they pursue and therefore can affect the course of events. Thus, we need to pay attention to personality characteristics and understand how individuals make decisions, how they employ various psychological mechanisms to process information, and what impact these processes have on individual and group behavior. Mass publics matter to liberals because liberals believe these publics help formulate the state's interests. Private individuals also matter, although they are clearly of secondary importance, even in liberal thinking. Constructivists, too, see individuals as important. Individuals form collective identities; elites can be key policy entrepreneurs who can promote change through ideas. But only in more recent postmodernist and some constructivist scholarship, especially in feminist scholarship, have private individuals' stories found salience.

Realists and radicals do not recognize individuals as important, independent actors in international relations. They see individuals primarily as constrained by the international system and the state. To realists, individuals are constrained by an anarchic international system and by a state seeking to project power consonant with its national interest. Similarly, radicals see individuals only as members of a class often misled or deluded by elites in the international capitalist system and within a state driven by economic imperatives. In neither case are individuals believed to be sufficiently unconstrained to be considered at the same level of analysis as either the international system or the state.

Individuals and states are not only important in themselves. They also form groups and operate in both international organizations and nongovernmental organizations, within a framework of international law. We turn to these topics in the next chapter.

Discussion Questions

1. Leaders such as Iran's former president Mahmoud Ahmadinejad, Equitorial Guinea's Teodoro Obiang Nguema Mbasogo, and North Korea's Kim Jong-Un are often dismissed as "crazy" or "nuts." What do we mean by these characterizations? What other explanations can be offered for their behavior?

2. You are a top decision maker in a government bureaucracy. What strategies would you use to try to minimize the effects of misperceptions in decision making?

3. If more women held major leadership positions in international affairs, would policies be any different? What theories would explain behavior by women leaders as similar to or different from that of male leaders?

4. Mass publics are often stimulated by the media and connected by new technologies. How? Show how the Internet, cell phones, and Twitter have made a difference to international relations.

Key Terms

belief system (p. 189)

cognitive consistency (p. 192)

evoked set (p. 193)

groupthink (p. 193)

mirror images (p. 193)

track-two diplomacy (p. 199)

07

Warming temperatures and melting ice allow both commercial and military ships to navigate in Arctic waters and have opened up previously unavailable territory for oil drilling. Competing claims over sovereignty of these contested spaces pit Canada, the United States, Russia, and others against each other.

INTERGOVERNMENTAL ORGANIZATIONS, INTERNATIONAL LAW, AND NONGOVERNMENTAL ORGANIZATIONS

The Arctic is changing, warming two times faster than the rate of the rest of the earth. The Arctic ice is melting, opening up new issues and bringing out new rivalries. A 3,000-mile Northern Sea passage connecting Europe and Asia is now a reality, at least in the short summer season and with expensive icebreakers; mineral and petroleum resources once thought unrecoverable now might be commercially viable.

Responding to the need for some kind of management of the Arctic, the Arctic Council was formed in 1996 with eight members—Canada, Denmark, Finland, Iceland, Norway, Russia, Sweden, and the United States. But many issues remain outside the purview of the council, namely, security and military issues. Is this intergovernmental organization (IGO) equipped to manage the dynamic issues facing the Arctic? Does a relevant international law govern areas like the polar regions, that were once considered the commons? Do nongovernmental organizations (NGOs), which might protect the interests of indigenous peoples living in the polar regions, have a role?

In this chapter, we explore the role of IGOs, their possibilities and their limitations. We illustrate the relevance of international law, then show how international law differs from domestic law and how both states and IGOs are embedded in that law. Understanding the international legal framework is central to understanding the liberal view of international politics. We then examine nongovernmental organizations (NGOs), which are relatively new but increasingly powerful actors. Finally, we explore the realist, radical, and constructivist responses.

Intergovernmental Organizations

The Creation of IGOs

Why have states chosen to organize themselves collectively? Liberalism provides the answer: within the framework of institutions and rules, cooperation is possible. International organizations are the arenas where states interact and cooperate to solve common problems. During the 1970s, neoliberal institutionalists, as described in Chapters 3 and 4, revived the study of international organizations; they argued that "even if . . . anarchy constrains the willingness of states to cooperate, states nevertheless can work together and can do so especially with the assistance of international institutions."[1]

Recall the prisoner's dilemma, explained in Chapter 3. If the situation between the two prisoners is played one time, both prisoners will defect (or confess) to minimize the possibility of real disaster. Consistent with realist expectations, each will serve a longer sentence than if they had cooperated and kept silent. But what happens when the interaction is repeated? Then, according to neoliberal institutionalists, multiple interactions lead to greater possibilities for cooperation. This continuous interaction among states provides the motivation for states to create international organizations. In turn, these organizations moderate state behavior, provide a framework for interactions, establish mechanisms to reduce cheating by monitoring others and punishing the uncooperative, and facilitate transparency for state actions. Organizations are the focal points for coordination and make state commitments more credible, specifying expectations and establishing reputations for compliance.

International organizations are particularly useful for solving two sets of problems. One set of problems arises from the need to cooperate on technical, often nonpolitical, issues where states are not the appropriate units for resolving these problems. As the scholar David Mitrany writes in *A Working Peace System*, units (states, subnational actors) need to "bind together those interests which are common, where they are common, and to the extent to which they are common."[2] This *functional* approach advocates building on and expanding the habits of cooperation nurtured by groups of technical experts outside of formal state channels. This notion explains why international cooperation began in specific, technical-issue areas such as health and communications during the nineteenth century. The expectation, according to functionalist thinking, was that solving problems in these technical areas (e.g., curbing epidemics, facilitating international mail and telegraphic services) would inspire cooperation or spill over into political and military affairs, and new international organizations would form.

International organizations also form around collective goods, the second type of problem. In "The Tragedy of the Commons," biologist Garrett Hardin tells the story

IN FOCUS   FUNCTIONALISM

- War is caused by economic deprivation.

- Economic disparity cannot be solved in a system of independent states.

- New functional units should be created to solve specific economic problems.

- People and groups will develop habits of cooperation, which will spill over from economic cooperation to political cooperation.

- In the end, economic disparities will lessen and war will be eliminated.

IN FOCUS

COLLECTIVE GOODS

- Collective goods are available to all members of a group, regardless of individual contributions.

- Some activities of states involve the provision of collective goods.

- Groups need to devise strategies to overcome problems of collective goods caused by the negative consequences of the actions of others—the "tragedy of the commons."

- Strategies include coercion, altering preferences by offering incentives, and altering the size of the group.

of a group of herders who share a common grazing area. Each herder finds it economically rational to increase the size of his own herd, allowing him to sell more in the market. Yet if all herders follow what is individually rational behavior, then the group loses: too many animals graze the land and the quality of the pasture deteriorates, leading to decreased output for all. As each person rationally attempts to maximize his own gain, the collectivity suffers, and, eventually, all individuals suffer.[3]

What Hardin describes—the common grazing area—is a **collective good**. The grazing area is available to all group members, regardless of individual contribution. The use of collective goods involves interdependent activities and choices. Decisions by one state have effects for other states—that is, states can suffer unanticipated negative consequences because of the actions of others. For example, the decision by wealthy countries to continue the production and sale of chlorofluorocarbons affects all countries through long-term depletion of the ozone layer. With collective goods, market mechanisms break down. Alternative forms of management are needed.

Hardin proposed several possible solutions to the tragedy of the commons. First, use coercion. Force nations or peoples to control the collective goods. States, for example, could force people to limit the number of children they have to prevent a population explosion that would harm the environment. Second, restructure the preferences of states through rewards and punishments. Offer positive incentives for states to refrain from engaging in the destruction of the commons; tax, or threaten to tax, those who fail to cooperate. Third, alter the size of the group. Smaller groups can more effectively exert pressure on their members because violations of the commons will be more easily noticed. China's long-time population policy of one child per couple was administered locally. Close monitoring, coupled with strong social pressure, is more likely to lead to compliance. These alternatives can also be achieved through international organizations. For many, they are the preferred way to address problems of the commons—the sea, space, the environment.

While all international problems are not collective-goods problems, most international issues require continuous interactions among parties—hence, over the long term, states find it mutually beneficial to cooperate, especially if the costs of ensuring transparency, reducing cheating, and punishing the uncooperative are relatively low.

The Roles of IGOs

Intergovernmental organizations, such as the United Nations, the World Bank, and the International Civil Aviation Organization, can play key roles at each level of analysis.[4] In the international system, IGOs contribute to habits of cooperation; states become socialized to regular interactions, such as through the United Nations. Some programs of IGOs, such as the International Atomic Energy Agency's nuclear-monitoring program, establish regularized processes of information gathering, analysis, and surveillance. Some IGOs, such as the World Trade Organization, develop procedures for making rules, settling disputes, and punishing those who fail to follow the rules. IGOs may also play key roles in international bargaining, facilitating the formation of transgovernmental and transnational networks, sometimes leading to common expectations of states' behavior. We know these rules and principles generally as **international regimes**. Charters of IGOs incorporate the norms, rules, and decision-making processes of regimes. By bringing members of the regime together, IGOs help to reduce the incentive to cheat and enhance the value of a good reputation.

For states, IGOs both enlarge the possibilities for foreign policy making and add to the constraints under which states conduct and, in particular, implement foreign policy. States join IGOs to use them as instruments of foreign policy. IGOs may legitimate a state's viewpoints and policies—thus, the United States sought the support of the Organization of American States during the Cuban missile crisis in 1962. IGOs increase available information about other states, thereby enhancing predictability in the policy-making process. Some IGOs, such as the UN High Commissioner for Refugees and UNICEF, may conduct specific activities that are compatible with, or augment, state policy.

But IGOs also constrain member states by setting international and hence national agendas and forcing governments to make decisions or develop implementation processes to coordinate IGO participation. Both large and small states may have to align their policies if they wish to benefit from their membership.

IGOs also affect individuals by providing opportunities for leadership. As individuals work with or in IGOs, they, like states, may become socialized to cooperate internationally.

Not all IGOs perform all of these functions, and the manner in and extent to which each carries out particular functions varies. Sometimes, the failure of one organization to perform its functions leads to its replacement by another organization that tries a

At the UN headquarters in New York City, political representatives from 193 member countries debate many critical issues, including whether to respond to civil strife in Mali and Syria and how to address environmental and health threats.

different approach. The United Nations, for example, reflects the successes and the failures of its predecessor organization the League of Nations.

The United Nations

The United Nations is a product of a historical process; it reflects processes during the nineteenth century when the European powers experimented with the Concert of Europe described in Chapter 2, when public international unions formed and when states established permanent mechanisms for conflict resolution through the Hague system. But, most of all, the United Nations is a product of the League of Nations.

Founded following World War I, the goal of the League was to end all wars; indeed, half of the League Covenant's provisions focused on preventing war. If dispute resolution failed, sanctions would follow, and should they fail, states would act against an aggression by all states acting together, under the idea of collective security, an idea Chapter 8 explains in depth.

The League did enjoy a number of successes, many of them on territorial issues. It conducted plebiscites in Silesia and the Saar and demarcated the German-Polish border.

It settled territorial disputes between Lithuania and Poland, Finland and Russia, and Bulgaria and Greece. However, the League failed to act decisively against the aggression of Italy and Japan in the 1930s. Britain and France pursued their national interests, causing collective security to fail. Voluntary sanctions carried little effect. The absence of great-power support for the League was evident in the failure even to attract the United States to join the organization. The League could not prevent the outbreak of World War II.

The United Nations built on the League's successes and tried to correct some of its weaknesses.

BASIC PRINCIPLES AND CHANGING INTERPRETATIONS

The United Nations, like the League of Nations, was founded on three fundamental principles. Yet, over the life of the United Nations, changing realities have significantly challenged each of these principles.[5]

First, the United Nations is based on the notion of the sovereign equality of member states, consistent with the Westphalian tradition. Each state—the United States, Lithuania, India, or Suriname, irrespective of size or population—is legally the equivalent of every other state. This legal equality is the basis for each state's having one vote in the General Assembly. However, the actual inequality of states is recognized in the veto power given to the five permanent members of the Security Council, the special role reserved for the wealthy states in budget negotiations, and the weighted voting system used by the World Bank and the International Monetary Fund.

Second is the principle that only international problems fall within the jurisdiction of the United Nations. Indicative of the Westphalian influence, the UN Charter does not "authorize the United Nations to intervene in matters which are essentially within the domestic jurisdiction of any state" (Article 2, Section 7). Over the life of the United Nations, the once-rigid distinction between domestic and international issues has weakened, leading to an erosion of sovereignty. Global telecommunications and economic interdependencies, international human rights, election monitoring, and environmental regulation all infringe on traditional areas of domestic jurisdiction and hence on states' sovereignty. War is increasingly civil war, which is not legally under the purview of the United Nations. Yet because international human rights are being abrogated, because refugees cross national borders, and because weapons are supplied through transnational networks, such conflicts are increasingly viewed as international, and the United Nations is viewed by some as the appropriate venue for action. These changes have led to a growing body of precedent for humanitarian intervention without the consent of the host country.

The third principle is that the United Nations is designed primarily to maintain international peace and security. This principle has meant that member states should refrain from the threat or the use of force; settle disputes by peaceful means, as detailed at the Hague conferences; and support enforcement measures.

Although the foundations of both the League of Nations and the United Nations focused on security in the realist, classical sense—protection of national territory and sovereignty—the United Nations is increasingly confronted with demands for action to support a broadened view of security. UN operations to feed the starving populations of Somalia and Niger, or to provide relief in the form of food, clothing, and shelter for Haitians and Nepalese forced out of their homes by natural disasters, are examples of this broadened notion of security—**human security**. Expansion into these newer areas of security collides head on with the domestic authority of states, undermining the principle of state sovereignty. The United Nations' founders recognized the tension between the commitment to act collectively against a member state and the affirmation of state sovereignty. But they could not foresee the dilemmas that changing definitions of security would pose.

STRUCTURE

The structure of the United Nations was developed to serve the multiple roles assigned by its charter, but incremental changes in that structure have accommodated changes in the international system, particularly the increase in the number of states. The central UN organs comprise six major bodies, as Table 7.1 shows.

The power and prestige of these various organs has changed over time. The **Security Council** was kept small to facilitate swift decision making in response to threats to international peace and security. Its five permanent members—the United States, Great Britain, France, Russia (successor state to the Soviet Union in 1992), and the People's Republic of China (replacing the Republic of China in 1971)—are key to council decision making, each having veto power on substantive issues where unanimity is required. In the early years of the Cold War, the Security Council became deadlocked by the Soviet Union's frequent use of the veto. Since the 1970s, the United States has used its veto more times than any other permanent member. The majority of these vetoes have concerned the Arab-Israeli-Palestinian conflict.

Since the end of the Cold War, the Security Council has regained power, because the use of the veto has dropped precipitously. The number of annual official meetings has risen, the number of resolutions passed has increased with consensus voting, and informal meetings among the permanent members have been more frequent. With greater cooperation among the permanent powers—especially since 1990, when the council authorized force against Iraq after its invasion of Kuwait—the Security Council has taken on more armed conflicts, imposed more types of sanctions in more situations, created war crimes tribunals to prosecute war criminals, authorized protectorates in Kosovo and East Timor, and, after 9/11, expanded involvement in antiterrorism activ-

TABLE 7.1

PRINCIPAL ORGANS OF THE UNITED NATIONS

ORGAN	MEMBERSHIP AND VOTING	RESPONSIBILITIES
Security Council	15 members: five permanent with veto, ten rotating members elected by region	Peace and security: identifies aggressor; decides on enforcement measures
General Assembly	193 members; each state has one vote; members work in six functional committees	Debates any topic within charter's purview; admits states; elects members to special bodies
Secretariat, headed by Secretary-General	Secretariat of 43,000; secretary-general elected for five-year renewable term by General Assembly and Security Council	Secretariat: gathers information, coordinates and conducts activities; secretary-general: chief administrative officer, spokesperson
Economic and Social Council (ECOSOC)	54 members elected for three-year terms	Coordinates economic and social welfare programs; coordinates action of specialized agencies (FAO, WHO, UNESCO)
Trusteeship Council	Originally composed of administering and nonadministering countries; now made up of five great powers	Supervision has ended; proposals have been floated to change function to that of forum for indigenous peoples, NGOs, or nation building
International Court of Justice	15 judges	Noncompulsory jurisdiction on cases brought by states and international organizations

ities and coped with the disruptions from the Arab Spring. But, although the Security Council has enormous formal power, it does not have direct control over the means to use that power. It depends on states for funding, personnel, and enforcement of sanctions and military action. A state's willingness to contribute depends on whether it perceives the council as legitimate.

The **General Assembly** is the main deliberative body of the United Nations and permits debate on any topic under its purview. All member states are represented in the General Assembly, which has grown in membership from 51 in 1946 to 193 in 2016. The bulk of the work of the General Assembly is done in six functional committees: Disarmament and Security; Economic and Financial; Social, Humanitarian, and Cultural; Political and Decolonization; Administrative and Budgetary; and Legal. Debate on resolutions emerging from the committees is organized around regionally based voting blocs, with member states using their one vote to coordinate positions and build support for them. Since the end of the Cold War, the General Assembly's work has been increasingly marginalized, as the epicenter of UN power has shifted back to the Security Council and a more active Secretariat. This marginalization has happened much to the dismay of various caucusing groups, including the **Group of 77**, the coalition of developing states; regional groups (Africa, Asia, Latin America); and some members of the **Group of 20**, a coalition of the emerging economies. Occasionally, the work of the General Assembly attracts public attention, as it did during the 2011 and 2012 debates over the status of Palestine, but generally, it provides a forum for member states to express positions and conduct the UN's housekeeping functions.

The Secretariat has expanded to employ a global staff of around 43,000 with about one-quarter located at UN headquarters. The role of the secretary-general has expanded significantly. Having few formal powers, the secretary-general depends on persuasive capability and an aura of neutrality for authority. With this power, the secretary-general, especially in the post–Cold War era, can potentially forge an activist agenda, as Secretary-General Kofi Annan did until his retirement in 2006. In 1998, he negotiated a compromise between Iraq and the United States over the authority, composition, and timing of UN weapon inspections in Iraq; he mediated between Iraq and the rest of the international community; he also implemented significant administrative and budgetary reforms and worked hard to establish a better relationship with the U.S. Congress. Annan used the office to push other initiatives, including the international response to the AIDS epidemic and the promotion of better relations between the private sector and the United Nations. A highly visible secretary-general, he was awarded the Nobel Peace Prize in 2001.

His successor, Ban Ki-moon of the Republic of Korea, was reelected to a second term in 2011. In the early years, he took initiatives on climate change, Darfur, and preventive diplomacy, and in the second term, violence against women, LGBT rights, natural-disaster risk reduction, as well as climate change. In pressing for management

reform, he appointed more women to top positions, eliminated patronage jobs, instituted internal competition for jobs, and reorganized major departments. However, he
is viewed generally as a weak leader, lacking in key communication skills, preferring to
operate below the radar. But, as one journalist acknowledged, "The fact is that when
the great powers squabble, there's little that anyone in the organization can accomplish, be they competent or not. . . ."[6]

Throughout the United Nations, when one organ has increased in importance,
others have diminished, most notably the Economic and Social Council (ECOSOC)
and the Trusteeship Council, albeit for very different reasons. ECOSOC was originally
established to coordinate the various economic and social activities within the UN
system through a number of specialized agencies. But the expansion of those activities
and the increase in the number of programs has made ECOSOC's task of coordination
a problematic one. In addition to covering such broad issues as human rights, the status of women, population and development, and social development, ECOSOC is
charged with coordinating the work of the family of UN-specialized institutions (discussed later). In contrast, the Trusteeship Council has worked its way out of a job. Its
task was to supervise decolonization and to phase out trust territories placed under
UN guardianship during the transition of colonies to independent states. Thus, the very
success of the Trusteeship Council has led to its demise.

KEY POLITICAL ISSUES

The United Nations has always mirrored what is happening in the world, and, in turn,
the United Nations and its organs have shaped the world. The United Nations played a
key role in the decolonization of Africa and Asia. The UN Charter endorsed the principle
of self-determination for colonial peoples, and former colonies such as India, Egypt,
Indonesia, and the Latin American states seized on the United Nations as a forum to
push the agenda of decolonization. By 1960, a majority of the United Nations' members
favored decolonization. UN resolutions condemned the continuation of colonial rule and
called for annual reports on the progress toward independence of all remaining territories. The United Nations was instrumental in the legitimation of the new international
norm that colonialism and imperialism are unacceptable state policies. By the mid-1960s,
most former colonies had achieved independence with little threat to international peace,
and the United Nations had played a significant role in this transformation.

The emergence of the newly independent states transformed the United Nations
and international politics more generally. These states formed a coalition of the South,
or Group of 77—developing states whose interests lie in economic development, a
group often at loggerheads with the developed countries of the North. The split
between the North and the South led to the Group of 77 calling for a New International
Economic Order (see Chapter 4). The North-South conflict continues to be a central

feature of world politics and of the United Nations, although the coalitions have become more fluid with the rise of the emerging economies.

PEACEKEEPING

Of the many issues the United Nations confronts, none is as vexing as peace and security. A new approach, labeled *peacekeeping*, evolved as a way to limit the scope of conflict and prevent it from escalating into a Cold War confrontation. Peacekeeping operations fall into two types, or generations. In **traditional peacekeeping**, multilateral institutions such as the United Nations seek to contain conflicts between two states through third-party military forces. Ad hoc military units, drawn from the armed forces of nonpermanent members of the UN Security Council (often small, neutral members), have been used to prevent the escalation of conflicts and to keep the warring parties apart until the dispute can be settled. Invited in by the disputants, the troops operate under UN auspices, supervising armistices, trying to maintain cease-fires, and physically interposing themselves in a buffer zone between warring parties. Table 7.2 lists some of these traditional UN peacekeeping operations.

TABLE 7.2	TRADITIONAL PEACEKEEPING OPERATIONS, REPRESENTATIVE CASES		
OPERATION	**LOCATION(S)**	**DURATION**	**STRENGTH**
UNEF I (First UN Emergency Force)	Suez Canal, Sinai Peninsula	Nov. 1956–June 1967	3,378 troops
UNMEE (UN Mission in Ethiopia and Eritrea)	Ethiopia/ Eritrean border	Sept. 2000–July 2008	3,940 troops; 214 police
UNFICYP (UN Peacekeeping Force in Cyprus)	Cyprus	March 1964–present	861 troops; 55 police; 151 civilians
UNIFIL (UN Interim Force in Lebanon)	Southern Lebanon	March 1978–present	10,521 troops; 848 civilians

Source: United Nations.

In the post–Cold War era, UN peacekeeping has expanded to address different types of conflicts and to take on new responsibilities. Whereas traditional peacekeeping activities primarily address interstate conflict, **complex (or multidimensional) peacekeeping** activities respond to civil war and ethnonationalist conflicts within states that may not have requested UN assistance. To deal with these new conflicts, peacekeepers have taken on a range of both military and nonmilitary functions. On the military side, they have aided in the verification of troop withdrawal (the Soviet Union from Afghanistan) and have separated warring factions until the underlying issues could be settled (Bosnia). Sometimes, resolving underlying issues has meant organizing and running national elections, as in Cambodia and Namibia; sometimes, it has involved implementing human rights agreements, as in Central America. At other times, UN peacekeepers have tried to maintain law and order in failing or disintegrating societies by aiding in civil administration, policing, and rehabilitating infrastructure, as in Somalia, East Timor, and Afghanistan. (This is often called **peacebuilding**.) And peacekeepers have provided humanitarian aid, supplying food, medicine, and a secure environment in part of an expanded conception of human security in Africa. Table 7.3 lists some representative cases of complex peacekeeping operations.

Complex peacekeeping has had successes and failures, as illustrated by the two African cases of Namibia and Rwanda. Namibia (formerly South-West Africa), a former German colony, was administered by South Africa following the end of World War I. Over the years, pressure was exerted on South Africa to relinquish control of the territory, but as long as Soviet-backed Cuban troops occupied neighboring Angola, South Africa refused to consider a change, citing security concerns. Finally, in 1988, Cuba and Angola agreed to withdraw Cuban troops as part of a regional peace settlement that included Namibian independence. The UN peacekeeping operation supervised the cease-fire, monitored the withdrawal of South African forces, supervised the civilian police force, secured the repeal of discriminatory legislation, and created conditions for free and fair elections. The UN Transition Assistance Group in Namibia (UNTAG) became the model for UN complex peacekeeping and nation building in Cambodia in the early 1990s and in East Timor in the late 1990s.

But not all UN peacekeeping operations have been successful. Rwanda is an example of a situation where a limited UN peacekeeping force proved to be insufficient and where genocide subsequently escalated as the international community watched and did nothing. Rwanda and neighboring Burundi have seen periodic outbreaks of devastating ethnic violence between Hutus and Tutsis since the 1960s. In the 1990s, intermittent fighting once again broke out. A 1993 peace agreement called for a UN force (the UN Assistance Mission in Rwanda, or UNAMIR) to monitor the cease-fire. Yet less than a year later, large-scale violence erupted following the death of the Rwandan president in a plane crash, with Hutu extremists in the Rwandan military and

TABLE 7.3	COMPLEX/MULTIDIMENSIONAL PEACEKEEPING OPERATIONS, REPRESENTATIVE CASES		
OPERATION	**LOCATION(S)**	**DURATION**	**MAXIMUM STRENGTH**
UNTAC (UN Transition Authority in Cambodia)	Cambodia	July 1991–Sept. 1993	15,900 troops; 3,600 police; 1,500 civilians
UNPROFOR (UN Protection Force)	Former Yugoslavia (Croatia, Bosnia and Herzegovina, Macedonia)	Feb. 1992–Dec. 1995	35,599 troops; 4,632 civilians
UNOSOM I, II (UN Operation in Somalia)	Somalia	April 1992–March 1995	28,000 troops; 2,800 civilians
UNAMIR (UN Assistance Mission in Rwanda)	Rwanda	Oct. 1993–March 1996	5,500 troops; 320 military observers; 90 police
Monusco (UN Organization Stabilization Mission in the Democratic Republic of Congo); Renamed from MONUC in 2010	Democratic Republic of Congo	Nov. 1999–present	16,938 troops; 454 military observers; 1,226 police; 3,470 civilians
UNAMID (African Union/United Nations Hybrid Operation in Darfur)	Darfur	July 2007–present	14,345 troops; 179 military observers; 2,929 police; 3,412 civilians

Source: United Nations.

police slaughtering minority Tutsis, resulting in 750,000 Tutsi deaths in a ten-week period. UNAMIR was not equipped to handle the crisis, and despite its commander's call for more troops, the UN Security Council failed to respond until it was too late. Although UNAMIR did establish a humanitarian protection zone and provided security for relief-supply depots and escorts for aid convoys, peacekeeping failed disastrously.

The UN's response to the crisis in Darfur, Sudan, has also proven problematic. When in 2003 thousands of people fled their villages to escape attacks from the government-based Arab militias (the Janjaweed), the UN system and NGOs responded with humanitarian aid, setting up refugee camps and providing emergency food and health care. The Security Council, however, issued only weak warnings to Sudan since both China and Russia opposed coercive measures, despite evidence that Darfur was witnessing a genocide. Between 2003 and 2008, estimates report that more than 300,000 were killed, 2.5 million were displaced within the country, and another 250,000 fled to neighboring Chad. Eventually, Sudan did accept a small African Union (AU) monitoring force, and in 2007, a stronger UN-AU peacekeeping force, just as the crisis has become more complex, with the number of factions increasing. By 2012, the worst of the mass killings had eased: the situation in Darfur more stabilized; the Sudan-Chad border relatively secure; and 100,000 refugees returned to an increasingly urbanized Darfur. But the Sudanese government continues to be hostile to the UN-AU peacekeeping forces, limiting their theater of operation and their ability to protect civilians. Thus, since 2014, more reports have surfaced about Sudanese troops engaged in more systematic killings and rape. Despite the independence of the Republic of South Sudan in 2011, permanent cessation of violence has come to neither the Darfur region nor the South Sudan, where a civil war between the Dinka and Nuer has led to another major UN operation.

Most problematic has been the UN's complex peacekeeping operation in the Democratic Republic of Congo. Since 1998, "Africa's first world war" has led to an estimated 5.4 million deaths and 1.4 million people displaced between 1998 and 2009, making it the deadliest conflict since World War II. The crisis is multidimensional: internationalized civil war with multiple belligerents; long-standing local conflicts over land, lootable resources, and political power; continuing violence; and humanitarian crises are all occurring within a weak and failing state. Despite being one of the largest UN forces ever mounted, the organization has been unable to craft an overall strategy, since the strategic interests of key member states and organizations diverge. And the logistical and operational difficulties are enormous due to the size of the country, the lack of transportation infrastructure, the inability to protect the civilian population, the lack of preparedness of UN troops, and the difficulty in managing the behavior of the UN troops who, themselves, have been accused of sex crimes and corruption. This operation has clearly tarnished the UN's reputation, leading many to wonder whether it is better to undertake a weak operation or perhaps to refrain from any operation lacking the will and resources for a more robust operation.

The United Nations has undertaken more than 70 peacekeeping missions since 1946. While some have successfully established peace, others, like the ongoing mission in the Democratic Republic of the Congo, are still struggling after a decade to prevent violence and rebuild state capacity.

ENFORCEMENT AND CHAPTER VII

Since the end of the Cold War, the Security Council has intervened in situations deemed threatening to international peace and security, as authorized in Chapter VII of the UN Charter. That provision enables the Security Council to take measures (economic sanctions, direct military force) to prevent or deter threats to international peace or to counter acts of aggression. Previously, the council had invoked such actions only twice because the UN preferred the more limited, traditional peacekeeping route. The disarmament provisions overseen by the U.S. Special Commission for the Disarmament of Iraq and the International Atomic Energy Agency (IAEA), one of the United Nations' specialized agencies, and the economic sanctions against Iraq during the 1990s were enforcement actions under Chapter VII. Indeed, the 1990s were known as the "sanctions decade" for the numerous times targeted sanctions were imposed.

Sanctions have been the major approach used by the UN, the European Union, and the United States to try to prevent Iran from developing nuclear weapons, its program seen as a threat to international peace and security. From 2006 to 2012, UN-based resolutions kept expanding the reach of the sanctions, while tightening monitoring and inspections. These sanctions isolated Iran from the international banking system and progressively targeted individuals, companies, and organizations for asset freezes.

Estimates show that the sanctions resulted in a 25 percent decline in Iran's GDP between 2012 and 2014. But getting agreement on when to impose sanctions, especially multilateral sanctions like those imposed on Iran, can be difficult, as explained in Chapter 5. In this case, those sanctions appeared to be a major factor leading Iran to the negotiating table with the P5+1 and EU in 2014 and 2015, culminating in the Joint Comprehensive Plan of Action announced in July 2015.

Taking military action is another enforcement mechanism. The 1991 Gulf War was an enforcement action under Chapter VII. The Security Council authorized members "to use all necessary means," a mandate that led to direct military action by the multinational coalition under U.S. command. In 2002, the United States went to the Security Council seeking Chapter VII enforcement against Iraq again, claiming that Iraq was in material breach of its obligations under previous UN resolutions. The Security Council was divided, with the United States and Great Britain supporting enforcement and France, Russia, and China opposing the action. When the stalemate solidified, the United States chose not to return to the Security Council to seek formal authorization for the use of force. Thus, the U.S.-led coalition in the 2003 Iraq War was not authorized by the United Nations, leading many to ponder whether the United Nations was still a relevant player in international politics.

PEACEKEEPING AND ENFORCEMENT: SUCCESS OR FAILURE?

What defines success in peacekeeping and enforcement? The end of fighting? The end of a humanitarian crisis? A peace agreement? For how long does the success have to last? Two years, five, or more? Does success include holding free elections? Establishing a viable record of human rights and achieving economic development? And who defines success? The local population, who may define success in being able to return home? The belligerents, who may be negotiating a cease-fire? The individuals who want to return home to the troop-contributing country? Or does the UN secretary-general, who wants to achieve the mission's stated mandates, define the success?

Case studies of specific conflicts tend to show that traditional peacekeeping has been successful. The Cyprus peacekeeping mission averted overt hostilities between Greeks and Turks on the island. For 11 years, the Arab and Israeli states were kept apart, and India-Pakistan hostilities over Kashmir were contained to intermittent intervals, thanks in large part to traditional peacekeeping operations. Unfortunately, in all three situations, traditional peacekeeping alone could make the peace but not keep it.

Scholarly studies using empirical data from multiple cases confirm that multidimensional complex operations have reduced the risk of war by half; the risk of another war occurring within five years ranged from 23 to 43 percent. But enforcement missions have been more associated with unstable peace. There is a disturbing rate of conflict recurrence, estimated at between 20 percent and 56 percent for all civil conflicts.[7]

When those complex operations involved verification of arms, monitoring, or election supervision, they were more successful. But, in the most difficult conflicts, with a long history of violence and multiple belligerents, peacekeeping and peacebuilding have been less successful, as the Democratic Republic of Congo case illustrates.

Because of the Congo quagmire, and more recently in UN operations in Mali, Central African Republic (CAR), and the Republic of South Sudan, significant concerns are being raised about the line between peacekeeping and enforcement. Does the UN's targeting of "an enemy" substantially reduce its impartiality and undermine its legitimacy? In the Congo, the authorization of the Force Intervention Brigade to "neutralize and disarm" a specific militia; the mandate to conduct war against Al Qaeda in the Islamic Maghreb and liberation movements and organized crime in Mali; and authorization in the CAR to stop the ethnic cleansing of Christian groups against Muslims may amount to a "doctrinal change," with multiple ramifications.[8]

The effectiveness of sanctions may be even more difficult to evaluate. Is it primarily sanctions, or something else, that induce compliance (see Chapter 5)? In a globalized economic system, for sanctions to be successful, they clearly need to be multilateral. If there is agreement among the permanent members of the Security Council, multilateral sanctions can be a powerful weapon.

UN REFORM: SUCCESS AND STALEMATE

Faced with escalating demands for the UN to act across a number of issues, confronted by the realization that the UN has rarely lived up to the expectations of all its members, and saddled with structures that no longer reflect the power realities of the international system, the United Nations has been confronted with persistent calls for reform. Although many reforms have been undertaken, the challenges remain critical. Because amending the charter is difficult—requiring ratification of two-thirds of the members, including all five permanent members of the Security Council—the UN has undertaken most reforms without actually amending the charter.

To address management problems—such as those publicized by the 2004 oil-for-food scandal, when UN officials were accused of taking bribes—new financial accountability mechanisms and internal oversight have been established. To address new transnational concerns, structures have been created or reorganized, including the High Commissioner for Human Rights in 1997 and the Counter-Terrorism Committee in 2001, to help countries become more effective in addressing terrorism. To manage peacekeeping operations more efficiently, the Department of Peacekeeping Operations has been expanded; a Department of Field Support has been organized to address financial, logistical, and information issues; military staff has been added from the troop-contributing countries; and rapid deployment teams have been organized. Since 2006, the Peacebuilding Commission had addressed post-conflict recovery issues, including monitoring economic stabilization, building government capacity, and coordinating economic-development activities by meeting with the heads of UN programs and agencies, including the World Bank, the International Monetary Fund, and the World Trade Organization.

Security Council reform remains the persistent reform issue critical to the legitimacy of the Security Council's role in enforcement. The five permanent members of the council, the victors of World War II who possess veto power over substantive issues, are an anachronism. Europe is overrepresented; China is the only emerging economy and the only Asian member; both Germany and Japan contribute more financially to the organization than the four permanent members other than the United States do. Virtually all agree that membership should be increased. But agreement ends there. What other countries should be admitted? Germany, Japan, and/or Italy? India, Pakistan, South Africa, and/or Nigeria from the developing world? Argentina or Brazil? Should the new members have the veto? Should the differentiation between permanent and nonpermanent membership be maintained? Contending proposals continue to be discussed and debated, but no agreement has been reached. As President Barack Obama has stated, the UN is both "flawed and indispensible."[9]

A COMPLEX NETWORK OF IGOS

The UN's perception as indispensable likely is attributable to the work of the 19 specialized agencies formally affiliated with the United Nations. Each organization reflects functionalist thinking, dedicated to specialized areas of activity that individual states cannot manage alone. Public health and disease do not respect national borders; neither do weather systems. Such phenomena require the monitoring of specialized expertise across states. Mail and telecommunications move across national borders; marine transport and airplanes fly between states; these areas need technical rules to govern them. Given the importance of these functional activities, it is not surprising that many of the specialized UN agencies actually predate the United Nations itself. The International Telecommunications Union dates from 1865, the Universal Postal Service from 1874, and international sanitary conferences from the middle of the nineteenth century. Others, such as the International Civil Aviation Organization and the International Maritime Organization, date from immediately after World War II.

Other specialized UN agencies and UN programs perform operational activities dedicated to limited tasks, although those tasks may be much more controversial: delivering food to those in need (World Food Programme), settling refugees and internally displaced people (UN High Commissioner for Refugees), or establishing labor standards (International Labour Organization). Many tasks these programs and agencies perform began under the auspices of the League of Nations. These organizations have separate charters, memberships, budgets, and secretariats. Although each reports directly or indirectly to the UN's Economic and Social Council, none can

TABLE 7.4	REPRESENTATIVE INTERNATIONAL AND REGIONAL ORGANIZATIONS	
UN SPECIALIZED AGENCIES	**INDEPENDENT ORGANIZATIONS**	
World Health Organization	Organization of the Petroleum Exporting Countries	
Food and Agriculture Organization	World Trade Organization	
International Labour Organization	Organisation of Islamic Cooperation	
International Atomic Energy Agency	North Atlantic Treaty Organization	
World Bank Group	Arctic Council	
REGIONAL ORGANIZATIONS	**SUBREGIONAL ORGANIZATIONS**	
European Union	European Free Trade Association	
African Union	Economic Community of West African States	
Organization of American States	Mercosur	
League of Arab States	Gulf Cooperation Council	

be instructed by it or by the General Assembly (see Table 7.4). Included under the specialized agencies are the Bretton Woods institutions—the International Monetary Fund and the World Bank—examined in Chapter 9.

The United Nations is not the only important IGO, of course, and numerous other intergovernmental organizations are not affiliated with the United Nations, including the World Trade Organization (Chapter 9) and the Arctic Council (see Behind the Headlines, p. 230–31). These IGOs perform critical functions arising from the need to take on new tasks. And they, like the plethora of regional and subregional organizations, are always changing.

The European Union—Organizing Regionally

Regional organizations also play an increasingly visible role in international relations. But none has been as visible, as strong, or as copied as the **European Union (EU)**.

The idea of a united Europe goes back centuries. Both Immanuel Kant and Jean-Jacques Rousseau presented plans on how to unite Europe.[10] After World War I, idealists dreamed that a united Europe could have forestalled the conflagration. World War II only intensified these sentiments. Hence, after the conclusion of World War II, vigorous debate ensued over the future organization of Europe. On the one hand were the federalists: drawing on the writings of Rousseau, they believed that because sovereign states instigated wars, peace was possible only if states gave up their sovereignty and invested in a higher federal body. States eventually could eliminate military competition, the root cause of war, if they joined with other states, each one surrendering some pieces of sovereignty to a higher unit. Advocates of federalism proposed the European Defense Community, which would have placed the military under community control, thus touching the core of national sovereignty.

On the other hand were the functionalists: their principal proponent, Jean Monnet, believed that the forces of nationalism, in the end, could be undermined by the logic of economic integration. Beginning with the creation of the European Coal and Steel Community (the predecessor of the European Economic Community, or EEC), he proposed cooperative ventures in nonpolitical issue areas. It was anticipated that these ventures would spill over eventually from the economic arena to issues of national security. The federalist European Defense Community was defeated by the French Parliament in 1954, and the functionalists' logic prevailed. No one at the time could have envisioned a union that in 2016 would bring together more than 500 million citizens in 28 countries, many of them able to travel freely with a burgundy EU passport. Nor could they have imagined the union enjoying an economy of more than $17.7 trillion (or 18 percent of the world's GDP), and 19 of its countries using a common currency, the euro.

HISTORICAL EVOLUTION

The impetus for the creation of the European Union grew not only from the devastation of the wartime experience but also from the security threat that remained. Urged on by the United States, an economically strong Europe (made possible by the reduction of trade barriers) knew it would be better equipped to counter the Soviet threat if it integrated. Europe also understood that if the Germans were enmeshed in such agreements, they would pose a lesser threat to other states. Of course, U.S.-based multinational corporations would also benefit from an expanded market. Thus, security threats, economic incentives, and a postwar vision all played a role in the drive of political elites for European integration.[11]

The European Coal and Steel Community, placing French and (West) German coal and steel production under a common "High Authority," was the first step toward realizing this idea. Although Germany was treated as an equal, its key economic sector supporting the arms industry was brought into a community with France, Italy, and

Who Governs the Arctic?

Russia, Canada, the United States, Denmark, Norway, Finland, Iceland, and Sweden joined together in the Arctic Council in 1996. With security and military issues specifically excluded from its mandate, the organization hoped to provide management of functional issues that affect all members. Permanent participants also include representatives of indigenous peoples, including the Saami Council, the Aleut International Association, and the Inuit Circumpolar Council, among others. Consistent with functionalist thinking, working groups agree on monitoring and assessment, flora and fauna, emergency preparedness, environmental protection, and sustainable development. Agreements have been reached on search-and-rescue operations and provisions for containment and cleanup of oil spills. And, in 2015, an agreement was signed regulating commercial fishing in international waters that includes the North Pole.

While a recent headline trumpeted the fact that the "U.S. Takes Helm of Arctic Council, Aims to Focus on Climate Change," politics has intervened.[a] Russia has expressed intense interest in the region, declaring in its 2014 rewritten military doctrine that the Arctic is Russia's top national security priority. Recent conflicts in Crimea and Ukraine have complicated negotiations on other Arctic issues, and boundary conflicts have become more salient as huge amounts of natural gas and petroleum resources become recoverable and economically profitable. Thus, the United States contests Russia's claims that part of the Northern Sea Route north of Siberia is within internal Russian waters. Both Denmark and Canada claim an uninhabited island in the Nares Strait. And several states claim part of the seabed underlying a mountain range under the Arc-

tic Ocean. Hence, given the potential resources and claims at stake, even observer member states like India, South Korea, and China are angling for a more formal role in the Arctic Council. When the United States assumed the chair of the council, its top priority was to address issues connected with climate change and global warming, but those issues are interdependent with, and connected to, all the other issues. The council has the complicated task of sorting them out.

Before the formation of the Arctic Council, no legal regime governed the Arctic. There was legal precedent in Antarctica. In 1961, the signatories to the Antarctic Treaty agreed that the continent should be used for peaceful purposes only—it prohibits bases, fortifications, military maneuvers, or testing of weapons. Scientific research may be pursued even by military authorities, but inspections are conducted to verify the peaceful nature of such activities. Preservation and conservation of living resources is encouraged. Yet absent from the treaty was any basis for "asserting, supporting or denying a claim to territorial sovereignty in Antarctica or create any rights of sovereignty." Since the Arctic, at the time, was only a piece of ice, no comparable legal agreement was deemed necessary.

The 1982 UN Convention on the Law of the Sea Law (UNCLOS) established some key rules that apply to states in proximity to this piece of ice. Territorial sea boundaries extend 12 miles offshore, freedom of navigation is assured, an exclusive economic zone extends up to 200 miles offshore, and continental shelf rights may be extended in some circumstances to 350 miles offshore. Thus, under UNCLOS, each coastal Arctic state is granted control over living and nonliving natural resources (both fish and hydrocarbons) within its exclusive economic zones. The miles of open water north of the five Arctic states' exclusive economic zones are considered high seas and outside national jurisdiction. Where exactly those boundaries are, especially in view of the melting of the ice sheets, is now contentious.

The Arctic Council is not the only IGO addressing polar issues. In 2015, the International Maritime Organization approved the Polar Code affecting navigation in waters 30 degrees of latitude from the North and South Poles. These rules affect discharges of residue from ships affecting mammal and sea life. The Nordic nations have partnerships on sustainable development issues relating to indigenous people in the Nordic Council. And the nonprofit Arctic Circle established in 2013 provides a venue for business groups and other interested parties to discuss Arctic issues.

Neoliberal institutionalists view these developments in the Arctic as a reflection of states choosing to cooperate in an area considered the global commons because it is in the self-interest of each to do so. For the Nordic states and the United States and Canada, such cooperation is long-standing and cooperation on other issues facilitates cooperation on this issue. With an institution, new issues can be brought to the fore, information flow can be improved, and potential conflicts become the subject of discussion.

Realists view recent conflicts over Arctic space as further affirmation of national interests taking priority over the interests of the commons. While realists may emphasize the divergent political interests of various states, radicals might point to the divergent economic interests—multinational energy companies seek access to the Arctic's potentially recoverable and lucrative resources, and that is their number one priority.

Meetings of the Arctic Council include both government delegates like U.S. secretary of state John Kerry, and representatives of indigenous peoples.

FOR CRITICAL ANALYSIS

1. As global climate change progresses, how will it affect issues in the Arctic? Are states likely to face more conflict, or will cooperation increase?

2. In your view, should the Arctic Council give more power to current observer states like India, China, and South Korea? Why or why not?

a. Carol J. Williams, "U.S. Takes Helm of Arctic Council, Aims to Focus on Climate Change," *Los Angeles Times,* April 24, 2015.

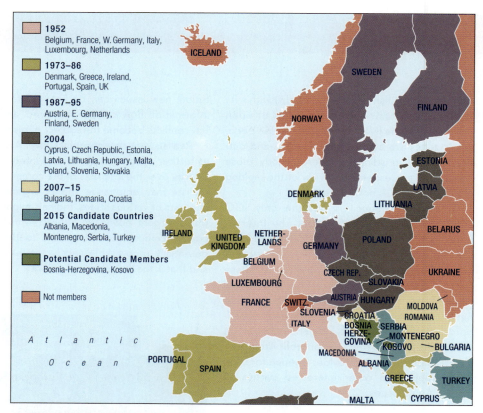

Legend:

1952
Belgium, France, W. Germany, Italy, Luxembourg, Netherlands

1973–86
Denmark, Greece, Ireland, Portugal, Spain, UK

1987–95
Austria, E. Germany, Finland, Sweden

2004
Cyprus, Czech Republic, Estonia, Latvia, Lithuania, Hungary, Malta, Poland, Slovenia, Slovakia

2007–15
Bulgaria, Romania, Croatia

2015 Candidate Countries
Albania, Macedonia, Montenegro, Serbia, Turkey

Potential Candidate Members
Bosnia-Herzegovina, Kosovo

Not members

Expansion of European Union, 1952–2016

the Benelux countries (Belgium, Netherlands, and Luxembourg). This functionalist experiment was so successful in boosting coal and steel production that the member states agreed to expand cooperation under the European Atomic Energy Community and the European Economic Community. Thus, the Treaties of Rome, signed in 1957, committed the six states to create a common market—removing restrictions on internal trade; imposing a common external tariff; reducing barriers to the movement of people, services, and capital; and establishing a common agricultural and transport policy. In 1968, two years ahead of schedule, most of these goals had been achieved.

New policy areas were gradually brought under the umbrella of the community, including health, safety, and consumer standards. As success in these areas waxed and waned, and economic stagnation hindered progress, action was taken. The first initiative was expanding the size of the community in the so-called widening process. The original six members were joined by three new members in 1973. Six successive enlargements followed, resulting in today's 28-state membership (see map, above). These enlargements have increased the organization's influence but complicated its decision making.

In 1986, the most important step was taken in deepening the integration process—the signing of the Single European Act (SEA), which established the goal of completing a single market by the end of 1992. Achieving this goal meant a complicated process of removing the remaining physical, fiscal, and technical barriers to trade; harmonizing national standards of health; varying levels of taxation; and eliminating the barriers to movement of peoples. The process also addressed new environmental and technological issues. Three thousand specific measures were needed to complete the single market.

Even before that process was completed, the Maastricht Treaty was signed in 1992. The European Community became the EU. Members committed themselves not only to an economic union but also to a political one, including the establishment of common foreign and defense policies, a single currency, and a regional central bank. Five years later, in 1997, the Amsterdam Treaty was signed, making some changes to the previous treaties, including granting more power to the European Parliament but generally putting more emphasis on the rights of individuals, citizenship, justice, and home affairs.

The increased power of the EU has not been without its opponents. As several national votes have illustrated, while the European public generally supports the idea of economic and political cooperation, it also fears a diminution of national sovereignty and is reluctant to surrender democratic rights by placing more power in the hands of bureaucrats and other nonelected elites. The debate over the proposed European Constitution brought that issue to a head. Pushed forward by elites, the European Constitution was signed by the heads of state in 2004, only to be rejected in two national referendums a year later. In its stead, in 2007, the Treaty of Lisbon replaced the Constitution. This treaty is another attempt to enhance the efficacy of the EU by creating the offices of president of the European Council and a High Representative for Foreign Affairs who leads a more united policy, and increasing the use of qualified majority voting in place of unanimity. The treaty is also aimed at improving the democratic legitimacy of the EU by increasing the authority of the European Parliament. The treaty became law on December 1, 2009 (see Table 7.5).

STRUCTURE

Table 7.6 provides the basic information about the EU's decision-making bodies, membership, voting, and responsibilities. Just as power has shifted among the UN organs, so, too, has power shifted in the EU. Initially, power resided in the European Commission, which represents the interests of the community as a whole. Although each state is entitled to one member, Commission members, who are not national representatives, must be impartial. Each is responsible for a particular policy area, known as a directorate-general, which, in turn, is divided into directorates that cover specific parts of that policy area. For much of its history, the EU Commission has

TABLE 7.5

SIGNIFICANT EVENTS IN THE DEVELOPMENT OF THE EUROPEAN UNION

YEAR	EVENT
1952	European Coal and Steel Community created by Belgium, France, Italy, Luxembourg, Netherlands, and West Germany.
1954	French National Assembly rejects proposal to form the European Defence Community.
1957	Treaties of Rome establish the European Economic Community (EEC) and the European Atomic Energy Community, comprising same six members.
1968	Customs union is completed; all internal customs, duties, and quotas are removed; and common external tariff is established.
1975	Lomé Convention between the EEC and 46 developing countries in Africa, the Caribbean, and the Pacific signed.
1979	High-level negotiations on European Monetary System are completed; first direct elections to the European Parliament.
1986	Signing of the Single European Act designed to ensure faster decisions; more attention to environmental and technological issues; list of measures compiled that need to be taken before achieving single market in 1992.
1992	Maastricht Treaty completed, committing members to political union, including the establishment of common foreign and defence policies, a single currency, and a regional central bank; name changed to European Union (EU); controversial referendums held in several countries.
1997	Treaty of Amsterdam extends competence on Justice and Home Affairs, defines European citizenship.
1999	Common monetary policy and single currency (the euro) launched.
2002	Euro in circulation.
2004	European Constitution negotiated.
2005	French and Dutch publics reject the proposed constitution; ongoing discussions.
2009	Lisbon Treaty authorizes institutional reforms.
2011–Present	Eurozone crisis.
2014–Present	Refugee crisis.

TABLE 7.6	PRINCIPAL INSTITUTIONS OF THE EUROPEAN UNION (2016)	
INSTITUTION	**MEMBERSHIP AND VOTING**	**RESPONSIBILITIES**
European Commission	28 members; four-year terms, approved by member states; plus 38,000 support staff (Eurocrats)	Initiates proposals; guards treaties; executes policies; responsible for common policies
Council of Ministers	Ministers of member states; unanimity or qualified majority voting depending on issue	Legislates; sets political objectives; coordinates; resolves differences
European Parliament	751 members, elected for five years by voters in member states; allocated by size of population; organized around political parties	Legislates; approves budget and the laws with the Council of Ministers
European Council	Heads of government; Council of Minister president; Commission president; High Representative for Foreign Affairs; summit meetings twice yearly	Defines policy agenda and priorities
European Court of Justice	Judges (28) and advocates-general; appointed by states for six-year terms	Adjudicates disputes over EU treaties; ensures uniform interpretation of EU laws; renders preliminary opinions to states

played this engine role, with the Council of Ministers ratifying, modifying, or vetoing proposals, even though the Commission formally reports to the Council. Increasingly, the Council, with its weighted voting system, has assumed more power; some policy decisions in foreign and security affairs, immigration, and taxation even require unanimous support.

The increasing power of the European Parliament is another change. Since the mid-1980s, the parliament has gained a greater legislative and supervisory role. Because members are elected by universal suffrage, this body has an element of democratic accountability not found in the other institutions. The relatively low turnout in the 2014 parliamentary elections, 43 percent, indicates that the legitimacy of the institutions remains a problem.

So, too, has the power of the European Court of Justice (ECJ) expanded. The court's wide-ranging responsibilities for interpreting and enforcing EU law include ruling on the constitutionality of all EU law; interpreting treaties; providing advisory opinions to national courts; and settling disputes among member states, EU institutions, corporations, and individuals. Member states are obligated to uphold EU law. If they fail to comply, the European Commission may undertake infringement proceedings that may include fines or imposition of sanctions. Virtually every member state has been brought before the court at some point for failing to fulfill its obligations. The 28 judges of the ECJ have heard nearly 15,000 cases and issued more than 7,500 judgments covering such diverse topics as disputes over customs duties, tax discrimination, elimination of nontariff barriers, agricultural subsidies, environmental law, consumer safety issues, and mobility of labor. More than its founders ever envisioned, the ECJ plays a major institutional role in European regionalism and the new legal order that is embodied in EU law. EU law represents the pooled sovereignty that makes the EU very different from other IGOs.

POLICIES AND PROBLEMS

The EU has moved progressively into more policy areas, from trade and agriculture to transport, competition, social policy, monetary policy, the environment, justice, and common foreign and security policy. Among the many controversial issues are the problems of trade, agriculture, and the euro, discussed in Chapter 9. The difficulties forging a common European foreign and security policy, the problem of immigration and asylum, and the disputes over membership are addressed below.

The functionalist aspiration was that the EU eventually would be able to forge a common foreign and security policy. But that has proven difficult. Indeed, on several major foreign policy issues, members of the EU were split. During the 2003 Iraq War, Great Britain, Spain, and Poland strongly supported the United States, sending in their military, while Germany and France opposed the policy, mainly because the UN Security Council had not given authorization. After Russia annexed the Crimea, European Union leaders again were divided over punishing Russia. Great Britain's prime minister David Cameron called for tough new sanctions to punish Russia, while Germany's Angela Merkel argued that Russia would have to send its military into eastern Ukraine to trigger stronger measures. Britain, Sweden, and East European members pushed for halting arms sales to Russia; France opposed the measure. Differences in the countries' positions tend to reflect economic ties. France has military contracts with Russia. Germany and Italy depend on imports of Russian gas and oil; Great Britain does not. While the record of unity on foreign policy is weak, the EU did negotiate in unity at the Iran nuclear negotiations, with the High Representative for Foreign Affairs playing a prominent role.

The difficulties in security policy have had repercussions in other arenas as well. The Amsterdam Treaty elevated the issue of the movement of persons and all border-management issues, including illegal immigration and asylum. But the 2014–16 refugee crisis, as discussed in Chapter 10, has bitterly divided EU members. The ten central European members have refused to accept refugee quotas, with Hungary, Slovakia, and the Czech Republic the most vehemently opposed. Germany and Sweden, two of the most generous countries toward the influx, want burden sharing, with other countries taking in a "fair share." And the terrorist acts committed in Paris in the fall of 2015 by the Islamic State have made every state more cautious about accepting large numbers of refugees without close vetting. The difficulty of arriving at an enforceable consensus on this issue suggests that the other problems, including the euro, will not be easily solved.

Equally problematic are the issues surrounding membership. Should the EU continue to expand its membership by reaching out to the newly democratic states of eastern Europe and the former Soviet Union, or to those in need, such as Iceland? How rapidly can new members come to adhere to the 80,000 pages of EU law and regulations currently in effect? How will the special concessions these countries won affect the functioning of the Union? Although new members such as Croatia, which joined in 2013, have been given extra time to phase in EU law, they also need to wait before receiving full benefits that range from agricultural subsidies to free movement of labor. Can Turkey, the first candidate state with a majority Muslim population, eventually meet the criteria for membership: stable democratic institutions, a functioning market, and a capacity to meet union obligations? Turkey has already made enormous improvements in its human rights record and minority protection, but its admission is still undecided. Will candidate member Serbia be accepted more rapidly? Will the EU governing institutions be able to change?

So far, the debates over the euro, foreign affairs, and membership suggest that the answers will not come easily. And those issues will be magnified when Great Britain votes in a referendum on its future relationship with the EU. Great Britain supports significant restructuring, including giving more power to national parliaments to block EU laws, restructuring social-welfare benefits for migrants, and eliminating the EU goal of an "ever closer union." The British government is carrying on two levels of negotiations: one with its own constituency and another with other member states of the EU.

Other Regional Organizations: The OAS, the AU, and the League of Arab States

For many years, the critical question was whether other regions would follow the European Union model: would the EU be a laboratory for others? Clearly, others would be unlikely to duplicate precisely the circumstances surrounding the development of the European Union, despite the attempts by such subregional groups as the Economic Community of West African States and the Caribbean Community. Most Asian leaders thought the European model inappropriate for that region. Two continent-wide regional organizations, the Organization of American States (OAS) and the African Union (AU), have followed a different path.

At its establishment in 1948, the OAS adopted wide-ranging goals: political (now promotion of democracy), economic (enhancing development, preferential treatment in trade and finance), social (promotion of human rights), and military (collective defense against aggression from outside the region and peaceful settlement of disputes within). No other regional organization includes such a North/South split between a hegemonic member such as the United States (and Canada) on the one hand and a "southern constituency" on the other. With that division, the OAS has adopted many of the foreign policy concerns of the hegemon: the defeat of communist/leftist factions during the Cold War and an emphasis on democracy promotion. In 1985, the OAS resolved to take action should an irregular interruption of democracy occur, declaring that a member should be suspended if its government is overthrown by force. The OAS has acted against coups or countercoups nine times, including, for example, in Haiti (1991–94), Peru (1992), Paraguay (1996, 2000), and Venezuela (1992, 2002). It instituted sanctions against Haiti and, in 2009, suspended Honduras from membership after that country's coup, lifting the suspension in 2011.

The overall record in achieving its political, economic, and social goals is mixed, however, constrained by a dearth of economic resources and political will. Unlike the EU, the OAS has played a limited role in economic development of the region. In recent years, the OAS has devoted more attention to transnational criminal threats like drugs, terrorism, money laundering, and human trafficking.

The African Union replaced the Organization of African Unity in 2002. The latter had been deliberately designed as a weak intergovernmental body at its founding in 1964. The newly independent countries at the time sought to protect their new sovereignty. They were in no mood to permit interference in domestic affairs, and they preferred sovereign equality of all states. Although the illegality of apartheid in South Africa remained a rallying cry of the OAU, members were largely silent on the major economic and development issues of the day.

The newly reconstituted AU is an attempt to give African states an increased ability to respond to the issues of economic globalization and democratization affecting the continent. Thus, the AU is committed to good governance and democratic principles, suspending illegitimate governments, pledging to intervene in the affairs of members should genocide and crimes against humanity occur, and adopting measures to strengthen monitoring under the African Peer Review mechanism. Such promises are predicated on the belief that better governance is key to economic development and necessary for external development funds. However, although the AU did suspend Mauritania from membership (2008), impose sanctions on Togo (2005), reverse a coup in the Comoros Islands (2008), and impose sanctions on and suspend Burkina Faso in 2014 following a coup, it has not taken additional measures. The AU also has not acted in the Zimbabwe crisis, despite its own findings of major human rights abuses in 2007 and evidence of election fraud in 2008.

But beginning in 2007, under UN Security Council authorization, the African Union Mission in Somalia has remained an AU operation with 22,000 uniformed personnel from Burundi, Ethiopia, Kenya, Djibouti, and Uganda, supplemented by NATO airlifts and UN and EU funding. While the force has helped to stabilize the transitional government and expanded the portions of the country under government control, it has suffered thousands of battlefield deaths, the precise figure being unknown. Following through on obligations and enforcement remains a problem not only for the OAS and the AU but also for most regional organizations because funding is limited and commitment waxes and wanes.

An example of varying commitment over time is illustrated by the League of Arab States. Established in 1945, the only action the league undertook for many years was to oppose Israel. Enforcement of the official boycott of Israeli goods and companies since 1948 has been lax and its effects on trade limited. Also, because of internal disputes among members, the league did not coordinate on policy regarding the wars with Israel in 1948, 1967, or 1973, and it stayed silent during the conflict between Israel and Hamas in Gaza in 2014.

Following the initial shock of the Arab Spring of 2011, the Arab League seized the opportunity and took initiative, taking the unprecedented step of suspending Libyan, Syrian, and Yemeni membership, calling for multilateral action, and condemning the respective governments for their use of force. In the case of Syria, the league sent in a multilateral observer mission and called for the peaceful transfer of power. When that mission failed, the league imposed sanctions on Syria, including freezing assets and halting bank transfers. Yet the league has had very little leverage over Syria as the war continues. These activities represent a major change in organizational behavior, as the league interfered in a member state's domestic politics and called for a democratic transition. In 2015, league members agreed in principle to form a joint military force.

In reality, today's more than 240 IGOs seldom act alone. Often they carry out their activities with the cooperation of other international or regional organizations, as well as with nonstate actors, including nongovernmental organizations. Furthermore, they are embedded in a structure of international law.

International Law

International law developed thousands of years before contemporary international organizations. Treaties between city-states and communities can be found in Mesopotamia; the Greeks and the Romans differentiated among different kinds of law, including international law; and during the Middle Ages, the authority of the Catholic Church developed canon law applying to all believers internationally. Yet, international law is largely a product of Western civilization. The man dubbed as the father of international law, the Dutch scholar Hugo Grotius (1583–1645), elucidated a number of fundamental principles that serve as the foundation for modern international law and international organization. For Grotius, all international relations are subject to the rule of law—that is, a law of nations and the law of nature, the latter serving as the ethical basis for the former. Grotian thinking rejects the idea that states can do whatever they wish and that war is the supreme right of states and the hallmark of their sovereignty. Grotius, a classic idealist, believed that states, like people, basically are rational and law abiding, capable of achieving cooperative goals.

The Grotian tradition argues that order in international relations is based on the rule of law. Although Grotius himself was not concerned with an organization for administering this rule of law, many subsequent theorists have seen an organizational structure as a vital component in realizing the principles of international order. The Grotian tradition was challenged by the Westphalian tradition, which established the notion of state sovereignty within a territorial space (see Chapter 2). A persistent tension arose between the Westphalian tradition, with its emphasis on sovereignty, and the Grotian tradition, with its focus on law and order. Did affirmation of state sovereignty mean that international law was irrelevant? Could international law undermine, or even threaten, state sovereignty? Would states join an international body that could challenge or even subvert their own sovereignty?

International Law and Its Functions

International law consists of a body of both rules and norms regulating interactions among states, between states and IGOs, and, in more limited cases, among IGOs, states, and individuals. As in domestic jurisdictions, laws serve several purposes: setting a body of expectations, providing order, protecting the status quo, and legitimating the use of force by a government to maintain order. Law provides a mechanism for settling disputes and protecting states from each other. It serves ethical and moral functions, aiming in most cases to be fair and equitable and delineating what is socially and culturally desirable. These norms demand obedience and compel behavior.

But what is the difference between domestic law and international law? At the domestic level, law operates in a hierarchical system. Established structures exist for both making law (legislatures and executives) and enforcing law (executives and judiciaries). Individuals and groups within the state are bound by law. Because of a general consensus within the state on the particulars of law, compliance with the law is widespread. To maintain order and predictability is in everyone's interest. But if the law is violated, the state authorities can compel violators to judgment and use the instruments of state authority to punish wrongdoers.

In contrast to domestic law, international law operates in a horizontal system. In the international system, authoritative structures are absent. There is no international executive, no international legislature, and no judiciary with compulsory jurisdiction. States themselves are largely the enforcers of law. For realists, that is the fundamental point: the state of anarchy. So can there be international law, given the absence of a sovereign body with enforcement power and the inability to compel compliance with effective physical coercion? The legal scholar Christopher C. Joyner argues yes: binding legal rules are created, states recognize their obligations, and resorting to force is not necessary for the international legal system to operate. After all, "international legal rules obtain their normative force not because any superior power or world government prescribes them but because they have been generally accepted by states as rules of conduct, with the expectation that states will follow suit."[12] To most liberals, international law not only exists but it also has an effect in daily affairs. They cannot imagine a world in which it was absent.

The Sources of International Law

International law, like domestic law, comes from a variety of sources. Virtually all law emerges from custom. Either a hegemon or a group of states solves a problem in a particular way; these habits become ingrained as more states follow the same custom, and eventually, the body codifies the custom into law. For example, Great Britain and later the United States were primarily responsible for developing the law of the sea. As great seafaring powers, each state adopted practices—establishing rights of passage through straits, methods of signaling other ships, conduct during war, and the like—that became the customary law of the sea and were eventually codified into treaties. The laws protecting diplomats and embassies likewise emerged from long-standing customs.

But customary law is limited. For one thing, it often develops slowly since multiple cases are needed to demonstrate the existence of a new customary practice. British naval custom evolved into the law of the sea over several hundred years. Sometimes customs become outmoded. For example, the three-mile territorial extension from shore was established because that was the distance a cannonball could fly. Eventually, law caught up with changes in technology, and states were granted a 12-mile extension of territory into the ocean. But even then, a period of conflict between advocates of the new and supporters of the old often follows. Occasionally, customs change more rapidly. Witness the norms and prohibition against genocide developing in just one generation, as discussed in Chapter 10. Furthermore, not all states participate in the making of customary law, let alone assent to the customs that have become law through European-centered practices. And the fact that customary law is initially uncodified leads to ambiguity in interpretation.

International law also arose from treaties, the dominant source of law today. Treaties, explicitly written agreements among states, number more than 25,000 since 1648 and cover myriad issues. When deciding cases, most judicial bodies look to treaty law first. Treaties are legally binding: only major changes in circumstances give states the right not to follow treaties they have ratified.

Authoritative bodies have also formulated and codified international law. Among these bodies is the UN International Law Commission, composed of prominent international jurists. That commission has codified much customary law: the Law of the Sea (1958), the Vienna Convention of the Law of Treaties (1969), and the Vienna Conventions on Diplomatic Relations (1961) and on Consular Relations (1963). The commission also drafts new conventions for which there is no customary law. For example, laws on product liability and on the succession of states and governments have been formulated in this way and then submitted to states for ratification.

Courts are also sources of international law. Although the International Court of Justice (ICJ) has been responsible for some significant decisions, the ICJ basically is a weak institution for several reasons. First, the court actually hears very few cases; between 1946 and 2015, the ICJ has had 161 contentious cases brought before it and has issued only 26 advisory opinions, although since the end of the Cold War, its caseload has increased. Ever since the small developing country of Nicaragua won a judicial victory over the United States in 1984, developing countries have shown greater trust in the court. Although procedures have changed to speed up the lengthy process, the court's noncompulsory jurisdiction provision still limits its caseload. Both parties must agree to the court's jurisdiction before a case is taken. This stands in stark contrast to domestic courts, which enjoy compulsory jurisdiction. A person accused of a crime is compelled to judgment. No state is compelled to submit to the ICJ.

Second, when cases are heard, they rarely deal with the major controversies of the day, such as the war in Vietnam, the invasion of Afghanistan, or the unraveling of the Soviet Union or of Yugoslavia. Those controversies are generally political and outside the court's reach, although interstate boundary disputes are major issues on the court's

The International Court of Justice occasionally rules on territorial disputes between countries. Here, in 2013, the ICJ ruled that the contested lands surrounding the Temple of Preah Vihear on the border between Cambodia and Thailand fell in Cambodian territory.

agenda. These have included cases concerning maritime disputes, including delimitation of the North Sea continental shelf, fisheries jurisdiction in the Gulf of Maine, and the maritime boundary between Cameroon and Nigeria. The court has also ruled on the legality of nuclear tests, environmental protection, and genocide, among other issues. Advisory cases, though they do not enjoy the force of law, have been on some consequential issues, including the construction of the barrier wall in the occupied Palestinian territories, and Kosovo's unilateral declaration of independence. Both of these were political issues.

Third, only states may initiate proceedings; individuals and nongovernmental actors such as multinational corporations cannot. This stipulation excludes the court from dealing with contemporary disputes involving states and nonstate actors, such as terrorist and paramilitary groups, NGOs, and private corporations.

State sovereignty limits the applicability of ICJ judgments, unlike the judgments of national courts, which use precedents from prior cases to shape future decisions. In reality, however, the ICJ has used many principles from earlier cases to decide later ones, and it draws increasingly from decisions rendered by national and regional courts.

The ICJ may not have been an important source of law except in a few cases, but with greater legalization of international issues, there has been an increase in international courts, and an increased willingness by developing countries to use international judicial bodies, especially since the Cold War's end. These new courts, some 20 permanent judicial institutions and more than 70 other international institutions that exercise judicial or quasi-judicial functions, are part of a group of "new-style" courts.[13] These courts enjoy compulsory jurisdiction and allow nonstate actors to litigate. They not only resolve disputes but also assess state compliance with international law and review the legal validity of state and international legislative and administrative acts. Thus, even without a central enforcer, they have a significant impact.

Likewise, the European Court of Justice of the European Union is a strong court, serving as a significant source of European law. It has a heavy caseload, covering virtually every topic of European integration, and it does have an enforcement mechanism, as discussed earlier in this chapter.

National and even local courts are also sources of international law. Such courts have broad jurisdiction: they may hear cases occurring on their territory in which international law is invoked, or cases involving their own citizens who live elsewhere; they may hear any case to which the principle of universal jurisdiction applies. Under **universal jurisdiction**, states may claim jurisdiction if an individual's conduct is sufficiently heinous to violate the laws of all states. Several states claimed such jurisdiction because of the genocide in World War II and, more recently, for war crimes in Bosnia, Croatia, Rwanda, and Sierra Leone, among others. In the European Union, national and local courts are a vital source of law. A citizen of an EU country can ask a national court to invalidate any provision of domestic law found to be in conflict with provisions of the EU treaty. A citizen can also seek invalidation of a national law found to be in conflict with self-executing provisions of community directives issued by the EU's Council of Ministers. Thus, in the European system, national courts are both essential sources of European community law and enforcers of that law.

Compliance and Enforcement of International Law

Why, then, in the absence of an international executive and an international legislature, and with only a weak international court having limited authority, do states voluntarily comply with international law? We can understand the answer in terms of self-interest. Both realists and liberals agree that international law compliance relies generally on states and their individual self-interest. States benefit from participating in making the rules through treaties, or else they would not participate in making or ratifying them; they can ensure, through participation, that those rules will be compatible with their interests. States benefit from knowing that other states generally respect territory, airspace, and property rights, that international products and people are safe to move across national borders, and that diplomats can safely carry out their duties with international protection. States find it beneficial to "lock in" their commitment, for both domestic and international tranquillity. And, thus, states comply most of the time.

Some liberals might point to the ethical argument that compliance occurs because it is the "right thing to do." States want to do what is right and moral, and international law reflects what is right. States want to be looked on positively, according to liberal thinking. They want to be respected by world public opinion, and they fear being labeled as pariahs and losing face and prestige in the international system.

Who, then, enforces international law in the absence of an international police force or international executive? The answer is that states enforce international law through self-help. Should states choose not to obey international law, other states have instruments at their disposal. Both realists and liberals point to states' reliance on self-help mechanisms, including the tools of diplomacy, economic statecraft, and use of force, as discussed in Chapter 5.

But liberals contend, rightly in many cases, that self-help mechanisms of enforcement by one state alone are apt to be ineffective. A diplomatic protest from an enemy or a weak state is likely to be ignored, although a protest from a major ally or a hegemon may carry weight. Economic boycotts and sanctions by one state will be ineffective as long as the transgressor state has multiple trading partners. And war is both too costly and unlikely to lead to the desired outcome. In most cases, then, for the enforcement mechanism to be effective, several states have to participate. For enforcement to be most effective, all states must join together in collective action against the violator of international law and norms. In the view of liberals, states find protection and solace in collective action and collective security. Hence, multilateral action, often organized through IGOs, is essential.

Sometimes, states do not comply with international law; scholars have conducted several studies to determine why. Is a deliberate decision to not comply always made because compliance was not in the state's national interest? Is it because states know there is no hierarchical enforcement and coercive mechanism? Is it because often times the wording of the law is ambiguous, either purposefully or accidentally? Or is it because some states lack the capacity to comply?[14] Recent empirical studies point to lack of bureaucratic or managerial capacity, especially in new states.

Lack of bureaucratic or state capacity was certainly not the explanation for U.S. noncompliance with the Geneva Conventions, or specifically, the UN Convention Against Torture. Issues arose over the U.S. treatment of individuals captured during the Afghanistan conflict. Were they prisoners of war and therefore protected under the Geneva Conventions? Was torture being committed? Based on the arguments of administration lawyers, the United States contended that since the prisoners did not represent a state, they were "enemy combatants," a category not found in the Geneva Conventions. And prisoners were not being tortured, according to the interpretation of the word "torture." Other states, most legal authorities, and most NGOs disagreed. The International Committee of the Red Cross, Human Rights Watch, and the Geneva Conventions, once known to only a few, have attained international visibility due to their revelations about U.S. actions.

Nongovernmental Organizations

Nonstate actors include nongovernmental organizations (NGOs), transnational networks, foundations, and multinational corporations, though they are not sovereign and do not have the same kinds of power resources as states. This chapter covers NGOs. We will examine multinational corporations in Chapter 9.

NGOs are generally private, voluntary organizations whose members are individuals or associations that come together to achieve a common purpose, often oriented to a public good. They are incredibly diverse entities, ranging from entirely local and/or grassroots organizations to those organized nationally and transnationally. Some are entirely private—that is, their funding comes only from private sources. Others rely partially on government funds or aid in kind. Some are open to mass membership; others are closed-member groups or federations. These differences have led to an alphabet soup of acronyms specifying types of NGOs. These include GONGOs (government-organized NGOs), BINGOs (business and industry NGOs), DONGOs (donor-organized NGOs), and ONGOs (operational NGOs), to name a few.

The number of NGOs has grown dramatically. The *Yearbook of International Organizations (2013–2014)* identifies 8,500 NGOs with an international dimension, and exclusively national NGOs number in the millions. Their exponential growth can be explained by the global spread of democracy, which provides an opening for NGO inputs; the explosion of UN-sponsored global conferences in the 1990s, where NGOs took on new tasks; and the electronic communication revolution, which enables NGOs to communicate and network both with each other and with their constituencies, providing a more forceful voice in the international-policy arena.

The Growth of NGO Power and Influence

Although NGOs are not new actors in international politics, they are growing in importance.[15] In Chapter 10, we discuss one of the earliest NGO-initiated efforts at transnational organization dedicated to the abolition of slavery. These NGOs took the first steps in the 1800s by defining the practice as inhumane and unjust, but they were not strong enough to accomplish international abolition. NGOs organizing on behalf of peace and noncoercive methods of dispute settlement also appeared during the 1800s, as did the International Committee of the Red Cross, which advocated for humanitarian treatment for wounded soldiers, and international labor unions fighting for better working conditions. During the first half of the twentieth century, these same groups were instrumental in lobbying for a "league of nations" and the International Labour Organization, and subsequently, in supporting the establishment of the United Nations and the related agencies protecting different groups of people, including refugees (UN High Commissioner for Refugees) and women and children (UNICEF), among others.

During the 1970s, as the number of NGOs grew, various groups formed networks and coalitions, and by the 1990s, these NGOs were able to mobilize the mass public effectively and influence international relations. A number of factors explain the remarkable resurgence of NGO activity and their increased power as actors in international politics. First, the issues NGOs have seized on have been increasingly viewed as interdependent, or transnational; states cannot solve these issues alone, and their solutions require transnational and intergovernmental cooperation. Airline hijackings during the 1970s; acid rain pollution and ocean dumping during the 1970s and 1980s; and global warming, land mines, and the AIDS epidemic during the 1990s are examples of issues that require international action and that are "ripe" for NGO activity. Some have been increasingly viewed as human security issues, an argument many NGOs have promoted.

Second, global conferences became a key venue for international activity beginning in the 1970s, each designed to address one of the transnational issues—the environment (1972, 1992, 2012), population (1974, 1984), women (1975, 1985, 1995), and food (1974, 1996, 2002). A pattern emerged when NGOs began to organize separate but parallel conferences on the same issues. These create opportunities for NGO representatives not only to network with each other and form coalitions on specific issues but also to lobby governments and international bureaucrats. In some cases, those linkages between the governmental and nongovernmental conferees enhance the power of the latter.

Third, the end of the Cold War and the expansion of democracy in the former communist world and developing countries have provided an unprecedented political opening for NGOs into parts of the world previously untouched by NGO activity.

Finally, the communications revolution also partly explains the newly prominent role of NGOs. First fax technology, and then the Internet, e-mail, Facebook, and Twitter have each enabled NGOs to communicate with core constituencies, build coalitions with other like-minded groups, and generate mass support. They can disseminate information rapidly, recruit new members, launch publicity campaigns, and encourage individuals to participate in ways unavailable two decades before. NGOs have benefited from these changes and have been able to capitalize on them to increase their own power.

Functions and Roles of NGOs

NGOs perform a variety of functions and roles in international relations. They advocate specific policies and offer alternative channels of political participation, as Amnesty International has done through its letter-writing campaigns on behalf of victims of human rights violations. They mobilize mass publics, as Greenpeace did in

By taking purposeful and public actions, NGOs can direct media attention to their cause, which in turn can result in pressure on politicians to change policy. Here, Greenpeace activists highlight the environmental degradation of palm oil production in Indonesia.

saving whales (through international laws limiting whaling) and in forcing the labeling of "green" (non-environmentally damaging) products in Europe and Canada. They distribute critical assistance in disaster relief and to refugees, as Catholic Relief Services and Oxfam have done in Somalia, Rwanda, Sudan, Haiti, and Democratic Republic of Congo. And Médecins Sans Frontières (Doctors Without Borders) has played a major role in addressing the HIV/AIDS epidemic and 2014 Ebola outbreak in Liberia and Sierra Leone, as well as helping to rebuild health infrastructure in conflict areas. NGOs are the principal monitors of human rights norms and environmental regulations, and they provide warnings of violations, as Human Rights Watch has done in China, Latin America, and elsewhere.

NGOs are also the primary actors at the grassroots level in mobilizing individuals to act. For example, during the 1990 meeting to revise the 1987 Montreal Protocol on Substances that Deplete the Ozone Layer, NGOs criticized the UN Environment Program secretary-general, Mostafa Tolba, for not advocating more stringent regulations on ozone-destroying chemicals. Friends of the Earth International, Greenpeace International, and the Natural Resources Defense Council held press conferences and circulated brochures to the public, media, and officials complaining of the weak regulations. The precise strategy of each group varied. Friends of the Earth approached the matter analytically, whereas Greenpeace staged a drama to show the effects of environmental degradation. But the intent of each was the same—to focus citizen action on strengthening the Montreal Protocol and, in more recent years, to focus on promoting climate change initiatives. By publicizing inadequacies, NGOs force discussion both within states and among states in international forums.

Nowhere has the impact of NGOs been felt more strongly than at the 1992 UN Conference on the Environment and Development (UNCED) in Rio de Janeiro. NGOs played key roles in both the preparatory conferences and the Rio conference itself, adding representation and openness (or transparency) to the process. They made statements from the floor; they drafted informational materials; they scrutinized working drafts of UN documents; they spoke up to support or oppose specific phrasing. The UNCED also provided extensive opportunities for NGO networking. Among the more than 400 accredited environmental organizations were not only traditional, large, well-financed NGOs, such as the World Wildlife Fund, but also those working on specific issues and those with grassroots origins in developing countries, many of which were poorly financed and had had few previous transnational linkages.

The persistence of the NGOs paid off. Agenda 21, the official document produced by the conference, recognized the unique capabilities of NGOs and recommended their participation at all levels, from policy formulation and decision making to implementation. What began as a parallel informal process of participation within the UN system evolved into a more formal role, which was replicated in other international conferences. But subsequent conferences have been disappointing, as illustrated by the Rio+20 conference in 2012: Rio+20 offered "no targets, no timelines, or specific objectives. It [did] not prioritize any areas or express a particular sense of urgency."[16] Both states and NGOs failed to generate enough consensus to move the agenda ahead.

NGOs play unique roles at the national level. In a few unusual cases, NGOs take the place of states, either performing services that an inept or corrupt government is not providing or stepping in for a failed state. Bangladesh hosts the largest NGO sector in the world, a response in part to that government's failure and the failure of the private for-profit sector to provide for the poor. Thus, NGOs have assumed responsibility in education, health, agriculture, and microcredit, originally all government functions. Other NGOs work to change various countries' public institutions, as illustrated by the Muslim Brotherhood in Egypt. Dating back to 1928, the brotherhood had a long, confrontational relationship with the Egyptian government until its political party successfully contested in the 2011 parliamentary elections and assumed the presidency. A year later, it was overthrown during mass protests, its leaders killed or imprisoned, its assets seized. The once NGO, then political party, was now pronounced a terrorist organization. Egypt is not the only government to crack down on NGOs. Russia and other states of the former Soviet Union, including Uzbekistan and Tajikistan, have limited the actions of international NGOs. Kenya is one of the latest.

NGOs: A View from Kenya

NGOs have been a vibrant sector in Kenya, particularly since the explosion of the numbers of NGOs during the 1990s. From more than 800 NGOs present in the mid-1990s, an estimated 4,200 existed a decade later. Kenya is known for having a liberal economic landscape, and NGOs, along with a strong and vibrant private sector, play a critical role. Moreover, the presence of NGOs represents a long tradition of philanthropy and volunteerism in that country.

Their dramatic increase in numbers and enhanced activities in virtually all sectors of social, economic, and political life in Kenya can be attributed to the shifts in international donors' economic development strategies. The World Bank and UN development agencies, as well as the northern bilateral donors like the U.S. Agency for International Development and Canada's Canadian International Development Agency, have increasingly turned to NGOs to implement policies at the grassroots level as the Kenyan state capacity to provide services and programs has diminished. It is estimated that the NGO sector brings more than $1.2 billion of external resources into Kenya, implementing projects in education, population and health, welfare, the environment, and, more recently, in gender empowerment. One of its own, Wangari Maathai, won the Nobel Peace Prize for her founding of a prominent NGO, Green Belt Movement, which focuses on environmental sustainability.

Both the government and NGOs have organized to try to make the charitable sector more responsible. Under the Non-Governmental Organizations Coordination Act of 1990, the government has tried to make the work in this sector more complimentary to its own, through regulation, capacity building, and advisory activities. For example, the board established by the act offers workshops to educate NGOs on government development policies. In turn, NGOs are required to submit annual reports, including audits on financing, human resources, projects undertaken, and governance. And the National Council of NGOs, whose members are NGOs themselves, facilitates coordination and advocacy among its thousands of members.

The liberal open environment in which the NGOs have traditionally operated has been stung by Kenyan government efforts to enhance security by targeting NGOs. These changes were precipitated by the 1998 twin bombings of the U.S. embassies in Kenya and Tanzania and the 2013 attack by al-Shabaab on the Westgate shopping center in Nairobi, an attack that killed 67 people. One of the actions taken in response, and justified in the name of national security, was to close more than 500 NGOs, including more than 15 NGOs that allegedly raised funds for terrorism. The NGO Coordination Board has deregistered these organizations for noncompliance with the law, accusing them of using their charitable status as a front for raising cash for terrorism. Of the organizations closed for failing to provide financial audits were orphanages, health NGOs, and Christian organizations.

Kenya is not the only East African country that has initiated anti-NGO policies. In 2009,

Nobel Prize winner Wangari Maathai planting trees in Kenya with volunteers of the Green Belt Movement.

Ethiopia tightened its regulations, passing a bill that any NGO receiving more than 10 percent of its funding from abroad was banned from activities concerning democracy, human rights, conflict resolution, or criminal justice. In 2015, Uganda's parliament debated a bill designed to, in the words of the country's internal affairs minister, provide greater transparency and accountability. This bill would strongly regulate NGO activity and allow the country to punish NGOs aggressively for noncompliance. At the same time, the minister admitted that NGOs provided key services in health, education, and water. Even the failing state of the Republic of South Sudan debated a law in the same year that no more than 20 percent of NGO staff could be foreigners.

Despite the many positive tasks undertaken by NGOs in developing countries, they are increasingly under intense scrutiny for their financial ties to foreign donors who may support policies different than those that the host state supports.

FOR CRITICAL ANALYSIS

1. NGOs are not independent actors; they exist by consent of host states. Explain.

2. How can NGOs use soft power? What other kinds of power do they have at their disposal?

3. How might realists and radicals justify a state's opposition to foreign-financed NGOs?

4. To constructivists, NGOs may be the conduit for transmitting or socializing norms. How might they do so in states such as Kenya and in the newly independent states of the former Soviet Union?

Yet NGOs seldom work alone. The communications revolution has linked NGOs with each other, formally and informally. Increasingly, NGOs are developing regional and global networks through linkages with other NGOs. These networks and coalitions create multilevel linkages among different organizations; each organization retains its separate organizational character and membership, but through the linkages, the organizations enhance each other's power. These networks have learned from each other, just as constructivists would have predicted. Environmentalists and women's groups have studied human rights campaigns for guidance in building international norms. Environmentalists seeking protection of spaces for indigenous peoples also increasingly use the language of human rights.

We usually associate NGOs with humanitarian and environmental groups working for a greater social, economic, or political good, but NGOs may also be formed for malevolent purposes—the Mafia, international drug cartels, and even Al Qaeda being prominent examples. The Mafia, traditionally based in Italy but with networks in Russia, Eastern Europe, and the Americas, is engaged in numerous illegal business practices, including money laundering, tax evasion, and fraud. International drug cartels, many with origins in Colombia, function with suppliers in such far-reaching states as Peru, Venezuela, Afghanistan, and Myanmar, while maintaining links with middlemen in Nigeria, Mexico, Guinea, and the Caribbean to deliver illegal drugs to North America and Europe (see Chapter 11). What these NGOs share is a loose series of networks across national boundaries that move illicit goods and services in international trade. Their leadership is dispersed and their targets ever changing, making their activities particularly difficult to contain.

Al Qaeda, too, is such an NGO—decentralized, dispersed, with individuals deeply committed to a cause, even at the price of death, and able and willing to take initiatives independent of a central authority. The organization has changed and expanded its goals over time, which has enabled it to recruit members willing to die for diverse causes. Osama bin Laden had forged broad links and alliances with various groups until his death in 2011. Like all NGOs, Al Qaeda has benefited from new communications technologies, using the Internet to collect information and train individuals and using e-mail to transfer funds and communicate messages, all virtually untrackable. Opponents of Al Qaeda and these other NGOs are waging a different battle: a war on organized crime, a war on drugs, and a war against terror.

The Power of NGOs

What gives NGOs the ability to play such diverse roles in the international system? What are their sources of power? Most NGOs rely on soft power, meaning credible information, expertise, and the moral authority that attracts the attention and admiration of governments and the public. This means that NGOs have resources such as flexibility to move staff rapidly depending on need, independent donor bases, and links with grassroots groups that enable them to operate in different areas of the world. This very flexibility enables them to create networks to increase their power potential, banding together with other like-minded NGOs and forming coalitions to promote their respective agendas. New communication technologies have facilitated this networking and coalition-building source of NGO power.

NGOs have distinct advantages over individuals, states, and intergovernmental organizations. They are usually politically independent from any sovereign state, so they can make and execute international policy more rapidly and directly, and with less risk to national sensitivities, than IGOs can. They can participate at all levels, from policy formation and decision making to implementation, if they choose. Yet they can also influence state behavior by initiating formal, legally binding action; pressuring authorities to impose sanctions; carrying out independent investigations; and linking issues together in ways that force some measure of compliance. Thus, NGOs are versatile and increasingly powerful actors, especially if they are able to network with other NGOs.

The International Campaign to Ban Landmines (ICBL) is an outstanding example of the power of an NGO network. Beginning in 1992, nine NGOs were eventually joined by more than 1,000 other NGOs and local groups (such as the Landmine Survivors Network, Vietnam Veterans of America Foundation, and Human Rights Watch) in more than 60 countries. They used electronic media to craft the message that land mines are a human rights issue and have devastating effects on innocent civilians. Not only was the issue framed to resonate with a large constituency but the leaders also formed a network. What became known as the Ottawa Process was bolstered by the death in 1997 of Diana, Princess of Wales, one of its vocal supporters. Jody Williams, a founder of the ICBL and winner of the 1997 Nobel Peace Prize for her efforts, coordinated the process, and Canada's foreign minister pushed the issue, hosted the conference, and provided financial support. The Convention to Ban Landmines was ratified in 1999. But not every attempt to forge such networks has been successful, as illustrated by the failure of the movement to curb small arm sales—NGOs have limits.

The Limits of NGOs

NGOs often lack material forms of power. Except for some of the malevolent groups, they do not have military or police forces as governments do, and thus, they cannot command obedience through physical means.

Most NGOs have very limited economic resources because they do not collect taxes, as states do. Thus, the competition for funding is fierce; NGOs that share the same concerns—for example, human rights organizations—often compete for the same donors. They have a continuous need to raise money, leading some NGOs to find new causes to widen their donor base. To expand their resources, NGOs increasingly rely on governments, an alternative that comes with its own set of limitations. If NGOs choose to accept state assistance, then their neutrality and legitimacy are potentially compromised. They may be forced continually to report "success" to renew their financing, even though success may be difficult to prove or even be an inaccurate description of reality. In short, NGOs are locked in a competitive scramble for resources.[17]

Do most NGOs succeed in accomplishing their goals? This question is difficult to evaluate, because the NGO community is itself diverse; it has no single agenda, and NGOs often work at cross-purposes, just as states do. Groups can be found on almost any side of every issue, resulting in countervailing pressures. In a world that is increasingly viewed as democratic, are NGOs appropriate? To whom are NGOs accountable if their leaders are not elected? How do they maintain transparency when they have no publicly accountable mechanism? Do NGOs reflect only liberal values?

Incomplete or unsatisfactory answers to these questions have led scholars to suggest that NGOs may be more like other actors and less altruistic than supposed—self-interested, self-aggrandizing, concerned with their own narrow agendas, hierarchical rather than democratic, more worried about financial gains than achieving progressive social purposes. This suggestion has led some critics to refer to NGOs as "wild cards" and "benign parasites."[18] Some case studies have found that NGOs' actions have led to unintended and detrimental consequences. In refugee camps in Rwanda run by NGOs such as Doctors Without Borders and the International Rescue Committee, the leaders of the genocide were actually being protected. When NGOs are active in war zones, are they becoming more like "force multipliers," expanding the capabilities of the military?[19] The roles NGOs play and the legitimacy they may or may not have depend in part on how they answer critical questions of accountability and transparency. Whether accountable and transparent or not, NGOs increasingly work with states, IGOs, and regional organizations.

Analyzing IGOs, International Law, and NGOs

The Realist View

Realists are skeptical about intergovernmental organizations, international law, and nongovernmental organizations, though they do not completely discount their place. Recall that realists see anarchy in the international system, wherein each state must act in its own self-interest and rely on self-help mechanisms. While it may be useful to use IGOs, states prefer not to do so out of distrust and skepticism. Realists doubt that collective action is effective and believe states will refuse to rely on the collectivity for the protection of their individual national interests. Realists can point to both the failures of the League of Nations and the weaknesses of the UN. They can legitimately point to the Cold War era, when the Security Council proved impotent in addressing the conflict between the United States and the Soviet Union. And the failure in 2003 of the United Nations to enforce Security Council resolutions against Iraq and its ineffectiveness in addressing the Syrian crisis are more reminders of the organization's weakness and supposed irrelevance.

To realists, international law may create some order, but they remind us that states can opt out of following international law, and if the more powerful do so, other states can do little about it.

In the state-centric world of the realists, NGOs are generally not on the radar screen at all. After all, most NGOs exist at the pleasure of states; states grant them legal authority, and states can take away that authority. To realists, NGOs are not independent actors.

The Radical View

Radicals in the Marxist tradition are also very skeptical about IGOs, international law, and many NGOs, albeit for very different reasons from those of the realists. Radicals see contemporary international law and organization as the product of a specific time and historical process. Emerging from Western capitalist state experiences, international law and organization serve the interests of the dominant capitalist classes. The actions by the United Nations following the Iraqi invasion of Kuwait in 1990, including a series of resolutions condemning Iraq and imposing sanctions on that country, were designed to support the position of the West, most notably the interests of the hegemonic United States and its capitalist friends in the international petroleum industry. To radicals, the UN-imposed sanctions provide an excellent example of hegemonic interests injuring the marginalized—Iraqi men, women, and children striving to eke out meager livings. Radicals also view NATO's actions in Kosovo as another example of hegemonic power harming the poor and the unprotected.

According to radicals, international law is biased against the interests of socialist states, the weak, and the unrepresented. For example, international legal principles, such as the sanctity of national geographic boundaries, were developed during the colonial period to reinforce the claims of the powerful. Attempts to alter such boundaries are, according to international law, wrong, even though the boundaries themselves may be unfair or unjust. Radicals are quick to point out these injustices and support policies that overturn the traditional order.

To most radicals, the lack of representativeness and the lack of accountability of NGOs are key issues. NGOs are largely based in the North and are dominated by members of the same elite that run the state and international organizations. They

| | THEORY IN BRIEF | | CONTENDING PERSPECTIVES ON IGOS, INTERNATIONAL LAW, AND NGOS | |

	LIBERALISM/ NEOLIBERAL INSTITUTIONALISM	REALISM / NEOREALISM	RADICALISM/ DEPENDENCY THEORY	CONSTRUCTIVISM
IGOs	Important independent actors for collective action; neoliberals see as forums	Skeptical of their ability to engage in collective action	Serve interests of powerful states; biased against weak states and the unrepresented	Both IGOs and NGOs can be norm entrepreneurs and socialize actors, which may change state behavior
INTERNATIONAL LAW	Key source of order in the international system; states comply because law ensures order	Acknowledges that international law creates some order, but stresses that states comply only when it is in their self-interest; states prefer self-help	Skeptical because origins of law are in Western capitalist tradition; international law only reaffirms claims of the powerful	Law reflects changing norms; shapes state expectations and behavior
NGOs	Increasingly key actors that represent different interests and facilitate collective action	Not independent actors; power belongs to states; any NGO power is derived from states	Represent dominant economic interests; unlikely to affect major political or economic change	Both IGOs and NGOs may lead to dysfunctional behavior, but may also represent new ideas and norms

see NGOs as falling under the exigencies of the capitalist economic system and as captive to those dominant interests. According to radicals, only a few NGOs have been able to break out of this mold and develop networks enabling mass participation designed to change the fundamental rules of the game. After all, radicals desire major political and economic change in favor of an international order that distributes economic resources and political power more equitably. Contemporary international law and organizations are not the agents of such change.

The Constructivist View

Constructivists place critical importance on institutions and norms.[20] Both IGOs and NGOs can be norm entrepreneurs that socialize and teach states new norms. Those norms may change state preferences, which in turn may influence state behavior. Constructivists acknowledge that new international institutions have been developing at a rapid rate and are taking on more tasks. But, as Michael Barnett and Martha Finnemore argue in *Rules for the World*, international organizations may produce conflict, acting in ways that are contrary to the interests of their constituency. They may pursue particularistic goals, creating a bureaucratic culture that tolerates inefficiency and lack of accountability. International institutions may become dysfunctional, serving the interests of international bureaucrats.[21]

Law plays a key role in constructivist thinking, not because law establishes precise rules, but because it reflects changing norms. Thus, both adherents of customary international law and constructivists see the critical role such norms play in providing shared expectations about appropriate state behavior. Over time, those norms are internalized by states themselves, they change state preferences, and they shape behavior. A number of key norms are of particular interest to constructivists, for example, multilateralism, the practice of joining with others in making decisions. Occurring both outside and within formal organizations, participants learn the value of this norm. Through multilateral participation, states have also learned other norms, including the emerging prohibition against the use of nuclear weapons, the norm of humanitarian intervention, and the increasing attention to human rights norms. Yet just as these norms and ideas affect state behavior, states also participate in shaping them. All of these norms are discussed in coming chapters. Thus, with the steady expansion of international institutions and international law and influence, constructivists have an active research agenda.

In Sum: Do IGOs, International Law, and NGOs Make a Difference?

Liberals and constructivists are convinced that IGOs, international law, and NGOs do matter in international politics, albeit with different emphases. To liberals, these organizations and international law do not replace states as the primary actors in international politics, although, in a few cases, they may be moving in that direction. They do provide alternative venues, whether intergovernmental or private, for states themselves to engage in collective action and for individuals to join with other like-minded individuals in pursuit of their goals. They permit old issues to be seen in new ways, and they provide both a venue for discussing new transnational issues and an arena for action. To constructivists, the emphasis is on how changing norms and institutions shape issues. Realists and radicals remain skeptical. And in the state-centered world of security, examined in the next chapter, that skepticism is warranted.

Discussion Questions

1. Everyone agrees that reform of the UN Security Council is necessary. What proposal for reform would you support? Why?

2. Do international organizations, NGOs, and international law threaten state sovereignty, or do they not? Substantiate your position.

3. Find two recent newspaper articles that give examples of states complying with international law and two other articles about states that are failing to comply. What explains the difference between the two sets of cases?

4. What problems arise when NGOs take over the tasks of states?

Key Terms

collective good (p. 212)

complex peacekeeping (p. 221)

European Union (EU) (p. 228)

General Assembly (p. 218)

Group of 77 (p. 218)

Group of 20 (p. 218)

human security (p. 216)

intergovernmental organizations (IGOs) (p. 213)

international regimes (p. 213)

peacebuilding (p. 221)

Security Council (p. 216)

traditional peacekeeping (p. 220)

universal jurisdiction (p. 244)

08

Relatives of civilians killed in a U.S. drone strike in Yemen mourn the loss of their family members. The United States has consistently denied deliberately targeting civilians in its drone strikes, but has acknowledged mistakes. Here it may be that one or more "high-value targets" was killed, but can we say the value of these deaths exceeds the harm likely to result from the resentment generated by the collateral death and injury to bystanders?

WAR AND STRIFE

I n October 2011, the U.S. Central Intelligence Agency identified and killed an American-born Al Qaeda leader named Anwar al-Awlaki. Two weeks later, al-Awlaki's 16-year-old son Abdulrahman al-Awlaki was also killed in a drone strike in Yemen. The killing of the younger al-Awlaki, a U.S. citizen, by executive order and without due process, marked a turning point in the use of armed drones in the war on terror. It may have set a dangerous precedent, especially as other states and possibly terrorists gain drone technology. Iran, for example, is close to being able to deploy its own long-range drones, and it has declared many of its former citizens, as well as some foreigners, guilty of crimes punishable by death. How might Britain respond should Iran use an armed drone to execute an Iranian citizen living in Oxford, England, especially if collateral damage would result?

Among the many issues engaging the actors in international relations, war is generally viewed as the oldest, the most prevalent, and, in the long term, the most important. Wars—in particular major wars between states—have been the focus of historians for centuries. Major works on war include Thucydides's *History of the Peloponnesian War* (431 BC) and Carl von Clausewitz's *On War* (1832). World War I and its aftermath (the founding of the League of Nations) led American diplomatic historians and legal scholars to create a new discipline called international relations. Since that time, prominent scholars in this field have addressed many of the critical and vexing issues surrounding war—its causes, its conduct, its consequences, its prevention, and even the possibility of its elimination. This attention to war and security is clearly warranted. Of all human values, physical security—security from violence, starvation, and the elements—comes first. All other human values that are crucially important to the quality of our lives—good government, economic development, a clean environment—presuppose a minimal level of physical security. Consider the difficulties the United States and its NATO allies have had in Afghanistan in trying to revive the economy, establish legal authority, and guarantee human rights, especially for women. In the absence of a minimum level of physical security (in this case, security from violence), these important goals have proven elusive.

Yet history suggests that a minimum level of security has not always been attainable. Historians have recorded approximately 14,500 armed struggles over time, with about 3.5 billion people dying either as a direct or an indirect result. Since 1816, between 224 and 559 international and intrastate wars have occurred, depending on how war is defined. As more and more states became industrialized, interstate war became more lethal and less controllable, and it engaged ever-wider segments of belligerents' societies. This new reality of interstate war culminated in two horrific convulsions: World Wars I (1914–18) and II (1939–45).

However, following the world wars and the Korean War (1950–53), and perhaps due to their destructiveness and potential to escalate to nuclear war, both the frequency and intensity of interstate war began a slow decline. The average number of interstate wars has shrunk every year: more than six in the 1950s and less than one in the 2000s. That is important since those wars often kill more people on average than civil wars. From the 1950s to the end of the Cold War, the total number of armed conflicts of all kinds has increased three times over, but most are low-intensity wars with a modest number of fatalities. Since the beginning of the 1990s to 2015, overall conflict numbers have declined by about 40 percent, while conflicts that have killed at least 1,000 persons a year have declined by more than half.[1] Yet, because our contemporary understanding of war remains incomplete, many international relations scholars worry that this trend could reverse itself. War therefore remains perhaps the most compelling issue in world politics, and theorists continue to analyze why international and intrastate conflicts occur.

- Define war and identify the different categories of war.

- Explain how the levels of analysis help us explain the causes of wars.

- Describe the key characteristics of conventional and unconventional warfare.

- Highlight the circumstances under which a war can be considered "just."

- Explain how realists and liberals differ in their approaches to managing insecurity.

What Is War?

International relations scholars maintain a healthy debate about how to define war, over what counts and does not count as a war. Over time, however, three features have emerged as agreed-upon standards. First, a war demands organized, deliberate violence by an identifiable political authority. Riots are often lethal, but they are not considered "war" because, by definition, a riot is neither deliberate nor organized. Second, wars are relatively more lethal than other forms of organized violence. Pogroms, bombings, and massacres are deliberate and organized but generally not sufficiently lethal to count as war. Currently, most international relations scholars accept that at least 1,000 deaths in a calendar year are needed in order for an event to count as a war. Third, and finally, for an event to count as a war, both sides must have some real capacity to harm each other, although that capacity need not be equal on both sides. We do not count genocides, massacres, terrorist attacks, and pogroms as wars because in a genocide, for example, only one side has any real capacity to kill, while the other side is effectively defenseless.

In sum, **war** is an organized and deliberate political act by an established political authority that must cause 1,000 or more deaths in a 12-month period and require at least two actors capable of harming each other.

These definitional issues are not simply academic. They have real-world consequences. An important case in point was the 1994 Rwandan genocide, in which over

750,000 men, women, and children were murdered in just four months. Had the international community named this violence properly as a genocide, the pressure to intervene militarily to halt it might have been greater, since in a genocide the side being murdered would have no chance of winning. However, the violence was instead characterized as a renewal of *civil war*, raising the legitimate question of whether international intervention should occur in Rwanda's internal affairs. So what began as a genocide—the organized mass murder of defenseless civilians sharing a particular characteristic—by government-supported extremists soon *escalated* to a civil war in which a former combatant, the Rwandan Patriotic Front, remobilized, rearmed, and attacked the government, systematically destroying the forces of the extremists and halting the genocide by forcing the government and its surviving *genocidaires* to flee.

Categorizing Wars

International relations scholars have developed many classification schemes to categorize wars. At the broadest level, we distinguish between wars that take place between sovereign states (**interstate war**) and wars that take place within states (**intrastate war**). Beyond this distinction, we tend to divide wars into total and limited (based on their aims and the proportion of resources dedicated to achieving these aims), and finally, the character of war fought, such as conventional or unconventional.

INTERSTATE AND INTRASTATE WAR

Since the advent of the state system in the years following the conclusion of the Thirty Years' War (1618–48), the state as a form of political association has proven ideal at organizing and directing the resources necessary for waging war. As Charles Tilly famously put it, "War made the state and the state made war."[2]

As a result, wars between states have captured the lion's share of attention from international relations theorists and scholars of war. Theorists are interested for two reasons. First, by definition, states have recognizable leaders and locations. When we say "France," we understand we are speaking about a government that controls a specific territory that others recognize as France. Therefore, states make good subjects for analysis and comparison. Second, states have formal militaries—some tiny and not much more than police forces; others vast and capable of projecting force across the surface of the globe and even into outer space. These militaries, and the state's capacity to marshal resources in support of them, make states very formidable adversaries. Thus, interstate wars are often characterized by relatively rapid loss of life and destruction of property. At the end of World War II, the world's states faced the prospect that a future interstate war might not only destroy them as such, but also, in a nuclear exchange, might destroy all human life.

Yet over time, the number of interstate wars has declined. After World War II, they dropped dramatically. The primary ones since 1980 have been the Iran-Iraq War (1980–88), the Ethiopia-Eritrea War (1999–2000), and the Russo-Georgia War (2008). Interstate wars have been increasingly replaced by intrastate war—violence whose origins lay within states, sometimes supported by neighboring or distant states—as the most common type of war. The First Indochina War (1946–54), the Greek civil war (1944–49), the Malayan Emergency (1948–60), and the Korean War (1950–53) were all examples of the new pattern.

Intrastate wars—civil wars—have decreased over time as well, but not nearly as rapidly as interstate wars have. Intrastate wars include those between a faction and a government fighting over control of territory (Boko Haram in Nigeria); establishment of a government for control of a failed or fragile state (Somalia or Liberia); ethno-nationalist movements seeking greater autonomy or secession (Chechens in Russia, Kachins in Myanmar); or wars between ethnic, clan, or religious groups for control of the state (Rwanda, South Sudan, Burundi, Yemen). The American and Russian civil wars stand as prime examples.

More recent civil wars include the civil war in Ukraine (2014) and those that followed the Arab Spring of 2011, especially those in Libya (February–October 2011) and Syria (June 2012–present). Both qualify as wars because well over 1,000 battle deaths resulted from conflict between an incumbent government and rebels, and because each side had military capacity, though government forces had the greater capacity, to harm the other. Both followed a similar course: government forces harshly repressed peaceful protests by mostly young people, which then led to an escalation of protests and international condemnation. That escalation led to a more harsh government response, with protests becoming both more widespread and more violent. After evidence of government murders, rapes, torture, and massacres, there were calls for international intervention. In Libya's case, both the incumbent government and its international supporters were caught by surprise, and limited military intervention by NATO on behalf of Libyan rebels accelerated the collapse of the incumbent government. In Syria, the incumbent government was better prepared, and more importantly, its allies (especially the Russian Federation) were prepared to offer military and diplomatic support. Finally, as if a civil war between rebel groups and Syria's government were not complicated enough, in 2013, the Islamic State began making territorial gains in eastern Syria. In 2015, the United States and its allies attempted to halt the advance of the IS into Syria by means of targeted air strikes, but these appear to have failed. In addition, as we learned in Chapter 4, the Russian Federation began targeted air strikes. However, these were aimed not at the IS but at opposition rebel groups in western Syria. Russia has said it cannot prevent "volunteer" ground forces from intervening, either. So currently, the civil war in Syria—which has also provoked a flood of desperate refugees seeking safe haven in Europe and neighboring countries—ranks among the world's most complicated and deadly civil wars.

Although some civil wars remain contained within state boundaries, civil wars are increasingly international—as we can see in Libya, Syria, and the Democratic Republic of Congo. The repercussions of civil wars are felt across borders, as refugees from civil conflicts flow into neighboring states and funds are transferred out of the country. States, groups, and individuals from outside the warring country become involved by funding particular groups, selling weapons to various factions, and giving diplomatic support to one group over another. Thus, although the issues over which belligerents fight are often local, once started, most civil wars quickly become internationalized.

TOTAL AND LIMITED WAR

Total wars tend to be armed conflicts involving massive loss of life and widespread destruction, usually with many participants, including multiple major powers. These wars are fought for high stakes: one or more belligerents seek to conquer and occupy enemy territory or to take over the government of an opponent and/or control an opponent's economic resources. Total wars are often fought over conflicts of ideas (communism versus capitalism; democracy versus authoritarianism) or religion (Catholic versus Protestant; Shiite versus Sunni Muslim; Hinduism versus Islam). In total war, decision makers marshal all available national resources—conscripted labor; indiscriminate weapons of warfare; economic, diplomatic, and natural resources—to force the unconditional surrender of their opponents. Importantly, even when opposing military forces are the primary target, in total war, opposing civilian casualties are accepted or even deliberately sought in pursuit of victory. The Thirty Years' War (1618–48), the longest total war ever fought, involved numerous great powers (England, France, Habsburg Austria, the Netherlands, Spain, and Sweden) and resulted in over 2 million battlefield deaths. The War of the Spanish Succession (1701–14) pitted most of the same powers against each other again and ended in over 1 million deaths. At the beginning of the nineteenth century, the Napoleonic Wars (1799–1815) resulted in over 2.5 million deaths in battle. In each war, civilian loss of life either equaled or dramatically exceeded battlefield deaths. For much of the seventeenth and eighteenth centuries, wars between and among great powers were common.

World War I and World War II were critical watersheds in the history of total war. The same great powers fought in both: Britain, France, Austria-Hungary, Germany, Japan, Russia/the Soviet Union, and the United States. But just as industrialization revolutionized agriculture and transport, it also revolutionized the killing power of states. Industrialization demanded workers, who moved from rural areas to concentrate in cities. The scope of the battlefield, once restricted to the physical areas over which soldiers fought, after World War I, soon expanded to include armaments and munitions workers, and eventually, even agricultural workers. Although total war had always imagined the mobilization of an entire society for war, industrialization—especially after World War I—made this ideal a reality. Casualties were horrific: most belligerents lost 4 to 5 percent of their pre-war population in World War I, and doubled their losses in World War II. After World War II, total war had become far too blunt and costly an instrument to enter into deliberately.

This increased devastation and cost may in part explain why since the end of World War II, interstate wars, particularly large-scale wars between or among the great powers, have become less frequent; the number of countries participating in such wars has fallen, and the duration of such wars has shortened. These factors have led several political scientists to speculate on whether or not extremely costly total wars like World Wars I and II are events of the past.

For example, John Mueller argues that such wars have become obsolete. Among the reasons he cites are the memory of the devastation World War II caused, the great powers' postwar satisfaction with the status quo, and the recognition that any war among the great powers, nuclear or not, could escalate to a level that would become too costly.[3] More recent scholarship has argued other causes of peace. Joshua Goldstein, for example, argues that a long decline in interstate war (including total war) is due to increasingly effective UN peacekeeping operations. Robert Jervis has offered an

From the perspective of the International Security Assistance Force, the war in Afghanistan was a limited one. From an Afghan point of view, however, the violence has been total and is certain to affect the country's recovery, security, and development for decades to come.

explanation embedded in the notion of a security community that combines thinking drawn from the best insights of realism (for example, NATO) and liberalism (for example, the UN, IMF, and GATT). In the security community composed of the United States, Western Europe, and Japan, Jervis argues, war is unthinkable.[4]

Realists explain the security community as arising from American economic, and especially military, hegemony. Since the end of World War II, the United States has had the world's largest economy, and in part because of that status, U.S. military spending on average has exceeded the combined spending of the next seven countries. Militarily, then, the United States has had no peer. That military dominance is magnified by the effect of nuclear weapons and by the continued recognition that an all-out, general war would be unwinnable and hence irrational, just as Mueller posits. In short, there was no World War III because the United States, in combination with support from its allies, was both willing and able to use its economic and military power to prevent it.

The liberal explanation has two parts. First, liberals argue that had it not been for the misguided economic policies of the 1920s, the economic depression that spread across the globe in the 1930s—and created fertile ground for extreme ideas and leaders such as Benito Mussolini—would never have happened. War would have either been entirely prevented, or at least contained. This notion explains the postwar liberal emphasis on trade openness and transparency, as represented by the IMF and GATT (now the WTO). Second, liberals argue that the steady proliferation of democratic states has expanded the European zone of peace globally. Not only are democracies unlikely to go to war with each other, but that effect also becomes magnified if they are economically interdependent and if they share membership in international organizations, as Chapter 5 explains.

Constructivists level an equally powerful set of propositions to explain the decline of interstate and total war since World War II. They posit that it is not change in the material conditions (American hegemony or economic interdependency) that matters, but rather change in the attitudes of individuals who are increasingly "socialized into attitudes, beliefs, and values that are conducive to peace."[5] As Robert Jervis—a self-identified realist who has made increasing use of constructivist arguments in his own theory—explains, "The destructiveness of war, the benefits of peace, and the changes in values interact and reinforce each other."[6] This explanation is effectively psychologist Steven Pinker's argument in *The Better Angels of Our Nature* (see Chapter 1). He argues that mutually reinforcing trends (the disciplinary power of states, the democratic peace, the empowerment of women) have led to a condition in which not just war but *all* interhuman violence has declined. Jervis and Pinker thus share the constructivist view that norms—such as the nature of security and the range of means permissible to pursue it—shift over time, creating new hazards and new opportunities.[7]

In contrast to total war, **limited wars** are often initiated or fought over less-than-critical issues (at least for one belligerent), and as such, tend to involve less-than-total national resources. Thus, for Austria-Hungary, World War I began as a limited war in which it sought to punish Serbia for its presumed support of the assassination of Archduke Franz Ferdinand. Yet by the end of August 1914, what had begun as a limited war had escalated into a total war, involving goals as ambitious as the complete conquest of adversaries (marked by their unconditional surrender) and the use of all national means available.

The Korean War (1950–53) is an excellent example of limited war. In the Korean War, U.S. and then UN forces were mobilized to prevent the outright conquest of South Korea by the North (the Democratic People's Republic of Korea, or DPRK). This goal made the war a limited one from the UN perspective. However, because both sides tended to view material outcomes as representative of the validity of their respective ideologies, the war between the communist North and the non-communist UN contained powerful incentives for escalation.

After the stunning success of General Douglas MacArthur's Inchon landing, for example, the DPRK's military collapsed, and its remnants were forced to retreat all the way to the country's frontier with the newly communist People's Republic of China (PRC). MacArthur and many in the United States and U.S. government viewed this victory as an opportunity to unify Korea under non-communist rule—a much more ambitious goal. So what began as war for limited aims on the UN side briefly escalated into a war of complete conquest. Then, in the winter of 1950, China intervened. The war could now only be thought of as "limited" in comparison to the real possibility that it might escalate to include the Soviet Union as well. U.S. president Harry S. Truman and his advisers decided to settle for a return to the status quo of 1950. China's leadership grudgingly agreed, effectively leaving the Korean peninsula divided. Although the United States possessed nuclear weapons and could have mobilized and deployed many additional combat forces, the fear of escalation to another—perhaps nuclear—world war led to an armistice instead of an outright victory.

In limited wars, because the aims of war are relatively modest, belligerents do not unleash all available armaments. In these two cases, conventional weapons of warfare were used—tanks, foot soldiers, aircraft, and missiles. But, despite their availability, nuclear weapons were never deployed.

There is no better illustration of limited war than the Arab-Israeli disputes from 1973 onward. Israel has fought six interstate wars against its neighbors—Egypt, Syria, Jordan, and Lebanon—and struggled against repeated Palestinian uprisings in the West Bank and Gaza. Since the conclusion of the 1973 Yom Kippur War (limited from the Egyptian perspective, total from the Israeli perspective), none of the opposing states have sought the complete destruction of their foes, and the conflict has blown hot and cold. Both sides have employed some of the techniques described later. With the increased destructiveness of modern warfare, limited war has become the most common option for states contemplating violence against other states.

While the number of interstate wars has declined precipitously, limited wars, and particularly civil wars that are total in nature, have not. Between 1846 and 1918, approximately 50 civil wars were fought. In contrast, in the decade following the end of the Cold War (1990–2000), the total number of civil wars was about 195. Although the number of civil wars has declined modestly between 2000 and 2015, two-thirds of all conflicts since World War II have been civil wars.

Civil wars share several characteristics. They often last a long time, even decades, with periods of fighting punctuated by periods of relative calm. Whereas the goals may seem relatively limited by the standards of major interstate wars—secession, group autonomy—the human costs are often high because in the context of the rivalry between incumbent governments and rebels, these stakes are often perceived to be total. Both combatants and civilians are killed and maimed; food supplies are interrupted; diseases spread as health systems suffer; money is diverted from constructive economic development to purchasing armaments; and generations of people grow up knowing only war.

Most total civil wars are now concentrated on the African continent. Ethiopia's war with two of its regions (Ogaden and Eritrea) lasted decades, as did the civil wars between the north and south in both Sudan and Chad. Liberia and Sierra Leone, likewise, have also been sites of civil conflict where various factions, guerrilla groups, paramilitary groups, and mercenaries have fought for control. The Democratic Republic of the Congo is another example of a civil war, but one that has become internationalized. In 1996, an internal rebellion broke out against the long-time dictator Mobutu Sese Seko. Very quickly, both Uganda, and Rwanda supported the rebellion, with the latter interested in eliminating Hutu militias that had fled Rwanda during the 1994 genocide. After Mobutu was ousted and replaced with a new leader, Laurent Kabila, a wider war erupted two years later. Powerful Congolese leaders and ethnic groups, supported by Rwanda and Uganda, opposed the new government. Angola and Zimbabwe supported Kabila's government, as did Chad and Eritrea. Over 5 million people were killed between 1998 and 2012, despite the efforts of a large UN peacekeeping force.

In virtually all these cases, the civil wars have been intensified by the availability of small arms, the recruitment of child soldiers, and financing from illicit trade in narcotics, diamonds, and oil. In all these cases, too, human rights abuses and humanitarian crises have captured media attention but rarely the political commitment or financial resources of the international community.

The Causes of War

In an analysis of any war—Vietnam, Angola, Cambodia, World War II, or the Franco-Prussian War, to take but a few examples—we will find more than one cause for the outbreak of violence. This multiplicity of explanations can seem overwhelming. How can we study the causes of war systematically, when the causes often seem idiosyncratic? To identify patterns and variables that might explain not just one war but war more generally, international relations scholars have found it useful to consider causes of war at the three levels of analysis Kenneth Waltz identified in *Man, the State, and War*[8]—the individual, the state, and the international system.

The Individual: Realist and Liberal Interpretations

Both the characteristics of individual leaders and the general attributes of people (discussed in Chapter 6) have been blamed for war. Some individual leaders are aggressive and bellicose; they use their leadership positions to further their causes. Others may be nonconfrontational by nature, perhaps avoiding commitments that might deter aggression, making war more likely. Thus, according to some realists and liberals, war occurs because of the personal characteristics of major leaders. It is impossible, however, to prove the general veracity of this position. Would past wars have occurred had different leaders—perhaps more pacifistic ones—been in power? What about wars that nearly happened but did not happen, due to the intervention of a charismatic leader? As we can see, the impact of individual leaders on war is difficult to generalize. We can identify some wars in which individuals played a crucial role, but if we are looking for a general explanation—one that might guide us across different periods or cultures—explanations based on individual characteristics or human nature will prove insufficient.

If the innate character flaws of individuals do not cause war, is it possible that leaders, like all humans, are subject to misperceptions that might lead to war? According to liberals, misperceptions by leaders—seeing aggressiveness where it may not be intended, attributing the actions of one person to a group—can indeed lead to the outbreak of war. Unlike individual characteristics such as charisma or the possession of extreme views, we can generalize about the human tendency toward misperception. Several types of misperceptions may lead to war. One of the most common is exaggerating the adversary's hostility, believing that it is more hostile than it may actually be or that it has greater military or economic capability than it actually has. This tendency may lead a state to build up its own arms or seek new allies, which its actual or potential rivals, in turn, may view as hostile acts. Misperceptions thus spiral, leading to costly arms races, new alliances, and potentially to war. The events leading up to World War I are often viewed as such a conflict spiral.

Beyond the characteristics of individual leaders, perhaps factors particular to the masses lead to the outbreak of war. Some realist thinkers—Saint Augustine and Reinhold Niebuhr, for example—take this position. Augustine wrote that every act is an act of self-preservation on the part of individuals. For Niebuhr, the link goes even deeper; the origins of war reside in the depths of the human psyche.[9] This approach is compatible with that of sociobiologists who study animal behavior. Virtually all species are equipped to use violence to ensure survival; it is biologically innate. Yet human beings are an infinitely more complex species than other animal species. If true, these presumptions lead to two possible alternative assessments. For pessimists, if war is the product of innate human characteristics or human nature, then there can be no reprieve. For optimists, even if war or aggression is innate, the only hope of eliminating war resides in changing social institutions, socializing or educating individuals out of destructive tendencies.

Of course, war does not happen constantly; it remains an *unusual* event. Thus, characteristics inherent in all individuals cannot be the only cause of war. Nor can the explanation be that human nature, indeed, has fundamentally changed, because wars still occur. Most experiments aimed at changing mass human behavior have failed miserably, and there is no visible proof that basic attitudes affecting insecurity, greed, aggression, and identity have been altered sufficiently to preclude war.

Thus, the individual level of analysis, though clearly implicated in some wars, is unlikely to stand as a good cause of war *in general*. Individuals, after all, do not make war. Only groups of political actors (for example, clans, tribes, nations, organizations, states, and alliances) make war.

State and Society: Liberal and Radical Explanations

A second level of analysis suggests that war occurs because of the internal characteristics of states. States vary in size, geography, ethnic homogeneity, and economic and government type. The question, then, is how do the characteristics of different states affect the possibility of war? Do some state characteristics have a higher correlation with the propensity to go to war than others do?

State and societal explanations for war are among the oldest. Plato, for example, posited that war is less likely where the population is cohesive and enjoys a moderate level of prosperity. Since the population would be able to thwart an attack, an enemy is likely to refrain from attacking it. Many thinkers during the Enlightenment, including Immanuel Kant, believed that war was more likely in aristocratic states.

Drawing on the Kantian position, liberals posit that republican regimes (those with representative governments and separation of powers) are least likely to wage war against each other; that is the basic position of the theory of the democratic peace introduced in Chapter 5. Democratic leaders hear from multiple voices, including the public, which tend to restrain decision makers, decrease the likelihood of misperceptions, and therefore lessen the chance of war. They also offer citizens who have grievances a chance to redress these complaints by nonviolent means. The ability to redress aids stability and prosperity. Ordinary citizens may be hesitant to support going to war because they themselves will bear the costs of war—paying with their lives (in the case of soldiers), the lives of friends and family, and taxes. Democratic states are thus especially unlikely to go to war with each other, because the citizens in each state can trust that the citizens in the other state are as disinclined to go to war as they are. According to liberals, this mitigates the threat that a democratic opponent represents, even one with greater relative power. But by this logic, the corollary is true also: citizens in democratic states tend to magnify the threat of nondemocratic states in which the government is less constrained by the public's will, even when such states appear to have a lesser capacity to fight and win wars. More broadly, democracies engage in war only periodically, and only when the public and their chosen leaders deem it necessary to maintain security.

Other liberal tenets hold that some types of economic systems are more susceptible to war than others are. Liberal states are likely to be states whose citizens enjoy relative wealth. Such societies feel little need to divert the attention of dissatisfied masses to an external conflict; the wealthy masses are largely satisfied with the status quo. And even when they are not satisfied presently, liberal economies are marked by the possibility of upward economic (and social) mobility: in a liberal state, even the poorest person may one day become one of the richest. Liberals argue that such conflicts as do arise can be limited by altering terms of trade, or by other concessions short of outright war. Furthermore, war interrupts trade, blocks profits, and causes inflation. Thus, liberal capitalist states are more likely to avoid war and promote peace.

But not every theorist sees the liberal state as benign and peace loving. Indeed, radical theorists offer the most thorough critique of liberalism and its economic counterpart, capitalism. They argue that capitalist, liberal modes of production inevitably lead to competition for economic dominance and political leadership between the two major social classes within the state—the bourgeoisie (middle classes) and the proletariat (workers). This struggle leads to conflict, both internal and external, because the state, dominated by an entrenched bourgeoisie, is driven to accelerate the engine of capitalism at the expense of the proletariat and for the economic preservation of the bourgeoisie.

This view attributes conflict and war to the internal dynamics of capitalist economic systems, which stagnate and slowly collapse in the absence of external stimulation. Three different explanations have been offered for why they must turn outward. First, the British economist John A. Hobson claimed that the internal demand for goods would slow down in capitalist countries, leading to pressures for imperialist expansion to find external markets to sustain economic growth. Second, according to Lenin and other Marxists, the problem is not underdemand but declining rates of return on capital. Capitalist states expand outward to find new markets; expanding markets increase the rates of return on capital investment. Third, Lenin and many later-twentieth-century radicals point to the need for raw materials to sustain capitalist growth; states require external suppliers to obtain such resources. So, according to the radical view, capitalist states inevitably expand, but radical theorists disagree among themselves about precisely why expansion occurs.

Although radical interpretations may help explain colonialism and imperialism, the link to war is more tenuous. One possible link is that capitalist states spend not only on consumer goods but also on the military, leading inevitably to arms races and eventually war. Another link points to leaders who resort to external conflict to divert public attention from domestic economic crises, corruption, or scandal. Such a conflict is called a **diversionary war** and is likely to provide internal cohesion, at least in the short run. For example, considerable evidence supports the notion that the Argentinian military used the Falkland/Malvinas Islands conflict in 1982 to rally the population around the flag and draw attention away from the country's economic contraction. Still another link suggests that the masses may push a ruling elite toward war. This view is clearly at odds with the liberal belief that the masses are basically peace loving. Adherents of this view point to the Spanish-American War of 1898 as an example in which the U.S. public, supported or inflamed by stilted reports in the new mass print media, pushed a reluctant McKinley administration into aggressive action. And many in the United States saw a clear three-way link between the terrorist attacks of September 11, 2001, the support for the attacks from Afghanistan's ruling Taliban, and Iraq's Saddam Hussein. As a result, both the Afghanistan and Iraq wars—the first, beginning in October 2001, named Operation Enduring Freedom; and the second, beginning in March 2003, named Operation Iraqi Freedom—enjoyed widespread popular support early on.

Those who argue that contests over the nature of a state's government are a basic cause of war have identified another explanation for the outbreak of some wars. Many civil wars have been fought over which groups, ideologies, and leaders should control a state's government. The United States' own civil war (1861–65) between the North and the South; Russia's civil war (1917–19) between liberal and socialist forces; China's civil war (1927–49) between nationalist and communist forces; and the civil wars in Vietnam, Korea, the Sudan, and Chad—each pitting north against south—are stark illustrations. In many of these cases, the struggle among competing economic systems and among groups vying for scarce resources within a state illustrates further the proposition that internal state dynamics are responsible for the outbreak of war. The American Civil War was fought not only over the institution of slavery and the question of which region should control policy, but also over the Southerners' belief that the government inequitably and unfairly allocated economic resources. China's civil war pitted a wealthy, landed elite supportive of the nationalist cause against an exploited peasantry struggling, often unsuccessfully, for survival. The intermittent Sudanese civil war pitted an economically depressed south against a northern government that poured economic resources into the region of the capital.

Yet, in virtually every case cited here, neither characteristics of the state nor state structures sufficiently explain the causes of war and peace. This is why neorealists such as Kenneth N. Waltz argue that we need to look for explanations at the level of the international system.

The International System: Realist and Radical Interpretations

If one key issue or argument distinguishes realists from their liberal and radical critics, it is that for realists, war is a natural, and hence an inevitable feature of interstate politics. War is as tragic and unpreventable as hurricanes and earthquakes. In advancing this argument, contemporary realists tend to focus on a single description of the international system as *anarchic*. Such an anarchic system is often compared with a "state of nature," after philosopher Thomas Hobbes's characterization, in which humans live without a recognized authority, and must therefore manage their own safety by themselves. In his most famous book, *Leviathan*, Hobbes argued that whenever men live without a common power that keeps them all in fear, they are in a condition of war: "every man against every man." This state leads to constant fear and uncertainty. By extension, because states in the international system do not recognize any authority above them, the international system is equivalent to a state of war, and Hobbes's description of that state perfectly characterizes the realist view. War, Hobbes continued, was not the same thing as battle or constant fighting. Instead, it was any tract of time in which war remained *possible*. Hobbes likened this situation to the relationship between climate and weather: it may not rain every day, but in some climates, rain is much more common than in others. Essentially, Hobbes concluded that so long as a single strong man (or state) was not more powerful than all the others combined, human beings would be forced to live in a climate of war.[10]

According to realists then, war breaks out in the interstate system *because nothing in the interstate system prevents it*. So long as there is anarchy, there will be war. War, in such a system, might even appear to be the best course of action that a given state can take. After all, states must protect themselves. A state's security is ensured only by its accumulating military and economic power. But one state's accumulation makes other states less secure, according to the logic of the security dilemma.

An anarchic system may have few rules about how to decide among states' contending claims. One of the major categories of contested claims is territory. For almost all of the previous century, the Arab-Israeli dispute rested on competing territorial claims to Palestine; in the Horn of Africa, the territorial aspirations of the Somali people remain disputed; in the Andes, Ecuador and Peru have competing territorial claims; and in the South China Sea, Japan, China, Taiwan, the Philippines, and Vietnam are all struggling over conflicting claims to offshore islands such as the Spratly Islands. According to the international-system-level explanation, these disputes tend to escalate to violence because there are no authoritative and legitimized arbiters of claims. John Mearsheimer calls this the "911 problem—absence of central authority, to which a threatened state can turn for help."[11]

Neither is there an effective arbiter of competing claims to self-determination. Who decides whether Tibetan, Chechen, Catalonians, or Quebecois claims for self-determination are legitimate? Who decides whether Kurdish claims against Turkey and Iraq are worthy of consideration? Without an internationally legitimized arbiter, authority is relegated to the states themselves, with the most powerful ones often becoming the decisive, interested arbiters.

In addition, several realist variants attribute war to other facets of the anarchic nature of the international system. One system-level explanation for war, advanced in the work of Kenneth Organski, is power transition theory. To Organski and his intellectual heirs, it is not only mismatched material power that tempts states to war, but also *anticipation* of shifts in the relative balance of power. War occurs because more power leads to expectations of more influence, wealth, and security. Thus, a power transition can cause war in one of two patterns. In one pattern, a challenger might launch a war to solidify its position: according to some power transition theorists, the Franco-Prussian War (1870–71), the Russo-Japanese War (1904–1905), and the two world wars (1914–18 and 1939–45, respectively) all share this pattern.[12] In a second pattern, the hegemon might launch a preventive war to keep a rising challenger down. Some have argued that current international pressure on Iran to halt its nuclear development fits this pattern. Either way, according to the theory, power transitions increase the likelihood of war.

A variant derived from power transition theory is that uneven rates of economic development cause war. George Modelski and William R. Thompson find regular cycles of power transition starting in 1494. They observe 100-year cycles between hegemonic wars—wars that fundamentally alter the structure of the international system. A hegemonic war creates a new hegemonic power; its power waxes and wanes, a struggle follows, and a new hegemon assumes dominance. The cycle begins again.[13]

Radicals also believe the international system structure is responsible for war. Dominant capitalist states within the international system need to expand economically, waging war with developing regions over control of natural resources and labor markets, or with other capitalist states over control of developing regions. According to radicals, the dynamic of expansion inherent in the international capitalist system is the major cause of wars.

Realist and radical reliance on one level of explanation may be overly simplistic, however. Because the international system framework exists all the time, to explain why wars occur at some times but not others, we also need to consider the other levels

| TABLE 8.1 | CAUSES OF WAR BY LEVEL OF ANALYSIS | |

LEVEL	CAUSE OF WAR
Individual ("First Image")	Aggressive leaders Misperceptions by leaders Human nature
State/Society ("Second Image")	Capitalist states, according to radicals Nonliberal/authoritarian states, according to liberals Domestic politics, scapegoating Struggle between groups for economic resources Ethnonational challengers
International System ("Third Image")	Anarchy (self-help) Power transitions (rising challengers or declining great powers) Aggressiveness of the international capitalist class (imperialism)

of analysis.[14] In actuality, most wars are caused by interactions between various factors at different levels of analysis. (See Table 8.1.)

How Wars Are Fought

Along with the aims of war, and the quality and quantity of resources states and other actors devote to winning, international relations theorists also argue there are important differences in *how* wars are fought. One important distinction is whether a war is fought conventionally or unconventionally. As the terms themselves denote, whether a war is conventional or unconventional depends a great deal on norms: what counts as conventional in 200 BCE might be considered dramatically unconventional today. In this chapter we introduce contemporary understandings—widely shared—of what counts as conventional or unconventional.

Conventional War

Throughout most of human history, wars were fought by people—almost invariably male—who were specially chosen, trained, and authorized to attack or defend against their counterparts in other political communities. Almost all societies have also considered some groups off limits, at least where killing is concerned. The tools of war reflected this restriction. Weapons of choice have ranged from swords and shields to bows, guns, and cannons; to industrialized armies fielding infantry and riding in tanks; to navies sailing in specialized ships; and to air forces flying fixed-wing aircraft. Such weapons are used to defeat the enemy on a territorial battlefield. The key attribute of conventional weapons is that their destructive effects can be limited in space and time to those who are the legitimate targets of war. Conventional wars are won or lost when the warriors of one group, or their leaders, acknowledge defeat following a clash of arms.

The two world wars challenged the prevalence of conventional war in three ways. World War I saw the first large-scale use of chemical weapons on the battlefield. Near the Flemish (Belgian) town of Ypres, in 1915, German forces unleashed 168 tons of chlorine gas against French positions. French troops suffered 6,000 casualties in just a few minutes as prevailing winds carried the poisonous gas across the fields and into the trenches. But German forces were unable to exploit the four-mile-wide gap in French lines that opened as a result. Many German troops had been wounded or killed in handling the gas or by moving through areas still affected and they were unable to exploit the temporary advantages gained. In addition, the effects of the weapons had proved difficult to restrict to combat. Chemicals leached into the soil and water table, affecting agriculture for months afterward. After the war, winners and losers signed a Geneva Protocol outlawing the use of chemical weapons in war.

World War II added two additional challenges to the prevalence of conventional weapons. First, the advent of strategic bombing led both to the possibility of large-scale harm to noncombatants and to a reexamination of who or what a "noncombatant" actually was. Prior to the war, the simple rule had been that civilians were to be protected from intentional harm. But the belligerents possessed large fleets of ships, armored vehicles, and planes, all of which demanded a constant supply of inputs. Were the civilians who made and supplied these great engines of war to be protected, too? What about the farmers who fed the soldiers, airmen, and sailors? As the war intensified, the dividing line between those who were to be protected from deliberate harm and those who could be legitimately targeted broke down. By the war's end, both sides had taken to using massive air strikes to deliberately target civilians. In March 1945, well before the atomic bombings of Hiroshima and Nagasaki in August, bombers from the U.S. Eighth Air Force targeted Japan's capital, Tokyo, with incendiary bombs. The ensuing flames killed over 100,000 Japanese in a single raid, most of them civilians. World War II also fast-forwarded the development of a nuclear weapon.

Weapons of Mass Destruction

The dropping of atomic bombs on Hiroshima and Nagasaki in 1945 did not have an immediate and dramatic impact on war-fighting capability. Conventional means, to some extent, had already matched the destructiveness of the atomic bomb and its capacity to kill hundreds of thousands without discrimination. Many in the U.S. military, for example, considered atomic weapons simply to be more economical extensions of conventional bombs. But these first steps into the nuclear age—the first and last time nuclear weapons were deliberately used against states in war—had already hinted at a key problem related to their use: the long-lasting effects of radiation. During the Cold War, both the United States and the Soviet Union constructed larger and more lethal weapons, and developed more accurate delivery systems, ballistic missiles, and cruise missiles, each capable of killing the earth's population many times over. Thermonuclear weapons led to the possibility that combatants could not limit the destruction of a nuclear exchange to a target only—nuclear weapons were now hundreds of times more powerful than those dropped on Hiroshima. A nuclear conflict might rapidly escalate into an exchange that could extinguish life on earth, either by radiation from fallout or by altering the climate in a "nuclear winter." This mutual assured destruction (or MAD) led the major antagonists to shelve plans to fight using nuclear weapons. Instead, they fought through proxies, using more conventional weapons (see Chapter 2).

The fact that nuclear weapons have never been employed in war since their use against Japan has prompted two important debates about the political effects of nuclear weapons. First, did nuclear deterrence prevent a third world war and therefore justify the risk and expense the Soviet Union, the United States, Britain, China, and France sustained through their development and deployment of nuclear weapons during the Cold War? Second, if nuclear deterrence causes peace—if the very destructiveness of nuclear weapons makes rational decision makers unlikely to use them or initiate a war that could escalate to their use—could the spread of nuclear weapons to other countries, called **nuclear proliferation**, cause peace? Scott Sagan and Kenneth Waltz debated these issues in the 1980s. They renewed the debate in the beginning of the twenty-first century after India and Pakistan—fierce rivals—had each acquired nuclear capability. Waltz argues that "more may be better," that under certain circumstances (namely, a rational government and a secure retaliatory capacity), the proliferation of nuclear weapons implies an expanding zone of deterrence and a lower risk of interstate war. Sagan strongly disagrees, arguing that the proliferation of nuclear weapons is more likely to lead to a failure in deterrence or an accidental war.[15] Sagan argues that the conditions Waltz cites for nuclear peace-causing are rare, and certainly not present in South Asia.

This debate over the threat the possession of nuclear weapons poses has gained a new salience as the technology to build nuclear weapons has proliferated. The tangled network of the Pakistani official A. Q. Khan, who provided elements of nuclear technology from Europe to Pakistan and then North Korea, has led many to reexamine the stabilizing effect of proliferation. More crucially, nuclear theorists have questioned whether a nuclear-capable Iran would make war in the region more or less likely. If Waltz is right, so long as Iran has a rational government and a number of weapons secure from a preemptive first strike, the risk of major conventional war in the Middle East would be dramatically reduced. If Sagan is right, even if Iran meets these minimal conditions (of which Sagan's argument is skeptical), the Middle East will be in increased danger of a nuclear exchange, an accidental launch or detonation, or perhaps an unauthorized launch. The Iran nuclear deal discussed below attempts to make sure that neither Sagan nor Waltz are correct.

Chemical and biological weapons, together with nuclear weapons, make up the more general category of **weapons of mass destruction (WMD)**. The key factor that separates WMD from conventional weapons is that *by their very nature*, their destructive effects cannot be limited in space and time. This is why they are often called "indiscriminate" weapons, a feature they share with antipersonnel land mines, depleted uranium munitions, and cluster bombs. Chemical and biological weapons have existed for many more years than nuclear weapons have. Although surreptitious testing and use of such weapons have persisted, many technical difficulties in their effective delivery persist. As noted earlier, chemical weapons were actually used on a large scale in World War I, but they proved useless strategically, and instead, only increased the suffering of war. Benito Mussolini's invasion of Ethiopia through Eritrea in 1935 must count as the only recent example of the effective use of chemical weapons in war; the aerial spraying of mustard gas on the mostly barefoot Ethiopian troops caused their rapid defeat. In that case, the Italians faced an adversary who had no possibility to retaliate in kind. In addition, the oily chemical tended to float on water and remained lethal on vegetation and bare ground for weeks. As a result, Fascist Italy's use of mustard gas killed and maimed thousands of Ethiopian noncombatants. For its part, Mussolini's government went to great lengths to hide its violation of the 1923 Geneva Accords' prohibition of the use of chemical weapons, in many cases, actually violating other laws of war to do so; the actions included strafing field hospitals marked with the red cross to eliminate evidence that Italy had used mustard gas. Possibly as a result of these costs, and of the likelihood of soon facing adversaries armed in kind, neither Fascist Italy nor any of the other belligerents used chemical weapons in World War II. Yet evidence suggests the use of chemical weapons by one or both adversaries during both the Iran-Iraq War during the 1980s, and by the Assad government in the current Syrian civil war.

Biological weapons—in particular, mutated strains of formerly common diseases such as plague and smallpox—have always suffered from the possibility that not only an adversary's troops and people but also one's own troops and people could be victims. In addition, their use as a weapon comes with the cost of a high probability of violating the norm of noncombatant immunity, something few states want to do. Today, most observers are more concerned with the possibility that rogue states or terrorists might obtain and deploy biological or other weapons of mass destruction; they are less concerned that states with rational leaders will do so.

In 2003, the George W. Bush administration, frustrated with Saddam Hussein's repeated refusal to abide by the terms of the cease-fire that had ended the first Gulf War in 1991, decided to prepare for a possible military invasion of Iraq. Among the U.S. government's many concerns was the possibility that Saddam Hussein was developing WMD. This concern proved to be the administration's main justification for war. The fear that Saddam's Iraq would either use such weapons against the United States or its allies or transfer such a weapon to a terrorist group helped gain sufficient U.S. public support for the invasion.

More recently, the realization that Iran is developing uranium-enrichment capacity and refuses to renounce a nuclear option has led to some of the most contentious political conflicts of the new millennium. In October 2015, Iran signed an agreement called the "Joint Comprehensive Plan of Action," limiting its development of components for a possible nuclear weapon for 15 years in exchange for an end to crippling economic sanctions. While this agreement may be an important step in stemming the tide of nuclear proliferation, it still leaves open the questions of whether Iran can cheat on the agreement and what will happen once the 15-year moratorium ends. Likewise, North Korea's tests of nuclear weapons since 2006, and more recently, new launch vehicles, have raised serious concerns in the international community.

Unconventional Warfare

Unconventional warfare is as old as conventional warfare and is distinguished in general by a willingness to flout restrictions on legitimate targets of violence or refuse to accept the traditional outcomes of battles—say, the destruction of a regular army, loss of a capital, or capture of a national leader—as an indicator of victory or defeat.

Two major changes progressively moved unconventional war from a side role to a prominent feature of war. First, the French Revolution unleashed the power of nationalism in support of large-scale military operations, enabling Napoleon Bonaparte's armies to make use of tactics that the older professional militaries of Europe at first could not counteract. Nationalism inflamed common people to resist "foreign" aggression and occupation, even when faced with receiving bribes or being penalized through torture and death. Nationalism has proven a double-edged sword ever since. Although Napoleon's forces initially swept aside the old order, the source of his greatest defeats lay in nationalist-inspired resistance in Russia and Spain (Spanish resistance came to be called "small war" or, in Spanish, **guerrilla warfare**). But nationalist-inspired resistance was not by itself sufficient to make unconventional warfare effective against the power of states or incumbent governments. That took a strategic innovation that combined the ancient doctrine of guerrilla warfare with explicit use of the power of nationalism.

Abu Sabaya (standing at left), a leader of Abu Sayyaf—a Muslim extremist group—poses with a group of rebels on Indonesia's Jolo Island in July of 2000 during the Sipadan Hostage Crisis. The group aims to establish a conservative version of Sharia Law throughout Indonesia.

That strategy was first called "revolutionary guerrilla war" by its chief innovator, Mao Zedong. It was specifically designed to counter a technologically advanced and well-equipped industrial adversary by effectively reversing the conventional relationship between soldiers and civilians. In conventional war, soldiers risk their lives to protect civilians. In guerrilla warfare, civilians risk their lives to protect the guerrillas, who hide among them and who cannot easily be distinguished from ordinary civilians when not actually fighting.[16]

Using revolutionary guerrilla warfare during the Chinese Civil War (1927–37, 1945–49) and in China's resistance to Japanese occupation during World War II (1937–45), Mao's Peoples Liberation Army was able to survive many setbacks. Eventually, it defeated the well-armed and U.S.-supplied Nationalist armies of Jiang Jieshi (Chiang Kai-shek), whose forces fled to the island of Formosa, now Taiwan. This unexpected outcome left Mao with a vast storehouse of captured weapons and, more importantly, led to the spread of revolutionary guerrilla warfare as a template for other insurgents, particularly in Asia.

The second half of the twentieth century witnessed a string of unexpected defeats of the major advanced industrial powers, each of which lost wars against "weak" or "backward" adversaries. Britain was forced to grant independence to India. France was defeated in Indochina and Algeria; Portugal in Mozambique and Angola; the United States in Vietnam; the Soviet Union in Afghanistan; and Israel in Lebanon. In each case, well-equipped, industrialized militaries had sought to overcome smaller, nonindustrial adversaries and lost. Ominously, both the French experience in Algeria and the Soviet experience in Afghanistan added a new element to the mix: religion as a means of inspiring and aggregating resistance.

Today, this pattern of advanced industrial states pitted against either nonstate actors or relatively weak states has become commonplace. International relations theorists now refer to such contests as **asymmetric conflict**.

Asymmetric conflict undercuts an important proposition of both conventional warfare and nuclear war: that conventional weapons and nuclear confrontations are more likely to occur among states having rough equality of military strength and using similar strategies and tactics. If one party is decidedly weaker, the proposition goes, fear of defeat makes that party unlikely to resort to war. Asymmetric conflicts, in contrast, are conducted between parties of very unequal strength. The weaker party seeks to innovate around its opponent's strengths, including its technological superiority, by exploiting that opponent's weaknesses.[17]

Like any strategy, revolutionary guerrilla warfare itself has weaknesses. In two asymmetric conflicts following World War II, the strong actors—Britain during the Malayan Emergency (1948–60) and the United States in the Philippines (1952–53)—devised a counterinsurgency strategy that effectively defeated revolutionary guerrilla wars. That strategy aimed not at insurgent armed forces (terrorists and guerrillas), or even their leaders, but instead focused on the real strength of successful guerrilla warfare: the people. As Mao recognized in his early writings, incumbent governments can defeat a well-led, well-organized guerrilla resistance in only two ways: either change the minds of the people (via a conciliation, or "hearts and minds," strategy) or destroy them utterly (a strategy one theorist calls "barbarism").[18] In either case, the social support of a guerrilla resistance is destroyed, and that resistance will collapse. Mao was confident that his "Western" and democratic adversaries were too arrogant in their own power to attempt to change minds and too squeamish in their ethical conduct to pursue a genocidal counterinsurgency. Yet in both Malaya and the Philippines, incumbent governments, supported by Britain and the United States, sought to redress the grievances that had led many of the country's poor or disaffected either to active support of guerrillas or to political apathy. Since World War II, "hearts and minds" strategies have proven the most effective method of counterinsurgency on the ground, but they are costly in political terms because they take a long time to work and, in most cases, they demand large numbers of troops.[19]

Yet guerrilla warfare is only one of several strategies a combatant might use to overcome a more materially powerful incumbent and its allies. Another such strategy is **nonviolent resistance**: resistance to authority that employs measures other than violence. Like revolutionary guerrilla warfare, nonviolent resistance deliberately places ordinary people at grave risk of harm in the pursuit of political objectives. Unlike guerrilla warfare or terrorism, however, nonviolent resistance avoids the use of violence as a means of protest. Prominent examples of nonviolent resistance include Mohandas Gandhi's resistance to British rule in the 1940s and the Reverend Dr. Martin Luther King Jr.'s civil rights movement of the 1960s. Another strategy for overcoming a materially more powerful adversary is terrorism.

Terrorism

Terrorism, a particular kind of asymmetric conflict, is increasingly perceived as a serious international security threat because the causes that motivate terrorists to murder defenseless civilians have become increasingly transnational rather than local, and because advances in WMD technology have made it theoretically possible for substate actors to cause state-level damage (say, with a nuclear bomb smuggled by a terrorist into a major metropolitan area). Though they did not involve WMD, Al Qaeda's attacks against U.S. embassies in Africa in 1998, against cities on U.S. soil in 2001, and in the London Underground and buses in 2005 were justified in the group's eyes as a religious imperative that recognized neither the state nor the international system of states.

Because a core feature of terrorism is the deliberate harm of noncombatants, "terrorists" are necessarily outlaws: by definition, outlaws neither observe the law nor are protected by it. Scholars of terrorism, a moribund subfield of international relations inquiry until 2001, today disagree on a universal definition of terrorism, but most definitions share three key elements:

1. It is *political* in nature or intent.
2. Perpetrators are *nonstate* actors.
3. Targets are *noncombatants*, such as ordinary citizens (especially young children or the elderly), political figures, or bureaucrats.

One contemporary terrorism expert, Audrey Kurth Cronin, adds a fourth element: terror attacks are unconventional and unpredictable.[20] Terrorism has often been called the strategy of the weak, but this argument begs the question of what "power" actually is. Is power only the material power to kill, or can it reside in the power of ideas? Gandhi, for example, did not overcome the British and win India's independence by means of violent revolution. The power of ideas proved decisive. Terrorists also hope to harness the power of ideas: they invariably justify their violence by reference to immortality imagery. This imagery tends to take one of three classic forms: nationalist, Marxist, or religious. In each case, terrorists intend their violent acts to preserve the nation, the proletariat, or the faithful, and ensure its immortality. In the Irish

Republican Army's long struggles with British rule in Ireland, all three immortality images came into play, as predominantly socialist, nationalist, and Catholic "terrorists" sought to coerce Britain into abandoning Ireland's Protestant minority, among other things.

Like guerrilla warfare, terrorism has a long history. During Greek and Roman times, individuals often carried out terrorist acts against their rulers. Interestingly, the contemporary sense of the word "terror" dates from the French Revolution, in which Robespierre's fragile government leveled extreme, and at times indiscriminate, violence against the French people. But neither state perpetration nor sponsorship of terror should be confused with terrorism as such, because, as observed earlier, a core element of terrorism is that it be perpetrated by nonstate actors. It is therefore difficult to say what to call the kind of mass killing perpetrated by states such as the United States against Native Americans, Hitler's Third Reich against Jews, Stalin's Soviet Union against Ukrainians, and Pol Pot's Cambodia against noncommunists. All terrorism may be barbarism, but not all barbarism terrorism.

Although terrorism involves physical harm, the essence of terrorism is psychological, not physical. Whatever the aims of the individual terrorist, killing is a by-product of terrorism as a strategy. The real aim of terrorism is to call attention to a cause, while at the same time calling into question the legitimacy of a target government by highlighting its inability to protect its citizens. For example, during the 1972 Summer Olympic Games in Munich, Germany, a group of Palestinian Arab terrorists styling themselves "Black September" took 11 Israeli athletes hostage in the Olympic Village. Two of the hostages were murdered immediately. During a botched rescue attempt by the surprised and ill-prepared Germans, the remaining nine hostages were murdered by their captors. Black September was a part of the Palestinian Liberation Organization (PLO), a group founded by Yasser Arafat in 1964 to advance the cause of Palestinian Arab statehood by means of violence. But until Munich, few outside the Middle East had ever heard of the PLO. After the games, the PLO (and "terrorists" more broadly) became a widespread topic of conversation and state action. Another method of gaining attention was hijacking commercial airplanes. In December 1973, Arab terrorists killed 32 people in Rome's airport during an attack on a U.S. aircraft. Hostages were taken in support of the hijackers' demand for the release of imprisoned Palestinian Arabs. In 1976, a Middle Eastern organization hijacked a French plane with mostly Israeli passengers and flew it to Uganda, where the hijackers threatened to kill the hostages unless Arab prisoners in Israel were released. In the aftermath of several such high-profile cases, the international community responded by signing a series of international agreements designed to tighten airport security, sanction states that gave refuge to hijackers, and condemn state-supported terrorism. The 1979 International Convention against the Taking of Hostages is a prominent example of such an agreement.

In January 2015, a young Jordanian fighter pilot named Muath Safi Yousef al-Kasasbeh was burned alive by the Islamic State after having been captured in Syria. His execution was videotaped by the IS and distributed on the Internet via a Twitter account. Al-Kasasbeh's execution provoked outrage in Jordan and worldwide.

Much recent terrorist activity has its roots in the Middle East—in the ongoing quest of Palestinian Arabs for self-determination and their own internal conflicts over strategy, in the hostility among various Islamic groups toward Western forces and ideas (in particular, what they perceive as Western support of Israel's persecution of Palestinian Arabs and the education and independence of women), and in the resurgence of extremist Islamic fundamentalism. Among terrorist groups with roots in the Middle East are Hamas, Hezbollah, and Palestine Islamic Jihad. After September 11, 2001, Al Qaeda was the most publicized of these groups. A shadowy network of extremist Islamic fundamentalists from many countries, including some outside the Middle East, Al Qaeda, led by the late Osama bin Laden, is motivated by the desire to install strict Islamic regimes in the Middle East, support radical Islamic insurgencies in Southeast Asia, and punish the United States for its support of Israel. When the United States and its allies began to seriously hurt Al Qaeda—as they did from 2009 to 2012—its leadership adapted by dispersing and forming new affiliates, such as Al Qaeda in Iraq and Al Qaeda in Yemen. But support for Al Qaeda has now diminished.

In its stead, as Chapter 5 explains, the Islamic State has emerged, with its roots in the 1979 Iran Shiite revolution and the 2003 invasion of Iraq. That invasion by the U.S.

empowered Shiites over the Arab Sunni minority, and the IS has taken up the radical Sunni cause. The IS broadcasts its terrorist acts through social media: the behead-ings of Westerners and Muslim opponents; mass executions; the rape of non-Muslim women like the Yazidi minority; the sexual slavery of non-Sunni Muslims; the taking of hostages for ransom; and the destruction of cultural antiquities. But it differs from most terrorist organizations in important respects, too. It seeks to control territory and has done so in parts of Syria and Iraq. It self-finances by controlling oil assets. And the IS claims religious authority centered in the proclamation of a caliphate, led by Abu Bakr al-Baghdadi. Many of its estimated 15,000 foreign recruits, from as many as 80 countries, are attracted by its utopian goals. As one scholar explains, the IS seeks to "create a 'pure' Sunni Islamist state governed by a brutal interpretation of *sharia*, to immediately obliterate the political borders of the Middle East that were cre-ated by Western powers in the twentieth century; and to position itself as the sole politi-cal, religious, and military authority over all of the world's Muslims."[21] Yet the very use of terror and its tactics, as well as its religious fundamentalism, has isolated the IS from virtually all of its neighbors, most Muslims, and the rest of the international community.

Though the examples above are from the Middle East, terrorism also has a long history in other parts of the world, reflecting diverse, often multiple, motivations. Some groups adhere to extreme religious positions, such as the Irish Republican Army, the protector of Northern Irish Catholics in their struggle against Protestant British rule. The Hindu-Muslim rivalry in India has led to many terrorist incidents. Other groups seek or have sought territorial separation or autonomy from a state. The Basque separatists (ETA) in Spain, the Tamil Tigers in Sri Lanka, Abu Sayyaf Group in the Philippines, and Chechen groups in Russia are all excellent examples.

Since the 1990s, terrorism has taken a new turn.[22] Terrorist acts have become more lethal, even as the groups responsible have become more dispersed. In the 1970s, about 17 percent of terrorist attacks killed someone, whereas in the 1990s, almost 25 percent of terrorist attacks resulted in deaths. Until 2000, the worst loss of life was the 1985 bombing of an Air India flight, in which 329 people were killed. That statistic changed dramatically on September 11, 2001, when over 3,000 civilians died and $80 billion in economic losses were incurred. Increasingly, terrorists have made use of a diverse array of weapons. AK-47s, sarin gas, shoulder-fired missiles, anthrax, back-pack explosives, and airplanes as guided missiles have all been used. The IS has made theater of executing prisoners by beheading, a particularly grisly form of execution in which the IS records the act and then distributes it online. The infrastructure that supports terrorism has also become more sophisticated. It is financed through money-laundering schemes and illegal criminal activities. Training camps attract not just young, single, and uneducated potential terrorists but also older, better-educated individuals who are willing to commit suicide to accomplish their objectives. Terrorist groups have also made increasingly effective use of the Internet and social media as a recruitment tool.

The groups practicing terrorism have become wider ranging, from nationalists and neo-Nazis to religious, left-wing and right-wing militants. (See Table 8.2.) State-sponsored terrorism, the support of terrorist groups by states, remains common. The United States and many of its allies (for example, Britain, Germany, and France) have repeatedly accused North Korea, Iran, Iraq, Syria, Libya, Sudan, and Cuba of having lent support to terrorist groups. Yet, while strong evidence of state complicity exists in each case, the accusing states are apt to overlook their *own* sponsorship of groups others might call "terrorists." In the U.S. case, U.S. support of *contras*—groups opposing communist rule in Nicaragua in the 1980s—could easily count as state-sponsored terrorism because the *contras* did not limit their targets to Nicaraguan police and soldiers, but also attacked civilians. Terrorists are increasingly launching attacks in developing countries. Turkey, Morocco, Indonesia, India, Kenya, and Pakistan are all examples.

TABLE 8.2 — SELECTED TERRORIST ORGANIZATIONS

GROUP	LOCATION	CHARACTERISTICS AND ATTACKS
Al Qaeda	Formerly in Afghanistan; now dispersed throughout Afghanistan, Pakistan, Iran, Indonesia, and Yemen	Formed by Osama bin Laden in the late 1980s among Arabs who fought the Soviets in Afghanistan; responsible for bombings in Africa (1998), Yemen (2000), United States (2001), Spain (2004), Great Britain (2005), India (2006), Pakistan (2008, 2009), Algeria (2010)
Hamas (Islamic Resistance Movement)	Israel, West Bank, Gaza Strip	Its leader signed bin Laden's 1998 *fatwa* calling for attacks on U.S. interests; elected in 2006 as governing authority in Gaza
Hezbollah (Party of God)	Lebanon	Also known as Islamic Jihad; often directed by Iran and suspected in the bombing of the U.S. embassy and marine barracks in Beirut in 1983; dominates Lebanon politically; fights against Israel

(CONTINUED)

GROUP	LOCATION	CHARACTERISTICS AND ATTACKS
Boko Haram (Western Ways Are Forbidden)	Nigeria's relatively impoverished northern states; some activities in neighboring states	Salafi jihadists who violently pursue the establishment of a strict version of Sharia law throughout Nigeria. Kidnapped 276 schoolgirls in Chibok, Nigeria, in April 2014. As of early 2016, none of the girls have been rescued.
Haqqani Network	Pashtunistan (eastern Afghanistan and western Pakistan)	Insurgent Islamist group; supported by U.S. CIA during Soviet occupation of Afghanistan; now allied with Taliban and tacitly supported by Pakistan; fought against ISAF in Afghanistan until 2010.
The Islamic State	Centered in Syria and Northern Iraq, but actively franchising to Yemen, Afghanistan, Libya, and possibly Chechnya	An outgrowth of Al Qaeda in Iraq, currently led by Abu Bakr al-Baghdadi, a former senior officer in Saddam Hussein's Iraqi Army and self-proclaimed Caliph; the world's wealthiest terrorist group; aims to establish an "Islamic" caliphate (no territorial boundaries) and is responsible for thousands of murders, including beheadings, rapes, and sexual slavery of any who oppose its restrictive interpretation of Sharia law.

Preventing terrorist activity has become increasingly difficult because most perpetrators have networks of supporters in the resident populations. Protecting populations from random acts of violence is an almost impossible task, given the availability of guns and bombs in the international marketplace. Pressure on governments is very strong because people worry disproportionately about terrorism, even though it kills a relatively small number of people, and because many people believe a violent response by state security forces will help protect them. Despite advances in detection technology like face-recognition software, committed individuals or groups of terrorists are difficult to preempt or deter. Indeed, such individuals may be seen as heroes in their community.

The international community has taken action against terrorists, first by creating a framework of international rules dealing with terrorism. The framework includes 12 conventions that address such issues as punishing hijackers and those who protect them; protecting airports, diplomats, and nuclear materials in transport; and blocking the flow of financial resources to global terrorist networks. Individual states have also taken steps to increase state security (the United States' controversial USA Patriot Act is one example); to support counterintelligence activities; and to promote cooperation among national enforcement agencies in tracking and apprehending terrorists. States have sanctioned other states they view as supporting terrorists, or as not taking effective enforcement measures. Libya, Sudan, Afghanistan, Syria, Iran, and Iraq are prominent examples. But it is important to recall that even developed states such as the United States,

In April 2014, terrorists affiliated with Boko Haram (or "Western ways are forbidden") kidnapped 276 schoolgirls at a secondary school in Chibok, Nigeria. To date, the Nigerian government has proven unable to find the girls, who many believe have since been forced to convert to Islam and in some cases marry Boko Haram fighters. Here, a student who escaped the school identifies some of her classmates.

Belgium, and France have had difficulty in "taking effective enforcement measures" against terrorists, although each has shut down many terrorist financial networks and enhanced security in airports and ports. After all, the terrorists who attacked New York's World Trade Center and the Pentagon on September 11, 2001, learned to fly commercial airplanes in Florida. And some of the terrorists responsible for the Paris bombings in 2015 were French citizens or were living in Belgium.

The Just War Tradition

When, if ever, is it just for states to go to war? Is war always an illegal and immoral act, or is it acceptable under certain conditions? What constitutes an appropriate justification—*jus ad bellum*—to enter into war? And what constitutes moral and ethical conduct—*jus in bello*—once a state decides to go to war? Normative political theorists draw our attention to the classical **just war tradition**. Although a Western and Christian doctrine dating from medieval times, just war theory draws on ancient Greek philosophy and precepts found in the Koran. As developed by Saint Augustine, Saint Thomas Aquinas, Hugo Grotius, and, more recently, the political philosopher Michael Walzer, just war theory asserts that several criteria can make the decision to enter a war a just one.[23] There must be a just cause (self-defense or the defense of others, or a massive violation of human rights) and a declaration of intent by a competent authority (which, since the formation of the United Nations, has been interpreted to mean the UN Security Council). The leaders need to have the correct intentions, desiring to end abuses and establish a just peace. They also need to have exhausted all other possibilities for ending the abuse, employing war as a last resort. Actors must rapidly remove forces after securing the humanitarian objectives. Because states choose war for a variety of reasons, however, it is rarely easy to assess the justness of a particular cause or particular intentions.

The just war tradition also addresses legitimate conduct in war. Combatants and noncombatants must be differentiated, with the latter protected from harm as much as possible. Violence must be proportionate to the ends to be achieved. Combatants should avoid causing undue human suffering and using particularly heinous weapons. Because mustard gas caused especially cruel deaths during World War I, it was subsequently outlawed, thus providing the basis for future chemical and biological warfare conventions. Many of the extended norms of the just war tradition were codified in the four 1949 Geneva Conventions and the two additional protocols concluded in 1977. These are designed to protect civilians, prisoners of war, and wounded soldiers, as well as to ban particular methods of war and certain weapons that cause unnecessary suffering.

Just war is an evolving practice. Key contemporary debates surround the question of how newer killing technologies—nuclear weapons, land mines, cluster munitions, fuel air explosives, and in particular drone strikes—affect our assessments of moral and ethical conduct during war. A key concern of just war theorists is the fact that some technological advances make the notion of **noncombatant immunity**, the protection of all civilians not using weapons and prisoners of war, among others, very difficult. The use of nuclear weapons has been viewed as a just war concern for two reasons. First, as observed earlier, unlike with most conventional weapons, the destructive effects of nuclear weapons are impossible to restrict in time and space. Although as many as 110,000 Japanese were killed in the first few hours after the atomic bombings of Hiroshima and Nagasaki, the Japanese government estimates that total fatalities directly attributable to the bombings today exceed 250,000. Second, the destructive potential of contemporary thermonuclear weapons is simply unprecedented. No one can say for certain what the impact of even a limited exchange of such weapons might be on the global ecosystem. An all-out exchange, in which hundreds of such weapons were deliberately detonated, might end all life on the planet (save perhaps insect life), damage the atmosphere, or plunge the earth into an extended "nuclear winter." Thus, the proportionality of means and ends, which stands as a second pillar of just war theory, would be violated.

Other weapons have also come under fire under the "nondiscriminatory nature" theory of unjust war. Two of particular note include antipersonnel land mines and cluster munitions. Although land mines originally were viewed as legitimate weapons, the International Campaign to Ban Landmines (ICBL) has succeeded in shifting perceptions of these weapons by emphasizing—as with other weapons of mass destruction—the indiscriminate effect of their capacity to harm. That approach and process has also been adopted by the Cluster Munitions Coalition, a coalition of NGOs present in over 100 countries. In 2008, the Convention on Cluster Munitions was signed, banning the use of weapons with a high potential to harm noncombatants and providing assistance for clearance and victim assistance.

The campaigns against antipersonnel land mines and cluster munitions reflect growing pressure to restrict or eliminate the use of various weapons and practices in accord with just war principles. Constructivists can rightly cite the power of norms and socialization to alter the behavior (and identity) of both state and nonstate actors in this regard. After 2001, for example, the George W. Bush administration sought guidance on whether certain interrogation techniques—in particular one called waterboarding, in which suspects are nearly suffocated repeatedly during questioning—were "torture." If waterboarding were torture, it would be illegal, even within the context of the war on terrorism. After being assured that waterboarding was not torture, the Bush administration approved its use in interrogations. The ensuing controversy proved fierce. Most interrogation and legal experts consider waterboarding both an ineffective interrogation technique and torture. The subject has been debated by U.S. presidential candidates in 2011 and 2016, when some Republican candidates supported waterboarding and other enhanced techniques. Others responded that waterboarding was torture, and therefore inherently un-American.

Another recent debate around morals and ethics in war has surfaced surrounding drone strikes. Initially, drones were used to place sophisticated eyes and ears over combat areas without risking pilots and expensive aircraft. But their use has increased radically since 2001. Many drones in the U.S. inventory are armed with missiles that operators thousands of miles away can aim and launch. From 2004 to 2015, an estimated 2,476–3,989 people were killed and 1,158–1,738 injured in U.S. CIA drone strikes in Pakistan alone. Of these, an estimated 423–965 were noncombatants, including 172–207 children. Yemen and Somalia have also seen the number of lethal drone strikes rise.

Two main questions currently surround the use of drone strikes in a just war. First, what safeguards ensure that those targeted by drone strikes are actually guilty of terrorism or of harming allied personnel? Most of those targeted do not wear uniforms, nor do they formally serve a state. The process by which U.S. intelligence agencies determine targets remains classified. Second, and related, is the harm caused by drone missile strikes justified? In the above statistics on Pakistan, for example, 17–24 percent of those killed in drone strikes were noncombatants.

The Debate over Humanitarian Intervention

No issue emerging from the just war tradition has been more critical or controversial than the debate over **humanitarian intervention**. The just war tradition asserts that military intervention by states or the international community may be justified or even obligatory to alleviate massive violations of human rights. Yet that position directly contradicts a hallmark of the Westphalian tradition—respect for state sovereignty. Historically, states selectively applied military intervention on behalf of humanitarian causes. In the nineteenth century, Europeans used military force to protect Christians in Turkey and the Middle East, though they chose not to protect other religious groups. And European nations did not intervene militarily to stop slavery, though they prohibited their own citizens from participating in the slave trade.[24]

Since the end of World War II, the notion has emerged that all human beings deserve protection—not just particular groups—and that states have an obligation to intervene. This idea is called the **responsibility to protect (R2P)**. The idea is that in cases of massive violations of human rights, when domestic avenues for redress have been exhausted and actions by other states might reasonably end the abuse, these states have a *responsibility* to intervene in the domestic affairs of the state in which the abuse is

::: BEHIND THE HEADLINES

The Difficult Trade-Offs of Drone Warfare

Since the September 11, 2001 attacks on the World Trade Center, Al Qaeda has been the target of a concerted effort by the United States and its allies to destroy or demobilize it, mainly by identifying Al Qaeda's leaders and killing them. In 2011, Osama Bin Laden, Al Qaeda's most famous leader and its chief architect, was killed in a raid by U.S. special operations forces in Abbottabad, Pakistan. But, like any organization under duress, Al Qaeda and affiliated groups responded by innovating new ways of planning and executing operations and new ways of avoiding detection and attack. Chief among these tactics are decentralizing leadership and physically dispersing either to countries that are too weak to arrest Al Qaeda operatives, or to countries that are hostile to the United States and its allies. When military interventions by U.S. ground forces in these countries seem likely to be either too costly or counterproductive, what means of self-defense might a state such as the United States consider?

One answer is highlighted in the headline "4 Yemen Al Qaeda leaders killed in suspected US drone strike."[a] Armed drone strikes give U.S. leaders a relatively low cost and highly effective tool for damaging or demobilizing terrorist groups, without putting American troops in harm's way. The material costs of sending an unmanned aerial vehicle over a target area are much less than even a small deployment of U.S. special operations forces

like Navy SEALs or Delta forces. Targets are killed in places like Yemen, Somalia, Libya, Syria, Afghanistan, and Pakistan with what is deemed an acceptable level of collateral damage. In none of those countries would an armed military intervention be cheap or practical. American decision makers remember from their experiences in 2001–13 that allied armed forces struggled in Afghanistan to defeat a variety of adversaries deemed "extremist" at great cost and to little ultimate positive effect.

Though drone warfare can be effective and relatively inexpensive, the use of drones to kill extremist leaders or other "high-value targets" suffers from several problems. The weapons

Wall mural in Sana'a, Yemen, depicts resentment of U.S. drone strikes and calls attention to the social construction of "targets" and "terrorists." A girl or boy who opposes U.S. intervention and plans or undertakes violence to oppose it will often become a target to the United States, whereas to her or his family, she or he will likely be seen as another victim of U.S. colonial or even religious aggression.

that most drones use in attacks have not been particularly discriminate. That is, targeted leaders often are found in their homes, or in the company of children, the elderly, or ordinary citizens who are likely to be killed. Survivors will be unlikely to forget or forgive the deaths of their children, even if those deaths were unintended. Declassified documents from the U.S. Air Force and U.S. Central Intelligence Agency, the two organizations most likely to use armed drones to kill high-value targets, show that they "do not always know who they are killing, but are making an imperfect best guess."[b] This admission, along with the reality of collateral damage, has led to vocal and persistent criticism of the use of armed drones, especially in the Muslim world. And that may explain the decline in the use of armed drones to kill high-value targets everywhere but Yemen.

Many states—including those not friendly to the United States and its allies—are pursuing drone development programs. Very soon, these states may target those *they* consider to be extremist, like artists, dissidents, or even nationals living in Western countries. Collateral damage would be expected to follow. Then those countries whose sovereign territory is being breached and their allies in the international system would be challenged to develop new laws and treaties to deal with this new technological capacity to view, target, and ultimately kill individuals and small groups with armed drones from thousands of miles away.

FOR CRITICAL ANALYSIS

1. The use of armed drones in predominantly Muslim states such as Pakistan, Yemen, and Somalia has led to a serious backlash against the United States not only in Muslim countries, but in Europe as well. Is the use of drones "worth" those costs?

2. Why is the use of drones popular in the United States? Do you support or oppose the continuation of drone strikes?

3. In what ways are armed drones similar to other weapons? In what ways are they different?

a. "4 Yemen Al Qaeda leaders killed in suspected US drone strike," *Associated Press*, May 12, 2015.
b. Scott Shane, "Drone Strikes Reveal Uncomfortable Truth: U.S. Is Often Unsure About Who Will Die," *New York Times*, April 23, 2015.

occurring. As two UN officials put it, this "marks the coming of age of the imperative of action in the face of human rights abuses, over the citadels of state sovereignty."[25] Though this belief emerged in the middle of the twentieth century, it gained prominence during the 1990s after humanitarian crises in Somalia and Rwanda, and following widespread murder, rape, and devastation in Darfur, Sudan (2003–05). Recently, Russia's President Vladimir Putin invoked a version of R2P in his justification for annexing Crimea in 2014. Putin argued a military intervention was part of Russia's responsibility to protect the lives and property of ethnic Russians in Crimea and parts of Eastern Ukraine.

Questions about R2P remain. How massive do the violations of human rights have to be to justify intervention? The Geneva Conventions specify that "genocide" is not about how *many* people are killed, but about the *intent* to kill an entire group. Who decides when to respond to the abuses? Might some states use humanitarian intervention as a pretext for achieving other, less humanitarian goals? Should states have an obligation to intervene militarily in these humanitarian emergencies? Why are some interventions justified (e.g., Kosovo and Libya), while others, in which equally heinous abuse is taking place (e.g., Rwanda and Syria), are ignored? As the same UN officials warn, military intervention can often be "devoid of legal sanction, selectively deployed and achieving only ambiguous ends."[26]

Given their experiences under colonial rule, many Asian and African countries are skeptical about humanitarian justifications for intervention by Western countries. Other states, such as Russia and China, have insisted that for a claim of humanitarian intervention to be legitimate, it must be authorized by the UN Security Council, where Russia and China are among the powers possessing a veto. In practice, humanitarian interventions are often multilateral, although they do not always receive authorization by the UN. For instance, when Western states sought military intervention in Kosovo, as discussed in Chapter 2, Russia opposed the measure, so Western powers turned to the North Atlantic Treaty Organization (NATO) instead. They also turned to NATO in the case of Libya because of operational expediency.

States that have supported humanitarian interventions in the past do not always support future interventions. This change in policy can occur for several reasons, including the perception of the success or failure of previous missions, as well as the nature of other interests at stake in the conflict. Having suffered a humiliating setback in Somalia in 1993, for instance, the United States (and the UN) opposed increased use of the military to protect civilians in Rwanda in 1994, despite clear evidence of genocide. Similarly, only a small military contingent from the African Union was originally mobilized for the Darfur region, despite 300,000 deaths and the culpability of the Sudanese government. In the Darfur case, other national interests were deemed more vital than support for humanitarian intervention: China cared about access to Sudanese oil; Russia cared about export arms markets; the United States was preoccupied with Iraq and the war on terrorism. In May 2012, a massacre in the Syrian village of Taldou of women, children, and even infants by the security forces of Syria's Bashar al Assad caused an international outcry, but China and Russia opposed UN-sanctioned military intervention. Both countries issued statements asserting that any foreign military intervention would only make the situation in Syria, and the region, worse. Russia's and China's positions on intervention ultimately failed to halt international military intervention in the civil war in Syria (2012–present). This outcome may be why Russia later determined that its own military intervention in Syria was both necessary to reverse the chaos caused by U.S. and allied interventions, and just.

So although support for R2P is an emergent norm, it remains the subject of ongoing controversy. Because states do not intervene in all situations of humanitarian emergency, state sovereignty remains intact. But when gross violations of human rights are obvious, and when military intervention does not conflict with other national interests, states increasingly view humanitarian intervention as a justifiable use of force.

Contending Perspectives on Managing Insecurity

Disparity in power between states, the inability to know the intentions of states and individuals, and the lack of an overarching international authority means that states—even powerful ones—are continually confronted by the need to manage their insecurity.

Four approaches to managing insecurity are well tested in international politics. Two of these approaches reflect realist thinking, requiring individual states themselves to maintain an adequate power potential. The other approaches reflect the liberal theoretical perspective and thus focus largely on multilateral responses by groups of states acting to coordinate their policies. Realists and liberals support different policy responses to arms proliferation, the resulting security dilemma, and managing insecurity more generally, as Table 8.3 on p. 300 describes.

Realist Approaches: Balance of Power and Deterrence

Realist approaches to managing insecurity come from the fact that for realists, war is a necessary condition of interstate politics: it can be managed but never eradicated. Classical realists, ranging from Thucydides to Machiavelli to Hobbes to Hans Morgenthau, argued that human nature made transcending war unlikely. Neorealists replaced the emphasis on human nature with an emphasis on structure, arguing that war will be a

Conflict in Ukraine, 2014: A View from Russia

Since Vladimir Putin's accession to the presidency of the Russian Federation in 2000, Russia has once again acted according to realist expectations, affirming its national interest by protecting Russian nationals in neighboring lands and reasserting the power and prestige of the Russian Federation after the demise of the Soviet Union.

After weeks of protest over the corrupt and ineffective leadership of Ukraine's president, Viktor Yanukovich, and over his suspension of the Ukraine-European Union Association Agreement, violent confrontations erupted between government security forces and Ukrainian protesters. Over a five-day period, these violent clashes culminated in the ouster of Yanukovich and his subsequent flight to Russia. In the weeks that followed, Russian president Vladimir Putin refused to recognize Ukraine's interim government. Then thousands of obviously trained soldiers in uniforms with no national insignia began to flood into Eastern Ukraine and Crimea. On February 23, pro-Russian demonstrations "spontaneously" broke out in the city of Sevastopol, and on February 27, soldiers stormed key sites across Crimea. This action was soon followed by a Crimean referendum where the population voted for independence by a wide electoral margin. In a subsequent petition, the newly independent Crimea joined the Russian Federation.

Crimea has a long association with Russia; beginning in 1802, it was included in the Russian Governorate. After the Soviet revolution in 1917, Crimea came under the jurisdiction of Moscow. But because of its close economic and cultural ties to the Ukrainian Soviet Socialist Republic, also part of the Soviet Union, Crimea was transferred to that jurisdiction in 1954. When Ukraine itself became independent in 1991, Crimea became an autonomous region within Ukraine—until the 2014 reversion to the Russian Federation. For the 84 percent Russian speakers in Crimea, this was a return to their ancestral home. Protecting nationals in other areas is the responsibility of states. Hence Russia' actions in Crimea and Eastern Ukraine to protect the 17 percent Russian minority in Ukraine, mainly located in the eastern region, are proper.

Russia's concern for protecting its borders is a logical extension of its history. Russia has been invaded many times from Western Europe—each time with fearful losses of life and property. Following World War II, the Soviet Union established the Warsaw Pact alliance with the states in central Europe to create a geographical buffer between Western Europe and the USSR, thus making it harder to invade the USSR. The USSR also maintained a very large military presence in East Germany and other Eastern European States. Russia's leaders remain consistently convinced that Western states have never given up on the idea of invading Russia and installing a "Western-style liberal government." Thus, even during the initial thaw of the immediate post–Cold War, Russia maintained hundreds of thousands of troops in Warsaw Pact countries primarily out of insecurity from an invasion.

During the 1990s, independent and neutral Ukraine established partnerships with Russia and other Commonwealth of Independent

States countries. It also established relationships with NATO and the European Union. To Russia, both organizations posed a threat. In Russian eyes, NATO had become an unnecessary military alliance since the Cold War had ended. Why did NATO not disband as the Warsaw Pact had done? Perhaps, Russia reasoned, NATO intended to expand as a military alliance right up to Russia's borders. And so it was with the EU. Is not the purpose of the ever-expanding EU to pose an economic wedge between Russia and its neighbors? Should neighboring states like Ukraine draw closer to the West and gain economic and military power and popular sovereignty governments, Russia itself would be threatened. Russian troops in Eastern Ukraine, joining with ethnic Russians fighting the Ukrainian government, send a clear message that becoming closer to the West is not to be tolerated.

Why had the West not learned the limits of what Russia tolerates along its borders? In 2008, Russian armed forces invaded South Ossetia and clashed with the armed forces of Georgia, a new NATO partnership member. Georgia's military was crushed. Russians had every reason to expect that this action would suffice to put the West on notice that it would not tolerate NATO expansion. But NATO expansion continued undaunted: from 1999 to 2009, NATO accepted 12 new member states and currently has 28 members in total.

After the breakup of the Soviet Union, the Russian people suffered a wrenching economic adjustment. People struggled; the state struggled. Part of the attraction of Vladimir Putin as leader is his belief that Russian power and influence can be restored. Aided by high petroleum prices beginning at the turn of the century, Putin has become popular by rebuilding the economy and reasserting Russia onto the

Russian-made battle tanks, fitted with reactive armor but not marked with Russian identification, on their way to Crimea. Russia annexed Crimea after a referendum among the Crimean population. The vote was condemned by the United Nations as invalid.

world stage. Most Russians today feel that Russia is not sufficiently respected in international affairs. Use of force may be a necessary condition of being respected as a great power. President Putin's commitment of armed forces to Ukraine and, in 2015, to Syria serve dual purposes: they enhance Russian security geopolitically, and they reassert Russia's prestige worldwide.

FOR CRITICAL ANALYSIS

1. Why did the West not react with military force when Crimea joined the Russian Federation?

2. How is the situation in Crimea different from that of Eastern Ukraine?

3. Both Ukraine and Russia were driven by domestic-level factors to act internationally. Explain.

TABLE 8.3	APPROACHES TO MANAGING INSECURITY	
	REALIST	**LIBERAL**
Approach	Reliance on force or threat of force to manage power	International institutions coordinate actions to manage power
Policies	Balance of power; Deterrence	Collective security; Trade liberalization; Arms control and disarmament

permanent feature of interstate politics so long as anarchy persists. This formulation at least hints at a possibility that states might eliminate war if a single state could amass sufficient power to defeat all other states. Because this possibility is remote, neorealists effectively share the pessimism of classical realists: as a prominent feature of interstate politics, war can never be transcended.

One key concept that informs realism is the prisoner's dilemma (see Chapter 3), a conflict of interest structured in such a way that rational actors choose to harm each other as a best strategy for avoiding a worse outcome. Another key concept is the **security dilemma**, in which even actors with no hostile or aggressive intentions may be led by their own insecurity into a costly and risky arms race. As the political scientist John Herz described it, "Striving to attain security from attack, [states] are driven to acquire more and more power in order to escape the power of others. This, in turn, renders the others more insecure and compels them to prepare for the worst. Since none can ever feel entirely secure in such a world of competing units, power competition ensues, and the vicious circle of security and power accumulation is on."[27] The security dilemma, then, results in a permanent condition of tension and power conflicts among states, even when none actually seek conquest and war.

Although realism itself imagines intra- and interstate warfare as enduring features of international politics, realists advance important arguments about how to decrease the frequency and intensity of wars once they break out. Power balancing is the first approach. The core logic of power balancing is simple: when power is unbalanced, stronger actors will be tempted to use their advantage to secure still more power. The greater the imbalance, the greater the temptation. This is because, for the stronger actor, the costs and risks of war seem low in comparison to potential gains, thus making war a *rational* strategy. But when aggressive, insecure, or greedy actors face others with relatively equal power, they are likely to hesitate to go to war because the costs of war are more likely to exceed expected benefits. Realism's logic therefore explains much of what we observe in interstate politics. It can provide an effective guide to policies aimed at preserving a status quo short of war. However, realist security-management strategies depend on the notion that adversaries share definitions of relevant costs and benefits and that they assign roughly equal values to both. When they do not, a realist strategy for security management can easily go awry, making warfare more rather than less likely, and more rather than less destructive.

BALANCE OF POWER

In Chapter 4, we saw that a balance of power is a particular configuration of a multi-polar international system. But theorists use the terms in other ways as well. So *balance of power* may refer to an equilibrium between any two parties, and *balancing power* may describe an approach to managing power and insecurity. The latter usage is relevant here.

Balance-of-power theorists posit that to manage insecurity, states make rational and calculated evaluations of the costs and benefits of particular policies that determine the state's role in a balance of power. All states in the system are continually making choices to maintain their position vis-à-vis their adversaries, thereby maintaining a balance of power. When that balance of power is jeopardized, as it was by the rise of German power in the early 1900s, insecurity leads states to pursue countervailing alliances or policies.[28] More recently, in October 2015, the United States sent warships to within 12 miles of a Chinese man-made island in the Spratly Island chain to demonstrate its ongoing commitment to the principles of the UN convention on the laws of the sea (UNCLOS), and, at the same time, reassure U.S. allies such as the Philippines and Japan that the United States would not permit unilateral territorial claims or the abrigment of the right of free transit through these contested waters, or unilateral claims to the wealth in mineral resources thought to lie under the sea bed nearby. In this context, the United States is attempting to balance against growing Chinese power in the Pacific by supporting the status quo and the principle that disputes over territory should be resolved through multilateral negotiations.

Alliances are the most important institutional tool for enhancing one's own security and balancing the perceived power potential of one's opponent. If an expanding state seems poised to achieve a dominant position, threatened states can join with others against the expanding state. This action is called external balancing. Formal and institutionalized military alliances play a key role in maintaining a balance of power, as the NATO and Warsaw Pact alliances did in the post–World War II world. States may also engage in internal balancing, increasing their own military and economic capabilities to counter potential threatening enemies.

Balancing power can be applied at both international and regional levels. At the international level during the Cold War, for instance, the United States and the Soviet

Union maintained a relative balance of power. If one of the superpowers augmented its power through the expansion of its alliances or through the acquisition of deadlier, more effective armaments, the other responded in kind. Absolute gains were not as critical as relative gains; no matter how much total power one state accrued, neither state could afford to fall behind the other. Gaining allies among uncommitted states in the developing countries through foreign aid or military and diplomatic intervention was one way to ensure they balanced the power. Not maintaining the power balance was too risky a strategy since both sides tended to believe their national survival was at stake.

Balances of power among states in specific geographic regions are also a way to manage insecurity. In South Asia, for example, a balance of power maintains a tense peace between India and Pakistan—a peace made more durable by the presence of nuclear weapons, according to realist thinking. In East Asia, Japan's alliance with the United States creates a balance of power with China. In the Middle East, a balance of power between Israel and its Arab neighbors continues. In some regions, a complex set of other balances has developed: between the economically rich, oil-producing states of Saudi Arabia and the Persian Gulf and the economically poor states of the core Middle East; and between Islamic militants (Iran), moderates (Egypt, Tunisia), and conservatives (Saudi Arabia). With the breakup of the Soviet Union, the newly independent states of Central Asia are struggling for position within a newly emerging regional balance of power that includes both Russia and China.

Realist theorists assert that balancing power is the most important technique for managing insecurity. It is compatible with human nature and the nature of the state, which is to act to protect one's self-interest by maintaining one's power position relative to that of others. If a state seeks preponderance through military acquisitions or offensive actions, then war against that state is acceptable under the balance-of-power system. If all states act similarly, the balance can be preserved without war.

One major limitation of the balance-of-power approach, however, is its requirement that states view established friendships with allies as expendable. According to the theory, should power shift, alliances should also shift to maintain the balance—regardless of friendship. But as liberals and constructivists observe, states exist in a kind of society and they resist giving up their "friends," even when power shifts. This idea may explain why, after the collapse of the Soviet Union in 1991, long-standing U.S. allies such as Britain did not abandon their alliance with the United States, even though the bipolar balance of power had collapsed.

A second limitation stems from the inability to manage security during periods of rapid change. A balance-of-power approach supports the status quo. When change occurs, or if the status quo comes to be perceived as unjust, how should other states respond? Rapid change occurred at the end of the Cold War, for example, with the dismemberment of the Soviet Union and the dissolution of the Warsaw Pact alliance. A balance-of-power strategy would have suggested that U.S. allies re-align to fill the power vacuum left by the USSR's demise. Instead, the United States attempted, with mixed success, to lead its allies into a series of escalating confrontations with what it considered "dictatorships" and "supporters of terror." After 2005, the United States' European allies began to balance against U.S. hegemony and unilateralism; however, their effort was stalled by the financial crisis of 2008 and the election of a more cir- cumspect U.S. president, Barack Obama, who preferred multilateral approaches.

DETERRENCE

Although the subject of deterrence has its own literature, it is best understood in rela- tion to the balance of power as the *mechanism* that enables a balance of power to cause peace. At its most basic level, deterrence is the manipulation of fear to prevent an unwanted action. If I am much bigger than you are, I can expect your fear of being hurt or killed to deter you from attacking me. The same is true of a balance of power: when power is balanced, fear of being defeated in war is expected to keep aggressive states from attacking. By contrast, when a rapidly rising state threatens the balance of power, its confidence of victory may tempt it to war. Thus, deterrence is *how* bal- ancing power works to reduce the likelihood of war.

Deterrence theory posits that the credible *threat* of the use of force can prevent vio- lence such as war. In its 2002 National Security Strategy, for example, the United States made the threat very explicit for those who may pursue global terrorism. The United States writes that it will defend "the United States, the American people, our interests at home and abroad by identifying and destroying the threat before it reaches our border. . . . We will not hesitate to act alone, if necessary, to exercise our right of self- defense by acting preemptively against such terrorists, to prevent them from doing harm against our people and our country."[29]

Deterrence theory, as initially developed, is based on several key assumptions.[30] First, the theory assumes that rational decision makers want to avoid resorting to war in those situations in which the anticipated cost of aggression is greater than the expected gain. Second, the theory assumes that nuclear weapons—one particularly intense form of harm—pose an unacceptable risk of mutual destruction, and thus, that decision makers will not initiate armed aggression against a nuclear state. Third, the theory assumes that alternatives to war are available to decision makers, irrespective of the issue of contention.

For deterrence to work, then, states must form alliances or build up their arsenals to present a credible threat. Information regarding the threat must be conveyed to the opponent. Knowing that a damaging reaction will counter an aggressive action, the opponent will decide not to resort to force and thereby destroy its own society.

IN FOCUS

ASSUMPTIONS OF DETERRENCE THEORY

- Decision makers are rational.

- The likelihood of escalation to mutual destruction from warfare is high.

- Alternatives to war are available.

- Attempts to deter insecure states may backfire.

As logical as deterrence sounds, and as effective as it seemed during the Cold War—after all, no nuclear war occurred between the superpowers—the very assumptions on which deterrence is based are frequently subject to challenge. Are all top decision makers rational? Might not one individual or a group of individuals risk destruction in deciding to launch a first strike? Might some states be willing to sacrifice a large number of people, as Germany's Adolf Hitler, Iran's Ayatollah Khomeini, and Iraq's Saddam Hussein were willing to do in the past? How do states credibly convey information about their true capabilities to a potential adversary? Should they? Or would it make more sense to bluff or to lie? For states without nuclear weapons, or for nuclear-weapons states that are launching an attack against a nonnuclear state, the risks of war may seem acceptable: when one's own society is unlikely to be threatened with destruction (as in most asymmetric conflicts), deterrence is more likely to fail.

The security environment makes deterrence even more problematic in the new millennium. First, the rise of terrorism conducted by nonstate actors appears to decrease the possibility that deterrence will work. Because nonstate actors do not hold territory, the threat to destroy such territory in a retaliatory strike cannot be a potent deterrent. Flexible networks—such as Al Qaeda—spread over different geographic areas, rather than an organizational hierarchy located within a particular state, make eliminating those networks very difficult. The increasing willingness of some groups to use suicide terrorism to achieve their objectives has made the logic of deterrence appear particularly shaky. Deterrence depends on the calculation that rational actors will never deliberately act to invite costly reprisals, yet suicide terrorists are willing to sacrifice their own lives. Since loss of life has traditionally been thought of as the highest of all costs, suicide terrorism appears to render deterrence meaningless.[31]

Second, in the changed security environment, the United States may be approaching nuclear primacy.[32] For the first time in nuclear history, the United States may be able to destroy the long-range nuclear arsenals of both Russia and China with a first strike because of improvements in U.S. nuclear capacity (including the ability to track submarines and mobile missiles) the declining capability of the Russian military, and the still slow pace of China's modernization. In fact, China has no long-range bombers and no advance-warning system. If true, U.S. nuclear primacy would deter other states from attacking the United States, but might tempt the United States to a preemptive nuclear strike against its enemies.

Realist approaches to managing insecurity rely mainly on fear, but as we have seen, they also imagine power in almost purely material terms. To the extent that changing norms, or a rise in the power of ideas, has changed world politics, can realist approaches to managing insecurity continue to be effective? If all realists have is bullets, it is hard to see how realist approaches to managing insecurity can succeed unaided. What is the liberal alternative?

Liberal Approaches: Collective Security and Arms Control/Disarmament

Unlike realists, liberals have a theory that imagines a world without war. The core logic of the liberal position acknowledges the structural constraint of anarchy and accepts the priority of state insecurity as a factor motivating interstate relations, but argues that states seeking power, including economic power, will be led by self-interest into successively deeper and broader cooperation with other states, even if at times that cooperation is punctuated by war. Over time, cooperation may be institutionalized, reducing the costs of transactions and increasing the costs and risks of cheating. Liberals also focus on the nature of a state's political system, arguing that, in contrast to the realist view, there are essentially "good" (liberal and open) and "bad" (authoritarian and closed) states. Over time, the rewards that accrue to good states will create pressures and incentives on more and more bad states to become responsible partners in an interstate system. Finally, liberal theorists argue that the democratic peace provides powerful empirical support for their arguments, because it is virtually impossible to cite an example of two democratic states going to war against one another. Given these theoretical underpinnings, liberal approaches to managing insecurity call on the international community or international institutions to coordinate actions to reduce the likelihood and destructiveness of war.

THE COLLECTIVE SECURITY IDEAL

Collective security is captured in the old adage "one for all and all for one." Based on the proposition that aggressive and unlawful use of force by any state against another must be stopped, collective security posits that such unlawful aggression will be met

IN FOCUS

ASSUMPTIONS OF COLLECTIVE SECURITY THEORY

- Wars are caused by aggressive states.

- Aggressors must be stopped.

- Aggressors are easily identified.

- Aggression is always wrong.

- Aggressors will be deterred from aggression by the credible threat of a collective response.

by united action: all (or many) states will unite against the aggressor. Potential aggressors will know this fact ahead of time, and thus, will choose not to act.

Collective security makes several fundamental assumptions.[33] One assumption is that the collective benefit of peace outweighs the individual benefits of war, even a successful war. Another assumption is that aggressors—no matter who they are, friends or foes—must be stopped. This assumption presumes that other members of the international community can easily identify the aggressor. Collective security also assumes moral clarity: the aggressor is morally wrong because all aggressors are morally wrong, and all those who are right must act in unison to meet the aggression. Finally, collective security assumes that aggressors know that the international community will act to punish an aggressor.

Of course, this idea is none other than deterrence, but with a twist. If all countries know that the international community will punish aggression, then would-be aggressors will be deterred from engaging in aggressive activity. The twist is that in liberal theory, states are more likely to calculate their interests collectively as shared interests rather than individually, as in the realist view. Both theoretical perspectives accept alliances as a fundamental aspect of interstate politics, but liberals put more faith in them than realists do. Hence, states will be more secure in the belief that would-be aggressors will be deterred by the prospect of united action by the international community. But for collective security to work, the threat to take action must be credible, and there must be cohesion among all the potential enforcers.

Collective security does not always work. In the period between the two world wars, Japan invaded Manchuria and Italy overran Ethiopia. In neither case did other states act as if it was in their collective interest to respond. Were Manchuria and Ethiopia really worth a world war? In these instances, collective security did not work because, as realists assert, the states capable of acting to halt the violence (particularly Britain and France) could not see sufficient national interest in doing so, especially when the threat of another war with Germany seemed increasingly likely. In the post–World War II era, two major alliance systems—NATO and the Warsaw Pact—arrayed states into two separate camps. States dared not engage in action against an ally or a foe, even if that state was an aggressor, for fear of causing another world war.

Collective security may also fail due to the problematic nature of a key assumption, that aggressors can be easily identified. Easy identification is not always the case. In 1967, Israel launched an armed attack against Egypt: clearly an act of aggression. The week before, however, Egypt had blocked Israeli access to the Red Sea, kicked the UN out of Sinai, and, in combination with Syria and Jordan, moved hundreds of tanks and planes closer to Israel. Clearly these, too, were acts of aggression. Twenty years earlier, the state of Israel had been carved out of Arab real estate. That, too, was an act of aggression. Where does the aggression "begin"? The George W. Bush administration argued in 2003 that its invasion of Iraq was a preemptive war because Saddam Hussein was preparing to operationalize and possibly use a nuclear weapon (or transfer one to a terrorist group). So who is the aggressor? Furthermore, even if an aggressor can be identified, is that party always morally wrong? Due to an understandable fixation on the individual and collective costs of war, collective-security theorists argue, by definition, yes. Yet trying to right a previous wrong is not necessarily wrong; trying to make just a prior injustice is not always unjust. Like the balance of power, at its best, collective security in practice supports the status quo at a specific point in time. If that status quo is unjust, then why isn't the collective security that supports it also unjust?

ARMS CONTROL AND DISARMAMENT

Arms control and general **disarmament** schemes have been the hope of many liberals over the years since the first Hague Convention of 1899. In the rich history of arms control and disarmament treaties since the nineteenth century—including hundreds of treaties limiting the militarization of the polar regions and space, the types of weapons that may be legitimately used (such as antipersonnel land mines, anti-ballistic-missile defenses, and cluster munitions), or even limiting the testing and development of certain weapons (such as nuclear weapons)—there have been two striking features overall: (1) most signatories to these treaties actually abide by their treaty obligations; cheating is rare; and (2) many of those who have been signatories have been of an avowedly "realist" orientation. This is counterintuitive because, as observed in Chapter 3, realists tend to conflate "security" with "capacity to do physical harm." Yet even at the very first Hague Convention in 1899, realist states such as Germany, France, Britain, and Russia all found themselves agreeing to limit the quantity and quality of arms they would manufacture and employ in war. Whatever the rationale for reductions in each individual case, the logic of this approach to security is both powerful and straightforward: fewer weapons means greater security. Regulating arms proliferation (arms control) and reducing the amount of arms and the types of weapons employed (disarmament) should logically reduce the costs of the security dilemma.

During the Cold War, many arms control agreements were negotiated to reduce the threat of nuclear war. For example, in the 1972 Treaty on the Limitation of Anti-ballistic Missile Systems (ABM treaty), both the United States and the Soviet Union agreed not to use a ballistic missile defense as a shield against a first strike by the other. The Strategic Arms Limitations Talks in 1972 and 1979 (SALT I and SALT II, respectively) put ceilings on the growth of both Soviet and U.S. strategic weapons. However, due to the Soviet invasion of Afghanistan in 1979, the U.S. Senate never ratified the second SALT treaty. The Nuclear Nonproliferation Treaty (NPT) was negotiated in 1968 at the United Nations in response to the Cuban missile crisis.

The NPT illustrates both positive and negative effects of such treaties. In force since 1970, the NPT spells out the rules of nuclear proliferation. In the treaty, signatory countries without nuclear weapons agree not to acquire or develop them; states with nuclear weapons promise not to transfer the technology to nonnuclear states and to eventually dismantle their own. During the 1990s, three states that previously had nuclear weapons programs—South Africa, Brazil, and Argentina—dismantled their programs and became parties to the treaty, along with three other states—Belarus, Kazakhstan, and Ukraine—that gave up nuclear weapons left on their territory after the dissolution of the Soviet Union. As with many of the arms control treaties, however, several key nuclear states and threshold non-nuclear states remain outside the treaty, including Cuba, India, Israel, and Pakistan.

The International Atomic Energy Agency (IAEA), a UN-based agency established in 1957 to disseminate knowledge about nuclear energy and promote its peaceful uses, is the designated guardian of the treaty. The IAEA created a system of safeguards, including inspection teams that visit nuclear facilities and report on any movement of nuclear material, in an attempt to keep nuclear material from being diverted to non-peaceful purposes and to ensure that states that signed the NPT are complying. Inspectors for the IAEA visited Iraqi sites after the 1991 Gulf War and North Korean sites in the mid-1990s. Their purpose in the first case was to verify that illegal materials in Iraq had been destroyed and, in the second case, to confirm that nuclear materials in North Korea were being used for nonmilitary purposes only. But the work of the IAEA has been constantly challenged. In 2009, Iran, which, as a signatory to the NPT was obligated to report any facility actively enriching fissile material, was discovered to have an unreported facility in violation of its treaty obligations. Iran's cheating in 2009 has called into question whether it will abide by the constraints of the Joint Comprehensive Plan of Action signed in 2015. This agreement calls upon Iran to cease enrichment of nuclear weapons-grade fuel in exchange for an end to international economic sanctions. In addition, signatories of the NPT that already possess nuclear weapons are expected to reduce their stockpiles, but they have proven reluctant, in most cases, to do so very quickly.

The end of the Cold War and the dismemberment of the Soviet Union resulted in major new arms control agreements. More arms control agreements between the United States and Russia and its successor states are likely as the latter are forced by economic imperatives to reduce their military expenditures. Yet the logic of arms control agreements is not impeccable. Arms control does not eliminate the security dilemma. You can still feel insecure if your enemy has a bigger or better rock than you do. And, as realists would argue, state policy toward such agreements is never assured. Verification is spotty and difficult to implement. For example, in 1994, the United States and North Korea signed the Agreed Framework: North Korea agreed to stop its nuclear weapons program in exchange for a U.S. package deal of energy supplies, light-water reactors, and security guarantees. The framework collapsed in 2002, when North Korea announced it was pulling out of the Nuclear Nonproliferation Treaty in response to U.S. decisions to halt shipments of fuel oil supporting North Korea's electric grid. On North Korea's restarting of the Yongbyon nuclear reactor, used to process weapons-grade nuclear material, the United States and Japan halted aid shipments.

In 2003, North Korea publicly admitted that it was engaged in a nuclear-weapons program; it has subsequently tested both long- and short-range missiles, causing great consternation in the region and in the United States. Is North Korea advancing a nuclear weapons program to enhance its own security? Or is North Korea simply bargaining for more aid in return for promising to halt its nuclear-weapons program? The agreement brokered in 2007 as a result of negotiations conducted among six parties—North Korea, China, Japan, the United States, South Korea, and Russia—directed that North Korea would close its main nuclear reactor in exchange for a package of fuel, food, and other aid. The agreement has proven highly unstable, however. In 2008, North Korea's leader, the late Kim Jong-Il, threatened to resume weapons development because the promised aid package was too small and had arrived too slowly. Later that year, further progress was stalled by rumors that Kim was near death. Kim reappeared in 2009, after which North Korea exploded a nuclear device underground, to widespread dismay and condemnation. Little progress has been made since that time. North Korea tested again in 2013 and in 2016, and in 2014, it tested a new long-range missile, capable, it claimed, of striking targets as far away as Japan.

Given how risky such a scheme would be, the complete disarmament envisioned by liberal thinkers is unlikely. Unilateral disarmament would place disarmed states in a highly insecure position, and cheaters could be rewarded. But incremental disarmament—as outlined in the Chemical Weapons Convention (CWC), which bans the development, production, and stockpiling of chemical weapons—remains a possibility. However, the increasing sophistication and miniaturization of chemical and biological weapons makes them difficult to detect, so it is hard to guarantee compliance. Liberals place their faith in a combination of the self-interest of states (these programs are expensive) and international institutions such as the IAEA to monitor adherence to such limited disarmament schemes.

NATO: Managing Insecurity in a Changing Environment

Managing insecurity is a particular challenge in times of transition in the international system. Such transitions can occur when major powers undergo a change in their actual or perceived ability to project power, protect allies, or threaten enemies. The end of the Cold War was such a moment of transition, as the Soviet Union dissolved and communist regimes were replaced with proto-democratic ones. The collapse of the Soviet Union brought an immediate end to the Warsaw Pact, leaving many countries in Eastern Europe without a major power ally. The end of the Cold War also affected NATO, the Western alliance whose purpose was to balance the now-defunct Warsaw Pact. With this change, some scholars predicted the imminent demise of NATO. What happened, however, was not the organization's demise but its reconfiguration in terms of both the tasks it undertakes and the expansion of its membership.

With the bloody civil war in Yugoslavia and attendant refugee crises in Europe, NATO increasingly took on peacekeeping and stabilization roles in Bosnia. In 1999, NATO undertook its largest military operation since its creation in 1949: Operation Allied Force, the air war over Serbia. Without UN authorization, NATO forces conducted a 78-day air war against the Federal Republic of Yugoslavia in an attempt to halt attacks against ethnic Albanians in the Serbian province of Kosovo. The war resulted in a popular uprising and the attendant overthrow of the Serbian leadership, the extradition of the Serbian strongman Slobodan Milošević to the Hague War Crimes Tribunal, and the petition by Serbia to join NATO's Partnership for Peace program.

Since the "global war on terrorism" began in September 2001, NATO has sought to maintain its relevance in the new security environment.[34] NATO has enhanced its operational capabilities to keep up with technology, created a rapid reaction force to respond to crises, and streamlined its military command structure. It has employed forces "out of area" in Afghanistan and Libya. Its members have helped train the Iraqi military, although the organization did not join the U.S.-led coalition in Iraq.

NATO membership has also expanded as its tasks have diversified. In 1999, the first wave of new members following the end of the Cold War, including Poland, Hungary, and the Czech Republic, were admitted. These new members were to be contributors to enhanced security in the region, not just the recipients of a security umbrella. It has proven more difficult than anticipated, however, to convince these states to make necessary defense reforms, increase defense expenditures, and modernize equipment and training. Yet despite these problems, a second wave of members was admitted in 2004. They included Estonia, Latvia, Lithuania, Slovakia, Slovenia, Romania, and Bulgaria. Albania and Croatia formally joined in 2009, bringing the total NATO membership to 28, along with 22 Partnership for Peace member states and 7 Mediterranean Dialogue states. This round of admissions was a reaction to the war on terrorism: a search by the United States and others for dependable allies who could maintain bases more proximate to the Middle East at a cheaper cost. The newer NATO members could curry favor with the United States and did not have to make reforms to be admitted to the organization.

During most of the 1990s, Russia opposed NATO enlargement, alarmed at seeing its old allies coming under NATO auspices. Russian concerns were reasonable. If NATO's reason for existence was the Soviet threat of invasion and conquest of Western Europe, and the Soviet Union no longer exists, why, asked the Russians, should NATO still exist, much less expand? This question may explain why, for many in Russia, the expansion of the alliance was viewed as a potential military threat. After 9/11, Russian opposition softened, especially once it realized that NATO's newest members were turning it into a kind of "toothless lion." But after the accession of Vladimir Putin to the presidency of the Russian Federation in 2000, opposition to NATO expansion has intensified to the point where Russia intervened militarily in Georgia (2008) and Ukraine (2014) to put NATO on notice that it would no longer tolerate further eastward expansion of NATO. Given that under Putin's leadership, Russia's military has become progressively more effective as compared to its neighbors, and given its unquestioned status as a nuclear superpower, there seems to be little NATO can do to counter Russia's opposition.

To most member states, particularly the United States, NATO expansion has been seen as a natural consequence of winning the Cold War, establishing a new post–Cold War security order, and more recently, trying to respond to new security threats posed by terrorism. Some realists see NATO expansion as a means of achieving relative gains over Russia and further enhancing Western security, while still others argue that NATO should have disbanded after 1991 when its main reason for being disappeared. Many liberals view expansion as a means of strengthening democracy in former communist states and bringing institutional stability to areas threatened with crises, and as a way to use a security institution to facilitate membership in a much more important set of economic and diplomatic institutions, in particular the European Union. But although NATO members have tried to convince Russia that NATO's growth is not an offensive threat, Russia has not viewed this expansion as benign.

For constructivists, the issue of NATO expansion powerfully engages issues of national identity. For states formerly dominated by the Soviet Union, accession to NATO reflected their resentment over that control. Russia opposed NATO expansion not only over security concerns, but also due to the implied insult. To a constructivist,

then, the politics of NATO expansion highlight the nonmaterial bases of interstate relations between the successor states of the former Soviet Union and the former Warsaw
Pact member states.

In Sum: A Changing View of International Security

Traditionally, international security has meant states' security and the defense of states'
territorial integrity from external threats or attack by other states. This was because
only states could master the technology of mass killing; as a result, interstate war proved
the most intense (in terms of deaths-per-unit-of-time) threat to life and property. Over
time, this definition has broadened to include intrastate conflicts as well. In both situations, conflicts arise not only over control of territory but also over control of government and ideas. Although major interstate wars, such as the last century's two world
wars, concentrate destruction in time, intrastate violence has resulted in just as much
or even more destruction. It has become progressively less likely that the destruction
civil wars cause can be contained within their states of origin. Instead, now more than
any time in world history, civil conflicts may involve regional and international actors.
This idea has been the major focus of this chapter.

But a new trend is occurring: the outsourcing of security from nationals in uniform to private security firms and robots.[35] Companies with such deliberately obscure
names as Blackwater (currently known as Academi, but now a part of Constellis Holdings), Sandline International, BDM, COFRAS, and Southern Cross are new actors in
security. G4S based in London is one of the largest, operating in 120 countries and
having more than 620,000 employees. These contracted private companies perform
diverse tasks: servicing military airplanes and ships, providing food for armies, de-
mining, protecting high-profile officials and their families, guarding and interrogat-
ing prisoners of war, training troops, and sometimes carrying out low-intensity military
operations on a client's behalf. Their "soldier" employees—the mercenaries of the
twenty-first century—come from all over the world, from the Ukraine to Fiji, Australia
to Chile and South Africa. Many are former government military personnel. They serve
in locations from Sierra Leone to Sri Lanka, from Bosnia to the Democratic Republic of
Congo, from Iraq to Afghanistan to South Sudan and Kenya.

The use of semi-intelligent or guided robots in war, as in the case of drones (previously discussed), is another form of "outsourcing" that offers a similar benefit to private-
security contracting: casualties will not be human beings who are representing the
state as nationals.

Today, the logistical, legal, and ethical problems emerging from each type of outsourcing remain unclear. Are private contractors merely mercenaries acting out of pecu-

Private security contractors, such as these Blackwater employees, were hired by the U.S. government after the start of the 2003 Iraq war to perform tasks such as protecting high-profile officials, transporting troops and materials, and engaging in occasional combat operations. The role of private contractors in international security has provoked troubling questions about accountability, lines of authority, and the rule of law.

niary self-interest? Or are they pragmatically solving problems that a state's military could not otherwise solve? Are they cost effective? Where do their loyalties lie? To what state or what ideology do they belong? What is their relationship with the organized military? Can they be held accountable for actions they take in war? In other words, do standard of ethics and morals in war apply to these forces? Should the international community employ them for UN-mandated peacekeeping? As regards robots such as drones, what safeguards exist to prevent their arbitrary or irresponsible use? As more and more states acquire this technology, how will they be regulated? Certain of its rectitude, the United States has already set dangerous precedents, reserving the right, for example, to target and kill terrorists—even U.S. citizens—on the sovereign territory of other states. How should the United States react if, say, China used a drone to target and kill a person in Nebraska it considered a dangerous terrorist?

In the waning years of the twentieth century, ideas among theorists have changed concerning who or what should be protected. Changing notions about what security is and who should be protected have been a key topic in constructivist discourse. Should only states be protected? Or should individuals be protected as well, not only from interstate rivalries but from failures of their own government to protect life, property, and ideas? The idea that states and the international community have the obligation, indeed the responsibility, to protect human beings, even if it means intervention in the affairs of another state, is the norm of humanitarian intervention.

But what should the individual be protected against? Should protection include more than that against the physical violence typically associated with interstate conflict, civil war, genocide, nuclear weapons, and terrorism, as discussed in this chapter? Should the concept of security be broadened? In 2004, the UN High-Level Panel on Threats, Challenges, and Change identified additional threats to what it labeled *human security*, a term that has increasingly been used since the early 1990s. Should individuals be protected from infectious diseases and environmental degradation? Should they be protected from the harmful effects of economic globalization or from poverty? We now turn to these economic issues.

Discussion Questions

1. How can we identify an aggressor in international conflicts? Is such identification important? Why or why not?

2. Before World War II, European colonial powers had relatively little difficulty controlling their large overseas empires with few troops. After World War II, this situation changed dramatically. What explains the change?

3. An American decision maker charged with U.S.–Russian Federation policy requests policy memos from realists (an offensive realist and a defensive realist), a liberal, a radical, and a constructivist. How might their respective recommendations differ?

4. North Korea has challenged the norm of nonproliferation, embodied in the Nuclear Nonproliferation Treaty. Is Iran's nuclear development also a challenge to the NPT? Or is it within the treaty's bounds? What are the legal issues? The political issues?

Key Terms

arms control (p. 307)

asymmetric conflict (p. 283)

disarmament (p. 307)

diversionary war (p. 274)

guerrilla warfare (p. 281)

humanitarian intervention (p. 293)

interstate war (p. 264)

intrastate war (p. 264)

09

Nicaraguan opposition to the building of the Chinese-financed canal is mounting among the rural poor, whose homes and livelihoods are threatened by the canal's proposed route. Graffiti and signs like this reading "Chinese get out" are common in areas that would be affected by the canal.

INTERNATIONAL POLITICAL ECONOMY

Nicaragua faces a huge and costly infrastructure project—a new canal linking the Pacific and Atlantic Oceans financed by a Chinese development group. While this effort might signal increased trade and an influx of investment in the Nicaraguan economy, rural Nicaraguans along the route of the proposed new canal fear eviction. In Chinese lettering, signs proclaim "Go Away Chinamen." To the rural population, the threat to their land and livelihood is real; others in Nicaragua and abroad are skeptical about whether a new canal will ever be built. For some, that skepticism comes from the slow reported progress and the difficulty of finding additional financing. Others question whether another canal in Central America is needed since the Panama Canal has been expanded to accommodate bigger ships. For still others in the countryside, their skepticism reflects a general distrust of government. As one rancher put it, "They always come with big plans. And they never do anything."

For the world's poor, is development elusive? Can development promoting the global good hurt local groups and individuals? Can the farmers and ranchers of Nicaragua benefit from economic globalization in 2016?

Few people would dispute that economic **globalization** accurately describes today's international political economy. As Thomas Friedman describes in *The Lexus* *and the Olive Tree*, globalization is the "inexorable integration of markets, nation-states and technologies to a degree never witnessed before in a way that is enabling individuals, corporations and nation-states to reach around the world further, faster, deeper and cheaper than ever before."[1] Economic liberalization and new technologies stimulate not only the increasing flows of capital and trade but also the decreasing territorialization of economic life both at the global and regional levels. But the international political economy was not always as globalized as it is today. How has the international economy changed? What ideas propelled these changes?

LEARNING OBJECTIVES

- Understand the core concepts of economic liberalism.

- Analyze the roles the major international economic institutions and multinational corporations play in the international political economy.

- Describe how the views of mercantilists/statists and radicals differ from those of economic liberals.

- Explain how the international economic system has become globalized in key areas: international finance, international trade, and international development.

- Explain how approaches to achieving economic development have changed over time.

- Show how the global economic crisis and the Eurozone crisis are connected.

- Explain how critics of international economic liberalism and economic globalization reflect differences in ideologies.

The Historical Evolution of the International Economy: Clashing Practices and Ideas

The era from the late Middle Ages through the end of the eighteenth century saw a number of key changes in technology, ideas, and practices that altered the international economy. Spurred by advances in ship design and navigation systems, European explorers opened up new frontiers in the Americas, Asia, and the Middle East to trade and commerce. Although Greek, Phoenician, and Mesopotamian traders had preceded them, the British East India Company, the Hudson's Bay Company, and the Dutch East India Company facilitated trade in goods (and people as slaves), provided capital for investments in the agricultural development of the new lands, and transported cotton, tobacco, and sugar to Europe. Settlers increasingly moved to these lands; linked to the motherland by economics, politics, and culture, they formed a nascent transnational class pursuing individual economic interests.

Writing during this time was the eighteenth-century British economist Adam Smith. As we noted in Chapter 2, Smith began with the notion that human beings act in rational ways to maximize their self-interest. When individuals act rationally, markets develop to produce, distribute, and consume goods. These markets enable individuals to carry out the necessary transactions to improve their own welfare. When there are many buyers and sellers, market competition ensures that prices will be as low as possible. Low prices result in increased consumer welfare. Thus, in maximizing economic welfare and stimulating individual (and therefore collective) economic growth, markets epitomize economic efficiency. Those markets need to be virtually free from government interference; only through a free flow of commerce will efficient allocation of resources occur. That is the rationale underpinning the theory of economic liberalism.

Yet the policies of many European governments at the time reflected an alternative view, **mercantilism**. The goal of a mercantilist government was to build economic wealth as an instrument of state power. Drawing on the views of the Frenchman Jean-Baptiste Colbert (1619–83), an adviser to Louis XIV, the mercantilist view held that states needed to accumulate gold and silver to guarantee power. A strong central government was needed for efficient tax collection and maximization of exports, both geared toward guaranteeing military prowess. Such governments encouraged exports over imports and industrialization over agriculture, protected domestic production against competition from imports, and intervened in trade to promote employment. The United States' first secretary of the treasury, Alexander Hamilton (1757–1804), advocated policies to protect the growth of the new nation's manufacturers. In his "Report on Manufactures" to Congress in 1791, he supported protectionist policies and investment in inventions. Mercantilist policies included high tariffs and discouraged foreign investment in the name of achieving national self-sufficiency.

From the beginning of the nineteenth century through World War I, the expansion of colonialism and the Industrial Revolution occurred as the result of major technological improvements in transoceanic communications, transportation, and manufacturing processes. The European states needed the raw materials found in the colonies, so international trade expanded, as did international investment; capital moved from Europe to the Americas as investors searched for higher profits. Often the creation of those economic links led to political and cultural domination. Britain, in particular, was the center of the

Industrial Revolution, the major trading state and source of international capital, as well as a political and cultural hegemon, contested only by France. Britain facilitated trade by lowering its own tariffs and opening its markets, policing the sea to provide safer transit, and encouraging investment abroad. It is no wonder that this period has been labeled the "Pax Britannica," when the hegemonic power of Great Britain, under the guise of economic liberalism, expanded so that "the sun never set on the British empire."

The excesses of that period gave rise to another economic perspective—radicalism—drawing on the body of Marxist and neo-Marxist writings. Having seen the harsh living conditions of the working class during nineteenth-century industrialization and imperialist expansion, and cognizant of the economic chasm between the developed and the developing worlds during the twentieth century, economic radicals blamed the capitalist system under liberalism. Although interpretations vary, the core belief found in Marxist and neo-Marxist writing is that society basically is conflictual. Conflict emerges from the competition among groups of individuals—namely, the owners of wealth and the workers—for scarce resources. The state tends to support the owners of the means of production. Finally, the owners of capital are determined to expand and accumulate resources at the expense of the working class and those in the developing world. As Marx himself argued, the constant expansion of capitalist markets leads to crises; dangerous speculation by those holders of capital only exacerbates these crises.

The worldwide depression of the 1930s saw a major decline in trade and investment, made worse by "beggar thy neighbor" policies, when states seeking to protect themselves from the effects of the economic crisis hurt others. Thus, at the end of World War II, the goal of the Western victors was to promote openness of trade and stimulate international capital flows while establishing a stable exchange-rate system. While multinational corporations (MNCs) would play a major role in stimulating growth, benefiting from innovations in transportation and communication, the Bretton Woods system, discussed below, is central to understanding the evolution of the international economy since the middle of the twentieth century.

Post–World War II Economic Institutions

At the end of World War II, policy makers established a set of intergovernmental organizations to support economic liberalism.[2] The so-called Bretton Woods institutions—the World Bank, the International Monetary Fund (IMF), and, to a lesser extent, the General Agreement on Tariffs and Trade (GATT), now the World Trade Organization (WTO)—have all played, and continue to play, key roles in the expansion of economic liberalism (see Figure 9.1).

THEORY IN BRIEF

CONTENDING PERSPECTIVES ON THE INTERNATIONAL POLITICAL ECONOMY

	ECONOMIC LIBERALISM	MERCANTILISM/ ECONOMIC REALISM	RADICALISM/ MARXISM
VIEW OF HUMAN NATURE	Individuals act in rational ways to maximize their self-interest	Humans are aggressive; conflictual tendencies	Naturally cooperative as individuals; conflictual in groups
RELATIONSHIP AMONG INDIVIDUALS, SOCIETY, STATE, MARKET	When individuals act rationally, markets are created to produce, distribute, and consume goods; markets function best when free of government interference	Goal is to increase state power, achieved by regulating economic life; economics is subordinate to state interests	Competition occurs among groups, particularly between owners of wealth and laborers; group relations are conflictual and exploitative
RELATIONSHIP BETWEEN DOMESTIC AND INTERNATIONAL SOCIETY	International wealth is maximized with free exchange of goods and services; on the basis of comparative advantage, international economy gains	International economy is conflictual; insecurity of anarchy breeds competition; state defends itself	Conflictual relationships because of inherent expansion of capitalism; seeks radical change in international economic system

The **World Bank** was initially designed to facilitate reconstruction in post–World War II Europe, hence its formal name: the International Bank for Reconstruction and Development. During the 1950s, the World Bank shifted its primary emphasis from reconstruction to development. It now generates capital funds from member-state contributions and from borrowing in international financial markets. Like any bank, its purpose is to loan these funds, with interest, and in the case of the World Bank, to loan them to states for their economic-development projects. Its lending is designed not to replace private capital but to facilitate the use of private capital. While a high proportion of the World Bank's funding has been used for infrastructure projects—hydroelectric dams,

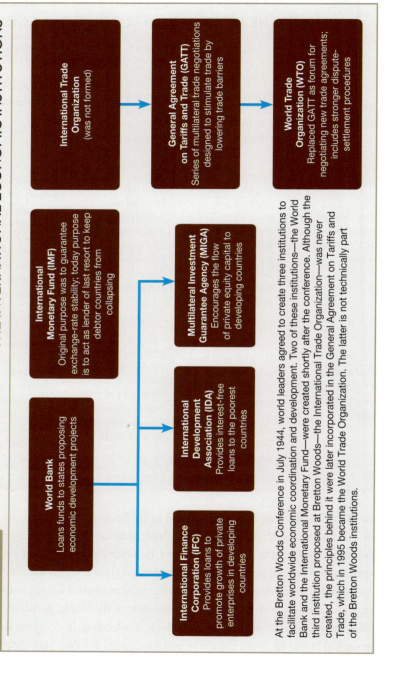

FIGURE 9.1

THE INTERNATIONAL ECONOMIC INSTITUTIONS

World Bank
Loans funds to states proposing economic development projects

International Finance Corporation (IFC)
Provides loans to promote growth of private enterprises in developing countries

International Development Association (IDA)
Provides interest-free loans to the poorest countries

International Monetary Fund (IMF)
Original purpose was to guarantee exchange-rate stability; today purpose is to act as lender of last resort to keep debtor countries from collapsing

Multilateral Investment Guarantee Agency (MIGA)
Encourages the flow of private equity capital to developing countries

International Trade Organization
(was not formed)

General Agreement on Tariffs and Trade (GATT)
Series of multilateral trade negotiations designed to stimulate trade by lowering trade barriers

World Trade Organization (WTO)
Replaced GATT as forum for negotiating new trade agreements; includes stronger dispute-settlement procedures

At the Bretton Woods Conference in July 1944, world leaders agreed to create three institutions to facilitate worldwide economic coordination and development. Two of these institutions—the World Bank and the International Monetary Fund—were created shortly after the conference. Although the third institution proposed at Bretton Woods—the International Trade Organization—was never created, the principles behind it were later incorporated in the General Agreement on Tariffs and Trade, which in 1995 became the World Trade Organization. The latter is not technically part of the Bretton Woods institutions.

basic transportation needs such as bridges and highways, and agribusiness ventures—the bank funds governments and the private sector to carry out a wide array of economic-development activities, including those in the social sector.

The **International Monetary Fund (IMF)** was designed to provide stability in exchange rates. Originally, the fund established a system of fixed exchange rates and, with the United States, guaranteed currency convertibility. From the 1940s to the 1970s, the United States guaranteed the stability of this system by fixing the value of the dollar against gold at $35 an ounce. In 1972, however, this system collapsed when the United States announced that it would no longer guarantee a system of fixed exchange rates. This decision was revised in 1976 when the International Monetary Fund formalized the system of floating exchange rates, a policy more consistent with economic liberalism. At that time, monetary cooperation became the responsibility of the **Group of 7 (G7)**, composed of the United States, Japan, Germany, Great Britain, France, Italy, and Canada. The IMF was to provide short-term loans for member states confronting temporary balance-of-payments difficulties. But, as it became increasingly apparent, "temporary" difficulties were rarely temporary. States needed to undertake structural changes, and the IMF expanded its functions to include policy advice on macroeconomic issues and economic restructuring.

The third part of the liberal economic order was the **General Agreement on Tariffs and Trade (GATT)**. This treaty enshrined important liberal principles:

- support of trade liberalization, because trade is the engine for growth and economic development
- nondiscrimination in trade—the **most-favored-nation (MFN) principle**—whereby states agree to give the same treatment to all other GATT members as they give to their best (most-favored) trading partner
- preferential access in developed markets to products from the South to stimulate economic development in the South
- support for "national treatment" of foreign enterprises—that is, treating them as domestic firms

GATT established these trade principles as well as procedures for moving toward free trade. Multilateral negotiations among those countries sharing major interests in the issue (major producers and consumers of a product, for example) were hammered out and then expanded to all GATT participants. Individual states could claim exemptions (called *safeguards*) to accommodate any domestic or balance-of-payments difficulties that might result from existing trade agreements. A weak dispute-resolution process was developed. Backed by U.S. hegemonic leadership, the Bretton Woods system led to postwar recovery and economic prosperity.

For 20 years after the end of World War II, economic growth occurred much as liberal economic theory had predicted. Growth rates in the developed and the developing world averaged more than 4 percent. Trade volume increased over sevenfold, and poverty rates fell dramatically worldwide. And the volume of international finance exploded, as the communication revolution expanded the possibilities for international financial transactions. The groundwork of economic globalization had been laid.

These changes in the international political economy are viewed differently by the major theories. Adherents of liberal economic theory, as introduced in Chapter 3 and expanded in this chapter, represent the majority of academics and policymakers in the Western world. They believe that internationalization of finance and free unfettered trade is a positive good, leading to greater economic welfare for all. Economic nationalists, the old mercantilists, are not so sure. Their goal is the accrual of individual state power; economic gain by one results in a diminution of power in others. Hence, trade, investment, and finance are all other arenas in the struggle for national power. Marxists see internationalization as leading to domination by a few and hence underdevelopment and exploitation of the poorer classes and states. Therefore, radical reforms are needed for the redistribution of power. By contrast, social constructivists recognize that polices are affected by historical and societal factors. Neither individual nor state preferences are stable or consistent; rather, there is a contestation over beliefs and ideologies.

How then does the international economy function in the twenty-first century? We examine three different areas: international finance, international trade, and economic regionalization. Then we turn to two of the major challenges of contemporary political economy—the gap between the rich and poor, both between states and within states, and contemporary global economic crises. Finally, we examine the arguments of the critics of international economic liberalism.

How the Globalized Economy Works Today

International Finance

Capital movements played a key role in the earlier development phases of the international political economy, as they do today. International capital traditionally moves in two ways. First, national currencies, like goods and services, are bought and sold in a free market system. In such a system of *floating exchange rates*, the market—individuals and governments buying and selling currencies—determines the actual value of one currency compared with other currencies. Just as for a tangible good, each national currency has a supply and demand, and the prices of each currency adjust continually in response to market supply and demand. According to liberal thinking, floating exchange rates will result in market equilibrium, in which supply equals demand. Second, capital frequently moves through investment. **Direct foreign investment (FDI)** includes the building of factories and investing in the facilities for extraction of natural resources. **Portfolio investment** includes investing in another country's stocks or bonds, either short or long term, without taking direct control of those investments.

MNCs play a major role in the movement of capital. Before World War II, most MNCs were in manufacturing—General Motors, Ford, Siemens, Nestlé, and Bayer were among the many MNCs in this category. Today, there are about 60,000 MNCs (depending on one's definition), with 51 MNCs among the largest 100 economies in the world. They account for 70 percent of worldwide trade. Of the largest, 60 percent have their headquarters in either the United States, Canada, or Western Europe with about 34 percent headquartered in Asia. Large MNCs include such well-known names as Walmart, Exxon Mobil, Royal Dutch Shell, Toyota, and General Motors, but also less well-known companies, like Sinopec, HSBC Holdings, Carrefour, Royal Bank of Scotland, Gazprom, and Tesco. Those MNCs provide both foreign direct investment and portfolio investments.

Indeed, between the 1960s and the 1980s, private international capital provided essential lending to the successful Asian "tigers," including Taiwan and South Korea. In fact, the infusion of private investment in particular emerging economies—China, Brazil, Argentina, Chile, South Korea, Mexico, Singapore, Turkey, and Thailand—has played a major role in their economic success. Yet the very volatility of private capital flows makes them unreliable for sustained development in some parts of the world, and private capital alone cannot explain economic outcomes in these countries.

The poorest of states typically have more difficulty attracting private investment. Until recently, African countries typically have received the least. Separate institutions within the World Bank were established to provide capital to states that were unable to attract private investment alone. The International Finance Corporation (IFC) and the International Development Association (IDA) were created in 1956 and 1960, respectively, for that purpose. The IFC provides loans to promote the growth of private enterprises in developing countries. The IDA provides capital to the poorest countries, usually in the form of interest-free loans. Repayment schedules of 50 years theoretically allow the developing countries time to reach economic takeoff and sustain growth. Funds for the IDA need to be continually replenished by major donor countries. In 1988, the Multilateral Investment Guarantee Agency (MIGA) was added to the World Bank group. This agency meets its goal—augmenting the flow of private-equity capital to developing countries—by insuring investments against losses. Such losses may result from expropriation, government currency restrictions, or civil war or ethnic conflict. Even with these changes, since the mid-1980s, the flows from both multilateral institutions (the World Bank institutions, regional development banks) and official bilateral donors (the United States, Germany, Japan) have declined as a percentage of total capital flows; at the same time, private capital flows from MNCs and other private sources have expanded. During the international financial crisis that began in 2008, however, the direction was reversed temporarily.

Beginning in the 1980s, international financial flows accelerated through several other mechanisms. Exchange rates were no longer fixed, so traders in currency exchange markets and in MNCs could capitalize on buying and selling currencies, often in very short periods, facilitated by increasing technological sophistication of communications. By the beginning of the new millennium, such currency transactions averaged more than $3 trillion a day. Markets developed new financial instruments, such as **derivatives** (options against the future in a variety of asset classes, including loans and mortgages). These instruments were packaged and sold around the world, spreading risk and accelerating the flow of capital. New economic actors, **sovereign wealth funds**—state-owned investment funds composed of financial assets, including stocks, bonds, precious metal, property, or other financial instruments—formed in capital-surplus countries such as China and in the major petroleum exporters such as Kuwait, the United Arab Emirates, Norway, Russia, and Canada. Those wealth funds have been able to move capital quickly across national boundaries, taking advantage of currency differentials and buying and selling new financial instruments to maximize long-term economic return for what many recognize may be a declining resource. Finally, economic liberalization has led to the emergence of **offshore financial centers**, such as the Cayman Islands, Bermuda, and the British Virgin Islands. These jurisdictions have low taxation and little or no regulation. Individuals, companies, and states can move capital in and out rapidly via electronic transfers, making millions of transfers daily.

The Asian financial crisis of the 1990s illustrates the possible outcomes of the globalization of finance. Beginning in Thailand in 1997, in a relatively short period, 2 percent of gross domestic product fled that country. Within weeks, the crisis spread to Indonesia, Malaysia, the Philippines, and beyond. Many countries were unable to adjust to the rapid withdrawal of capital. Exchange rates plummeted to 50 percent of precrisis values, stock markets fell 80 percent, and real GDP dropped 4 to 8 percent. Individuals lost their jobs as companies went bankrupt or were forced to restructure. Millions of people were forced into poverty. In Thailand, then spreading to South Korea and Taiwan, and eventually, to Brazil and Russia, economies that had previously depended on external trade experienced an unparalleled sense of economic vulnerability. Fueled by instantaneous communication, the capacity to move trillions of dollars daily, and the power of MNCs, traders, and financial entrepreneurs, economic globalization quickly displayed its pitfalls. The largely unregulated market had melted down, and states and individuals appeared helpless.

The IMF responded to the social and political upheaval with large, controversial bailout packages to three of the affected countries (Thailand, $17 billion; Indonesia, $36 billion; and South Korea, $58 billion); lengthy sets of conditions that each country was supposed to follow; and monitoring devices to ensure compliance. Extensive structural reforms would transform their economies from semimercantilist to more market-oriented ones. In South Korea, for example, the government lifted restrictions on capital movements and foreign ownership, permitted companies to lay off workers, and adopted measures to restructure the country's financial institutions. Budget cuts eliminated more social services and pushed more families below the poverty line, leading to a backlash against governments and the IMF. Solutions that the international financial institutions implemented in one country proved counterproductive in others, and marginalized groups suffered. Dissatisfaction with IMF policies led many in developing countries to conclude that these institutions were captive to the interests of the developed world.

Yet following two years of economic stress and the wounded credibility of the IMF, none of the countries involved retreated from globalization or the international financial markets, and all resumed a path of strong economic growth. Critics of the IMF response focus on the so-called **moral hazard** problem: states were rescued from the consequences of their reckless behavior, providing little incentive for them to change that behavior. Later in this chapter we will examine the international economic crises beginning in 2008 and see similar kinds of responses: the contraction of some key economies, the spillover of economic hardship around the world because of globalization, the reaction of governments and international institutions, and reminders of the moral hazard dilemma.

International Trade

Economic growth is fueled by both financial and trade flows. This idea was the key contribution of liberal economic theorists beginning with Adam Smith. Liberal economics recognizes that states differ in their resource endowments of land, labor, and capital. Under these conditions, worldwide wealth is maximized if states engage in international trade.

The British economist David Ricardo (1772–1823) developed a theory that states should engage in international trade according to their **comparative advantage**. Because each state differs in its ability to produce specific products—because of differences in natural-resource bases, labor force characteristics, and land values—each state should produce and export that which it can produce most efficiently and import goods that other states can produce more efficiently. Thus, states maximize gains from trade. However, individual actors can be hurt in this process, necessitating periodic government intervention to ensure that all people gain.

Consider the production of cars and trucks in the United States and Canada. The United States can produce both cars and trucks using fewer workers than Canada would use, making production less expensive in the United States. Under the principle of *absolute* advantage, the United States would manufacture both cars and trucks, and then export both to Canada. However, under *comparative* advantage, each country should specialize; the United States should produce the car, for which it has a relative advantage in production, and Canada, the truck. By trading cars for trucks, each country gains by specialization. Each state minimizes its opportunity cost. Each gives up something to get something else. The United States gives up the production of trucks to gain car production; Canada gives up the production of cars to gain more truck production. Each country gains by shifting resources to manufacture more of the commodity it produces more efficiently and by trading for the other commodity. Both countries can consume more than if they remained in isolation, consuming only what they produced domestically. Liberal economics posits that under comparative advantage, production is oriented toward an international market. Efficiency in production is increased, and worldwide wealth is maximized.

According to the principle of comparative advantage, labor-intensive production will move to countries where labor is cheap, while capital-intensive production (such as research and development in technology or pharmaceuticals) will move to countries with abundant capital. China's large population makes it attractive to labor-intensive manufacturers like Nike, although that may be changing as Chinese wages increase.

While international trade based on comparative advantage may result in economic growth of the collectivity, individual states also have other policy objectives. They want to maintain domestic employment levels and minimize unemployment. They want to enforce their own domestic labor and environmental standards. They may want to help subsidize emerging sectors to enable them to be competitive. They often view some economic sectors as vital for national security reasons and thus seek to protect domestic production or prevent exports. Therefore, negotiations over trading arrangements must consider not only the anticipated economic gains from opening up the economy to competition from others, but also the costs of achieving the other objectives. It is no wonder trade negotiations have been so contentious.

INTERNATIONAL TRADE NEGOTIATIONS

The negotiating parties in GATT, the forerunner of the World Trade Organization, sought to expand international trade by lowering trade barriers. That work occurred over the course of eight negotiating rounds, with each round progressively cutting tariffs, giving better treatment to the developing countries, and addressing new problems (subsidies and countervailing duties). For example, in the Kennedy Round, between 1963 and 1967, tariff cuts averaged 35 percent on $40 billion of trade among 62 countries. In the following Tokyo Round, between 1973 and 1979, 102 states negotiated tariff cuts, again amounting to more than 35 percent on $100 billion of trade. In addition, more favorable arrangements were negotiated for developing countries. Overall, between 1946 and the mid-1990s, tariffs were reduced in the major trading countries from an average of 40 percent to 5 percent on imported goods.

The final round, called the Uruguay Round, began in 1986. The Uruguay Round covered new items such as services (insurance), intellectual property rights (copyrights, patents, trademarks), and, for the first time, agriculture. Previously, agriculture was seen as too contentious an issue, complicated by both U.S. agricultural subsidies and the European Union's protectionist Common Agricultural Policy (CAP). Agreement was reached to begin to phase out agricultural subsidies. In late 1994, the most comprehensive trade agreement in history was finally reached, a 400-page document covering everything from paper clips to computer chips. Tariffs on manufactured goods were cut by an average of 37 percent among members. The developing countries that participated in these tariff cuts—the liberalizers—enjoyed a full percentage point per year boost in growth compared with the nonliberalizers.

In 1995, GATT became a formal institution, renaming itself the **World Trade Organization (WTO)**. The WTO incorporated the general areas of GATT's jurisdiction and expanded jurisdiction in services and intellectual property. Regular ministerial meetings give the WTO a political prominence that GATT lacked. Representing states that conduct over 90 percent of the world's trade, the WTO has the task of implementing the Uruguay Round, serving as a forum for trade negotiations and providing a venue for trade review, dispute settlement, and enforcement.

Two important procedures were initiated in the WTO. First is the Trade Policy Review Mechanism (TPRM), which conducts periodic surveillance of the trade practices of member states. Under this procedure, there is a forum where states can question each other about trade practices. Second is the Dispute Settlement Body, designed as an authoritative panel to hear and settle trade disputes. With the authority to impose sanctions against violators, this body is more powerful than earlier GATT arrangements.

Getting global participation in the WTO has proved a painstaking task. China's accession to the WTO in 2001, after 15 years of negotiations, illustrates the long process and significant concessions that some countries must make to participate. WTO rules require domestic legislation and clarification. China revised its laws to permit foreign ventures in previously restricted areas, leading to a significant inflow of foreign investment in telecommunications, tourism, insurance, and banking. China continues to dismantle barriers to trade, relaxing tariffs and quotas. Special domestic courts hear WTO-related disputes. China is now proactive in the WTO itself. The country is a regular party to disputes, having acted as a complainant in 12 cases, a respondent in 33, and a third party in 116 as of early 2015, even though it has lost a majority of the cases. The difficulties have been enormous. Since China's laws governing foreign investment and joint ventures were rudimentary, its security markets were not prepared for liberalization. China still lags on intellectual property-rights issues, long a source of contention. Vietnam, which joined the WTO in 2007, is undergoing some of the same reforms. In 2012, Russia joined as well, following 18 years of contentious negotiations, largely over industrial subsidies. In each case, disentangling the government from the economy has proven to be a difficult task.

The WTO process remains contentious, as illustrated by the Doha Round launched in 2001. The negotiations ended in stalemate, pitting the United States and the EU against emerging economies, such as India, Brazil, and China. The main sticking point has been the liberalization of agricultural markets. Neither the United States nor the EU was willing to reduce farm subsidies significantly, which would have made agricultural products from developing countries more competitive in international markets. India and China, in particular, sought, if not an end to farm subsidies, then special safeguard mechanisms for their own poor farmers to ensure food security. Many blamed the WTO's director-general Roberto Azavedo for not exercising more leadership to iron out disagreements. More generally, however, the Doha Round failed over the perception of fairness in trade. Already dissatisfied with new rules that opened competition in investment and government procurement, the developing countries sought more advantages in the politically sensitive areas of agriculture and other labor-intensive sectors.

In 2013 and 2014, negotiators finally broke the impasse. India and the United States agreed that India and other developing countries would not incur penalties for imposing subsidies greater than the WTO's cap of 10 percent on grain produced for food in their own country, nor for stockpiling grain to guarantee food security for impoverished citizens. That agreement paved the way for a trade-facilitation agreement to streamline customs procedures and upgrade border and port infrastructure. In actuality, as *The Economist* reports, Doha seems to have "fizzled out. The WTO is still good at enforcing existing trade agreements, but has not managed to bring in a comprehensive new deal for two decades."[3]

Negotiating agreements among 161 countries at varying levels of development and with diverse national objectives is a challenge. Meanwhile, as discussed later, the United States, the European Union, ASEAN, and others are pursuing regional and bilateral trade agreements, often with mutually incompatible rules, that will make future global agreements even harder to conclude. Not at the negotiating table as independent actors, but key interests, nonetheless, are multinational corporations.

THE ROLE OF MULTINATIONAL CORPORATIONS

Multinational corporations play a key role as engines of economic growth, providing both international finance and items to trade. To many economic liberals, MNCs are the vanguard of the liberal order. They are the "embodiment par excellence of the liberal ideal of an interdependent world economy. [They have] taken the integration of national economies beyond trade and money to the internationalization of production. For the first time in history, production, marketing, and investment are being organized on a global scale rather than in terms of isolated national economies."[4] To liberals, MNCs are a positive development: economic improvement happens through the most efficient mechanism. MNCs invest in capital stock worldwide, they move money to the most efficient markets, and they finance projects that industrialize and improve agricultural output. MNCs are the transmission belt for capital, ideas, and economic growth. In the liberal ideal, MNCs prefer to act independently of states; the market itself will regulate behavior. Any abuses of the market by MNCs can be best corrected by other market actors, or at worst by government regulation.

MNCs take many different forms and engage in many different activities:

- importing and exporting goods and services
- making significant investments in a foreign country
- buying and selling licenses in foreign markets
- engaging in contract manufacturing—permitting a local manufacturer in a foreign country to produce their products
- opening manufacturing facilities or assembly operations in foreign countries

Whatever the specific form that their business takes, MNCs choose to participate in international markets for a variety of reasons. They seek to avoid tariff and import barriers, as many U.S. firms did in the 1960s when they established manufacturing facilities in Europe to circumvent the external barriers of the newly established European Economic Community. They may seek to reduce transportation costs by moving facilities closer to consumer markets. Some MNCs are able to obtain incentives such as tax advantages or labor concessions from host governments; these incentives can cut production costs and increase profitability. Others go abroad so they can meet the competition and the customers, capitalize on cheaper labor markets (e.g., Chinese firms moving production to Vietnam or Laos), or obtain the services of foreign technical personnel (e.g., computer firms in India). These reasons are based in economics, but rationales based on the political policies of the host state may also play a role. MNCs may move abroad to circumvent tough governmental regulations at home, such as banking rules, currency restrictions, or environmental regulations. In the process, MNCs become not only economic organizations but also political ones, potentially influencing the policies of both home and host governments.

Some liberal economists go further than extolling the economic benefits of liberalism or the virtues of MNCs. They see a positive relationship between the international liberal economy and peace. We saw one aspect of this view in our discussion of the democratic peace in Chapter 5. Norman Angell, recipient of the 1933 Nobel Peace Prize, argued in favor of stimulating free trade among liberal capitalist states, in the belief that enhanced trade would be in the economic self-interest of all states. But, more than that, Angell argued that national differences would vanish with the formation of an international market. Interdependence would lead to economic well-being and eventually to world peace; war would become an anachronism.[5] Although not all liberals agree with this formulation, economic liberalism does suggest specific economic policies (open markets, free trade, free flow of goods and services). Liberals also posit that government's role should be as limited as possible, merely protecting property rights and providing a functioning legal system. Under this formulation, liberals view international competition as healthy and desirable, with the potential to lead to more peaceful interactions.

Economic Regionalization

Despite the efforts of the World Trade Organization and multinational corporations to support internationalization or globalization of economic life, economic regionalization has seen a resurgence. Since the 1990s, more regional economic arrangements have been negotiated, and those already operational have been strengthened. What is the relationship between globalization and regionalism? Is regionalism another step toward enhanced globalization, or is regionalism really an obstacle to globalization?

EUROPEAN ECONOMIC INTEGRATION

The establishment of the European Union (discussed in Chapter 7) and the accompanying economic integration have had a major impact on the international political economy and have become models for other regions. European economic integration was predicated on the notion that a larger market, along with the free movement of goods and services, would permit economies of scale and specialization to stimulate growth, competition, and innovation while enhancing opportunities for investment—all goals compatible with liberal economics. The European Union has generally proven successful in achieving some of these objectives, creating a single market and developing a monetary union. Yet to achieve these objectives, the EU has relied on some protectionist measures, and in doing so, may have only diverted trade from one group to another.

The impetus for expanded European economic integration lay in part in Europe's sluggish economic growth in the 1970s and 1980s, a time when the United States and Japan were increasingly competitive. To stimulate Europe's growth, and hence its international competitiveness, the Single European Act of 1987 accelerated the integration process, setting the goal of achieving a single market by 1992. That effort involved removing physical, fiscal, and technical barriers to trade and harmonizing national standards by adopting more than 300 community directives. Some parts of the goal—the elimination of customs barriers—were quickly achieved; other areas—labor mobility—have proved more problematic. Although most countries eliminated passport controls and adopted similar visa rules, recognition of education and professional qualifications has proven a thorny issue. Abolishing technical barriers to trade has been difficult because of differing health and safety standards, but the process is ongoing, as is the effort to break state monopolies and eliminate state aids to specific sectors.

The overall results have been positive, with the growth of all types of economic transactions across state borders deepening integration among the national economies of the 28 member states. Exports of goods and services constitute more than one-third of the GDP for the average EU member. More than 70 percent of total trade in goods is conducted with other EU members. Not only is trade integrated but so are capital flows; cross-border mergers and acquisitions have accelerated. The broad consensus is that European integration has resulted in greater trade creation and had a positive welfare effect on member and nonmember states.[6]

The EU is more than a regional trading area or a single market. During the discussions for the single market, the outlines of a monetary union were also negotiated. With monetary stability and a single currency, the union would grow and prosper even more. The European Monetary Union, set forth in the Maastricht Treaty in 1991, called for the establishment of a single currency, the euro; it became the unit of exchange for businesses in 1998 and for consumers in 2002. Thereafter, the individual 17 members of the Eurozone could no longer use exchange rates or interest rates as instruments of economic policy. Most observers agree that the euro has facilitated business transactions and eliminated the uncertainty caused by fluctuations in exchange rates. But the euro has come under unprecedented pressure since 2009, creating a financial crisis and a situation that jeopardizes the future of the whole European integration project. This situation is discussed below.

The European Union very early recognized, just as international trade negotiators did, that agriculture was different from other economic sectors. First, agricultural prices dramatically fluctuate with weather and disease, so there has long been a strong incentive to moderate the price fluctuations caused by supply volatility. Second, foodstuffs are viewed as vital for national security; in emergencies, no state wants its population to depend on others for food. Third, in many countries, the well-organized farm sector enjoys disproportionate political power. For all these reasons, the EU adopted the Common Agricultural Policy (CAP). The CAP has changed over time, moving gradually away from a production-oriented policy in which the EU purchases surplus crops from farmers at guaranteed prices and then either stores the surplus, anticipating higher prices in the future, or donates it to food aid programs, absorbing the losses. Since the 2003 reforms, the EU has moved toward a Single Payment Scheme, where each country chooses whether the EU payment goes to the farm or the region. Farmers choose to produce any commodity, except fruit, vegetables, or potatoes. Price interventions by the EU are limited to wheat, butter, and types of milk. Large farmers are being phased out of the program.

The CAP's total budget is 42 percent of the EU budget, down from 71 percent in 1984. The CAP has proved to be one of the most controversial EU policies. Not only has it been a major issue for states seeking membership and wanting their share of the agricultural budget, but it is also a critical issue in multilateral negotiations because nonmembers pay more for EU agricultural products.

Have the EU's policies contributed to economic globalization or proved an impediment? Most economists agree that the openness of the European markets has benefited Europeans and become increasingly compatible with the goals of the multilateral global system. Indeed, the EU has developed a web of preferential agreements with its neighbors in the Mediterranean area and with former colonies having shared histories in Africa, as well as with other regional trade agreements, including the North American Free Trade Agreement and Mercosur in Latin America. In general, the EU has enhanced that region's global economic power, making it more competitive with both the United States and China.

But are conditions in Europe—similarity of economic, political, and social systems; a history of post–World War II cooperation; and the development of nascent community political institutions—also present in other parts of the world?

THE NORTH AMERICAN FREE TRADE AGREEMENT

The free-trade area negotiated by the United States, Canada, and Mexico in 1994 differs substantially from the European Union and other regional schemes. It comprises one dominant economy and two dependent ones: Mexico's and Canada's combined economic strength is one-tenth that of the United States. The driving force behind NAFTA was not political elites but business interests (including multinational corporations) seeking larger market shares than their Japanese and European competition and free-trade advocates in all countries. It was opposed by labor, environmental, and other groups. The phasing out of many restrictions on foreign investment and most tariff and nontariff barriers, as well as the many restrictions on foreign investment, has allowed MNCs to shift production to low-wage labor centers in Mexico and to gain economically by creating bigger companies through mergers and acquisitions.

The social, political, and security dimensions we saw in the European Union are absent from NAFTA. Cooperation in trade and investment is not intended to lead to the free movement of labor, as the European Union championed. The goal is quite the opposite; the United States expects that Mexican workers will *not* seek employment in the United States, because economic development in Mexico will provide ample employment opportunities. And economic cooperation does not mean political integration in NAFTA. With NAFTA, economic integration is to remain just that—confined to specific economic sectors.

The phased elimination of tariff and nontariff barriers has resulted in expansion of trade, particularly for Mexico. Mexico's exports increased from $60 billion in 1994 to almost $400 billion in 2013. With the completion of the free-trade area and the dismantling of both trade and investment barriers, trade among the three partners increased to almost $1 trillion in 2010, a 218 percent increase since 1993. Foreign direct investment among the three countries has increased tenfold. Since 2005, the rate of growth in trade has slowed, however, largely because of the growth of trade with China and the latter's admission to the WTO in 2001.

Other provisions of NAFTA deal with property rights of companies making investments in the three countries and with protection of some domestic producers, notably the Mexican oil and gas industry and the U.S. shipping industry. NAFTA's sanitary and phytosanitary measures are designed to protect people and animals from health risks, although such protective measures may not be imposed for economic reasons alone. NAFTA's flexible standards permit national and local governments to impose stricter standards. Export subsidies are eventually to be eliminated, though they are permitted in the Mexican market. There are also incentives for buying within the region. Committees have been established to monitor and promote these various provisions.

Yet the economic controversies generated by NAFTA continue to be profound, illustrating that the state is not a unitary actor. Labor unions in the United States estimate that hundreds of thousands of workers have lost their jobs to Mexico. Environmental groups point to firms in the United States relocating to Mexico to take advantage of weak environmental regulations. Canadian labor contends that the country is becoming too dependent on natural resources exports, while manufacturing has lagged. Mexican supporters point to major increases in labor productivity and growth of exports, while critics point to the slide in real manufacturing wages with lower-skilled jobs moving to China. And as Jorge Castañeda, Mexico's former foreign minister reports, "If the purpose of the agreement was to spur economic growth, create jobs, boost productivity, lift wages, and discourage emigration, then the results have been less clear-cut."[7] Mexico has failed to develop backward linkages in its export sector, namely because of foreigners' unwillingness to invest in Mexico. Foreign investment in Mexico has increased from $4.4 billion in 1993 before NAFTA to about $22 billion annually. But that is well below foreign investment in such countries as Brazil, Chile, and Colombia, among others—not members of NAFTA. To radical opponents, NAFTA is yet another example of U.S. expansionism and exploitation of the Mexican workforce.

The NAFTA case illustrates that, as in all regional economic arrangements, there will be winners and losers. In NAFTA, agriculture and manufacturing in general may well be the winners. Agricultural markets are better integrated, and consumers enjoy lower prices with virtually all tariffs eliminated. Both Canada and Mexico are now large markets for U.S. agricultural exports. The share of Canadian exports absorbed by the United States has expanded, and agricultural exports from Mexico have boomed. Tariffs on manufactured goods have been almost entirely eliminated. But some manufacturers and some groups of individuals have also been losers in all countries, just as the critics argued. Both radicals and economic nationalists have ample evidence to support their analyses.

Believing that there will be more winners than losers, other regions have developed regional trading arrangements. Asia is a relative newcomer.

ASIA: ASEAN FREE TRADE AREA

Individual East Asian countries have experienced phenomenal economic growth through competitive exports; prior to the 1990s, most of the exports went to either the United States or European countries. In 1992, the Association of Southeast Asian Nations (ASEAN) established the ASEAN Free Trade Area (AFTA). Its goal is twofold: to attract foreign investment to the region, taking advantage of economies of scale, and to increase members' competitive edge in the global market by eliminating tariff and nontariff barriers within ASEAN. The exception to these reductions is rice—the food staple of the region—and certain other highly sensitive products. And like the EU, AFTA has also emphasized nontariff barriers, quantitative restrictions, and harmonizing customs rules. By the end of 2014, 70 percent of ASEAN intraregional trade incurred no tariffs, and the average tariff rate was less than 5 percent. Unlike in the EU, however, the goal is not to create a common external tariff.

Compared to either the EU or NAFTA, the original AFTA agreement is relatively brief, with no binding commitments. Under the ASEAN Charter adopted in 2007, the organization has legal personality, giving it authority to conclude trade agreements with countries and regional, subregional, and international organizations. ASEAN has agreements with India, Japan, China, and South Korea, among others. Although AFTA members signed agreements to form an integrated ASEAN Economic Community by 2015 (minus a common currency), that has not occurred. The hope is that closer regional economic integration will boost growth. Whether ASEAN members can bridge their large differences in levels of development and national standards, however, remains to be seen. China has voiced interest in joining AFTA—a step apt to complicate regional economic integration.

TRANSREGIONAL ECONOMIC ARRANGEMENTS

The United States is negotiating on both trade and investment issues with both Asia and Europe. In late 2015, the United States, Japan, and ten Pacific Rim countries (including both developed and developing states such as Canada, Chile, Mexico, Vietnam, and Australia) reached agreement on provisions affecting 40 percent of the world's economy through the Trans-Pacific Partnership (TPP). Proponents claim it is a standard setter for global commerce. Import tariffs on 18,000 American products, including automobiles, machinery, technology, and agricultural products, would be phased out. Macroeconomic cooperation would be strengthened, although there is no enforceable currency provision. There are provisions for protection for labor and the environment, going well beyond what is found in other trade agreements. Stricter rules are included for protection of copyrights and patents. One estimate concludes that the agreement would boost the world economy by $223 billion in the next decade, but absent the final details, that estimate is just that—an estimate.[8]

The key question is China. For some, the purpose of TPP is to contain China's rise. To others, the expectation is that China will eventually join, as will others like South Korea. With China occupying such a key position of the global supply chain, it is hard to see the viability of the agreement without China. Both U.S. congressional skepticism and public concern for the loss of jobs and stagnant incomes means that U.S. passage of the agreement through Congress is not guaranteed.

The United States and the European Union are also negotiating a series of trade and investment agreements that would knit together their economies even more closely.

In 2013, one-fifth of U.S. exports went to the EU, while the EU exported one-eighth of its goods to the United States. The proposed Transatlantic Trade and Investment Partnership (TTIP) is intended to reduce obstacles to trade and investment, such as EU barriers to genetically modified foods, and empower U.S. firms to sue in local European courts. Some Europeans are concerned about granting more rights to U.S. firms, which could lead to weakened worker protections, but some economists predict the deal could result in economic gains equivalent to an extra $700 per year for each European family of four.[9] The negotiations continue.

THE DEBATE OVER REGIONAL AND PREFERENTIAL TRADE AGREEMENTS

Since 1990, the number of regional and preferential trade agreements has exploded from roughly 50 in 1990 to nearly 400 in 2014, and another 200 are pending. With this proliferation, three debates regarding regionalization of economics have emerged. First, do regional trade agreements improve the economic welfare of their members through trade creation, or is trade actually diverted and economic welfare reduced? With regional trade agreements, some trade is created in goods produced efficiently relative to the rest of the world. Trade is also diverted from efficient nonmembers because of the preferences states grant to each other, and hence, state welfare is reduced.

Second, are regional trade agreements a stepping-stone or a stumbling block to global trade arrangements? On the one hand, they clearly reduce the number of actors in international negotiations and enhance competitiveness of some domestic industries, making it easier to argue for liberalization. On the other hand, under regional trade agreements, larger economies can impose their will and interest groups may find it easier to lobby for their interests, inhibiting freer global trade. Economist Jagdish Bhagwati, a prominent opponent of regional trade agreements, calls this patchwork of agreements "termites in the trading system."[10] Regional agreements make states less likely to agree to global tariff cuts; freer trade may erode the narrow gains already won.

Third, does economic regionalization in broad areas of economic and social policy enhance the position of labor and improve environmental arrangements? Or, does economic regionalization force a downward pressure on wages and environmental standards as countries and regions actively compete for trade and foreign direct investment? While this may not be an issue for most of the trade agreements, it is a critical issue for the major agreements discussed above.

The economic challenges of the twenty-first century are actually challenges whose origins we can trace to the last century. The issues of how best to achieve international development and how to cope with economic crises in the era of globalization have risen to the top of the agenda.

Economic Challenges in the Twenty-First Century

International Development

The end of colonialization following the end of World War II and through the mid-1960s led not only to the geopolitical competition between the United States and the Soviet Union (as Chapter 2 discusses) but also to the emergence of newly independent states who were poor, lacking the material resources and expertise to deliver economic goods to their citizens. Very quickly, international programs developed to begin to meet the needs of these states. These included the UN's Expanded Programme of Technical Assistance, which in the 1950s became the primary UN development agency, the regional commissions, and other programs pushed by the coalition of the South or the Group of 77 developing countries, as explained in Chapter 7. And the World Bank's affiliates, the International Finance Corporation and the International Development Association, as discussed earlier, were designed to address the issues of the developing world. GATT itself adopted the idea of more favorable treatment for developing countries. Even the Doha Round of trade negotiation was labeled a "development" round, although, as one cynic put it, the round "has not filled any bellies."[11]

Despite these efforts, the most developed countries, largely in the North, average $40,046 gross national income (GNI) per capita and still bask in relative wealth, with high consumption habits, high levels of education and health services, and social-welfare safety nets. In contrast, the least developed countries, mainly in the South, still struggle to meet basic caloric needs, with poor educational and health services and no welfare nets to meet the needs of the poorest of the poor, averaging only $2,904 GNI per capita. The Human Development Index (HDI) in Table 9.1 shows these stark contrasts across several indicators. Caused by many factors—colonialism, earlier industrialization of Europe, geography, poor government policies, unaccountable governments—this is the development gap, or for the poorest, the development trap.[12] In actuality, the divisions between the poor and the rich have become more complex since the 1990s. As exemplified during the Doha Round, the G7 major economic powers are faced by both the **BRICS** (Brazil, Russia, India, China, and South Africa) and Group of 20 collective of emerging powers, which includes the G7, the BRICS, and Australia, Mexico, South Korea, Turkey, Argentina, Indonesia, and Saudi Arabia.

STRATEGIES TO ACHIEVE ECONOMIC DEVELOPMENT

Ideas about how development occurs have evolved from the work of state policy makers, officials within the UN system, and analysts within such institutions as the World

TABLE 9.1	HUMAN DEVELOPMENT INDEX, 2015				
	LIFE EXPECTANCY AT BIRTH (YEARS)	MEAN YEARS OF SCHOOLING (YEARS)	EXPECTED YEARS OF SCHOOLING (YEARS)	GROSS NATIONAL INCOME PER CAPITA (2011 PPP$)[a]	HUMAN DEVELOPMENT INDEX VALUE[b]
Arab States	70.6	6.4	12.0	15,722	0.686
East Asia and the Pacific	74.0	7.5	12.7	11,449	0.710
Europe and Central Asia	72.3	10.0	13.6	12,791	0.748
Latin America and the Caribbean	75.0	8.2	14.0	14,242	0.748
South Asia	68.4	5.5	11.2	5,605	0.607
Sub-Saharan Africa	58.5	5.2	9.6	3,363	0.518
World	71.5	7.9	12.2	14,301	0.711

a. PPP is purchasing power parity. It is a way to compare levels of economic data cross-nationally, free of price and exchange-data distortions.

b. The HDI combines indicators for life expectancy, educational attainment, and income into a composite value, ranging between 0 (low development) and 1 (high development).

Source: United Nations Human Development Report, 2015.

Bank. Most of the debates over the best approach have focused on variations or adaptations of the liberal economic model, but other critiques are more fundamental. As constructivists assert, there is a real conflict over ideas.

During the 1950s and 1960s, the development institutions, including the World Bank and major donors such as the United States, adopted a strategy for development that emphasized financially large infrastructure projects—such as dams, electric power, and telecommunications—as necessary for providing the foundations of development.

In the 1970s, realizing that not all groups were benefiting from such investments, the aid agencies began to fund projects in health, education, and housing, designed to improve the economic life of the poor. The 1980s saw a shift toward reliance on private-sector participation to meet the task of restructuring economies and reconstructing states torn apart by ethnic conflict. When areas of the economy are privatized, the government's fiscal burden is reduced, and state spending in education and health can then increase. This approach to economic growth has become known as the **Washington Consensus**, a version of liberal economic ideology. Its adherents hold that only with certain economic policies—including privatization, liberalization of trade and foreign direct investment, government deregulation in favor of open competition, and broad tax reform—will development occur. The World Bank and its sister institution, the International Monetary Fund, have been the leaders in advocating these policies.

Although the IMF was not originally charged with development, it realized very quickly that many countries' seemingly temporary balance-of-payments problems were actually long-term structural problems that prevented those countries from developing, and the IMF's short-term loans could not address these problems. Thus, during the early 1980s, the IMF began to provide longer-term loans if states adopted **structural adjustment programs** consistent with the Washington Consensus. If a state adopted those policies—economic reforms (limiting money and credit growth, forcing currency devaluation, reforming the financial sector, introducing user fees, eliminating subsidies), trade liberalization reforms (removing tariffs, rehabilitating export infrastructure), government reforms (privatizing public enterprises), and private-sector policies (ending government monopolies)—then the IMF gave its stamp of approval, leading other multilateral lenders and bilateral and international private banks to lend as well.

In the 1990s, **sustainable development**, an approach to economic development that incorporates concern for renewable resources and the environment, became part of the bank's rhetoric, although that rhetoric did not always translate into its practices. During the 1990s, however, it became apparent that even under structural adjustment, some countries could not get out from under the weight of their debt and begin to develop. That debt had been escalating; developing countries owed $2.2 trillion in 2000; 20 years earlier, it had been $577 billion. There was also mounting pressure to adopt a more systematic approach to debt. Buoyed by Jubilee 2000, a social movement that promoted changes in the name of social justice and supported by radicals who thought debt doomed states to permanent underdevelopment, a major policy shift occurred. Sponsored by the IMF, the World Bank, and the G7 economic powers, the Heavily Indebted Poor Countries (HIPC) Initiative was a historic one, for never before had foreign national debt been canceled or substantially rescheduled. While implementation of the plan and its attendant conditions has been slow and controversial, by mid-2015, 36 countries had received debt relief, 30 of them in Africa. Countries receiving such relief had to submit plans to channel debt savings into poverty-reduction programs. These programs have alleviated debt burdens in recipient countries and enabled them to increase their poverty-reducing expenditures by 3.5 percent of GDP.

Uganda is one beneficiary, working with both local and international NGOs to develop debt-reduction strategies. A Poverty Eradication Action Plan beginning in the 1990s made major poverty issues top priorities. Resources for school construction, feeder roads, and water systems were developed by local communities during the consultative process. Debt relief proved to be part of the answer for some countries as a way to direct scarce resources for development purposes.

Another change occurred in the international financial institutions beginning in 2009, following a study by the World Bank's Commission on Growth and Development. The institutions discontinued structural performance criteria for loans, even for loans to low-income countries, in response to both their critics and the 2008 global financial crisis. This represents a substantial overhaul of the lending framework. The amount of the loans can be greater than previously allowed, and loans are to be tailored according to the respective state's needs, a direct response to criticism of the "cookie-cutter" approach of structural adjustment lending. Monitoring of the loans will be done more quietly to reduce the stigma attached to conditionality. Also in response to previous criticism, the IMF has urged lending to programs that encourage social safety nets for the most vulnerable within the populations. Ideas that were previously unacceptable to the IMF—that capital flows may need regulation and that states might take a proactive role in coordinating economic development—became more acceptable in response to the market failures of the global financial crisis.[13]

A broad consensus has emerged among virtually all states on the utility of market-oriented economic policies that lead to sustainable economic development. Scarce natural resources cannot be exploited as in the past; sustainability means that growth can be ensured for future generations. There must be more emphasis on human development, particularly education and health. The targets of development—the people—should have a say in how funds are allocated. And there is much more attention being paid to the political dimension of development. Daron Acemoglu and James Robinson, among others, argue that successful development demands strong economic and political institutions that protect private property, foster competition, and ensure the rule of law to prevent corruption. In short, the current thinking is that institutions play a more critical role in successful development than the liberal economic model suggests.[14]

NGOs organized at the grassroots level to carry out locally based projects play a critical role in this new approach. Involving NGOs in development was one approach for improving both accountability and effectiveness of both multilateral and bilateral donor programs. NGOs such as World Catholic Relief, Oxfam, and Doctors Without Borders not only deliver food and medical assistance during emergencies but also distribute seeds, drill wells, and plan local-level projects that they hope will bring economic development.

NGOs can also be an alternative channel for finance to individuals and small groups that are often neglected by the national or international banks; many of these programs are subcontracted to NGOs from national and international development institutions.

One well-publicized effort, now duplicated many times over, has been microfinance. Grameen Bank in Bangladesh, created in 1983 by an academic-turned-banker, Muhammad Yunus (who won the Nobel Peace Prize in 2006), provides small amounts of funding for individuals and groups to invest in an economically productive enterprise. The Grameen Foundation has aided 9.4 million of the world's poor with the support of its national and local partners. Using a variety of funds, programs have been incubated in India, Indonesia, the Philippines, and Ethiopia, among others. The purpose is to empower women, who are typically ignored by multilateral institutions, by providing them with income that they are expected to use for productive purposes.

Microfinance institutions have grown exponentially, becoming bigger, more competitive, and more diverse. Some are not-for-profit, such as the Grameen Bank, while others are for-profit institutions; some offer just credit, while, increasingly, others offer a variety of saving alternatives. But do microfinance institutions lift individuals out of poverty? Do they foster economic development and growth more generally, as the Grameen Bank has claimed?

Recent studies show a more nuanced result on whether microfinance alleviates poverty. One study finds that microfinance has no overall impact on the borrower's household welfare after 18 months, measured by income, spending, or school attendance. However, when the borrower already owned a small business, then the new credit infusion improved income and spending. In other words, microcredit helps those who are already better off.[15] Another study of six randomized evaluations of programs across four continents finds some evidence that expanded credit increased business activity, but did not result in a statistically significant increase in total household income. Microcredit is not a panacea.[16] Clearly, the verdict about the effectiveness of microcredit in improving living standards awaits further refinement.

IS DEVELOPMENT BEING ACHIEVED? GOALS FOR THE NEXT 15 YEARS

Are the benefits of the many forms of economic globalization being distributed across the continents? Are the goals of sustainable development being met? In general, proponents of economic liberalism point to success in closing the development gap. Beginning in the 1990s, growth in emerging markets increased, followed after 2000 by an acceleration in the developing world. Average per-capita incomes in both emerging markets and developing economies in general have grown at a faster rate than in the developed economies.

The UN has undertaken the tasks of goal setting and monitoring a broad set of development goals that emphasize not just GNI per capita but also other indicators of human development, like education and health. In 2001, the UN-sponsored Millennium Summit set forth eight goals known as the Millennium Development Goals (MDGs). These goals were designed to reduce poverty by 2015 and promote sustainable human development in direct response to globalization. Each substantive goal (e.g., poverty reduction, better education, improved health, environmental sustainability, and global partnerships) had specific targets, time frames, and performance indicators, along with an implementation plan. The goals have clearly raised public awareness and helped to direct aid flows to the poorer countries in targeted sectors like health and education.

Substantial progress toward achieving these goals has been made.[17] Extreme poverty, defined as living on less than $1.25 a day, has declined significantly, both in terms of the percentage of (from 50 percent to 14 percent) and the absolute number of people, from 1.9 billion in 2001 to 836 million in 2015. Primary school enrollment has reached 91 percent in the developing regions, and the number of out-of-school children of primary school age has fallen by half. Most improved in this category is sub-Saharan Africa. Many more girls are now in school compared to 15 years ago, with Southern Asia improving the most. Under-five mortality rates have declined by more than half. The maternal mortality ratio has declined by 45 percent worldwide, with major reductions in both Southern Asia and sub-Saharan Africa. New HIV infections fell by 40 percent, and the malaria incidence rate has fallen by 37 percent. Globally, 147 countries have met the drinking water target, 95 countries the sanitation target, and 77 countries both. Official development assistance from the developed countries is $135.2 billion per year, an increase of 66 percent in real terms since 2000. But, as one critic points out, there are methodological problems with attributing these advancements to the MDGs: "progress toward the Goals is not the same as progress because of the Goals."[18]

Yet it is widely acknowledged that, while progress on many indicators was made, the actual goals were not achieved. Major gaps persist between the rural and urban areas, and between the poorest and richest households within countries. Climate change is undermining progress, and millions still live in poverty without access to basic services.

The Sustainable Development Goals (SDGs) for 2030 were passed by the UN General Assembly in 2015. More ambitious and broad-ranging than the MDGs, the SDGs include 17 goals such as ending poverty and hunger, ensuring healthy lives in safe and inclusive cities, and developing reliable and sustainable modern energy supplies. Associated targets number 169. An estimated $90 to $120 trillion is needed for those goals to be achieved—through partnerships among governments, the private sector, and NGOs, rather than through traditional foreign aid. Skeptics are legitimately concerned that these goals are too encompassing and too unwieldy to measure. Some commentators predict their "impending failure," even before they have begun.[19]

Detractors of economic liberalism, including many economic radicals and some working within the UN development community, point to a different set of indicators to argue that the gap between rich and poor is actually increasing and that more radical change is needed. The changes that the dependency school of radical political economy has advocated include more regulation of MNCs, improved means of technology transfer, better terms of trade through commodity pricing, more debt relief, and radical restructuring of international financial institutions. Only debt relief and restructuring of the financial institutions actually remain subjects of discussion.

Meanwhile, during the 1980s and early 1990s, the East Asian "tigers"—South Korea, Singapore, and Taiwan—saw the results of a statist approach to development. States actually supported key industries through subsidies to enhance their international competitiveness. With internationally strong industries, economic wealth would accrue.

More recently, a variation on this thinking has been labeled the **Beijing Consensus**, pointing to China's rapid, state-driven growth as a model for development and an alternative to economic liberalism. While there is no precise definition, the Beijing Consensus implies experimentation with policies that may be compatible with a state's political structure and cultural experience. Using capitalist tools—the stock market and professional managers—state capitalism and state enterprises invest capital in their own markets and abroad. At the same time, private companies are permitted to function. This approach had been viewed quite favorably since China continued to have high growth rates—as much as 9.5 percent annually—and had apparent success in weathering the global financial crisis. In the emerging markets of China, Russia, and Brazil, 80 percent, 62 percent, and 38 percent, respectively, of the value of the stock market is held by state enterprises. As *The Economist* reports, "The invisible hand of the market is giving way to the visible, and often authoritarian, hand of state capitalism."[20] But, by 2015, China's economic slowdown, its rapidly increasing debt load from $7 trillion in 2007 to $28 trillion in 2014, its oversold real estate market, and unregulated banking have led critics to question the sustainability of that model. Further proof came in 2015 with the stunning stock market declines, not only in China itself but also in New York, Frankfort, Tokyo, Singapore, and beyond. Although China accounts for only 15 percent of global output, the country has contributed up to half of recent global growth—hence, markets worldwide respond to China's economic problems.

Crises of Economic Globalization

International crises like those connected with the Chinese decline have been a recurrent feature of the global economic system, ranging from the 1982 Mexican debt crisis to the Asian financial crisis (1997–99). The booms and busts of international petroleum markets have been particularly volatile. As a key commodity necessary for economic growth in the industrial era, a major driver of economic success for the oil-exporting countries that depend on revenue for foreign exchange, and the financier of sovereign wealth funds, petroleum plays a key role. Yet in one year, 2008, oil prices ranged between a high of $145 a barrel to a low of $33 a barrel, disrupting markets and economies worldwide. Although Marx saw such crises and volatility as a fatal weakness of the capitalist system, economic liberal theory predicts that the market will regain its equilibrium; it will heal. The booms and busts will self-correct; they will not bring down the global system.

Indeed, reforms were undertaken after many of the historic crises to ensure that the underlying conditions would not recur. For example, after the depression of the 1930s, the banking system was reformed. When new states emerged, global financial standards in accounting, bank regulations, and ratings agencies, among others, were developed to improve information and transparency. When new and developing states encountered economic difficulties, the Bretton Woods institutions were available for temporary fixes. And the volatility of petroleum markets was met for a time by the establishment of the Organization of Petroleum Exporting Countries in 1960 to try to manage production and hence stabilize prices.

THE 2008–2009 GLOBAL FINANCIAL CRISIS

For all the reforms undertaken during past economic crises, the Bretton Woods institutions did not include actual surveillance and temporary fixes for the richer countries or the economically strong United States. The 1980s and 1990s saw an explosion of unregulated (and little understood), highly leveraged financial instruments, including oil futures and derivatives markets. U.S.-based financial institutions and governmental units at all levels were participating in those markets. Excess credit against insufficient equity prevailed across a number of sectors—in the housing market, the financial sector, and consumer-credit markets. That spending spree was accompanied by the importation of cheap goods from China, causing an unsustainable trade imbalance with China and the oil-exporting countries. By 2007, it was clear the U.S. economy itself was exhibiting fundamental structural weaknesses, although few policy makers were ready to take action. First to feel the impact was the subprime mortgage market. With financial companies and international banks carrying unsustainable debt, defaults increased, and there were no assets to back up those loans. Credit became more difficult to acquire. Private investment to build factories and produce goods dried up.

What began as a financial crisis centered in the United States rapidly became a global economic crisis. The U.S.-based financial instruments that had spawned the excess lending had been sold abroad to investors ranging from local communities in Norway to banks in Europe and East Asia and investors in Japan and China. What safer place to invest, they thought, than in the United States? That proved not to be the case. Financial institutions were unable to meet their obligations. Credit became almost impossible to obtain in the United States and Europe. Businesses cut expenditures and workforces. Consumer demand plummeted. States such as China, South Korea, and Japan, dependent on exports to the United States and Europe, saw their markets shrink and export earnings fall, forcing companies to curb production further. Oil prices dropped by 69 percent between July and December 2008, severely affecting such oil-exporting countries as Russia, Angola, and Venezuela. In emerging markets (especially Eastern Europe and states of the former Soviet Union) dependent on private foreign investment, investment plummeted; in 2008, it was less than half that of a year earlier. In late 2008, Iceland became the first state victim when its banking system collapsed. The Baltic states, the Ukraine, and Eastern European economies virtually collapsed. As international trade declined, world shipping plummeted, with ships languishing in the ports of Singapore and Hong Kong. The crisis rippled outward to developing countries that faced the prospect of sharply reduced or negative growth and the erosion of gains from globalization-driven growth. The speed and depth of the collapse in global financial and international trade markets surprised even the experts; the self-correcting mechanisms were not working as economic liberals had theorized.

Initial responses to the financial crisis were mostly unilateral. Both the United States and various EU member governments took unprecedented steps, bailing out banks and insurance companies to get credit markets functioning again and stimulate investor confidence. The United States, many EU governments, Japan, and China each responded with substantial economic stimulus packages to encourage economic growth. Some coordinated actions were taken among central bankers. The U.S. Federal Reserve, the European Central Bank, and the Bank of England engaged in currency swaps.

The IMF also responded to the crisis by making available almost $250 billion for credit lines. Iceland became the first Western country to borrow from the IMF since 1976. Substantial loans were made to Ukraine, Hungary, and Pakistan. The IMF, with an infusion of $750 billion, created the Short-Term Liquidity Facility for emerging-market countries suffering temporary liquidity problems. It reorganized the Exogenous Shocks Facility, designed to help low-income states by providing assistance more rapidly and streamlining conditions. Unfortunately, the IMF's capacity had already been weakened by those preferring market solutions over greater regulation and those wanting to abolish the Bretton Woods system itself. In addition, the International Development Association of the World Bank increased its resources for lending to some of the poorest developing countries. Both short-term responses were needed, though, as well as better long-term cross-border supervision of financial institutions, standards for accounting and banking regulations, and an early warning system for the world economy. But these were not yet in place for the subsequent Eurozone crisis.

THE 2009 EUROZONE CRISIS

As growth within the states in the EU began to slow or reverse because of the global economic crisis, a crisis closer to home magnified the disequilibrium. In the early years of the new millennium, easy credit had ushered in a decade of risky borrowing and profligate spending in some EU countries. International banks were eager to oblige credit-hungry governments and individuals with low interest rates. In Greece, high public-sector wages and long-term pension obligations fueled public-sector borrowing. In Ireland and Spain, private-sector borrowing accelerated, similar to the U.S. housing bubble. Then, when the global economic crisis hit, households faced underwater mortgages, foreclosures, and even bankruptcy. Many individuals whose net worth had dramatically declined now faced the possibility of unemployment and declining wages, only deepening the debt trap. And governments dependent on borrowing in international markets were turned away, deepening their debt obligations.

But the crisis was not just a debt problem. It was also caused by an imbalance of trade. After the turn of the century, Germany's export trade grew, while that of the so-called PIGS (Portugal, Italy, Greece, and Spain) had worsening balance-of-payments positions. Wages rose faster than gains in productivity, making their exports uncompetitive, while Germany's wage restraint made German exports even more competitive. Germany's trade surplus is the world's largest at $200 billion; 40 percent of that surplus comes from trade within the Eurozone.

The arrangements within the European monetary union and within the Eurozone itself made addressing the twin problems of unsustainable debt and trade imbalances even more difficult. As its critics warned in the early days, how could the euro work with no fiscal union and no treasury? How could the Eurozone deal with economic shocks affecting different subregions? Individual states do not have the ability to manage their monetary policy: they could not print more money, and they could not devalue their currency to make their exports more competitive. Labor mobility was constrained, and there were no agreed-upon procedures for transferring funds between states.[21] When the banks, including German ones, that had lent money liberally during the credit explosion became stressed, they demanded higher interest rates from the PIGS, making it more difficult for those governments to finance budget deficits and service the existing debt, a problem compounded by low growth rates.

There have been more than 25 summits to address the Eurozone crisis. In response, the PIGS undertook numerous reforms to reduce government debt, slashing expenditures, increasing the retirement age, promising to improve the tax collection system, and using financial transfers to avert bankruptcy. Greece has been the government in the most severe crisis. The Global Perspectives box on p. 350–51 charts the Eurozone crisis from the viewpoint of Greece.

Domestic constituencies affected by the economic distress include not only Greeks who have stood in line at soup kitchens but also Cypriots whose bank depositors are subject to capital controls, Spanish youth who face an unemployment rate of 50 percent, and the Germans who are paying the bailout costs. These constituencies are pressuring their democratically elected leaders for outcomes favorable to their own interests. And what is best for sectoral or national interests may not be consistent with Eurozone stability or the viability of the EU.

The future of the Eurozone specifically and the EU more generally is being debated. Commentators differ on the prognosis. Economist C. Fred Bergsten acknowledges that fundamental reforms of the Eurozone are necessary, including imposing tighter constraints on government budgets—and enforcing them. If those goals are accomplished, then the Eurozone will survive, but integration will probably slow down. As Bergsten forecasts, "If the history of the continent's integration is any guide . . . Europe will emerge from its current turmoil not only with the euro intact but also with stronger institutions and far better economic prospects for the future."[22] Others predict that the crisis will lead to a "leveling off of European integration," where policy makers are neither widening nor deepening the EU.[23] And still another analyst points to a different future: "Without some new driving forces, without a mobilization among its elites and peoples, the EU, while probably surviving as an origami palace of treaties and institutions, will gradually decline in efficacy and real significance, like the Holy Roman Empire of yore."[24]

RESPONSES TO ECONOMIC CRISES

Crises do not affect all states equally and in the same way. While the Eurozone crisis adversely affected Greece, Italy, Portugal, and Spain, forcing them to take austerity measures, the global financial crisis did not have its anticipated effect in many countries of Africa. Prior to the crisis, many African economies had been experiencing a resurgence in terms of growth of real GDP, increase in private capital investments, unprecedented Chinese economic activity, and even several multilateral debt-relief initiatives.

Neither Ghana nor Kenya, for example, were directly affected by these crises. Ghana, a long-time world leader in both cocoa and coffee production, had been increasing cocoa production, earning $2 billion annually from international trade, a 32-year high. Because Ghana was also a major gold producer, it benefited from higher prices as consumers moved into gold to protect themselves from declining currencies. In 2007, the country discovered a large petroleum field off its coast, and by 2011, the first oil flowed, helping to spur its 7.7 percent annual growth rate. Private equity is now investing in projects, and Ghanaians from the diaspora are returning.

Kenya, too, has not experienced the dire effects of the economic crises. Kenya, like other East African states, is benefiting from private equity, including investment in

The Eurozone Crisis: A View from Greece

The economic problems in Greece have historical origins. Although the country has been a member of the European Economic Community since 1981, Greece was unable to adopt the euro in 1999 when 11 other members implemented the Maastricht Treaty and agreed to use the euro as a common currency. The country did not meet the fiscal criteria—inflation rates, its budget deficit, and its debt to GDP ratio were all too high.

In 2001, Greece joined the Eurozone, hoping that membership would promote liberalization of the economy and modernization of state institutions. But, as is now widely acknowledged, leaders at the time misrepresented the country's financial condition: its budget deficit was still well above the 3 percent of GDP ceiling required for membership in the EU and its debt level was above 100 percent of GDP. By the time Greece hosted the Olympic Games three years later, its deficit had risen to 6.1 percent of GDP. However, the early years of the new millennium brought what seemed like a stronger economy. Both the Greek government and the private sector went on a borrowing binge. The country grew, but it was debt-fueled growth.

The 2008 global financial crisis exacerbated Greece's economic problems. The cost of borrowing escalated, and financing by international banks dried up. Greece struggled to service its debt. By 2009, its budget deficit had risen to 15.4 percent, as public-sector borrowing was fueled by a bloated government bureaucracy, high public-sector wages, and exorbitant pension costs. But it was not just a debt problem. Greece's worsening balance-of-payments problems and its high wages and low productivity made its exports uncompetitive, and earnings from trade dropped precipitously.

Greece was forced to turn to the EU, the European Central Bank, and the International Monetary Fund for bailouts. In return for bailouts, the Greek government was obligated to take multiple steps to slash public spending by cutting services and laying off workers, improving tax collection by going after delinquent taxpayers and increasing tax rates, and renegotiating labor contracts (including cutting social welfare benefits) and ending subsidies. In the view of the international economists of the EU, IMF, and ECB, those painful measures were necessary to get Greece's financial house in order.

These measures resulted in a dramatic decline in the standard of living for the Greek population. Public opposition and antigovernment and anti-EU demonstrations escalated, just as they had in Ireland, Spain, and Italy. But the conditions in Greece proved the most dire. Despite several EU–IMF bailouts, domestic opposition grew as government spending was slashed, taxes increased, pensions were cut, and government employment fell by 25 percent.

In 2015, the left wing Syriza party won election on a platform of opposing the austerity measures and standing up to the EU and the IMF. Midway through the year, the prime minister closed banks and the stock exchange and imposed controls limiting how much capital could be moved. ATMs emptied. While the immediate crisis was alleviated, Greece, the EU, the European Central Bank, and the

Greek citizens in Athens attend a "No" rally against accepting bailout conditions. While the population voted in 2015 to stand up to the demands of the EU and the IMF, the government continued negotiations.

IMF continue negotiations over how best to get Greece on the road to economic recovery while preserving the Eurozone and the EU more generally. At each step, to receive another round of bailout funds, Greece is forced to take increasingly stringent measures. These measures must be taken before there is actual debt relief from the 240 billion euros owed. The banks themselves remain a major concern, as 40 percent of the loans they have issued are in arrears. The country cannot rebound if the banks are failing. Greek economists fear that their country may not be able to recover. At stake is Greece's membership in the EU and its European identity.

CRITICAL THINKING QUESTIONS

1. What leverage does Greece have to thwart the demands of the international lenders?

2. If you were a Greek citizen, what recommendations would you make to your government?

3. Should Greece stay in the EU and the Eurozone? Why or why not?

railways that link East African states, tripling intraregional exports among these regional economies. Kenya has emphasized education, building more schools and requiring compulsory education. And, more than in other countries, indigenous technology companies are bringing new communication devices to educational, agriculture, and service sectors. Kenya is penetrated by increasing numbers of cell phone users, who are able not only to connect with each other but also to use the devices for key banking services. The technology has improved access to international markets and expedited transfers between urban workers and rural families. The mobile company M-Pesa, for example, allows users to transfer money easily through their mobile device. Finally, civil society activists are playing an increasingly vital role, and democratic elections occur in a peaceful manner.

While investments from the United States, Europe, and MNCs declined during the global financial crisis, investments from China and other emerging economies like India were growing at an unprecedented rate. China alone increased foreign investment from $9.5 billion in 2005 to $86.3 billion in 2013. In Ghana, Chinese loans and investments have gone to roads, communications systems, rural electrification, and dam building. In Kenya, about one-third of Chinese investments are in manufacturing. Chinese companies are carrying out construction of roads, bridges, and airports.

As the World Bank optimistically predicted in 2011, "Africa could be on the brink of an economic take-off, much like China was 30 years ago and India 20 years ago." But much of this optimism assumes China as the driver of world economic growth, an assumption that is increasingly being tested.

Critics suggest the need for some reforms of the global economic system. What is needed: "a scalpel or a hatchet"?[25] Scalpel-like reforms are being implemented: giving China and other BRICS a greater role in the IMF, hoping that China will channel its foreign-currency savings through the IMF to stabilize markets and promote development; improving the surveillance functions of the IMF to anticipate risks and threats; reinvigorating the G7 with greater participation by China; rethinking the role of the G20, including its finance ministers, central bank officials, and member state heads of state, both in terms of membership and their shifting coalitions; and reworking the rules and regulations of the private financial institutions, although the latter has proven more difficult than anticipated. Reforms in the Eurozone state have been granting more authority to the European Central Bank to act as a regulator of banks in member countries and giving more authority to an IMF-like institution—namely, the European Stability Mechanism—to handle bailouts and work with the European Central Bank. Economic liberals believe that modest reforms can preserve the system, giving more transparency to market transactions. They point to the promising economic recovery after 2010 as evidence that an equilibrium can reemerge.

Those critics who argue that the crises demand the hatchet wonder: Do these crises portend the end of economic globalization as now practiced? Perhaps not the end, some economic liberals admit, but certainly an end to the expectation that individuals will act rationally and that markets will always be stable, efficient, and eventually recover at a higher level. Mercantilists and economic realists might applaud the return to the state-level policies protecting their own citizens and the rise of state-controlled enterprises. Radicals recognize that delivering the hatchet to economic globalization would be necessary to achieve their goals of a more just and equitable international economic system. Social constructivists regard the contestation over ideas about the economy as an ever-evolving process.

Critics of International Economic Liberalism and Economic Globalization

The triumph of economic liberalism in the twenty-first century has not been without its critics. These include both traditional critics of the theory of economic liberalism and critics of particular policies, most notably of the international financial institutions.

As they did in the seventeenth and eighteenth centuries, old-style mercantilists, with their interpretation of economic nationalism, argue that economic policy should be subservient to the state and its interests; for them, politics determines economics. This mercantilist thinking dominated explanations of the economic success of Japan, as well as that of the newly industrializing countries of East Asia during the 1960s and 1970s, as discussed earlier. Those states used their power to stimulate industrial growth. Those governments could then harness the power of the MNCs in the state's interest. Setting national economic and political objectives above international economic and political objectives, statists see MNCs as economic actors to be controlled. They suggest imposing national controls on MNCs, including denying market entry to some of them, using the power of taxation to control repatriation of profits, and imposing currency controls. Mercantilists, like realists, believe that the international system is dominated by competition among states for power. States will take any action necessary to survive, protecting their self-interests.

Radical theorists have also been critical of the liberal economic path, just as they were in the nineteenth century. Development has not occurred, and for dependency theorists particularly, MNCs and their facilitators are the culprit; they exploit the resources of the poor, and they perpetuate the dominance of the North and the dependency of the South. This view is taken by some in the "Behind the Headlines" study of the new canal project in Nicaragua, courtesy of Chinese capital.

So whereas economic liberals value the interdependencies that MNCs create, radicals see them as instruments of dependency, exploitation, and even imperialism. Decisions made in the economic and financial centers of the world—Tokyo, London, New York, Seoul—create an inherently unequal and unfair international economic system.

::: BEHIND THE HEADLINES

The Nicaraguan Canal: Good Economics, Bad Politics?

While the construction of the Panama Canal to connect the Pacific and Atlantic Oceans was hailed in the early 1900s as both a major engineering feat and a facilitator of international commerce and trade, a Chinese billionaire's proposal to build the Nicaragua Intraoceanic Grand Canal has not been as universally praised. The Nicaragua Canal may have some of the same benefits, but also poses many troubling issues. A headline in *Al Jazeera America* reads, "Titanic Canal Project Divides Nicaragua."[a] Why are Nicaraguans divided about this big infrastructure project? And why is China even interested in Nicaragua, which is more than 9,000 miles away?

After the Panama Canal was built, commerce through the canal expanded, but peoples within Panama and neighboring countries saw few direct benefits. Rather, the canal embodied U.S. hegemony in the western hemisphere. The United States operated the canal and even had a long-term lease of that piece of American territory. Panamanians and those from many Latin American countries saw the canal as a symbol of American neocolonialism and imperialism—a view often reinforced by U.S. military interventions in Guatemala, the Dominican Republic, Cuba, and El Salvador.

The proposal to build the Nicaraguan Canal is raising some of the same issues. President Ortega of Nicaragua sees the 172-mile project as an engine of development, citing the promise that more than 50 percent of the 50,000 jobs created will go to his country's citizens. He projects that Nicaragua will be transformed into a regional economic power, with annual growth at 15 percent. Ortega's view is that the project will serve as a symbol of national progress and sovereignty.

Skeptics wonder about the lack of transparency surrounding the project. Little is known about Wang Jing, the telecom magnate who was granted the 50-year concession to build the canal (with another 50-year option). The company established for the project, the Hong Kong Nicaragua Development Group, needs to raise $50 billion in five years, five times the annual economic output of Nicaragua. But how and from whom is unknown, and the final anticipated cost is $100 billion. The enterprise's precise relationship with the Chinese government is unknown, although several Chinese companies are involved

Chinese businessman Wang Jing, promoter of the canal across Nicaragua, celebrated the inauguration of the canal's construction in December 2014.

in the planning and construction. Secrecy has prevailed in Nicaragua itself since the project was fast-tracked through the National Assembly in one day. There was little public debate and scant information.

Environmentalists also warn of the potential negative side effects. Although the exact route of the canal has not been revealed, the country's rich biodiversity would be threatened by whatever path it takes. The shallow Lake Nicaragua through which the canal must pass would need to be dredged and 700 metric tons of rock and soil removed, threatening the integrity and survival of its ecosystems. The land would be taken from the local indigenous communities that live there. Yet there has not been an environmental impact assessment and indigenous people have not been consulted.

Is this project another indication of China's push into the Western hemisphere? Between 2000 and 2013, Chinese trade with Latin America grew from $12 billion to $262 billion. China is involved in financing major infrastructure projects, including hydroelectric projects in Argentina and Ecuador and a Brazil-to-Peru rail system. In 2015, China promised to support a $50 billion overhaul of Brazil's infrastructure—roads, rail, airports—before the Olympic Games.

Liberal economic theory asserts that competition will both lower prices and lead to more goods flowing within the markets. But will the enormous costs of the canal be competitive with the Panama Canal? Will a competitor canal lead to higher levels of trade at lower cost?

Dependency theorists would argue that the canal represents nothing more than another example of a rich state, or a rich individual or company, co-opting leaders in a country with promises of riches for themselves or for their countries, of which there are no guarantees. And the poor people whose lands are being confiscated and who have lost their ability to earn a livelihood will be the ones who suffer if the project is completed.

CRITICAL THINKING QUESTIONS

1. How important is the unknown relationship between the Chinese investor and the Chinese government?

2. President Ortega was once a Marxist before he became president. What explains his dramatic change in views about economic development?

3. Would a new canal actually be competitive with the Panama Canal? How would you research that question?

a. Alfonso Serrano, "Titanic Canal Project Divides Nicaragua," *Al Jazeera America*, April 6, 2015.

That system must be altered significantly. Because developing states cannot adequately control multinational corporations, and because many of the leaders of these states have been co-opted by those very MNCs, radicals have sought international regulations in many forums.

Not all the critics of the current international economic system are radicals. Reformers both outside and within the international financial institutions question both governance and specific policies.[26] In terms of governance, reformers propose altering the weighted voting system the IMF and the World Bank now use in favor of greater representation for the emerging economies. In the current system, the major donors are guaranteed voting power commensurate with their contributions. The largest shareholders in each institution—the United States, the European Union states, Japan, and Canada—hold about 60 percent of the total votes. Reformists believe a more representative voting structure might lead to the promotion of different policies. While incremental changes have been proposed, including giving more weight to China by increasing its weight-voting share from 3.66 percent to 6.06 percent, fundamental voting power has not shifted. Further, hiring a more diverse group of bureaucrats, instead of the current predominance of economists trained in Western developed countries, might bring new, innovative solutions to development dilemmas.

Failing fundamental changes in these organizations, there is a movement to create alternative institutions that reflect changing power relations. The BRICS created two new financial institutions in 2014: the New Development Bank, a potential rival to the World Bank with $50 billion in capital, and the Asian Infrastructure Investment Bank, a rival to the Asian Development Bank with 50 members (including 13 states within NATO) with paid-in capital of $20 billion. In both cases, China is the major financial contributor, the membership is broad, and each state has a vote, with no veto power. With a $40 billion Silk Road Fund also backed by China, China seeks to become an alternative banker to the world. The BRICS countries differ with the West over many issues, and they share little in common, making it unclear how soon and how well the new institutions could begin operating.

Other reformers are critical of specific policies; here, the critics differ. On the one hand, some argue that both the IMF and the World Bank have strayed too far from their liberal economic foundations, taking on too many different tasks (trying to promote an environmental agenda or gender equality) and deviating from actions promoting market liberalization. In fact, some maintain that aid and loans themselves should be allocated by competition, creating a liberal market for aid funds. On the other hand, radical political economists claim the institutions promote the interests of private international capital, pointing to the economic returns to those firms that provide the services for the dams and power plants. Other bank policies that have been rigidly developed without considering local conditions and local knowledge end up disproportionately affecting the disadvantaged sectors of population: the unskilled, women, and the weak.

The World Trade Organization has also become a lightning rod for domestic groups from many countries. They feel that the WTO, a symbol of economic globalization, is usurping local decisions and degrading the welfare of individuals. NGOs are some of the major critics of WTO activities. Some of them oppose the idea that the WTO has the power to make regulations and settle disputes in high-handed ways that intrude on or jeopardize national sovereignty. Still others fear that promotion of unregulated free trade undermines the application of labor and environmental standards; they believe that the WTO sets economic liberalization above other social values.

Some of the challenges to economic globalization and the triumph of economic liberalism have developed at the local level. In 1994, for example, an army of peasant guerrillas seized towns in the southern Mexican state of Chiapas to protest against an economic and political system that they viewed as biased against them. The date of the protest coincided with the beginning of NAFTA. Feeling that economic decisions were beyond their control, the peasants protested against the structures of the international market, the state, and economic globalization. This rebellion alerted the world to the challenges of globalization. The protesters were able to tell their side of the story, ironically enough, through the Internet, one of the by-products of the globalization they opposed.

A wider antiglobalization movement has grown in response to several issues, one being labor mobility. At the outset, the EU had adopted the goal of free movement

Farmers in Manila protest the WTO's regulation of agricultural trade in advance of a speech by WTO secretary general Roberto Azavedo. The liberalization of agricultural markets has been a major point of contention between developed and emerging economies in recent rounds of trade negotiation.

of goods, services, *and* labor. Though the last has not been achieved, the Schengen Agreement adopted in 1985 allowed the free movement of nationals from member states without needing visas or showing passports. Individuals from non-EU states have found that once they arrive in an EU country, by whatever means, they can move more easily among countries. This situation has resulted in a flood of refugees seeking political asylum, illegal aliens seeking better-paying jobs in EU countries, as well as a new market in human trafficking, including women and children for the sex trade. Some of those arriving may even be terrorists who seek to conduct illegal activities against a receiving country, as the terrorist attack in Paris, France, in late 2015 revealed. In NAFTA, too, the porousness of the U.S.-Mexican border has fueled antiglobalist sentiments and political debates over how to solve the problem.

Another unanticipated effect of globalization is the rise of illicit markets.[27] These markets can include the illegal movement of commodities, such as arms or even money, to evade tariffs, trade restrictions, and sanctions. Or it can mean the illegal movement of banned commodities, such as drugs, human organs, endangered species, or even protected intellectual property. These transnational crimes pose a threat to security of the individual and a challenge to the viability of states, as explained in Chapter 5 and as further discussed in Chapter 11.

Many in the antiglobalization movement have their own agenda—jobs, environment, better labor conditions, alternative energy strategies, control of big capital. Stimulated by unanticipated repercussions resulting from the openness of economic markets, they have forged unity in seeking more local control and more meaningful participation in economic governance. However, there has been no greater stimulus to the antiglobalization movement and to the pitfalls of economic globalization than the global economic crisis of 2008 and the Eurozone crisis of 2009.

But globalization is not only a characteristic of the international political economy, it is also reflected in the emergence of international human rights, discussed in the next chapter.

Discussion Questions

1. You are a citizen in rural Mexico. In what ways does the international political economy *directly* affect you?

2. Liberals, mercantilists, and radicals see multinational corporations in different ways. What are those differences?

3. Does economic regionalization lead to globalization? Why or why not? Provide evidence.

4. How has your belief in the economic liberal model been modified by the global economic crises?

Key Terms

Beijing Consensus (p. 345)

BRICS (p. 339)

comparative advantage (p. 327)

derivatives (p. 326)

direct foreign investment (FDI) (p. 325)

General Agreement on Tariffs and Trade (GATT) (p. 323)

globalization (p. 317)

Group of 7 (G7) (p. 323)

International Monetary Fund (IMF) (p. 323)

mercantilism (p. 319)

moral hazard (p. 327)

most-favored-nation (MFN) principle (p. 323)

offshore financial centers (p. 326)

portfolio investment (p. 325)

sovereign wealth funds (p. 326)

structural adjustment programs (p. 341)

sustainable development (p. 341)

Washington Consensus (p. 341)

World Bank (p. 321)

World Trade Organization (WTO) (p. 329)

10

Activists from a coalition of African women's organizations demonstrate in Nairobi, Kenya, demanding the release of 200 school girls abducted by Boko Haram in northern Nigeria, in solidarity with the global #BringBackOurGirls movement.

HUMAN RIGHTS

Since 2009, over 10,000 people have been killed and 1.5 million people displaced due to Boko-Haram related violence in northern Nigeria. Boko Haram, whose name means "Western ways are forbidden," is a radical Islamist guerrilla group fighting the Nigerian government. Since 2014, the group has kidnapped over 2,000 women and children from towns and villages. World attention was drawn to the situation when more than 200 girls were kidnapped from one boarding school, leading to an international media campaign #BringBackOurGirls that drew the support of activists worldwide. The kidnapping and the subsequent campaign dominated the airwaves and social media for several months, only to die a slow death as the girls remained in captivity, more were kidnapped, and the Nigerian military floundered in its efforts to right the wrong.

The actions of Boko Haram and other groups committing such atrocities are no longer viewed as acceptable during war, any more than using child soldiers or torturing prisoners of war is viewed as acceptable. And in peacetime, trafficking of people and illicit goods by states and criminal organizations and maltreating refugees are no longer deemed to be defensible. International human rights has emerged as another key issue in world politics.

For several centuries after the Treaties of Westphalia, state sovereignty remained unchallenged. How states treated individuals and groups within their own jurisdiction was their own responsibility. In the twenty-first century, that is no longer true. What happens in Asian cities, African towns, European streets, and American halls of government is not only heard around the world but also watched carefully. State authorities who take coercive actions against individuals and groups are widely condemned by other states and the media, even if no others choose to act. Even what happens within the family (e.g., violence against spouses, children, to people of a different sexual orientation) is now viewed as a public issue.

While these issues have only relatively recently risen to a prominent place on the international agenda, the ethical treatment of individuals and groups of individuals—or human rights—has a long historical genesis. Over the ages, both philosophers and theologians have waxed eloquent over proper treatment of individuals and groups, while novelists and essayists have called attention to the evils of slavery, forced servitude, and the degradation of women and children. Individuals who have been prevented from freely expressing themselves or practicing their religion have emigrated, finding new homes far away from offending authorities. Civil wars are fought over acceptable treatment of individuals and groups. That people care about other people comes from religious, philosophical, and historical traditions. We briefly explore those traditions and then trace how the notion of responsibility for protection of rights of individuals and groups has become internationalized.

LEARNING OBJECTIVES

- Describe the religious, philosophical, and historical foundations of human rights.

- Explain the roles that states, IGOs, and NGOs perform in the protection and monitoring of human rights.

- Identify what human rights have been protected under international law.

- Analyze why the international community so often has failed to respond to allegations of genocide.

- Analyze why women's human rights in the private sphere are so difficult to address.

- Explain why refugees are both a human rights and a humanitarian issue.

Religious, Philosophical, and Historical Foundations

All of the world's great religions—Hinduism, Judaism, Christianity, Buddhism, Islam, and Confucianism—assert the dignity of individuals and people's responsibilities to fellow human beings. Different religions emphasize different facets: Confucianism, the social group; Judaism, the responsibility to help those in need; and Buddhism, the rejection of government policies that cause suffering.[1] But do these religions assert the inalienable rights of human beings to a standard of treatment? Or are these merely duties or responsibilities of the faithful? Who protects these rights and enforces the duties? Who acts on behalf of those whose rights are violated? Do these religions support human rights for all? The answers are not clear.

Like the world's religions, philosophers and political theorists have also conceptualized the rights of humans, each with different emphases. Liberal political theorists assert individual rights that the state can neither usurp nor undermine. John Locke, for example, wrote that individuals are equal and autonomous beings whose natural rights predate both national and international law. Public authority is designed to secure these rights. Key historic documents such as the English Magna Carta in 1215, the French Declaration of the Rights of Man in 1789, and the U.S. Bill of Rights in 1791 lay out these rights. Political and civil rights, including freedom of speech, religion, and press, deserve protection. Neither authoritarian governments nor arbitrary actions should deprive individuals of these freedoms, known as political and civil human rights.

Theorists in the radical tradition heavily influenced by Karl Marx and other socialist writers identify social and economic rights for individuals, which they believe the state should provide. Individuals, according to this view, enjoy material rights—rights to education, decent work, an adequate standard of living, housing—that are critical for sustaining and improving life. Without these guarantees of socioeconomic rights, socialist theorists believe that political and civil rights are meaningless.

What is included as a human right has continually been reconceptualized in the last two centuries, expanding into the realm of group rights. These include both group rights for marginalized peoples and collective rights for all. Group rights include protection for indigenous peoples, refugees, and, more recently, the disabled and those of different sexual orientations. Collective rights include rights necessary for the collectivity to survive—namely, the right to development and the right to a clean environment. These rights are highly contested within states and in the international arena. This process itself has led to a debate—whether the expansion of what is included as a fundamental human right actually dilutes the very rights that others are trying to protect.

Four major debates emerge from these foundations. First, are these really human rights? That is, are they inalienable—fundamental to every person? Are they necessary to life? Are they nonnegotiable—that is, are the rights so essential that they cannot be taken away? If human rights are inalienable, are they not, by definition, universal rights?

Second, if human rights are universal, are they really applicable to all peoples, in all states, religions, and cultures, without exception? Or are rights dependent on culture? Some scholars have argued for **cultural relativism**, the idea that some rights are culturally determined, and hence, that different rights are relevant in different cultural settings. Particularly sensitive have been the debates on women's status, child protection, family planning, and practices such as female circumcision. Other scholars like political scientist Jack Donnelley see both universal and contextual elements, which he calls "relative universality."[2] The Vienna Declaration adopted at the 1993 World Conference on Human Rights stated, "All human rights are universal, indivisible and interdependent and interrelated." But the same document qualified the statement, saying "the significance of national and regional particularities and various historical, cultural and religious backgrounds must be borne in mind."

Third, should some rights be prioritized over others? Just because political-civil rights have a longer historical genesis, are those rights more important than the others are?

The Dharavi neighborhood is one of the biggest slums in Mumbai, India. Many of its residents lack decent work, education, housing, and health. Although human rights are often debated in lofty terms, the absence of socioeconomic rights protections has real consequences for people.

Some writers from East Asia, for example, argue that advocating the rights of the individual over the welfare of the community as a whole is unsound and potentially dangerous.[3] The socialist states of the former Soviet bloc, as well as many European social-welfare states, rank economic and social rights as high priorities, even higher than political and civil rights. Other states in the West prioritize political-civil rights. And, indeed, many of the international initiatives in articulating and enforcing rights have been on behalf of political-civil rights. Yet, to many, human rights are interdependent; the purpose of each type of human right is to treat people with respect and dignity.

Fourth, who has the responsibility and the "right" to respond to violations of human rights? And is this response an absolute obligation or merely an opportunity? Traditionally, it was the state's responsibility to protect its citizens, but if the state is the abuser, who should and can respond? How? Does state sovereignty trump protection of human rights?

The first global human rights movement, the antislavery movement, illustrates the long struggle in responding to these questions.[4] In the eighteenth century, abolitionists (including religious groups, workers, housewives, and business leaders) in the United States, Great Britain, and France organized to advocate for an end to the slave trade. In 1815, when the Final Act of the Congress of Vienna was signed, it stated that the slave trade was "repugnant to the principles of humanity and universal morality." The act was framed in terms of morality, not in human rights language. But the act did not declare that slavery was illegal, nor did it provide mechanisms for supporting that aspiration. At that point, states did not view freedom as an inalienable right, fundamental to every person.

Nor did the right apply universally to all states and cultures. States responded individually to the actions of what were generally domestic constituencies: letter writing, petition signing, and public advocacy, among other actions. Responding to these pressures, both the British and American governments banned the slave trade in their territories in 1807 (i.e., new slaves could not be imported from abroad). But it was not until a half-century later that the U.S. Civil War was fought to free the slaves. Elsewhere, Spain abolished slavery in Cuba in 1880, and Brazil ended the practice in 1888. The International Convention on the Abolition of Slavery was not ratified until 1926. The antislavery movement suggests that political-civil rights and social-economic rights are intertwined. Since slaves were owned by other humans as property, they had no rights, indeed no human dignity at all. Even after political and civil rights were won, the former slaves and their descendants had, and still have, a long struggle to acquire full social-economic rights, rights often denied because of discrimination and racism.

Recently, the Islamic State seems to have revived the institution of slavery. In 2014, the group forced Yazidi women by the thousands into sex slavery. Contrary to prevailing norms, the IS claims that the practice is a religious one approved by the Koran, even as other Muslim scholars refute that association and affirm the universal consensus that slavery is both morally repugnant and illegal. Yet the Global Slavery Index, compiled by an NGO, finds that in 14 states, over 1 percent of the population is enslaved; half of these states are Muslim states.[5]

Generally, slavery is reconceptualized in modern-day terms. In 1990, the renamed Anti-Slavery International included as part of its agenda the prohibition of human trafficking, child labor, and forced labor, each representing contemporary notions of slavery. The Kafala system in the Gulf states is an example of ties between employers and migrants seeking employment that border on servitude. Over time, the notion of who is human expanded to include slaves and others in economically enforced servitude.

Recognition of who should take responsibility to protect rights has also expanded over time. States remain primarily responsible. But since World War II, the notion of an international community responsibility to protect human rights has developed.

Human Rights as Emerging International Responsibility

Human rights only gradually became an international issue. Just as nongovernmental organizations (NGOs) propelled the antislavery initiatives, another nongovernmental group, the International Committee of the Red Cross, worked for protection of wounded soldiers, prisoners of war, and civilians caught in the midst of war. With states unable to guarantee protection, a third party was poised to act on behalf of those special groups. That protection was legally codified in 1864 in the first Geneva Convention for the Amelioration of the Condition of the Wounded and Sick in Armed Forces in the Field, aimed at protection of people during wartime. From that beginning of international humanitarian law in the nineteenth century came three other conventions and several protocols during the twentieth century. These are known collectively as the Geneva Conventions, rules that apply in times of conflict, including noncombatant immunity (discussed in Chapter 8).

Internationalization of human rights in other sensitive areas was slower to evolve. At the Congress of Versailles, which ended World War I, the Japanese government tried to convince other delegates, principally U.S. president Woodrow Wilson, to adopt a statement on human rights. As a victorious and economically advanced power, Japan felt it had a credible claim that such basic rights as racial equality and religious freedom would not be rejected. Yet the initiative was blocked, with the U.S. representatives recognizing that such a provision would doom Senate passage of the peace treaty.

The League of Nations Covenant made little explicit mention of human rights, although it noted protection of certain groups. For example, the Mandates Commission was authorized to protect the treatment of dependent peoples with the goal of self-determination, but it could not carry out independent inspections. Likewise, the 1919

Minorities Treaties required states to provide protection to all inhabitants, regardless of nationality, language, race, or religion. The League also established principles for assisting refugees, the precedent for the protected status of refugees under the 1951 Convention Relating to the Status of Refugees.

President Franklin Roosevelt's famous "Four Freedoms" speech in 1941 called for a world based on four essential freedoms. However, that new moral order would not take shape until after World War II, when the full extent of the Holocaust was shockingly revealed. With that recognition came the demand for international action. Thus, at the conference founding the UN, civil society groups, churches, and peace societies successfully pushed for inclusion of human rights in the charter. In the end, the UN Charter (Article 55c) gave a role to the organization in "promoting and encouraging respect for rights and for fundamental freedoms for all without distinction as to race, sex, language, or religion."

Drawing on the religious, philosophical, and historical foundations discussed earlier, the UN General Assembly approved the Universal Declaration of Human Rights in 1948, a statement of human rights aspirations. The statement identified 30 principles incorporating both political and economic rights. These principles were eventually codified in two documents, the International Covenant on Economic, Social, and Cultural Rights and the International Covenant on Civil and Political Rights, approved in 1966 and ratified in 1976. Together, the three documents are known as the **International Bill of Rights**. The conflict between Western and socialist views blocked conclusion of a single treaty.

Subsequently, the UN and its agencies have been responsible for setting human rights standards in numerous areas, as Table 10.1 shows. But, at the same time that the Charter gave human rights a prominent place and states that ratified the conventions a standard to follow, the Charter (Article 2[7]) acknowledges the primacy of state sovereignty: "Nothing contained in the present Charter shall authorize the United Nations to intervene in matters which are essentially within the domestic jurisdiction of any state." So who protects human rights and how?

States as Protectors of Human Rights

States, as the Westphalian tradition and realists posit, are primarily responsible for protecting human rights standards within their own jurisdiction. Many liberal democratic states have based human rights practices on political and civil liberties. The constitutions of the United States and many European democracies give pride of place to freedom of speech, freedom of religion, and due process. And those same states have tried to internationalize these principles. That is, it has become part of their foreign policy agenda to support similar provisions in newly emerging states. U.S. support for

TABLE 10.1

SELECTED UN HUMAN RIGHTS CONVENTIONS

CONVENTION	OPENED FOR RATIFICATION	ENTERED INTO FORCE	RATIFICATIONS (AS OF 2015)
General Human Rights			
International Covenant on Civil and Political Rights	1966	1976	168
International Covenant on Economic, Social, and Cultural Rights	1966	1976	164
Racial Discrimination			
International Convention on the Elimination of All Forms of Racial Discrimination	1966	1969	177
International Convention on the Suppression and Punishment of the Crime of Apartheid	1973	1976	109
Rights of Women			
Convention on the Elimination of All Forms of Discrimination against Women	1979	1981	189
Human Trafficking and Other Slave-like Practices			
UN Convention for the Suppression of the Traffic in Persons and of the Exploitation of the Prostitution of Others	1949	1951	82
International Convention on the Abolition of Slavery and the Slave Trade (1926), as amended in 1953	1953	1955	99
UN Convention against Transnational Organized Crime: Protocol to Prevent, Suppress, and Punish Trafficking in Persons, Especially Women and Children	2000	2003	169

(CONTINUED)

CONVENTION	OPENED FOR RATIFICATION	ENTERED INTO FORCE	RATIFICATIONS (AS OF 2015)
Refugees and Stateless Persons			
Convention Relating to the Status of Refugees	1951	1954	145
Children			
Convention on the Rights of the Child	1989	1990	196
Physical Security			
Convention on the Prevention and Punishment of the Crime of Genocide	1948	1951	147
Convention against Torture and Other Cruel, Inhuman, or Degrading Treatment or Punishment	1984	1987	158
Convention for the Protection of All Persons from Enforced Disappearance	2006	2010	51
Other			
Convention Concerning Indigenous and Tribal Peoples in Independent Countries	1989	1991	20
International Convention on the Protection of the Rights of All Migrant Workers and Members of Their Families	1990	2003	48
Convention on the Rights of Persons with Disabilities	2007	2008	160

Sources: University of Minnesota Human Rights Library and UN High Commissioner for Human Rights.

such initiatives is evident in both Iraq and Afghanistan, where specific human rights guarantees were written into the new constitutions. And the European Union has made candidate members show significant progress toward improving political and civil liberties records before granting them membership in the EU. Consistent with the constructivist view, states may accept these new norms of international behavior through gradual socialization.

Why do liberal democratic states support political and civil rights in their foreign policy? One explanation is based on realist self-interest: states sharing those values are better positioned to trade with one another and will, according to the democratic peace theory discussed in Chapters 3 and 5, be less likely to go to war with one another. The second explanation is based in liberalism: liberal democracies believe strongly in the protection of individuals from unsavory governments and desire those values and beliefs to be projected abroad.

Some European socialist states have taken up the mantle of protecting economic and social rights because they see it as the role of government to play a positive role in providing those rights. In this view, governments need to do as much as possible to ensure access to education, adequate health care, and employment. But how much should the government actually do? What is an adequate level? Economic and social rights are achieved only gradually and over time, and thus, the crux of the discussion is whether the state is acting in good faith and doing enough to protect the economic and social welfare of its citizens.

What can states do if they believe that the human rights of individuals in another state are not being protected? A number of instruments are available. States may try to engage the other state to change its human rights practices. Recall Chapter 5's discussion of how states exercise power. Diplomatic engagement rests on the idea that linking multiple other interests—economic, security, and/or diplomatic—to human rights may be a way of getting a state to change the latter. For example, a state may be granted trade concessions if human rights abuses decline. Linking may work because of the notion that better economic relations and a more open economic system can create domestic pressure for more political freedom, including less offensive human rights practices. This approach has been used at times with China. With Cuba, the United States now expresses the same hope. By engaging with Cuba in trade, commerce, and cultural exchanges, the United States will be better able to monitor and pressure Cuba to stop its abusive human rights practices.

States like the United States and European donor states can tie better human rights policies to more foreign or military aid, or reduce or take away that aid should a state's human rights record be particularly egregious. In 1976, under pressure from Congress, the U.S. Department of State began writing annual country reports on human rights. Over time, those reports have become increasingly comprehensive. Along with annual reports from NGOs like Amnesty International and Freedom House, they are used as one element in the process of deciding whether the United States should allocate foreign aid to a country or engage in a relationship. Just hours before Secretary of State John Kerry left for Vienna to conclude the Iran nuclear deal in 2015, the U.S. Department of State released a negative assessment of Iran's human rights record. However, these reports are not the only criteria, and sometimes, major human rights violators do receive aid because of other overriding strategic or political interests.

Punishing states through sanctions, as Table 5.1 shows (p. 157), is also a possibility. Following China's crackdown on dissidents and the Tiananmen Square massacre in June 1989, the United States instituted an arms embargo against China and cancelled new foreign aid; it was joined by Japan and members of the European Union. Some estimate that the coercive action may have cost China over $11 billion in bilateral aid over a four-year period. But, as Chapter 5 discusses, imposing sanctions to try to pressure a state to reverse its egregious policy (or policies) often punishes the population more than the state, impinging further on individual rights.

In cases of particularly severe violations, like genocide or mass atrocities, states may choose to use force against offending states, although as discussed in a later section, resorting to force for human rights violations is controversial, selective, and usually carried out through multilateral actions.

States as Abusers of Human Rights

States are also violators of human rights. Both regime type and forms of real or perceived threats to the state are explanations for state abuse. In general, authoritarian or autocratic states are more likely to abuse political and civil rights, while less developed states, even liberal democratic ones, may be unable or unwilling to meet basic obligations of social and economic rights due to scarce resources or lack of political will.

All states, including democratic ones, threatened by civil strife or terrorist activity are apt to use repression against foes, domestic or foreign. State security usually prevails over individual rights. In fact, the International Covenant on Civil and Political Rights acknowledges that heads of state may revoke some political-civil liberties when national security is threatened.

Nowhere is the potential clash between human rights and national security more focused than the issue of torture, prohibited in the Convention against Torture and Other Cruel, Inhuman, or Degrading Treatment or Punishment. May states, fearing imminent attack or grave harm, use torture to coerce those they believe have relevant knowledge? If states restrain themselves and avoid coercive interrogations, some citizens may die. Which, then, is the greater harm—violation of the rights of the detained, or loss of the lives of innocent citizens? In 2009, former U.S. vice president Dick Cheney argued publicly that political leaders had a greater responsibility to the nation's security. Others responded by questioning whether less violent methods might not have achieved the same results. Still others, like U.S. senator John McCain, argued that Americans should not use torture because it is wrong and violates what it means to be an American. Indeed, the Convention against Torture is clear: freedom from torture is a right never to be revoked. But what acts are considered torture remains a controversial question, as Chapters 7 and 8 discuss.

Economic conditions also influence a country's adherence to human rights standards. Poor states or states experiencing deteriorating economic conditions are apt to repress political-civil rights, in an effort by the elite to maintain authority and divert attention from economic disintegration. But even economically developed states may have difficulty meeting the demands of economic and social rights for all members of their population. And, in some cases, those rights may be deliberately undermined or denied due to discrimination by race, creed, national origin, or gender.

Finally, culture and history affect a state's human rights record. Where there is a long history of communal violence, ethnic hatred, and mobilizing ideologies (like Nazism), then human rights are more apt to be abused. High degrees of factionalization along ethnic, religious, or ideological lines bring out the worst abuses.

The Role of the International Community—IGOs and NGOs

What can the international community do to protect human rights? What can the United Nations and other intergovernmental organizations do when they are themselves composed of the very sovereign states that threaten individual and group rights?[6]

IGOs in Action

The human rights activities of the United Nations and other intergovernmental organizations (IGOs) involve, first and foremost, setting the international human rights standards articulated in the many international treaties. (See Table 10.1.) With standards set, even though some may be aspirational, the IGOs can then move on to problems connected with implementation.

Second, the United Nations and the European Commission on Human Rights have worked to monitor state behavior by establishing procedures for complaints about state practices, compiling reports from interested and neutral observers about state behavior, and investigating alleged violations. Monitoring state behavior is a sensitive undertaking because it impinges directly on state sovereignty. Yet special bodies have been established to examine, advise, and publicly report on the human rights situation in a given country or on worldwide violations.

Beginning in 2006, the UN Human Rights Council initiated a new approach, the Universal Periodic Review, wherein every member state participates in evaluating the strengths and weaknesses of its own human rights record every four years. Based on that assessment, other states make recommendations, such as calling for the state to request assistance in a particular area, offering new approaches, suggesting that the state share its best practices with others, or even taking specific actions. For example, both Cuba and Burkina Faso have been pressured to abolish the death penalty. Recent data suggests that almost two-thirds of recommendations have been accepted; states recognize that reform "must be largely evolutionary, rather than revolutionary."[7]

The third area in which IGOs have operated is in taking measures to promote human rights and improve levels of state compliance. In the UN system, that responsibility rests with the coordinating office and person of the High Commissioner for Human Rights. Among the most visible of those promotional activities is ensuring fair elections. For example, since 1992, the United Nations has provided electoral assistance—election monitors, technical assistance—in over 100 countries. The role of the UN varies, from certifying the electoral process in Côte d'Ivoire in 2010, to providing expert monitoring, sometimes sharing that responsibility with states as in Afghanistan in 2004 and 2005 and in the Republic of South Sudan in 2011. In 2014, the UN oversaw the counting of votes in the contested Afghanistan election. While not eliminating cheating and fraud, states gain legitimacy by having external monitors, often UN and other IGO monitors. Enforcement actions by IGOs for human rights violations are also a possibility, but rare. In the case of apartheid—legalized racial discrimination against the majority black population in South Africa and a comparable policy in Southern Rhodesia (now Zimbabwe)—the international community took coercive economic measures. But, as Chapter 5 discussed, the South African government did not immediately change its human rights policy, nor was the government immediately ousted from power.

In a few cases, enforcement action may involve the use of military force. In the case of the humanitarian emergency in northern Iraq after the 1991 Gulf War, as well as in reaction to the crises in Somalia in 1992, Bosnia in the mid-1990s, and Libya in 2011, the UN Security Council explicitly linked human rights violations to security threats and undertook enforcement action without the consent of the states concerned. Yet the cases where IGOs intervene are few. Many states are suspicious of strengthening international organizations' power to intervene in what they still regard as their domestic jurisdiction.

NGOs' Unique Roles

NGOs have been particularly vocal and sometimes very effective in the area of human rights. Of the hundreds of human rights organizations with interests that cross national borders, a core group has been the most vocal and attracted the most attention, including Amnesty International (AI) and Human Rights Watch (HRW). These organizations publicize the issues, put pressure on states (both offenders and enforcers), and lobby international organizations. Furthermore, these organizations have often formed coalitions, leading to advocacy networks and social movements.[8]

With the Internet and Twitter, individuals and groups can voice their grievances swiftly to a worldwide audience and solicit sympathizers to take direct actions. These technologies are particularly effective for shaping discourse surrounding an issue and generating interest among multiple constituencies. For example, during the 1970s, disability rights groups formed first in Europe and North America, generally organizing along lines of disability type. Activists were fragmented, and there was no overarching approach. Over time, these various groups adopted a rights-based approach. By 1992, seven of the groups had merged into a loose network, the International Disability Alliance. As new communication technologies were coming into the mainstream, disability activists began to elicit the support of established NGOs like HRW and AI. With the backing of HRW, AI, and funding from the Open Society Institute, a disability convention was brought to the UN General Assembly. In 2006, the Convention on the Rights of Persons with Disabilities was adopted.[9] By the end of 2015, 160 states had become party to the treaty, which obligates signatories to prohibit all discrimination on the basis of disability. This example illustrates how concerted NGO action can result in substantive international law.

Students in Seattle distribute a poster in support of controversial group Invisible Children's Kony 2012 campaign. The campaign was designed to bring Joseph Kony, leader of the Lord's Resistance Army, to justice.

While new communication technologies have often facilitated the campaigns of NGOs, one example of a media-driven effort illustrates both the promise and the problems of the approach. For over two decades, the Lord's Resistance Army and its leader, Ugandan Joseph Kony, has kidnapped children in northern Uganda and used them as child soldiers, creating fear and intimidation among the population. Invisible Children, founded in 2004, is an NGO organized to call attention to this abuse through film and organized political activity. Over the years, it has presented a simplistic but graphic message aimed at Western audiences to fight against Kony. In 2012, a half-hour video piece called "Kony 2012" went viral, attracting 80 million hits. While all agree that the abuse represents an egregious violation of human rights, not everyone, including many in Uganda itself, agrees with Invisible Children's solution, which supports military action. So, in constructivist discourse, NGOs can aid in the spread of ideas, and in the age of new media, they often use material resources for effect. Yet NGOs also have the power to distort the message, oversimplify a complex problem, and offer slick solutions. And, as Chapter 7 outlines, NGOs may not be representative of all those most directly concerned. Remember, they have no independent legal standing, have few material resources compared to states, and exist at the discretion of states in which they are operating.

Evaluating the Efforts of the International Community

How effective are the efforts of the international community in the area of human rights? Setting the standards as exemplified in treaty setting is critical—without a standard, there is no benchmark for assessment. But of the various activities discussed, perhaps none is as effective as monitoring. NGOs have also been particularly useful in monitoring activities. Amnesty International, founded in 1961, has become perhaps the most effective human rights monitor. AI was involved in efforts to end the abuse of human rights in Uruguay and Paraguay in the 1970s. It was instrumental in bringing international attention to the Argentinian military abuses involving abductions and disappearances in the early 1980s, using its research and publicity expertise. While the organization originally emphasized the protection of individual political prisoners, its agenda has now broadened to include multiple issues, including systematic abuses of economic and social rights, women's rights, and LGBT rights. AI and organizations like it provide information for the UN's own monitoring activities and for the United States.[10]

Of course, monitoring is not an end in itself, so it is important to ask whether monitoring by either IGOs or NGOs through investigations, reports, resolutions, and naming and shaming ultimately makes a difference for rights protection. The evidence is mixed. One study of over 400 human rights organizations on shaming governments between 1992 and 2004 found that states targeted by NGOs do improve their human rights practices. But shaming is not enough. Shaming is effective when both domestic NGOs on the ground and advocacy by other third parties and individuals are present.[11] Another study of monitoring by the UN, NGOs, and the media between 1975 and 2000 found that governments identified as violators often "adopt better protections for political rights afterward, but they rarely stop or appear to lessen acts of terror."[12] Only when NGOs actively took up issues did practices improve.

Thus, IGO and NGO monitoring over time, as well as the Universal Periodic Review, is not necessarily enough to alter practices. Achieving compliance with international human rights norms can be a long process. Moreover, when states fail to comply with existing norms, it may not be a deliberate act. Obstacles may prevent willing states from readily complying, as explained in Chapter 7.

All of these activities of the international community on behalf of human rights are fraught with difficulties. A state's signature on a treaty is no guarantee of its willingness or ability to follow the treaty's provisions. Monitoring state compliance through self-reporting systems presumes a willingness to comply and be transparent, a major caveat that cannot necessarily be taken for granted. Taking direct action by imposing economic embargoes may not achieve the announced objective—a change in human rights policy—and may actually be harmful to those very individuals whom the embargoes are trying to help. Reports suggest that the international community's economic sanctions against Iraq after the first Gulf War resulted in a lower standard of living for the population and an imposition of real economic hardship on the masses, while the targeted elites remained unaffected. The sanctions did not have the intended effect of securing the elimination of Iraq's weapons of mass destruction.[13]

Despite these difficulties, the international community is moving toward the **soft law** position or norm of responsibility to protect (R2P) that, first, states have a responsibility to treat their own people humanely. It is the second part associated with protection of populations in other countries that is more controversial. Intervening in the affairs of other states even for humanitarian purposes, as Chapter 8 introduces, comes with its own set of problems. Can intervention be a legitimate response if it is used only selectively, in some cases and not in others? In 2011, for example, why did the international community (the UN, NATO, and the League of Arab States) all voice support for military action against Libya's Colonel Muammar Qaddafi? Qaddafi's predictions of "rivers of blood" against his opponents and his threats to "cleanse Libya house by house" provided the justification for internationally sanctioned intervention.[14] But mass atrocities attributed to the Syrian regime of Bashar al Assad against the Syrian people since 2011 have not led to the same response. Might the danger be that all interventions in another state's affairs can ultimately be justified by R2P? After all, the American government, when no weapons of mass destruction were found in Iraq, justified the invasion by pointing to the ruthless regime of Saddam Hussein. When does use of the term become a justification for a state or group of states to act only in their national interest?

Indeed, states differ over interpretation of the norm. When the UN Security Council approved the resolution authorizing measures to protect civilians in Libya, Brazil, India, China, and Russia abstained. When NATO acted to end Qaddafi's four-decade rule, Brazil joined with Russia and China in expressing public outrage. As Brazil argued, the Libyan intervention acted against humanitarian purposes because it created conditions that accelerated the terrorist threat and resulted in more civilian deaths. Brazil later supported an alternative concept "Responsibility While Protecting." They argued that a case-by-case assessment of the consequences of military actions was needed so that more civilians would not be put at risk.[15]

International and national actions on behalf of human rights objectives remain a very tricky business. This idea becomes all the more apparent when we delve into specific human rights problems.

Specific Human Rights Issues

Generally, international human rights treaties address separate issues, each of which is worthy of study. In this section, we first turn to a study of genocide and mass atrocities. Protecting humans from physical violence has been a preeminent religious value over the ages. Since the reaction to the atrocities of World War II is what led to the internationalization of human rights, focusing on these issues is appropriate. At the same time, crimes against humanity and war crimes have led to new ways of punishing violators. Then we take up the issue of protection of two specific groups. First, the issue of women's rights is instructive, as it involves the expansion of rights across time and space. Second, we consider the issue of refugees, both a human rights and a humanitarian concern.

The Problem of Genocide and Mass Atrocities

The twentieth century saw millions of deaths from deliberate acts of warfare, ethnic cleansing, crimes against humanity, and physical violence against individuals. Yet the word to describe one kind of physical violence—**genocide**—did not even exist during the first half of the century. A Polish lawyer, Raphael Lemkin, became so incensed by the destruction of Armenians in 1915 that he devoted his life to the human rights cause, penning the word *genocide* and then traveling around the world in support of an international law prohibiting it.

It took the genocide of Jews and other "undesirables" during World War II before the international community was ready to act. In 1948, the Convention on the Prevention and Punishment of Genocide was adopted. Genocide is defined in the convention (see Box 10.1). While the convention was signed, ratified, and recognized as an advance in international human rights, like most legal conventions, it is both precise on some questions and vague on others. Such ambiguity often reflects real disagreement among the parties during the negotiating process or an inability of the negotiators to reach a compromise. From one perspective, the convention is precise in terms of defining what constitutes genocide. The perpetrator of the genocide must have the intention to kill; the killing or maiming is not an unintended result of violence or a random act. The targets of the violence must be a national, ethnical, racial, or religious group. But from another view, the convention is vague. It does not specify how many people must be killed to be considered genocide. Nor does it specify what evidence is necessary to prove intentionality. The convention provides no permanent body to monitor potential genocides or any system for early warnings. How the international community should respond is vague, but respond it should.

Despite the convention and the good intentions of "never again," the international community has failed to act decisively in cases of purported genocide. One million Bangladeshis were killed in the 1970s; India intervened but did not stop the carnage. Two million Cambodians were killed in the same era, but Vietnam's intervention, undertaken for different reasons, was too late and the rest of the world was silent.

In the 1990s, over 750,000 Rwandans were killed while the small UN contingent on the ground sat back and watched. In the states of the former Yugoslavia, including

---

BOX 10.1

The Genocide Convention

ARTICLE 1   The Contracting Parties confirm that genocide, whether committed in time of peace or in time of war, is a crime under international law which they undertake to prevent and punish.

ARTICLE 2   In the present convention, genocide means any of the following acts committed with intent to destroy, in whole or in part, a national, ethnical, racial or religious group, as such:

(a)   Killing members of the group;
(b)   Causing serious bodily or mental harm to members of the group;
(c)   Deliberately inflicting on the group conditions of life calculated to bring about its physical destruction in whole or in part;
(d)   Imposing measures intended to prevent births within the group;
(e)   Forcibly transferring children of the group to another group.

ARTICLE 3   The following acts shall be punishable:

(a)   Genocide;
(b)   Conspiracy to commit genocide;
(c)   Direct and public incitement to commit genocide;
(d)   Attempt to commit genocide;
(e)   Complicity in genocide.

Bosnia-Herzegovina, Croatia, Serbia, and Kosovo, people of one ethnic group were forced to move, sometimes killed or placed in concentration camps, and raped, but the reaction by the United Nations and NATO proved ineffective in stopping the carnage. In Darfur in the early 2000s, as many as 200,000 people were killed and millions forced to move. While the NGOs provided humanitarian relief, states failed to act decisively. A UN/African Union peacekeeping force was approved later, but it was too weak, as Chapter 7 discusses.

In the Rwanda and Darfur cases, there was a concerted policy of major states not to use the word *genocide*, clearly aware that admitting it was genocide would necessitate an international response. Instead, at the outset these were framed as "ordinary" ethnic conflicts; in retrospect, it is clear they were anything but ordinary. Even when the NATO-backed coalition organized to stop the ethnic cleansing of Serbs in Kosovo, NATO never used the word *genocide* to describe what was happening. Neither is the word *genocide* used by many states for the 1.5 million Armenian Christians killed in 1915 because of Turkish policy. A century later, the dispute continues.

BOX 10.2

Crimes against Humanity

Article 7 of the Rome Statute of the International Criminal Court reads as follows: For the purpose of this Statute, "crime against humanity" means any of the following acts when committed as part of a widespread or systematic attack directed against any civilian population, with knowledge of the attack:

(a) Murder;

(b) Extermination;

(c) Enslavement;

(d) Deportation or forcible transfer of population;

(e) Imprisonment or other severe deprivation of physical liberty in violation of fundamental rules of international law;

(f) Torture;

(g) Rape, sexual slavery, enforced prostitution, forced pregnancy, enforced sterilization, or any other form of sexual violence of comparable gravity;

(h) Persecution against any identifiable group or collectivity on political, racial, national, ethnic, cultural, religious, gender as defined in paragraph 3, or other grounds that are universally recognized as impermissible under international law, in connection with any act referred to in this paragraph or any crime within the jurisdiction of the Court;

(i) Enforced disappearance of persons;

(j) The crime of apartheid;

(k) Other inhumane acts of a similar character intentionally causing great suffering, or serious injury to body or to mental or physical health.

Along with the prohibition against genocide came the codification of other crimes against humanity and crimes committed during warfare. These **crimes against humanity** are now incorporated in Article 7 of the Rome Statute of the International Criminal Court (see Box 10.2).

The former Yugoslavia illustrates the dilemmas associated with the application of these conventions. During the war in the early 1990s, the term *ethnic cleansing* was coined to refer to systematic efforts by Croatia and the Bosnian Serbs to remove peoples of another group from their territory, but not necessarily to wipe out the entire group.

But was this genocide or crimes against humanity? During 1992 and 1993, the UN Commission on Human Rights undertook several investigations, concluding that there were "massive and grave violations of human rights" and that Muslims were the principal victims. The Security Council Commission of Experts concluded that all sides were committing war crimes, but only the Serbs were conducting a systematic campaign of genocide. But some states and many NGOs disagreed. In 2007, the International Court of Justice ruled that Serbia neither committed genocide nor conspired or was complicit in the act of genocide. The judges pointed to insufficient proof of intentionality to destroy the Bosnians. In 2015, the same court ruled that both Serbia and Croatia committed crimes, but the intent to commit genocide had not been proven.[16]

Other cases of possible genocide and war crimes continue to occur. In 2015, the UN High Commissioner for Human Rights reported that the Islamic State may have committed genocide and war crimes against the Yazidi community in Iraq and called for the Security Council to refer the case to the ICC. But since Iraq is not a signatory state to the ICC, the ICC has not yet seized the issue.

As this discussion shows, international efforts to prevent or stop mass human rights abuses have been fitful. When prevention isn't possible, for practical or political reasons, the next issue is whether and how to punish the individuals responsible.

PUNISHING THE GUILTY INDIVIDUALS

A key trend in the new millennium is that individuals responsible for genocide and crimes against humanity should be held accountable. This idea is not new. After World War II, the allies convened trials to punish German and Japanese leaders for their wartime actions. However, because these trials were the victor's punishment, they were not seen as legitimate precedents. Following the atrocities in Yugoslavia and Rwanda, the United Nations established two ad hoc criminal tribunals, the International Criminal Tribunal for the Former Yugoslavia, in 1993, and the International Criminal Tribunal for Rwanda, in 1994. These ad hoc tribunals, approved by the UN Security Council, have developed procedures to deal with the issues of jurisdiction, evidence, sentencing, and imprisonment. Because of the need to establish procedures and the difficulty in finding the accused, the trials have proceeded very slowly. As of the end of 2015, the Yugoslav tribunal had completed proceedings for 141 out of 161 persons indicted, with 80 sentences rendered. The Rwanda court had indicted 95 individuals and convicted 55. The tribunal was closed officially on December 1, 2015.

Judges of the International Criminal Court render an acquittal in February 2015 for Congolese ex-militia boss Ngudjolo Chui.

In light of the difficulties with the ad hoc tribunals, in 1998, states under UN auspices concluded the Rome Statute for the International Criminal Court (ICC), an innovative international court having both compulsory jurisdiction and jurisdiction over individuals.[17] Four types of crimes are covered: genocide, crimes against humanity, war crimes, and crimes of aggression. No individuals (save those under 18 years of age) are immune from jurisdiction, including heads of states and military leaders. The ICC functions as a court of last resort, hearing cases only when national courts are unwilling or unable to deal with prosecuting grave atrocities.

In 2003, the work of the ICC began; in 2016, the almost 25 cases on the docket address war crimes or crimes against humanity. Most of these cases involve crimes committed in African countries, and few have been given extensive attention in the Western media. The arrest warrants for Sudanese president Omar Hassan al-Bashir and Joseph Kony of the Lord's Resistance Army are prominent exceptions. In 2014, Congolese warlord Bosco Ntaganda was captured and accused of war crimes including rape, murder, and use of child soldiers.

Yet the ICC is controversial. Many of its supporters see the court as essential for establishing international law and enforcing individual accountability for actions taken during conflict. Others, including the United States, China, India, and Turkey, are critical. Specifically, the United States objects to provisions of the statute that might make U.S. military personnel or the U.S. president subject to ICC jurisdiction, believing that the United States has "exceptional" international responsibilities as a hegemon that should make its military and leaders immune from the ICC's jurisdiction. The

United States also objects more generally, asserting that the ICC infringes on U.S. sovereignty. While the controversy continues, the United States, as a member of the Security Council, voted in favor of referring Libya to the ICC in 2011. Yet African states, once supporters of the ICC, are increasingly skeptical of its neutrality since so many cases on the court's docket target African leaders.

Punishment of instigators, whether through international or regional courts, is controversial because of the trade-off between peace and justice. Is it more critical to try individuals for wrongdoing committed during war, or is it more critical to ensure peace? Bringing individuals to justice might jeopardize the long-term peace because those facing future prosecution may try harder to stay in power. The ICC's indictment of Sudan's al-Bashir, for war crimes and his "essential role" in murder and atrocities in Darfur, illustrates the dilemma. Would the war have ended sooner had his case not been referred to the ICC by the Security Council? Did the indictment complicate any potential political settlement to the Darfur conflict? And does al-Bashir's open defiance of the court undermine the court's legitimacy? For some, there is a better way to proceed.

RECONCILING AND REBUILDING: TRUTH COMMISSIONS

Truth commissions are another approach that has gained popularity since their use in South Africa following the end of apartheid. The idea behind such commissions is to examine in an open forum what happened during the time of crisis, to uncover the truth, and in the process, move forward with the reconciliation process. This approach is seen as appropriate in countries emerging out of civil war where violence is widespread, where blame is apportioned to all sides, and where all parties must now live side by side. Increasingly, truth commissions are used in conjunction with other legal mechanisms, such as local courts (as in Rwanda and Bosnia) or hybrid courts (as in Sierra Leone or Cambodia). The establishment of these mechanisms illustrates a movement in the direction of accepting individuals like present and former heads of state and nonstate groups as subjects of international law, where previously only states have had such a status.

Women's Rights as Human Rights: The Globalization of Women's Rights

The case of women's rights illustrates how human rights have moved from the national to the international agenda, how different types of rights have become interconnected, and how women's human rights touch directly on cultural values and norms. Gradually becoming a global issue, a UN poster prepared for the Vienna Conference in 1993 headlined: "Women's Rights Are Human Rights." But this view has not always been the case.

FROM POLITICAL AND ECONOMIC RIGHTS TO HUMAN RIGHTS

Women first took up the call for political participation within national jurisdictions, demanding their political and civil rights in the form of women's suffrage. Although British and U.S. women won that right in 1918 and 1920, respectively, women in many parts of the world had to wait until after World War II. Then the immediate priority of the UN and its Commission on the Status of Women following the 1949 Universal Declaration of Human Rights was getting states to grant women the right to vote, hold office, and enjoy legal rights. More than a decade later, the 1979 Convention on the Elimination of All Forms of Discrimination against Women (CEDAW) further articulated the standard, positing that discrimination against women in political and public life is illegal.

During the 1960s and 1970s, states paid more attention to economic and social rights for women. The development community had believed for many years that all individuals, including women, could participate and benefit equally from the economic-development process. Yet as experts began to examine statistics on economic and social issues relevant to women, they found that not to be the case. Men benefit disproportionately from the introduction of technology; women need policies specifically aimed at them.

The result was the women in development (WID) movement—a transnational movement concerned with systematic discrimination against women and the failure of development to make an impact on the lives of the poor. The movement gained steam through four successive UN-sponsored world conferences on women, where women mobilized and networks developed enabling them to set a critical economic agenda affecting women, including equal pay remuneration, maternity protection, and non-discrimination in the workplace. Under WID, the World Bank and virtually the entire UN system initiated programs for women's economic enhancement. Today, the WID agenda is well integrated in most international assistance programs, under the rubric of gender and development and gender mainstreaming.[18]

CEDAW addresses both political-civil and a wide range of socioeconomic rights. Although 188 states have signed the treaty, these signatories have included significant reservations or understandings that illustrate differences in how states are interpreting the treaty. Many of those reservations concern the rights of women. States like Algeria and Egypt, along with many others, each expressed reservations on provisions that conflict with their own domestic and family law codes, which reflect religious and cultural values.

Most controversial has been protection against human rights abuses in the private sphere, notably gender-based violence against women. The latter includes violence against women in the family and domestic life; gendered division of labor in the workplace; and violence against women in war, particularly rape and torture. In short, violence against

In Afghanistan under the Taliban, women risked death by meeting clandestinely to receive education. Discrimination against women in education is prohibited under the UN Declaration of Human Rights and CEDAW. Afghanistan signed CEDAW in 1980 but did not ratify the treaty until after the Taliban was overthrown.

women and other abuses in all arenas were identified as breaches of both human rights and humanitarian norms.

CONTINUING VIOLENCE AGAINST WOMEN

In 2015, the UN reported that violence against women and girls "persists at alarmingly high levels"—more than one in three have experienced physical violence. Two examples illustrate this widespread and often controversial problem.

Rape is a prime example of violence against women. In Chapter 2, we discussed the massacres in Nanking by Japanese soldiers in 1937. Those atrocities included the systematic rape of thousands of Chinese women. Several contemporary events highlight the extent of this unique form of violence against women: the rape of 2,000 Kuwaiti women by Iraqi soldiers during the 1991 Gulf War, of 60,000 Bosnian women in 1993 by Serb and Croat forces, of 250,000 women in Burundi's and Rwanda's ethnic conflicts in 1993–94, of an estimated 200,000 women during the violence in the Democratic Republic of Congo, and of over 200 women and girls in Darfur in 2014. At earlier wartime trials, rape was not brought up as a war crime, even though states systematically employed it as an instrument of war during World War II.

During the 1990s, rape as a systematic state policy was increasingly viewed as a human rights issue, and NGOs urged the ad hoc international criminal tribunals to consider the crime of rape. At the ad hoc tribunal for Rwanda, Jean-Paul Akayesu was accused of gang rape and genocide. In a controversial 1998 decision, the judges issued the unprecedented ruling that rape constitutes not only a crime against humanity but also genocide. Now the statute for the International Criminal Court includes rape, sexual slavery, and forced prostitution among crimes against humanity, when such actions are part of a widespread and systematic attack against a civilian population.

Rape is not just a wartime issue. In South Asia and the Middle East, the problem is particularly acute even during peacetime. In some places, rape against women may be seen as an acceptable act of revenge against a prior wrong. The raped women, being dishonored, may be subsequently killed. Or prosecution of the crime may be difficult, as in Pakistan when a woman who has been raped may be convicted of adultery unless four male witnesses corroborate her rape story. The case of the gang rape of an Indian student in 2012 and her subsequent death has brought the issue into the international limelight in a country where the definition of rape is vague, local police and government authorities fail to investigate, and prosecutors do not pursue cases vigorously. Under widespread public pressure, the Indian government fast-tracked the prosecution of that case and gave four death sentences.

Physical assault against women is a problem in many parts of the world, as well. Beginning in the 1990s, Ciudad Juarez, Mexico, experienced a wave of attacks against women, about a third of which involved sexual assault, resulting in 304 deaths in 2010 alone. Like in Pakistan and India, Mexican authorities have been criticized for their lax investigations and failure to bring perpetrators to justice. In the U.S. military, rape of female soldiers by their male counterparts attracted widespread attention in 2012–13. While the military has taken measures to curb this abhorrent behavior, Congress left prosecution in the hands of the military itself, much to the dismay of those wanting civilian authorities to handle cases.

Increasingly, human rights NGOs like Human Rights Watch and Amnesty International bring violations of women's rights to the attention of the international community, and public pressure is brought to bear. If state authorities fail to take these cases seriously, then the state, too, becomes complicit. But given different cultural norms, private-sphere activities are much easier to hide and more resistant to change.

Trafficking in women and children is another form of gender-specific human rights violations. While prohibited under the CEDAW convention, the practice has become more prevalent, facilitated by open borders, pressures to keep labor costs low, and poverty that drives women and families to seek any kind of employment (including working in the sex trade). The number of women forced into bonded sweatshop labor

The Victims of War

The plight of the victims of the actions of Boko Haram described at the beginning of the chapter is not unique. Women and children are often the victims of war and civil strife. While some may take up arms and become warriors themselves, most have become victims by other means, losing their spouses and family members, their homes, and their livelihood. Some have been raped, tortured, and forced into providing sexual services for troops. Headlines around the world have been shocking—"Most of the Girls Rescued from Boko Haram Are Now Pregnant" read one.[a]

Sometimes, women and children become pawns in political strife. In Uganda, the Lord's Resistance Army has, since the 1980s, been responsible for the abduction of over 30,000 children in northern Uganda, using them as child soldiers and creating fear and intimidation. Similar to the #BringBackOurGirls movement in Nigeria, the campaign mounted by the nongovernmental organization Invisible Children on behalf of the child soldiers drew the attention of the global community, only to be later discredited for its recommendations. In both cases, social media was unable to right the wrongs or keep the world's attention.

In Nigeria, about 1,000 of the girls and children abducted by Boko Haram have been freed. When they talk about their captivity, they report

Women and children gather in the UN's Assaga refugee camp in southeast Niger in 2015. They have fled from Boko Haram violence in their home country, Nigeria.

extreme brutality, insufficient food, forced marriages, coerced conversion to Islam, sexual slavery, and rape. Of 234 women rescued by the Nigerian army in one raid, 214 of them were pregnant. These figures suggest that rape was a widespread weapon of war. Is rape an incidental by-product of strife—just what soldiers do and have done—from the rape by Japanese soldiers in Nanking, China, in 1937 to American rape in Vietnam? This was the view of the international community for many years. Or is rape a deliberate strategy of war, designed to destroy a national group or perpetuate another group? The rape of Bosnian women in 1993 by Serbian and Croatian forces and the rape of women in Burundi's and Rwanda's ethnic conflicts in 1993–94 suggest a deliberate strategy. Indeed, according to The Genocide Convention, forcibly transferring children, imposing measures intended to prevent births, or causing serious bodily harm in a deliberate fashion is genocide.

The Nigerian government has been unable to stop Boko Haram's insurgency; the violence has spread to neighboring Cameroon, Chad, and Niger. Despite the United States deploying military advisers to help locate the girls, French efforts to coordinate military activities, and the African Union force, Boko Haram continues rape, pillaging, and killing.

The human costs of the war remain. The international community through UN agencies and NGOs is engaged in treating those affected and trying to heal those who have suffered from the indignations and violence. Liberals might point to these positive programs. Violence against women has moved from the private sphere to the public sphere, and both international institutions and states are responding. In 1994, the Inter-American Convention on Violence against Women was signed, and in Europe, the European Women's Lobby has pushed the agenda. States, too, have taken a variety of actions, creating rape-crisis centers and targeting vulnerable populations like immigrants, refugees, and persons stuck in war and strife.

For radical feminists, as long as a gendered division of labor exists, the international community is going to be slow to respond to abuses against women, whether it be for sweatshop labor conditions, prostitution, trafficking in women's bodies, or abuses during war. Indeed, the persistence of economic forces continues to place women in a disadvantaged position.

For realists, many of these issues will never be issues of "high politics," essential to national security. But the actions of Boko Haram are a threat to the national security of not only Nigeria but also of others in the region and the greater international community. Clearly, they are a threat to human security.

FOR CRITICAL ANALYSIS

1. Why are women and children especially vulnerable to the horrors of war?

2. What is the new government in Nigeria doing to confront Boko Haram?

3. What can the international community do to ameliorate the consequences of the violence committed by Boko Haram?

a. Karyn Polewaczyk, "Most of the Girls Rescued from Boko Haram Are Now Pregnant," *Jezebel*, May 6, 2015.

and domestic servitude is unknown, ranging between 12 and 27 million persons; about one-quarter of these are trafficked, many for the sex trade. This problem is especially vexing, because unlike rape, where consent is not given, women may choose to be trafficked for economic reasons. Yet the international community, speaking through several treaties, has made this kind of exploitation illegal (see Table 10.1).

Although international standards against trafficking in women and children exist, monitoring and enforcement remain difficult. First, despite the international agreements, disagreement remains on the local level about what constitutes trafficking. Second, the clandestine nature of the problem complicates enforcement. Furthermore, the issue has been framed as both a human rights problem and a transnational crime issue. Various UN-related groups, including special rapporteurs responsible for monitoring and pressuring states and anti-trafficking NGOs, are involved. They employ a variety of different strategies, from providing alternative employment opportunities to women, to educating women on the dangers of trafficking, to punishing the traffickers through incarceration, to stricter law enforcement across national boundaries.

In the long term, the solution to fully address discrimination against women, be it political, economic, or social, is to elevate women from their historically subordinate status to men. Liberal feminists see that progress has been made, as women have secured privileges that were once exclusively male prerogatives. The fact that both public and private abuses are the subject of media attention, concerted NGO activity, and state action denotes progress. However, radical (socialist) feminists do not see as much progress as they point to the economic forces that continually place women in a disadvantaged position. Encouragingly, virtually all condemn the various forms of both public and private violence against women, though their remedies for relief vary.

While the legal stage has been set by the protection provided in various human rights treaties under the auspices of international organizations, the mainstay of enforcement will continue to be at the state level. States, prodded by the strong advocacy and mobilization of autonomous domestic feminist groups and the gradual regional diffusion of norms addressing violence, support specific policies—funding shelters, creating rape crisis centers, adopting legislation protecting vulnerable populations, and funding prevention programs.[19] And states, unilaterally or multilaterally, undertake punitive action against offending states. Yet the dilemma remains that states can be not only the protectors but also the abusers.

Refugees and IDPs: A Human Rights and Humanitarian Crisis

Another protected class of individuals are **refugees**. Once thought to be a temporary problem at the end of World War II, the refugee problem has increased dramatically from Europe, to the Middle East, Southeast Asia, and the Americas. This challenge is both a human rights issue and humanitarian problem: people flee from civil war, genocide, and devastating economic conditions in one state and move to another. It is also a crisis of asylum, as receiving states adopt increasingly restrictive asylum policies and have sought to keep refugees in their area of origin.[20]

The 1951 Convention Relating to the Status of Refugees defines a refugee as a person who, because of a "well-founded fear of being persecuted for reasons of race, religion, nationality, membership of a particular social group or political opinion, is outside the country of his nationality and is unable or, owing to such fear, is unwilling to avail himself of the protection of that country." By convention, it now includes those moving because of internal conflicts. The international community, namely the UN High Commissioner for Refugees (UNHCR) working with NGOs, is responsible for protecting those people by providing temporary refuge until another state grants them asylum or they can return home. The right of the refugee is **non-refoulement**: refugees cannot be forced to return to their country of origin.

The civil wars of the 1990s, ethnic strife in the new millennium, and the repercussions of the Arab Spring mean that the lives of millions of people have been disrupted. The numbers are overwhelming, almost 60 million, more than at any point since the end of World War II. One group are the **internally displaced people** (or IDPs): those who have been uprooted from their homes but remain in their home country. While not legally awarded international protection, they represent a humanitarian crisis. They need shelter, food, medical care, and the state where they are living either is unable to provide those necessities or is unwilling. They still are technically under their state's protection. However, since the mid-1990s, the UNHCR has gradually assumed responsibility for assisting many of the IDPs, working with humanitarian agencies like the World Food Programme and UNICEF, and NGOs like the International Committee of the Red Cross and Doctors without Borders.

Another group are those estimated 19.5 million people who have left their home country and seek either temporary protection in another country or permanent asylum in another country: the refugees. While international agencies can try and meet the refugees' humanitarian needs and provide legal documentation, states themselves have authority to accept or reject actual refugees or would-be refugees. Only states can grant permanent residency, permission to work, or citizenship.

In Southeast Asia, it is a crisis brought about by the plight of the Rohinyga people of Myanmar. And the receiving states—Malaysia, Thailand, and Indonesia—are all developing countries with socioeconomic problems and scarce resources. (See the Global Perspectives feature on p. 390–91.)

Nowhere has the refugee/asylum crisis and humanitarian crisis become as visible as with the ongoing civil war in Syria. As of early 2016, there are over 4 million refugees from Syria and over 7 million IDPs present in Syria itself. The refugees fled to the

Refugees: A View from Southeast Asia

Since 2013, Malaysia, Thailand, Indonesia, and Singapore have seen a massive influx of undocumented persons trying to land in their territory. Most of those fleeing their homeland for other shores are Rohingyas—Muslims fleeing Buddhist-dominated Myanmar.

Rohingyas have lived in Myanmar for hundreds of years. Yet in 1974, the country's military government asserted that Rohingyas were but economic migrants from Bangladesh who traveled to Burma during the period of colonial British rule. They were subsequently stripped of Burmese citizenship. In the early 1990s, extremist Buddhist teaching within Myanmar and repression by the military leadership intensified, targeting the Rohingyas. Hatred and discrimination became more prevalent and overt, as colonial legacies were blamed.

Since Myanmar became more democratic in 2011, the plight of the Rohingyas has worsened. Their personal security is threatened and their livelihood in fishing curbed. Neither the Myanmar government nor the opposition political party National League for Democracy, led by Aung San Suu Kyi, has spoken out on the issue.

The refugee problem is now regional. Several countries of Southeast Asia have been faced with huge numbers of people trying to reach their shores. Smugglers established routes for the transport of human beings, setting up temporary camps in Thailand and sending Rohingyas in rickety boats across the seas. Most countries in the region are not party to the 1951 Convention on Refugees, and states lack the national legal frameworks for dealing with refugees, asylum seekers, and stateless people. Those states have authorized the UN High Commission of Refugees to protect these individuals until their ultimate status is determined.

Malaysia, a Muslim country and the preferred destination of Rohingyas, had for many years accepted small numbers of those fleeing. Authorities worked quietly with the UN High Commission for Refugees and other international organizations to handle refugees and asylum seekers, but those who made it to the shores illegally were treated more harshly. But as the numbers swelled in 2015, Malaysia's views hardened against the refugees.

Similarly, Indonesia, in the past, had quietly taken in small numbers requesting assistance. But with the explosion in the numbers of boats plying the sea to escape Myanmar, Indonesia's military began to send back smuggler boats, pushing them out of their territorial waters, and even initiating refoulement—returning people who have the right to be recognized—an action prohibited under international humanitarian law. Singapore, too, argued they did not have the resources to deal with the onslaught.

Thailand has intercepted migrants at sea, providing fuel and food to force the boats to other waters. But smugglers have also set up camps in Thai territory to hold people in deplorable conditions before they are put on boats for other parts. The Thai military has been breaking up these camps, however, accelerating the numbers of people put on boats adrift to find more welcoming land.

None of the largest or richest Asian countries has accepted responsibility. Australia and Japan have offered some financial assistance,

Rohingya migrants pass food provisions dropped by the Thai military to those adrift in the Andaman Sea in May 2015. The Rohingya are attempting to find refuge in other Southeast Asian countries.

but not resettlement. Rumors abound that Australia actually paid off the smugglers to leave Australian territorial waters, in direct violation of international law. Neither India nor China has stepped up. China's position is that this is an internal Myanmar problem yet it has not used its political influence to try to alter the conditions within Myanmar. The problem also reflects the reality that many of these people are not refugees in the legal sense of the term: because of their race, religion, or nationality, they fear being persecuted if they return to their place of origin. Many would be unable to prove they would be persecuted if they returned. Many have fled because of poverty or unemployment, and they do not have a legal right to asylum. They are subject to the laws and regulations of the receiving country—hence, the strategy of the Southeast Asian countries is not to let them land on their shores.

In 2015, the Association of Southeast Asian Nations (or ASEAN) began to coordinate action. ASEAN members have agreed to launch a fund to share the costs of host governments for victims of human trafficking. And Indonesia, Malaysia, and the Philippines have agreed to take in 7,000 individuals each.

International humanitarian agencies like the World Food Programme, UNICEF, UNESCO, the International Organization for Migration, International Committee of the Red Cross, and Doctors without Borders thus have the responsibility to support orderly and humane migration.

FOR CRITICAL ANALYSIS

1. Why would Muslim countries like Malaysia and Indonesia be unwilling to accept more refugees?

2. What could a regional organization like ASEAN do to address the refugee crisis?

3. What pressures could be applied on the Myanmar regime to accept the Rohingyas as citizens with full civil and political rights?

neighboring countries of Turkey, Lebanon, Jordan, and Iraq. Each country has handled the situation differently—Turkey provides temporary protection for about 30 percent of the displaced in refugee camps. But Turkey, although a signatory to the Convention on Refugees, does not permit those from outside of Europe to apply for asylum. While Jordan and Lebanon are not signatories, they have allowed Syrians entrance but prevented them from working. Unable to work, the people have run out of patience and money and both Lebanon and Jordan are at a breaking point. This explains the surge of refugees making the journey to Europe.

Since 2015, the refugees and IDPs have risked dangerous sea voyages, paying traffickers to navigate the route, and walking the roads north through the Balkans. Their hope is that they will be granted refugee status and perhaps permanent asylum in an EU member state, mainly the richer and more welcoming states of Germany and Sweden. But, as Chapter 7 describes, this situation has led to a crisis in the EU itself. The European Commission proposes compulsory relocation of persons across various member states, but most states have refused to consider taking in sufficient numbers or have only taken in certain categories (primarily Christians). The significant numbers, their images projected on the 24-hour news cycle, their desperate hopes of a better life, despite the lack of resources, have made this a humanitarian emergency of unprecedented proportions. The resources and administrative capacity of even the richer countries are stretched thin and domestic backlash is mounting. Yet their obligation under the international human rights regime is to offer temporary protection, until refugees' individual cases are heard. And they cannot be repatriated as long as the wars continue and persecution is feared.

The refugee crisis can be considered a key test of the R2P norm. The R2P norm not only obligates states to take coercive action against state offenders, but it also obligates states to protect people by providing asylum and refuge. As Alex Bellamy notes, "The granting of safe passage and asylum is without doubt one of the most effective, if not the most effective, ways of directly protecting people from atrocity crimes."[21] But the least developed states, where 86 percent of the world's refugees are housed, do not have adequate financial resources and many Western developed states have national security concerns.

Contending Perspectives on Responding to Human Rights Abuses

What explains the lack of decisive action in responding to human rights abuses? Realists say that states have determined that it is not in their national interest to respond, since human rights abuses do not usually threaten a state's own security. If genocide committed by one state does jeopardize another state's national interest, including intruding on its core values, then it could act. As former U.S. national security adviser

Henry Kissinger has warned, a wise realist policy maker would not be moved by sentiment alone or by personal welfare, but by the calculation of the national interest.[22] How else can we explain why, on specific issues, one or more of the five permanent UN Security Council members has exercised its veto, or has asserted that it would exercise its veto, to prevent a concerted international response to egregious violations of human rights, as occurred with the United States regarding Rwanda, China regarding Darfur, and Russia regarding Syria?

While national interest is generally viewed in terms of security, it may be broader than that, encompassing historical tradition or domestic values. The United States has historically fought for human rights consistent with its domestic values. President Franklin Roosevelt in 1941 affirmed, "Freedom means the supremacy of human rights everywhere. Our support goes to those who struggle to gain those rights and keep them." After World War II, Americans advocated punishing the guilty and, at the UN's founding conference, there was strong American support for including human rights as a key area of responsibility. Yet, other U.S. actions have not followed. During the Cold War, the United States supported anti-communist regimes, even those having abusive human rights records; the United States supported the South African white regime. It failed to ratify many key human rights documents, including the statute on the International Criminal Court. The realist explanation is that these actions were in the national interest and consistent with protection of sovereignty.

Liberals would be more likely to advise state intervention in response not only to genocide but also to less dramatic abuses. Liberals' emphasis on individual welfare and on the malleability of the state makes such intrusions into the actions of other states more appealing to them. Like the realists, they may prefer that nongovernmental actors or humanitarian agencies take the initiative. Hence, sending in the UN humanitarian agencies is often the first response. But liberals generally see it as a state's duty to intercede in blatant cases of human rights abuse. However, that interest may conflict with other contending interests—preserving an alliance, hamstringing an enemy, or putting resources into domestic policy initiatives. U.S. justification can also be found in the liberal thinking: the U.S. domestic imperative is the primacy of the U.S. Constitution, and the division of power between the federal government and states often makes it difficult to incorporate international law.

Radicals have different reasons for not intervening. To them, the injustices in the international system stem from an unfair economic system—namely, the international capitalist system, where some groups and individuals are exploited. If intervention is justified, it must be applied without discrimination. And radicals do not believe that will occur, because the economic interests of the most powerful states will drive the interventions.

While human rights may be "the single most magnetic political idea of the contemporary time,"[23] other transnational issues are emerging—and that is the subject of the next chapter.

Discussion Questions

1. Which rights do you think should have priority? Political-civil rights? Socioeconomic rights? Collective rights of groups? Why?

2. Find two newspaper articles that provide examples of state officials abusing the rights of their citizens. Do these citizens have any recourse?

3. Genocide is sometimes difficult to prove. Choose a specific case of state-sponsored violence (e.g., Turkey against the Armenians; Sudan against the Darfurians; the Assad government in Syria against its citizens). Does the violence qualify as genocide? What evidence would you have to collect?

4. If you are a woman whose human rights are being abused, what avenues of recourse might you use to make your case?

5. What is the conflict between the rights of refugees and the right of states to protect borders and national security?

Key Terms

crimes against humanity (p. 379)

cultural relativism (p. 364)

genocide (p. 377)

internally displaced people (p. 389)

International Bill of Rights (p. 367)

non-refoulement (p. 389)

refugees (p. 388)

soft law (p. 376)

Only 12 feet above the current sea level, Dhaka, Bangladesh, is often hit by floods and tropical cyclones. It is estimated that as many as 20 million people would be displaced by the sea level rising due to global warming. Some of those individuals may be this man and his family.

TRANSNATIONAL ISSUES: THE ENVIRONMENT, GLOBAL HEALTH, AND CRIME

The reality of climate change has already begun to affect some groups of people. In small island states and low-lying areas of particular states, the rise of the oceans is already shrinking land available for agriculture. Bangladesh is one of the most vulnerable states. As many as 1.5 million in Dhaka, the capital, are estimated to have moved from near the Bay of Bengal, where rising tides affect areas in the river delta and where salty rivers now poison the agricultural fields. In Pacific islands like Kiribati and Fiji, governments have been relocating residents from outlying islands after saline water has ruined crops and contaminated freshwater supplies. And, in Alaska, 30 native villages are about to disappear as sea ice and the permafrost melt. As President Barack Obama noted in 2015, "Climate is changing faster than our efforts to address it."[1]

States and peoples are interconnected and interdependent to a degree never previously experienced, thanks in large part to new technologies. Climate change is but one example. Economic globalization is another. Human rights, both as norms and as emerging international law, are another. As the world shrinks and its population expands, environmental, health, and crime problems (and solutions) once limited by geography and climate are becoming increasingly shared or "transnational."

In this chapter, we introduce three representative transnational issues: the environment, global health, and transnational crime. For each issue, we highlight interconnectedness, the interactions among various international actors, and the impacts of these changes on core concepts and the study of international relations. What is new is that these are now *global* interests, and they often demand global responses. How can we think conceptually about transnational issues? How do these issues intersect with traditional conceptions of sovereignty, security, and economics? Who are the various actors with interests in these issues? How would a realist, a liberal, a radical, and a constructivist address these issues?

LEARNING OBJECTIVES

- Explain what makes the environment, health, and crime *transnational issues*.

- Analyze how the concepts of collective goods and sustainability help us think about environmental issues.

- Analyze how environmental issues might lead to armed conflict.

- Identify the factors that make communicable diseases a particularly difficult transnational issue to manage.

- Describe what technologies facilitate the spread of transnational organized crime.

- Explain what prescriptions international relations theories might offer to possibly reverse the detrimental consequences of transnational threats.

The Environment—Protecting the Global Commons

The environment powerfully affects the quality of our individual and collective lives. Every person, regardless of age, national origin, culture, or level of education, needs access to clean air and water, and beyond these needs, access to physical space in which to live and prosper. Wherever they live, human beings convert some portion of the natural world to energy or objects. Many of these natural resources, such as timber, are renewable, and others, such as many metals, are recyclable; but some—in particular petroleum—are nonrenewable: once they are gone, they are gone. Given our universal dependence on the environment both for our very existence and as a resource for our broader welfare, how did the environment come to be so threatened and why have the efforts of individuals, states, and international organizations to protect the environment not been more successful? If states' shared interest in peace can lead to a dramatic decline in the likelihood and destructiveness of interstate war, why cannot their shared interest in a clean environment lead to a reduction in the rate of its consumption or destruction? In this chapter, we see that issues of pollution, climate change, natural resources, population change, and energy are all intertwined, such that trends in one of these areas affect trends in each of the others. Costly policy decisions made to address one issue can have unintended consequences. The complexity of the global ecosystem and the difficulty of predicting the interaction of its many parts is one partial answer to the question of why more has not already been done to slow or reverse harm to the global environment.

Conceptual Perspectives

Two conceptual perspectives help us think critically about the interrelation of environmental issues. These perspectives augment each other. First is the notion of collective goods. (See Chapter 7.) Collective goods help us conceptualize how to achieve shared benefits that depend on overcoming conflicting individual interests. How can individual herders in the commons be convinced to abridge their own self-interest (which is for each to increase the number of sheep he or she allows to graze on the commons) in the interest of preserving the commons for the collectivity? How can individual polluters of the global air and water commons be likewise convinced to abridge their self-interest to preserve these commons for the collectivity? One difficulty is that our most influential economic theories had their origins at a time when the global air, sea, and natural resources commons seemed truly infinite. Published in 1776, Adam Smith's *Wealth of Nations*, for example, suggested that individual self-interest was moved "as if by an invisible hand" to a collective good in the form of ever-cheaper and more plentiful consumer goods. Yet by the close of the nineteenth century, this seemingly infinite supply of space and resources had become bounded. Since the end of World War II, we have come to understand that our planet itself is a commons, and as such, we must reassess the collective impact of our individual self-interests. Collective-goods theory helps us understand these problems and, at the same time, suggests solutions.

The second conceptual perspective is sustainability, or sustainable development, introduced in Chapter 9. Sustainability is a crucial perspective because it helps us think about advancing our survival and welfare without doing lasting damage to our environment and thereby abridging the health and welfare of our descendants. As a conceptual perspective, then, sustainability reminds us that it is possible, desirable, and even necessary to value the future quality of the earth's air, water, and land. Both perspectives underline the most fundamental problem facing those committed to slowing and ultimately reversing damage to the global ecosystem: because the costs of harm to the environment are diffused across both space and time, and the benefits of pollution and unsustainable resource consumption are concentrated, each individual state, corporation, or person has a strong incentive to enjoy a "free ride" and hope others will bear the costs of restraint. A pernicious logic takes root: if we do not poach the elephants, someone else will. If we install pollution controls, our competitors who did not will achieve a competitive edge. Furthermore, free-riding and cheating are very difficult to detect and monitor; worse still, the effects of cheating may last for years, even after it has been detected and halted.

But, as in the example of the grazing commons, real-world evidence of harm has forced today's "farmers" to acknowledge an interest in acting to slow or halt further damage to our shared air, water, and land resources. The influence of this evidence is why principles and norms concerning the environment have evolved considerably in customary international law in the past few decades. One core principle is the *no significant harm principle*, meaning a state cannot initiate policies that cause significant environmental damages to another state. Another is the *good neighbor principle* of cooperation. Beyond these are soft-law principles, often expressed in conferences, declarations, or resolutions, which, although currently nonbinding, often informally describe acceptable norms of behavior. These include the *polluter pays principle*, the *precautionary principle* (action should be taken based on scientific warning before irreversible harm occurs), and the *preventive action principle* (states should take action in their own jurisdictions). New emerging principles include sustainable development and intergenerational equity, both linking economics and the environment to future generations.

The level of attention accorded to the environment is reflected in the international treaties and agreements that have been ratified on a host of different issues. These include the protection of natural resources, such as endangered species of wild fauna and flora, tropical timber, natural waterways and lakes, migratory species of wild animals, and biological diversity in general, as well as protection against polluting in marine environments, on land, and in the air. Each of these treaties sets standards for state behavior, and some provide monitoring mechanisms. In so doing, they are very controversial because they affect core political, economic, and human rights interests, and because, ultimately, individual states must guarantee them, even in circumstances where abiding by the treaty means a short-term cost or missed opportunity.

By studying three key environmental topics—pollution and climate change, natural resources, and population—we can see how interests in economic development, promoting human rights, and protecting the environment often conflict. Although each topic may be treated separately, and often is, they are all integrally related, and each has transnational implications.

Pollution and Climate Change

As pressures on the global commons mount, the quality of geographic space diminishes. In the 1950s and 1960s, several events dramatically publicized the deteriorating quality of the commons. The oceanographer Jacques Cousteau warned of the degradation of the ocean, a warning made prescient by the 1967 Torrey Canyon oil spill off the coast of England. Rachel Carson's best-selling 1962 book *Silent Spring* warned of the impact of pesticides and chemicals on the environment.[2] Carson highlighted the paradoxical effect of pesticides such as DDT—which could dramatically reduce the spread of diseases like malaria, but at the same time, devastated the reproductive cycle of wildfowl and ultimately caused cancer in humans. Millions of Americans and many others worldwide, who had never thought about the links between pesticides, the ecosystem, and human health outcomes were suddenly aware of these connections and became concerned about the damage. More people became aware that human activity associated with agricultural and industrial practices is degrading the natural world, and that humans do not exist separately from the natural world. Economic development in agriculture and industry has **negative externalities**—costly unintended consequences—for everyone, as well as positive consequences.

Although many negative externalities may be local, some have national and international implications. Take the case of energy. To meet a rising demand for oil, the United States and China have turned to the oil sands of Alberta, Canada. In times of high oil prices, it becomes economically profitable to convert those sands to oil for refinement into gasoline. Multinational corporations have heavily invested in the operation. Deleterious environmental externalities are, however, increasingly evident. The extractive process, for example, requires a massive withdrawal of water, disturbing fish populations and adversely affecting water quality. Tailing ponds containing toxic extraction residues have proliferated, imperiling wildlife. And forests are cut—the same forests that provide carbon sinks to slow the escalation of global warming.

Halfway around the world, China's thirst for energy has led to increased coal usage. Coal-burning power plants emit soot, toxic chemicals, and gases, which, with weather inversions, create air pollution not only over China, neighboring Korea, and Japan but also over the west coast of the United States. These sulfur dioxide emissions carry known health risks, including respiratory and heart disease and certain kinds of cancer. China is now taking critical initiatives to replace polluting plants, but air pollution alerts in major Chinese cities are frequent.

In addition, the rivers that facilitate the transport of ships and commerce and that provide water for industry and human consumption can carry pollution across state boundaries. On October 4, 2010, for example, the wall of a storage pond used for toxic "red sludge" near the town of Kolontar in Hungary ruptured, and a massive wall of caustic red slime flooded nearby towns—killing four people and injuring more than

100—before making its way into rivers. Once in the water, the sludge killed fish and poisoned drinking water along the way. Hungary reacted quickly in an effort to contain the damage, but in three days, a much-reduced flow of sludge reached the Danube River, a major European waterway linking Hungary to Croatia, Slovenia, Romania, and Bulgaria. Thus, an industrial accident in one state became a threat to the health and well-being of at least four states downstream.

Nothing affects our globe more than the pollution issues of the twenty-first century: ozone depletion and global warming. Both issues have characteristics in common. Both concern pollution in spaces that belong to no single state. Both result from negative externalities associated with rising levels of economic development. Both pit groups of states against one another. Both have been the subjects of highly contested international negotiations.

OZONE DEPLETION AND GLOBAL WARMING

Thrust onto the international agenda in 1975, ozone depletion illustrates a relative success story of international cooperation. States recognized this environmental problem, caused by the emission of chlorofluorocarbons (CFCs), before it grew to crisis proportions, and they reacted with increasingly strong measures. Both the developed and the developing worlds became involved, with the latter receiving financial aid from the former to finance changes in technology. Substitutes were developed, and multinational corporations eventually supported the prohibition of CFCs in the 1987 Montreal Protocol on Substances that Deplete the Ozone Layer. As a result, the depletion of the ozone layer was reversed. The story is a success story; consumption of ozone-depleting substances has dropped 75 percent since the Montreal Protocol. Outside the polar zones, the ozone layer is recovering, but at the poles, the loss is variable. Complete recovery could take decades after the harm has stopped.

The issue of global climate change has proved much more complicated. There are no inexpensive substitutes for agricultural, communications, and industrial processes that emit greenhouse gases; the costs of reducing emissions are high and must be paid now, while the benefits are diffuse and may only emerge after decades. But scientific facts are indisputable. The preponderance of greenhouse gas emissions comes from the burning of fossil fuels in the industrialized countries of the North, and increasingly from China and India's growing use of fossil fuels. Greenhouse gases are also emitted by the developing countries, most notably from deforestation of the tropics for agriculture and the timber industry. (See Table 11.1.) These greenhouse emissions have consequences.

The earth is warming, with an increase of between 1.9 and 3 degrees Celsius estimated by the end of the twenty-first century, relative to temperatures recorded between 1986 and 2005. "The atmosphere and ocean have warmed, the amounts of snow and ice have

TABLE 11.1

WORLD CARBON DIOXIDE EMISSIONS BY REGION (MILLION METRIC TONS CARBON DIOXIDE)

REGION	2010	2015*	2020*	2030*	2040*	AVERAGE ANNUAL PERCENT CHANGE (2010–2040)
OECD Americas	6,657	6,480	6,627	6,880	7,283	0.3
United States	5,608	5,381	5,454	5,523	5,691	0.0
Canada	546	551	574	609	654	0.6
Mexico/Chile	503	548	599	748	937	2.1
OECD Europe	4,223	4,054	4,097	4,151	4,257	0.0
OECD Asia	2,200	2,287	2,296	2,341	2,358	0.2
Japan	1,176	1,243	1,220	1,215	1,150	−0.1
South Korea	581	600	627	666	730	0.8
Australia/ New Zealand	443	444	449	460	478	0.3
Total OECD	13,079	12,821	13,020	13,373	13,897	0.2
Non-OECD Europe and Eurasia	2,645	2,750	2,898	3,250	3,526	1.0
Russia	1,595	1,650	1,749	1,945	2,018	0.8
Other	1,050	1,100	1,149	1,340	1,508	1.2
Non-OECD Asia	11,538	13,859	15,812	19,392	21,668	2.1
China	7,885	10,022	11,532	14,028	14,911	2.1
India	1,695	1,856	2,109	2,693	3,326	2.3
Other	1,958	1,981	2,171	2,671	3,431	1.9
Middle East	1,649	1,959	2,126	2,419	2,756	1.7
Africa	1,070	1,123	1,224	1,474	1,815	1.8
Central and South America	1,202	1,306	1,366	1,556	1,793	1.3
Brazil	450	506	547	632	771	1.8
Other	752	800	819	924	1,022	1.0
Total Non-OECD	18,104	20,996	23,426	28,092	31,558	1.9
Total World	31,183	33,817	36,446	41,464	45,455	1.3

*Estimate.

Note: The U.S. numbers include carbon dioxide emissions from electricity generation using nonbiogenic municipal solid waste and geothermal energy.

Sources: History: U.S. Energy Information Administration (EIA), International Energy Statistics Database (as of November 2012), www.eia.gov/ies. Projections: EIA, Annual Energy Outlook 2013, DOE/EIA-0383(2013) (Washington, DC: April 2013); AEO2013 National Energy Modeling System, run REF2013. D102312A, www.eia.gov/aeo; and World Energy Projection System Plus (2013).

diminished, sea level has risen, and the concentrations of greenhouse gases have increased," the Intergovernmental Panel on Climate Change reported in 2013. A year later, the same group affirmed once again that the human influence on climate change is clear.[3] The scientific community finds the evidence compelling.

Although scientists increasingly agree on the problem—that contemporary industrial, agricultural, and communications processes have strongly accelerated global warming—politicians and economists struggle to find solutions. This struggle is not surprising, given the competing interests of various parties. Industrialized countries seek continued growth, and the South wants to become industrialized and enjoy the North's consumer lifestyle; both are made possible by converting oil and gas to energy. The parties disagree on whether voluntary restraints or market-based responses will be sufficient for both "worlds" to reach their economic objectives while at the same time reducing greenhouse emissions (that is, achieve *sustainable* growth). If the global response proves insufficient, might authoritative regulations be needed, and if so, what authority should be invoked to monitor and enforce them—international, state level, subnational, or even local?

The international community has made several attempts to respond to climate change through negotiated state action. One of those efforts was the Kyoto Protocol of 1997, which provided for stabilizing the concentration of greenhouse gases and delineated international goals for reducing emissions by 2010. The protocol came into force in 2005, ratified by 156 states, including Russia, Canada, China, India, and Japan, but not the United States. The George W. Bush administration argued that the economic costs of moving away from a fossil fuel–based economy would be too high and an unacceptable number of U.S. jobs would be lost. Furthermore, the developed northern countries would be forced to comply with restrictions, whereas rapidly developing economies like India and China were not obligated under Kyoto, giving them an unfair economic advantage. Markets would be the best way to bring about the necessary changes, with higher prices leading to decreased consumption and, possibly, a system for trading emission quotas. But U.S. views began to change as the private sector realized that climate change was affecting their operations, and the U.S. military recognized growing security threats as rising sea levels resulted in the vulnerability of people and food supplies. Some kind of new approach was necessary.

European states and Japan did sign the Kyoto Protocol and established the EU Emissions Trading System as a way to reduce industrial greenhouse gas emissions. States that use less than their allowance may sell credits to others who are not meeting their obligations. However, with the economic recession and the Eurozone crisis, demand for the permits has dropped, and there is overcapacity in the carbon market.

Three lines of thinking have emerged from difficulties with Kyoto. First, perhaps by seeking a comprehensive global treaty, the individuals, groups, states, and coalitions of states seeking to slow, halt, and reverse global warming have aimed too high. As Robert Keohane and David Victor have argued, perhaps what is needed is a kind of middle-ground: a "regime complex" for climate change that focuses on key *parts* of the climate change problem rather than the whole.[4] Many have concluded that the process of trying to accomplish many goals simultaneously is impractical and dysfunctional. Thus, negotiators have examined issues in a piecemeal fashion for about a decade. Forests were the priority in 2008, with states agreeing to get credit for saving forests; a fund was established to help poor countries adapt. Technology and financing were the topics in 2009, when the parties agreed to focus on new technologies and increase financing to mitigate the effects of climate change.

A second approach has been to get the top three emitters—China (the top emitter), the United States, and India—to come to agreement. In 2013, India agreed to take on legally binding obligations, but not until after 2020, fearful that such obligations would inhibit growth. In late 2014, China agreed for the first time to stop its emissions from growing by 2030, and the United States announced new targets for reducing carbon emissions. These commitments proved to be a critical impetus for commitments by other states in the 2015 UN climate change talks.

For still others, given the reality of global warming and the likely continued failure of efforts to slow or halt it, a third approach is to shift resources into preparing for and remediating its effects. For example, 80 percent of the world's population lives near a coastline and some states are already vulnerable, so mitigation efforts must become a major priority. However, financial commitments by the wealthy states are clearly lacking.

In December 2015, following two weeks of intensive negotiations, the 195 participants in the Paris climate change talks reached an accord replacing the Kyoto Protocol. In a grand bargain, which includes numerous compromises, the states agree to aim to keep the increase in global average temperature to "well below" 2 degrees Celsius and to pursue efforts to limit warming to 1.5 degrees Celsius. This agreement is different from Kyoto in several ways. First, the target is aspirational, requiring both significant cuts in emissions *and* growth in renewable sources of energy. Second, states agree to achieve a balance between greenhouse gases and carbon-absorbing sinks like forests. And third, and perhaps most importantly, states agree to publish climate plans every five years from 2020. The submission of plans is mandatory, but meeting the targets is not legally binding. Fourth, key developed countries *should* take the lead. In the end, the breakthrough was the agreement between the U.S. and China reached prior to the Paris meetings.

Global warming and climate change are not solved by this agreement, but supporters assert that a structure now exists to tackle the problem in an effective way. Climate change clearly will continue to be a high-priority agenda item across a wide spectrum

The Human Cost of Climate Change

If climate change continues, small island states and states with low elevations near the seas may see their land subsiding and their national territory shrinking. Their populations may be more susceptible to higher rates of waterborne diseases, caused by increased temperatures and changes in rainfall. Many states already are located in tropical areas, where diseases such as dengue, schistostomiasis, and malaria are rampant. It is no surprise that recently we have seen headlines like "As Seas Rise, Millions Cling to Borrowed Time and Dying Land."[a] We are likely to see more such headlines.

Climate change can have an outsized effect on small island nations. Their economies often depend largely on tourism (in the Maldives, for example, 95 percent of the labor force is involved in tourism, as is 70 percent in the Bahamas), and

The 10,000 residents of the South Pacific island of Tuvalu collect fresh water made from desalinated sea water daily. The rising sea levels have resulted in a water shortage caused by contaminated ground water. Financial assistance for the desalination plants is being provided by the governments of Australia, New Zealand, and the United States.

when beaches erode, coral reefs are polluted, and the quality of drinking water declines, tourists stay away.

Some of these states have begun mitigation efforts. Kiribati has bought land on neighboring islands of Fiji to protect its food supply and possibly to relocate its population. Panama's government is planning to relocate residents from islands off the mainland, although those groups are resisting relocation. Other states, like Antigua and Barbuda and Saint Kitts and Nevis, are taking hazard monitoring more seriously, while still others with more resources, such as the Federated States of Micronesia and Malta, have begun desalination of sea water. Islands in the Caribbean like Barbados, Grenada, and Saint Lucia are paying particular attention to protecting essential tourist facilities.

For most of the approximately 40 small island states, however, it will be virtually impossible to forestall the effects of climate change. As a group, they share characteristics that make them particularly vulnerable: limited natural resources; a high density of population and socio-economic activities along the coastal zone; susceptibility to intense tropical storms and storm surge; limited land area, which prevents some adaptation strategies; and insufficient financial resources.

These small island states have come together around their shared challenges in the Alliance of Small Island States. While they have no formal charter or institutions, they have become a forceful group at the United Nations in New York in lobbying for concrete action. But even though developed states have pledged economic and technical aid to these states during annual conferences on climate change, the gap remains wide between what the small states need and how the developed nations have pledged to help.

FOR CRITICAL ANALYSIS

1. What financial commitments have been made to developing states adversely affected by climate change under the 2015 Paris Accord?

2. What power resources does the Alliance of Small Island States have at its disposal?

3. What mitigation efforts have begun in the United States?

a. Gardiner Harris, "As Seas Rise, Millions Cling to Borrowed Time and Dying Land," *New York Times,* March 29, 2014.

of state interests, including economic development and national security. Climate change is an issue that brings with it both very real threats and opportunities in the twenty-first century, and any change will occur slowly.

Natural Resource Issues

The belief in the infinite supply of natural resources was not unreasonable throughout much of human history, as people migrated to uninhabited or only sparsely inhabited lands. Trading for natural resources became a mainstay of economic activity once people recognized that natural resources were not uniformly distributed. Radical Marxist thinkers challenged the assumption of an infinite supply of key economic resources. According to Lenin, one of the reasons for imperialism was the inevitable quest for new sources of raw materials. Capitalist states depended on overseas markets *and* resources, precisely because resources are unevenly distributed. From this assertion, Lenin also drew his explanation for why imperialism necessarily resulted in war: capitalist states would be compelled to use armed force to secure the natural resources their factories demanded.

Nowadays, we are keenly aware that natural resources *are* limited and that states do compete for resources. The example of freshwater, linked to pollution, climate change, and population, helps highlight the importance of natural resources as a transnational issue.

Perhaps *the most crucial* transnational resource issue is freshwater because it is necessary for all forms of life—human, animal, and plant. Only 3 percent of the earth's water is fresh (one-third lower than in 1970). Freshwater is political because it is unevenly distributed; by 2025, two-thirds of the world's people will live in countries facing moderate or severe water-shortage problems. Others live in states with abundant supplies. Water is unequally used: agriculture accounts for about two-thirds of the use of water, industry about one-quarter, and human consumption slightly less than one-tenth. But 1.1 billion people have no access to improved drinking water, and one-third of those live in Africa. Climate change is apt to make the situation worse since 70 percent of the world's total supply of freshwater is leaking away from the polar ice caps. And some new technologies may be using freshwater faster than it is replenished, leading to unanticipated consequences. The use of water as an aid to natural gas and petroleum extraction (a process most commonly known as "fracking") threatens shortages in some locales and has caused contamination issues.

Three examples illustrate the international controversies and repercussions of the limited supply of freshwater. The Middle East has long been a geographic area where freshwater is a contested resource. Since the 1960s, Israel has adopted methods to preserve scarce water resources, adopting drip irrigation, reusing treated household sewage for agriculture, and piping water long distances from the north to the parched

Mediterranean coast. And the country has been a leader in desalination: now half of the country's drinking water comes from seawater. With the exception of the rich Gulf states like Saudi Arabia, Kuwait, and Qatar, who have installed desalination plants, other states lag behind. The World Bank predicts that in the twenty-first century, water could be the major political issue between Israel and Jordan, since Israeli authorities control access to scarce water on the West Bank of the Jordan River. Exacerbating the conflict is the Israeli and Palestinian fight over water. Israel permits its own settlers greater access to the resource, restricting access to the Palestinians in the occupied West Bank and occasionally cutting off supplies to express political dissatisfaction. In the Gaza Strip, where the population is growing 4.6 percent annually, resources have been depleted and the water is polluted, intensifying the conflict with Israel. There is no solution to the water crisis in either the West Bank or Gaza without Israel's participation.

Another brewing conflict over water surrounds the Grand Renaissance Dam, currently under construction in Ethiopia, the source of the Nile River. When completed in 2018 or 2019, it will be Africa's largest hydropower dam, encompassing 685 square miles. Egypt, the downstream state, relies totally on the waters of the Nile, and is not pleased by the anticipated lower river flows. With agriculture threatened, Egypt sees access to river water as an issue of national security. Under an agreement reached during the colonial era, Egypt and Sudan got most of the Nile's waters for their own use. The Grand Renaissance Dam would change that historic allocation. No wonder during 2013 talks on the issue, Egyptian authorities reported that Egypt was keeping all options open. While not calling for war, Egypt has made it clear that its water security cannot be violated.

The story is much the same in Central Asia, where two upstream countries with relatively poor land, Tajikistan and Kyrgyzstan, are the water source for areas downstream with good land. Under the old system in the Soviet Union, water was freely available for downstream users. Now, conflict has arisen because water systems are in decay and no new system for water allocation has been developed. Disputes over freshwater resources are related to population trends.

Population Issues

Recognition of the potential world population problem occurred centuries ago. In 1798, Thomas Malthus posited a key relationship. If population grows unchecked, it will increase at a geometric rate (1, 2, 4, 8, . . .), whereas food resources will increase at an arithmetic rate (1, 2, 3, 4, . . .). Very quickly, he postulated, population increases will outstrip food production. This scenario is called the **Malthusian dilemma**. Although Malthus did not think productivity would keep up with population growth rates, he did acknowledge wars, famine, or moral restraint as ways to check excessive population.[5] Three centuries later, *The Limits to Growth*, an independent report issued by the Club of Rome in 1972, systematically investigated trends in population, agricultural production, natural resource utilization, and industrial production, as well as pollution and the intricate feedback loops that link these trends. Its conclusion was pessimistic: the earth would reach natural limits to population growth within a relatively short time.[6]

Neither Malthus nor the Club of Rome proved to be correct. Malthus did not foresee the technological changes that would lead to much higher rates of food production, nor did he predict the **demographic transition**—that population growth rates would not proceed unchecked. Although improvements in economic development led at first to lower death rates and hence to a greater population increase, over time, as the lives of individuals improved, women became more educated, people moved to urban areas, and birthrates dropped dramatically. The advent of safe, reliable birth-control technologies also led to a decline in birthrates. Likewise, the Club of Rome's predictions proved too pessimistic, as technological change stretched resources beyond the limits predicted in its 1972 report.

Although Malthus and the Club of Rome missed some key trends, their prediction that the world's population would increase dramatically has proved correct. The population has increased from 800 million in 1776 to 7.3 billion in 2015. The UN estimates that by the end of the twenty-first century, the global population will reach 11.2 billion. (See Table 11.2.) In fact, the relative rate of growth of the world's population has declined, much faster than expected.

Several key observations make population and population growth rates cause for concern. First, the population increase is not uniformly distributed. Women in low-income countries averaged 4.8 births in 2013; in middle-income areas, fertility was 2.4 births, and in high-income states, fertility averaged 1.7 births per female, due to the demographic transition. There are significant differences among low- and middle-income geographic regions, from 1.9 births in East Asia and the Pacific; 2.7 births in the Middle East and North Africa; to 5.1 births per female in sub-Saharan Africa. Clearly, a significant demographic divide exists between the rich with low population growth rates and the poorer states, particularly in Africa, with higher population growth rates. These divides have politically sensitive consequences, as poor states labor under the burden of the population explosion while attempting to meet the economic consumption standards of the rich states of North America and Europe.

Realists see two threats emerging from these demographic trends that could destabilize the balance of power. First, states with burgeoning populations and insufficient food might seek to expand their territory or acquire food by means of war. Second, surplus males, who might otherwise turn to domestic crime or destabilize the state from within, might be channeled into state militaries and "expended" in aggressive interstate

TABLE 11.2	POPULATION OF THE WORLD AND MAJOR AREAS, 2015, 2030, 2050, AND 2100, ACCORDING TO THE MEDIUM-VARIANT PROJECTION (IN MILLIONS)			
MAJOR AREA	2015	2030	2050	2100
World	7,349	8,501	9,725	11,213
Africa	1,186	1,679	2,478	4,387
Asia	4,393	4,923	5,267	4,889
Europe	738	734	707	646
Latin America and the Caribbean	634	721	784	721
Northern America	358	396	433	500
Oceania	39	47	57	71

Source: United Nations, Department of Economic and Social Affairs, Population Division (2015), *World Population Prospects: The 2015 Revision* (New York: United Nations).

wars. Both liberals and radicals see these possibilities as confirming that the South needs economic development for more than simply material needs. This is because wherever economic life improves (especially when that improvement has resulted from greater educational and workplace opportunities for women), women tend to have fewer and healthier babies, more of whom survive to adulthood. As a state's economic fortunes improve, so does access to health care and family planning. Better education for parents and their children, in turn, opens up more economic opportunity, and the cycle reinforces itself. Thus, for these theorists, closing the development gap leads to a self-reinforcing spiral of economic improvement and demographic balance.

In addition, both rapid rates of overall population growth and high levels of economic development mean increased demands for natural resources—in particular, arable land and freshwater. For countries that already have large populations, such as China, India, and Bangladesh, the problem is severe. In Bangladesh and Nepal, the growing population is forced onto increasingly marginal land. In Nepal, human settlements at higher elevations have resulted in deforestation, as people cut down trees for fuel, leading to hillside erosion, landslides, and other "natural" disasters. In Bangladesh, population pressures have led to settlements on deltas, which are vulnerable to monsoonal flooding; this settlement strips topsoil, decreases agricultural productivity, and, especially when coupled with rising sea waters, dislocates millions of individuals.

Accelerating demand for natural resources occurs in the developed world as well. As the smaller (even slightly declining) population becomes more economically affluent, it increasingly demands more energy and resources to support its higher standards of living. People clamor for more living space, larger houses, and more highways, creating more demand for energy and resources. Wealthier people, especially those in the United States, also produce more garbage per person than in the developing world, and much is not recycled, leading to a high demand for domestic landfill space and a profitable business in exporting garbage to the developing world.

High population growth rates lead to numerous ethical dilemmas for state and international policy makers. How can population growth rates be curbed without infringing on individual rights to procreate? How can cultural barriers to birth control or to the value of female children be overcome? How can the developed countries promote lower birthrates in the developing world without sounding racist or ethnocentric? Can policies be developed that both improve the standards of living for those already born and guarantee equally high standards and improvements for our descendants?

Population becomes a classic collective-goods problem. It is eminently rational for a couple in the developing world to have more children: children provide valuable labor and often earn money in the wage economy, contributing to family well-being. Children are the social safety net for families in societies where no governmental programs exist. But what is economically rational for each couple is not environmentally sustainable for the collectivity. The amount of land in the commons shrinks on a per capita basis, and the overall quality of the resource declines. Over time, the finite resources of the commons have a decreasing capacity to support the population: Adam Smith's famous "invisible hand," when considered in the context of a commons, may therefore lead not to collective benefit but to collective disaster.

What actions can be taken with respect to population to alleviate or mitigate these dilemmas? The biologist Garrett Hardin's solution, using coercion to prohibit procreation, is politically untenable and pragmatically difficult, as China discovered with its one-child policy. Relying on group pressure to force individual changes in behavior is also unlikely to work in the populous states.[7] Leaving coercion aside, even if individuals may desire smaller families, family-planning methods may be unavailable to them.

But like the global environment, the connections, causes, and consequences of global population growth and decline have proven not only interlinked but complex. In many Western states, including Europe and Russia, as well as Japan, Korea, and China, the population growth has not only slowed, but it is in decline, and the population is aging.

These regions all share in a remarkable trend of increasing women's access to education and career employment outside the home. As a result, one of the world's most powerful demographic trends—women having fewer babies and having babies later in life—can be explained by the extraordinary demands of education and career. The aggregation of these individually rational decisions is a declining birthrate. In China, this dramatic decline may not have been by individual choice, but by the government policy of one child per couple. But in 2013, the Communist Party Central Committee announced that couples could have two children if either husband or wife is an only child; rural families were already permitted to have two children. In 2015, China rescinded the one-child policy, recognizing the deleterious economic consequences of a declining population.

In China and India as well, the problem is also a surplus of males, since males are still preferred for cultural reasons and sex-selective abortions have become increasingly common. From 2010 to 2015, the sex ratio at birth was 116 boys to 100 girls in China and 111 boys to 100 girls in India, above the 105 to 100 natural rate, leading to what is called the "marriage squeeze"—many males in search of too few females. This imbalance (bare branches) leads to brides for sale, prostitution, and, some scholars suggest, actually threatens domestic and international security.[8]

In Russia, characterized by one demographer as a "demographic disaster," there has been a steep decline in population, due to a combination of two decades of dramatic underinvestment in health care and education, widespread alcoholism, and heart disease. This decline has occurred despite significant immigration into Russia from the Central Asian states.[9]

One exception to the pattern of population growth decline is the Nordic countries (in particular Norway and Sweden), where parental leave and strongly enforced anti-discrimination policies make it possible for women to avoid having to choose between becoming mothers and obtaining higher education and lifetime employment.

What is clear about world population growth and decline, and the disparities among regions, is that the problems and opportunities they create are international. Decisions affect not just states with high rates of population growth but also their neighbors, as people on overcrowded land contend for scarce resources, seek a better life in other countries through migration, or may turn to violence to get more desirable space.

States are not the only actors affected by population pressures: this issue affects individuals, couples, and communities, along with their deepest-held religious and humanistic values. Population pressures also involve the nongovernmental community, including groups such as Population Connection or the Population Council that try to change public attitudes about population and procreation, as well as the Catholic Church and fundamentalist Islamic sects that oppose artificial restrictions on family size. They involve intergovernmental organizations such as the World Bank, charged with promoting sustainable development and yet hamstrung by the wishes of some member states to refrain from directly addressing the population issue. Perhaps most important, the population issue intersects inextricably with other environmental issues. Populations put demands on land use for enhanced agricultural productivity; they need natural resources and energy resources. Thus, ironically, population may well be the pivotal global environmental issue, but it may also be the one that states and other international actors can do the least about resolving.

Environmental NGOs in Action

Nongovernmental organizations (NGOs) have played a vital role in environmental issues since the 1960s. Their numbers have grown, and their interests are diverse. They range from the Nature Conservancy and the Rainforest Action Network to the Earth Island Institute and the Climate Coalition.

NGOs perform a number of key functions in environmental affairs. First, they often act as international critics, using the media to publicize their dissatisfaction and get environmental issues onto international and state agendas. For example, Greenpeace's

Human action has caused significant damage to our environment, but the political response has rarely proved commensurate with the harm. Many well-intentioned efforts, like cleaning landfills, fail to address the larger problems of overconsumption and pollution of natural resources.

condemnation of Brazil's unsustainable cutting of mahogany trees led that country to stop all mahogany exports until forestry practices could be improved. Second, NGOs may function through intergovernmental organizations, working to change the organizations from within. For example, NGOs transformed the International Whaling Commission from a body that limited whaling through quotas into one that banned whale hunting altogether. Third, NGOs can aid in monitoring and enforcing environmental regulations, by either pointing out problems or actually carrying out onsite inspections. For example, TRAFFIC, the wildlife-trade-monitoring program of the World Wildlife Fund and the International Union for the Conservation of Nature (IUCN), is authorized to conduct inspections under the Convention on International Trade in Endangered Species of Wild Fauna and Flora (CITES). Fourth, NGOs may function as part of transnational communities of experts, serving with counterparts in intergovernmental organizations and state agencies to try to change practices and procedures on an issue. One such **epistemic community** formed around the Mediterranean Action Plan of the UN Environmental Program. Experts gathered to discuss ways to improve the quality of seawater, share data, and, ultimately, establish monitoring programs. These same individuals also became active in domestic-bargaining processes, fostering learning among government elites. Finally, and perhaps most important, NGOs can attempt to influence state environmental policy directly, providing information about policy options, sometimes initiating legal proceedings, and lobbying directly to a state's legislature or bureaucracy. For climate change, several epistemic communities have been active. Yet in the long run, despite the increased roles for NGOs and epistemic communities, it is still states that have primary responsibility for taking action.

A Theoretical Take

What has made many environmental issues so politically controversial at the international level is that states have tended to divide along the developed/developing—North/ South—economic axis, although some developed states have been more accommodating than others have. From the perspective of some in the developed world, many environmental issues appear to stem from the population explosion, which they take to be a problem of the developing world, and furthermore, a problem over which governments in those parts of the world have some control. In this view, the developing world's governments must enact policies that slow population growth rates, leading to a decrease in the pressure on scarce natural resources and diminishing the negative externality of pollution locally, regionally, and internationally.

States of the developing South perceive the environmental issue differently. These states correctly point to the fact that many environmental problems—including the overuse of natural resources and the pollution issues of ozone depletion and greenhouse gas emissions—are the result of the industrial world's excesses. By exploiting the environment in an unsustainable way, by misusing the commons, the developed countries were able to achieve high levels of—depending upon one's point of view—either economic development or consumption. Putting restrictions on developing countries by not allowing them to exploit their natural resources or by limiting their use of fossil fuels may impede *their* development. Thus, because the developed states have been responsible for most of the environmental excesses, it is they who should bear the burden of reduced energy consumption and environmental cleanup.

The challenge in addressing transnational environmental issues is to negotiate a middle ground that reflects the fact that both sides are, in fact, correct. High population growth rates are a problem in the South—one that will not be alleviated until higher levels of economic development are achieved. Overuse of natural resources is primarily a problem of the North. Powerful economic interests in the North are continually reminding us that changes in resource use may lead to a lower standard of living. Pollution is a by-product of both problems, which in the South tends to be in the form of land- and water-resource overuse because of excessive population, whereas in the North, it stems from the by-products and negative externalities of industrialization. Thus, more than the other transnational issues, the environmental issue involves trade-offs with economic interests. Economic security is more likely to lead to environmental security. Realists, liberals, radicals, and constructivists do not all have the same degree of concern for environmental issues, although each group has modified its perspectives in response to external changes.

Realists' principal emphasis has been on state security, although some have identified human-security concerns. Both types of security require a healthy and strong population base, near self-sufficiency in food, and a dependable supply of natural resources. Making the costs of natural resources or the costs of pollution abatement too high diminishes a state's ability to make independent decisions. So, for example, Iceland's dependency on cod fishing as an industry made it much more vulnerable to unsustainable harvesting practices by its own fisheries and those of Britain and the United States, and to issues surrounding the rise in sea temperatures caused by global warming, which have caused cod populations to move to deeper or more northerly waters. The deeper implication is that for countries like Iceland, sovereignty is necessarily abridged, and the security of Iceland's citizens cannot be guaranteed by the state. Thus, realists fit environmental issues into the theoretical concepts of the state, power, sovereignty, and the balance of power.

Radicals are also concerned with the economic costs of the environmental problem. Radicals are apt to see the costs borne disproportionately by those in the South and by the poorer groups in the developed North. What remains striking about the most recent decade is how the most cogent part of radical—in this case, Marxist—theory has been revived by a resurgent transnational corporatism. Marxism predicts that capital must necessarily capture the state, which will then place corporate (commercial) interests above those of the state's citizens, its weakest and poorest. Thus, a Marxist critique of the current period would hold that the United States—epicenter of global capitalism—gutted regulations governing health care, food safety, worker safety, and environmental protection in the wake of the global financial crisis. The hammer blow of environmental harm (among others) then fell hardest on the poorest in the United States, its trading partners, and neighboring countries.

Both realists and radicals clearly recognize that controversies over natural resources and resource scarcity may lead to violence and even war. Drawing on Malthusian logic, political scientist Thomas Homer-Dixon, as part of the Toronto Group, modeled how the degradation of renewable natural resources may lead to violence: as resources such as freshwater or arable land decline in quality or quantity, individuals and groups will compete for these vital resources, resulting in violent conflict.[10] Many years later, he added that climate change may also lead to insecurity and violence. This view is consistent with the popular wisdom expressed by President Obama: "the long-term threat of climate change, which, if left unchecked, could result in violent conflict."[11] Yet the empirical evidence does not yet confirm the link. The very complexity of the model(s) with multiple intervening variables makes them difficult to test. And so far, scholars have not found a relationship between climate change and conflict.[12] Even lacking the empirical evidence, realists legitimately point to the possible security threat.

Liberals have typically seen environmental issues as appropriate for the international agenda in the twenty-first century. Their broadened view of security, coupled with the credence they give to the notion of an interdependent international system—perhaps even one so interconnected as to be called an international society—make environmental issues ripe for international action. Because liberal theory can accommodate a greater variety of different international actors, including nongovernmental actors from global civil society, they see environmental and human rights issues as legitimate, if not key, international issues of the twenty-first century. Unlike realists and radicals, who fear dependency on other countries because it may diminish state power and therefore limit state action, liberals welcome interdependence and have faith in the technological ingenuity of individuals to be able to solve many of the natural-resource dilemmas.

Constructivists, too, are comfortable with environmental issues as an arena for international action because environmental issues bring out salient discourse on environmentalism and sustainability. Constructivists are interested in how political and scientific elites define the problems and how these definitions change over time as new ideas become rooted in their belief sets. Constructivists also realize that environmental issues challenge the core concepts of sovereignty. One of the major intellectual tasks for constructivists has been to uncover the roots and practices of sovereignty.[13]

Health and Communicable Disease— Protecting Life in the Global Commons

Public health and communicable disease are ancient issues that have never respected national boundaries. But, when thinking about disease as a transnational threat, we should remember that, like other threats, global health also provides opportunities for cooperation.

The threat of plagues crossing state boundaries cannot be ignored. Around 1330, for example, the bubonic plague began in China, transmitted from rodents and fleas to humans. Moving rapidly from China to Western Asia and then to Europe, by 1352 the plague had killed one-third of Europe's population, about 25 million people. The epidemic, like others before and after, followed trade routes. During the age of discovery, Europeans carried smallpox, measles, and yellow fever to the distant shores of the Americas, decimating the indigenous populations. Expanding trade and travel in the nineteenth century within Europe and between Europe and Africa accelerated the spread of deadly diseases such as cholera and malaria, leading to the first International Sanitary Conference in 1851.

Between 1851 and 1903, a series of 11 International Sanitary Conferences developed procedures to prevent the spread of contagious and infectious diseases. As economic conditions improved and medical facilities expanded, the prevalence of diseases such as cholera, plague, yellow fever, and, much later, polio declined in the developed world.

Other diseases have continued to ravage the developing world. The World Health Organization (WHO), founded as one of the specialized UN agencies in 1948, tackled two of the most deadly diseases with its 1955 malaria eradication program and its 1965 smallpox campaign. Malaria eradication proved successful in the United States, the Soviet Union, Europe, and a few developing countries, using a combination of the insecticide DDT and new antimalarial drugs. Yet in most of the developing world, the program failed to curb the disease, as the number of cases of malaria soared in Burma (Myanmar), Bangladesh, Pakistan, India, and much of Africa. Efforts in malaria eradication focus today on low-cost mosquito netting to protect sleeping children, the most vulnerable victims. In contrast, the smallpox campaign was a stunning success. When the vaccination campaign began, there were an estimated 10 to 15 million smallpox cases a year, including 2 million deaths and 10 million disfigurements in the developing world. The last reported case of smallpox occurred in 1977.

Buoyed by the success of smallpox eradication, WHO tackled polio. In 1988, when the campaign began, this disease was estimated to paralyze 350,000 children a year. By working with state officials, WHO has immunized most of the world's population using an effective and inexpensive vaccine, leading to a 99 percent reduction in cases, with but a few cases reported. In 2010, when it was revealed that the U.S. Central Intelligence Agency had been using health workers administering inoculations to take blood samples to locate Osama bin Laden via DNA analysis, many health workers came under attack. Polio resurged in Afghanistan, Pakistan, and later Syria because of civil war disruptions. Since then, the availability of more effective vaccines and new emergency inoculation initiatives has brought the number of new cases to nearly zero. But some public health officials have criticized the practice of targeting specific diseases on grounds that funds might be better used to improve public health systems more generally.

No one doubts, however, that one of the tasks of state and international authorities is to report quickly and honestly on the outbreaks of transmissible diseases. Twenty-first-century mobility has posed major problems for containing these outbreaks as individuals and communities become vulnerable to disease through migration, refugees, air and truck transport, trade, and troop movements. The importance of these responsibilities became all the more apparent in the SARS outbreak of 2002–03. China initially suppressed information, was slow to permit WHO officials to visit affected areas, and

As a result of globalization, goods and services are not the only items traded around the world more quickly than ever before; communicable diseases too can spread rapidly, as humans hop airplanes to distant destinations more and more frequently. Here, passengers at Mohammed V International Airport in Casablanca, Morocco, are checked for possible signs of Ebola during the outbreak in West Africa.

failed to take preventive measures for several months. While fewer than 1,000 indi-viduals died, the potential for a global pandemic was widely recognized and the economic repercussions on the most affected states, including China, Vietnam, Sin-gapore, and Canada, were significant. When the avian flu broke out in 2005–06 and H1N1 virus in 2009, the new Strategic Operations Center for the Global Out-break Alert and Response Network was in place; WHO regulations were revised in 2007 to address global health emergencies in a more effective, better-coordinated manner.

Ebola and HIV/AIDS as Transnational Issues

The outbreak of Ebola in the West African states of Liberia, Sierra Leone, and Guinea tested the new system of quick response and alerts, and the system failed. Ebola was not new; there had been known outbreaks in 1976 and in 1995, both in Zaire (now the Democratic Republic of Congo). In each case, the outbreaks occurred in a rural area, there was high mortality, and the disease died out relatively quickly. This time, in the words of global health specialist Laurie Garrett:

> There was still no vaccine, no treatment, no field diagnostic tools, limited supplies of protective gear, nearly non-existent local health-care systems and trained medical personnel, no clear lines of national and global author-ity for epidemic response, few qualified scientists capable of and inter-ested in being deployed, no international law governing actions inside countries lacking the capacity to stop epidemics on their own, and no money.[14]

With broken domestic health systems unable to contain the outbreak, Doctors With-out Borders and a few other NGOs found themselves the primary international groups organizing assistance on the ground. They had stocks of protective gear and well-trained personnel immediately available. Neither the WHO nor governments were in charge. WHO itself did not issue its Public Health Emergency of International Concern until over four months after the outbreak! Budget cuts affecting outbreak- and crisis-response programs—20 percent in a two-year period—and poor adminis-trative practices at the regional level explains the poor international response. Over 11,000 people died; the economies of the affected states have been damaged. The dif-ficulty of dealing with Ebola is an order of magnitude different from the problems faced with the decades-long battle against HIV/AIDS.

Of all communicable diseases, the history of HIV/AIDS is the most illustrative of the challenges facing the world's peoples in the twenty-first century. Since the begin-ning of the epidemic, 78 million people have been infected. HIV/AIDS is the quintessential transnational issue. Originally transmitted from animals to humans in Central Africa, it then spread from person to person through the exchange of bodily fluids. Then those infected carried it to others around the globe as they travelled among states, all long before any symptoms appeared. HIV/AIDS rapidly became a major health and humanitarian problem, with an estimated 36.9 million people living with the disease at the end of 2014 (see Figure 11.1). The number of AIDS-related deaths has dropped from about 2 million annually in 2005 to 1.2 million in 2014. Africa still is the epicenter, with about 70 percent of the cases. HIV/AIDS is also an economic issue, disproportionately affecting those in their primary productive years, between the ages of 15 and 45. As teachers, workers, military personnel, and civil servants are infected, economic development is stymied and the viability of the military as an institution is threatened. And HIV/AIDS is a social issue, as families are torn apart and children are orphaned and left to fend for themselves. These children are often then forced to turn to prostitution or crime to survive. As the International Crisis Group explains, "it destroys the very fibre of what constitutes a nation: individuals, families and communities; economic and political institutions; military and police forces. It is likely then to

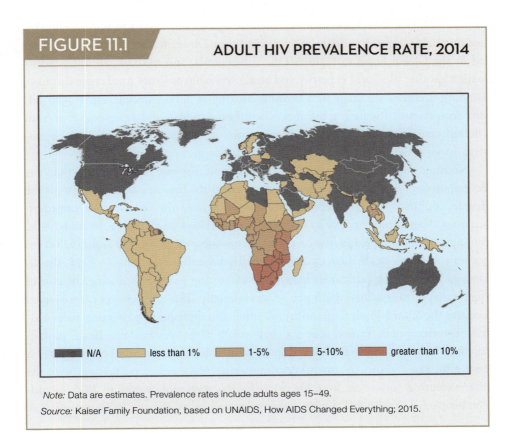

FIGURE 11.1   ADULT HIV PREVALENCE RATE, 2014

N/A   less than 1%   1-5%   5-10%   greater than 10%

Note: Data are estimates. Prevalence rates include adults ages 15–49.

Source: Kaiser Family Foundation, based on UNAIDS, How AIDS Changed Everything; 2015.

have broader security consequences."[15] Thus, in 2000, the UN Security Council identified HIV/AIDS as a threat to global security, the first time that a health issue has been so recognized.

While many different actors have responded to the HIV/AIDS problem, individual states are key. Some states and leaders seized on the issue very rapidly, launching major public-relations campaigns to inform their populations of risky practices leading to transmission of the virus, distributing condoms, and, eventually, facilitating the distribution of life-extending drugs. Uganda, Botswana, and Brazil are examples of states that took initiatives very early. Other states, like South Africa, India, and China, were slow to acknowledge the problem. But states have now responded, constrained by financial resources and technical expertise and sometimes social conventions. Without the willingness to act and respond openly, programs initiated by the international community cannot penetrate national borders.

Intergovernmental organizations took the leadership role at the early stages of the HIV/AIDS epidemic, though that response was too slow and disorganized. Beginning in 1986, WHO took steps to help states create national HIV/AIDS programs and made recommendations for drug treatments, adding antiretroviral drugs to its essential drug list in 2002. But WHO and other UN-related agencies struggled to find an effective institutional framework to address the various issues. Dissatisfaction with UN leadership led to the Global Fund to Fight AIDS, Tuberculosis, and Malaria, an independent institution that uses local expertise and local ownership of issues to advance its cause. Funding decisions are made by a board consisting of donors, recipients, NGOs, private sector actors (including businesses and foundations), and representatives from affected communities. The Global Fund continues to support and deliver antiretroviral drugs as well as help in the fight against tuberculosis and malaria.

Nothing was more critical to reducing the mortality rate of HIV/AIDS than the development of antiretroviral drugs used to extend the lives of people living with the disease. Multinational pharmaceutical companies became the saviors, albeit controversial ones. These drugs became available in the developed countries in the mid-1990s, but in the developing world, the cost of the drugs—between $10,000 and $15,000 per person annually—made them essentially unaffordable. But beginning in 1998, Brazilian and Indian drug companies began manufacturing generics, reducing the cost of the treatment to less than $500 per person annually. This activity was controversial because the World Trade Organization's intellectual-property protection rules prohibit internationally traded generics that violate patent restrictions. Brazil took its case to UN human rights bodies and to the international media, arguing that patients have a human right to treatment. A compromise was reached on pricing, with the pharmaceutical companies lowering prices for the developing world; in 2015, 15 million people living with AIDS were accessing antiretroviral therapy, or 41 percent of all patients. Successful use of antiretrovirals explains why the number of people living with HIV/AIDS has increased and the mortality rate has dropped. NGOs have led the public campaigns in both developed and developing countries to make these antiretrovirals available to those infected and to change the behavior of those not yet infected. The international community also raises funds for a variety of prevention strategies, including targeting pregnant women for antiretroviral treatment to prevent transmission to infants and supporting male circumcision programs that reduce the risk of infection.

No organization has been more influential in global health than the Bill and Melinda Gates Foundation. Since its establishment in 2000, it has devoted considerable resources to global health initiatives, including combating HIV/AIDS. It supports basic research on prevention as well as national programs. Many NGOs, likewise, have been actively involved with this issue, including Doctors Without Borders, CARE (Cooperative for Assistance and Relief Everywhere), the Global Network of People Living with HIV/AIDS, as well as scores of local NGOs. Some work at the grassroots level, treating victims and helping families and communities survive. Others train health-care workers in HIV/AIDS care, so they can then spread out around the world to provide for HIV/AIDS patients.

As with other technical issues in international politics, such as environmental protection, another new group of actors has become increasingly important for HIV/AIDS and other health-related issues—transnational communities of experts, or epistemic communities. Such groups are composed of experts and technical specialists from international organizations, nongovernmental organizations, and state and sub-state agencies. Besides sharing a set of beliefs, these communities share expertise, notions of validity, and a set of practices organized around solving a particular problem.[16] Major research institutes, such as the U.S. Centers for Disease Control and Prevention, the U.S. National Institutes of Health, and France's Pasteur Institute, are important contributors to the global health epistemic communities. The heads of these institutes became familiar to American and European actors during the 2014 Ebola crisis as they sought not only to contain the epidemic in West Africa but also to help Western national medical authorities develop procedures to protect domestic audiences terrified by the transmission of cases across state borders. These institutions also conduct research; in fact, the Public Health Agency of Canada has developed the most promising vaccine against Ebola, now in trials in West Africa. Members of epistemic communities can influence the behavior of both states and international organizations and have done so on the issues of HIV/AIDS and Ebola.

Both the Ebola epidemic and the continuing HIV/AIDS epidemic are development issues. The World Bank estimated that the regional economic drain caused by Ebola might be as high as $3.8 billion at the end of 2015, severely impacting Liberia, Sierra Leone, and Guinea. Liberia's economy alone is likely to decline by at least

21 percent and the effects will probably continue, even if the crisis is abated. Clearly, the economic development gap and the quality of individual lives cannot change without improvements in health conditions. That is why the Millennium Development Goals related to improving health (reducing child mortality and improving maternal health) and the new Sustainable Development Goals have even a broader conception of healthy lives (with goals related to nutrition, mortality, tobacco, and alcohol). The fact that during the 1980s the World Bank became the largest multilateral financier of health programs in developing countries confirms the health-development connection. The Bank uses a sector approach, funding programs to increase the capacity of national and local health facilities, facilities that were lacking in many African states. Without a doubt, health is a transnational issue affecting politics, economics, society, and individuals.

A Theoretical Take

Health is an example of a quintessential functionalist issue. (See Chapter 7.) Virtually everyone agrees that prevention of disease is critical and good health is desired by all. This consensus extends to the belief that we should rely on technical experts and highly trained medical personnel to prevent the spread of infectious disease. Given these two functionalist criteria, it is not surprising that one of the first historical areas of international cooperation was health, as states sought to harmonize quarantine practices and address the spread of communicable diseases such as the plague. This was the narrow purpose of the First International Sanitary Conference of Paris in 1851. But interstate cooperation to manage communicable disease has dramatically expanded since that time. On this issue, realists, liberals, radicals, and constructivists can all find common ground.

Differences remain, however. Because most realists focus on states and define security narrowly (as physical security), realists tend to reduce a broad array of global health issues to such goals as responding to outbreaks of communicable disease or preparing against the possibility of the deliberate use of bioweapons by state or nonstate actors. Once conceptualized as a threat, relevant questions tend to get reduced to the capacity of the state to defend itself against the threat of infectious disease or a biological weapons attack. The result is a paradox in two respects. First, because it privileges states as independent political actors, threat rhetoric tends to attract considerable organizational and financial resources. Yet the likelihood that any single state, however powerful, can succeed in mitigating the "threat" is low. Not all transnational issues demand a multilateral response, but health care is one of them. Second, the privileging of short-term, direct threats like terrorism over longer-term indirect threats like a compromised global health-care infrastructure can lead to seemingly irrational policies. Jeopardizing the polio immunization program in Pakistan and Afghanistan by using it to locate Osama bin Laden would only make sense if Al Qaeda had killed and maimed more human beings worldwide than polio had, but the reverse is true.

For liberals, world health presents great opportunities along with real threats. Because liberal theory's basic unit of analysis is the state as a member of a *community* of states, concerns about acute threats of plague are no more or less important than chronic threats or preventive action. Liberals are more likely to focus on international responsibility for dealing with health issues and to be willing to utilize all groups possible, including local, substate, state, international, and nongovernmental organizations, when appropriate.

Perhaps no issue clarifies these disparate approaches to world health as a transnational issue more than the 2011 announcement that a Dutch scientist in Malta had successfully modified a strain of the H5N1 virus so that it could infect humans. The team that modified the virus wanted to publish its findings. But publication was stalled by a demand from the U.S. National Science Advisory Board for Biosecurity. The board worried that publishing the information would make it easier for a bioterrorist to create a lethal bioweapon. Virologists (an epistemic community) were appalled: publication of the information would make it much easier to stop an H5N1 pandemic in its tracks because researchers would be able to study the virus and how to treat it. In this situation, who is right?

Even among radicals, important differences remain. Marxists, for example, might argue that challenges to world health stem from capitalism's tendency to concentrate wealth and the power of multinational corporations. By forcing many of the earth's peoples into poverty, and compromising the health-care infrastructure of states in the developing world, the eventual emergence of a lethal pandemic that slays the owners of the means of production along with workers is yet another way that capitalists "dig their own graves."

Constructivists would focus our attention on key features of how we think we know what world health means, and how that meaning came to be established. For example, as noted earlier, the resources a state may be able to extract from its citizens to engage health as an issue may depend on whether, in a given state, threat rhetoric is a more successful framing than cooperation and prevention rhetoric. For some feminist international relations theorists, the argument might be that women and men understand the world differently: women may think of world health in terms of long-term prevention and health-care infrastructure, and men may think of world health in terms of short-term responses to acute threats. The fact that most epistemic communities and states' bureaucracies are staffed by males means that world health issues are too often addressed as reactions to periodic health crises. More women in positions of authority, or a more humanistic (as opposed to masculinist) perspective, might therefore be needed before world health outcomes improve.

Transnational Crime

Over the last two decades, transnational crime has emerged alongside global health as a major issue of international relations, leading Moisés Naím to posit, "Global criminal activities are transforming the international system, upending the rules, creating new players, and reconfiguring power in international politics and economics."[17] As the frequency, intensity, and likelihood of interstate war declines, we can begin to focus on other persistent issues. And the capacity of transnational criminal organizations (TCOs) to cause harm to people (and, by extension, states) has increased over time in proportion to the continual drop in the costs of communication between places. In 2015, the data analysis firm Havocscope identified the economic value per year of the top 50 categories of organized crime worldwide.[18] The numbers are staggering: the top six categories alone—counterfeit drugs ($200 billion), prostitution ($186 billion), counterfeit electronics ($169 billion), marijuana ($141.8 billion), illegal gambling ($140 billion), and cocaine ($85 billion)—total nearly a trillion U.S. dollars. Beyond the examples of human and sex trafficking discussed in Chapter 10, two additional examples of transnational crime are narcotrafficking and cyber crime.

Narcotrafficking

Trafficking in illegal drugs—in particular highly addictive narcotics—is one form of transnational crime that garnered international attention following the end of the Cold War. **Narcotrafficking**—the transportation of large quantities of narcotics such as heroin or cocaine across state borders—has always been a problem. By the early 1970s, it had become severe enough in the United States that President Richard Nixon declared a "war on drugs," reasoning that lives lost to drug abuse were akin to casualties of war. In NATO countries alone, over 10,000 people die annually from heroin overdoses.[19] The other advantage of declaring a war on drugs was that "war" implies a shared undertaking that mobilizes all sectors of society to victory in a just cause. It also implied that the best way to address the problem was to cut off the *supply* of drugs to potential customers. But the problem is that such a "war" can never be won. Even if the destruction of major tracts of land where opium poppies or coca plants are grown can temporarily reduce the supply, the costs of shipping large quantities of product long distances are so low that new areas of cultivation can quickly be found to replace the lost supply.

Another challenge in preventing narcotrafficking is that the production, refinement, and shipment of narcotics contributes substantially to gross national product in many countries, including those that supply the raw materials for illegal narcotics, like Colombia and Afghanistan, and countries that are transit routes for narcotics, like Tajikistan. Thus, destroying poppy fields in Afghanistan or coca fields in Bolivia would be tantamount to destroying the economies of each of these states. Afghanistan, for example, produces an estimated 70 percent of the world's heroin, most of which is consumed in the Russian Federation. The economic value to Tajikistan of heroin smuggling from Afghanistan to the Russian Federation is equivalent to 30 to 50 percent of its GDP. A similar fate has befallen the West African state of Guinea-Bissau, whose offshore islands and miles of coastland have been too costly for the relatively poor country to police adequately. Narcotraffickers have established a collection-and-distribution base in Guinea-Bissau that may be responsible for the transit of 2,200 pounds of cocaine *per night*, with the complicity of some in the national military.

Moreover, once a narcotics transport infrastructure is established, it can be used to transport other illicit goods, ranging from copied software, movies, music, and designer clothing to the much more horrific trafficking in humans.

A final challenge is that because drug profits are often recycled into the purchase of arms, intelligence, and bribes for use by terrorist organizations, the harm of narcotrafficking is not restricted to destabilized countries, violent and property crime, broken families, and shattered lives. It also takes the form of organized terrorist attacks against ordinary people all around the world. (See Chapter 8.)

This situation has led to an increasing use of the term *narcoterrorism*, which highlights the links between terrorism as a political strategy and narcotrafficking as an effective method of funding terrorists. The term also serves to increase the availability of resources to counter narcotrafficking, because in much of the advanced-industrial world, framing an issue as an element of "national security" makes it more important, and thus more effective in competing for resources against "less-than-vital" threats.

One important shared feature of human and narcotrafficking is that the damage each does is relatively slow and may not always result in death. States usually pay the most attention to violence that results in death. This may explain why TCOs are again gaining the attention of policy makers and publics: since 2010, a rapid escalation in drug cartel violence in Mexican towns and cities bordering the United States has pushed the salience of narcotrafficking to the forefront of public-policy debates. The dramatic escapades of the Mexican drug lord Joaquin "El Chapo" Guzman and his Sinaloa cartel provide an accessible face to what otherwise might seem dry policy debates.

Cyber Crime or Netcrime

Cyber crime is increasingly familiar to people in the developed world. The Internet had its origins in a U.S. Department of Defense project aimed at making the U.S. nuclear command and control structure less vulnerable to a first strike. The concern was that the structure was too hierarchical, making command and control of a nuclear counterstrike problematic: What if the president and his cabinet were killed in a first strike? What if they were not killed, but their ability to communicate to the military in control of a U.S. counterstrike was disrupted?

The Internet's networked structure offered a solution. Unlike in a hierarchy, when a node in a network is destroyed, "traffic" (in this case, commands) can instantly reroute around the compromised node. Networks, as a form of communication, are extremely resilient to damage. Once computing hardware technology became sufficiently inexpensive for households to own in the early 1980s, the number of nodes that could be connected in an "internet" increased dramatically. From there, the development of the Internet was exponential. As more and more personal computer users began to link to the Net, the value of the Net increased, providing incentives for additional households to buy computers and devices to access the Net. Entrepreneurs began to offer "content" in the form of text, and later, music, video files, and applications or "apps." The evolution of the Internet also made it possible to implement electronic or "e-commerce." The rapid evolution of the Internet and e-commerce also created a lucrative potential for criminal activity. Anyone with a computer and access to the Internet can vandalize or steal. Identity and credit card fraud remain common hazards of e-commerce, as does the compromise of sensitive personal data like credit scores and social security numbers. Thus, two categories of cyber crime, or **netcrime**, have become major transnational issues: (1) cyber vandalism and (2) cyber theft.

Cyber vandalism is most often associated with "hackers," who delight in compromising state or corporate information and communications networks or stealing private information. Cyber vandalism tends to be transnational because there is a great deal of variation in the degree to which access to the Internet is monitored and controlled around the world. Two kinds of states do a good job of policing access to the Internet: (1) advanced-industrial states with major e-commerce stakes, and (2) authoritarian governments anxious to surveil their citizens and control public access to extrastate sources of information. Thus, many of the perpetrators of netcrime prefer to base themselves in urban areas in the developing world with weak state capacity to monitor their behavior. Cyber vandalism remains a serious problem because the viruses hackers create often propagate well beyond initial targets and can threaten power grids and emergency services. Every year, cyber vandals cause millions of dollars of lost revenue in the form of remediation costs.

Even more serious is cyber theft. In cyber theft, banking and financial networks can be attacked and large sums of money can be stolen, though this remains rare. More prevalent, and more costly, is corporate espionage. Estimates of the threat vary, largely because companies prefer not to report it for fear of stockholder lawsuits. But it is estimated that the yearly losses from Chinese cyber espionage and theft are between $800 million and $1 billion in intellectual property value. While many states, including the

United States, engage in some form of cyber espionage, China has so far been the most expansive, sophisticated, and successful. While experts disagree about the magnitude of the theft, they do not dispute where these attacks originate: China (95 percent), Russia (3 percent), and Iran (2 percent). In 2011, a U.S. nonprofit monitoring group, U.S. Cyber Consequences Unit, characterized the theft from China alone as representing "the biggest transfer of wealth in a short period of time that the world has ever seen."[20] Because it takes time to evaluate and duplicate stolen designs, the damage of such a theft today may not be truly felt for five or ten years.

A good example of netcrime that straddled the lines between vandalism, espionage, and deliberate harm was the Sony Pictures Entertainment attack in 2014. Sony Pictures Entertainment was attacked by a group calling itself the "Guardians of Peace." The group demanded that Sony halt the release of a film titled *The Interview*, which was meant to be a comedy about a plot to assassinate North Korea's leader, Kim Jong-Un. The North Korean government did not find the film funny, and the "hack" resulted in an estimated 100 terabytes of stolen data from Sony. Beyond the disclosures released by the Guardians—many unflattering—Sony has had to set aside $15 million to secure itself against future cyber attacks. To make matters worse, subsequent investigation could not confirm the identity of the hackers, and most experts do not believe that North Korea—itself a major cyber power—was actually behind the attack. The lack of capacity to identify attackers is one feature of cyber crime that sets it apart from many other types of organized criminal activity.

Finally, the same capacity to steal can be turned into the capacity to disrupt communications, water, electricity, and emergency services operations in major metropolitan areas of a target state. Military networks can potentially be compromised as well. Because each of these actions has a high potential to result in loss of life in a target community, these capabilities generally fall under the heading of cyber terror or cyber warfare. (See Chapter 8.)

In 2013, the UN group of Governmental Experts on Developments in the Field of Information and Telecommunications wrote a report supporting norms to govern state behavior in cyberspace. States should be held responsible for cyberattacks coming from within their territory and provide assistance to stop such attacks. Yet finding the culprits behind cyber attacks in any form is itself difficult. And for the United States, a state that ranks high as an origin country of malicious cyber activity, the stakes are high. Great Britain's approach to cyber security is instructive (see the Global Perspectives box, p. 430–31).

A Theoretical Take

Because the motive of most crime is by definition profit, international relations theory tends to treat issues such as cyber crime and human and narcotrafficking as peripheral

Cyber Security: A View from the United Kingdom

Cyber security has become a major global issue in the twenty-first century as more and more of the world's population gains access to the Internet and e-commerce. As an island nation with a long maritime tradition and a colonial legacy, the United Kingdom (UK) maintains an important independent perspective on increasing its cyber security.

Like many of the world's advanced industrial economies, the United Kingdom has benefitted greatly from the growth in the distribution and sophistication of the networked computers that make up most of cyberspace. In 2011, when the UK government published its cyber-security strategy, there were already 2 billion Internet users around the world.[a] As of 2015, there were just over 3 billion, many of whom do not even own a computer, but instead access cyberspace from an Internet-enabled mobile phone or tablet. From 2014 to 2015, the number of British citizens accessing the Internet with mobile phones, for example, rose 4 percent. British broadband use has risen at a similar rate, and the speed of connections has risen in a single year from 17.8 Mbps to 22.8 Mbps.

Because most software for computers and Internet devices is written in places such as the United Kingdom, the economic value to trade and commerce in cyberspace is immense and growing. With each new application, businesses and individuals in the UK and abroad are able to accomplish more tasks using fewer resources, including time and money. According to the data analysis firm Ofcom, the Internet in the UK accounts for about 6 percent of GDP, and as high as 21 percent of GDP growth.[b] In short, the economic value of cyberspace to Britain is critical.

But along with the increasing reliance on cyberspace have come increasing threats and vulnerabilities. Cyber crime, cyber attacks and espionage from other states, and the use of cyberspace to finance and recruit terrorists, top a long list of concerns. Britain's response to these concerns has been circumspect, creative, and above all, collaborative.

Britain has been careful in its efforts to make cyberspace more secure while not jeopardizing freedom of expression or other civil liberties—a difficult balancing act. Britain's view is that any support it gives in the form of cyber security–capacity assistance must be guided by Britain's own conception of human rights, a view widely shared in the European Union and North America. This precludes the use of cyber-facilitated censorship of free expression or the use of cyber-security technology to identify and persecute minority communities.

Like most other developed economies taking cyber security seriously, the UK started by tasking its communications and security ministries with securing the UK against cyber threats believed to originate from another state. The task of protecting the UK's critical national infrastructure (e.g., rail and communications networks, energy storage and delivery systems, and water sanitation and delivery) remains complicated, however, by a need to engage key players in the private sector: the businesses that own the power plants, storage facilities, and the like.

Britain recognized early on that its own efforts to secure UK cyberspace could not succeed without collaboration and cooperation, not just from individual citizens, groups and organizations, and businesses but also from other states. In thinking through the broader issues, Britain recognized that not only could it not succeed unless all other developed countries collaborated, but that it could not succeed unless developing countries succeeded as well. In Britain's view, unlike that of the United States, for example, no one is secure unless everyone is secure; or, in other words, UK cyber security will only be as strong as its weakest link. In a world in which cyberspace links virtually everything, this is no small challenge.

In meeting that challenge, the UK government initiated a Conference on Cyberspace in London in 2011. Since then, the newly titled Global Conference on Cyberspace has convened in Hungary, Seoul, and The Hague. It will meet next in Mexico City in 2017. The conferences bring together senior government officials, ministers, industry leaders, and representatives of both the cyber technical community and civil society in a truly global forum.

Beyond this global strategy, the UK continues to advance its cyber-security agenda across eight linked domains: (1) setting up a National Cyber Crime Unit; (2) establishing a cyber-security, information sharing partnership; (3) identifying and analyzing threats and strengthening its networks; (4) building cyber-security capacity internationally; (5) providing cyber-security advice for business and the public; (6) promoting economic growth in the cyber-security sector; (7) working with industry on minimum standards and principles; and (8) improving cyber skills, education, and professional opportunities.[c]

At the London Cyberspace Conference on November 2, 2011, Foreign Secretary William Hague argues for Internet freedom. The global conference was designed to set up the "rules of the road" for cyberspace.

FOR CRITICAL ANALYSIS

1. What conflicting choices does Britain face in implementing cyber security?

2. How are the UK's cyber-security concerns also transnational issues?

3. Are threats to global cyber security a tragedy of the commons? If so, how?

4. Should the developing world jump into cyberspace before it is secure? Why or why not?

a. UK Cabinet Office. "The UK Cyber Security Strategy: Protecting and promoting the UK in a digital world," November 2011, www.gov.uk/government/uploads/system /uploads/attachment_data/file/60961/uk-cyber-security -strategy-final.pdf.

b. Ofcom, "Facts & figures," 2015, http://media.ofcom.org .uk/facts/.

c. "2010 to 2015 government policy: cyber security," May 8, 2015, www.gov.uk/government/publications/2010-to -2015-government-policy-cyber-security/2010-to-2015 -government-policy-cyber-security.

issues. What makes organized crime increasingly likely to come into international relations theory nowadays is the violence that very often accompanies organized criminal activities, and the fact that many of these activities cross international borders in ways that cause states to treat them more as foreign policy issues over time.

Realists, for example, only care about transnational crime to the extent that crime might diminish a state's military or economic power or a state's ability to manage its military or economic power. Counterfeiting is an older example of a crime that affects state power, and cyber crime is more recent. Either sort of crime might harm a state's economy, its credit rating, and, in the case of cyber crime, even a state's capacity to direct its military. But it is only in cases where crime affects state power that realism recognizes crime as a problem of theoretical interest.

By contrast, liberals share a deep concern about transnational crime precisely because it affects a central pillar of liberal theories of cooperation and peace: trust. When cyber criminals in, say, Ukraine hack into a financial network in London, the British government is likely to consider Ukraine's government partly responsible, even though Britain itself hosts hackers and net criminals, and recognizes a need to do more to identify and stop domestic netcrime. The same goes for human trafficking and narcotrafficking. The existence of each causes states to worry that only "they" are working to really control and stop the crime, and that others are likely either passively or actively condoning such criminal activity. This potential harm to trust in commerce and security cooperation would count as a serious threat to the liberal ideal of incremental improvement in global security and prosperity.

Radicals argue that transnational organized crime has its roots in a system of inequality and violence embedded in the system of states as such, and is caused ultimately by the institution of private property, which acts to systematically impoverish the masses so that a few might enjoy vulgar consumption and an unsustainable standard of living. The state may tolerate crime itself because the state represents the interests of wealthy elites, including their security interests.

Constructivists, by contrast, might argue that transnational "crime" tends to be defined in ways that serve the interests of particular classes of international actors like multinational corporations. Why is a corporation charging too much for a given product like prescription drugs not classified as criminal, when a hacker who steals a formula enabling a poor country to make a generic version of a costly prescription drug *is* classified as a criminal? Constructivists, in short, focus on the political implications of the meanings given to phenomena rather than accepting those meanings as universal.

For many feminist international relations scholars, the lack of serious engagement at the international level with transnational crime confirms a narrow masculinist view of what does and what does not matter politically. Domestic abuse, economic and educational discrimination against women, and sex trafficking "do not matter" in this account because they allegedly neither enhance nor diminish state "power." But when we look more deeply at how economic and military power are generated within states, we see that these transnational crimes deeply affect state power, especially including public health systems and economic and military power.

In sum, international relations theorists increasingly recognize that transnational crime has more than a marginal impact on the interstate system, although they may disagree about the root causes of this transnational issue and its relative significance.

The Impact of Transnational Issues

As an unexpected consequence of advances in communications technology, transnational issues like the environment, world health, and organized crime have advanced from tertiary and moral issues to primary and vital interests. Before World War II, developed states might have viewed more active economic, health infrastructure, and human rights interventions as morally desirable but either risky or unnecessary for reasons of state. Since the late 1970s, however, transnational issues such as organized crime, terrorism, pandemics, natural disasters, and refugees from these disasters have tended to affect the developed world much more directly. Transnational issues have *become* issues because morality-based arguments for intervention to redress damages have increasingly transitioned into interest-based arguments for undertaking the same interventions. Transnational issues have effects on four major areas of international relations theory and practice.

First, the interconnectedness of the many sub-issues within health, environment, human rights, and transnational law enforcement affects international bargaining. When states choose to go to the bargaining table, a multiplicity of issues is often at stake, and states may be willing to make trade-offs between issues to achieve a desired result. For example, in the aftermath of the 1973 oil embargo and in the face of supply shortages, the United States was willing to negotiate with Mexico on cleaning up the Colorado River. The United States built a desalination plant at the U.S.-Mexico border and helped Mexican residents reclaim land in the Mexicali Valley for agriculture. To win an ally in the supply of petroleum resources, the United States made this major concession and also accepted responsibility for past legal violations.

Other issues, however, are less accommodating to negotiation, particularly if key concerns of national security are at stake. The United States was unwilling to compromise by signing the Anti-Personnel Land Mine Ban Convention because of the security imperative to preserve the heavily mined border between North and South Korea. Supporters of the treaty framed the argument in human rights terms: innocent individuals, including vulnerable women and children, are being killed or maimed by such weapons, which must be eliminated. Yet in this case, the United States decided not to sign the treaty because of Korean security. Although some states, eager for U.S.

participation, were willing to make concessions, others, afraid that the treaty would be weakened by too many exceptions, were not. Bargaining is a much more complicated process in the age of transnational issues.

Second, transnational issues themselves may be the source of conflict, just as the Marxists predicted in the nineteenth century. The need to protect the petroleum supply, for example, was a primary motivation for the West's involvement in the 1991 Gulf War. Jared Diamond's book *Collapse: How Societies Choose to Fail or Succeed* documents how the struggle for scarce resources led to the collapse of empires in the past and to state failure in Rwanda and Burundi, resulting in the abrogation of human rights.[21] The relationship between environmental and resource issues and conflict is a complex one, just as we have seen with the discussion of resource depletion and degradation; it is usually worsened by population increase, which is likely to result in conflicts when some groups try to capture use of scarce resources. Nonrenewable resources such as oil may lead to particularly violent conflicts, because such resources are vital for industry, economic health and welfare, and national security, and there are few viable substitutes. How else can we explain the conflict over remote and uninhabited islands in the China Seas? Only with the possibility of oil or other natural resources beneath the waters surrounding the islands does the conflict make sense. Changes in the distribution of these resources may lead to a shift in the balance of power, creating an instability that may lead to war, just as realists fear. In contrast, issues such as ozone depletion or global warming are not particularly conducive to violent interstate conflict. In these cases, the commons and responsibility for its management are diffuse.

Third, transnational issues pose direct challenges to state sovereignty, setting off a major debate about the nature of sovereignty. In Chapter 2, we traced the roots of sovereignty in the Westphalian revolution. The notion developed that states enjoy internal autonomy and cannot be subjected to external authority. That norm—noninterference in the domestic affairs of other states—was embedded in the UN Charter.

Yet the rise of nonstate actors—multinational corporations, nongovernmental organizations, and supranational organizations such as the European Union—and the forces of globalization, whether economic, cultural, or political, undermine Westphalian ideals of state sovereignty. Communicable diseases, the environment, human rights, and transnational crime were traditionally sovereign state concerns, and interference by outside actors was unacceptable. After World War II, those norms began to change, a process that continues today. The problems raised by transnational terrorism, for example, necessitate a multinational response: by transnational terrorism's very nature, single states, no matter how powerful, cannot solve these problems on their own. This is one of the main reasons that discussion has turned to a power shift, an erosion of state authority and the severe weakening of state power overall. Issues that once were the exclusive hallmark of state sovereignty are increasingly susceptible to scrutiny and intervention by global actors.

Part of the problem is that in many areas of the world, particularly since the end of the Cold War, states themselves have become fragile or have failed. These so-called states then become sites for transnational crime, terrorist organizations, and disease, all of which may be exported at relatively low cost to neighboring states and even around the world. Consider the fate of Zimbabwe under Robert Mugabe's heavy hand. In 2008, Zimbabwe's collapsed health-care infrastructure was unable to prevent or control the outbreak of a cholera epidemic. The disease soon spread to affect (and infect) the citizens of neighboring states, just as Ebola spread beyond its epicenter. Yet traditions of sovereignty mitigate against interventions aimed at restoring a state to full functionality. Who is to judge whether an intervention will simply restore a state or become a kind of twenty-first-century neocolonialism, as debated in Chapter 8?

How then should we reconceptualize sovereignty? How has sovereignty been transformed? Mainstream theories in the realist and liberal traditions tend to talk of an erosion of sovereignty. Constructivists go further, probing how sovereignty is and always has been a contested concept. There have always been some issues where state control and authority are secure and others where authority is shared or even undermined. After all, sovereignty is a socially constructed institution that varies across time and place. Transnational issues such as health, the environment, and human rights permit us to examine in depth long-standing but varying practices of sovereignty. These issues give rise to new forms of authority and new forms of governance, stimulating us to reorient our views of sovereignty.[22]

Fourth, transnational issues pose critical problems for international relations scholars and for the theoretical frameworks introduced at the beginning of this book. Adherents of each framework have been forced to rethink key assumptions and values, as well as the discourse of their theoretical perspective, to accommodate transnational issues.

IN FOCUS   EFFECTS OF TRANSNATIONAL ISSUES

- On international bargaining: More policy trade-offs; greater complexity

- On international conflict: May increase at international and substate levels

- On state sovereignty: Traditional notion challenged; need for reconceptualization

- On study of international relations: Core assumptions of theories jeopardized; theories modified and broadened

Transnational Issues from Different Theoretical Perspectives

The very core propositions of realist theory—the primacy of the state, the clear separation between domestic and international politics, and the emphasis on state security— are made problematic by transnational issues. Issues of health and disease, the environment, human rights, drug and human trafficking, transnational terrorism, and international crime are problems that no single state can effectively address alone. These issues have broken down the divide between the international and the domestic. They may threaten state security, but have no traditional military solution, even for a great power or superpower.

Responding to transnational issues, realists have generally adopted a nuanced argument consonant with realist precepts. Although most realists admit that other actors have gained power relative to the state, they contend that state primacy is not in jeopardy. Competitive centers of power at the local, transnational, or international level do not necessarily or automatically lead to the erosion or elimination of state power. Most significant, the fundamentals of state security are no less important in this age of globalization than they were in the past. What has changed is that the decreasing salience of interstate and nuclear war as challenges to state and interstate security has forced a broadening of security discourse to encompass numerous aspects of human security. For humans to be secure, not only must state security be ensured, but economic security, environmental security, human rights security, and health and well-being must be secured as well. One form of security does not replace another; each augments the rest. Thus, although transnational issues have forced realists to add qualifications to their theory, they have preserved it and enhanced its theoretical usefulness.

Transnational issues can be more easily integrated into the liberal theoretical picture. After all, at the outset, liberals asserted the importance of individuals and the possibility of both cooperative and conflictual interests. They introduced the notion that many other issues may be as important as physical security. They see power as a multidimensional concept. Later versions of liberal thinking, such as neoliberal institutionalism, recognized the need for international institutions to facilitate state interactions, to ensure transparency, and to add new issues to the international agenda. Though not denying the importance of state security, they quickly embraced the notion of other forms of security compatible with health, environmental, and human rights issues.

Radicals have never been comfortable with the primacy of the state or the international system that the dominant coalition of states created. For them, a shift in power away from the state and that international system is a desired transition. Marxists, for example, imagined a transnational revolution that would sweep away the state because the state's only function was the use of violence to maintain the power of capital over labor. With their pronounced emphasis on economics over security, radicals may be able to accommodate such transnational issues as communicable diseases, the environment, human rights, and transnational crime. A prominent radical interpretation of both communicable disease and the environment is that economic deprivation and perceived relative economic deprivation are the root causes of disparities in health care and environmental degradation. Human rights violations, according to radical thought, are caused by elites and privileged groups trying to maintain their edge over the less fortunate.

Constructivists have presented a different approach for analyzing transnational issues. They have alerted us to the nuances of the changing discourse embedded in discussions of health, the environment, and human rights. They have illustrated how both material factors and ideas shape debates over these issues. They have called attention to the importance of norms in influencing and changing individual and state behavior. More directly than other theorists, constructivists have begun to explore the varying impacts of these issues on the traditional concepts of the state, national identity, and sovereignty.

Some feminist international relations theorists make a similar but different argument: like constructivists, they interrogate the origins and content of terms like *threat*. But feminists go on to ask whether greater participation of women in scientific, academic, and policy-making processes might not lead to a more productive understanding not only of threats but also of solutions to transnational challenges. Why, for example, do "we" tend to respond to threats that are acute and direct but ignore those that are chronic and indirect, irrespective of the magnitude of potential harm? Why privilege harm that results in death as opposed to harm that abridges the quality of an affected person's life? Why speak of "threats" at all?

As transnational issues assume greater salience in the twenty-first century, all international relations theories will need modification and reformulation.

Will Transnational Issues Lead to Global Governance?

Recognition of transnational issues and their effects has led some scholars and pundits to conclude that we need to conceptualize governance processes differently than we have in the past. The processes of interaction among the various actors in international politics are now more frequent and intense, ranging from conventional ad hoc cooperation and formal organizational collaboration to nongovernmental and network collaboration and even virtual communal interaction on the Internet. These changes imply an increasing role for the regulatory capacity of norms. **Global governance** implies that through various structures and processes, actors can coordinate interests and needs in the absence of a unifying political authority.

As noted throughout this book, the core nature of international relations has changed over time. Perhaps the most important component of that change has been variation in the *demand* for governance and, in addition, a widening variety in the forms that global governance can take. Perhaps the key example of the problem and potential of global governance is the Internet.

As noted earlier, the Internet had its origins in U.S. state security as a way to increase the resilience of communications after a nuclear attack. Yet by the late 1980s, it had evolved into a way for researchers to share information across national and disciplinary boundaries. As the capacity of the Internet to carry information expanded, the types of information that could be exchanged—images, and in particular video—expanded as well. Yet the Internet remained almost entirely ungoverned. For many, this characteristic was its chief virtue. But the economic and political implications of the unregulated exchange of information proved too much to remain independent of governance or the depredations of commerce. States and private corporations began to weigh in, particularly states whose governments depended for their very survival on control of public access to information (for example, China, Saudi Arabia, Russia, Iran, North Korea), and corporations whose technology had facilitated the Internet's growth and capacity (Google, Apple, Cisco). The Internet proved a double-edged sword. On the one hand, it had the potential to bring its users closer together and to dramatically facilitate international collaboration in solving tough problems. On the other hand, that same openness created vulnerabilities, which prompted states to attempt to capture and regulate that openness.

What makes the Internet so important as an example of a transnational issue is that it incorporates both a horizontal component (geographic space) and vertical components (local to global and interest heterogeneity). In a way, the complexity of the Internet stands as a perfect metaphor for the complexity, and positive potential, of global governance. The European Commission, for example, defines "Internet governance" as "the development and application by governments, the private sector and civil society, in their respective roles, of shared principles, norms, rules, decision-making procedures, and programmes that shape the evolution and use of the Internet."[23]

The implications of the Internet example for global governance are crucial. Global governance, in its idealized form, presupposes a global civil society. The political scientist Ronnie Lipschutz describes the essential component of global civil society:

> While global civil society must interact with states, the code of global civil society denies the primacy of states or their sovereign rights. This civil soci-

ety is "global" not only because of those connections that cross national boundaries and operate within the "global, nonterritorial region," but also as a result of a growing element of global consciousness in the way the members of global civil society act.[24]

Some liberals would find this a desirable direction in which to be moving—a goal to be attained—whereas others fear that global governance might undermine democratic values: as the focus of governance moves further from individuals, democracy becomes more problematic. Others worry that a global civil society implies cultural convergence. If convergence is to happen, in other words, some cultures may become extinct and others dominant. Who is to say which cultures should be favored? In December 2012, for example, 89 of the UN's 193 members at an International Telecommunications Union conference in Dubai voted to approve a treaty giving states new powers to close off Internet access to their countries.[25] While countries like France and the United Kingdom were disappointed, others such as Iran and the Russian Federation were delighted. Each has argued that a perfectly open Internet fundamentally abridges state sovereignty, or each state's right to manage its own domestic affairs as it sees fit. Many of the 89 states who voted for the treaty see an open Internet as a proxy for the imposition of "Western" values on their own, different values.

Skeptics of global governance do not believe that anything approaching it, however defined, is possible or desirable. For realists, there can never be global governance because the more closely it is approached, the more dangerous it is perceived, and the more likely a countervailing authority or alliance is to halt or reverse the process of convergence. Outcomes are determined by relative power positions rather than by law or other regulatory devices, however decentralized and diffuse those devices might be. For Kenneth Waltz, the quintessential neorealist, the anarchic structure of the international system is the core dynamic. For other realists, such as Hans Morgenthau, there is space for both international law and international organization. His textbook includes chapters on both, but each is relatively insignificant in the face of power politics and the national interest. Few realists would talk in global governance terms. Radicals are also uncomfortable with global governance discourse. Rather than seeing global governance as a multiple-actor, multiple-process, decentralized framework, radicals fear domination by hegemons that would structure global governance processes to their own advantage. Skepticism about the possibility of global governance does not diminish the fact that there may be a need for it in the age of globalization.

In Sum: Changing You

In these eleven chapters, we have explored the historical development of international relations, from the development of the state system to notions of an international system and community and global governance. We have introduced different theories—realism, liberalism, radicalism, and constructivism—that help us organize our perspectives about the role of the international system, the state, the individual, and intergovernmental and nongovernmental organizations in international relations. From these perspectives, we have examined the major issues of the day and analyzed how these issues affect interstate bargaining, conflict, sovereignty, and even the study of international politics.

A citizenry able to articulate these arguments is better able to explain the whys and hows of events that affect our lives. A citizen who can understand these events is better able to make and support informed policy choices. In the transnational era of the twenty-first century, as economic, political, social, and environmental forces both above the state and within the state assume greater saliency, the role of individuals becomes all the more demanding—and all the more important.

Discussion Questions

1. Before World War II, crises and disasters in distant parts of the world stayed there. This is no longer the case today. What are two important implications of this new reality?

2. Global warming is a problem of the global commons, but not all environmental problems are. How should different environmental issues be approached?

3. Select two news accounts that address the trade-off between economic development and environmental sustainability. Can these two objectives be harmonized in the twenty-first century?

4. International cooperation on health has traditionally been viewed as a functionalist issue, but increasingly the issue has been politicized. What has changed? With what effect? Cite specific examples.

5. Explain why you agree or disagree with the following statement: too many policies aimed at redressing problems such as narcotrafficking, sex trafficking, illegal immigration, and netcrime focus on the supply of harmful effects (say, narcotics, or enslaved women and children) rather than the demand for such "goods."

Key Terms

demographic transition (p. 410)

epistemic community (p. 415)

global governance (p. 438)

Malthusian dilemma (p. 409)

narcotrafficking (p. 426)

negative externalities (p. 401)

netcrime (p. 428)

NOTES

Chapter 01

1. Stephen M. Walt, "International Relations: One World, Many Theories," *Foreign Policy* 110 (Spring 1988): 30.

2. Thucydides, *History of the Peloponnesian War,* trans. Rex Warner, rev. ed. (Harmondsworth, UK: Penguin, 1972).

3. See Jeffrey Record and W. Andrew Terrill, "Iraq and Vietnam: Differences, Similarities, and Insights" (Carlisle, PA: Strategic Studies Institute, U.S. Army War College, 2004), www.strategic studiesinstitute.army.mil/pubs/display.cfm?pubID=377 (accessed 9/18/15).

4. Stephen Krasner, "Israel: Munich or Helsinki," *Omphalos: Middle East Conflict in Perspective* (August 28, 2015). For more on the use of historical analogies, see Yuen Foong Khong, *Analogies at War: Korea, Munich, Dien Bien Phu, and the Vietnam Decision of 1965* (Princeton, NJ: Princeton University Press, 1992).

5. Plato, *The Republic*, trans. Desmond Lee (Harmondsworth, UK: Penguin, 1955).

6. Aristotle, *The Politics,* ed. Trevor J. Saunders, trans. T. A. Sinclair (Harmondsworth, UK: Penguin, 1981).

7. Thomas Hobbes, *Leviathan,* ed. C. B. Macpherson (Harmondsworth, UK: Penguin, 1968).

8. Jean-Jacques Rousseau, "Discourses on the Origin and Foundations of Inequality among Men," in *Basic Political Writings of Jean-Jacques Rousseau,* ed. and trans. Donald A. Cress (Indianapolis, IN: Hackett Publishing, 1987).

9. Jean-Jacques Rousseau, "On the Social Contract," bk. 2, chap. 1, in *Basic Political Writings of Jean-Jacques Rousseau*, p. 153.

10. Rousseau, "Social Contract," bk. 1, chap. 6, p. 148.

11. See Immanuel Kant, *Idea for a Universal History from a Cosmopolitan Point of View* (1784) and *Perpetual Peace: A Philosophical Sketch* (1795), both reprinted in *Kant Selections*, ed. Lewis White Beck (New York: Macmillan Co., 1988).

12. See, for example, Michael Walzer, *Just and Unjust Wars. A Moral Argument with Historical Illustrations* (New York: Basic Books, 1977); Jack Donnelly, *Universal Human Rights in Theory and Practice*, 2nd ed. (Ithaca, NY: Cornell University Press, 2003).

13. J. David Singer and Melvin Small, *The Wages of War, 1816–1965: A Statistical Handbook* (New York: Wiley, 1972).

14. Wade M. Cole, "Mind the Gap: State Capacity and the Implementation of Human Rights Treaties," *International Organization* 69 (Spring 2015): 410.

15. Meredith Reid Sarkees, "Defining and Categorizing Wars," in *Resort to War: A Data Guide to Inter-State, Extra-State, Intra-State, and Non-State Wars, 1816–2007*, ed. Meredith Reid Sarkees and Frank Whelon Wayman (Washington, DC: CQ Press, 2010).

16. Emilie M. Hafner-Burton and James Ron, "Seeing Double: Human Rights Impact through Qualitative and Quantitative Eyes," *World Politics* 61:2 (April 2009): 360–401.

17. Peter J. Katzenstein, ed., *The Culture of National Security: Norms and Identity in World Politics* (New York: Columbia University Press, 1996).

18. Cynthia Weber, *Simulating Sovereignty: Intervention, the State, and Symbolic Interchange* (Cambridge, UK: Cambridge University Press, 1994).

19. Karen T. Litfin, ed., *The Greening of Sovereignty in World Politics* (Cambridge, MA: The MIT Press, 1998).

20. Christine Sylvester, "Emphatic Cooperation: A Feminist Method for IR," *Millennium: Journal of International Studies* 23:2 (1994): 315–34.

21. See articles in Clifford Bob, ed., *The International Struggle for New Human Rights* (Philadelphia: University of Pennsylvania Press, 2009).

Chapter 02

1. Jean Bodin, *Six Books on the Commonwealth*, trans. M. J. Tooley (Oxford: Basil Blackwell, 1967), p. 25.

2. Bodin, *Commonwealth*, p. 28.

3. Bodin, *Commonwealth*, p. 28.

4. Adam Smith, *An Inquiry into the Nature and Causes of the Wealth of Nations* (New York: Modern Library, 1937).

5. John Locke, *Two Treatises on Government* (Cambridge, UK: Cambridge University Press, 1960).

6. Hilaire Belloc, as quoted in John Ellis, *A Social History of the Machine Gun* (New York: Random House, 1975), p. 18.

7. Quoted in A. C. Walworth, *Woodrow Wilson* (Baltimore, MD: Penguin, 1969), p. 148.

8. E. H. Carr, *The Twenty Years' Crisis, 1919–1939: An Introduction to the Study of International Relations* (New York: Harper Torchbooks, 1939, rep. 1964), p. 224.

9. P. M. H. Bell, *The Origins of the Second World War in Europe* (New York: Longman, 1986), pp. 151–52.

10. John Dower, *War Without Mercy: Race and Power in the Pacific War* (New York: Pantheon Books, 1986).

11. George F. Kennan ["X"], "The Sources of Soviet Conduct," *Foreign Affairs* 25 (July 1947): 566–82.

12. Quoted in Charles W. Kegley Jr. and Eugene R. Wittkopf, *World Politics: Trend and Transformation*, 5th ed. (New York: St. Martin's, 1995), p. 94.

13. Joseph Stalin, "Reply to Comrades," *Pravda*, August 2, 1950.

14. Mikhail Gorbachev, "Reality and Guarantees for a Secure World," as reported in Foreign Broadcast Information Service, Daily Report, Soviet Union, September 17, 1987, p. 25.

Chapter 03

1. Helen Benedict, "The Nation: The Plight of Women Soldiers," May 6, 2009, www.npr.org /templates/story/story.php?storyId=103844570.

2. Kenneth N. Waltz, *Man, the State, and War* (New York: Columbia University Press, 1954); and J. David Singer, "The Levels of Analysis Problem," in *International Politics and Foreign Policy,* ed. James N. Rosenau, rev. ed. (New York: Free Press, 1961), pp. 20–29.

3. Thucydides, *History of the Peloponnesian War,* trans. Rex Warner, rev. ed. (Harmondsworth, UK: Penguin, 1972).

4. Augustine, *Confessions* and *City of God,* in *Great Books of the Western World,* ed. Robert Maynard Hutchins, vol. 18 (Chicago: Encyclopedia Britannica, 1952, 1986).

5. Thomas Hobbes, *Leviathan,* ed. C. B. Macpherson (Harmondsworth, UK: Penguin, 1968), p. 13.

6. Hans J. Morgenthau, *Politics among Nations: The Struggle for Power and Peace,* 5th ed., rev. (New York: Knopf, 1978).

7. John J. Mearsheimer, *The Tragedy of Great Power Politics* (New York: W. W. Norton, 2001), pp. 19–22.

8. Kenneth N. Waltz, *Theory of International Politics* (Reading, MA: Addison-Wesley, 1979).

9. Kenneth N. Waltz, "Realist Thought and Neorealist Theory," in *Controversies in International Relations Theory: Realism and the Neoliberal Challenge,* ed. Charles W. Kegley Jr. (New York: St. Martin's, 1995), pp. 67–82.

10. John J. Mearsheimer, "The False Promise of International Institutions," *International Security* 19:3 (Winter 1994–95): 5–49.

11. Robert Gilpin, *War and Change in World Politics* (Cambridge, UK: Cambridge University Press, 1981), p. 29.

12. Gilpin, *War and Change,* p. 210.

13. Montesquieu, *The Spirit of the Laws,* vol. 36, ed. David Wallace Carrithers (Berkeley: University of California Press, 1971), p. 23.

14. Immanuel Kant, *Perpetual Peace,* ed. Lewis White Beck (New York: Macmillan, 1957).

15. Robert Axelrod and Robert O. Keohane, "Achieving Cooperation under Anarchy: Strategies and Institutions," in *Cooperation under Anarchy,* ed. Kenneth Oye (Princeton, NJ: Princeton University Press, 1986), pp. 226–54.

16. G. John Ikenberry, *After Victory: Institutions, Strategic Restraint, and the Rebuilding of Order after Major Wars* (Princeton, NJ: Princeton University Press, 2003).

17. Robert O. Keohane and Joseph Nye, *Power and Interdependence,* 3rd ed. (New York: Longman, 2001); Keohane and Nye, "Transnational Relations and World Politics," *International Organization* 25:3 (Summer 1971): 329–50, 721–48.

18. Francis Fukuyama, "The End of History?" *National Interest* 16 (Summer 1989): 4.

19. John Mueller, *Retreat from Doomsday: The Obsolescence of Major War* (New York: Basic Books, 1989).

20.   Steven Pinker, *The Better Angels of Our Nature: Why Violence Has Declined* (New York: Viking Penguin, 2011); and Joshua S. Goldstein, *Winning the War on War: The Decline of Armed Conflict Worldwide* (New York: Dutton, 2011).

21.   Karl Marx, *Capital: A Critique of Political Economy*, trans. Ben Fowkes (New York: Random House, 1977).

22.   John A. Hobson, *Imperialism: A Study*, ed. Philip Siegelman (Ann Arbor: University of Michigan Press, 1965).

23.   Tony Smith, "The Underdevelopment of the Development Literature: The Case of Dependency Theory," *World Politics* 31:2 (January 1979): 247–88.

24.   Stephen M. Walt, "International Relations: One World, Many Theories," *Foreign Policy* 110 (Spring 1998): 29–46.

25.   Ted Hopf, "The Promise of Constructivism in International Relations Theory," *International Security* 23:1 (Summer 1989): 172.

26.   Alexander Wendt, "Anarchy Is What States Make of It: The Social Construction of Power Politics," *International Organization* 46:2 (Spring 1992): 396. For a more complete analysis, see Wendt, *Social Theory of International Politics* (Cambridge, UK: Cambridge University Press, 1999).

27.   Wendt, "Anarchy Is What States Make of It."

28.   Ann Tickner, "Hans Morgenthau's Principles of Political Realism: A Feminist Reformulation," *Millennium: Journal of International Studies* 17:3 (1988): 429–40.

29.   Cynthia Enloe, *Bananas, Beaches, and Bases: Making Feminist Sense of International Politics,* 2nd ed. (Berkeley, CA: University of California Press, 2014).

30.   John J. Mearsheimer and Stephen M. Walt, "An Unnecessary War," *Foreign Policy* 134 (January–February 2003): 50–59.

Chapter 04

1.   See especially Morton Kaplan, *System and Process in International Politics* (New York: Krieger, 1976).

2.   Kenneth N. Waltz, "International Structure, National Force, and the Balance of World Power," *Journal of International Affairs* 21:2 (1967): 229.

3.   Kenneth N. Waltz, "Why Iran Should Get the Bomb," *Foreign Affairs* 91:4 (July/August 2012): 5.

4.   John J. Mearsheimer, "Back to the Future: Instability after the Cold War," *International Security* 15:1 (Summer 1990): 52.

5.   Paul M. Kennedy, *The Rise and Fall of the Great Powers: Economic Change and Military Conflict from 1500 to 2000* (New York: Random House, 1987).

6.   Robert O. Keohane, *After Hegemony: Cooperation and Discord in the World Political Economy* (Princeton, NJ: Princeton University Press, 1984).

7.   J. David Singer and Melvin Small, "Alliance Aggregation and the Onset of War," in *Quantitative International Politics,* ed. J. David Singer (New York: Free Press, 1968), pp. 246–86.

8.   Michael C. Webb and Stephen D. Krasner, "Hegemonic Stability Theory: An Empirical Assessment," *Review of International Studies* 15 (1989): 183–98.

9. Robert Gilpin, *War and Change in World Politics* (Cambridge, UK: Cambridge University Press, 1981).

10. Robert O. Keohane and Joseph S. Nye, *Power and Interdependence*, 3rd ed. (New York: Longman, 2001).

11. G. John Ikenberry, *After Victory: Institutions, Strategic Restraint, and the Rebuilding of Order After Major Wars* (Princeton, NJ: Princeton University Press, 2001), p. 50.

12. Martha Finnemore, *The Purpose of Intervention: Changing Beliefs about the Use of Force* (Ithaca, NY: Cornell University Press, 2003), p. 94.

13. See Alexander Wendt, *Social Theory of International Politics* (Cambridge, UK: Cambridge University Press, 1999).

14. Finnemore, *Intervention*, p. 95.

15. Hedley Bull and Adam Watson, eds., *The Expansion of International Society* (Oxford: Oxford University Press, 1984).

16. Samuel Huntington, *The Clash of Civilizations: The Remaking of the World Order* (New York: Simon & Schuster, 1996).

Chapter 05

1. James N. Rosenau, *Turbulence in World Politics: A Theory of Change and Continuity* (Princeton, NJ: Princeton University Press, 1990), pp. 117–18.

2. Graeme Wood, "Limbo World," *Foreign Policy* (January–February 2010): 49.

3. Quoted in Yaroslav Trofimov, "The Stateless Nation," *The Wall Street Journal*, June 20–21, 2015, C2.

4. Minxin Pei, "The Paradoxes of American Nationalism," *Foreign Policy* 134 (May–June 2003): 31–37.

5. See Martha Finnemore, *National Interests in International Society* (Ithaca, NY: Cornell University Press, 1996), chap. 1.

6. Alfred T. Mahan, *The Influence of Seapower upon History 1660–1783* (Boston: Little, Brown, 1897).

7. Halford Mackinder, "The Geographical Pivot of History," *Geographical Journal* 23 (April 1904): 434.

8. Joseph S. Nye Jr., *Soft Power: The Means to Success in World Politics* (New York: Public Affairs, 2004).

9. David Shambaugh, *China Goes Global. The Partial Power* (New York: Oxford University Press, 2013), p. 207.

10. Andrew Mack, "Why Big Nations Lose Small Wars: The Politics of Asymmetric Conflict," *World Politics* 27:2 (January 1975): 175–200.

11. Joseph S. Nye Jr., *The Future of Power* (New York: PublicAffairs, 2011).

12. Robert D. Putnam, "Diplomacy and Domestic Politics: The Logic of Two-Level Games," *International Organization* 42:3 (Summer 1988): 427–69.

13. Putnam, "Two-Level Games," 434.

14. Raymond Cohen, *Negotiating across Cultures: Communication Obstacles in International Diplomacy*, 2nd ed. (Washington, D.C.: U.S. Institute of Peace, 1997).

15. John Avlon, "A 21st Century Statesman," *Newsweek* (February 28, 2011), p. 16.

16. David A. Baldwin, *Economic Statecraft* (Princeton, NJ: Princeton University Press, 1985).

17. Biersteker, Thomas, Sue E. Eckert, Marcos Tourinho, and Zuzana Hudakova, *The Effectiveness of United Nations Targeted Sanctions: Findings from the Targeted Sanctions Consortium*, http://graduateinstitute.ch/un-sanctions (accessed 10/10/15).

18. Thomas C. Schelling, *Arms and Influence* (New Haven, CT: Yale University Press, 1966).

19. Immanuel Kant, *Perpetual Peace: A Philosophical Sketch* (1795), reprinted in *Kant Selections*, ed. Lewis White Beck (New York: Macmillan, 1988).

20. See, for example, William J. Dixon, "Democracy and the Peaceful Settlement of International Conflict," *American Political Science Review* 88 (1994): 14–32; Joe D. Hagan, "Domestic Political Systems and War Proneness," *Mershon International Studies Review* 38:2 (October 1994): 183–207; Erik Gartzke, "The Capitalist Peace," *American Journal of Political Science* 51:1 (2007): 166–91; Seung-Whan Choi, "Beyond Kantian Liberalism: Peace through Globalization?" *Conflict Management and Peace Science* 27:3 (2010): 272–95.

21. Norman M. Naimark, *The Russians in Germany: A History of the Soviet Zone of Occupation, 1945–1949* (Cambridge, MA: Harvard University Press, 1995).

22. Brendon O'Connor and Srdjan Vucetic, "Another Mars-Venue Divide? Why Australia said 'yes' and Canada said 'non' to involvement in the 2003 Iraq War," *Australian Journal of International Affairs* 64:5 (November 2010): 526–48.

23. See Monica Duffy Toft, Daniel Philpott, Timothy Samuel Shah, *God's Century: Resurgent Religion and Global Politics* (New York: W. W. Norton, 2011).

24. Samuel P. Huntington, *The Clash of Civilizations and the Remaking of World Order* (New York: Simon & Schuster, 1996).

25. Audrey Kurth Cronin, "ISIS Is Not a Terrorist Group: Why Counterterrorism Won't Stop the Latest Jihadist Threat," *Foreign Affairs* 94:2 (March–April 2015): 87–98.

26. Jack Snyder, *From Voting to Violence: Democratization and Nationalist Conflict* (New York: W. W. Norton, 2000).

27. See Moisés Naím, *Illicit: How Smugglers, Traffickers, and Copycats Are Hijacking the Global Economy* (New York: Doubleday, 2005).

28. Defined by Fund for Peace. "Fragile States Index 2015," www.fundforpeace.org/fsi15-report (accessed 10/12/15).

Chapter 06

1. Robert G. Herman, "Identity, Norms, and National Security: The Soviet Foreign Policy Revolution and the End of the Cold War," in *The Culture of National Security: Norms and Identity in World Politics*, ed. P. J. Katzenstein (New York: Columbia University Press, 1996), pp. 271–316.

2. Hans J. Morgenthau, *Politics among Nations: The Struggle for Power and Peace*, brief ed., ed. Kenneth W. Thompson (New York: McGraw-Hill, 1993), p. 5.

3. Quoted in Mijib Marshall, "After Karzai," *The Atlantic*, July/August 2014, 56.

4. Margaret G. Hermann, "Explaining Foreign Policy Behavior Using the Personal Characteristics of Political Leaders," *International Studies Quarterly* 24:1 (March 1980): 7–46.

5. Stephen Benedict Dyson, "Personality and Foreign Policy: Tony Blair's Iraq Decisions," *Foreign Policy Analysis* 2:3 (July 2006): 289.

6. Betty Glad, "Personality, Political, and Group Process Variables in Foreign Policy Decision Making: Jimmy Carter's Handling of the Iranian Hostage Crisis," *International Political Science Review* 10 (1989): 58.

7. Betty Glad, "Why Tyrants Go Too Far: Malignant Narcissism and Absolute Power," *Political Psychology* 23:1 (2002): 6.

8. Jerold Post, quoted in Peter Carlson, "The Son Also Rises," *Washington Post National Weekly Edition*, May 26–June 1, 2003, 10–11.

9. Ole Holsti, "The Belief System and National Images: A Case Study," *Journal of Conflict Resolution* 6 (1962): 244–52.

10. Harvey Starr, *Henry Kissinger: Perceptions of International Politics* (Lexington: University Press of Kentucky, 1984); and Stephen Walker, "The Interface between Beliefs and Behavior: Henry Kissinger's Operational Code and the Vietnam War," *Journal of Conflict Resolution* 21:1 (March 1977): 129–68.

11. John Lewis Gaddis, *George F. Kennan. An American Life* (New York: Penguin, 2012). See also George F. Kennan and Frank Costigliola, *The Kennan Diaries* (New York: W. W. Norton, 2014).

12. See Niall Ferguson, *Kissinger. The Idealist 1923–1958* (New York: Penguin, 2015).

13. Irving L. Janis, *Victims of Groupthink: A Psychological Study of Foreign-Policy Decisions and Fiascoes* (Boston: Houghton Mifflin, 1972), p. 9.

14. Dina Badie, "Groupthink, Iraq, and the War on Terror: Explaining US Policy Shift Toward Iraq," *Foreign Policy Analysis* 6 (2010): 285.

15. Herbert Simon, "A Behavioral Model of Rational Choice," in *Models of Man: Social and Rational Mathematical Essays on Rational Human Behavior in a Social Setting* (New York: John Wiley, 1957).

16. Robert Jervis, "Hypotheses on Misperception," *World Politics* 20:3 (April 1968): 454–79.

17. Malala Yousafzai, *I Am Malala: The Story of the Girl Who Stood Up for Education and Was Shot by the Taliban* (New York: Little, Brown and Co., 2013).

18. David Makovsky, *Making Peace with the PLO: The Rabin Government's Road to the Oslo Accord* (Boulder, CO: Westview, 1996).

19. Cynthia H. Enloe, *Bananas, Beaches, and Bases: Making Feminist Sense of International Politics* (Berkeley: University of California Press, 1990).

20. Pamela Johnston Conover, Karen A. Mingst, and Lee Sigelman, "Mirror Images in Americans' Perceptions of Nations and Leaders during the Iranian Hostage Crisis," *Journal of Peace Research* 17:4 (1980): 325–37.

21. Swanee Hunt and Cristina Posa, "Women Waging Peace," *Foreign Policy* 124 (March–June 2001): 38–47.

22. Pew Research Center, Global Attitudes and Trends, Global Attitudes Survey Q 84 (May 2014).

23. Johanna McGeary, "The End of Milošević," *Time,* October 16, 2000, 60.

24. "Top Global Thinkers: Mohamed ElBaradei, Wael Ghonim,*" Foreign Policy* (December 2011): 36.

Chapter 07

1. Joseph M. Grieco, "Anarchy and the Limits of Cooperation: A Realist Critique of the Newest Liberal Institutionalism," in *Neorealism and Neoliberalism: The Contemporary Debate*, ed. David A. Baldwin (New York: Columbia University Press, 1993), p. 117.

2. David Mitrany, *A Working Peace System* (London: Royal Institute of International Affairs, 1946), p. 40.

3. Garrett Hardin, "The Tragedy of the Commons," *Science* 162 (December 13, 1968): 1243–48. See also Mancur Olson Jr, *The Logic of Collective Action: Public Goods and the Theory of Groups* (New York: Schocken, 1968).

4. Margaret P. Karns and Karen A. Mingst, "The United States and Multilateral Institutions: A Framework," in *The United States and Multilateral Institutions: Patterns of Changing Instrumentality and Influence*, ed. Margaret P. Karns and Karen A. Mingst (Boston: Unwin Hyman, 1990), pp. 1–24.

5. See Karen A. Mingst and Margaret P. Karns, *The United Nations in the 21st Century,* 4th ed. (Boulder, CO: Westview, 2012).

6. Jonathan Tepperman, "Where Are You, Ban Ki-moon?" *International New York Times*, September 24, 2013, www.nytimes.com/2013/09/25/opinion/tepperman-where-are-you-ban -ki-moon.html.

7. See, for example, Virginia Page Fortna, "Does Peacekeeping Keep Peace? International Intervention and the Duration of Peace after Civil War," *International Studies Quarterly* 28:2 (June 2004): 269–92; Virginia Page Fortna, *Does Peacekeeping Work? Shaping Belligerents Choices After Civil War* (Princeton: Princeton University Press, 2008).

8. John Karlsrud, "The UN at War: Examining the Consequences of Peace-Enforcement Mandates for the UN Peace-Keeping Operations in the CAR, the DRC, and Mali," *Third World Quarterly* 36:1 (2015): 41.

9. Quoted by Ambassador Joseph Torsella in speech delivered at Council on Foreign Relations (January 20, 2012).

10. Immanuel Kant, "Idea for a Universal History from a Cosmopolitan Point of View" (1784), reprinted in *Kant Selections*, ed. Lewis White Beck (New York: Macmillan, 1988); and Jean-Jacques Rousseau, "State of War," "Summary," and "Critique of Abbé Saint-Pierre's Project for Perpetual Peace," in *Reading Rousseau in the Nuclear Age,* trans. and ed. Grace G. Roosevelt (Philadelphia: Temple University Press, 1990), pp. 185–229.

11. This section draws on Margaret P. Karns and Karen A. Mingst, *International Organizations: The Politics and Processes of Global Governance*, 3rd ed. (Boulder, CO: Lynne Rienner, 2015), chap. 5.

12. Christopher C. Joyner, *International Law in the 21st Century: Rules for Global Governance* (Lanham, MD: Rowman & Littlefield, 2005), p. 6.

13. Karen Alter, *The New Terrain of International Law: Courts, Politics, Rights* (Princeton: Princeton University Press, 2014).

14. Abram Chayes and Antonia Handler Chayes, *The New Sovereignty: Compliance with International Regulatory Agreements* (Cambridge: Harvard University Press, 1995).

15. This section on NGOs draws on Karns and Mingst, *International Organizations*, 3rd ed., chap. 6.

16. Maria Ivanova, "The Contested Legacy of Rio + 20," *Global Environmental Politics* 13:4 (November 2013): 4.

17. See Alexander Cooley and James Ron, "The NGO Scramble: Organizational Insecurity and the Political Economy of Transnational Action," *International Security* 27:1 (Summer 2002): 5–39.

18. See, for example, William DeMars, *NGOs and Transnational Networks: Wild Cards in World Politics* (London: Pluto, 2005); Volker Heins, *Nongovernmental Organizations in International Society: Struggles over Recognition* (New York: Palgrave Macmillan, 2008).

19. Fiona Terry, *Condemned to Repeat? The Paradox of Humanitarian Action* (Ithaca, NY: Cornell University Press, 2002); and Sarah Kenyon Lischer, "Military Intervention and the Humanitarian 'Force Multiplier,'" *Global Governance* 13:1 (January–March 2007): 99–118.

20. For pathbreaking theoretical and empirical work, see Martha Finnemore, *National Interests in International Society* (Ithaca, NY: Cornell University Press, 1996) and Finnemore, *The Purpose of Intervention: Changing Beliefs about the Use of Force* (Ithaca, NY: Cornell University Press, 2003); and Margaret E. Keck and Kathryn Sikkink, *Activists beyond Borders: Advocacy Networks in International Politics* (Ithaca, NY: Cornell University Press, 1998).

21. Michael Barnett and Martha Finnemore, *Rules for the World: International Organizations in Global Politics* (Ithaca, NY: Cornell University Press, 2004). Also Barnett and Finnemore, "The Politics, Power, and Pathologies of International Organizations," *International Organization* 53:4 (Autumn): 699–732.

Chapter 08

1. Data on war frequency and number of deaths can be found in several, sometimes divergent, sources. These include Quincy Wright, *A Study of War,* rev. ed., 2 vols. (Chicago: University of Chicago Press, 1942, 1965); J. David Singer and Melvin Small, *The Wages of War, 1816–1965: Statistical Handbook* (New York: Wiley, 1972); Jack S. Levy, *War in the Modern Great Power System, 1495–1975* (Lexington: University Press of Kentucky, 1983); Ruth Leger Sivard, *World Military and Social Expenditures, 1996* (Washington, DC: World Priorities, 1996); Human Security Group, "The Human Security Report 2012," www.hsrgroup.org/human-security-reports/2012/overview.aspx (accessed 2/27/13); and Human Security Report Project (March 2015), www.hsrgroup.org.

2. Charles Tilly, "Reflections on the History of European State-Making," in *The Making of National States in Western Europe* (Princeton, NJ: Princeton University Press, 1975), p. 42.

3. John Mueller, "The Essential Irrelevance of Nuclear Weapons: Stability in the Postwar World," *International Security* 13:2 (Fall 1988): 55–79; and Mueller, *Retreat from Doomsday: The Obsolescence of Major War* (New York: Basic Books, 1989). See also Gregg Easterbrook, "The End of War?" *New Republic*, May 30, 2005, 18–21.

4. See Joshua S. Goldstein, *Winning the War on War: The Decline of Armed Conflict Worldwide* (New York: Dutton, 2011); and Robert Jervis, "Theories of War in an Era of Leading Power Peace," *American Political Science Review* 96:1 (March 2002): 1–14.

5. Jervis, "Theories of War," 11.

6. Jervis, "Theories of War," 9.

7. Steven Pinker, *The Better Angels of Our Nature: The Decline of Violence in History and Its Causes* (New York: Viking Penguin, 2011).

8. Kenneth N. Waltz, *Man, the State, and War: A Theoretical Analysis* (New York: Columbia University Press, 1954).

9. Augustine, *Confessions* and *The City of God*, in *Great Books of the Western World*, ed. Robert Maynard Hutchins, vol. 18 (Chicago: Encyclopedia Britannica, 1952, 1986); and Reinhold Niebuhr, *The Children of Light and Children of Darkness* (New York: Scribner, 1945).

10. Thomas Hobbes, *Leviathan*, rev. student ed. (New York: Cambridge University Press, 1996), pp. 88–89.

11. John J. Mearsheimer, *The Tragedy of Great Power Politics* (New York: W. W. Norton, 2001), p. 32.

12. F. K. Organski, *World Politics* (New York: Knopf, 1958), chap. 12; and Organski and Jacek Kugler, *The War Ledger* (Chicago: University of Chicago Press, 1980).

13. George Modelski and William R. Thompson, "Long Cycles and Global War," in *Handbook of War Studies,* ed. Manus I. Midlarsky (Boston: Unwin Hyman, 1989).

14. For a more comprehensive approach, see Jack S. Levy, "The Causes of War: A Review of Theories and Evidence," in *Behavior, Society and Nuclear War*, ed. Philip E. Tetlock et al., vol. 1 (New York: Oxford University Press, 1989), pp. 209–333.

15. Scott D. Sagan and Kenneth N. Waltz, *The Spread of Nuclear Weapons: A Debate Renewed* (New York: W. W. Norton, 2003).

16. Michael Walzer, *Just and Unjust Wars* (New York: Basic Books, 1992), p. 185.

17. Andrew Mack, "Why Big Nations Lose Small Wars: The Politics of Asymmetric Conflict," *World Politics* 27:2 (January 1975): 175–200.

18. Ivan Arreguín-Toft, *How the Weak Win Wars: A Theory of Asymmetric Conflict* (New York: Cambridge University Press, 2005).

19. Ivan Arreguín-Toft, "How the Weak Win Wars: A Theory of Asymmetric Conflict," *International Security,* 26:1 (Summer 2001): 105.

20. Audrey Kurth Cronin, "Behind the Curve: Globalization and International Terrorism," *International Security* 27:3 (Winter 2002/3): 33.

21. Audrey Kurth Cronin, "ISIS Is Not a Terrorist Group. Why Counterterrorism Won't Stop the Latest Jihadist Threat," *Foreign Affairs* 94 (March–April 2015): 90.

22. See, for example, Dan Caldwell and Robert E. Williams Jr., *Seeking Security in an Insecure World* (Lanham, MD: Rowman & Littlefield, 2006); and Walter Enders and Todd Sandler, "Distribution of Transnational Terrorism among Countries by Income Classes and Geography after 9/11," *International Studies Quarterly* 50:2 (June 2006): 367–68.

23. For contemporary views, see Michael Walzer, *Just and Unjust Wars*, 4th ed. (New York: Basic Books, 2006).

24. Martha Finnemore, *The Purpose of Intervention: Changing Beliefs about the Use of Force* (Ithaca, NY: Cornell University Press, 2003), pp. 52–84.

25. Shashi Tharoor and Sam Daws, "Humanitarian Intervention: Getting Past the Reefs," *World Policy Journal* 18:2 (Summer 2001): 23.

26. Tharoor and Daws, "Humanitarian Intervention," 23.

27. John Herz, "Idealist Internationalism and the Security Dilemma," *World Politics* 2:2 (January 1950): 157–80.

28. Hans J. Morgenthau, *Politics among Nations: The Struggle for Power and Peace*, 4th ed. (New York: Knopf, 1967), pp. 161–215.

29. George W. Bush, "The National Security Strategy of the United States of America," September 17, 2002, http://georgewbush-whitehouse.archives.gov/nsc/nss/2002/index.html (accessed 2/1/10).

30. See Glenn Snyder, *Deterrence and Defense* (Princeton, NJ: Princeton University Press, 1961); and Alexander L. George and Richard Smoke, *Deterrence in American Foreign Policy: Theory and Practice* (New York: Columbia University Press, 1974).

31. For a good analysis of suicide terrorism, see Robert A. Pape, "The Strategic Logic of Suicide Terrorism," *American Political Science Review* 97:3 (August 2003): 343–61. On the discounted power of credible threats to kill as a challenge to deterrence, see Ivan Arreguín-Toft, "Unconventional Deterrence: How the Weak Deter the Strong," in *Complex Deterrence: Strategy in the Global Age*, ed. T. V. Paul, Patrick Morgan, and James Wirtz (Chicago: University of Chicago Press, 2009), pp. 204–21.

32. Keir A. Lieber and Daryl G. Press, "The Rise of U.S. Nuclear Primacy," *Foreign Affairs* 85:2 (March–April 2006): 42–54.

33. For a complete treatment, see Inis Claude, *Power and International Relations* (New York: Random House, 1962), pp. 94–204.

34. Zoltan Barany, "NATO's Post–Cold War Metamorphosis: From Sixteen to Twenty-Six and Counting," *International Studies Review* 8:1 (March 2006): 165–78.

35. Deborah Avant, *The Market for Force: The Consequences of Privatizing Security* (New York: Cambridge University Press, 2005).

Chapter 09

1. Thomas L. Friedman, *The Lexus and the Olive Tree: Understanding Globalization* (New York: Farrar, Straus, and Giroux, 1999), p. 257.

2. Some of the material in this chapter is drawn from Margaret P. Karns, Karen A. Mingst, and Kenneth W. Stiles, *International Organizations. The Politics and Processes of Global Governance* (Boulder, CO: Lynne Rienner Publishers, 2015).

3. "The Sticky Superpower," *The Economist*, Oct. 3, 2015, 8.

4. Robert Gilpin, "Three Models of the Future," *International Organization* 29:1 (Winter 1975): 39.

5. Sir Norman Angell, *The Great Illusion* (New York: Putnam, 1933).

6. See John McCormick and Jonathan Olsen, *The European Union: Politics and Policies* (Boulder, CO: Westview, 2014).

7. Jorge G. Castañeda, "NAFTA's Mixed Record: The View from Mexico," *Foreign Affairs* 93:1 (Jan.–Feb. 2014): 134.

8. "Weighing the Anchor: The Trans-Pacific Partnership," *The Economist*, Oct. 10, 2015, 72.

9. Joseph Francois et al., *Reducing Transatlantic Barriers to Trade and Investment. An Economic Assessment. Final Project Report* (London: Center for Economic Policy Research, March 2014), http://trade.ec.europa.eu/doclib/docs/2013/march/tradoc_150737.pdf.

10. Jagdish Bhagwati, *Termites in the Trading System: How Preferential Agreements Undermine Free Trade* (New York: Oxford University Press, 2008).

11. David S. Christy Jr., "Round and Round We Go," *World Policy Journal* 25:2 (Summer 2008): 24.

12. Paul Collier, *The Bottom Billion: Why the Poorest Countries Are Failing and What Can Be Done about It* (New York: Oxford University Press, 2007).

13. Nancy Birdsall and Francis Fukuyama, "The Post-Washington Consensus: Development after the Crisis," *Foreign Affairs* 90:2 (2011): 45–53.

14. Daron Acemoglu and James A. Robinson, *Why Nations Fail. The Origins of Power, Prosperity, and Poverty* (New York: Crown Business, 2012).

15. David Roodman, *Due Diligence: An Impertinent Inquiry into Microfinance* (Washington, DC: Center for Global Development, 2012).

16. Abhijit Banerjee, Dean Karlan, and Jonathan Zinman, "Six Randomized Evaluations of Microcredit: Introduction and Further Steps," *American Economic Journal: Applied Economics* 7:1 (2015): 1–21.

17. United Nations, *The Millennium Development Goals Report 2014*, www.un.org/millenniumgoals /2014%20MDG%20report/MDG%202014%20English%20web.pdf.

18. John McArthur, "Seven Million Lives Saved: Under-5 Mortality since the Launch of the Millennium Development Goals" (Brookings Institution, 2014), www.brookings.edu/research /papers/2014/09/under-five-child-mortality-mcarthur.

19. Scott Wisor, "The Impending Failure of the Sustainable Development Goals," *Ethics and International Affairs* (Sept. 30, 2014), www.ethicsandinternationalaffairs.org/2014/the-impend ing-failure-of-the-sustainable-development-goals (accessed 10/19/15).

20. Quoted in "Special Report, State Capitalism: The Visible Hand," *The Economist*, January 21, 2012, 5.

21. C. Fred Bergsten, "Why the Euro Will Survive: Completing the Continent's Half-Built House," *Foreign Affairs* 91:5 (September/October 2012): 16–17; and Timothy Garton Ash, "The Crisis of Europe: How the Union Came Together and Why It's Falling Apart," *Foreign Affairs* 91:5 (September/October 2012): 7–8.

22. Bergsten, "Why the Euro Will Survive," 22. For a more general assessment of the viability of the EU, see Wallace J. Thies, "Is the EU Collapsing?," *International Studies Review* 14 (2012): 225–39.

23. Ash, "The Crisis of Europe," 15.

24. Andrew Moravcsik, "Europe after the Crisis: How to Sustain a Common Currency," *Foreign Affairs* 91:3 (May/June 2012): 67.

25. Roger Altman, "The Great Crash, 2008: A Geopolitical Setback for the West," *Foreign Affairs* 88:1 (January/February 2009): 13.

26. William Easterly, *The White Man's Burden: Why the West's Efforts to Aid the Rest Have Done So Much Ill and So Little Good* (New York: Penguin, 2006); and Joseph E. Stiglitz, *Globalization and Its Discontents* (New York: W. W. Norton, 2002).

27. Moisés Naím, *Illicit: How Smugglers, Traffickers, and Copycats Are Hijacking the Global Economy* (New York: Doubleday, 2005).

Chapter 10

1.   See Paul Gordon Lauren, *The Evolution of International Human Rights. Visions Seen*, 3rd ed. (Philadelphia: University of Pennsylvania Press, 2011), chap. 1.

2.   Jack Donnelly, *International Human Rights*, 4th ed. (Boulder, CO: Westview, 2013). See esp. chap. 3.

3.   See, for example, Amartya Sen, "Universal Truths: Human Rights and the Westernizing Illusion," *Harvard International Review* 20:3 (Summer 1998): 40–43.

4.   See Paul Gordon Lauren, *Power and Prejudice: The Politics and Diplomacy of Racial Discrimination* (Boulder, CO: Westview Press, 1996).

5.   "The Persistence of History," *The Economist*, August 22, 2015, 50.

6.   See Karen A. Mingst and Margaret P. Karns, *The United Nations in the 21st Century*, 4th ed. (Boulder, CO: Westview, 2012), chap. 6.

7.   See Edward McMahon and Marta Ascherio, "A Step Ahead in Promoting Human Rights? The Universal Periodic Review of the UN Human Rights Council," *Global Governance* 18:2 (April–June 2012): 239.

8.   See Margaret E. Keck and Kathryn Sikkink, *Activists beyond Borders: Advocacy Networks in International Networks* (Ithaca, NY: Cornell University Press, 1998); and Charles Tilly, *Social Movements, 1768–2004* (Boulder, CO: Paradigm, 2004).

9.   Janet E. Lord, "Disability Rights and the Human Rights Mainstream: Reluctant Gate Crashers?" in *The International Struggle for New Human Rights*, Clifford Bob, ed. (Philadelphia: University of Pennsylvania Press, 2009), pp. 83–92.

10. On Amnesty International, see Stephen Hopgood, *Keepers of the Flame. Understanding Amnesty International* (Ithaca, NY: Cornell University Press, 2006); Ann Marie Clark, *Diplomacy of Conscience: Amnesty International and Changing Human Rights Norms* (Princeton, NJ: Princeton University Press, 2001).

11. Amanda M. Murdie and David R. Davis, "Shaming and Blaming: Using Events Data to Assess the Impact of Human Rights INGOs," *International Studies Quarterly* 56:1 (March 2012): 1–16.

12. Emilie Hafner-Burton, "Sticks and Stones: Naming and Shaming the Human Rights Enforcement Problem," *International Organization* 62:4 (2008): 706.

13. David Cortright and George A. Lopez, *The Sanctions Decade: Assessing UN Strategies in the 1990s* (Boulder, CO: Lynne Rienner, 2000).

14. Jonas Claes, *Libya and the "Responsibility to Protect"* (Washington, DC: United States Institute of Peace, 2011). See also Alex J. Bellamy, "The Responsibility to Protect Turns Ten," *Ethics and International Affairs* 29:2 (2015): 161–85.

15. Paul Wojcikiewicz Almeida, "From Non-Indifference to Responsibility While Protecting: Brazil's Diplomacy and the Search for Global Norms," South African Institute of International Affairs Occasional Paper No. 138 (April 2013).

16. International Court of Justice, *Case Concerning Application of Convention on the Prevention and Punishment of the Crime of Genocide* (Bosnia and Herzegovina v. Serbia and Montenegro), ICJ

Reports 2007, p. 43. International Court of Justice, *Application of the Convention on the Prevention and Punishment of the Crime of Genocide* (Croatia v. Serbia, 2015), www.icj-cij .org/docket/files/118/18422.pdf.

17. For an excellent study on the International Criminal Court, see Benjamin N. Schiff, *Building the International Criminal Court* (Cambridge, UK: Cambridge University Press, 2008). For an updated analysis related to U.S. position, see David Bosco, *Rough Justice: International Criminal Court in a World of Power Politics* (New York: Oxford University Press, 2014).

18. See Devaki Jain, *Women, Development and the UN: A Sixty-Year Quest for Equality and Justice* (Bloomington: Indiana University Press, 2005).

19. Mala Htun and S. Laurel Weldon, "The Civic Origins of Progressive Policy Change: Combating Violence Against Women in Global Perspective, 1975–2005," *American Political Science Review* 106:3 (August 2012): 548–69.

20. Gil Loescher and James Milner "UNHCR and the Global Governance of Refugees," in *Global Migration Governance*, ed. Alexander Betts (New York: Oxford University Press, 2011), pp. 189–209.

21. Alex J. Bellamy, "Safe Passage and Asylum Key to Fulfilling the Responsibility to Protect," International Peace Institute: Global Observatory (Sept. 8, 2015).

22. Henry Kissinger, *Diplomacy* (New York: Simon and Schuster, 1994).

23. Zbigniew Brzezinski, *The Grand Failure: The Birth and Death of Communism in the Twentieth Century* (New York: Scribner's, 1989), p. 256.

Chapter 11

1. Barack Obama, quoted in "Tales of Atlantis," *The Economist*, September 5, 2015, 36.

2. Rachel Carson, *Silent Spring* (Boston: Houghton Mifflin, 1962). See also Jacques Yves Cousteau with Frederick Dames, *The Silent World* (New York: Harper & Row, 1953); and Cousteau with James Dugan, *The Living Sea* (New York: Harper & Row, 1963).

3. Intergovernmental Panel on Climate Change (IPCC) Working Group I, "Summary for Policymakers," 2013, www.climatechange2013.org/images/report/WG1AR5_SPM-FINAL .pdf; IPCC Working Group II, "Summary for Policymakers," 2014, http://ipcc-wg2.gov/AR5/.

4. Robert Keohane and David Victor, "The Regime Complex for Climate Change," *Perspectives on Politics* 9:1 (March 2011): 7–23.

5. Thomas Malthus, *An Essay on the Principle of Population: Text, Sources, and Background Criticism,* ed. Philip Appleman (New York: W. W. Norton, 1976).

6. Donella H. Meadows et al., *The Limits to Growth* (New York: Signet, 1972).

7. Garrett Hardin, "The Tragedy of the Commons," *Science* 162 (December 13, 1968): 1243–48.

8. Andrea den Boer and Valerie M. Hudson, "A Surplus of Men, a Deficit of Peace: Security and Sex Ratios in Asia's Largest States," *International Security* 26:4 (Spring 2002): 5–38. For extended argument, see Valerie M. Hudson and Andrea M. den Boer, *Bare Branches: The Security Implications of Asia's Surplus Male Population* (Cambridge, MA: The MIT Press, 2005).

9. Nicholas Eberstadt, "The Dying Bear: Russia's Demographic Disaster," *Foreign Affairs* 90:6 (March 2011): 95–108.

10. Thomas F. Homer-Dixon, "Environmental Scarcities and Violent Conflict: Evidence and Cases," *International Security* 19:1 (Summer 1994): 5–40.

11. Barack Obama, "Remarks by the President on Jobs, Energy Independence, and Climate Change," January 26, 2009, www.whitehouse.gov/blog/2009/01/26/peril-progress-environment.

12. Emily Meierding, "Climate Change and Conflict: Avoiding Small Talk About the Weather," *International Studies Review* 15:2 (June 2013): 185–203.

13. See Karen T. Litfin, *Ozone Discourses: Science and Politics in Global Environmental Cooperation* (New York: Columbia University Press, 1994).

14. Laurie Garrett, "Ebola's Lessons: How the WHO Mishandled the Crisis," *Foreign Affairs* 94:5 (Sept./Oct. 2015): 82.

15. International Crisis Group, "HIV/AIDS as a Security Issue," June 19, 2001, www.crisisgroup .org/home/index/cfm?1=1&id=1831.

16. Peter M. Haas, "Introduction: Epistemic Communities and International Policy Coordination," *International Organization* 46:1 (Winter 1992): 3.

17. Moisés Naím, *Illicit: How Smugglers, Traffickers, and Copycats Are Hijacking the Global Economy* (New York: Anchor Books, 2006), p. 5.

18. www.havocscope.com.

19. www.unodc.org/unodc/en/press/releases/2009/october/unodc-reveals-devastating-impact-of -afghan-opium-.html.

20. See "China-Based Hacking of 760 Companies Shows Global Cyber War," *The Washington Examiner*, December 13, 2011.

21. Jared Diamond, *Collapse: How Societies Choose to Fail or Succeed* (New York: Penguin, 2005).

22. See Stephen D. Krasner, *Sovereignty: Organized Hypocrisy* (Princeton, NJ: Princeton University Press, 1999); and Karen T. Litfin, ed., *The Greening of Sovereignty in World Politics* (Cambridge, MA: The MIT Press, 1998).

23. See http://ec.europa.eu/information_society/policy/internet_gov/index_en.htm.

24. Ronnie Lipschutz, "Reconstructing World Politics: The Emergence of Global Civil Society," *Millennium: Journal of International Studies* 21:3 (1992): 398–99.

25. L. Gordon Crovitz, "America's First Big Digital Defeat," *The Wall Street Journal*, December 16, 2012.

GLOSSARY

anarchy the absence of governmental authority

arms control restrictions on the research, manufacture, or deployment of weapons systems and certain types of troops

asymmetric conflict war between political actors of unequal strength, in which the weaker party tries to neutralize its opponent's strength by exploiting the opponent's weaknesses

balance of power any system in which actors (e.g., states) enjoy relatively equal power, such that no single state or coalition of states is able to dominate other actors in the system

bandwagoning strategy in which weaker states join forces with stronger states

behavioralism an approach to the study of social science and international relations that posits that individuals and units like states act in regularized ways; leads to a belief that behaviors can be described, explained, and predicted

Beijing Consensus an alternative to the Washington Consensus; experimenting with economic policies in state capitalism; government plays a more active role in picking economic winners and losers

belief system the organized and integrated perceptions of individuals in a society, including foreign policy decision makers, often based on past history, that guide them to select certain policies over others

bipolar an international system in which there are two great powers or blocs of roughly equal strength or weight

BRICS an informal group of emerging economic powers, including Brazil, Russia, India, China, and South Africa

bureaucratic politics the model of foreign policy decision making that posits that national decisions are the outcomes of bargaining among bureaucratic groups having competing interests; decisions reflect the relative strength of the individual bureaucratic players or of the organizations they represent

capitalism the economic system in which the ownership of the means of production is in private hands; the system operates according to market forces whereby capital and labor move freely; according to radicals, an exploitative relationship between the owners of production and the workers

celebrity diplomacy use of popular individuals to bring attention to an issue and/or to try to influence both the public and decision makers to pursue a course of action

cognitive consistency the tendency of individuals to accept information that is compatible with what has previously been accepted, often by ignoring inconsistent information; linked to the desire of individuals to be consistent in their attitudes

Cold War the era in international relations between the end of World War II and 1990, distinguished by ideological, economic, political, and military rivalry between the Soviet Union and the United States

collective good a public good that is available to all regardless of individual contribution—e.g., the air, the oceans, or Antarctica—but that no one owns or is individually responsible for; with collective goods, decisions by one group or state have effects on other groups or states

collective security the concept that aggression against a state should be defeated collectively because aggression against one state is aggression against all; basis of League of Nations and United Nations

colonialism the 15th–20th century practice of founding, maintaining, and expanding colonies abroad. Colonialism, now universally delegitimized, was marked by two main motivations: (1) showing indigenous peoples how best to live (a "civilizing mission"); and (2) exploiting indigenous people and their territory for labor and material resources in order to increase the power of the colonial authority

comparative advantage the ability of a country to make and export a good relatively more efficiently than other countries; the basis for the liberal economic principle that countries benefit from free trade among nations

compellence the use of threats to coerce another into taking an action it otherwise would not take

complex (or multidimensional) peacekeeping multidimensional operations using military and civilian personnel, often including traditional peacekeeping and nation-building activities; more dangerous because not all parties have consented and because force is usually used

constructivism an alternative international relations theory that hypothesizes how ideas, norms, and institutions shape state identity and interests

containment a foreign policy designed to prevent the expansion of an adversary by blocking its opportunities to expand, by supporting weaker states through foreign aid programs, and by the use of coercive force only to oppose an active attempt by an adversary to physically expand; the major U.S. policy toward the Soviet Union during the Cold War era

crimes against humanity international crimes, including murder, enslavement, ethnic cleansing, and torture, committed against civilians, as codified in the Rome Statute

cultural relativism the belief that human rights, ethics, and morality are determined by cultures and history and therefore are not universally the same

democratic peace theory supported by empirical evidence that democratic states do not fight wars against each other, but do fight wars against authoritarian states

demographic transition the situation in which increasing levels of economic development lead to falling death rates, followed by falling birth rates

dependency theorists individuals whose ideas are derived from radicalism, and who explain poverty and underdevelopment in developing countries based on their historical dependence on and domination by rich countries

derivatives financial instruments often derived from an asset (mortgages, loans, foreign exchange, interest rates) which parties agree to exchange over time; a way of buying and selling risk in international financial markets

détente the easing of tense relations; in the context of this volume, détente refers to the relaxation and reappraisal of threat assessments by political rivals, for example, the United States and Soviet Union during the later years of the Cold War

deterrence the policy of maintaining a large military force and arsenal to discourage any potential aggressor from taking action; states commit themselves to punish an aggressor state

diplomacy the practice of states trying to influence the behavior of other states by bargaining, negotiating, taking specific noncoercive actions or refraining from such actions, or appealing to the foreign public for support of a position

direct foreign investment (FDI) investing in another state, usually by multinational corporations, by establishing a manufacturing facility or developing an extractive industry

disarmament the policy of eliminating a state's offensive weaponry; may occur for all classes of weapons or for specified weapons only; the logic of the policy is that fewer weapons leads to greater security

diversionary war the theory that leaders may start conflicts to divert attention from domestic problems

domino effect a metaphor that posits that the loss of influence over one state to an adversary will necessarily lead to a subsequent loss of control over neighboring states, just as dominos fall one after another; used by the United States as a justification to support South Vietnam, fearing that if that country became communist, neighboring countries would also fall under communist influence

epistemic community community of experts and technical specialists who share a set of beliefs and a way to approach problems

ethnonational movements the participation in organized political activity of self-conscious communities sharing an ethnic affiliation; some movements seek autonomy within an organized state; others desire separation and the formation of a new state; still others want to join with a different state

European Union (EU) a union of twenty-eight European states, formerly the European Economic Community; designed originally during the 1950s for economic integration, but since expanded into a closer political and economic union

evoked set the tendency to look for details in a contemporary situation that are similar to information previously obtained

extremist Islamic fundamentalism groups seeking to change states and societies through violent and coercive means to support imposition of Sharia law

first-strike capability the ability to launch a nuclear attack capable of completely preventing a retaliatory strike

fragile state state which has ineffective or nonexistent government, widespread lawlessness, often accompanied by insurgency and crime; situation where state authorities are not protecting their own people

General Assembly one of the major organs of the United Nations; generally addresses issues other than those of peace and security; each member state has one vote; operates with six functional committees composed of all member states

General Agreement on Tariffs and Trade (GATT) founded by treaty in 1947 as the Bretton Woods institution responsible for negotiating a liberal international trade regime that included the principles of nondiscrimination in trade and most-favored-nation status; re-formed as the World Trade Organization in 1995

genocide the systematic killing or harming of a group of people based on national, religious, ethnic, or racial characteristics, with the intention of destroying the group

global governance structures and processes that enable actors to coordinate interdependent needs and interests in the absence of a unifying political authority

globalization the process of increasing integration of the world in terms of economics, politics, communications, social relations, and culture; increasingly undermines traditional state sovereignty

Group of 7 (G7) group of the traditional economic powers (U.S., Great Britain, France, Japan, Germany, Italy, Canada) who meet annually to address economic problems; when Russia joins, the G8 discussions turn to political issues

Group of 77 a coalition of about 125 developing countries that press for reforms in economic relations between developing and developed countries; also referred to as the South

Group of 20 group of finance ministers and heads of central banks (recently heads of state) of major economic powers, including China, Russia, Australia, Argentina, Brazil, Indonesia, Mexico, South Africa, South Korea, Turkey, as well as representatives from the G7; meets periodically to discuss economic issues

groupthink the tendency for small groups to form a consensus and resist criticism of a core position, often disregarding contradictory information in the process; group may ostracize members holding a different position

guerrilla warfare the use of irregular armed forces to undermine the will of an incumbent government (or its foreign support) by selectively attacking the government's vulnerable points or personnel over a prolonged period of time; guerrillas hide among the people they aim to represent, and as such tend to place ordinary citizens at great risk; guerrillas require both social support (or at a minimum, social apathy) and sanctuary (either a remote base in a rugged environment or a weakly defended international border) in order to survive, and by surviving, to win

hegemon a dominant state that has a preponderance of power; often establishes and enforces the rules and norms in the international system

humanitarian intervention actions by states, international organizations, or the international community in general to intervene, usually with coercive force, to alleviate human suffering without necessarily obtaining consent of the state

human security a concept of security broadened to include the protection of individuals from systematic violence, environmental degradation, and health disasters; the concept gained ground after the Cold War due to the inability or unwillingness of states (see also "responsibility to protect") to adequately protect their own citizens

hybrid warfare a new term used to describe a strategy that deliberately mixes elements and techniques of conventional warfare (e.g., national uniforms, heavy weapons) and unconventional warfare (e.g., guerrilla, paramilitary, information, or cyber war) as a way to coerce adversaries while avoiding attribution and retribution

hypotheses tentative statements about causal relationships put forward to explore and test their logical and usually their empirical consequences

imperialism the policy and practice of extending the domination of one state over another through territorial conquest or economic domination; in radicalism, the final stage of expansion of the capitalist system

institutions processes and structures of social order around which relatively stable individual and group expectations and identities converge; for example, in most places the contemporary institution of marriage is a simultaneously social, political, and economic one

intergovernmental organizations (IGOs) international agencies or bodies established by states and controlled by member states that deal with areas of common interest

internally displaced people individuals who are uprooted from their homes, often due to civil strife, but remain in their home country

International Bill of Rights the collective name for the Universal Declaration of Human Rights, the International Covenant on Civil and Political Rights, and the International Covenant on Economic, Social, and Cultural Rights

International Monetary Fund (IMF) the Bretton Woods institution originally charged with helping states deal with temporary balance-of-payments problems; now plays a broader role in assisting debtor developing states by offering loans to those who institute specific policies or structural adjustment programs

international regimes the rules, norms, and procedures that are developed by states and international organizations out of their common concerns and are used to organize common activities

international relations the study of the interactions among various actors (states, international organizations, nongovernmental organizations, and subnational entities like bureaucracies, local governments, and individuals) that participate in international politics

international society the states and substate actors in the international system and the institutions and norms that regulate their interaction; implies that these actors communicate, sharing common interests and a common identity; identified with British school of political theory

interstate war organized violence between internationally-recognized states which results in at least one thousand deaths from combat in a calendar year; since 1900, wars between states have been responsible for the greatest concentration of deaths in a relatively short period of time in world history—for example, World War II resulted in from fifty to seventy million casualties from 1939 to 1945

intrastate war organized and deliberate violence within a state which results in at least one thousand battle-related deaths per year; civil wars are by far the most common form of intrastate war, but some terrorist attacks within states have exceeded the one-thousand deaths threshold, and might therefore be counted as wars

just war tradition the idea that wars must be judged according to two categories of justice: (1) *jus ad bellum*, or the justness of war itself; and (2) *jus in bello*, or the justness of each actor's conduct in war

League of Nations the international organization formed at the conclusion of World War I for the purpose of preventing another war; based on collective security

legitimacy the moral and legal right to rule, which is based on law, custom, heredity, or the consent of the governed

levels of analysis analytical framework based on the ideas that events in international relations can be explained by looking at individuals, states, or the international system and that causes at each level can be separated from causes at other levels

liberalism the theoretical perspective based on the assumption of the innate goodness of the individual and the value of political institutions in promoting social progress

limited wars armed conflicts usually between states in which belligerents acknowledge limits on both the resources applied to an armed conflict, and on the political objectives sought by means of war (namely, some objective less than the total defeat of the adversary or its unconditional surrender)

Malthusian dilemma the scenario in which population growth rates will increase faster than agricultural productivity, leading to food shortages; named after Thomas Malthus

mercantilism economic theory that international commerce should increase a state's wealth, especially gold; state power is enhanced by a favorable balance of trade

mirror images the tendency of individuals and groups to see in one's opponent the opposite characteristics as those seen in one's self

moral hazard problem when states or individuals are not made to pay the consequences of reckless behavior; they have little incentive to change that behavior

most-favored-nation (MFN) principle principle in international trade agreements when one state promises to give another state the same treatment in trade as the first state gives to its most-favored trading partner

multilateralism the conduct of international activity by three or more states in accord with shared general principles, often, but not always, through international institutions

multinational corporations (MNCs) private enterprises with production facilities, sales, or activities in several states

multipolar an international system in which there are several states or great powers of roughly equal strength or weight

narcotrafficking the transportation of large quantities of illegal narcotics like heroin or cocaine across state borders

nation a group of people sharing a common language, history, or culture

national interest the interest of the state, most basically the protection of territory and sovereignty; in realist thinking, the interest is a unitary one defined in terms of the pursuit of power; in liberal thinking, there are many national interests; in radical thinking, it is the interest of a ruling elite

nationalism devotion and allegiance to the nation and the shared characteristics of its peoples; used to motivate people to patriotic acts, sometimes leading a group to seek dominance over another group

nation-state the entity formed when people sharing the same historical, cultural, or linguistic roots form their own state with borders, a government, and international recognition; trend began with French and American Revolutions

negative externalities economies term for costly (harmful) unintended consequences of exchange; in political terms, a negative externality of a failed government might be refugees; in counterinsurgency, a negative externality for an incumbent government fighting insurgents might be increased terrorist group recruitment as a result of deliberately or inadvertently harming noncombatants in disputed areas

neoliberal institutionalism a reinterpretation of liberalism that posits that even in an anarchic international system, states will cooperate because of their continuous interactions with each other and because it is in their self-interest to do so; institutions provide the framework for cooperative interactions

neorealism a reinterpretation of realism that posits that the structure of the international system is the most important level to study; states behave the way they do because of the structure of the international system; includes the belief that general laws can be found to explain events

netcrime criminal use of the Internet; may include such diverse activities as use of e-mail or chat to bully a peer, manipulation of computer code to steal another's identity, propagation of child pornography, or theft of intellectual property

New International Economic Order (NIEO) a list of demands by the Group of 77 to reform economic relations between the North and the South, that is, between the developed countries and the developing countries

noncombatant immunity a core principle of international humanitarian law (formerly, "the laws of war") that holds that people not bearing arms in a conflict may not be deliberately targeted or systematically harmed; this category includes unarmed civilians, soldiers who have surrendered, and soldiers who are too severely injured to defend themselves

nongovernmental organizations (NGOs) private associations of individuals or groups that engage in political, economic, or social activities, usually across national borders

non-refoulement principle that refugees cannot be forced to return to their country of origin because of fear of persecution on the grounds of race, ethnicity, or membership in a social group

nonviolent resistance resistance to established authority that systematically precludes the use of violence as a tactic; common examples include strikes, sit-ins, and protest marches

normative relating to ethical rules; in foreign policy and international affairs, standards suggesting what a policy should be

North the developed countries, mostly in the Northern Hemisphere, including the countries of North America, the European countries, and Japan

North Atlantic Treaty Organization (NATO) military and political alliance between Western European states and the United States established in 1948 for the purpose of defending Europe from aggression by the Soviet Union and its allies; post–Cold War expansion to Eastern Europe

nuclear proliferation the geographic diffusion of the capacity to manage a controlled nuclear chain reaction; originally restricted to the United States and the Soviet Union, this technology—which includes peaceful nuclear power facilities as well as nuclear weapons—has spread to include the United Kingdom, France, Japan, Argentina, Germany, Switzerland, Pakistan, India, and Israel, among others

offshore financial centers states or jurisdictions with few regulations on banking and financial transactions, often with low taxation; used by individuals and international banks to transfer funds

organizational politics the foreign policy decision-making model that posits that national decisions are the products of subnational governmental organizations and units; the standard operating procedures and processes of the organizations largely determine the policy; major changes in policy are unlikely

peacebuilding post-conflict political and economic activities designed to preserve and strengthen peace settlements; includes civil administration, elections, and economic development activities

portfolio investment private investment in another state by purchasing stocks or bonds, without taking direct control of the investments

power the ability to influence others and also to control outcomes so as to produce results that would not have occurred naturally

power potential a measure of the power an entity like a state could have, derived from a consideration of both its tangible and its intangible resources; states may not always be able to transfer their power potential into actual power

prisoner's dilemma a theoretical game in which rational players (states or individuals) choose options that lead to outcomes (payoffs) such that all players are worse off than under a different set of choices

public diplomacy use of certain diplomatic methods to create a favorable image of the state or its people in the eyes of other states and their publics; methods include, for example, goodwill tours, cultural and student exchanges, and media presentations

radicalism a social theory, formulated by Karl Marx and modified by other theorists, that posits that class conflict between owners and workers will cause the eventual demise of capitalism; offers a critique of capitalism

rational actors in realist thinking, an individual or state that uses logical reasoning to select a policy; that is, it has a defined goal to achieve, considers a full range of alternative strategies, and selects the policy that best achieves the goal

realism a theory of international relations that emphasizes states' interest in accumulating power to ensure security in an anarchic world; based on the notion that individuals are power seeking and that states act in pursuit of their own national interest defined in terms of power

refugees individuals who flee from their country of nationality because of fear of persecution on the grounds of race, ethnicity, or membership in a social group

responsibility to protect (R2P) emerging norm that the international community should help individuals suffering at the hands of their own state or others

rollback a strategy of using, or threatening the use of, armed force to aggressively coerce an adversary into abandoning occupied territory

sanctions economic, diplomatic, and even coercive military force used to enforce an international policy or another state's policy; sanctions can be positive (offering an incentive to a state) or negative (punishing a state)

satisficing in decision-making theory, the tendency of states and their leaders to settle for the minimally acceptable solution, not the best possible outcome, in order to reach a consensus and formulate a policy

second-strike capability in the age of nuclear weapons, the ability of a state to respond and hurt an adversary after a first strike has been launched against that state by the adversary; ensures that both sides will suffer an unacceptable level of damage

Security Council one of the major organs of the United Nations charged with the responsibility for peace and security issues; includes five permanent members with veto power and ten nonpermanent members chosen from the General Assembly

security dilemma the situation in which one state improves its military capabilities, especially its defenses, and those improvements are seen by other states as threats; each state in an anarchic international system tries to increase its own level of protection leading to insecurity in others, often leading to an arms race

smart power using a combination of coercion (hard power) with persuasion and attraction (soft power)

smart sanctions limited sanctions targeted to hurt or support specific groups; used to avoid the humanitarian costs of general sanctions

socialism an economic and social system that relies on intensive government intervention or public ownership of the means of production in order to distribute wealth among the population more equitably; in radical theory, the stage between capitalism and communism

soft law nonbinding norms of state behavior; may or may not eventually become hard or obligatory law

soft power ability to change a target's behavior based on the legitimacy of one's ideas or policies, rather than on material (economic or military) power

South the developing countries of Africa, Latin America, and Southern Asia

sovereignty the authority of the state, based on recognition by other states and by nonstate actors, to govern matters within its own borders that affect its people, economy, security, and form of government

sovereign wealth funds state-controlled investment companies that manage large foreign exchange reserves; located in China or in petroleum-exporting countries (Norway, the Gulf states, Saudi Arabia)

state an organized political unit that has a geographic territory, a stable population, and a government to which the population owes allegiance and that is legally recognized by other states

stratification the uneven distribution of resources among different groups of individuals and states

structural adjustment programs IMF policies and recommendations aimed to guide states out of balance-of-payment difficulties and economic crises

summits talks and meetings among the highest-level government officials from different countries; designed to promote good relations and provide a forum to discuss issues and conclude formal negotiations

superpowers highest-power states as distinguished from other great powers; term coined during the Cold War to refer to the United States and the Soviet Union

sustainable development an approach to economic development that tries to reconcile current economic growth and environmental protection with the needs of future generations

system a group of units or parts united by some form of regular interaction, in which a change in one unit causes changes in the others; these interactions occur in regularized ways

terrorism the use of organized political violence by nonstate actors against noncombatants in order to cause fear as a means to achieve a political or religious objective; a form of asymmetric warfare

theory generalized statements about political, social, or economic activities that seek to describe and explain those activities; used in many cases as a basis of prediction

Third Reich the German state from 1933–45; a time which coincides with the rule of Adolf Hitler and his National Socialist Workers Party, or "Nazis"; this period followed the Second Reich (1871–1918), and the First Reich (962–1806)

total wars armed conflicts usually among multiple powerful states involving widespread destruction and major loss of life in which participants acknowledge no limits on the use of force to achieve their political aims, and in which those aims encompass an adversary's unconditional surrender

track-two diplomacy unofficial overtures by private individuals or groups to try and resolve an ongoing international crisis or civil war

traditional peacekeeping the use of multilateral third-party military forces to achieve several different objectives, generally to address and contain interstate conflict, including the enforcement of cease-fires and separation of forces; used during the Cold War to prevent conflict among the great powers from escalating

transnational across national or traditional state boundaries; can refer to actions of various nonstate actors, such as private individuals and nongovernmental organizations

transnational movements groups of people from different states who share religious, ideological, or policy beliefs and who work together to change the status quo

Treaties of Westphalia treaties ending the Thirty Years War in Europe in 1648; in international relations represents the beginning of state sovereignty within a territorial space

unconventional warfare wars in which either the means used (e.g., deliberately harming noncombatants) or the ends sought (e.g., genocide) violate the expectations of traditional practice

unipolar an international system in which a single actor exercises the most influence

unitary actor the state as an actor that speaks with one voice and has a single national interest; realists assume states are unitary actors

universal jurisdiction a legal concept that permits states to claim legal authority beyond their national territory for the purpose of punishing a particularly heinous criminal that violates the laws of all states or protecting human rights

war organized political violence by a recognized political authority intended to coerce another polity, and which results in at least one thousand battle deaths per calendar year. All parties involved must have some real capacity to harm one another; this definition makes war distinct from terrorism, riots, massacres, genocides, and skirmishes

war on terrorism a powerful rhetorical call to exploit a given society's total available resources (both material and nonmaterial) in order to defeat a political tactic; a key implication of declaring "war on terrorism" is that few if any limits on the use of a society's resources either should or will be observed

Warsaw Pact the military alliance formed by the states of the Soviet bloc in 1955 in response to the rearmament of West Germany and its inclusion in NATO; permitted the stationing of Soviet troops in Eastern Europe

Washington Consensus the liberal belief that only through specific liberal economic policies, especially privatization, can development result

weapons of mass destruction (WMD) chemical, biological, and radiological weapons distinguished by an inability to restrict their destructive effects to a single time and place; they therefore share a quality of irrationality in their contemplated use because attackers can never be entirely protected from the harm of any attacks they initiate with such weapons

World Bank a global lending agency focused on financing projects in developing countries; formally known as the International Bank for Reconstruction and Development, established as one of the key Bretton Woods institutions to deal with reconstruction and development after World War II

World Trade Organization (WTO) intergovernmental organization designed to support the principles of liberal free trade; includes enforcement measures and dispute settlement mechanisms; established in 1995 to replace the General Agreement on Tariffs and Trade

CREDITS

Chapter 01: Pg. 2: EPA/Georgi Licovski/Landov; Pg. 5: Maya Hautefeuille/AFP/Getty Images; Pg. 8: Steve Liss/Time Life Pictures/Getty Images; Pg. 14: Getty Images/Universal Images Group

Chapter 02: Pg. 20: Masashi Kato/Getty Images; Pg. 27: Bonhams, London, UK/The Bridgeman Art Library; Pg. 32: Giraudon/The Bridgeman Art Library; Pg. 33: 'Countries that have been under European control' from "Map: European colonialism conquered every country in the world but these five," by Max Fisher. Vox.com, February 24, 2015. http://www.vox.com/2014/6/24/5835320/map-in-the-whole-world-only-these-five-countries-escaped-european. Reprinted by permission of Vox Media, Inc.; Pg. 53: AFP/Getty Images; Pg. 59: David Turnley/Getty Images; Pg. 63: Christopher Furlong/Getty Images; Pg. 64: The Asahi Shimbun/Getty Images

Chapter 03: Pg. 70: AP Photo/Branden Camp; Pg. 73: Q. Sakamaki/Redux; Pg. 86: Thomas Niedermueller/Getty Images; Pg. 93: Gamma-Keystone via Getty Images; Pg. 99: Reuters/Lance Cpl. Marionne T. Mangrum/U.S. Marine Corps/Handout; Pg. 103: Bernard Weil/Toronto Star/Getty Images

Chapter 04: Pg. 106: Reuters/Alaa Al-Faqir; Pg. 112: Popperfoto/Getty Images; Pg. 121: EPA/Alexey Druzhinyn/RIA Novosti/Pool/Landov; Pg. 122: Jacob Silberberg/Panos Pictures; Pg. 127: Thomas Lekfeldt/Moment/Redux

Chapter 05: Pg. 132: Abbas Momani/AFP/Getty Images; Pg. 135: The Asahi Shimbun/Getty Images; Pg. 141: Rina Castelnuovo/The New York Times/Redux; Pg. 150: Justin Guariglia/Redux; Pg. 153: Manjunath Kiran/AFP/Getty Images; Pg. 171: Louisa Gouliamaki/AFP/Getty Images

Chapter 06: Pg. 180: Ed Jones/AFP/Getty Images; Pg. 184: Hulton-Deutsch Collection/Getty Images; Pg. 191: Mandel Ngan/AFP/Getty Images; Pg. 195: Klimentyev Mikhail Tass/Newscom; Pg. 200: AP Photo/Korean Central News Agency via Korea News Service; Pg. 204: Marco Longari/AFP/Getty Images

Chapter 07: Pg. 208: George Steinmetz/Getty Images; Pg. 214: Doug Armand/Getty Images; Pg. 224: Junior D. Kannah/AFP/Getty Images; Pg. 231: Reuters/Chris Wattie; Pg. 243: AFP/Stringer/Getty Images; Pg. 248: Marta Nascimento/REA/Redux; Pg. 251: Micheline Pelletier/Getty Images

INDEX

Page numbers in *italics* refer to boxes, figures, maps, and tables.